NEW STUDIES IN

The temple and the church's mission

Titles in this series:

NEW STUDIES IN BIBLICAL THEOLOGY 17

Series Editor: D. A. Carson

The Temple and the Church's Mission

A BIBLICAL THEOLOGY OF THE DWELLING PLACE OF GOD

G. K. Beale

InterVarsity Press
Downers Grove, Illinois

Apollos
Leicester, England

InterVarsity Press
P.O. Box 1400, Downers Grove, IL 60515-1426
World Wide Web: www.ivpress.com
Email: email@ivpress.com

APOLLOS (an imprint of Inter-Varsity Press, England)
Norton Street, Nottingham NG7 3HR, England
Website: www.ivpbooks.com
Email: ivp@ivpbooks.com

InterVarsity Press® is the book-publishing division of InterVarsity Christian Fellowship/USA®, a movement of students and faculty active on campus at hundreds of universities, colleges and schools of nursing in the United States of America, and a member movement of the International Fellowship of Evangelical Students. For information about local and regional activities, write Public Relations Dept., InterVarsity Christian Fellowship/ USA, 6400 Schroeder Rd., P.O. Box 7895, Madison, WI 53707-7895, or visit the IVCF website at <www.intervarsity.org>.

Inter-Varsity Press, England, is closely linked with the Universities and Colleges Christian Fellowship (formerly the Inter-Varsity Fellowship), a student movement linking Christian Unions in universities and colleges throughout Great Britain, and a member movement of the International Fellowship of Evangelical Students. For information about local and national activities write to UCCF, 38 De Montfort Street, Leicester LE1 7GP, email them at email@uccf.org.uk, or visit the UCCF website at www.uccf.org.uk.

All Scripture quotations, unless otherwise indicated, are taken from the New American Standard Bible *copyright 1960, 1962, 1963, 1968, 1971, 1972, 1973, 1975, 1977, 1995 by The Lockman Foundation. Used by permission.*

US ISBN 978-0-8308-2618-6
UK ISBN 978-1-84474-022-2

Printed in the United States of America ∞

Library of Congress Cataloging-in-Publication Data
Beale, G. K. (Gregory K.), 1949-
 The temple and the church's mission: a biblical theology of the
 temple/Gregory K. Beale.
  p. cm.—(New studies in biblical theology; 18)
 Includes bibliographical references and index.
 ISBN 0-8308-2618-1 (pbk.: alk. paper)
 1. Temple of God. 2. bible—Theology. I. Title. II. New studies in
biblical theology (InterVarsity Press)
  BS680.T4B42 2004
  220.6'4—dc22

British Library Cataloguing in Publication Data
A catalogue record for this book is available from the British Library.

P	21	20	19	18	17	16	15	14	13	12	11
Y	24	23	22	21	20	19	18	17	16	15	14

Contents

CONTENTS

Series preface

New Studies in Biblical Theology is a series of monographs that address key issues in the discipline of biblical theology. Contributions to the series focus on one or more of three areas: 1. the nature and status of biblical theology, including its relations with other disciplines (e.g. historical theology, exegesis, systematic theology, historical criticism, narrative theology); 2. the articulation and exposition of the structure of thought of a particular biblical writer or corpus; and 3. the delineation of a biblical theme across all or part of the biblical corpora.

Above all, these monographs are creative attempts to help thinking Christians understand their Bibles better. The series aims simultaneously to instruct and to edify, to interact with the current literature, and to point the way ahead. In God's universe, mind and heart should not be divorced: in this series we will try not to separate what God has joined together. While the notes interact with the best of the scholarly literature, the text is uncluttered with untransliterated Greek and Hebrew, and tries to avoid too much technical jargon. The volumes are written within the framework of confessional evangelicalism, but there is always an attempt at thoughtful engagement with the sweep of the relevant literature.

Of the three approaches to biblical theology listed above, this volume follows the third. Dr Greg Beale traces out the theme of the tabernacle/temple across the Bible's story-line, illuminating text after text as he goes. But more, he shows that the significance and symbolism of the temple draw on cultural assumptions, with the result that his theology is well grounded not only in exegesis but also in history. And beyond that, he ventures some suggestions about the meaning of the temple in both the Old and the New Testaments that break new ground, enabling thoughtful readers to perceive connections in the text of Scripture that doubtless escaped them in the past. The importance of this book therefore lies not only in the competent handling of its chosen theme, but also in three other things: its evocative unpacking of the theme of the temple in its relations to broader structures of thought, including the kingdom of God; its modelling of the way biblical theology is to be done; and its capacity to cause readers to perceive fresh and wonderful things in the Scriptures, and bow in worship and gratitude.

D. A. Carson
Trinity Evangelical Divinity School

Author's preface

This book had its birth as a three-page excursus to Revelation 22:1–2 in my commentary on Revelation (see Beale 1999a: 1109–1111). In 2001 I expanded the excursus into an extended paper, which was read at the Tyndale Fellowship Study Group on Biblical Theology in Cambridge, England (whose topic was on 'The Biblical Theology of the Temple'). The paper, along with other papers at that conference, was subsequently published (see Beale 2004). I am thankful to the conveners of the Tyndale Study Group for giving me opportunity to deliver this paper and for including it in the published volume of papers from the conference.

The extended paper was still only the barest thumb-nail sketch of what I had in mind as a biblical theology of the temple. Therefore, I set out to write a fuller-scale work. I have discovered that some of the book's chapters themselves need even further elaboration, but one has to stop somewhere.

This book has been the most exciting research project on which I have ever worked. It has opened my eyes to themes that I had seen only dimly before. In particular, I have seen more clearly than ever that the themes of Eden, the temple, God's glorious presence, new creation and the mission of the church are ultimately facets of the same reality! It is my hope that the biblical-theological perspective of this book will provide greater fuel to fire the church's motivation to fulfil its mission to the world.

I am indebted beyond words to my wife, Dorinda, who has discussed the theology of the temple with me for the past couple of years, and who remains as excited as I am about the subject. She has been one of the main instruments through which I have been able to understand this topic in more depth.

I also owe a great debt to Don Carson, the editor of this series. Don made a significant investment in reading and carefully evaluating the manuscript. His suggestions for revision were invaluable and have definitely made this a better book than it would have been! In addition, his encouragement about the project's viability throughout the editorial process has motivated me to finish it. Along with Don Carson, I must mention Philip Duce, Theological Books Editor at IVP in England, who has also read the manuscript and offered suggestions for improvement and encouragement. I am thankful to both Don and Philip for accepting this book for publication. I am similarly indebted to Jeff Niehaus, Gordon Hugenberger, Dan Master, John Monson and John Walton for reading and commenting on parts of this book, as well as alerting me to some OT and ANE sources.

I am likewise grateful to College Church (in Wheaton), which asked me to deliver the Fall 2001 Missions Sunday sermon on the subject of this book (and invited me to teach in other venues in the church on the theme). Attempting to distil the material for the church community has been essential in helping me to understand it even better. In addition, being able to teach the subject at Park Woods Presbyterian Church (Kansas City), Wheaton College Graduate School, The Greek Bible School of Athens (Greece), the Evangelical Theological College of Addis Ababa (Ethiopia) and the Bethlehem Theological Institute (Minneapolis) has been an enormous benefit, especially with respect to student questions that have sharpened my perspectives.

I also want to offer appreciation to the following research students who either helped do research or double-checked and edited the manuscript of this book: John Kohler, Ben Gladd, Stephen Webster, Kevin Cawley (particularly his research in early Judaism) and Todd Wilson. I am especially indebted to Greg Goss for his stylistic comments and other suggestions to improve the clarity of the book. Thanks must also be given to David Lincicum for creating the indices for the book.

Above all, I am thankful to God for enabling me to conceive the idea for this book and giving me the energy and discipline to write it. It is my prayer that God's glory will more greatly be manifested as a result of the reading of this book.

A few comments about some stylistic aspects of the book are in order. English translations follow the New American Standard Bible, unless otherwise indicated or, when different, represent my own translation. With respect to all translations of ancient works, when the translation differs from the standard editions usually referred to, then it is my translation or someone else's (in the latter case I indicate whom).

References to the Greek New Testament are from the NA[27]. In making references to the Septuagint, I refer to the Greek text of *The Septuagint Version of the Old Testament and Apocrypha with an English Translation*, which is dependent on Codex B. This will enable those not knowing Greek to follow the Septuagint in a readily available English edition. Occasionally, reference is made to A. Rahlfs (ed.), *Septuaginta*, which is the standard eclectic text for the Septuagint.

My references to the Dead Sea Scrolls come primarily from A. Dupont-Sommer, *The Essene Writings from Qumran*; reference to more recently published materials comes from the new edition of F. G. Martínez, *The Dead Sea Scrolls Translated*, and sometimes reference is made to F. G. Martínez and E. J. C. Tigchelaar (eds.), *The Dead Sea Scrolls Study Edition*. In addition, other translations of DSS were consulted and, sometimes, preferred in quotations, though at other times variations from Dupont-Sommer or Martínez are due to the author's own translation.

The primary sources of various Jewish works were ordinarily referred to, and sometimes quoted, in the following English editions: I. Epstein (ed.), *The Babylonian Talmud*; J. Neusner (ed.), *The Talmud of the Land of Israel* (the Jerusalem Talmud), Vols. 1–35; J. Z. Lauterbach (ed.), *Mekilta de-Rabbi Ishmael*, Vols. 1–3; *The Fathers According to Rabbi Nathan*, translated by J. Goldin; *The Midrash on Proverbs*, translated by B. L. Visotzky; W. G. Braude (ed.), *The Midrash on Psalms*; H. Freedman and M. Simon (eds.), *Midrash Rabbah*, Vols. 1–10; P. P. Levertoff (ed.), *Midrash Sifre on Numbers* in *Translations of Early Documents*, Series 3, Rabbinic Texts; J. T. Townsend (ed.), *Midrash Tanhuma*, Vols. 1–2; *Midrash Tanhuma-Yelammedenu*, translated by S. A. Berman; A. Cohen (ed.), *The Minor Tractates of the Talmud*, Vols. 1–2; H. Danby (ed.), *The Mishnah*; J. H. Charlesworth (ed.), *The Old Testament Pseudepigrapha*, Vols. 1–2 (though sometimes reference was made to R. H. Charles [ed.], *Apocrypha and Pseudepigrapha of the Old Testament*, Vol. 2 [Pseudepigrapha]); W. G. Braude and I. J. Kapstein (eds.), *The Pesikta de-rab Kahana*; W. G. Braude (ed.), *Pesikta Rabbati*; G. Friedlander (ed.), *Pirke de Rabbi Eliezer*; R. Hammer (ed.), *Sifre: A Tannaitic Commentary on the Book of Deuteronomy*; W. G. Braude and I. J. Kapstein (eds.), *Tanna debe Eliyyahu*; J. W. Etheridge (ed.), *The Targums of Onkelos and Jonathan Ben Uzziel on the Pentateuch, with the Fragments of the Jerusalem Targum, on Genesis and Exodus*; the available volumes published in M. McNamara (ed.), *The Aramaic Bible: The Targums*.

References to ancient Greek works, especially those of Philo and Josephus (including English translations), are from the Loeb Classical Library. References and some English translations of the apostolic fathers come from M. W. Holmes (ed.), *The Apostolic Fathers*.

Publication details of all works cited in this preface are given in full in the Bibliography at the back of this book.

G. K. Beale

Preface by
Mary Dorinda Beale

Have you ever wondered about some of the people described in the Bible? Some of them frankly seem superhuman, not quite real. For example, it seems odd that Paul and Silas sang in prison. Would I sing if I were in prison? Would I have the attitude expressed in Hebrews 10:34, where it portrays Christians as accepting 'joyfully' the seizure of their property? Would I be joyful if the authorities came and seized my house? In Acts 5:40–41, it says they flogged the apostles and told them not to speak in the name of Jesus any more. Their response is not what I consider a 'normal' reaction. They went away rejoicing because 'they had been considered worthy to suffer shame for His name'.

Would I rejoice if I suffered shame and was beaten? Why is their response so different? How can they act so totally different from most of us? It is as though their reality was different or they were seeing things that the natural eye cannot see. In 2 Kings 6, Elisha prays for his servant. The two men are surrounded by the army of Syria. The servant of Elisha is, naturally, distressed. Elisha comforts him with these words: 'Do not fear, for those who are with us are more than those who are with them' (v. 16). I have never been very good at arithmetic, but I do know that a Syrian army outnumbers two men! Elisha then prays that God would open his servant's eyes. We discover that the servant 'sees' 'the mountain [is] full of horses and chariots of fire all around'. What happened? He was given eyes to see true reality!

What is this true reality that can so alter all that we say and do? When one becomes a Christian, real truth is seen. True reality is the fact that humanity is drowning in a sea of sin with no way to save itself. The only hope is to cry out to God. Only Jesus, the Messiah, can save. If you cling to him as your Saviour, you will not be carried away in the sea of sin because he is the rock of our salvation (Acts 4:10–12).

Second Corinthians 5:17 says, 'if any man is in Christ, he is a new creature; the old things have passed away; behold, new things have come'. How is this 'newness' of life as a Christian manifested? It seems as though Nicodemus's question to Jesus is understandable: 'how can a man be born when he is old? He cannot enter a second time into his mother's womb' (John 3:4). Jesus answers this perplexing question in verse 6, 'That which is born of the flesh is flesh, and that which is born of the Spirit is spirit.' The significance seems to be that the Spirit is different. It is not at all like the flesh. So, how can we still remain in our fleshly bodies and yet 'walk' in 'newness of life' (Rom. 6:4)? First Peter 2:11 tells us that we are 'aliens and strangers' on earth, which means earth is not our home. Instead, Ephesians 2:19–22 explains, our home is in heaven, and we are *now* 'of God's household' (see also 1 Tim. 3:15). How can we really be part of God's household *now*? We live on earth. Are we not just in a 'holding pattern' until we actually die or the world ends? Aren't we only looking forward to the future time when we will be part of 'God's household'?

Since Scripture tells us that we are *now* part of God's household and are not just wandering around as 'aliens' on earth, where is God's household, who is there, and what difference does it make anyway? Hebrews 12:22–24 explains very clearly where we are and who is there with us:

> But you have come to Mount Zion and to the city of the living God, the heavenly Jerusalem, and to myriads of angels, to the general assembly, and the church of the first-born who are enrolled in heaven, and to God, the Judge of all, and to the spirits of righteous men made perfect, and Jesus, the mediator of a new covenant, and to the sprinkled blood, which speaks better than the blood of Abel.

When we, like Elisha's servant, have our eyes of faith opened, the awesome fact is that we are in the presence of God, and Jesus the mediator of a new covenant. 'He delivered us from the domain of darkness, and transferred us to the kingdom of His beloved Son' (Col. 1:13). We are there now. Christians are 'living stones', 'being built up as a spiritual house' (1 Pet. 2:5).

When my oldest daughter Nancy was three years old, our family lived in England. In the spring of that year, Nancy and I were invited to a picnic at a very large country estate. As we walked around the house and grounds, I realized that she was hardly fazed by the splendour and beauty of this magnificent estate. I pulled her aside and said, 'Nancy, I know you are very young, but this is a special place. Try to remember this day.'

We, like my daughter, need to be pulled aside and told that we are in the most special place of all – *now* – God's palatial mountain-temple.

This book will explain in detail where we are and the beauty and splendour of the new Jerusalem, the temple of the living God. Israel's physical temple which was seen by the naked eye was a mere shadow of the heavenly reality (Heb. 9:24)! May God open our eyes to understand:

> How blessed is the one whom Thou
>   dost choose, and bring near to Thee,
> To dwell in Thy courts.
> We will be satisfied with the goodness
>   of Thy house,
> Thy holy temple.
>
> (Ps. 65:4)

Abbreviations

Ancient sources: standard abbreviations are used; authors and titles are given in full in the 'Index of ancient sources' on p. 450.

AB	Anchor Bible
ABD	*Anchor Bible Dictionary*
AnBib	*Analecta Biblica*
ANE	Ancient Near East
ArBib	The Aramaic Bible
ASOR	American School of Oriental Research
AV	Authorized (King James) Version
b.	*Babylonian Talmud*
BA	*Biblical Archaeologist*
BAGD	W. Bauer, W. F. Arndt, F. W. Gingrich, and F. W. Danker, *A Greek-English Lexicon of the New Testament* (2nd ed.)
BAR	*Biblical Archaeology Revue*
BBR	*Bulletin for Biblical Research*
BDAG	W. Bauer, F. W. Danker, W. F. Arndt, and F. W. Gingrich, *A Greek-English Lexicon of the New Testament and Other Early Christian Literature* (3rd ed.).
BDB	F. Brown, S. R. Driver and C. A. Briggs, *A Hebrew and English Lexicon of the Old Testament*
BECNT	Baker Exegetical Commentary on the New Testament
BETL	Bibliotheca ephemeridum theologicarum lovaniensium
Bib	*Biblica*
BibO	Biblica et Orientica
BJS	Brown Judaic Studies
BNTC	Black's New Testament Commentaries
BRev	*Bible Review*
BSac	*Bibliotheca Sacra*

BZNW	Beihefte zur Zeitschrift für die neutestamentliche Wissenschaft
c.	circa
CBC	Cambridge Bible Commentary
CBQ	*Catholic Biblical Quarterly*
CBQMS	Catholic Biblical Quarterly Monograph Series
CE	*Critical Enquiry*
ConB	Coniectanea biblica
CT	*Cuneiform Texts from Babylonian Tablets in the British Museum*
CTM	*Concordia Theological Monthly*
DSD	*Dead Sea Discoveries*
DSS	Dead Sea Scrolls
EBC	Expositor's Bible Commentary
ErIs	*Eretz-Israel*
ExpT	*Expository Times*
frag(s).	fragment(s)
FS	Festschrift
HNT	Handbuch zum Neuen Testament
HSMS	Harvard Semitic Monograph Series
IBD	*The Illustrated Bible Dictionary*, ed. J. D. Douglas
IBS	*Irish Biblical Studies*
ICC	International Critical Commentary
JATS	*Journal of the Adventist Theological Society*
JBL	*Journal of Biblical Literature*
JEH	*Journal of Ecclesiastical History*
JETS	*Journal of the Evangelical Theological Society*
JJS	*Journal of Jewish Studies*
JR	*Journal of Religion*
JSNTS	Journal for the Study of the New Testament Supplement Series
LXX	Septuagint
m.	*Mishnah*
MNTC	Moffatt New Testament Commentary
MT	Masoretic Text
NA^{27}	Nestle-Aland, *Novum Testamentum Graece* (27th ed.), Stuttgart: Deutsche Bibelgesellschaft, 1993.
NAC	The New American Commentary
NASB	New American Standard Bible
NCB	New Century Bible
n.d.	no date

Neot	*Neotestamentica*
NICNT	The New International Commentary on the New Testament
NICOT	The New International Commentary on the Old Testament
NIDOTTE	*New International Dictionary of Old Testament Theology and Exegesis*, ed. W. A. VanGemeren
NIGTC	New International Greek Testament Commentary
NIV	New International Version of the Bible
NIVAC	NIV Application Commentary
NLH	*New Literary History*
NT	New Testament
NTS	*New Testament Studies*
NumSup	Numen Supplements
OLA	Orientalia lovaniensia analecta
OT	Old Testament
RevQ	*Revue de Qumran*
RSMS	Religious Studies Monograph Series
SacP	Sacra Pagina
SBLA	Society of Biblical Literature Abstracts
SBLDS	Society of Biblical Literature Dissertation Series
SBLEJL	Society of Biblical Literature Early Judaism and its Literature
SBLSP	Society of Biblical Literature Seminar Papers
SBLWAW	Society of Biblical Literature Writings from the Ancient World
SHR	Studies in the History of Religions
SNTS	Society for New Testament Studies
SNTSMS	Society for New Testament Studies Monograph Series
SPB	Studia Post-Biblica
SubB	Subsidia Biblica
TDNT	*Theological Dictionary of the New Testament*, ed. G. Kittel and G. Friedrich
TDOT	*Theological Dictionary of the Old Testament*, ed. J. Botterweck and H. Ringgren
Tg.	*Targum*
Them	*Themelios*
TNTC	Tyndale New Testament Commentary
TynB	*Tyndale Bulletin*

VT	*Vetus Testamentum*
VTSup	Vetus Testamentum Supplement
WBC	Word Biblical Commentary
WC	Westminster Commentaries
WTJ	*Westminster Theological Journal*
WUNT	Wissenschaftliche Untersuchungen zum Neuen Testament
y.	Jerusalem Talmud
ZAW	Zeitschrift für die alttestamentliche Wissenschaft

Chapter One

Introduction

The final vision of the Apocalypse and its implications for a biblical theology of the temple

Revelation 21:1 – 22:5 contains the well-known and much discussed final vision of the entire Bible. There is, however, a major problem that has barely been noticed. Why does John see 'a new heaven and a new earth' in Revelation 21:1 and yet in 21:2–3, 10 – 22:3 he sees a city that is garden-like, in the shape of a temple? Why does John not see a full panorama of the new heavens and earth? Why does he not see the many forests, rivers, mountains, streams, valleys and the many other features of a fertile worldwide new creation. Some might attribute the apparent discrepancy to the irrational nature that ancient apocalyptic visions and dreams could have, though this would be hard to accept for a vision that John claims has its origin in God (cf. 21:9 with Rev. 1:1 and 22:6, for example). Also, how does this vision relate to Christians and their role in fulfilling the mission of the church, an issue with which John has been absorbed throughout Revelation?

Thus, after initially saying that he saw 'a new heaven and a new earth', John focuses only on an arboreal city-temple in the remainder of the vision. The dimensions and architectural features of the city in these verses are drawn to a significant extent from Ezekiel 40 – 48, a prophecy of the dimensions and architectural features of a future temple (so vv. 2, 10–12; 21:27 – 22:2). The precious stones forming the foundation in Revelation 21:18–21 reflect the description of Solomon's temple which also was overlaid with gold and whose foundation was composed of precious stones: see respectively 1 Kings 6:20–22 (and 5:17) and 7:9–10, and note that the dimensions of Revelation 21:16 ('its length and width and height are equal') are based on the dimensions of the 'holy of holies' in 1 Kings 6:20 (where the 'length . . . and the breadth . . . and the height' of the holy of holies were equal in measurement).

How can one explain the apparent discrepancy that John, in verse 1, saw a new creation, yet in the remainder of the vision observed only a city in the shape and structure of a temple? It is possible, of course, that he first sees the new world and then sees a city-temple *in* that world. But this is not likely because it is apparent that he equates the 'new heavens and earth' with the following description of the 'city-temple'.

This equation of the new world with the city-temple becomes clearer when one begins to reflect on Revelation 21:27, which declares that 'nothing unclean ... shall ever come into' the urban temple. In this respect, it is significant to remember that in the Old Testament any uncleanness was to be kept out of the temple precincts (e.g., 2 Chr. 23:19; 29:16; 30:1–20). That the perimeters of the new city-temple will encompass the whole of the new creation is suggested then by the fact that Revelation 21:27 says that no uncleanness was allowed into this unusual temple. This observation probably means that no uncleanness will be allowed into the new world. The equation of the city-temple with the new world is further evident from the exclusion of the unclean from the new city in 22:15, which means they will also be excluded from dwelling in the new creation, since they will be in the lake of fire for ever (see ch. 10 in this book).

Another observation points to the equation of the new cosmos with the city-temple. Revelation 21:1 commences, as we have seen, with John's vision of 'a new heaven and a new earth', followed by his vision of the 'new Jerusalem, coming down out of heaven' (v. 2), after which he hears a 'loud great voice' proclaiming that 'the tabernacle of God is among men, and he shall dwell among them'. It is likely that the second vision in verse 2 interprets the first vision of the new cosmos, and that what is heard about the tabernacle in verse 3 interprets both verses 1 and 2. If so, the new creation of verse 1 is identical to the 'new Jerusalem' of verse 1 and both represent the same reality as the 'tabernacle' of verse 3.

The 'seeing–hearing' pattern elsewhere in Revelation suggests that verses 1–3 refer to the same reality. At other points in the book either what John sees is interpreted by what he then hears or vice versa. A good example is Revelation 5:5, where John *hears* about a 'Lion that is from the tribe of Judah' who 'conquered'. John *sees* a slain lamb possessing sovereign authority in verse 6, which interprets how the messianic lamb conquered: he won victory ironically by dying as a 'slain lamb'.

That the 'new heaven and new earth' of 21:1 is defined by and equated with the paradisal city-temple of 21:2 and 21:9 – 22:5 is also supported by J. D. Levenson's observation that 'heaven and earth' in the Old Testament may sometimes be a way of referring to Jerusalem or its temple, for which 'Jerusalem' is a metonymy.[1] He quotes Isaiah 65:17–18 in support: *'For behold, I create new heavens and a new earth;/*And the former things shall not be remembered or come to mind./*'But be glad and rejoice forever in what I create;/For behold, I create Jerusalem* for rejoicing' (emphasis mine).[2] These two new-creation statements in these verses appear to be in a synonymously parallel relationship. Since Isaiah 65:17 is alluded to in Revelation 21:1, it is most natural to understand that the new Jerusalem of 21:2 is equated with the 'new heaven and earth' of 21:1. That the new creation in verse 1 and new Jerusalem in verse 2 are interpreted in verse 3 to be 'the tabernacle of God' among all humanity, would also be a natural equation, as Levenson noted above, and as we will see throughout this book.

Consequently, the new creation and Jerusalem are none other than God's tabernacle. This tabernacle is the true temple of God's special presence portrayed throughout chapter 21.

As I have continued to reflect on the Apocalypse, and especially my conclusion about the temple of Revelation 21, since the writing of my commentary on Revelation (published in 1999), I have noticed even more connections between the various temple texts in the Old and New Testaments. My purpose in this book is to explore in more depth the significance of the temple in John's Apocalypse and especially in this final vision of the book. My beginning point is a brief answer to the above question about why John equates the new creation with an arboreal city-temple in his last vision of the book. I formulated a brief answer to this in my Revelation commentary a few years ago.[3]

In this book I will attempt to amplify the evidence adduced in support of this answer in order to enhance its plausibility. My thesis is that the Old Testament tabernacle and temples were symbolically designed to point to the cosmic eschatological reality that God's tabernacling presence, formerly limited to the holy of holies, was to be extended throughout the whole earth. Against this background, the Revelation 21 vision is best understood as picturing the final end-time temple that will fill the entire cosmos. If correct, the thesis provides

---

[1] A metonymy is the substitution of what is meant with something associated with what is meant.

[2] Levenson 1988: 89–90; 1984: 294–295.

[3] Beale 1999a: 1109–1111.

not only the answer to the above problem in chapter 21, but also gives crucial insight into an understanding of the biblical theology of the temple in both testaments.

In attempting to substantiate this thesis, I will survey the evidence for the cosmic symbolism of Old Testament and Ancient Near Eastern temples. Then I will argue that the Garden of Eden was the first archetypal temple, and that it was the model for all subsequent temples. Such an understanding of Eden will enhance the notion that the Old Testament tabernacle and temples were symbolic microcosms of the whole creation. As microcosmic symbolic structures they were designed to point to a worldwide eschatological temple that perfectly reflects God's glory. It is this universally expanded eschatological temple that is pictured in Revelation's last vision. Other relevant passages about the temple in the New Testament will be adduced in further support of this contention.

A brief comment on the interpretative approach of this book

An important presupposition underlying this study is the divine inspiration of the entire Bible, both Old and New Testaments. This foundational perspective means that there is unity to the Bible because it is all God's word. Therefore, there is legitimacy in attempting to trace common themes between the testaments. Though interpreters differ about what are the most significant unifying themes, those who affirm the ultimate divine authorship of Scripture have a common data-base with which to discuss and debate.

Another important presupposition is that the divine authorial intentions communicated through human authors are accessible to contemporary readers. Though no-one can exhaustively comprehend these intentions, they can be sufficiently understood, especially for the purposes of salvation, sanctification and glorification of God. Of this subject, especially as it bears on the subject of the book, we will speak more in a concluding chapter (see ch. 12).

Finally, a typical strategy of argumentation throughout this book will be to adduce several lines of evidence in favour of a particular interpretation. Some of these lines will be stronger than others, but when all of the relevant material is viewed as a whole, the less convincing material should become more significant than when seen by itself. Therefore, it will sometimes be true that some of the arguments in favour of an interpretation will not stand on their own but are intended to take on more persuasive power when viewed in light of the other angles of reasoning. And, even when this may not be the case, the design is that the overall weight of the cumulative arguments points to the plausibility or probability of the main idea being contended for.

Chapter Two

Cosmic symbolism of temples in the Old Testament

Some of the best clues to solving the problem posed above about the relation of the new creation to the city-temple of Revelation 21 are to be found in the conception of Israel's temple. We will also look at the symbolic meaning of other ancient temples to enhance the understanding of Israel's sanctuary in the midst of its ancient environment. Though these were pagan temples, it is not likely that their resemblances to Israel's temple were due to coincidence or to Israel's mere dependence on her pagan neighbours for religious ideas. Rather, this resemblance of pagan temples to Israel's temple probably was due, at least in part, to a refracted and marred understanding of the true conception of the temple that was present from the very beginning of human history. As history unfolded, God's special revelation about the temple continued only with the faithful remnant of humanity. The recollection of the true temple by those outside God's covenant community probably continued, but its memory became dim over time. Nevertheless, refracted glimmers of truth may have continued, so that some temples were designed that still retained features corresponding to God's own view.[1] God's people, on the other hand, continued building temples that represented the pristine view of the true cult.[2] One could say that just as God's image in unbelieving humanity has not been erased but blurred, so their continuing conception of the structure where God should be worshipped was likewise blurred.

Some commentators disagree that the design and symbolism of ancient pagan temples reflected glimmers of God's truth. Even granting such a view, however, it is apparent that Israel intentionally alluded to facets of the pagan religion surrounding them (e.g., Egyptian, Canaanite and Babylonian) in order to affirm that what the pagans thought was true of their gods was true only of Israel's God

---

[1] In contrast, see Fairbairn 1863a: 219–220, who rejects the notion that symbolic aspects of pagan temples could have significant overlap with that of Israel's temple.

[2] See Rodriguez 2001: 58–59, who has a similar analysis of Israel's temple in relation to pagan sanctuaries.

(e.g., Ps. 29 is a well-known example of applying the sovereign attributes of the fertility god Baal to Yahweh in order to demonstrate that only Yahweh possesses such characteristics). The same polemical intention was likely part of Israel's depiction of their temple. Hence, there is a sense in which Israel may have borrowed religious notions and imagery from her neighbours, but it was for polemical reasons and not for lack of religious creativity. That pagan nations, however, could depict their gods with attributes like those of the true God and their temples along the lines of the true God's dwelling probably shows they had some sense of the true God, though certainly in a non-salvific and confused form (as, e.g., in Rom. 1:19–25).

There is, at least, a third way in which pagan cultural ideas could have been related to Israel and even her temple. Some of Israel's ideas were merely shared with pagan peoples because they simply shared a general common culture, though often when Israel employed the concept, it became filled with theological significance. For example, it was likely a widespread custom in the Ancient Near East that certain ceremonies involving the donning of clothes or the removal or leaving of clothes indicated respectively the acquisition of inheritance rights or disinheritance. This may explain a whole host of passages involving clothing in the Old Testament (and the New Testament): the divine provision of clothing to Adam and Eve in Genesis 3:21 appears to indicate a gracious reaffirmation of their inheritance rights over creation, despite their former rebellion.[3] It is possible that some kind of relationship like this may have existed between the clothing of pagan and Israel's priests and even the adornment of the respective temples.

With these possible relationships between the thought of the ancient Israelites and the peoples surrounding them, we now turn primarily to a study of Israel's temples. After looking at the Old Testament evidence, reflection on Jewish interpretations of Israel's temple may also prove helpful for understanding the Old Testament material. We will also survey pertinent parallels in the Ancient Near East, where examination of the sanctuaries of Israel's neighbours may also shed some light on the subtle symbolism of the Israelite holy place.

Our study of ancient materials outside the Bible to gain a better

---

[3] Cf. also Gen. 9:23 (Noah's garment); 37:3 (Joseph's tunic); Deut. 24:17; Luke 15:22 (the father's robe given to the prodigal son); Gal. 3:27 ('clothed' with Christ); Rev. 21:2–3, 7. For this meaning of 'clothing' in the ANE and biblical literature, cf. Hugenberger 1997. See also Hugenberger 1994: 390, n. 130.

understanding of the temple does not mean that this material is equal in authority to the Bible. Rather, it indicates that the Bible was written in very specific historical circumstances and the better one understands these surrounding circumstances, the more rich one's understanding of the Bible may become. Christians often use commentaries on the Bible in order to understand the biblical text better. Sometimes such commentaries provide a perspective on a text, which sheds new light and helps us to understand the text better. The new perspective is validated over other previous ones because it makes more sense of the details of the text. Sometimes, however, these commentaries are clearly wrong and are not helpful, and, at other times, these commentaries merely resummarize the biblical text, saying nothing new nor wrong.

The documents of the Ancient Near East and of Judaism function comparably to modern commentaries. Should we not also make use of this ancient commentary material, for example early Jewish interpretations of Old Testament texts, themes, and so on? Such Jewish commentary material has the same potential use (and misuse) as do contemporary commentaries, though they have the potential of picking up early oral interpretative tradition that may stem from Old Testament times itself. We will see that there may be some early Jewish interpretation of the temple that sheds helpful light on the Old Testament notion of the temple. We will propose the same thing for some Ancient Near Eastern views of temples.

Though the discussion of this chapter is rather detailed, it is absolutely crucial to work through and understand it as a basis for the later part of this book.

The Old Testament view of Israel's earthly temple as a reflection of the heavenly or cosmic temple

The rationale for the worldwide encompassing nature of the paradisal temple in Revelation 21 lies in the ancient notion that the Old Testament temple was a microcosm of the entire heaven and earth.[4] One of the most explicit texts affirming this is Psalm 78:69: 'And He built His sanctuary like the heights,/Like the earth which He has

[4] For OT, and, especially, Jewish perspectives, see Patai 1967: 54–139; Barker 1991: 104–132; Levenson 1984: 283–298; 1985: 111–184; Hayward 1996; Koester 1989: 59–63; Fletcher-Lewis 1997: 156–162. The discussion in the section below, 'Judaism's view of the symbolism of the temple', is based partly on these works, which should be consulted.

founded *forever* (or from eternity)'.[5] The psalmist is saying that, in some way, God designed Israel's earthly temple to be comparable to the heavens and to the earth. Similarly, the earlier 'pattern of the tabernacle and the pattern of all its furniture' was made 'after the [heavenly] pattern . . . which was shown . . . on the mountain' (Exod. 25:9, 40; cf. Exod. 26:30; 27:8; Num. 8:4; Heb. 8:5; 9:23–24). The following study will attempt to demonstrate that the symbolism of the tabernacle is essentially the same as that of Israel's subsequent temple. This equivalence is implied by their many overt similarities and by comparing Exodus 25:9, 40 with 1 Chronicles 28:19, which say that both the plan of the tabernacle and of the temple came from God.[6]

Jewish tradition, as we will see, also reaffirms the truth of Psalm 78 and Exodus 25, that the earthly temple corresponded in some significant manner to the heavens, especially a heavenly temple.[7] The primary task of this chapter is to elaborate on how Israel's tabernacle and temple were comparable in symbolic design to the heavens and earth.

General symbolism of the temple

Our thesis is that Israel's temple was composed of three main parts, each of which symbolized a major part of the cosmos: (1) the outer court represented the habitable world where humanity dwelt; (2) the holy place was emblematic of the visible heavens and its light sources; (3) the holy of holies symbolized the invisible dimension of the

---

[5] On which see further Levenson 1988: 87–88, and Hurowitz 1992: 335–337. Ps. 78:69 has a striking parallel in the *Enuma Elish* 6.112, where it is said concerning the building of Marduk's temple, 'A likeness of what he made (?) in heaven [let him make (?)] on earth' (the translation of the *Enuma Elish* follows Heidel 1942: 50. Cf. also the translation of Foster 1997: 402: 'He shall make on earth the counterpart of what he brought to pass in heaven.' Jer. 17:12 is another text possibly parallel to Ps. 78:69: 'A glorious throne on high from the beginning is the place of our sanctuary.' There is debate about whether the whole verse refers only to a heavenly temple or only an earthly temple. Is it not possible that both are in mind as in the psalm? If so, God's glorious throne in his heavenly temple is being compared to the earthly temple that was to reflect the former.

[6] The equivalence was also made by early Judaism (so *Wisdom of Solomon* 9:8: the temple was 'an imitation of the holy tabernacle which you prepared from the beginning'); see Haran 1978: 189–204 on the organic correspondences between the tabernacle and temple; cf. also Clifford 1984: 112–115. For the close link between the tabernacle and the temple, see 1 Kgs. 8:1–6 (= 2 Chr. 5:2–5), which may imply that the tabernacle was even incorporated into the temple (on which cf. Cross 1977: 175).

[7] See *Tg. 2 Chronicles* 6:2; likewise, *Tg. Pseudo-Jonathon Exodus* 15:17; *Midrash Rabbah Numbers* 4:13; 12:12; *Midrash Psalms* 30:1; *Tanhuma Yelammedenu Exodus* 11:1–2. See also, Ego (1989), who elaborates on the correspondence between the earthly and heavenly temples in rabbinic Jewish tradition.

cosmos, where God and his heavenly hosts dwelt. In this connection, M. Haran has observed an increasing gradation in holiness beginning with the outer court and proceeding to the holy place and then into the holy of holies. Furthermore, he notes that this gradation corresponds to a gradation in dress and furnishings dependent on the position of the person in the temple (respectively worshipper, priest or high priest) or the location of the furnishings (curtains, furniture, etc.).[8] This observation about increasing gradation indicating increasing holiness may not be inconsistent with A. A. de Silva's view that Old Testament temple-building narratives reflect a three-tiered structure with God at the top, kings (and, I would add, priests) in the middle, and Israel and the rest of the cosmos at the bottom (de Silva 1994: 11–23).

The identification of the outer court as the visible earth and sea is suggested further by the Old Testament description, where the large molten wash-basin and altar in the temple courtyard are called respectively the 'sea' (1 Kgs. 7:23–26) and the 'bosom of the earth' (Ezek. 43:14; the altar also likely was identified with the 'mountain of God' in Ezek. 43:16).[9] The altar was also to be an 'altar of earth' (in the early stages of Israel's history) or an 'altar of [uncut] stone' (Exod. 20:24–25), thus identifying it even more with the natural earth.[10] Thus both the 'sea' and 'altar' appear to be cosmic symbols that may have been associated in the mind of the Israelite respectively with the seas and the earth[11] (enhancing the water imagery were the

---

[8] Haran 1978: 158–188, 205–221, 226–227, followed by Dumbrell 1985: 43.

[9] See further Levenson 1988: 92–93. Translations of Ezek. 43:14 typically have 'from the base on the ground' but literally it is 'from the bosom of the earth [or ground]'; among the reasons for associating 'the altar hearth' (literally 'Ariel') of Ezek. 43:16 with 'the mountain of God' is Levenson's observation that the same mysterious word 'Ariel' occurs also in Is. 29:1, where it refers to 'the city where David camped' and is equated by synonymous parallelism to 'Mount Zion' (cf. Is. 29:7a with 29:8h), so that it resonates with 'mountain' imagery (on the ambivalent meaning of the Hebrew word, see further BDB, 72). See also Barrois 1980: 65–66, who renders the respective phrases in Ezek. 43:14, 16, as 'bosom of the earth' and 'the mountain of God', which he sees to be symbolic cosmic names. For virtually identical conclusions, see Mitchell 1980: 36, who observes that Ezekiel's altar resembled a Babylonian ziggurat, which, as we will see later, was designed to resemble a mountain and was considered the top of a temple.

[10] The altar's association with the earth may be enhanced by noticing that it is repeatedly described as having a 'foundation' (Exod. 29:12; Lev. 4:7, 18, 25, 30, 34), imagery typical elsewhere of structures rooted to the earth (e.g., Ezek. 30:4; Mic. 1:6; Ps. 137:7; Job 4:19; Lam. 4:11) and sometimes used of mountains (Deut. 32:22; Ps. 18:7). I am indebted to G. P. Hugenberger for these observations.

[11] On which see Terrien 1970: 323 for additional bibliography in support. See also Bloch-Smith 1994: 26–27, on Solomon's 'bronze sea' as representing the primordial sea

ten smaller wash-basins, five on each side of the holy place enclosure [1 Kgs. 7:38–39]). The arrangement of the twelve bulls 'entirely encircling the sea' and the 'lily blossom' decorating the brim would also seem to present a partial miniature model of land and life surrounding the seas of the earth (2 Chr. 4:2–5). The twelve bulls also supported the wash-basin and were divided into groups of three, facing to the four points of the compass, which could well reflect the four quadrants of the earth (Levenson 1988: 92–93, and Levenson 1985: 139, 162). That twelve oxen were pictured holding up the 'sea' and designs of lions and oxen were on the wash-basin stands points further to an 'earthly' identification of the outer courtyard (though cherubim were also depicted on the basin stands). That the outer court was associated with the visible earth is also intimated by recalling that all Israelites, representing humanity at large,[12] could enter there and worship.

There is also reason to view the second section of the temple, the holy place, to be a symbol of the visible sky. The seven lamps on the lampstand may have been associated with the seven light-sources visible to the naked eye (five planets, sun and moon). This identification is pointed to by Genesis 1 which uses the unusual word 'lights' (*mě'ōrōt*, 5 times) instead of 'sun' and 'moon', a word that is used throughout the remainder of the Pentateuch (10 times) only for the 'lights' on the tabernacle lampstand. On the same basis, a contemporary commentator on Genesis has made virtually the same observation and proposed that this is the first hint also that the cosmos itself was conceived of as a huge temple.[13] In addition, John's Apocalypse

---

or waters of Eden, though some see it representing the primeval chaos waters that were overcome at creation. Cf. Bloch-Smith (1994: 20–21) and C. Meyers (1992a: 1060–1061), who note both connotations of the 'sea', and underscore its symbolic significance, the latter especially pointing out that Solomon's 'bronze sea' was over seven feet high and fifteen feet in diameter, holding about 10,000 gallons of water and weighing between 25 and 30 tons when empty. Priests would have had to climb a ladder to wash in it.

[12] Later we will see that Israel was a 'corporate Adam', thus being designed ideally to represent humanity.

[13] So Walton 2001: 148. Among the three other uses elsewhere in the OT, two also refer to the 'lights' of the heaven. The only other use is Ps. 90:8 ('the light of your presence'), which may suggest that the lampstand 'lights' also symbolized the light of God's glorious presence, just as the stars were held to reflect God's glory (Pss. 19:1; 148:3–4; cf. Pss. 8:1; 50:6; 57:5). Such an identification may be represented in the Qumran *Hymn Scroll* (1QH 7.24): 'I [the Teacher of Righteousness] will shine with a *seven-fold li*[*ght*] in the E[den which] Thou has [m]ade for Thy glory' (for justification of the translation 'Eden', see below at the end of this chapter).

also closely identifies the seven lamps on the lampstand with stars by saying that each of the seven churches that are symbolized by a 'lampstand' are represented in heaven by an 'angel' who is symbolized by a 'star' (Rev. 1:20) (Beale 1995a: 211–219).

Vern Poythress also contends along similar lines that the lamps signify the seven main lights of the heaven:

> The lampstand is placed on the south side of the Holy Place. Perhaps this placement is intended to correspond to the fact that from Israel's point of view, north of the equator, the circuit of the heavenly lights would be primarily to the south. That there are seven of the lamps correlates not only with the seven major lights of heaven ... but with the general symbolism for time within Israel. The heavenly bodies were made in order to 'serve as signs to mark seasons and days and years' (Gen. 1:14). The whole cycle of time marked by the sun and moon and stars is divided up into sevens: the seventh day in the week is the Sabbath day; the seventh month is the month of atonement (Lev. 16:29); the seventh year is the year of release from debts and slavery (Deut. 15); the seventh of the seven-year cycles is the year of jubilee (Lev. 25). Fittingly, the lampstand contains the same sevenfold division, symbolizing the cycle of time provided by the heavenly lights. (Poythress 1991: 18–19)

That the holy of holies represented the unseen heavenly dimension of the world is apparent from its descriptions. Just as the angelic cherubim guard God's throne in the heavenly temple (e.g., Rev. 4:7–9), the sculpted cherubim around the ark of the covenant in the holy of holies (1 Kgs. 6:23–28), and the figures of the cherubim woven into the curtain that guards the holy of holies reflects the real cherubim in heaven who presently and in the future will stand guard around God's throne in the heavenly temple (cf. 2 Sam. 6:2; 2 Kgs. 19:15; 1 Chr. 13:6; Pss. 80:1; 99:1, all of which may have double reference to the earthly and heavenly cherubim). Furthermore, no human could enter the inner sanctum and look upon the luminous divine glory. Even the high priest, who could enter only once a year, offered incense which formed a 'cloud' so thick that he could not see God's glorious appearance (Lev. 16:13). The 'cloud' itself could easily have been associated with the visible heaven that pointed beyond to the unseen heaven, where God dwelt. Finally, the ark itself was understood to be the footstool of God's heavenly throne (1 Chr. 28:2; Pss. 99:5; 132:7–8; Is.

66:1; Lam. 2:1). For example, 1 Chronicles 28:2 asserts that 'King David rose to his feet and said, "Listen to me, my brethren and my people; I had intended to build a permanent home for the ark of the covenant of the LORD and for the footstool of our God. So I had made preparations to build it."'

Hence, the ark is part of God's heavenly throne-room, and, appropriately, the space directly above the ark is empty. God cannot be seen, and no images of him are to be placed there, because he has no human form and his special glorious dwelling is primarily in heaven and not on earth (Poythress 1991: 15). Thus, the holy of holies was a representation of God's unseen heavenly dwelling in his temple amidst ministering angels and spirits (Is. 6:1–7; Ezek. 1; Rev. 4:1–11).[14]

Heavenly symbolism of the temple

The Old Testament highlights particularly the heavenly symbolism of the temple, both with respect to the visible and invisible heavens. One of the best examples of this is the account of the dedication of Solomon's temple. The 'cloud' that filled Israel's temple when it was completed and dedicated by Solomon (1 Kgs. 8:10–13; cf. 2 Chr. 5:13b – 6:2) may partly be associated with the clouds in the visible heavens that pointed beyond themselves to God's unseen heavenly dwelling place.[15]

Two different Hebrew words for 'cloud' are used in this passage, but they are generally synonymous. The repeated mention of the 'cloud' and that the temple was 'a lofty place' points more clearly to an attempt to identify it in some way with the heavens. 'Cloud' obviously refers elsewhere to a constituent part of the visible heavens or sky. For example, Job 26:8–9 says, 'He wraps up the waters in His clouds;/And the cloud does not burst under them./He obscures the face of the full moon,/And spreads His cloud over it' (cf. also Gen. 9:13–14, 16; Job 7:9). And just as 'lightning' is part of literal 'clouds' (Job 37:11, 15), so Ezekiel portrays God's theophanic 'glory' as 'radiance [like] a great cloud with fire flashing forth' and as 'the appearance of a rainbow in the clouds on a rainy day' (Ezek. 1:4, 28). That Ezekiel views such

---

[14] So also Poythress 1991:31, who cites also in this respect 1 Kgs. 8:30; Job 1:6; Ps. 89:7.

[15] That the visible heavens pointed beyond themselves to the unseen heavens is apparent from Dan. 7:13, where the 'Son of Man' approaches God's unseen heavenly presence 'with the *clouds of heaven*'; likewise, 2 Sam. 22:10: God 'bowed the heavens . . . and came down with thick darkness under his feet'.

heavenly descriptions of God's presence as occurring in the temple is also clear from the cloud that hides the divine presence in the temple (cf. 10:3–4).

The visible 'cloud' that filled the temple was certainly identified with the visible heaven but likely also pointed to the invisible heaven. The preceding references to the 'cloud' in Ezekiel's vision confirms this, since there the word refers both to a visible meteorological phenomenon and the invisible presence of God in the unseen heaven. Furthermore, it is well known that the same Hebrew word for 'heaven' in the Old Testament is used for both the seen and unseen dimensions.[16] The upper part of the visible cosmos came to represent God's dwelling place, pointing beyond the physical to the divine transcendence and an 'invisible spiritual created order' (cf. 2 Kgs. 6:17; Job 1:1, 16; Ps. 2:4; Zech. 3:1) (Lincoln 1981: 140–141). Thus, again the temple is associated with the physically created firmament and the invisible heavenly dwelling of God to which that firmament pointed.

The same luminescent 'cloud' mixed with darkness that filled Solomon's temple had also hovered over and covered Sinai and the tabernacle during Israel's wilderness wanderings, suggesting that the earlier forms of the temple were also reflective of or associated with the heavens.[17] Hence, the visible bright aspect of the clouds of the heavens came to be appropriate vehicles to express the invisible heavenly, radiant presence of God in the tabernacle and subsequent temple (Exod. 16:10; 40:35; Num. 16:42; Is. 4:5; Ezek. 1:28; 10:3–4).

Solomon's reference to his building of 'a lofty house' in 1 Kings 8:13 refers to an elevated dwelling. The word 'lofty' (*zĕbul*) occurs only three times elsewhere in the Old Testament, and always refers to the 'elevated places' in the visible heavens where the 'sun and moon stood' (Hab. 3:11) and to the invisible 'holy and glorious *elevated place*' where God 'looks down from heaven' (Is. 63:15).[18] It is this

---

[16] Poythress 1991: 17–18, who cites Ps. 19:1–6 as an example where the inaccessibility and majesty of the visible sky points to God's glory.

[17] For Sinai, cf. Exod. 19:16; 24:15–16; for the tabernacle, cf., e.g., Exod. 13:21–22; 14:19; note the 'cloud' descending and covering the tabernacle in Exod. 33:9; 40:35; Num. 9:15–16; 16:42; for the luminosity of the cloud at Sinai and the tabernacle, cf. respectively Exod. 19:16 and 14:20, 24; 40:38; Num. 9:15. For Sinai as a mountain-temple, see pp. 105–107.

[18] The only other usage is in Ps. 49:14, which refers to earth as an 'elevated place' above Sheol; in Qumran the word occurs four times, all pertaining to God's heavenly dwelling. The cloud in 1 Kgs. 8:12 is likely mixed with brightness and darkness, apparently like a dark thunder cloud containing lightning (like that on Sinai, e.g., Exod.

invisible place that Solomon sees being symbolized in 1 Kings 8 by the earthly temple. Accordingly, he describes the temple figuratively as being in the visible heavens, so that the bright clouds appropriately surround it.[19]

The reference to 'winged' figurines around the ark of the covenant in the above-cited 1 Kings passage (8:6–7) may add further to an upper atmospheric symbolism. This symbolism appears to have been enhanced in the tabernacle where its numerous curtains (including the veil before the holy of holies) were all made of the variegated colours resembling the sky ('blue and purple and scarlet material', Exod. 26:31) and had woven into them figures of flying 'cherubim' (i.e., winged bird-like creatures; so Exod. 26:1, 31; 36:8, 35). Apparently the 'scarlet' colour was intended to resemble the fiery colour of lightning and, perhaps of the sun, with the 'blue and purple' resembling sky blue and the dark blue of dark clouds.[20] So also the 'screen' for the 'gate of the court' and 'doorway of the tent' was to be made of 'blue and purple and scarlet material' (Exod. 26:36; 27:16; 36:37; 38:18). Even the 'loops' 'on the edge' of some of the curtains were to be of 'blue' (Exod. 36:11). Likewise, the priests were to cover all the furniture of the tabernacle with 'blue' material when dismantling the tabernacle for transport (Num. 4:5–13). All of the colours of these inner tabernacle furnishings were likely reproduced in Solomon's temple, since it was the permanent establishment of the mobile tabernacle and since the first-century historian Josephus testifies that the later Herodian temple of Jesus' day, modelled on Solomon's, contained the numerous curtains that the tabernacle also had (see *War* 5.210–214; *Ant.* 3.132, 183).

19:16; 20:18–21). In this respect, 1 Kgs. 8:53b (LXX) adds to the Hebrew text the following, evidently as an interpretative expansion of 1 Kgs. 8:12–13: 'Then spoke Solomon concerning the house, when he had finished building it – He [God] manifested the sun in the heaven; the Lord said he would dwell in darkness; build thou my house, a beautiful house for thyself to dwell in anew.'

[19] The Jews living in Qumran went so far as to believe that the heavenly light-sources, such as the moon, actually retired to God's unseen 'lofty' temple when they retreated from visible sight at dawn and shone out from it at night: 'When the lights of the holy vault [or lofty place = zĕbul] shine out, when they retire to the abode of glory; at the entry of the constellation in the days of the new moon . . . it is a great day for the Holy of Holies' (1QS 10.2–4 [Martinez 1994]). This Qumran passage may have been inspired by Ps. 19:4–5.

[20] More overtly, Josephus (*Ant.* 3.183) says the 'blue' of the 'tapestries' symbolized 'the air' (so also *War* 5.212), and Philo (*Vit. Mos.* 2.88) interprets 'dark blue' [hyakinthos] to be 'like the air, which is naturally black'.

Symbolism of the priest's robe in relation to the temple

It is apparent that aspects of the priest's robe contained cosmic symbolism. Like the tabernacle curtains, the various parts of the high priests' attire were also woven of 'blue and purple and scarlet material' because it was also to reflect the cosmos. The square shape of the breast-piece corresponded to the square shape (*tetragōnos*) of 'the holy place and temple', the 'altar', and the 'mercy seat' (see LXX of Exod. 27:1; 30:2; Ezek. 41:21; 43:16; and LXX [Alexandrinus] of Ezek. 43:17). Interestingly, the Greek Old Testament even applies the word 'four-square' to the high priest's 'breast piece of judgment' (Exod. 28:16; 36:16). If this symbolic identification of the priest with parts of the temple is correct, then it is natural that the priest's clothing was also of the same colour as the various inner furnishings of the temple (about 12 times parts of his attire are said to be of 'blue and purple and scarlet' and his robe was all 'blue', phrases also used to describe the curtains of the tabernacle; cf. also 'a blue cord' on the turban [Exod. 28:37; 39:31]).

I have argued in an earlier work that the jewels on the priest's breast-piece, which were a small replica of the holy of holies, symbolized the earthly or heavenly cosmos, and the same jewels are part of the new city-temple in Revelation 21.[21] Accordingly, one needs to picture the precious stones on the priest's breast-piece set within the larger background of the long blue robe as an apt model of the stars set within the cosmic tent of the dark bluish heavens. Correspondingly, the same scene on a larger scale was depicted with the seven 'luminaries' on the lampstand placed within the broader backdrop of the sky-coloured curtains covering the inside of the tent-like tabernacle. The seven lamps on the lampstand especially stood out in the holy place since the four thick curtains so thoroughly covered the tabernacle that no natural light would have come in unless the curtain at the entrance were pulled back (Longman 2001: 55). Both the priest and the tabernacle were designed to represent the creative work of God 'who stretches out the heavens like a curtain and spreads them out like a tent to dwell in', and 'who has created ... [the] host' of stars to hang in (Is. 40:22, 26; similarly, Ps. 19:4b–5a: in the 'heavens' God 'has placed a tent for the sun, which is as a bridegroom coming out of his chamber').

It is, in fact, discernible that there are broadly three sections of the priest's garment that resemble the three sections of the temple. First,

---

[21] See Beale 1999a: *in loc.*, 'The High Priest's Breastpiece', following the discussion of 21:18–20.

the outermost part at the bottom (the outer court), on which were sewn 'pomegranates of blue and purple and scarlet' along 'with variegated flowers'[22] represented the fertile earth. Secondly, the main body of the bluish robe (the holy place), within which and on the upper part of which are set the jewels, symbolized the stars that are set in the sky. Thirdly, the square ephod resembles the square holy of holies, within which were placed the Urim and Thumim, stones representing God's revelatory presence (the priest's crown with 'holy to the LORD' inscribed on it may represent the divine presence in heaven or above the ark in the temple's sanctuary that the ephod symbolized). Given all this symbolism, one can well understand the assertion in the *Letter of Aristeas* that anyone who saw the fully attired high priest 'would think he had come out of this world into another one' (99).

If the precious stones on the priest's breast correspond partly to the lamps on the lampstand, as suggested above, then this identifies them further with the heavenly luminaries, since we have seen that the lampstand lights are likewise identified with the heavenly stars. This link of the precious stones with the starry heavens may provide an important clue to the significance of the precious stones and metals that compose the temple itself. Why is the temple so heavily adorned with these extremely valuable and shiny materials? Before answering this question, it is important to highlight just how much the temple was adorned with these expensive items.

The 'foundation' of the temple building (containing the holy place and holy of holies) was laid with 'gold', 'silver', and 'precious stones': 'they quarried great stones, costly stones, to lay the foundation of the house' (1 Kgs. 5:17); 'and the inner sanctuary ... he overlaid ... with pure gold ... So Solomon overlaid the inside of the house with pure gold' (1 Kgs. 6:20–21). He also covered with gold the altar (1 Kgs. 6:20), the cherubim around the ark (1 Kgs. 6:28), the floor of the temple (1 Kgs. 6:30), and the engraved work on the temple doors (1 Kgs. 6:35; see similarly 2 Chr. 3 – 4). Indeed, '100,000 talents of gold and 1,000,000 talents of silver' were 'prepared' for the construction of the temple house (1 Chr. 22:14; likewise 1 Chr. 22:16; 29:2–7). First Chronicles 29:1–7 refers to 'gold ... silver ... onyx stones and inlaid stones, stones of antimony, and stones of various colors, and all kinds of precious stones' to be used for all the various parts, pieces of furniture, and utensils of the temple.[23]

---

[22] *Letter of Aristeas*, 96 adds the phrase 'with variegated flowers' to the biblical description.

[23] See 2 Chr. 3:6 also for 'precious stones and the gold'.

Thus, the same precious stones and metals used in the construction of the temple were also used in the fashioning of the priest's clothing (e.g., in Exod. 28), enhancing the connection between the two.[24] Furthermore, the same precious stones are used to describe the heavenly dwelling of God, further associating the same stones of the temple and of the priestly raiment with the heavenly sphere.[25]

How does the connection between the precious stones and the starry heavens provide an important clue to the significance of the precious stones and metals that were used to adorn the holy place and holy of holies? It is likely that part of the reason for so many precious stones and metals in one place is that they were intended to remind one of the luminous splendour of the starry sky, which, we have seen, itself pointed to God's transcendent glorious dwelling place that was concealed from human sight (indeed, even today one of the main uses of our English word 'metallic' is to indicate that which is 'shiny, glossy, gleaming, lustrous', etc.).[26]

Another aspect of the stones on the priest's robe also suggests that the function of such gems in the temple is to reflect divine, heavenly glory. God commands Moses to 'make holy garments for Aaron ... for *glory and for beauty*' (Exod. 28:2; cf. likewise 28:40). The description of the garments (Exod. 28:4–43) is dominated by descriptions of precious stones or of gold cloth or metal that adorned the robes.[27] Certainly, therefore, the goal of the gold and stone-work of the robe was included in the purpose of reflecting the 'glory and beauty', presumably of God. The word for 'glory' (*kābôd*) is the typical word for God's glorious theophanic revelation of himself to Israel at Sinai, at the tabernacle and at the end of time. The word for 'beauty' (*tip'ārâ*)

---

[24] 1 Chr. 29 mentions only gold, antimony and onyx specifically, whereas Exod. 28 mentions explicitly by name each of the various metals and gems. Nevertheless, Chronicles does mention 'inlaid stones ... and stones of various colors, and all kinds of precious stones', which probably included all the specific stones noted in Exod. 28.

[25] Cf. 'sapphire' as a part of the heavenly temple (Exod. 24:10; Ezek. 1:26; 10:1; Rev. 21:19), likely included in the earthly temple (1 Chr. 29:2), and a facet of the priest's clothing (Exod. 28:18; 39:11); cf. onyx as a part of the priestly clothing (Exod. 25:7; 28:9, 20; 35:9, 27; 39:6, 13) and of the temple (1 Chr. 29:2), though not mentioned explicitly in the heavenly visions; cf. 'jasper' as a part of the priest's attire (Exod. 28:20; 39:13) and of the appearance of the heavenly temple (Rev. 4:3; 21:11, 18–19), the latter of which also suggests that 'jasper' (or a stone essentially identical to it) was included among the precious stones of Solomon's temple; cf. 'beryl' as part of the priestly apparel (Exod. 28:20; 39:13) and of the structure of the heavenly temple (Ezek. 1:16; Rev. 21:20; cf. Dan. 10:6), which shows again that it was presumably included among the 'precious stones' of Solomon's temple.

[26] E.g., see Rodale 1978: 726.

[27] Of the 39 verses, 24 include such description.

is less often used. Not insignificantly, in the midst of a description of the gems and valuable metals composing the temple (2 Chr. 3:4–10), this word is chosen to explain why the precious stones were so heavily used in constructing Solomon's temple: Solomon 'adorned the house with precious stone for the purpose of *beauty*' (2 Chr. 3:6).[28] The common use of this word for the purpose of the stones on the priest's clothing and the stones of the temple further indicates the same function of the two: they were to reflect glorious beauty.

Interestingly, this word 'beauty' is also associated with description of the heavenly light-sources as metaphors for God's beauteous glory. The Isaiah 60 prophecy of Israel's restoration in the new creation is significant in this respect, since it combines the mention of precious metals in relation to 'beautifying' the temple and God, whose lustrous beauty is compared to the light of the sun and moon. God's end-time glorious presence over Israel is described as 'light' that 'has risen' in the midst of 'darkness', so that Israel might experience 'the brightness of ... rising' (Is. 60:1–3). At this time, the nations will bring riches (including 'gold') in order to 'beautify' God's 'glorious house' (60:5–7), and they will bring 'their silver and their gold with them, for the name of the LORD your God [i.e., the temple where God dwelt][29] ... because *he has beautified* you' (i.e., caused his splendorous beauty to reflect on Israel; 60:9). The 'wealth of the nations' will pour in to Israel '*To beautify* the place of My sanctuary .../And *make* the place of My feet *glorious*' (Is. 60:11–13).[30] Isaiah 60:16–17 reiterates the same theme: 'You will also suck the milk of nations ... Instead of bronze I will bring gold, and instead of iron I will bring silver', which, again, contributes to the goal of divine 'beautification' (Is. 60:19: 'you will have God ... for your *beauty*'). However, instead of explicitly viewing this divine beauty as being centred in the end-time temple, as earlier in the chapter, it is spoken of as replacing the sun and the moon and shining on Israel in a greater way than these former light-sources had ever done:

[28] Likewise, part of the purpose of the elaborate description of the precious stones and metals used in the temple in 1 Chr. 29:2–8 is twice stated to be for Yahweh's 'beauty' (29:11, 13; similarly, cf. 1 Chr. 22, where the verbal form in 22:5 occurs).

[29] So also in Hag. 2:7–9, God will bring the 'wealth of all nations' to 'fill this house with glory ... silver ... and the gold ... The latter glory of this house will be greater than the former'.

[30] Note here the combined use of 'beautify' and 'make glorious', as in Exod. 28:2 (though verbal forms of the respective noun forms found in Exod. 28:2 occur; verbal forms of 'beauty' appear also in 60:7, 9).

[19]'No longer will you have the sun for light by day,
Nor for brightness will the moon give you light;
But you will have the LORD for an everlasting light,
And your God for your *beauty*.
[20]'Your sun will set no more,
Neither will your moon wane;
For you will have the LORD for an everlasting light,
And the days of your mourning will be finished.'

(Is. 60:19–20)

Here we find God's 'beauty' explicitly compared to the splendour of the sun and moon, though his brightness is incomparably greater, so that the chapter ends with astronomical metaphors as it began (note 'light', 'brightness', and 'rising' in 60:1–3). And, again, the result of this will be that God 'may be beautified' (verbal form of *tip'ārâ*; 60:21). Thus, Isaiah 60 repeatedly refers to God's 'beauty' being expressed as a supernova-like sun and moon primarily in his eschatological sanctuary and outwards, *toward which the bringing in of precious metals contributes*.[31] The main light sources of the old creation were representations, though only faintly, of the glorious light that God would shine in the new creation.

It is unlikely to be a coincidence that the precious metals of the new creational temple listed in Revelation 21:18–20, which allude partly to the jewels of the priestly attire in Exodus 28:17–20 (see Beale 1999a: 1080–1088), function to reflect God's glory (especially in light of 4:3, 9–11 and 21:11), and that they are directly followed by allusions to the same Isaiah texts crucial to the directly preceding discussion (Is. 60:3, 5, 11, 19) (see Beale 1999a: 1093–1101). Revelation 21 makes the same connections that we have pursued within the Old Testament itself. Accordingly, Isaiah appears to have considered that Israel's earthly temple could be called 'beautiful' (Is. 64:11) because

---

[31] In this context, the wealth and valuable metals ultimately find their fulfilment in more than physical metallic reality in a glorious new creation, whereby the ultimate wealth they bring is themselves as worshippers and reflectors of God's end-time glorious presence (on which, see Beale 1999a: 1093–1101, for how Is. 60:3, 5, 11, 19 is fulfilled in the new cosmos). The word 'beauty' is also contextually associated with astronomical phenomena in Is. 62:1, 3 ('brightness . . . a torch that is burning') and Ps. 110:3 ('Thy people will volunteer . . . in the *beauty* of holiness, from the womb of the dawn'). Ps. 96:5–9 strikingly combines elements of the heavens, beauty, the temple, and priestly attire: directly following mention of the created 'heavens', it says, 'splendor and majesty are before Him, strength and *beauty* are in His *sanctuary*', followed by a command to 'bring an offering into His courts' and to 'worship the LORD in the splendor of holiness' (NASB renders 'holy attire').

it was a reflection of God's 'beautiful habitation' that was in 'heaven' (Is. 63:15), which would eventually descend to fill the earth with divine glory (Is. 64:1–3; 66:1–2)[32] and of which Revelation is the fuller explanation.

The following considerations further support the conclusion that the metals in the temple were intended to recall the starry heavens and, ultimately, the luminous glory of God to which the stars themselves pointed. First, the precious materials adorn only the temple house proper and not any part of the courtyard. This fits with our identification of the holy place with the starry sky and inner room there as the unseen heavenly domain. On the other hand, the only metal used in the courtyard is the less expensive and less radiant bronze (e.g., the altar is made of bronze), which is also the only area of the temple complex that common Israelite worshippers could enter (Poythress 1991: 16).

Secondly, Scripture itself describes part of God's glory in his heavenly palace or temple through portrayals of precious stones. The first such depiction occurs at the Sinai theophany: when Moses and the elders of Israel saw God in the cloud at the top of Mount Sinai, 'under his feet there appeared to be constructed tile-work of sapphire, *as clear as the body of the heavens*'[33] (Exod. 24:10; cf. 19:16–20). Here we find a conglomeration of precious stone describing the divine environment of God's heavenly temple that had temporarily descended to the top of Sinai (and we shall propose in a following chapter that Sinai was conceived of as a temple).[34] Furthermore, this gem-like pavement is said to be 'as clear [or 'pure' blue] as the body of the heavens'. Thus, the blue colour of the stone is comparable to the majestic appearance of the heavens (see also Cassuto 1967: 314).

Likewise Ezekiel's description of the heavenly dimension that corresponded to the earthly temple includes virtually the same reference as found in the Exodus 24 passage: 'now above the vault of heaven [firmament] that was over the heads' of the living cherubim 'there was something resembling a throne, like sapphire in appearance', which itself was under a human-like depiction of God (Ezek. 1:26). Ezekiel 10:1 has an almost identical description, though there 'something like a sapphire stone ... resembling a throne' was not

---

[32] For discussion of which, see ch. 4. This discussion of 'beauty' in relation to precious stones on the priestly attire and in the temple has been inspired by the discussion of Kline 1980: 43.

[33] My translation of the Hebrew. LXX reads, 'under his feet there was the likeness of a sapphire slab, and it was just as the appearance of the firmament of heaven in purity'.

[34] On which see ch. 3.

above but '*in* the vault of heaven that was over the heads of the cherubim'. Ezekiel 1:27–28 describes the divine figure itself 'like glowing metal that looked like fire … and there was a radiance around Him. As the appearance of the rainbow in the clouds on a rainy day, so was the appearance of the surrounding radiance. Such was the appearance of the likeness of the glory of the LORD.' It is clear that the sapphire is not only directly compared to the appearance of the heavens but is associated with another startling feature of the sky: the brilliant colours of a rainbow reflective of the sun. Furthermore, the sapphire is part of the immediate heavenly surroundings that, like the 'glowing metal', reflected the radiance of the divine glory.[35] The precious stones in Revelation also describe the radiant glory of God's dwelling in the heavenly temple (Rev. 4:3; 21:11, 18–20).

Therefore, though every part of the preceding analysis about the astronomical significance of the precious metals and stones will not necessarily be equally persuasive, it is plausible to understand that the gleaming stones and metals composing the temple and the priest's garments functioned to remind one of the sparkling stars in the heavens, which themselves pointed to God's glorious presence in his invisible heavenly temple-court.

Judaism's view of the symbolism of the temple

Jewish interpreters of the Old Testament reflect on the temple and understand it and develop it in ways that are similar to and consistent with our above analysis. What was more implicit in the Old Testament portrayal of the temple becomes explicitly drawn out by commentators in Judaism.

Symbolism of particular parts of the temple

Somewhat similar to our above analysis of the symbolism of the three parts of the temple, Josephus understood the tripartite structure of the tabernacle to signify 'the earth [= outer court] and the sea [= inner court], since these … are accessible to all; but the third portion [= holy of holies] he reserved for God alone, because heaven also is inaccessible to men' (*Ant.* 3.181; cf. 3.123). Likewise, in support of the

---

[35] Ezek. 1:16 also refers to the 'workmanship' of the 'wheels' that accompanied the cherubim to be 'like sparkling beryl'. The words 'workmanship' and 'sapphire' also describe the heavenly environment of the theophanic presence in Exod. 24:10, which links the Ezekiel portrayal even more closely to the earlier Exodus appearance.

idea that the outer court was associated with the visible sea, *Midrash Rabbah Numbers* 13:19 says, 'the court ... encompassed the Tabernacle as the sea encompasses the world'.[36] In support of the idea that the outer court represented the earthly habitation, one of the early Aramaic Bibles says that Moses was to 'set up the courtyard round about for the sake of the merits of the fathers of the world who surround the people of the house of Israel round about' (Exod. 40:8 of *Tg. Pseudo-Jonathon Exodus*).

Early Judaism also makes explicit the biblical implication about the lampstand by directly asserting that the seven lamps on the lamp-stand symbolized the planets (Josephus, *Ant.* 3.145; *War* 5.217; Philo, *Rer. Div. Her.* 221–225; *Vit. Mos.* 2.102–105; *Quaest. Exod.* 2.73–81; Clement of Alexandria, *Stromata*, 5.6) or heaven (Philo, *Rer. Div. Her.* 227). These lamps are also equated with the 'lights in the expanse of heaven' from Genesis 1:14–16.[37]

In addition, Josephus and Philo discuss a number of ways in which the tabernacle or temple, or parts of it, symbolically reflect the cosmos (Philo, *Vit. Mos.* 2.71–145; cf. *Plant.* 47–50; *Spec. Leg.* 1.66; Josephus, *Ant.* 3.123, 179–187). They also observe that the outer veil of the holy place and curtains of the tabernacle and temple were made to reflect the four elements of the cosmos: earth, air, water and fire (Philo, *Quaest. Exod.* 2.85; *Vit. Mos.* 2.87–88; Josephus, *War* 5.212–214; *Ant.* 3.183).[38] Furthermore, the 'tapestry' hanging over the outer entrance into the temple 'typified the universe' and on it 'was portrayed a panorama of the heavens' (Josephus, *War* 5.210–214). Indeed, all of the curtains in the temple contained 'colours seeming so exactly to resemble those that meet the eye in the heavens' (Josephus, *Ant.* 3.132). Likewise, the veil symbolizes the airy covering of the earth that separates the changeable part of the world beneath from the unchanging heavenly region (Philo, *Quaest. Exod.* 2.91). The curtains of the temple were woven of things

---

[36] Likewise cf. a saying attributed to Rabbi Pinhas ben Ya'ir, a talmudic sage of the second century AD: 'The house of the Holy of Holies is made to correspond to the highest heaven. The outer holy house was made to correspond to the earth. And the courtyard was made to correspond to the sea' (cited in Patai 1967: 108); *b. Sukkah* 51b says the variegated blue and white marbled walls of the temple were comparable to sea waves. There is also depiction of a tripartite heavenly temple like that of the earthly Jerusalem in *1 Enoch 14*.

[37] *Tg. Pseudo-Jonathon Exodus* 39:37 and 40:4; *Midrash Rabbah Numbers* 12:13; 15:7; cf. Keel 1985:171–176 and Goppelt 1972:256–257.

[38] Likewise, *Tg. Numbers* 24:6; *Midrash Rabbah Exodus* 35:6; *Midrash Rabbah Numbers* 4:13; *Midrash Rabbah Song of Songs* 3:10 § 4. Cf. *3 Enoch 45*, where the curtain 'before the Holy One' had printed on it all the events throughout world history.

that resembled the elements of which the world was made, since the created world itself was the macrocosmic temple after which Israel's small temple was modelled (Philo, *Quaest. Exod.* 2.85). These observations support the larger point strongly suggested in the Old Testament descriptions that the temple is a small-scale image of the entire universe, especially the visible and invisible heavenly dimensions.

In reflecting on the overall significance of the tabernacle, Josephus says, 'every one of these objects [of the tabernacle] is intended to recall and represent the nature of the universe' (*Ant.* 3.180).

Symbolism of the priest's robe in relation to the temple

Just as Judaism further developed the Old Testament perspective on the heavenly significance of the temple curtains, so likewise do Jewish commentators develop further the biblical notion of the meaning of the priest's attire. Both Josephus and Philo understand the jewels on the priestly breast-piece to be symbolic of the twelve constellations.[39] Josephus (*War* 4.324) affirms that priests are referred to as leading the 'cosmic worship' (*tēs kosmikēs thrēskeias*). Likewise, both Josephus and Philo understand the garments of the high priest to symbolize the whole cosmos (Philo, *Vit. Mos.* 2.117–126, 133–135, 143; Josephus, *Ant.* 3.180, 183–187). For example, Philo says explicitly that the high priest 'represents the world' and is a 'microcosm' (or 'small world', *brachys kosmos*; so *Vit. Mos.* 2.135). In addition, he states that the priest's 'long robe and ephod' were 'woven ... to represent the universe' (*Vit. Mos.* 2.143), and the 'sacred vesture was designed' to be 'a copy of the universe' (Philo, *Spec. Leg.* 1.95). The 'garments' that the priest 'puts on as raiment are the world' (*Fug.* 110) and 'is a copy and replica of the whole heaven' (*Som.* 1.215).

Other sectors of Judaism held virtually the same view of the priest's clothing. *Wisdom of Solomon* 18:24 (2nd century BC – 1st century AD) likewise understands the high priest's garment and jewels to be symbolic of the entire cosmos: 'in the long garment was the whole world, and in the four rows of the stones was the glory of the fathers'. The reference to the 'glory of the fathers' is also an allusion to the blessing upon Abraham's seed that would result in blessing to the whole world (so also 18:22). One of the Aramaic translations of Exodus 28:17 and 39:10 affirms a cosmic symbolism of the stones: the

---

[39] Philo, *Spec. Leg.* 1.84–94; *Vit. Mos.* 2.122–126, 133; *Quaest. Exod.* 2.107–114; *Som.* 1.214–215 (cf. also *Fug.* 184–185); Josephus, *Ant.* 3.186–187; cf. Clement of Alexandria, *Stromata* 5.6.

'four rows of precious gems [were] corresponding to the four corners of the world'.[40]

Comparable to the emblematic meaning of the curtains of the tabernacle and temple, Philo held that the priest's 'gown is all of violet, and is thus an image of the air; for the air is naturally black' (*Vit. Mos.* 2.118). Josephus similarly says the 'blue' of the 'high priest's tunic ... signifies' the 'arch of heaven' and his 'head-dress appears ... to symbolize heaven, being blue' (*Ant.* 3.184, 186).

Therefore, early Judaism clearly understood the priests' clothing to be a microcosm of the entire creation. The most likely reason for this is because they also believed the priestly attire was a microcosm of the temple itself, which was also a small model of the entire cosmos.

Conclusion: symbolism of the temple in the Old Testament and Judaism

Taking all of the preceding data into consideration, the three parts of Israel's temple represented the three parts of the cosmos: the outer court symbolized the visible earth (both land and sea, the place where humans lived); the holy place primarily represented the visible heavens (though there was also garden symbolism); the holy of holies stood for the invisible heavenly dimension of the cosmos where God dwelt[41] (apparently not even the high priest who entered there once a year could see because of the cloud from the incense which he was to put on the fire; cf. Lev. 16:32).[42] As we will see more fully later, this understanding of the temple as a small model of the entire cosmos is part of a larger perspective in which the temple pointed forward to a huge worldwide sanctuary in which God's presence would dwell in every part of the cosmos. The conception also is a linchpin for better understanding why John later pictures the entire new heavens and earth to be one mammoth temple in which God dwells as he had formerly dwelt in the holy of holies.

[40] *Tg. Pseudo-Jonathon.* See Patai 1967: 112–113, for a helpful synoptic overview of Josephus's various cosmic perspectives of the temple; see also Koester 1989: 59–63, for a synoptic overview of both Josephus and Philo on the same topic.

[41] See more generally Spatafora (1997: 31), who proposes only a twofold symbolism: outer court = the earth, and sanctuary proper = the heaven (he makes no distinction between the visible and invisible dimension of the heavens).

[42] Philo (*Spec. Leg.* 1.72) expands on the Leviticus text by saying, 'the great quantity of vapour which this naturally gives forth covers everything around it, beclouds the eyesight and prevents it from being able to penetrate to any distance'.

This cosmic perspective of the temple is discernible in the Old Testament, and it is developed in Judaism. Before concluding this section, a word is in order about the evidence adduced from the Jewish authors Philo and Josephus. While it is true that Philo and Josephus had varying interpretations of the temple symbolism, their views intersect at significant points. Furthermore, they both testify to a general cosmological understanding of the temple held by mainstream contemporary Jewish thought, especially where their views overlapped. Philo himself says that his symbolic understanding of the lampstand was generally acknowledged during his time (*Quaest. Exod.* 2.78; cf. also *Rer. Div. Her.* 224).[43] That their perspective was probably not idiosyncratic is suggested also by recalling that other Jewish sources testify to the same cosmic viewpoint (the earliest being Wisdom, followed by the Targum and then the profusion of references in the later midrashic and Talmudic literature). Though every one of their detailed symbolic identifications is unlikely to be correct, their approach generally represented an accurate understanding of the Old Testament temple's emblematic meaning.

Among the admittedly few *explicit* biblical passages supporting the cosmic temple thesis (Levenson 1984: 289–298), Levenson offers Isaiah 6:3: 'Holy, Holy, Holy, is the LORD of hosts, The whole earth is full of His glory.' He contends that this 'glory' is the divine radiance by which God manifests his presence in the temple. The significance of Isaiah's vision of the luminescent smoke filling the temple (6:4) is explained by the seraphim to mean that the whole world manifests Yahweh's cultic heavenly glory that has unique correspondence in the earthly temple. Isaiah 6:3b could well be rendered 'the fullness of the whole earth is his glory' (an alternative rendering proposed by Levenson and the NASB), that is, the entire world reflects God's glory in the temple.[44] In the same way that God's glory (*kābôd*) filled both the tabernacle and temple at the conclusion of their construction, Isaiah 6:3 affirms with the same terms that God's glory fills the entire cosmos (Levenson 1984: 289). While Levenson grants that the biblical evidence is 'muted and implicit', the Old Testament 'evidence is not quite so lacking as one would think at first glance' (Levenson 1984: 286).

---

[43] See Levenson 1988: 96–99 for additional striking examples of the cosmic symbolism of the tabernacle or temple in rabbinic Judaism; see also Kline (1980: 41–47) and Poythress (1991: 13–35), who, as modern commentators, make many similar observations about the temple and the priestly garments.

[44] Though Levenson later more speculatively interprets this to mean 'the world in its fulness is the temple' (1984: 296).

In the light of all the above evidence, R. E. Clements's conclusion about similar evidence is cautious and judicious:

> Not all of these supposed symbolic references of features of the temple are convincing, but the essential claim that the temple and its furnishings did possess cosmic, or naturalistic, symbolism must be upheld. Such features were designed to stress the divine power over the created order, and to establish the temple as a source of blessing for the land and people of Israel. The underlying idea was that the temple was a microcosm of the macrocosm, so that the building gave visual expression to the belief in Yahweh's dominion over the world ... We need not suppose that every Israelite worshipper was conscious of this ... Thus the temple building ... signified the cosmic rule of God who was worshipped there ...[45]

I have tried to discuss the symbolic meaning of the temple as a miniature model of the cosmos by observing features of the structure itself and by tracing the use of words and concepts about the temple that occur elsewhere in the Old Testament in other contexts. As Vern Poythress has concluded at the end of his study of the temple, 'we must of course recognize that some associations and connections are more obvious than others, and that we may possibly be wrong about some details. But the overall picture emerges clearly' (Poythress 1991: 39).

Israel's temple in the light of the Ancient Near Eastern view of the earthly temple as a reflection of the heavenly or cosmic temple

Some scholars like de Vaux (1965: 328–329) allege that early Judaism's explicit cosmic understanding of the temple was a late

---

[45] Clements 1965: 67; see also his larger discussion (pp. 64–75), where especially he cites texts from the Psalms underscoring God's rule from the temple; e.g., Ps. 11:4, 'The LORD is in His holy temple, the LORD's throne is in heaven.' Levenson gives the same qualified assessment as Clements that the temple was conceived as an institution representing the cosmos (1984: 286). The assessments of Clements and Levenson are partly a response to R. de Vaux who concludes that in the Bible there is 'feeble support for these theories' about the cosmological significance of the temple (1965: 328; see Levenson 1988: 82, for further response to de Vaux). He was anticipated a century earlier by Fairbairn (1863a: 220), who asserted that a cosmological view of Israel's temple 'is never once distinctly brought out' in the OT.

allegorical development. A good response to this may be found not only in the evidence from the Old Testament itself but also the observation that Ancient Near Eastern archaeology and texts portray ancient temples as microcosms of heavenly temples or of the universe in a manner similar to that of the Old Testament.[46] It is now widely known that archaeological ruins and texts from the Ancient Near East portray ancient temples as small models of heavenly temples or of the universe conceived of as a temple.

As noted in the introduction to this chapter, we should not think that Israel's temple was like her pagan neighbours because she merely copied the religious traditions around her. The likeness should be viewed, at least, from two perspectives. First, the similarity is intended at times to be a protest statement that, while the pagan nations think that they have cornered the market on divine revelation from their gods who dwell in their temples, in fact, their gods are false and their temples purely idolatrous institutions, which are really the den of demons (Deut. 32:17; Ps. 106:37; 1 Cor. 10:19–20). From another angle, it is appropriate to ask whether or not there was anything in ancient pagan religion and its institutions that resembled the truth about the true God and his designs for humanity. Certainly, there was not special revelation that these nations had received in order that they would come into saving relation to the true God. Nevertheless, just as the image of God is not erased but distorted in unbelieving humanity, it is plausible that some of the affinities in ancient pagan beliefs and religious institutions to that of Israel's may be due to the fact that they are garbled, shadowy representations about the being of the biblical God and of his design for his dwelling place.

Reminding ourselves about these perspectives, we proceed to investigate the Ancient Near Eastern beliefs about the temples that housed their gods.

General symbolism of the temple

One of the best examples of cosmic symbolism of temples is the notion in the *Enuma Elish* 6.113, where it is said concerning the building of Marduk's temple, 'He shall make on earth the counterpart of what he brought to pass in heaven.'[47] Likewise, the Egyptian Pharaoh Thutmose III restored a temple for the god Amon and made it 'like the

---

[46] See, e.g., Hurowitz 1992: 335–337; Meyers 1992b: 359–360; Keel 1985: 171–176 (cf. also 113–115); Levenson 1984: 285–286; Niehaus, forthcoming: ch. 5; and Fletcher-Lewis 1997: 159, n. 47.

[47] Following the translation of Foster in Hallo and Lawson-Younger 1997: 402.

heavens' (Breasted 1906: 2:239 §601; see also 240 §604). And Ramses III (1195–1164 BC) affirmed about his god: 'I made for thee an august house in Nubia ... the likeness of the heavens' (Breasted 1906: 4:123 §218; see also 2:240 §604). The same Pharaoh said of an Amon temple, 'I made for thee an august palace ... like the great house of [the god] Atum which is in heaven.'[48] It was not unusual for Egyptian temples to be called 'heaven' on earth (see Keel 1985: 172 for several examples).

One of the earliest Mesopotamian accounts of a temple being closely associated with the heavens is that found in the commemoration of King Gudea's building and dedication of a temple in Lagash for the god Ningirsu (c. 2112–2004 BC). 'The building of the temple' was done 'according to its holy star(s)' (Averbeck 2000: 421) and the builders 'were making the temple grow (high) like a mountain range; making it float in mid-heaven like a cloud ...' (428). The new temple was like 'brilliant moonlight ... shining. It illuminated the land, (and) ... rivaled the newborn Suen (the moon god)' (430). This is a theme that spans the centuries in the ancient world. Almost two millennia later, in a hymn to Mar, the god of the kingdom of Rashu and Arashu (near Babylonia and Elam, third century BC), there is the exhortation 'Oh, let them build, in heaven, your house, concealed, with stars.'[49] Similarly, the Sumerian *Keš Temple Hymn* portrays the 'temple, at its top rising like the sun, at its bottom setting like the moon', and it refers to the 'temple' as that 'which sketches the outlines of heaven and earth' (lines 50 [cf. 87], 5, in Sjöberg et al. 1969: 170, 172, 176).

The most explicit Old Testament parallel to these references is Psalm 78:69, noted earlier: 'And He built His sanctuary like the heights,/Like the earth which He has founded *forever* [or from eternity].' Similarly, Solomon's description of the temple is quite similar to that of King Gudea's temple, which was clearly compared to the heavens and its light sources: 'the LORD has said that He would dwell in the thick cloud. I have surely built Thee a lofty house' (1 Kgs. 8:12–13; recall the comparable portrayal of the builders of Gudea's temple, who 'were making the temple grow (high) ... making it float in mid-heaven like a cloud'). Like Israel's temple, in some way the temples of Marduk, Amon and other gods were designed to symbolize not merely heaven but the entire cosmos.

---

[48] Breasted 1906: 4:115 §192; see directly below for similar phraseology concerning Egyptian temples being made in 'the likeness of the heaven' (with respect to the temples built by Thutmose III, Ramses I and Seti I).

[49] Steiner 1997: 315; the hymn was likely composed by exiles from Rashu, living in Egypt.

Symbolism of particular parts of the temple

Not only were temples as a whole designed to portray the cosmos, but various parts of earthly temples were made to resemble aspects of the entire earth, conceived of as a huge cosmic temple. For instance, the arboreal lampstand of Israel's temple was analogous to the portraits of and actual presence of trees in ancient temples that were viewed as 'cosmic trees', symbolizing the life-essence of the entire world. In particular, taken together with other cultic appurtenances of cosmic symbolism, the tree image pointed to the temple as 'the cosmic center of the universe, at the place where heaven and earth converge and thus from where God's control over the universe is effected'.[50] The metaphorical picture is that of a huge tree atop a cosmic mountain whose height reaches heaven, whose branches encompass the earth, and whose roots sink down to the lowest parts of the earth.[51] This tree was the central life-giving force for the entire creation (there is portrayal of such trees in Dan. 4; Ezek. 17; 19; 31).[52]

Similarly, the bronze 'sea' basin in the courtyard of Israel's temple finds striking correspondence to ancient temples of the Levant, which also have artificial replicas of seas, symbolizing either the chaotic forces stilled by the god or the waters of life at the cosmic centre.[53] In still other respects ancient temples reflected cosmic symbolism.[54] Temples were symbolically the 'embodiment of the cosmic mountain' representing the original hillock first emerging from the primordial waters at the beginning of creation; these waters themselves were symbolized in temples together with fertile trees receiving life from such waters.[55]

The names of various Mesopotamian temples also express specific

---

[50] Meyers 1992: 6:359–360; 1976: e.g., 169–172, 177, 180; see Terrien 1970: 318 for additional sources supporting this idea.

[51] For actual representations of cosmic trees on mountains from oriental seals, see Henning von der Osten 1934: 106–109.

[52] On which see citation and further discussion below (pp. 126–129).

[53] Meyers 1992a: 1060–1061. Gudea, king of Lagash, furnished the temple of Eninnum with a limestone basin, decorated with designs of heavenly vases pouring water down to the earth (Frankfort 1954: 490). Quite interestingly, Marduk's temple, Esagil, is said in *Enuma Elish* 6.62 to be 'the counterpart of Apsu' (the cosmic subterranean waters) (see Horowitz 1998: 122–123 for this translation and discussion).

[54] E.g., see Lundquist 1983: 205–219; 1984b: 33–55; the latter showing how the ANE notion is reflected in Isaiah's description of Israel's temple.

[55] So Lundquist 1984a: 53–76, on which see other relevant secondary sources cited. Also, see Janowski 2001: 229–260 for a survey in Mesopotamia and Egypt of temples that were designed to depict the cosmos and 'heaven on earth', as well as the primeval hill that rose out of the ancient chaos sea (see also his relevant bibliography in this respect).

notions about their 'cosmological place and function' and hence symbolic significance (George 1993: 59). There are many examples of temples repeatedly being called such names as 'House like Heaven', 'House of Heaven and Underworld', 'House, Bond of the Land', 'Apsu ['fresh water or sea']-House', 'House of the Mountains', 'House of the Pure New Moon', etc.[56] That 'Apsu' was 'appointed ... for shrines' (*Enuma Elish* 1.76) suggests that cultic places typically were intended to derive their sacred water from rivers but likely also that temples were to be closely associated and symbolically identified with cosmic water.

One of the famous Mesopotamian inscriptions, portraying the Babylonian King Nabuapaliddin entering a temple, combines some of the prominent symbolic elements noted so far in identifying the temple with the cosmos: the seven main light-sources seen by the naked eye (sun, moon, Venus, and four other planets), a palm pillar and an ocean (Keel 1985: 172–174). Similarly, a wall painting from Mari pictures a temple containing trees, four cherubim, two mountains at its base, four streams and plants growing out of the streams (Keel 1985: 142–143). There is thus abundant evidence from the ancient world that temples symbolized the cosmos in various ways.

Temples in the Ancient Near East also generally exhibited the same three-part structure as found in Israel's temple,[57] often with the similar symbolic significance: outer court = the visible sea and earth where humans live; an inner court inside a building = the visible heavens (and also garden terrain); and a holy of holies = the dwelling of the god. For example, Egyptian cult complexes from the New Kingdom period (1570 BC) onwards exhibited an increasing gradation in sacredness beginning with the outer court and proceeding to a zone of greater holiness and then climaxing in an inner womb-like sanctuary. For the Egyptians 'the temple was ... the cosmos in microcosm'.[58] The

---

[56] George 1993: 63–161, where a profusion of examples are listed; see also Horowitz 1998: 122–123 for a similar reference in the *Enuma Elish* 6.55–68.

[57] See Mazar 1992: 161–187 for examples of tripartite temple structures. If the porch ('*ûlām*) is considered a separate section, then, including the courtyard, Solomon's temple and some of the other examples of temples would have four sections. See n. 70 for further discussion. Cf. also Frankfort (1954: 107, plates 12 and 154), who shows examples of tripartite temples.

[58] Shafer 1997: 5, on which see also Finnestad (1997: 203, 212, 215), who also discerns a broader cosmic bipartite structure in later Egyptian temples. Though Finnestad focuses on a later stage of Egyptian temples (from c. 323 BC onwards), his evidence for the most part is in continuity with that of earlier temples: e.g., he says, 'what scholarship has to say about the conceptual framework of Egyptian temples has in large part been deduced from the late temple's lavish source material and its extensive reflection of earlier traditions' (1997: 202; see also, e.g., pp. 185, 194).

outer court had its outer wall constructed of mud bricks from the Nile that were patterned to look like waves of sea or lake water. There was also a pond or small lake for ceremonial washing, representing primeval waters (Wilkinson 2000: 72). There were scenes on the gateways of the Pharaoh's victories over enemies and of his skill in hunting, typical scenes of the world and the king's rule over it. All Egyptians, regardless of societal rank, could come into this outer section, as was also the case in Israel's temple courtyard (this likely included women,[59] who were later sequestered into an additional court outside the original outer court in Herod's redevelopment of the temple).

The second zone of sacredness in Egyptian temples was ornamented with solar images. The two trapezoidal pylon towers forming the gateway leading into it symbolized the peaks of mountains that were on the eastern horizon where the sun rose daily (could this be the symbolism of the two mammoth pillars leading into the Israelite temple's holy place? See 1 Kgs. 7:15–22). Battle and hunting scenes were on the inside of the outer courtyard wall and on the external side of the gate leading into the second court. All of these images were transitional indicators between the earthly symbolism of the outer region to that of the next inner sphere, which apparently symbolized the visible heavens (stars, moon and sun were also inscribed on ceilings, though whether this included the most holy sanctum is not clear).[60] Likewise, the east–west orientation of the axial path, which led to the innermost sanctum, signified the daily circuit of the sun and had solar images along its route. The entire temple complex also symbolized the horizon, where the sun rose and set.

Intriguingly, like the holy place in Solomon's temple, so the second section of Egyptian temples contained garden imagery: bases of walls symbolized the swamp, columns represented plants, ceilings signified the sky, and the floors the earth.[61] The temple façade had designs of lily and papyrus plants and its columns were adorned with images of palms, papyrus, lotus and reeds.[62] If the two big columns at the outer porch of the holy place did not symbolize mountains at the horizon, then, in the light of the Mesopotamian and Assyrian

[59] Which is implied by Ezra 10:1 and Exod. 35:22, 25, 26, 29, and especially Exod. 38:8.

[60] Finnestad 1997: 204. See Wilkinson (2000: 76), who notes that ceilings were 'decorated with stars and flying birds' in order to symbolize the heavens.

[61] This paragraph and the preceding on Egypt are mainly based on Shafer 1997: 5–8.

[62] Finnestad 1997: 204. In this respect, see also Nelson 1944: 48, and Wilkinson 2000: 66–67, 76–77.

(see Bloch-Smith 1994: 19, 22–27), as well as Egyptian, Persian[63] and Syro-Phoenician[64] evidence, perhaps they represented giant trees, since they were ornamented with vegetation (clusters of pomegranates and lilies) at the top.

Depictions of garden imagery in the second part of the temple might seem to contradict the prior conclusion that the second sacred space in both Israel's and pagan temples primarily symbolized the visible heaven. As we will see at the conclusion of this chapter, especially with respect to Israel's temple, this is not necessarily inconsistent with the star imagery of the holy place, since it was also intended to mimic the Garden of Eden, which we will argue was the 'holy place' in the first primeval temple (e.g., the lampstand with seven lamps representing luminaries also alluded to the 'tree of life' in Eden). Nevertheless, there probably was some overlap of symbolism in the various sections of these temples for other reasons, so that while it is difficult to draw hard and fast distinctions between them, the broad symbolic divisions probably remain valid.

Symbolism of precious metals in temples

As we have discussed above, the precious metals used in the construction of Israel's temple had a sheen that reflected light, apparently designed in part to remind one of the reflection of the sun, moon and stars in the heavens (see the discussion above and 1 Chr. 29:2–8; 2 Chr. 3:3–9; 4:20–22; for all the precious metals used; likewise for the inner furnishings of the tabernacle, see Exod. 26:32; 31:4; 35:32; 36:36).

Descriptions of other temples in the ancient orient suggest further that the precious metals in Israel's temple possessed cosmic significance. Royal inscriptions of Assyria regularly compare the inside of renovated or newly built temples to the heavenly abode of the deities.[65] Assyrian kings used precious metals to decorate the interiors of temples in order to produce a shining glimmer like the heavens above (Niehaus forthcoming). The Assyrian king Tiglath-pileser I (1115–1077 BC) declared that 'the great gods ... commanded me to rebuild their shrine ... Its interior I decorated like the interior of

---

[63] Frankfort (1954: 22–224) cites Persian evidence of columns in various buildings ornamented with plant or flower designs.

[64] Stager (1999: 186, 193) notes that columns with palmette captials in the Levant 'signified the sacred, or cosmic, tree'.

[65] Niehaus 1995: 118, citing, among others, in support, Grayson 1987: 1:254–255; 2:15–57.

heaven. I decorated its walls as splendidly as the brilliance of rising stars ...'[66] A later Assyrian king, Ashurbanipal (668–627 BC), said, 'The sanctuaries of the great gods, my lords, I restored with gold (and) [silver] I decked ... Esarra ... I made shine like the writing of heaven. Every kind of gold (and) silver adornment of a temple I [ma]de ...' (Peipkorn 1933: 28–29 [i. 16–23]).

Nearly identical descriptions are found of the interior of Egyptian temples. Thutmose III (1490–1436 BC) built an inner sanctuary for the god Amon and called it, 'His-Great-Seat-is-Like-the-Horizon-of Heaven'. Likewise, 'its interior was wrought with electrum' in order to serve as an imitation of the light reflected from the heaven itself (Breasted 1906: 2:64 §153). Even the liturgical furniture of this sanctuary was composed of precious metals for the same purpose: 'a great vase of electrum ... silver, gold, bronze, and copper ... the Two Lands were flooded with their brightness, like the stars in the body of Nut [i.e., the sky goddess], while my statue followed. Offering-tables of electrum ... I made ... for him ...' (2:68 §164; likewise, with respect to Amen-hotep II [1439–1406 BC], on which see 2:318 §806). Similarly, the Pharaoh Pi-ankhi I (720 BC) created court furnishings of a temple composed 'of gold like the horizon of heaven' (4:495 §970) (recall that the inside furniture and utensils of Israel's temple were covered with precious metal according to 1 Kgs. 6:20–28; 7:48–51).

Queen Hatshepsut (1486–1468 BC) constructed a temple for Amon with a floor of silver and gold, and said, 'its beauty was like the horizon of heaven' (2:156 §375).[67] Along virtually identical lines, Amen-hotep III (1398–1361) built a temple in Karnak for the deity Amon and constructed it 'of gold ... unlimited in malachite and lazuli; a place of rest for the lord of gods, made like his throne that is in heaven' (2:355 §881); and about the temple of the same god in Thebes, the same Pharaoh said, 'it resembles the horizon in heaven when Re rises therein' (2:356 §883). The temple 'ceiling is painted blue for the sky and is studded with a multitude of golden stars' (Nelson 1994: 47, 48).

So also Ramses I (1303–1302 BC) constructed 'a temple like the horizon of heaven, wherein Re [rises]' (Breasted 1906: 3:36 §79). The Pharaoh Seti I (1302–1290 BC) built for the underworld god Osiris 'a temple like heaven; its divine ennead are like the stars in it; its

---

[66] Grayson 1976: 2:18 [vii.71–114]); I am indebted to Niehaus (forthcoming) for alerting me to this reference and the following ones in this section.

[67] Recollect here that Solomon 'overlaid the floor of the house [temple] with gold, inner and outer sanctuaries' (1 Kgs. 6:30).

radiance is in the faces (of men) like the horizon of Re rising therein at early morning' (3:96–97 §232 and §§236–237). This temple was also referred to as 'a house like the heavens, its beauty illuminating the Two Lands' (3:98 §240.12; see also Ismail 2002: 158, with respect to a temple at Karnak). Ramses II, a successor to Seti, observed about the temple at Karnak that 'its august columns are of electrum, made like every place that is in heaven. (It is) mistress of silver, queen of gold, it contains every splendid costly stone' (3:218 §512; sim. 3:217 §510).[68] Similarly, Ramses III built doors to a temple with precious stones 'like the double doors of heaven' (4:122 §216).

This evidence from Mesopotamia and Egypt suggests to some degree that just as Ancient Near Eastern temples used precious metals to adorn their temples, the precious metals of Israel's temple also had heavenly symbolism. Interestingly, even the clothing of Egyptian priests was like that of Israel's priests, representing both the inner sanctuary and the heavens (Bryan 2002: 130).[69]

Conclusion

Evidence from the ancient cultures surrounding Israel points further in the direction that Israel's tabernacle and temple reflect the cosmos and that the cosmos itself appears to be a massive temple or will become such in the future. The Ancient Near Eastern temples are also compatible with the earlier conclusion that the three sections of Israel's temple represented the three parts of the cosmos.[70] The outer court

---

[68] See Finnestad 1997: 213 for gold covering in temples being metaphorical for sun-light.

[69] I am grateful to G. P. Hugenberger for bringing this source to my attention.

[70] Greek Orthodox churches also reflect the tripartite structure and symbolism of Israel's temple: an outer section, often with wall paintings of war scenes and other depictions of activities in the world; an inner court with two lampstands (with seven light-bulbs) on either side of the central entrance to the next section (stars are some-times depicted as surrounding an image of Christ on the ceiling and a figure of ivy is around the outside of the central door to the next section); an inner sanctum, separated off from the middle room by a wooden curtain, within which I have been told is an emblem of shewbread and a copy of the Bible (e.g., note a basilica in one of the monasteries in Meteora, Greece). Likewise, ancient Greek temples were typically divided into three sections: outer court (with an altar and, sometimes, a wash-basin); an inner section; an inmost sanctuary where the idol of the god was placed. The tomb of Phillip of Macedon was apparently considered a temple: an outside paved section called 'the road', where the king's body was burned and burnt offerings were made for forty days; a section entered by huge marble doors, where Phillip's wife was buried, where also was found a large gold disc and smaller ones, all of which had stars in the middle; the innermost section of the cultic burial site held Phillip's remains, who was considered to be divine. For other examples of tripartite Greek temples, see Tomlinson 1976, though see the qualification in the next note.

symbolized the visible earth (land, sea, the place of human habitation); the holy place primarily represented the visible heavens (though garden imagery was included to recall Eden, which, we will see, was the primeval equivalent of the later holy place); the holy of holies stood for the invisible heavenly dimension of the cosmos where God dwelt.[71]

These commonalities with Israel's temple reflected partial yet true revelation, though insufficient for a personal knowledge of God. Yet Israel's temples are not like her neighbours merely because they reflected some degree of perception about the true reality of God's dwelling, but because Israel's temple was intended to be viewed as the true temple to which all other imperfect temples aspired. Israel's temple was likely a protest statement against all other pretenders, of whom she was quite aware. In order to make an effective polemical statement there had to be similarities with the temples of her neighbours, but there also had to be differences. We have discussed the similarities above. It is appropriate here briefly to highlight the differences.

One of the major differences is that, whereas in the inner sanctuary of the pagan temple there was an idol, there was no such thing in the holy of holies, since God's being cannot be seen, much less an image of it reproduced by human craft. In addition, while there were a variety of temples for various gods in each pagan nation, in Israel there was only one temple, since there was only one true God. Furthermore, in contrast to priests of other religions who practised magic rituals (incantations, divination etc.) to manipulate the gods, Israel's priests, indeed all Israelites, were forbidden to participate in such practices, since God could not be manipulated. The pagan priests' main function revolved around caring for and feeding their god in the temple, but Israel's God had no needs, so that priests only served God through various rituals designed for worship of the sovereign, self-existing deity that he was.[72]

Similarly, the gods of the nations needed 'housing' for rest but God himself says that no human-made structure could adequately be a

[71] Some contend that the temple consisted of three sections in addition to the outer courtyard by including the 'forecourt' (*'ûlām*) or porch to the holy place and that this was in contrast to the earlier three-part tabernacle (Homan 2000: 24). The porch may just as easily be viewed as a sacred entryway into the holy place and not a separate room with distinct significance. The gateways into the second sections of ancient Greek temples may well offer corroboration of this. Such gateways could be part of temple complexes or sometimes they were absent. When they were present, they served as mere transitional passageways; they were 'important not just for themselves' but functioned primarily as entrances into the next sacred room and, thus, helped to 'enhance the sense of drama, of movement into and through the sanctuary' (Tomlinson 1976: 40).

[72] I am thankful to my colleague, John Walton, for this observation.

dwelling for him (cf. 1 Kgs. 8:27; Is. 66:1, on the latter of which see the next chapter). One reason for this is that, as we have already hinted and will see later, Israel's temple pointed to the end-time goal of God's presence residing throughout the entire cosmos, not merely in one little, isolated structure. The pagan temples had no such eschatological purpose as a part of their symbolism.

Finally, though parts of Israel's temple, like the neighbouring pagan temples, symbolized the starry heavens, that symbolism is not highlighted as much. Why? We believe the reason to be that Israel wanted to make it clear that she did not worship the stars as gods. Therefore, while the stellar symbolism is discernible in Israel's temple, it is not as ornate and ostentatious as in temples dedicated to the sun god and other astronomical deities. Nevertheless, the cosmic symbols that are present indicate that Israel's temple was a small model of the heavens and earth, which points to the end-time goal of God's presence dwelling throughout the creation and no longer only in the back room of the temple.

Divine 'rest' after creating the cosmos and after constructing the sanctuary

Levenson summarizes previous research on the Pentateuch and observes that the creation of the cosmos, the making of the tabernacle and the building of the temple 'are all described in similar, and at times identical language'. The reason for the similarity is to indicate 'that the temple and the world were considered congeneric' (Levenson 1984: 286). Levenson even notes that the similarity is a distillation 'of a long tradition in the ancient Near East, which binds Temple building and world building' (1984: 287–288).[73] Such a connection is also linked to divine 'rest', which occurs subsequently to the work of creating.

God's 'rest' after creating the world, the tabernacle and the temple

John Walton has observed a link between creation and the tabernacle. In this respect, he cites M. Fishbane, following M. Buber, who observes significant parallels between the creation account and that of the construction of the tabernacle (Walton 2001: 149) (e.g., cf.

---

[73] So also Weinfeld 1981: 501–512. Cf. also Janowski 1990: 37–69, especially with respect to a depiction of the establishment of the tabernacle according to the thematic lines of the creation narrative in Gen. 1:1 – 2:4.

respectively Gen. 1:31; 2:1; 2:2; 2:3 with Exod. 39:43; 39:32; 40:33; 39:43). Fishbane notes that Moses' work of constructing the tabernacle is patterned after God's creation of the cosmos, using the same language: 'Thus, "Moses saw all the work" which the people "did" in constructing the tabernacle; "and Moses completed the work" and "blessed" the people for all their labors' (Fishbane 1979: 12). Fishbane concludes that the tabernacle's construction was intentionally portrayed in the image of the world's creation.

More specifically, both accounts of the creation and building of the tabernacle are structured around a series of seven acts: cf. 'And God said' (Gen. 1:3, 6, 9, 14, 20, 24, 26; cf. vv. 11, 28, 29) and 'the LORD said' (Exod. 25:1; 30:11, 17, 22, 34; 31:1, 12) (Sailhamer 1992: 298–299). In the light of observing similar and additional parallels between the 'creation of the world' and 'the construction of the sanctuary', J. Blenkinsopp concludes that 'the place of worship is a scaled-down cosmos' (1992: 217–218).[74]

Levenson also suggests that the same cosmic significance is to be seen from the fact that Solomon took seven years to build the temple (1 Kgs. 6:38), that he dedicated it on the seventh month, during the Feast of Booths (a festival of seven days [1 Kgs. 8]), and that his dedicatory speech was structured around seven petitions (1 Kgs. 8:31–55). Hence, the building of the temple appears to have been modelled on the seven-day creation of the world, which also is in line with the building of temples in seven days elsewhere in the Ancient Near East (Levenson 1988: 78–79). Just as God rested on the seventh day from his work of creation, so when the creation of the tabernacle[75] and, especially, the temple are finished, God takes up a 'resting place' therein.[76] For example, Psalm 132:7–8, 13–14 says,

> [7]Let us go into His dwelling place;
> Let us worship at His footstool.
> [8]Arise, O LORD, to Thy resting place;
> Thou and the ark of Thy strength . . .

---

[74] Cf. also 62–63. One later Jewish tradition similarly identifies the creation with the tabernacle by saying, 'the Tabernacle is equal to the creation of the world', and then substantiates the claim by comparing the various things created on each day of creation to seven similar items created in the tabernacle (*Tanhuma Yelammedenu Exodus* 11:2).

[75] With respect to the tabernacle, Exod. 25:8 of *Tg. Onqelos* quotes God as saying that the Israelites were to 'make before Me a sanctuary and I will let My presence rest among them'.

[76] I am indebted to Walton 2001: 149–155 for the discussion about the link between the temple and divine 'rest' here and below.

> [13]For the LORD has chosen Zion;
> He has desired it for his habitation.
> [14]'This is My resting place forever;
> Here I will dwell, for I have desired it.'

Therefore, 'the temple and the world stand in an intimate and intrinsic connection. The two projects cannot ultimately be distinguished or disengaged. Each recounts how God brought about an environment in which he can rest' (Levenson 1984: 288).

Indeed, in addition to the clear affirmation of Psalm 132, there are other Old Testament passages indicating that part of the purpose of the temple is as a divine resting place. Among other references in this respect are 1 Chronicles 28:2 (David intended 'to build a house of rest for the ark ... of the LORD'), Isaiah 66:1 ('Where then is a house you could build for Me?/And where is My resting place?'), 2 Chronicles 6:41 ('arise, O LORD God, to Thy resting place, Thou and the ark of Thy might'; cf. also the apocryphal Judith 9:8, 'Thy sanctuary ... the tabernacle where Thy glorious name rests').[77]

God's rest both at the conclusion of creation in Genesis 1 – 2 and later in Israel's temple indicates not mere inactivity but that he had demonstrated his sovereignty over the forces of chaos (e.g., the enemies of Israel) and now has assumed a position of kingly rest further revealing his sovereign power. Similarly, as we will also see below in citations of the *Enuma Elish* and other sources, the building of a shrine for divine rest occurs only after the powers of chaos have been defeated.

Accordingly, it is likely not coincidental that David initially conceived of building God a temple only after 'the LORD had given him rest on every side from all his enemies' (2 Sam. 7:1–6; following Levenson 1988: 107). David prepares for the building of the temple (1 Chr. 21:18 – 29:30), but he does not construct it because he had been 'a man of war' and had 'shed blood' (1 Chr. 22:8; 28:3); furthermore, he did not build the temple because, while there was 'rest' externally, there was still political unrest internally that needed to be quelled before Solomon could assume the throne and then build the temple (1 Kgs. 1 – 2).

---

[77] See also Is. 57:15 (LXX): 'the Most High, who dwells on high for ever, Holy in the Holies, is his name, the Most High resting in the holies'. This appears to be a reference not only to God's cultic heavenly resting place but may include the temple in Zion which is the extension of or symbol of the heavenly dwelling. Cf. also Num. 10:33–36; 1 Chr. 6:31; Ps. 95:11.

Consequently, Solomon decides to 'build a house for the name of the LORD' when he recognizes that 'now the LORD my God has given me rest on every side' (1 Kgs. 5:4–5; so almost identically 1 Chr. 22:9–10, 18–19; 23:25–26; cf. 1 Kgs. 8:56). And, in fact, when God promises that Solomon 'will build a house for My name', it is directly preceded and followed by the phrase 'I will establish ... his kingdom' (2 Sam. 7:12–13), thus underscoring the close relation of temple building and complete sovereign rest as a result of defeating all enemies.[78]

Exodus 15:17 confirms this by saying that God would bring Israel to 'the place, O LORD, which Thou hast made for Thy dwelling, the sanctuary, O LORD, which Thy hands have established. *The LORD shall reign forever and ever.*' God's dwelling in Israel's temple was conceived as the rest of a divine king who had no worries about opposition. God's *sitting* in the temple is an expression of his sovereign rest or reign. This is underscored by the repeated phrase 'who is enthroned above the cherubim' (2 Sam. 6:2; 2 Kgs. 19:15; 1 Chr. 13:6; Pss. 80:1; 99:1), which includes reference to God's actual presence in the temple as a reflection of his reign in the heavenly realm. Psalm 99:1 even more clearly asserts, 'The LORD reigns ... He is enthroned above the cherubim.' Just as God 'ascended and sat in the heights of the universe [to reign]', after he completed the creation (*The Fathers According to Rabbi Nathan* 1), so he would ascend to the temple and reign from there, after he subdued all Israel's enemies (Levenson 1988: 108).[79] In like manner, the repeated image of God 'sitting on a throne' is another picture of the sovereign who is resting (the phrase occurs approximately 35 times in the Old Testament, usually with respect to Israel's human kings; cf., e.g., Ps. 47:8: 'God reigns over the nations, God sits on His holy throne').

The Ancient Near Eastern concept of tabernacles in relation to temples, overcoming opposition and consequent divine 'rest'

With respect to the overcoming of opposition followed by temple-building, the reason for the transition from Israel's tabernacle to the

---

[78] See Uhlschöfer (1977), who shows well the relationship of Israel's temple construction to the ANE background of 'rest' being accomplished by putting down external and internal political opposition, followed by temple building; once there is no need to go out and conquer, then one can focus on constructing a permanent temple to signify 'rest'.

[79] The image of 'resting' as connoting a position of sovereign reign is also conveyed by the description of Solomon's throne which had 'arms on each side of the seat, and two lions *resting* beside the arms', picturing sovereign guardianship.

temple is important. It has become apparent that the tabernacle was modelled for polemical purposes, at least in part, on mobile Egyptian military tent camps that consisted of almost exactly the same three-part structure with the same measurements and that was oriented eastward (courtyard, inner reception area and the innermost chamber, where an image of the divine Pharaoh was flanked by two winged creatures!) There is even evidence that the Egyptian military tent was surrounded by troops divided into four units similar to the four distinct units of Israel's tribes that camped around the tabernacle (Num. 2). Just as the divine Pharaoh led his army into battle, so likewise did Yahweh, though he was the true god dwelling in his tabernacle in contrast to Pharaoh's idolatrous tent. Therefore, Israel's tabernacle may well have been conceived to be a travelling war headquarters from where the Lord directed the troops until all opposition was put down.[80] When the enemies are defeated, then a more permanent dwelling can be built to signify God's sovereign 'resting' from opposition, as happened during Solomon's reign.

The Ancient Near Eastern concept of gods 'resting' after creating the world and the temple

Walton notes how well God's 'rest' in Israel's temple corresponds to the purpose of temples in the Ancient Near East, which enhances the conclusions of the preceding discussion. In particular, the *Enuma Elish* narrates that the lack of rest among the gods results in a battle. The 'higher' god Apsu complains to Tiamat about the lower gods:

> Their ways have become very grievous to me,
> By day I cannot rest, by night I cannot sleep.
> I shall abolish their ways and disperse them.
> Let peace prevail, so that we can sleep.
> (*Enuma Elish* 1.37–40)[81]

After defeating Tiamat, Marduk reorganizes the cosmos and the lesser gods under his sovereignty, concluding with the building of Babylon conceived as a shrine-like temple in which the gods can find rest:

---

[80] The paragraph on the Egyptian background of the tabernacle is based on Homan 2000.

[81] Here Walton follows the translation of Dalley 1991: 234; see also the translation of Heidel 1942: 19.

> We will make a shrine, which is to be called by name
> 'Chamber that shall be Our Stopping Place,'
> we shall find rest therein.
> We shall lay out the shrine, let us set up its emplacement,
> when we come thither ... we shall find rest therein.
> When Marduk heard this,
> His features glowed brightly, like the day,
> Then make Babylon the task that you requested,
> Let its brickwork be formed, build high the shrine.
>
> (*Enuma Elish* 6.51–58)[82]

Similarly, in the Sumerian narrative of Gudea's building a temple for the god Ningirsu, the purpose of the temple was to establish a place of rest for the god and his consort (Walton 2001: 151).[83] And when the Sumerian god Ningirsu enters the temple built for him, he is portrayed as a 'warrior' and 'king' (Cyl. B 5.1–19) (Averbeck 2000: 431). His majestic inactivity shows that the powers of chaos have been ruled over, that stability in his kingdom has been achieved, and no further exertion on his part is needed to achieve victory.

After the Egyptian Pharaoh Ramses had built a temple for the god Ptah, he made an image of the deity, set it in the most inner holy chamber, and exclaimed that now the god was 'resting upon its [the temple's] throne' (Breasted 1906: 3:181 §412). This theme occurs repeatedly in Egypt.[84] Another passage in the *Enuma Elish* (1.73–76) pertaining to divine rest, not apparently noticed by commentators, explains that after the god Ea defeats other divine opponents, he rests in a shrine:

> After Ea had vanquished (and) subdued his enemies,
> Had established his victory over his foes,
> (And) had peacefully rested in his abode,
> He named it *Apsu* and appointed (it) for shrines.[85]

---

[82] Here Walton follows the translation of Foster 1995: 39–40. See also the translation of Heidel (1942: 48), who translates with 'sanctuary' instead of 'shrine' in lines 51 and 58. Like Walton, J. Laansma cites the same two segments from Tablets 1 and 6 of the *Enuma Elish* in order to make the same point (1977: 71).

[83] See Cyl. B 14.21–23 (for the text, see Jacobsen 1987: 438, as well as Averbeck 2000: 430: 'O Ningirsu, I have built your temple for you ... O my Baba, I have set up your bed-chamber [?] for you, [so] settle into it comfortably').

[84] For temples as the 'resting' place of a deity, see Breasted 1906: 2:355 §881 and 3:217 §510; 220 §517; 221 §521.

[85] Following Heidel 1942: 21.

Similarly, another text (6.8, 35–36) in the same work affirms that 'after Ea ... had created mankind ... they had imposed the service of the gods upon them' for the purpose that the gods 'may be at rest'.

Consequently, 'in the Ancient Near East as in the Bible, temples are for divine "rest", and divine rest is found in sanctuaries or sacred space' (Walton 2001: 151).[86] The pagan religious material suggests further that after God overcame chaos and created the world and after he overcame Israel's enemies and built the temple, he 'rested' as a true sovereign on his throne in contrast to the pretending, false deities whom pagan worshippers believed had done the same.

Israel's earthly tabernacle and temple as reflections and recapitulations of the first temple in the Garden of Eden

In addition to the notion that the earthly temple reflected the heavenly, cosmic temple, Revelation 22:1ff. appears to be aware of an earlier interpretation of Eden as a sanctuary. Following the lead of John's allusion to Genesis 2 – 3 that is woven into his depiction of the city-temple, it will be instructive to go back and study this beginning narrative of sacred history. Such a study will reveal hints that the Garden of Eden was the first archetypal temple in which the first man worshipped God.[87]

The Garden as the unique place of God's presence

Israel's temple was the place where the priest experienced God's unique presence, and Eden was the place where Adam walked and talked with God. The same Hebrew verbal form (stem) *mithallēk* (hithpael) used for God's 'walking back and forth' in the Garden (Gen. 3:8), also describes God's presence in the tabernacle (Lev. 26:12; Deut. 23:14 [15]; 2 Sam. 7:6–7).

The Garden as the place of the first priest

Genesis 2:15 says God placed Adam in the Garden 'to cultivate [i.e., work] it and to keep it'. The two Hebrew words for 'cultivate and keep' are usually translated 'serve and guard [or keep]' elsewhere in the Old

---

[86] See further Levenson 1988: 100–111 for expanded discussion of the 'rest' of gods in temples, both in the ANE and the OT.

[87] Following to a significant extent Kline 1989: 31–32, 54–56; 1980: 35–42; as well as Wenham 1994; Barker 1991: 68–103; Parry 1994: 126–151; and, to lesser degree, Poythress 1991: 19, 31, 35; see further Davidson 2000: 109–111.

Testament.[88] It is true that the Hebrew word usually translated 'culti-vate' can refer to an agricultural task when used by itself (e.g., 2:5; 3:23). When, however, these two words (verbal ['ābad and šāmar] and nominal forms) occur together in the Old Testament (within an approximately 15-word range), they refer either to Israelites 'serving' God and 'guarding [keeping]' God's word (approximately 10 times) or to priests who 'keep' the 'service' (or 'charge') of the tabernacle (see Num. 3:7–8; 8:25–26; 18:5–6; 1 Chr. 23:32; Ezek. 44:14).[89]

The Aramaic translation of Genesis 2:15 (*Tg. Neofiti*) underscores this priestly notion of Adam, saying that he was placed in the Garden 'to toil in the Law and to observe its commandments' (language strik-ingly similar to the above Numbers' references; likewise *Tg. Pseudo-Jonathon Genesis* 2:15). Verse 19 of this Aramaic translation also notes that in naming the animals Adam used 'the language of the sanctuary'.[90] Later Jewish and early Christian tradition make affir-mations consistent with the notion that part of Adam's function was to worship God.[91]

---

[88] Cf. Cassuto (1989: 122–123), who prefers these meanings in Gen. 2:15.

[89] See likewise Wenham 1987: 67; cf. also Is. 56:6; cf. Kline (1989: 54), who sees this only with respect to the priestly 'guarding' of the temple from the profane (e.g., Kline cites Num. 1:53; 3:8, 10, 32; 8:26; 18:3ff.; 1 Sam. 7:1; 2 Kgs. 12:9; 1 Chr. 23:32; 2 Chr. 34:9; Ezek. 44:15ff.; 48:11); so similarly, Wenham 1987: 67. Similarly, Walton (2001: 173) concludes that Adam's tasks were of a priestly nature because of the use of the two Hebrew verbs elsewhere and the temple atmosphere of Eden (see further pp. 172–174, for his excellent discussion). It is a well-known grammatical problem that the word for 'garden' is masculine but the pronominal suffix on the infinitives is femi-nine. Cassuto (1989: 122) and Sailhamer (1992: 100–101), followed by Hafemann (2001: 228), note the possibility that the two infinitives could be translated as 'serving [or worshipping] and guarding' rather than 'work it and guard it'; i.e., that the forms are infinitival gerunds and not infinitives with a feminine pronominal suffix. The ques-tion is whether or not the mappiq in the final *he* was originally intended; if not, then Cassuto and Sailhamer would be right (Cassuto claims there are some Hebrew manu-scripts where the mappiq, indeed, is missing, but he does not list them). Probably, the traditional translation is correct, especially since the two verbs in the surrounding context bear such a sense (2:5; 4:2, 9, 12; esp. note the two verbs close together in 3:23–24, on which see Hugenberger ([n.d.])). Hugenberger notes that there are abun-dant examples of the infinitive construct of both verbs throughout the OT but the forms proposed by Cassuto and Sailhamer would be unique. Nevertheless, the two verbs should be viewed as painted with 'cultic colors'. Cf. also Hendel 1998: 44.

[90] Indeed, *Tg. Pseudo-Jonathon Genesis* 2:7 says that God created Adam partly of 'dust from the site of the sanctuary'. See Scroggs (1966: 51) for other references in Judaism that Adam was created at the location where Israel's temple was later built: e.g., see *Tg. Pseudo-Jonathon Genesis* 3:23; cf. also *y. Nazir* 7:2, IV.L, *Pirke de Rabbi Eliezer* 11 and 12, and *Midrash Rabbah Genesis* 14:8, which all affirm that Adam was created at the site of the later temple, which was also at Eden or was apparently close to it (as the latter text would imply).

[91] *Midrash Rabbah Genesis* 16:5 interprets Adam's role in Gen. 2:15 to be one of offering the kinds of 'sacrifices' later required by the Mosaic Law. Early Christian

The best translation of Adam's task in Genesis 2:15 is 'to cultivate (work) it and to keep it [the Garden]'. Regardless of the precise translation, however, the preceding observations suggest that the writer of Genesis 2 was portraying Adam against the later portrait of Israel's priests, and that he was the archetypal priest who served in and guarded (or 'took care of'[92]) God's first temple.[93] While it is likely that a large part of Adam's task was to 'cultivate' and be a gardener as well as 'guarding' the garden, that all of his activities are to be understood primarily as priestly activity is suggested not only from the exclusive use of the two words in contexts of worship elsewhere but also because the garden was a sanctuary, as we will argue throughout this segment. If this is so, then the manual labour of 'gardening' itself would be priestly activity, since it would be maintaining the upkeep and order of the sanctuary.

After telling Adam to 'cultivate' and 'guard/keep' in Genesis 2:15, God gives him a specific 'command' in verse 16. The notion of divine 'commanding' (*ṣāwâ*) or giving of 'commandments' (*miṣwôt*) not untypically follows the word 'guard/keep' (*šāmar*) elsewhere, and in 1 Kings 9:6, when both 'serving' and 'keeping' occur together, the idea of 'commandments to be kept' is in view. The 1 Kings passage is addressed to Solomon and his sons immediately after he had 'finished building the house of the LORD' (1 Kgs. 9:1): if they do 'not *keep* My commandments ... and *serve* other gods ... I will cut off Israel from the land ... and the house [temple] ... I will cast out of My sight' (1 Kgs. 9:6–7). Is this a mere coincidental connection with Genesis 2:15–16?

Hence, it follows naturally that after God puts Adam into the Garden for 'cultivating/serving and keeping/guarding' (v. 15) that in the very next verse God would command Adam to keep a commandment: 'and the LORD God commanded the man ...' The first 'torah' was that 'From any tree of the Garden you may eat freely; but from the tree of the knowledge of good and evil you shall not eat, for in the day that you eat from it you shall surely die' (Gen. 2:16–17). Accordingly, Adam's disobedience, as Israel's, results in his being cut

---

interpretation comports with the same point of view. In a context of warning the church against the 'sneak attacks' of the devil, *Barnabas* 4:11 exhorts, 'let us become a complete temple for God. To the best of our ability, let us *cultivate* [*meletaō*] the fear of God and strive *to guard* [*phylassō*] his commandments' (*Barnabas* 6 then links this temple with Adam's commission in Gen. 1:28).

[92] So the rendering of Walton 2001: 172–173.

[93] As we will see reiterated more explicitly by Jewish commentators in a following section at the end of this chapter.

off from the sacred land of the Garden. This is an indication that the task of Adam in Genesis 2:15 included more than mere spadework in the dirt of a garden. It is apparent that priestly obligations in Israel's later temple included the duty of 'guarding' unclean things from entering (cf. Num. 3:6–7, 32, 38; 18:1–7), and this appears to be relevant for Adam, especially in view of the unclean creature lurking on the perimeter of the Garden and who then enters. Interestingly, priests of ancient pagan temples were also to 'guard the temple' and to kill intruders,[94] as well as 'guard' and pass on sacred texts (Finnestad 1997: 228).

Adam's priestly role of 'guarding' (*šāmar*) the garden sanctuary may also be reflected in the later role of Israel's priests who were called 'guards' (1 Chr. 9:23) and repeatedly were referred to as temple 'gatekeepers' (repeatedly in 1 and 2 Chronicles and Nehemiah: e.g., 1 Chr. 9:17–27) who 'kept watch [*šāmar*] at the gates' (Neh. 11:19), 'so that no one should enter who was in any way unclean' (2 Chr. 23:19). Consequently, the priestly role in both the Garden and later temple was to 'manage' it by maintaining its order and keeping out uncleanness. The picture is that of a 'warden' who 'keeps charge of the temple' (cf. Ezek. 40:45; 44:14) or manages a sacred ward (indeed, the AV of Neh. 12:45 says that temple priests '*kept* the *ward* of their God').[95]

Interestingly, when the second temple is destroyed, the priests are portrayed as saying to God, 'Guard your house yourself, because, behold, we have been found to be false stewards' (*2 Baruch* 10:18; so also *Midrash Rabbah Leviticus* 19:6). One early Jewish commentary summarizes Adam's role accordingly: 'And you [God] said that you would make a man for this world as a guardian over your [God's] works' (*2 Baruch* 14:18, apparently alluding to Gen. 2:15).

There may also be significance that the word used for God 'putting' Adam 'into the garden' in Genesis 2:15 is not the usual Hebrew word for 'put' (*śûm*) but is the word typically translated as 'to rest' (*nûaḥ*).

---

[94] See McMahon 1997: 219, a text from a pre-New-Hittite period. *Sifre on Deuteronomy*, Piska 41 interprets 'work it' of Gen. 2:15a as study of Torah and 'guard it' of v. 15b as guarding the commandments. See *Books of Adam and Eve* (Armenian version), pericope 10.32(7).3; pericope 16[44](15).2; pericope 19[44](17).2d–3, which describe Adam and Eve as guarding Eden.

[95] Both words 'kept' and 'ward' in Neh. 12:45 are forms of *šāmar*, the same word used for Adam's task in Gen. 2:15 and of the cherubim's task in Gen. 3:24. Priests outside of Israel also were administrators of temples, participating in decoration and construction, as well as 'managing . . . land registered to the temples' (Finnestad 1997: 228).

The selection of a word with overtones of 'rest' may indicate that Adam was to begin to reflect the sovereign rest of God discussed above and that he would achieve a consummate 'rest' after he had faithfully performed his task of 'taking care of and guarding' the garden. This is in line with the 'rest' that God promises later to Israel if they live faithfully in the Promised Land (which, as we will see, is repeatedly compared to the Garden of Eden).[96] That this verb (in its hiphil or hophal causative form) was intentionally chosen is pointed to further by the observation that it is used elsewhere to refer to the installation of sacred furniture (2 Chr. 4:8) and divine images into temples (2 Kgs. 17:29; Zech. 5:5–11) and especially of God's 'resting place' (so the noun form) in his heavenly palace-temple (Ps. 132:7–8, 14; Is. 66:1).[97] Thus, the implication may be that God places Adam into a royal temple to begin to reign as his priestly vice-regent. In fact, Adam should always best be referred to as a 'priest-king', since it is only after the 'fall' that priesthood is separated from kingship, though Israel's eschatological expectation is of a messianic priest-king (e.g., see Zech. 6:12–13).

The Garden as the place of the first guarding cherubim

When Adam failed to guard the temple by sinning and letting in a foul serpent to defile the sanctuary, he lost his priestly role, and the cherubim took over the responsibility of 'guarding' the Garden temple: God 'stationed the cherubim ... *to guard* the way to the tree of life' (so Gen. 3:24; see also Ezek. 28:14, 16).[98] The guarding function of the cherubim probably did not involve gardening but keeping out the sinful and unclean, which suggests that Adam's original role stated in Genesis 2:15 likely entailed much more than cultivating the soil, but also 'guarding' the sacred space.

The guarding role of the cherubim plausibly became memorialized in the tabernacle when God commanded Moses to make two statues of cherubim and stationed them on either side of the 'ark of the

---

[96] So Exod. 33:14; Deut. 3:20; 12:10; 25:9; 2 Sam. 7:1–6; Ps. 95:11; cf. Heb. 4:3–5. I am indebted to Ross (1988: 124) for the connotations of the verb in Gen. 2:15. Notice that Heb. 4 compares God's rest after creation to that of Israel's rest, which may suggest that the same analogy could be drawn between God's rest and Adam's.

[97] This has been argued by Beckerleg who also shows that cognates for 'rest' appear in Ugaritic (the Kirta Epic) and the Egyptian pyramid texts to refer to a place of enthronement (1999: 310).

[98] Not only does the Greek OT identify the figure who 'guards' in Ezek. 28 as Adam but *possibly,* so does the Hebrew text as well (as, e.g., argued by Callender 2000: 87–135, 179–189).

covenant' in the 'holy of holies' (Exod. 25:18–22). The same arrangement was also part of the design of Solomon's temple (1 Kgs. 8:6–7).
The reliefs of carved cherubim together with ornamental palm trees
and calyxes that were on the inner walls of the holy place of
Solomon's temple (1 Kgs. 6:29) and on its doors (1 Kgs. 6:32–35) may
also reflect the primeval cherubim whose duty it was to patrol the
entrance leading to 'the tree of life' (Ezek. 41:18 is even more explicit:
at the entrance of and on the walls of the holy place there were carved
'cherubim and palm trees; and a palm tree was between cherub and
cherub'). This point becomes more significant if our following point
is viable: that the lampstand in the holy place was intended to represent the ancient 'tree of life'.[99]

The Garden as the place of the first arboreal lampstand

The 'tree of life' itself is a good candidate to be considered as the model
for the lampstand placed directly outside the 'holy of holies'.[100] The
lampstand in the tabernacle and temple looked like a small, flowering
tree with seven protruding branches from a central trunk, three on one
side and three on the other, and one branch going straight up from the
trunk in the middle. Exodus 25:31–36 pictures the lampstand having a
flowering and fructifying appearance of a tree with 'bulbs and flowers',
'branches', and 'almond blossoms' (likewise, Josephus, *Ant.* 3.145).

The Garden as formative for garden imagery in Israel's temple

That the Garden of Eden was the first sacred space is also suggested
by observing that Solomon's temple was described with botanical and
arboreal imagery that gave it a garden-like appearance. The account
in 1 Kings 6 – 7 of the temple construction includes a proliferation of
garden-like descriptions of the interior, much of which are descriptions of carvings, structures or pieces of furniture covered with precious metals: wood-carved 'gourds and open flowers' (1 Kgs. 6:18),
'palm trees and open flowers' (1 Kgs. 6:29, 32, twice mentioned),
'pomegranates numbered two hundred in rows around both capitals'
on the two doorway pillars (1 Kgs. 7:20; cf. likewise, 7:18–19), on the
top of which were a 'lily design' (1 Kgs. 7:22); the bronze sea in the
courtyard had two rows of 'gourds' under its brim, which was 'made

---

[99] See Bloch-Smith (1994: 22–27), who has observed this significance of the cherubim carvings and lampstand in relation to Eden. She also confirms this by document-
ing depictions of cherubim-like figures flanking sacred trees in the Ancient Near East.
[100] On which see Beale 1999a: 234–236; Longman 2001: 57.

... like a lily blossom' (1 Kgs. 7:24–26); 'four-hundred pomegranates' around the two capitals of the pillars (1 Kgs. 7:42); ten (!) lampstands that were configured like trees with blossoms (1 Kgs. 7:49), thus resembling a small orchard (note the later *Testament of Adam* 4:7, which says that in Zech. 1:8–11 the prophet saw 'trees' in the heavenly 'tabernacle'; cf. also Ps. 74:3–7 which includes portrayal of a 'thicket of trees' in Israel's sanctuary; cf. similarly *y. Yoma* 4:4).[101]

Accordingly, subsequent Old Testament literature identifies Solomon's temple (Pss. 52:8; 92:13–15; Lam. 2:6) and Israel's eschatological temple (Is. 60:13, 21) with a 'garden' or garden-like depictions in order to identify them with Eden.[102] Appropriately, Solomon himself is portrayed as an Adamic figure, the ideal botanist, who lectured about 'trees, from the cedar that is in Lebanon even to the hyssop that grows on the wall' (1 Kgs. 4:33a).

Eden as the first source of water

Just as a river flowed out from Eden (Gen. 2:10), so the post-exilic temple (*Letter of Aristeas*, 89–91) and the eschatological temple in both Ezekiel 47:1–12 and Revelation 21:1–2 have rivers flowing out from their centre (and likewise Rev. 7:15–17 and probably Zech. 14:8–9).[103] Indeed, Ezekiel generally depicts latter-day Mount Zion (and its temple) with descriptions of Eden in an attempt to show that the promises originally inherent in Eden would be realized in the fulfilment of his vision (Levenson 1976: 25–53). Fertility and 'rivers' are also descriptions of Israel's temple in Psalm 36:8–9:

---

[101] For Solomon's temple as an intentional replication of the Garden of Eden, especially in its arboreal likeness, see Stager 2000: 36–47, 66; 1999: 183–193 (though, because of his view of dating OT sources, he actually sees the temple as the model for Eden in the latter article and is unclear in the former); he also notes likenesses with other ANE temples containing gardens or garden depictions on their walls that also reflect the essential characteristics of the Garden of Eden (on which likewise see Keel [1985: 124–151] and Yarden [1971: 38], where iconographic examples are found). See also Josephus (*Ant.* 3.124–126), who observed that the curtain separating the holy of holies from the holy place in the 'second temple' was woven 'with every manner of flower that earth produces'; likewise, 'the gate opening into the [temple] building . . . had . . . above it those golden vines from which depended grape-clusters as tall as a man . . .' (Josephus, *War* 5.210; almost identically, see Josephus, *Ant.* 15.395). *Midrash Rabbah Numbers* 13:2 identifies the tabernacle as a replication of God's dwelling in the Garden of Eden.

[102] See Stordalen 2000: 411, 413–414, 435–436; likewise, see Fishbane 1979: 111–120, though he speaks more in terms of 'sacred space' than of 'temple'.

[103] Later Judaism understood that from 'the tree of life' streams flowed (*Midrash Rabbah Genesis* 15:6; *2 Enoch* [J] 8:3, 5).

They drink their fill of the abundance of Thy house [temple];
And Thou dost give them to drink of *the river of Thy
delights* [literally, 'the river of your Edens'].
For with Thee is *the fountain of life;*[104]
In Thy light we see light [perhaps a play of words on the light
from the lampstand in the holy place].

Jeremiah 17:7–8 also compares those 'whose trust is the LORD' to 'a
tree planted by the water, that extends its roots by a stream', with the
result that 'its leaves will be green' and it will not 'cease to yield fruit'
(cf. also Ps. 1:2–3). Then verses 12–13 refer to 'the place of our
[Israel's] sanctuary' and virtually equates it with 'the fountain of
living water, even the LORD'.[105]

The Garden as the place of precious stones

Genesis 2:12 says that 'good gold' and 'bdellium and onyx stone' were
in 'the land of Havilah', apparently where Eden was or, at least, to
which it was close. Of course, various items of tabernacle furniture
were made of gold, as were the walls, ceiling and floor of the holy of
holies in Solomon's temple (1 Kgs. 6:20–22; for 'gold' in the tabernacle
see Exod. 25:11–39). Furthermore, the onyx stones decorated both the
tabernacle and temple, as well as the high priestly garments (Exod.
25:7; 28:9–12, 20; 1 Chr. 29:2). Gold and onyx are also found together
on the priest's clothing (Exod. 28:6–27) and are mentioned together as
composing parts of the temple (1 Chr. 29:2). Thus, the common feature
of precious stones further associates the Garden with the later temple.

The Garden as the place of the first mountain

The prophet Ezekiel portrays Eden as being on a mountain (Ezek.
28:14, 16). Israel's temple was on Mount Zion (e.g., Exod. 15:17), and
the end-time temple was to be located on a mountain (Ezek. 40:2;
43:12; Rev. 21:10).

The Garden as the first place of wisdom

The ark in the holy of holies, which contained the Law (that led to
wisdom), echoes the tree of the knowledge of good and evil (that also

---

[104] Levenson (1976: 28) sees this phrase as an allusion to the 'flow [which] welled up
from the earth and watered the whole surface of the soil' from which Adam was created
in Gen. 2:6–7.

[105] Among other commentators, D. Callender especially cites Ps. 36 and Jer. 17 as
examples of Israel's temple being likened to Eden (2000: 51–52).

led to wisdom). Both the touching of the ark and the partaking of the tree's fruit resulted in death.

The Garden as the first place with an eastern facing entrance

The entrance to Eden was from the east (Gen. 3:24), which was also the direction from which one entered the tabernacle and later temples of Israel, and would be the same direction from which the latter-day temple would be entered (Ezek. 40:6).

The Garden as part of a tripartite sacred structure

It may even be discernible that there was a sanctuary and a holy place in Eden corresponding roughly to that in Israel's later temple. The Garden should be viewed as not itself the source of water but adjoining Eden because Genesis 2:10 says, 'a river flowed out of Eden to water the garden'.

Therefore, in the same manner that ancient palaces were adjoined by gardens, 'Eden is the source of the waters and [is the palatial] residence of God, and the garden adjoins God's residence.'[106] Similarly, Ezekiel 47:1 says that water would flow out from under the holy of holies in the future eschatological temple and would water the earth around. Similarly, in the end-time temple of Revelation 22:1–2 there is portrayed 'a river of the water of life ... coming *from the throne of God and of the Lamb*' and flowing into a garden-like grove, which has been modelled on the first paradise in Genesis 2, as has been much of Ezekiel's portrayal.

If Ezekiel and Revelation are developments of the first garden-temple, which we will argue later is the case, then Eden, the area where the source of water is located, may be comparable to the inner sanctuary of Israel's later temple and the adjoining garden to the holy place.[107] Even aside from these later biblical texts, Eden and its adjoining garden formed two distinct regions. This is compatible with our further identification of the lampstand in the holy place of the temple with the tree of life located in the fertile plot outside the inner place of God's presence. Additionally, 'the bread of the presence', also in the holy place, which provided food for the priests, would

---

[106] Walton 2001: 167, citing also Gleason 1997: 2:383 and Cornelius 1997: 1:875–878 for sources showing that ancient temples had gardens adjoining them.

[107] Discussion of the distinction between Eden and its garden is based on Walton 2001: 167–168, 182–183.

appear to reflect the food produced in the Garden for Adam's sustenance (Walton 2001: 182).

I would add to this that the land and seas to be subdued by Adam outside the Garden were roughly equivalent to the outer court of Israel's subsequent temple, which would lend further confirmation to the above identification of Israel's temple courtyard being symbolic of the land and seas throughout the earth.[108] Thus, one may be able to perceive an increasing gradation in holiness from outside the garden proceeding inward: the region outside the garden is related to God and is 'very good' (Gen. 1:31) in that it is God's creation (= the outer court); the garden itself is a sacred space separate from the outer world (= the holy place), where God's priestly servant worships God by obeying him, by cultivating and guarding; Eden is where God dwells (= the holy of holies) as the source of both physical and spiritual life (symbolized by the waters).

Ezekiel's view of the Garden of Eden as the first sanctuary

In the light of these numerous conceptual and linguistic parallels between Eden and Israel's tabernacle and temple, it should not be unexpected to find that Ezekiel 28:13–14, 16, 18 refer to 'Eden, the garden of God ... the holy mountain of God', and also alludes to it as containing 'sanctuaries', which elsewhere is a plural way of referring to Israel's tabernacle (Lev. 21:23) and temple (Ezek. 7:24; so also Jer. 51:51). The plural reference to the one temple probably arose because of the multiple sacred spaces or 'sanctuaries' within the temple complex (e.g., courtyard, holy place, holy of holies).[109] It is also probable that the Greek Old Testament version of Ezekiel 28:14 and 16 views the glorious being who had 'fallen' to be Adam: 'From the day that you were created you were with the cherub' (v. 14); 'you sinned; therefore, you have been cast down wounded from the mount of God [where Eden was]' (v. 16). Ezekiel 28:13 pictures Adam dressed in bejewelled clothing like a priest (28:13), which corresponds well to the reference only five verses later to Eden as a holy sanctuary. Ezekiel 28:18 is probably, therefore, the most explicit place

---

[108] See Stordalen 2000: 307–312 for a discussion of other commentators who, in various ways, have identified the Garden of Eden with a temple or sanctuary, in favour of which he offers further evidence (457–459).

[109] There were even smaller sacred areas in the temple complex: e.g., of Solomon's temple (1 Chr. 28:11) and of the second temple (1 Maccabees 10:43). Philo can refer to 'the Holy of Holies' as 'the Holies of Holies' (*Leg. All.* 2.56; *Mut. Nom.* 192) or 'the innermost places of the Holies' (*Som.* 1.216).

anywhere in canonical literature where the Garden of Eden is called a temple.[110]

The Ancient Near Eastern concept of temples in association with garden-like features

Gardens not untypically were part of temple complexes in the Ancient Near East (Stager 1999: 193). For example, Ramses III of Egypt created 'gardens' in the deity's 'house' (Breasted 1906: 4:148 §274) and 'made to grow the pure grove of thy [the deity's] temple . . . with gardeners to cultivate it . . .'[111]

The earlier-mentioned elements of a garden-like atmosphere, rivers and precious stones in common between Eden and Israel's temple occur also in the Ancient Near East. There one can find the combined mention of a temple, trees, rivers, subterranean waters, jewels and divine activity as a description of one cultic place. An apt example comes from a Sumerian-Akkadian text:

> In Eridu the black tragacanth tree grew in a pure place it was created. Its appearance is lapis lazuli stretched out on the Apsu [fresh water or sea] of [the god] Ea-his promenade in Eridu filled with abundance . . . its shrine is the bed of Nammu. In the holy temple in which like a forest it casts its shadow, into which no one has entered, in its midst are [the gods] Shamash and Tammuz, in between the mouths of the two rivers.[112]

This ancient pagan text shows that Ancient Near Eastern gods were also conceived of as dwelling in watery abodes or at the source

---

[110] On this identification of Eden as a temple, see further the section below on Num. 24:5–6 (pp. 123–126) and Dan. 2 (pp. 145–147) and the discussion there summarizing the work of Stordalen 2000: 352. See also Greenberg 1997: 591, who sees that Ezek. 28:11–19 fuses together the Garden of Eden and the temple; he sees that the passage strongly evokes the Jerusalem temple because of the following elements: (1) reference to 'the holy mountain of God', which Zion was sometimes called; (2) reference to the 'cherub who guards' (Ezek. 28:14, 16) reflects the cherub figures around the ark of the covenant and woven into the temple's curtains (e.g., 1 Kgs. 6:23–35); (3) the cherubim in the midst of coals of fire (cf. Ezek. 1:13; 10:2 and 28:14, 16). See also *Books of Adam and Eve* (Armenian version), pericope 5.16.2–3, where Satan is cast out of Eden, which is referred to as the *dwelling* of light.

[111] Breasted 1906: 4:148 §272; likewise, 3:236–237 §567 and 4:122 §215, 147 §271. See Brown 1999: 250–251 for further references and discussion of the inextricable link between gardens and temples in Egypt.

[112] The text (= *CT* 16, 46:183–198) is cited by Callender 2000: 50, who is dependent on the translation of Thompson (1976: 1:200, lines 183–198) and who also notes other translations.

of headwaters from which fertile areas were watered: the gods Shamash and Tammuz dwelt in the 'midst' of 'the holy temple' 'in between the mouths of the two rivers'. The Canaanite god El is also a good example of this (see Walton 2001: 167): the god's permanent 'tent' dwelling was at 'the headwaters of the Euphrates River'.[113]

A further observation can be made with particular reference to common tree-like images in both Eden and Israel's temple. In the light of Mesopotamian, Assyrian,[114] Egyptian, Persian[115] and Syro-Phoenician[116] evidence about columns in ancient buildings and temples having a tree-like appearance, the two large columns at the outer porch of the holy place, perhaps represented giant trees, since, as we saw above, they were ornamented with vegetation (clusters of pomegranates and lilies at the top). Possibly, they corresponded to the two well-known trees of 'life' and 'knowledge' in the Garden of Eden.[117] The Sumerian *Keš Temple Hymn* depicts the temple not only as 'green in its fruit' but also 'a boxwood tree bearing its crown to the sky, like a poplar ... like the Mountain, green as the sky' (Sjöberg et al. 1969: 169, 171, lines 40, 67–69).

Possibly, these affinities between Eden and pagan garden-like divine dwellings were intended to indicate that God's depiction in Eden is a polemic against the similar depiction of pagan gods. More precisely, the polemical force may focus on the original description of the first garden-like temple for the true God, of which the pagan versions are faint imitations.

Early Judaism's view of the garden as the first sanctuary

Judaism in various ways also understood the Garden to be the first sanctuary in line with the above Old Testament evidence. Comment has already been made on a little of this evidence in the preceding paragraphs.

First, Adam was considered to be a priest, serving God in the sanctuary of Eden. The book of *Jubilees* (160 BC) represents an early Jewish interpretation of Adam as a priest in an arboreal temple. When he was cast out of the garden, he offered the sweet savoury offering

---

[113] This is found in a Hittite version of the Canaanite myth 'Elkunirsa and Ashertu', in Hoffner 1990: 90–91.

[114] See Bloch-Smith 1994: 19, 22–27.

[115] Note again, Frankfort 1954: 22–224, who cites Persian evidence of columns in various buildings ornamented with plant or flower designs.

[116] See once more, Stager 1999: 186, 193, who notes that columns with palmette captials in the Levant 'signified the sacred, or cosmic, tree'.

[117] As proposed by Bloch-Smith 1994: 27.

(composed of the very same elements used only in the later temple) that he apparently had formerly been offering (*Jubilees* 3:27). *Jubilees* 4:23–25 likewise portrays Enoch offering 'the incense which is acceptable ... in the evening (at) the holy place', after he was caught up 'into the Garden of Eden'. Rabbinic interpretation also links Adam's expulsion from the garden to being cast out of the temple and to the destruction of Israel's later temple (*Midrash Rabbah Genesis* 21:8).[118]

Perhaps the earliest (160 BC) and clearest example of Judaism's identification of Eden as a sanctuary is *Jubilees* 8:19: 'And he [Noah] knew that the Garden of Eden was the holy of holies and the dwelling of the Lord. And Mount Sinai (was) in the midst of the desert and Mount Zion was in the midst of the navel of the earth. The three of these were created as holy places, one facing the other.' This is quite interesting because it links the Garden as a temple with, not only Sinai, but also the temple in Jerusalem. *Testament of Levi* 18:6, 10 and *1 Enoch* 24 – 27 also closely associate God's temple with imagery of the Garden of Eden.[119]

Similarly striking is the Qumran community's identification of itself as the 'Temple of Adam [or Temple of Humankind]' (*miqdaš 'ādām*[120] in 4QFlor 1, 6, referring to a future time in the community's history) and 'an Eden of glory [bearing] fruits [of life]' (1QH 8.20, though cf. 8.4–23).[121] Similarly, 1QS 8.5 identifies the community as 'the House of holiness for Israel' and 'the company of the Holy of Holies for Aaron' and 'an everlasting planting', the latter a reference to the Garden of Eden.[122] Another Dead Sea Scroll text (4Q418, frag. 81 = 4Q423 8 + 24?) refers to Adam's descendants who, in contrast to him, will obey and walk in an 'eter[nal] plantation' (lines 13–14). They will serve him 'by consecrating yourself to him, in accordance to the fact that he has placed you as a Holy of Holies

---

[118] See Barker 1991: 68–72 for these and like references; in this respect, see further van Ruiten 1999: 218–220. Other sectors of rabbinic Judaism also understood that Adam was a priest (*Midrash Rabbah Genesis* 20:12; *Midrash Rabbah Numbers* 4:8; *Midrash Rabbah Genesis* 34:9; see further Hayward 1996: 44–47, 88–95).

[119] So see van Ruiten 1999: 223; see also Baumgarten (1989: 1–6), who discusses some early and later Jewish sources identifying Israel's temple with Eden; see also Himmelfarb 1991: 72–75 for *Sirach*'s identification of the temple with Eden; for the notion of Sinai as a temple, see Lundquist (1983), and especially Parry (1990: 482–500).

[120] Following the translation of Wise et al. 1996: 227.

[121] See Schwartz 1979: 83–91, on the debate about how many temples are in mind in 4QFlor 1.2–6 and on the translation of *miqdaš 'ādām*. The expression could be translated 'sanctuary of man' or 'of humanity' or 'consisting of men'. On the debated translation of 4QFlor 1.6, see also Gärtner 1965: 34–35, and Brooke 1999: 292. On the debated translation of 1QH 8.20 see Brooke 1999: 292.

[122] Similarly, see CD 3.19–20, on which see Brooke 1999: 292–293.

[over all][123] the earth, and over all the angels . . .' (line 4). This passage closely associates a cultivated garden-like plot of land with those who dwell in it, who have been placed there as a 'holy of holies' and who are to extend their holy sphere over all the earth.

Early Jewish commentators also compared either the tree of life with Israel's temple or Eden with the later lampstand. The early Jewish book of *1 Enoch* says the tree of life would be transplanted from Eden, which was on a 'high mountain', to the 'Holy Place beside the temple of the Lord' in Jerusalem (*1 Enoch* 24 – 25), implying that the tree's former location in Eden was also a sanctuary.[124] This also comes close to identifying the tree with the lampstand that was also in the 'Holy Place'. The Qumran *Hymn Scroll* makes a similar identification: 'I will shine with a *seven-fold li[ght]* in the *E[den*[125] which] Thou has [m]ade for Thy glory' (1QH 7.24, my italics). The righteous person of Qumran is compared to the seven lamps of the lampstand shining in the Garden of Eden.

Jewish sources also associate the precious stones in Havilah, where Eden was or was near, with Israel's later priests and temple.[126]

Conclusion

The cumulative effect of the preceding parallels between the Garden of Genesis 2 and Israel's tabernacle and temple indicates that Eden

[123] The Martínez–Tigchelaar Hebrew–English edition rightly supplies the lacunae with 'over all' because of the following parallelism with 'over all the angels' [literally 'gods'], though in Martínez's earlier English edition he did not do so and gave an otherwise quite different translation, which does not reflect the Hebrew as well as the later translation.

[124] In this respect, see Black 1985: 38–39, 171. That the tree is located in Eden is apparent also from the mention of 'stones . . . priceless for their beauty' nearby the mountain where the tree was (cf. the precious stones in the land of Havilah in Gen. 2:11–12).

[125] Our translation follows Dupont-Sommer, who is the only translator who supplies the second lacuna of the line with 'Eden.' The translations of Martínez, Gaster and Wise et al. supply 'light' instead of 'Eden'. If 'Eden' is not explicitly referred to here, the setting of the 'seven-fold light' is still most probably understood to be Eden, since descriptions of the Garden of Eden together with 'fire' and 'light' are close by in the context, where 'Eden' *is* explicitly mentioned (1QH 6.15–18 and 8.4–22); cf. also God causing 'salvation to flower and the Shoot to grow' in the directly preceding lines of 7.19. Such a context may point, indeed, to the plausibility of Dupont-Sommer's translation, but our point is not dependent on it.

[126] Pseudo-Philo, *Biblical Antiquities*, 25–26, asserts that twelve precious stones almost identical to those composing the vestments of the high priest (see Exod. 28) were originally taken by the Amorites 'from the land of Havilah', and used for idolatry until they were taken by Israel and placed in the ark of the temple. At the time of Israel's latter-day redemption one will come and 'build a house for my [God's] name' (26:12) and then the stones will be restored to all of the righteous.

was the first archetypal temple, upon which all of Israel's temples were based. Some of the similarities drawn may not be as strong as others, but when all are viewed together they have a significant collective effect, pointing to Eden as the first temple in garden-like form. We are not left, however, with a collection of similarities that show how comparable Eden is to a temple. Indeed, Ezekiel 28 explicitly calls Eden the first sanctuary, which substantiates that Eden is described as a temple because it is the first temple, albeit a 'garden-temple'. Early Judaism confirms this identification. Indeed, it is probable that even the similar Ancient Near Eastern temples can trace their roots back to the original primeval garden.

Chapter Three

The expanding purpose of temples in the Old Testament

Humanity's kingly and priestly role in serving God in the temple

It is particularly interesting that among the preceding cultic affinities drawn between Eden and Israel's temple was the observation that the word-pair usually translated as 'cultivate' (*'ābad*) and 'keep' (*šāmar*) occur together in the Old Testament elsewhere referring only either to Israelites 'serving' God and 'guarding' (keeping) God's word (approximately 10 times), or to priests who 'keep' the 'service' (or 'charge') of the tabernacle (5 times). Genesis 1 – 2 not only portrays Adam as a kingly gardener and watchman but does so in language that rings with the notion of worshipful obedience. Consequently, we concluded in the last chapter that Adam is being portrayed as a priest in this task.

The cosmic expansion of the garden sanctuary through Adam's rule as a priest-king in God's image

Not only was Adam to serve as a priest-king in the initial stage of the Edenic sanctuary, but Genesis 1:28 affirms that he was also to subdue the entire earth: 'And God blessed them ... "Be fruitful and multiply, and fill the earth, and subdue it; and rule over the fish of the sea and over the birds of the sky, and over every living thing that moves on the earth."' Genesis 1:27 provides the means by which the commission and goal of verse 28 was to be accomplished: humanity will fulfil the commission by means of being in God's image.[1] They were to reflect God's kingship by being his vice-regents on earth. Because Adam and Eve were to subdue and rule 'over all the earth', it is plausible to suggest that they were to extend the geographical boundaries of the

[1] The same relationship exists between 1:26a and 1:26b; see also, in this respect, Dumbrell 1994: 18–20.

garden until Eden covered the whole earth.[2] They were on the primeval hillock of hospitable Eden, outside of which lay the inhospitable land. They were to extend the smaller liveable area of the garden by transforming the outer chaotic region into a habitable territory.

In actuality, Adam, as God's vice-regent, and his progeny were to put 'the finishing touches' on the world God created in Genesis 1 by making it a liveable place for humans. The penultimate goal of the Creator was to make creation a liveable place for humans in order that they would achieve the grand aim of glorifying him. This penultimate goal of making the whole earth habitable would appear to be confirmed by Isaiah 45:18: 'God ... formed the earth and made it ... and did not create it a waste place, but formed it *to be inhabited*' (likewise cf. Ps. 115:16). God's ultimate goal in creation was to magnify his glory throughout the earth by means of his faithful image-bearers inhabiting the world in obedience to the divine mandate.

As we will see below, this is consistent with the notion in Babylonian and Egyptian tradition of people being created to serve their god in a temple and extend that god's glorious light by building more temples or widening the borders of an original temple. In Adam's case, however, it is more probable that he was to spread God's luminescent presence by extending the boundaries of the original Edenic temple outward into the earth. Furthermore, in contrast to Ancient Near Eastern accounts, God did not create Adam and Eve because he was tired of the drudgery of providing for himself, but that humanity would reflect his glorious image in extending his sacred presence outward into the wider regions of the earth (Walton 2001: 186).

In this regard, Genesis 1:26–27 says four times that God made Adam in his 'image' or 'likeness', and Genesis 2 says God placed him into the garden-like sanctuary. Ancient kings would set up images of themselves in distant lands over which they ruled in order to represent their sovereign presence. For example, after conquering a new territory, the Assyrian king Shalmanesar 'fashioned a mighty image of my majesty' that he 'set up' on a black obelisk, and then he virtually equates his 'image' with that of 'the glory of Assur' his god (Frankfort 1954: 90 and plate 93). Likewise, Adam was created as the image of the divine king to indicate that earth was ruled over by Yahweh (von Rad 1962: 146–147). In the light of Genesis 1:26–28,

[2] See Kline 1989: 55–56. The plausibility of this suggestion will be enhanced by the cumulative evidence of the remainder of this chapter and the following chapters of the book, especially chs. 3 – 4 and the discussions of Rev. 21 (e.g., see chs. 10 and 12).

this meant the presence of God, which was initially to be limited to the garden temple of Eden, was to be extended throughout the whole earth by his image bearers, as they themselves represented and reflected his glorious presence and attributes.

The following parallels from Assyria and Egypt (discussed below) show that typically images of gods were placed in the god's temple and that kings were viewed as living images of a god. Against this background and in the light of Genesis 1:26–28, Adam's commission to 'cultivate' (with connotations of 'serving') and 'guard' in Genesis 2:15 as a priest-king is probably part of the commission given in 1:26–28.[3] Hence, Genesis 2:15 continues the theme of subduing and filling the earth by humanity created in the divine image.[4] This 'ruling' and 'subduing' 'over all the earth' is plausibly part of a functional definition of the divine image in which Adam was made, though there is likely an additional ontological aspect of the 'image' by which humanity was enabled to reflect the functional image.[5] Just as God, after his initial work of creation, subdued the chaos, ruled over it and further created and filled the earth with all kinds of animate life, so Adam and Eve, in their garden abode, were to reflect God's activities in Genesis 1 by fulfilling the commission to 'subdue' and 'rule over all the earth' and to 'be fruitful and multiply' (Gen. 1:26, 28).[6]

In the light of the above, one can conclude that Adam's kingly and priestly activity in the garden was to be a beginning fulfilment of the commission in 1:28 and was not to be limited to the garden's original earthly boundaries but was to be extended over the whole world. In particular, for example, Adam's speaking and naming of the animals (Gen. 2:19) expresses part of his rule over the creation and reflects God's naming of parts of creation in Genesis 1 through his creative speech.[7]

---

[3] I have found support for this link in Cohen (1989: 18), who also cites James Barr and Claus Westermann in support.

[4] So also Dumbrell 1994: 24–26.

[5] See Cohen 1989: 22–23 for evidence that God's 'image' in Gen. 1:26a, 27 has both an ontological and functional aspect, though it is likely that the latter is the emphasis in Gen. 1, which is also the emphasis of Walton 2001: 130–131.

[6] Following Gage 1984: 27–36. Though there is debate about whether or not Gen. 1 depicts God first creating the chaos from nothing or portrays the chaos already present before God's work of creation, the former, traditional view is assumed here, for which limits of space do not allow argumentation.

[7] Gage 1984: 31. Interestingly, *Midrash Rabbah Genesis* 17:4 says that the way Adam expressed being in the image of God (Gen. 1:26a) was by his ability to name the animals in Gen. 2:20. See Cohen 1989: 99 for other Jewish traditions making the same link between Gen. 1 and Gen. 2.

Similarly, that Adam and Eve were to become 'one flesh' in 2:24 is certainly part of the beginning of the commission to be 'fruitful and multiply, and fill the earth', further underscoring that humanity's function in the image of God as 'male and female' (Gen. 1:27)[8] was to be extended until the earth was filled with people performing this function. Accordingly, a significant increase in population would necessitate an expansion of the original sacred habitable dwelling of the first primal couple.[9] In this regard, Matthew 19:4–6 (= Mark 10:6–9) is one of the earliest texts relating Genesis 1:27 to Adam and Eve in Eden:[10]

> [4]And He [Jesus] answered and said, 'Have you not read, that He who created them from the beginning made them male and female [Gen. 1:27], [5]and said, "For this cause a man shall leave his father and mother, and shall cleave to his wife; and the two shall become one flesh"? [Gen. 2:24] [6]"Consequently they are no longer two, but one flesh. What therefore God has joined together, let no man separate.'

Jesus identifies humans as 'male and female' in the image of God (Gen. 1:27) who were to begin to fulfil their commission in the Garden by maintaining their unity. Reproducing offspring in God's image is a natural implication of the first couple's unity.

John Walton, I have found, corroborates this link between Genesis 1:26–28 and Genesis 2:15ff., contending that Adam was much more than a gardener but was to maintain the created order of the sacred space of the sanctuary. He also concludes that such maintenance indicates that the 'cultivating' and 'guarding' of Genesis 2:15 is an expression of the 'subduing and ruling' of chapter 1 (Walton 2001: 174).[11]

Consequently, as observed earlier, Adam's priestly role in the

---

[8] Cf. Ross 1988: 113, 126.

[9] This finds some support from Josephus, *Ant.* 1.110, who says that God wanted the people at the tower of Babel to spread out over the earth in fulfilment of the Gen.1:26, 28 commission 'because of increasing population'.

[10] Another early text linking Gen. 1:26, 28 to Gen. 2 is the Qumran passage of 4Q504 = 4QWords of the Luminaries (frag. 8 Recto, lines 4–6): 'You molded [Adam], our [fa]ther, in the image of [your] glory . . . [in the gard]en of Eden, which you planted, y[ou] made him to rule . . . in order that he would walk in a glorious earth', and 'he guarded'; so also 4Q423 = 4Q *Instruction*ᵍ (frag. 2, line 2): 'is it not a garden . . . to rule . . . And over it he made you (Adam) to rule, to till it and to guard it'. Likewise, though not quite as clearly, 4Q418, frag. 81 (= 4Q423 8 + 24?) links Gen. 1:26, 28 with Gen. 2:15 (see discussion in ch. 4, pp. 157–158).

[11] This view supported by Gorman 1990: 28–29 and Hornung 1982: 183.

Garden was to 'manage' or 'care' for it by maintaining its order and keeping out uncleanness. This included 'gardening' but likely went beyond it to managing the affairs of the sacred place where God's presence dwelt and maintaining its orderliness in contrast to the disordered space outside. This management included 'guarding' Eden from the threat of unclean things entering into it and corrupting it. And would not this management also logically include Adam's teaching of God's Law (from Gen. 2:16–17) to Eve in order that they both would help one another to obey, so that spiritual chaos might not set in? The picture, therefore, is that of a 'warden' managing a sacred ward. As the first couple had children, it is certainly plausible to suggest that the management of the Garden extended to teaching them God's Law and serving God by obeying it. Furthermore, Walton observes that

> if people were going to fill the earth [according to Genesis 1], we must conclude that they were not intended to stay in the garden in a static situation. Yet moving out of the garden would appear a hardship since the land outside the garden was not as hospitable as that inside the garden (otherwise the garden would not be distinguishable). Perhaps, then, we should surmise that people were gradually supposed to extend the garden as they went about subduing and ruling. Extending the garden would extend the food supply as well as extend sacred space (since that is what the garden represented). (2001: 186)

The intention seems to be that Adam was to widen the boundaries of the Garden in ever increasing circles by extending the order of the garden sanctuary into the inhospitable outer spaces.[12] The outward expansion would include the goal of spreading the glorious presence of God. This would occur especially by Adam's progeny born in his image and thus reflecting God's image and the light of his presence, as they continued to obey the mandate given to their parents and went out to subdue the outer country. The original purpose of an expanding Eden will be supported by our next chapter which will be exclusively dedicated to tracing other passages primarily in the Old Testament and, secondarily, in early Judaism, both of which interpret the Garden in this manner.

---

[12] This may be implied by Is. 45:18: God 'did not create it [the earth] a waste place, but formed it to be inhabited [as Eden was initially inhabited]'.

The psalmist, commenting on the purpose of Adam and humanity in Psalm 8, also indicates that the ultimate goal of humanity was to fill the whole earth with God's glory. The psalm begins in verse 1 and concludes in verse 9 with the same stated goal: 'O LORD, our Lord, How majestic is Thy name in all the earth.' This 'majesty' is God's glorious 'splendor' (cf. v. 1). The goal of divine splendour is to be achieved 'in all the earth' by humanity whom God 'has crowned with glory and majesty' by making him in his image (v. 5). In particular, Psalm 8 says God's glory is to be spread throughout the earth by humanity 'ruling' over all 'the works of Thy [God's] hands' (vv. 6–8). Included in this rule was making 'the enemy and revengeful cease' (v. 2), which the Aramaic translation of the psalm identifies with the 'author of enmity', the devil.

Genesis 1:28 is best taken as a command, possibly with an implied promise that God will provide the ability to humanity to carry it out.[13] A medieval rabbinic commentary expresses well the aspect of 'mandate' involved in the verse:

the rationale of the commandment is that the world should be settled, because God ... desires its settlement, as it is written, 'He did not create it a waste but formed it for habitation' [Is. 45:18]. And this is a great commandment for whose sake there

[13] We are not able here to enter into the problem of whether Gen. 1:28 is merely a 'blessing . . . delineating a privilege' (Walton 2001: 134) or whether it is a blessing that includes a mandate or command. Traditionally, it has been called a 'creation mandate', and with this we essentially agree. Joüon concludes that in Gen. 1:28 all 'five imperatives are direct imperatives', with the explicit sense of a direct command (1993: 373). Gesenius et al. construe Gen. 1:28 as command, 'the fulfillment of which is altogether out of the power of the one addressed', which has the force of an 'assurance' or 'promise' (1970: 324). Wenham combines the two preceding views: 'This command . . . carries with it an implicit promise that God will enable man to fulfill it' (1987: 33). Wenham's conclusion is pointed to by observing that imperatives are used as commands in the restatement of Gen. 1:28 to Abraham (Gen. 12:1–2: 'Go forth from your country . . . and you will be a blessing') and to Jacob (Gen. 35:11, 'be fruitful and multiply'). Some see the verb 'bless' in Gen. 12:2 to be a basic imperative (so Carroll 2000: 22, who cites others in support). Some grammarians see Gen. 12:2 as part of a promise (e.g., see Gesenius et al. 1970: 325), while others view it as an 'indirect imperative' expressing purpose or result (Joüon 1993: 385; cf. Carroll 2000: 22, who cites others who view the construction to be conveying consequence or purpose). But the context of such 'indirect' uses of the imperative may indicate that they retain a notion of 'command' (e.g., Exod. 3:10, an example adduced in Gesenius et al.: 'Therefore, come now, and I will send you to Pharaoh, *so that you may bring out* my people'; cf. in light of Exod. 3:11; 4:21–23; 6:10–13) (1970: 325). Apparently, on this basis, Ross (1988: 263) sees that the last imperative of 12:2 emphasizes the purpose of the divine blessing yet still 'retains an imperatival force' (Carroll's discussion approaches the same conclusion).

exist all of the other commandments, for they were given to human beings and not to the ministering angels ... And he who does not fulfill it annuls a positive commandment ... because he himself demonstrates that he does not wish to fulfill God's desire to settle his world (Sefer ha-Hinnukh).[14]

Adam, however, failed in the task with which he was commissioned, which includes permitting entrance into the Garden to an antagonistic and unclean being. Though Genesis 2 – 3 does not explicitly say that Adam's 'ruling and subduing' task was to guard the garden from the satanic snake, our overall discussion so far in this chapter together with the conclusion of the preceding chapter points to this (see Kline 1989: 54–55, 65–67). Thus, Adam did not guard the Garden but allowed entrance to a foul snake that brought sin, chaos and disorder into the sanctuary and into Adam and Eve's lives. He allowed the Serpent to 'rule over' him rather than 'ruling over' it and casting it out of the Garden. Rather than extending the divine presence of the garden sanctuary, Adam and Eve were expelled from it. Consequently, Adam and Eve disobey God's mandate in Genesis 1:28 (and, if 1:28 includes an implicit promise to provide them ability to obey, it is not fulfilled).

The Ancient Near Eastern concept of the cosmic expansion of temples through the rule of priest-kings in the image of a deity

As we commented in the last chapter, it should not be surprising to find some parallels to biblical ideas in the literature of ancient cultures surrounding Israel. The biblical writers were sometimes aware of the ideas reflected in this literature and sometimes intentionally presented their versions as the true ones in contrast and even contradiction to the others. The narrative of creation, especially the creation of humanity, would have been a prime place to point out the unique witness of biblical revelation. On the other hand, the very fact that this revelation is being set against the same general pagan conceptions means that there will also be some similarities between the two

---

[14] As cited by Cohen 1989: 195, who also summarizes Luther's perspective of Gen. 1:28a with similar import: 'Defiance of the instruction to reproduce not only contravenes the will of God but subverts the order of God's creation, whose natural imperative our verse bespeaks' (1989: 307–308).

which mutually interpret one another. And, as we have noted earlier, the fact that unbelieving humanity is still in the image of God, distorted as that image is, indicates that their conceptions about the nature of deity and of humanity contains some truth. That unregenerate humanity can still have some glimmers of such truths is part of God's grace in natural revelation (e.g., see Rom. 1:20, in the context of idolatry).

For example, the notion that Adam was set in a sanctuary as a royal 'image' of his God is an ancient concept found even outside Israel. The following examples of this show how natural it is that images of a god are placed in a temple after it has been constructed.[15] Ashurbanipal II (883–859 BC) 'created an icon of the goddess Ishtar ... from the finest stones, fine gold ... (thus) making her great divinity resplendent', and he 'set up in (the temple) her dais [throne platform] (with the icon) for eternity (Grayson 1996: 296–297).' The resplendent glory of the image was to reflect the luminescent glory of the goddess herself. Accordingly, the light of the deity was to shine out from the temple into the faces of humanity. Consequently, the idols in Assyria were made of precious metals in order to reflect the heavenly glory of the god they represented.[16]

We have already had occasion to observe that Pharaoh Seti I (1302–1290 BC) built for the underworld god Osiris 'a temple like heaven; its divine ennead are like the stars in it; its radiance is in the faces (of men) like the horizon of Re rising therein at early morning'.[17] The Egyptians believed that the sun god, Re, would empower other lesser deities to enter stone images placed in temples (Budge 1951: 164–166). Accordingly, an inscription from the Pyramid Age affirms that the Creator Ptah 'fashioned the [lesser] gods ... He installed the gods in their holy places ... he equipped their holy places. He made likenesses of their bodies ... Then the gods entered into their bodies of every wood and every stone and every metal' (Breasted 1959: 46).[18] Ramses III (1195–1164 BC) said that in the temple of the sun god, Re, he 'fashioned the gods in their mysterious forms of gold, silver, and every costly stone ...' (Breasted 1906: 4:143 §250).[19] Indeed, 'the King

---

[15] I am indebted to J. Niehaus for alerting me to the sources cited below on 'images' in the Ancient Near East.

[16] As argued by Niehaus (forthcoming).

[17] Breasted 1906: 3:96–97 §232; 2:156 §375: 'it [the temple] illuminated the faces [of people] with its brightness', and almost identically 3:97 §236.

[18] Cf. also Budge 1951: 72, 82, 87, 93–94, 98, 102, 106, 304.

[19] So also with respect to the same Pharaoh, see Breasted 1906: 4:114 §190; 15 §26 and 491 §958K.

is a sacred image, the most sacred of the sacred images of the Great One . . .' (Faulkner 1969: 82 [Utterances 273–274, §407]).

The Egyptian king is not merely a 'sacred image' of the deity (Faulkner 1969: 82), but he is a *living* image of the god.[20] Furthermore, other Egyptian texts say that the god 'Horus has acted on behalf of his spirit in you [the Pharaoh]' (Faulkner 1969: 122 [Utterance 370, §647]), and one king is recorded as saying, 'I am the essence of a god, the son of a god, the messenger of a god' (Faulkner 1969: 160 [Utterance 471, §920]).[21] Perhaps most striking, because of its similarity to Genesis 1:26, is the statement by Ramses II (1290–1224 BC) about his relationship to his god:[22] 'I am thy son whom thou hast placed upon thy throne. Thou hast assigned to me thy kingdom, thou hast fashioned me in thy likeness and thy form, which thou hast assigned to me and has created' (Breasted 1906: 3:181 §411). In addition, Ramses II was even to build temples for the gods: the creator god Ptah said to the same Pharaoh, 'thou buildest their [the lesser gods] holy places . . .' (1906: 3:179 §406). In this task, as well as others in relation to the temple, the Egyptian king also served as a priest performing rituals (Shafer 1997: 22–23; Finnestad 1997: 229). In the context of an inscription about a temple for the god Amun, the god is recorded as calling the king Amenhotep 'My son . . . My living image' (Lichtheim 1976: 46).

The Genesis portrayal of humans being created in the image of God and being placed in the sanctuary of Eden is even generally in line with the Ancient Near Eastern practice in which images of the god were placed in a *garden-like* temple. There is a fascinating parallel from Mesopotamia, where 'the creation, animation and installation of divine images followed a strictly specified set of rites' (Beckerleg 1999: 310). A series of rituals were acted out in the workshop of a craftsman, at a riverbank, in an arboreal garden and finally, in a temple. Through the rituals the inert image of a god was born, brought to life, clothed and changed into a living manifestation of the god. The image was then installed in a temple. Likewise, God formed Adam in his 'workshop' (Gen. 2:7a), he was transmuted into a living person by God's breath (Gen. 2:7b), and was fully brought to life (Gen. 2:7c). Next, he was installed in the Garden (Gen. 2:15) (Beckerleg 1999: 310). Such a background suggests further that

---

[20] Similarly, the Sumerians not only believed that a god inhabited images but that human kings were living images of a god (so Jacobsen 1976: 37–40, 66, 71).

[21] So almost identically Faulkner 1969: 242 (Utterance 589, §1609).

[22] So following here, in particular, Niehaus (forthcoming).

Adam was a living 'image' of the true God, not of a false pagan deity and, as such, was placed into the garden temple.

As an image of the true God, in contrast to Ancient Near Eastern priest-kings, Adam's royal and priestly service in the Eden temple and his temple-expanding task also find further striking parallel in Ancient Near Eastern literature. Again, these similarities are only imperfect shadows of the genuine task described in Genesis 1 – 2. With regard to Adam's role as a human priest-king, the notion of a human king created for the purpose of serving gods in a temple appears in an Akkadian prayer employed in dedicating the foundation stone of a temple:

> When Anu, Enlil and Ea had a first idea of heaven and earth,
> They found a wise means of providing support for the gods:
> They prepared, in the land, a pleasant dwelling,
> And the gods were installed in this dwelling: their principal
> temple.
> Then they entrusted to the king the responsibility
> of assuring them their regular choice offerings.
> And for the feast of the gods, they established the
> required food offering!
> The gods loved this dwelling!
>
> (Clifford 1994: 61)

The Babylonian *Enuma Elish* asserts that Marduk would 'create Man! (Upon him) shall the services of the gods be imposed'[23] (6.7–8; twice more in the immediate context it is said that Ea 'had created mankind' and 'imposed the services of the gods upon them that they may be at rest' [6.33–36]) (Heidel 1942: 46). Such 'services' most likely are conceived of as being performed within the gods' temple, since the 'service' enables the gods to be at 'rest', a rest that we have seen occurs uniquely in a temple (on which see the above discussion of *Enuma Elish* 6.51–58). Another cosmological Akkadian text affirms that Ea 'created the king, for the mainten[ance of the temples]; [He created] mankind for the doi[ng of the service of the gods (?)].'[24] A similar passage says, 'let us create mankind. The service of the gods be their

---

[23] Ramses II said of himself, 'I have built it [Egypt] up with temples' (1906: 3:181 §411), and 'I made thee an august temple . . .' (1906: 3:181 §412). So also with respect to Ramses III (1906: 4:143 §250).

[24] Lines 37–38 of an Akkadian text that Heidel titles 'When Anu Had Created the Heavens' (1942: 65–66).

portion.' Then the kind of 'service' humanity is to perform is explained:

> To place the hoe and the basket
> Into their hands
> For the dwelling of the great gods,
> Which is fit to be an exalted sanctuary,
> To mark off field from field . . .
> To water the four regions of the earth (?),
> To raise plants in abundance . . .
> To fill (?) the granary . . .
> To make the field of the Anunnaki produce plentifully,
> To increase the abundance in the land . . .
> To pour out cold water
> In the great house of the gods, which is fit to be an exalted
> sanctuary.
>
> (Heidel 1942: 69–70)

This text may refer to agricultural work within a temple or to an actual construction of a temple. The former appears to be the case because 'the exalted sanctuary' is in existence before humanity's creation (1942: 69, line 10) and because the directly following context of the quotation describes only horticultural tasks. It is not clear whether humanity performs this 'service' both inside and outside the sanctuary, or whether the whole earth is considered a sanctuary in which the work on earth is performed. If the latter, the service in the sanctuary is to be performed throughout the entire earth. If the former, the work on earth is in some way inextricably linked with service in the sanctuary. Thus, these Babylonian texts provide background consistent with the notion that Adam's agricultural role in Eden, as the first human, was a kingly and priestly function associated with service in a temple.

A similar text to the preceding, again from the Babylonian *Enuma Elish* (6.107–130), clarifies that cultic 'service' in an initial sanctuary was to be widened to include 'service' within other sanctuary-shrines throughout the land and likely beyond:

> Let him [Marduk] exercise shepherdship over mankind, [his] crea[tures(?)].
> Let them provide for their maintenance (and) let them take care of their sanctuaries . . .

A likeness of what he made (?) in heaven [let him make (?)]
   on earth.
Let him teach mankind to fear him (?).
Let the subjects be ever mindful of their god (and) their
   goddess ...
Let offerings be brought for their god and goddess;
Let their god not be forgotten, (but) let them support (him).
Let them make their land shine by building shrines for
   themselves.
Let mankind stand (in awe) before our god ...
Let his ways shine forth in glory ...
In the brightness of his [Marduk's] bright light let them walk
   about constantly.
(upon) the people, whom he created ...
He imposed the services of the gods ...

Not only was humanity's 'temple service' to extend beyond only
one sanctuary-shrine to others but, as this occurred, the glorious light
of the god would shine forth further because the human servants continued to perform their cultic tasks in 'fear' of and faithfully in the
presence of their god.

Perhaps not coincidentally, a similar extension of temple boundaries is observable in Egypt from the First Intermediate Period (c. 2200)
and onward; unlike the preceding Babylonian example of extending
by building numerous sanctuaries, this involves the extension of the
boundaries of only one temple:

> 'We find the yearning for limitation side by side with the desire
> to transcend and dissolve all boundaries.' By expanding a
> divine cult complex, a king [Pharaoh] resolved this tension cre-
> atively, simultaneously transcending old limits and establishing
> new ones. As each king pushed the perimeter of walls and
> courtyards farther and farther in to what had previously been
> secular space, the area of the sacred was greatly extended.[25]

The process of temple expansion represented an attempt to extend
the space of existing order into the outer chaotic sphere (Hornung
1992: 116–118). In addition to widening a temple horizontally, the
Egyptians also built various levels skyward as well as into subterra-

---

[25] Shafer 1997: 7, who summarizes the work of E. Hornung.

nean areas (Shafer 1997: 7). Such a phenomenon of outward extension may be due to the Egyptian belief that at the beginning of creation a small hillock arose, from which grew the entire creation. Since,
as we saw in chapter 1, the temple symbolized the entire cosmos, and
in particular the holiest place was conceived of as resting on this primordial mound,[26] it would have made sense for kings to want to continue to extend the boundaries of their temples ever outward, in
imitation of the cosmos that was expanded in the beginning by the
Creator. The floor level of the temple gradually got higher as one
approached the sanctuary in order to signify the primeval mound
(Wilkinson 2000: 77).

The Egyptians employed other architectural features to portray
the temple as a kind of expanding new creation. The temple pylons
pictured the divine Pharaoh defeating his enemies, just as the Creator
of the world had overcome chaos and 'expanded the territory of
cosmos' (Finnestad 1997: 210). Imitation of the original cosmic
expansion was also reflected by making the holiest place the narrow-
est and smallest part of the temple complex, with ever-widening
sacred spaces as one proceeded into the outer courts (1997: 210). Just
as light flashed over the earth at the beginning of creation, so the
king-priest's representation of the god in relation to the temple was
to shine out divine light increasingly throughout the earth (1997:
205–206, 213). The divine light of Isis is said to illumine 'the Two
lands with her radiance, and fill[s] the earth with gold-dust', so that
'her radiance [is] inundating the faces' (1997: 213).

These examples of expanding temples were imperfect echoes of the
original commission to the first human priest-king to subdue and rule
over the earth and fill it with God's glory by widening the primal
garden sanctuary. Genesis 1 – 2 also stands as a polemic against all
imperfect attempts to fulfil this commission apart from faithful
service to the true God.

Adam's commission as a priest-king to rule and expand the temple is passed on to others

As we will see, after Adam's failure to fulfil God's mandate, God
raises up other Adam-like figures to whom his commission is passed
on. We will find that some changes in the commission occur as a
result of sin entering into the world. Adam's descendants, like him,

---

[26] Shafer 1997: 8, though he does not draw the directly following conclusion.

however, will fail. Failure will continue until there arises a 'Last Adam' who will finally fulfil the commission on behalf of humanity.

The nature of the commission and temple building

Some commentators have noticed that Adam's commission was passed on to Noah, to Abraham and on to his descendents:

Gen. 1:28	And God blessed them; and God said to them, 'Be fruitful and multiply, and fill the earth, and subdue it; and rule over the fish of the sea and over the birds of the sky, and over every living thing that moves on the earth.'
Gen. 9:1, 7	And God blessed Noah and his sons ... 'Be fruitful and multiply, fill the earth ... be fruitful and multiply; populate the earth abundantly and multiply in it.'
Gen. 12:2	'And I will make you a great nation,/And I will bless you,/And make your name great;/And so you shall be a blessing.'
Gen. 12:3	'And I will bless those who bless you, and the one who curses you I will curse. And in you all the families of the earth shall be blessed.'
Gen. 17:2, 6, 8	'And I will establish My covenant between Me and you, and I will multiply you exceedingly ... And I will make you exceedingly fruitful ... And I will give to you and to your descendants after you, the land of your sojournings, all the land of Canaan ...'
Gen. 22:17–18	'... indeed I will greatly bless you, and I will greatly multiply your seed as the stars of the heavens, and as the sand which is on the seashore; and your seed shall possess the gate of their enemies. And in your seed all the nations of the earth shall be blessed, because you have obeyed My voice.'
Gen. 26:3	'Sojourn in this land and I will be with you and bless you, for to you and to your descendants I will give all these lands, and I will establish the oath which I swore to your father Abraham.'
Gen. 26:4	'And I will multiply your descendants as the stars of heaven, and will give your descendants all these lands; and by your descendants all the nations of the earth shall be blessed ...'
Gen. 26:24	And the LORD appeared to him the same night and

said,/'I am the God of your father Abraham;/Do not fear, for I am with you./I will bless you, and multiply your descendants,/For the sake of My servant Abraham.'

Gen. 28:3–4   'And may God Almighty bless you and make you fruitful and multiply you, that you may become a company of peoples. May He also give you the blessing of Abraham, to you and to your descendants with you; that you may possess the land of your sojournings, which God gave to Abraham.'

Gen. 35:11–12   God also said to him,/'I am God Almighty;/Be fruitful and multiply;/A nation and a company of nations shall come from you,/And kings shall come forth from you./And the land which I gave to Abraham and Isaac,/I will give it to you,/And I will give the land to your descendants after you.'

Gen. 47:27   Now Israel lived in the land of Egypt, in Goshen, and they acquired property in it and were fruitful and became very numerous.

In fact, the same commission given to the patriarchs is restated numerous times in subsequent Old Testament books both to Israel and the true eschatological people of God. Like Adam, Noah and his children also failed to perform this commission. God then gave the essence of the commission of Genesis 1:28 to Abraham (Gen. 12:2; 17:2, 6, 8, 16; 22:18), Isaac (26:3–4, 24), Jacob (28:3–4, 14; 35:11–12; 48:3, 15–16), and to Israel (see Deut. 7:13 and Gen. 47:27; Exod. 1:7; Ps. 107:38; and Is. 51:2, the latter four of which state the beginning fulfilment of the promise to Abraham in Israel).[27] The commission of Genesis 1:28 involved the following elements:

[27] This was first brought to my attention by N. T. Wright 1992a: 21–26, upon which the above list of references in Genesis is based. Wright sees that the command to Adam in Gen. 1:26–28 has been applied to the patriarchs and Israel; he also cites other texts where he sees Gen. 1:28 applied to Israel (Exod. 32:13; Lev. 26:9; Deut. 1:10f.; 7:13f.; 8:1; 28:63; 30:5, 16). I have subsequently likewise discovered that Cohen (1989: 28–31, 39) makes the same observation in dependence on G. V. Smith (1977: 207–319), who both include Noah. See also Dumbrell 1994: 29–30, 37, 72–73, 143 for the notion that the blessings conditionally promised to Adam are given to Israel. Likewise, Gage affirms only generally that the 'divine command (or creative mandate) originally pronounced to Adam . . . (Gen. 1:28), is formalized covenantally through three administrations (i.e., three mediators: Noah, Abraham and David)' (1984: 29). Cf. also Carroll 2000: 27, who says only briefly that the divine intention to bless humankind is reaffirmed in Gen. 12:1–3. Cf. similarly Fishbane 1979: 112–113. Jewish tradition applies the Gen. 1:28 commission to Noah and Abraham (Midrash Tanhuma Genesis 3:5; likewise Tanhuma Yelammedenu 2:12).

1. 'God blessed them';
2. 'be fruitful and multiply';
3. 'fill the earth';
4. 'subdue' the 'earth';
5. 'rule over ... all the earth' (so Gen. 1:26, and reiterated in 1:28).

The commission is repeated, for example, to Abraham: (1) 'I will greatly *bless you*, and (2) I will greatly *multiply your seed* ... (3–5) and *your seed shall possess the gate of their enemies* [= 'subdue and rule']. And in your seed all the nations of the earth shall be *blessed* ...' (Gen. 22:17–18).[28] God expresses the universal scope of the commission by underscoring that the goal is to 'bless' 'all the nations of the earth'. It is natural, therefore, that in the initial statement of the commission in Genesis 12:1–3 God commands Abraham, 'Go forth from your country ... and so be a blessing ... and in you all the families of the earth shall be blessed.'

Commentators apparently have not noticed something very interesting: that the Adamic commission is repeated in direct connection with what looks to be the building of small sanctuaries. Just as the Genesis 1:28 commission was initially to be carried out by Adam in a localized place, enlarging the borders of the arboreal sanctuary, so it appears to be not accidental that the restatement of the commission to Israel's patriarchs results in the following:

1. God appearing to them (except in Gen. 12:8; 13:3–4);
2. they 'pitch a *tent*' (literally a 'tabernacle' in LXX),
3. on a mountain;
4. they build 'altars' and worship God (i.e., 'calling on the name of the LORD', which probably included sacrificial offerings and prayer [Pagolu 1998: 62]) at the place of the restatement;
5. the place where these activities occur is often located at 'Bethel' – the 'House of God' (the only case of altar-building not containing these elements nor linked to the Genesis 1 commission is Gen. 33:20).

The combination of these five elements occurs elsewhere in the Old Testament only in describing Israel's tabernacle or temple![29]

---

[28] Notice that the ruling aspect of the commission is expressed to Abraham elsewhere as a role of 'kingship' (Gen. 17:6, 16), and likewise with respect to Jacob (Gen. 35:11).

[29] The combination of 'tent' (*'ōhel*) and 'altar' (*mizbēaḥ*) occur in Exodus and Leviticus only with respect to the tabernacle and associated altar (e.g., Lev. 4:7, 18). 'Altar' (*mizbēaḥ*) and 'house' (*bayit*) occur 28 times in the OT with reference to the

Therefore, though 'occasions for their sacrifices were usually a theophany and moving to a new place' (Pagolu 1998: 85), there seems to be more significance to the construction of these sacrificial sites. The patriarchs appear also to have built these worship areas as impermanent, miniature forms of sanctuaries that symbolically represented the notion that their progeny were to spread out to subdue the earth from a divine sanctuary in fulfilment of the commission in Genesis 1:26–28.[30] Though they built no buildings, these patriarchal sacred spaces can be considered 'sanctuaries' along the lines comparable to the first non-architectural sanctuary in the Garden of Eden. It will also be important to recall later that a holy piece of geography or a sacred area can be considered a true 'sanctuary' or 'temple' even when no architectural building is constructed there.

These informal sanctuaries in Genesis pointed then to Israel's later tabernacle and temple from which Israel was to branch out over all

---

temple and its altar. Rarely do any of the words in these two combinations ever refer to anything else other than the tabernacle or temple. The building of these worship sites on a mountain may represent part of a pattern finding its climax in Israel's later temple that was built on Mount Zion (the traditional site of Mount Moriah), which itself becomes a synecdoche of the whole for the part in referring to the temple (pp. 145–146). We do not mean to say that 'tent' in the patriarchal episodes is equivalent to the later tabernacle, only that it resonates with tabernacle-like associations because of its proximity to the worship site.

[30] Later midrashic exegesis on the temple may have been partly inspired by Gen. 1:26–28 in its understanding that the temple brought the blessing of fertility, even of children. While some of these references are speculative and fanciful, they show, nevertheless, an awareness of some kind of a relationship between Gen. 1:28 and the temple. For example, one midrashic source says, 'Why was the Sanctuary compared to a couch? Because just as this couch serves fruitfulness and multiplication (i.e. sexual intercourse), even so the Sanctuary, everything that was in it was fruitful and multiplied' (cited in Patai 1967: 90). In addition, the same Jewish source affirms, 'just as the forest is fruitful and multiplies, even so the Sanctuary, everything that was in it was fruitful and multiplied' (cited in Patai 1967: 90). So also *Midrash Rabbah Numbers* 11:3; *b. Yoma* 39b. 'During the three months in which the Ark of the Lord was kept in the house of Obed Edom, each one of the wives of his eight sons gave birth to a child every two weeks. It was the Ark then, in which lay the power of fertility' (Patai 1967: 90, citing *y. Yebamot* 6b.; cf. *b. Berakoth* 63b–64a; *Midrash Rabbah Numbers* 4:20; *Midrash Rabbah Song of Songs* 2:5). Likewise, the existence of the temple and the rites performed therein procured blessing and fruitfulness for Israel (and implicitly the earth in general; so Patai 1967: 122–128). For example, 'The world stands . . . on the temple service: how so? So long as the Temple service is maintained, the world is a blessing to its inhabitants and the rains come down in season . . . But when the Temple service is not maintained, the world is not a blessing to its inhabitants and the rains do not come down in season . . .' (*The Fathers According to Rabbi Nathan* 4; I am grateful to Patai for alerting me to the preceding Jewish sources). That these sources are developing a biblical concept is evident from Hag. 1:9–11 that says Israel was unfruitful because they had been disobedient by not building the temple. *Midrash Rabbah Song of Songs* 1:16 §3 notes that building the first and second temple resulted in a radical increase of Israel's population.

the earth. Not many commentators hold this view. After writing the first draft of this chapter, I found that A. Pagolu is perhaps most clearly in agreement (1998: 70). He says that Isaac's building of an altar at Beersheba was because that place already 'had a tradition as a patriarchal sanctuary', as a result of Abraham's similar earlier cultic activities, and, Pagolu contends, Jacob's subsequent similar activities appear to confirm this (for Abraham's activities at Beersheba, see Gen. 21:33; 22:19, and for Jacob's, see Gen. 46:1–14). Pagolu adds that, in addition to Isaac building this site because of a divine theophany and moving to a new area for the purpose of worship, 'it is possible to suggest that building an altar at Beer-sheba, the southernmost border of the promised land, may have represented not only a claim to the land but also a legitimation of the sanctuary for later Israel' (1998: 70).[31]

G. Vos agrees that the theophanies at these altar sites prepared for the more permanent theophany at the Jerusalem temple. He makes the astounding and, as far as I can tell, unique claim that these episodes not merely point to a future and greater temple but represent 'the renewal of the paradise-condition and as such presages a full future paradise. It points to the new world' (2001: 85–86).[32]

That these miniature sanctuaries adumbrated the later temple is also suggested by the facts that 'before Moses the altar was the only architectural feature marking a place as holy' and that later 'altars were incorporated into the larger [structural] sanctuaries, the tabernacle and the temple' (Longman 2001: 16).[33] The small sanctuary in Bethel also became a larger sanctuary in the northern kingdom of

---

[31] Similarly, with respect to Gen. 12:6–8 see Cassuto 1964: 328–329. Cassuto (1964:325–326) argues that the worship site at the 'oak of Moreh' in Shechem that Abraham established had become a 'sanctuary', at least by the time Jacob went there and performed cultic rituals in preparation for re-establishing another similar site at Bethel (Gen. 35:1–15; Cassuto also identifies the site with the place where Israel later set up an altar in Deut. 27:5–7, which is inextricably linked there with Israel's tabernacle (on which cf. Josh. 8:30–35). A. Dillmann says with respect to Gen. 12:7 (and implicitly of the other patriarchal altar building episodes) that 'the building of a sanctuary (subsequently in Jerusalem or Bethel) was a less simple form of the same practice' performed by the patriarchs and that these patriarchal activities 'were regarded as patterns for a later time' (1892: 15). See also Driver 1904: 143, who says that these sites 'in later times were regarded as sanctuaries' because of the earlier altar building activities of the patriarchs.

[32] Though he gives no exegetical evidence, I have subsequently found that his approach is almost identical to the one being forged in this section.

[33] While some commentators acknowledge that some of these patriarchal episodes involve the construction of small sanctuaries, they do not associate them with Israel's later large-scale temple (so, e.g., Leupold 1960: 781, 918, with respect to Gen. 28 and 35).

Israel, though it subsequently became idolatrous and was rejected as a true shrine of Yahweh worship.[34]

The result of Abraham, Isaac and Jacob building altars at Shechem, between Bethel and Ai, at Hebron, and near Moriah was that the terrain of Israel's future land was dotted with shrines. This pilgrim-like activity 'was like planting a flag and claiming the land' (Longman 2001: 20; sim. Pagolu 1998: 70)[35] for God and Israel's future temple, where God would take up his permanent residence in the capital of that land.[36] Thus, all these smaller sanctuaries pointed to the greater one to come in Jerusalem.[37] The patriarchs were like people climbing a tall mountain for the first time and planting the national flag to indicate that the climber's native land had first conquered the mountain.

---

[34] See Amos 7:13: Amos is told, 'no longer prophesy at Bethel, for it is a sanctuary of the king . . .' (so see Gunkel 1997: 313; Vawter 1997: 311; and Towner 2001: 139. Cf. also 1 Kgs. 12:28–29 and Hos. 10:5).

[35] The Talmud affirmed of Gen. 28:13 that God 'rolled up the whole of the land of Israel and put it under . . . Jacob, [to indicate to him] that it would be very easily conquered by his descendants' (b. Chullin 91b).

[36] Later Judaism held the similar view that the patriarchal altar building sites were the place of the future temple or that at these sites the patriarchs had visions of Solomon's temple and of the eschatological temple: for Abraham cf. *Tg. Genesis* 22:14; *Sifre on Deuteronomy*, Piska 352; *Midrash Tanhuma Genesis* 4:41; *Midrash Rabbah Genesis* 56:10; *Pesikta Rabbati*, Piska 39; for Jacob see *Sifre on Numbers* §119; *Midrash Tanhuma Genesis* 7:9; *Midrash Rabbah Genesis* 69:7; *Pirke de Rabbi Eliezer* 35. Cf. *Ladder of Jacob* 5:8: 'around the property of your [Jacob's] forefathers a palace will be built, a temple in the name of . . . (the God) of your fathers'.

[37] In addition to the subsequent temple built in Bethel, Israel's tabernacle subsequently came to rest for a long time in Shiloh, which was located near Bethel and Shechem (so Judg. 21:19), locations where Abraham had set up shrines. The tabernacle remained there, at least, during the time of Joshua and the Judges (on which see the references to 'Shiloh' in Joshua, Judges and 1 Samuel). This would be another example of a smaller sanctuary being succeeded by a bigger one. There is some debate about whether or not an actual temple structure was built there, since 1 Samuel employs language apparently more fitting for a temple than a tabernacle: e.g., 1 Sam. 1:9, 'Now Eli the priest was sitting on the seat by the doorpost of the temple of the LORD' (so likewise 1 Sam. 3:3; the word is *hêkāl*, used predominately of Israel's temple structure or God's heavenly temple but never of the tabernacle). Most likely, though, there was only a tabernacle in Shiloh, since the phrase 'house of the Lord' and 'house of God' is also used in 1 Sam. 1:7, 24 and 3:15 and the same phrase was also used of the tabernacle (Exod. 23:19; 34:26; Deut. 23:18; Josh. 6:24; 1 Chr. 6:48; cf. 'house of my God' in Josh. 9:23). Also, 1 Sam. 2:22 speaks of 'the doorway of the tent of meeting', likely the same location referred to in 1:9. Furthermore, Ps. 78:60 summarizes God's dwelling in Shiloh as being a tabernacle: God 'abandoned the dwelling place at Shiloh, the tent which He had pitched among men'. Even if there were some kind of temple structure, 1 Sam. 2:35 says that God's dwelling in Shiloh was not an 'enduring house' but was to be succeeded by one which would be.

Abraham at the mountains of Bethel and Moriah

Abraham, after receiving the Genesis 1 promissory commission, went 'to the mountain on the east of Bethel ['House of God'], and pitched his tent ... and there he built an altar to the LORD and called upon the name of the LORD' (Gen. 12:8; so likewise Gen. 13:3–4). Sometimes mention is made only of the commission and of the tent and altar (Gen. 13:18; 26:24–25). Only an altar is cited together with the promise in Gen. 22:9–18, though there the site is also called 'the mountain of God', a name often attached by synecdoche to Israel's temples.[38] That 'Mount Moriah' is the site of Abraham's aborted sacrifice of Isaac and apparently also the site of the Solomonic temple (2 Chr. 3:1) suggests 'that God had long intended that the temple would eventually be placed in the vicinity of Jerusalem' (Longman 2001: 45).[39] The observation that Mount 'Moriah' is mentioned elsewhere in the Old Testament only in 2 Chronicles 3:1 serves to enhance this point: 'Then Solomon began to build the house of the Lord in Jerusalem on Mount Moriah ...' (Vawter 1977: 257).

Jacob at the mountain of Bethel

Though a 'mountain' or 'hill' is not explicitly associated with Bethel in the Jacob narratives, it is likely the same or, at least, near the same location of Abraham's earlier similar experiences (notice that 'go up to Bethel' occurs twice in Gen. 35:1, 3 in the introduction to the narrative of Jacob's experience at Bethel). When the divine promises of blessing are first made to Jacob (28:13–14), they are preceded by his dream of a 'stairway' connecting heaven and earth and angels ascending and descending on it and God appearing beside it (28:12). Jacob responds by saying, 'This is none other than the house of God, and this is the gate of heaven' (28:17). He then sets up a 'pillar, and poured oil on its top' (equivalent to building an altar) and names the place 'Bethel' (28:18–19). He concludes by declaring that 'this stone,

---

[38] E.g., Is. 2:2 refers to 'the mountain of the house of the LORD', and then 2:3 refers to the same thing with the phrase 'let us go up to the mountain of the LORD, to the house of the God of Jacob' (so identically Mic. 4:1–2). The precise phrase 'the mountain of God' refers elsewhere in the OT only five times to Mount Sinai (Exod. 3:1; 4:27; 18:5; 24:13; 1 Kgs. 19:8) and twice to the Garden of Eden (Ezek. 28:14, 16), both, as we have seen, being sanctuary-like sacred locations; in Dan. 9:20 'the holy mountain of my God' focuses on Israel's temple (though Pagolu demurs on identifying Moriah with Mount Zion in Jerusalem [1998: 67]).

[39] This point may be enhanced by rabbinic tradition that held that Eden was located near Mount Moriah (*Pirke de Rabbi Eliezer* 20; *Midrash Psalms* 92:6).

which I have set up as a pillar, will be God's house' (28:22). This state-ment indicates that from the stone a sanctuary, indeed, a temple would arise (Westermann 1995: 459).[40] He returns to 'Bethel' later (Gen. 35:1–15), and the text notes three times that Jacob builds an 'altar' there (35:1, 3, 7, and 14; Jacob also establishes a sacred 'pillar' in v. 14).

This episode further links the altar construction of the patriarchs with the notion of 'temple', since Israel's later temple was the place in all of the world where heaven was linked to the earth, particularly the 'holy of holies' that represented God's invisible presence in heaven. It is helpful in this respect to recall that the ark of the cov-enant in the holy of holies was considered God's 'footstool', conjur-ing up the picture of God sitting on his throne in heaven with his legs extending to Israel's temple on earth (Is. 66:1; Acts 7:49; cf. also Ps. 99:5; 110:1; a 'footstool' was attached to Solomon's 'throne' in imita-tion of God's throne [2 Chr. 9:18]). Indeed, Bethel became the site of 'the ark of the covenant of the LORD' during the time of the judges, continuing apparently into the time of Samuel. This means, of course, that the tabernacle was likewise there, since Phineas, Aaron's grandson, served as high priest at Bethel, and Israel 'offered burnt offerings and peace offerings' during his tenure (see Judg. 20:18–28; 1 Sam. 7:16; 10:3).

The holy site established by Jacob at 'Bethel' near 'Haran' in Genesis 28 and 35 is the clearest of the patriarchal sanctuary build-ing episodes, which is enhanced by its location at or near the second altar built by Abraham (cf. Gen. 12:8, where the vicinity of 'Bethel [House of God]' and 'Haran' [Gen. 12:4] are also mentioned). In this respect, Genesis 28:11 introduces the narrative there by saying, Jacob 'came to *the* place [*māqôm*]', which may indicate that this site was already considered holy because of Abraham's repeated earlier worship there, which itself is twice referred to as 'the place [*māqôm*]' in Genesis 13:3–4 (e.g., note 'the place of the altar' in 13:4).[41]

---

[40] That this episode points to the building of a large temple is further apparent from noticing that Gen. 28:22 directly links the 'stone' of 'God's house' with Jacob pledg-ing that 'of all that you give me I will surely give a tenth to you'. Israelites are later to give a 'tenth' to the temple or to those who serve in the temple (so approximately 18 times, mostly in Lev., Num. and Deut., as well as in Heb. 7:5). Notable exceptions to this are Abraham giving a 'tenth' to Melchizedek (Gen. 14:20; Heb. 7:6) and the Israelites giving a 'tenth' to their king (1 Sam. 8:15, 17).

[41] In support of this point, see also Gamberoni, '*Māqôm*', *TDOT*, 8:538; the same word is used of the first place that Abraham set up an altar probably with the same notion of 'sacred place' (following Driver 1904: 146). This suggestion is enhanced by

The associations with a temple in Genesis 28 are enhanced by the Ancient Near Eastern associations of 'stairway-like' structures that connected heaven to earth, allowing heavenly beings to descend and dwell in a temple.[42] The tower of Babel in Genesis 11 may well have been an example of such temple-like towers. In fact, the similarities between the tower of Babel and Genesis 28 suggest that the latter is the true 'counterpoint' to the former, which was a vain attempt to experience God's presence.[43]

In keeping with the thesis that the patriarchal shrines both recalled the original temple in Eden and anticipated the tabernacle and temple, it is not likely coincidental that in the seven instances where the patriarchs build their holy places, 'tree[s]' are present or close by on four occasions (Gen. 12:6; 13:18; 22:13; 35:8),[44] though all of them probably had a significant arboreal feature in their midst.[45] In the light of the links with Genesis 1 – 2 noted above, the common feature of a tree next to these worship sites, where humans experience God's

---

observing that, after 28:11, the Hebrew word 'place' occurs seven more times in Gen. 28 and 35 with reference to God appearing to Jacob there or with reference to Jacob calling the site 'Bethel' ('House of God'). This use of 'place' as a special sanctuary site takes on even more significance when it is remembered that the same word not untypically refers to the tabernacle and temple, or things related to the temple, later in the OT (on which see Gamberoni, 'Māqôm', TDOT, 8:537–543).

[42] In Mesopotamian mythology, a messenger of the gods would use a stairway to move from a heavenly realm to an earthly or netherworld sphere. 'It is this same stairway that is architecturally depicted in the famous ziggurats that adjoined temples in Mesopotamian cities, designed to offer a way for the gods to descend to the temple [on earth] to be worshipped' (Walton 2001: 571; likewise, Skinner 1910: 377–378, and Speiser 1982: 219–220). Typically, at the stairway's top was a gate to heaven and at the bottom was a temple for the divine being to rest in and be refreshed after the journey down from heaven (Speiser 1982: 373–374). Indeed, the Hebrew word 'stairway' (sullām) is cognate to the Akkadian simmiltu that was used to refer to a heavenly 'stairway' linked to a temple (Ross 1988: 488–489).

[43] Cf. Fishbane 1979: 115, who sees the Gen. 28 episode as a 'counterpoint' to the 'temple-tower' of Babel. B. K. Waltke adds to Fishbane's conclusion by observing that 'the Semites understood the name Babylon to have been derived from bābili, "gate of God"' (11:9)' (2001: 392). The identification of Bethel as 'gate of heaven' may be intended as a counterpoint to 'Babylon', which apparently had its origin in connection with the 'tower of Babel' episode, where the name 'Babel' in Gen. 11:9 occurs.

[44] The Hebrew word for 'thicket' in Gen. 22:13 occurs six other times in the OT, three of which refer to a 'thicket of the forest [or tree]' (Ps. 74:5; Is. 9:18 [MT = 9:17]; 10:34).

[45] The 'oak' in Gen. 35:8 may be at the site of Bethel or more probably in its vicinity. Though Gen. 12:8, 13:3–4, and 28:11–22 do not mention a tree at (or in the vicinity of) Bethel, there may well have been one there because of the mention of a tree at the site in Gen. 35:6–15. Similarly, Isaac's building of an altar in Beersheba (Gen. 26:25) must also have been placed directly next to a tree, since Abraham had 'planted a tamarisk tree at Beersheba' and worshipped there.

presence, might well evoke 'the tree of life' in the Garden of Eden (Longman 2001: 21).[46]

Jewish views of Jacob's temple-building activities in Genesis 28

Jubilees 32:16–32 is the earliest Jewish commentary (2nd century BC) identifying Jacob's building activities at Bethel as temple construction: 'Jacob planned to build up that place and to build a wall around the court, and to sanctify it, and make it eternally holy.'[47]

With respect to the expectation of Israel's eschatological temple, the Qumran Temple Scroll says, 'during the day of [the new] creation ... I [God] shall create my temple, establishing it for myself for ever, *in accordance with the covenant which I made with Jacob at Bethel*' (11Q19 29:8–9, my translation)! The 'covenant' refers to the three-fold promise God made to Jacob at Bethel, which, as we have seen, is the reapplication of the Adamic commission: (1) that God would 'be with' Jacob and his seed and 'keep' them and 'bring them back' (2) in order to possess the promised land (Gen. 28:13, 15); (3) that his seed would 'spread out' to the four points of the compass, so that 'in you and your seed shall all the families of the earth be blessed' (28:14).

Thus, Qumran interprets that the future establishment of Israel's eschatological temple will be the fulfilment of this threefold promise and repeated Adamic commission.[48] Furthermore, this will take place at the time of the new 'creation', as a recapitulation of the primal Edenic temple within which Adam and his seed should have carried out their commission by spreading out over the earth. Quite intriguingly, Philo, the first-century philosophical theologian, understands the incipient sanctuary building episode at Bethel to have fulfilment throughout the earth in *all saints* who become cleansed by

---

[46] Westermann contends that the trees at these sites indicate an 'early type of sanctuary' but not a temple, since there is no 'cultic institution, personnel, or building' (1995: 154–157, 181). Nevertheless, there can still be the essence of a 'temple' without these latter three formal elements, as we have argued above in our attempt to demonstrate that Eden was functionally a temple. Indeed, just as Adam was a priestly figure, so likely are the patriarchs. Hence, it is better to view the patriarchal worship sites, like Eden, as inchoate or embryonic sanctuaries or informal temples, pointing to Israel's later tabernacle and temple.

[47] The *Jubilees* passage goes on to say that an angel told him, 'Do not build this place, and do not make it an eternal sanctuary', since it was not the precise place nor the time for the permanent temple to be built.

[48] See Kampen 1994: 85–97 for debate about whether or not one or two temples is spoken of in this Qumran text.

God's word and, consequently, 'become a house of God, a holy temple, a most beauteous abiding-place' (*Som.* 1.148–149).[49]

For all or some of these reasons, the Aramaic translation of the Old Testament identifies the place of God's appearance to Jacob as a 'sanctuary' (*Tg. Pseudo-Jonathon Genesis* 28:11, 17; *Tg. Neofiti 1 Genesis* 28:22 [literally, 'a house of holiness']). Later Judaism identified the stone that Jacob set up as a sacred 'pillar' to be the foundation stone of Solomon's temple (*Pirke de Rabbi Eliezer* 35) and of the temple to be built at the time of Israel's restoration (cf. *Midrash Tanhuma Genesis* 6:20; likewise *b. Pesachim* 88a).[50]

Thus, Judaism even more explicitly identifies Jacob's building activities in Genesis 28 to be the beginning stages of temple contruction.

Noah on Mount Ararat

Though Noah precedes Abraham and his sons, it is more instructive for our purposes to discuss his significance now, rather than earlier, against the background of what took place with Abraham and his descendants. That 'Noah built an altar to the LORD' (Gen. 8:20), also in direct connection with God's reapplication of the Adamic commission (Gen. 9:1, 7; cf. 8:17), indicates that this also may have been an even earlier inchoate temple-building event. The following observations enhance this suggestion. First, he 'offered burnt offerings on the altar'. Second, these offerings were a 'soothing aroma' before the Lord. The only other place where 'burnt offerings' (in singular) are a 'soothing aroma' to God are the offerings in the tabernacle.[51] Third, Noah offers these sacrifices on a mountain (in the mountain range of Ararat). Fourth, the distinction between 'clean and unclean' animals is made for the first time here in the Bible (Gen. 7:2, 8), and only 'clean' animals could be offered as a sacrifice (Gen. 8:20). The only other situation where a distinction between 'clean and unclean' animals is made is in the context of requirements of those who want to gain access to the outer court of the tabernacle (Lev. 11:47; 20:25; Deut. 12:15, 22).[52]

---

[49] On which see Michel, *'naos'*, *TDNT*, 4:886.

[50] *b. Pesachim* 88a explains 'the house of the God of Jacob' by Gen. 28:19. Some Jewish traditions contend that either the mid-point or the top of the heavenly ladder was over the site of the future Jerusalem temple (Zlotowitz and Scherman 1977: 1238, 1240).

[51] So 13 times in Exodus, Leviticus, and Numbers, though a different Hebrew word for 'burnt offering' is used; offerings as a 'soothing aroma' [*rêaḥ nîḥôaḥ*] is found over 40 times with respect to the tabernacle and temple in the Pentateuch and Ezekiel.

[52] For the idea, intriguingly, that Noah's ark was a temple, see Holloway 1991: 328–354. For the LXX's intention to present the ark in the temple in the light of Noah's

Israel at the mountain sanctuary of Sinai

Israel's encounter with God at Mount Sinai also appears to be another experience of worship at a sacred location that approximates a temple site. First, some of the same things seen with the sanctuary building of the patriarchs appear here too. For example, Israel is to worship on a mountain (Exod. 3:12), though Sinai is never called 'house of God'. In addition, the Sinai episode exhibits other features typically associated with Israel's later tabernacle or temple.

First, Sinai is called 'the mountain of God' (Exod. 3:1; 18:5; 24:13), a name associated with Israel's temple on Mount Zion.[53]

Second, just as with the tabernacle and temple, so Mount Sinai was divided into three sections of increasing sanctity: the majority of the Israelites were to remain at the foot of Sinai (Exod. 19:12, 23), the priests and seventy elders (the latter functioning probably as priests) were allowed to come some distance up the mountain (Exod. 19:22; 24:1), but only Moses could ascend to the top and directly experience the presence of God (Exod. 24:2).

Third, just as an altar was in the outermost section of the temple, so an altar was built at the lowest and least sacred part of Sinai, where Israel 'offered burnt offerings and sacrificed young bulls as peace offerings to the LORD. And Moses took half of the blood and ... sprinkled [it] on the altar' (Exod. 24:5–6). The temple atmosphere of this text is apparent from observing that the phrase 'burnt offering[s]' occurs approximately thirty-eight times together with 'peace offerings' in the Old Testament, and the vast majority refer to sacrifices in the tabernacle or temple (though even some of the remaining uses may be linked to a sanctuary setting: e.g., Judg. 20:26; 21:4; 1 Sam. 10:8; 13:9). Likewise, the majority of the numerous uses of each of the two phrases by themselves refer to the same temple context.

Fourth, not only does the top part of Sinai approximate the holy of holies because only Israel's 'high priest', Moses, could enter there, but it was the place where God's theophanic 'cloud' and presence 'dwelt' (Exod. 24:15–17; for Moses as a 'high priest' see Philo, *Vit. Mos.* 2.75). Significantly, the only other times in all of the Old

---

ark by translating both by *kibōtos*, see Haywood 1999: 37. Furthermore, Noah's ark was divided into three storeys or levels, just as was Israel's later tabernacle and temple. Likewise, detailed architectural plans elsewhere in the OT describe only the tabernacle or temple (e.g., cf. Exod. 25ff. and Ezek. 40 – 48; on which see Kline 1989: 156–159).

[53] E.g., see 'mountain of the LORD' as a virtual synonym for 'house of God' in Is. 2:2 and Mic. 4:2; for almost identical names, see below.

Testament that God's presence is spoken of as a 'cloud dwelling' is with respect to God's presence above the tabernacle (Exod. 40:35; Num. 9:17–18, 22; 10:12). Even the word 'dwell' (*šākan*) could be rendered 'to tabernacle' (*miškān*) and the word 'tabernacle' is the noun form of this verb (which is used with the verb in three of the four preceding texts). So also, 1 Kings 8:12–13 says that God 'would dwell in the thick cloud' in the temple completed by Solomon. Furthermore, the 'ten commandments' and the 'ark' are created at the top of Sinai (Deut. 10:1–5), just as later they find their place in the inner sanctum of the temple, once again in God's presence.

Fifth, earlier in Exodus God's presence at Sinai was depicted as a 'cassia tree [*sĕneh*, or 'bush'] burning with fire, yet the cassia tree was not consumed' (Exod. 3:2). In the light of the parallels already adduced, this 'unconsumed burning tree' may be the proleptic equivalent to the lampstand-like tree in the holy place on Mount Zion, whose lamps burned continually.[54] Correspondingly, the ground around the burning tree is called 'the place' of 'holy ground' (Exod. 3:5). The correspondence of this small area at Sinai to the later 'holy place' is seen from the only other uses of 'holy place' in Hebrew, four of which refer to the section of the sanctuary directly outside the 'holy of holies' (Lev. 7:6; 10:17; 14:13; 24:9) and the remaining two refer to the temple in general (Ezra 9:8; Ps. 24:3).

As in the case of the temporary patriarchal shrines, so the Siniatic holy place is linked to development of the themes found in Genesis 1:28. God sends Moses to deliver Israel out of Egypt's womb because the embryonic seed of Jacob has come to full term, in fulfilment not only of the Abrahamic promises but also of the promissory Adamic commission: 'But the sons of Israel were *fruitful* and *swarmed* greatly, and *multiplied*, and became exceedingly numerous, so that *the land was filled* with them.'[55]

In this respect, subduing the land of Canaan is also mentioned (Exod. 3:8, 17). Not surprisingly, there is also a link with the promise to 'Abraham, Isaac and Jacob' (Exod. 3:6, 15–16).[56]

---

[54] G. P. Hugenberger in private communication; supported by Longman 2001: 57. Could the tree-like image on Sinai also have some degree of correspondence to the tree of life in Eden, which was on a mountain (Ezek. 28:13–16), and to the trees at the various patriarchal sanctuary sites that were also on mountains?

[55] See Exod. 1:7, where the italicized words represent the same Hebrew as Gen. 1:28; 'swarmed' comes from the development of Gen. 1:28 in Gen. 9:7, where the commission is passed on to Noah; cf. similarly Exod. 1:12.

[56] See Spatafora 1997: 28, 31, who, on the basis of some of the above observations, recognizes that Israel's temple was symbolic of Mount Sinai.

In the light of the association of Sinai as a temple, it may not be accidental that Revelation 11:19 later alludes to the theophanic phenomena at Sinai in describing the opening of the heavenly holy of holies at the end of history, when 'the ark of his covenant' will be revealed ('there came about lightnings and sounds and thunders').[57]

In this light, Sinai was an appropriate place for God to show to Moses 'the pattern of the tabernacle and the pattern of all its furniture' in order that they would construct it exactly as it was 'shown' to Moses (Exod. 25:9; cf. 25:40). Hence, once Israel leaves the stationary sanctuary of Sinai, the commission is passed on to them to build the mobile tabernacle in order that God's glorious presence would continue to 'dwell among them' during their wilderness wanderings (Exod. 25:8). Indeed, it has been observed by others that the building of the tabernacle itself appears to have been modelled on the tripartite pattern of Sinai.[58] The building of the tabernacle would be a step towards the construction of the immovable temple in Jerusalem.

David and Solomon at Mount Moriah

What appears implicit with the patriarchs and with Moses at Sinai, becomes explicit with Israel's tabernacle and temple. The first book of Chronicles narrates David's preparations for building the temple that Solomon will accomplish. David's preparatory actions include all the same elements found with the small-scale temple building activities of Abraham, Isaac and Jacob, which confirms that their building activities were, indeed, miniature versions of, or pointers to, a later sanctuary.

1. David begins the preparations on a mountain (Mount Moriah);
2. David experiences a theophany (he sees 'the angel of the LORD standing between earth and heaven'; so 1 Chr. 21:16; 2 Chr. 3:1).
3. At this site 'David built an altar to the LORD . . .
4. 'and offered burnt offerings . . . And he called to the LORD' (1 Chr. 21:26).
5. Furthermore, David calls the place 'the house of the LORD God' (1 Chr. 22:1) because this is the site of Israel's future temple to be prepared by David and built by Solomon (1 Chr. 22; 2 Chr. 3:1).

[57] For the allusion to Sinai in Rev. 11:19, see Bauckham 1993: 202–204. Similarly, Jewish tradition believed that at the final resurrection, 'the ark will be the first to be resurrected . . . and be placed on Mount Sinai' (*Lives of the Prophets* 2:15), implying that this author viewed Sinai itself to be a mountain temple.

[58] See Douglas 1999: e.g., 59–64.

Now we can see more clearly that the altar-building activities of the patriarchs were constructions of small-scale sanctuaries that find their climax with the larger-scale construction of Israel's temple. The episode in 1 Chronicles 21 particularly mirrors the one with Jacob, where also God and angels appear to him and a link between 'earth' and 'heaven' is underscored.[59] The reason why David performed priestly activities at this site was twofold: first, because from that very site the temple of Israel was to be built; second, because the 1 Chronicles 21 passage goes on to say that 'the tabernacle ... which Moses had made ... and the altar of burnt offering were in ... Gibeon at that time' (21:29). This latter point implies not only that David was not able to travel there to offer sacrifices at the properly designated cultic place, but that a transition from the movable tabernacle to the permanent temple has begun. Mount Moriah was now becoming the designated place for sacrifice because the temple would soon be built there.[60]

As with the patriarchs, there are also links in the Davidic narrative with Genesis 1:28, though not as explicitly. In direct connection with David's preparations for the building of the temple in 1 Chronicles 29:10–12, he praises God: '*Blessed* art Thou, O Lord ... Thine ... is the greatness and the power and the glory and the victory and the majesty, indeed everything that is in *the heavens and the earth*; Thine is the *dominion* ... Thou dost exalt Thyself as head over all ... Thou dost *rule over all* ... and it lies in Thy hand to make great, and to strengthen everyone.'

David uses language synonymous to that of Genesis 1:28 to praise God himself because he is the one who 'makes great and strengthens' his human vice-regents to rule under his hand. Then Solomon is designated in the following verses as the example *par excellence* of such a vice-regent: 'Then Solomon sat on the throne of the Lord as king ... And the Lord highly exalted Solomon ... and bestowed on him

---

[59] *Tg. 1 Chronicles* 21:23–24 together with *Tg. 2 Chronicles* 3:1 identifies the place with Jacob's experience in Gen. 28 as well as the place where Abraham prepared Isaac for sacrifice. The former Targumic text identifies a heavenly 'sanctuary-house' that existed above the place apparently, at least, since the time of Jacob's small-scale building activities recorded in Gen. 28. David and Solomon were completing a temple-building process begun with the patriarchs wherein the earthly temple was to reflect the heavenly (accordingly, *Tg. 2 Chronicles* 6:2 says that Solomon 'built a sanctuary house ... corresponding to the throne of the house where you dwell, which is for ever in the heavens').

[60] *Tg Pseudo-Jonathon Genesis* 2:7 says that God created Adam partly of 'dust from the site of the sanctuary', which he then identifies with Mount Moriah (*Tg. Pseudo-Jonathon Genesis* 3:23).

royal majesty which had not been on any king before him in Israel' (29:23–25). It is probably not accidental that a few verses earlier David refers explicitly to the nation's identification with the patriarchs: he petitions 'the God of Abraham, Isaac, and Israel, our fathers' to preserve the peoples' godly desires and 'give to my son Solomon a perfect heart to keep ['guard'] Thy statutes . . . and to build the temple, for which I have made provision' (29:18–19), perhaps echoing the first temple context of Genesis 2:15–16: to 'guard' the garden sanctuary by following what God 'commanded'. Solomon completed the foundation-laying activities of his father: 'Then Solomon began to build the house of the LORD in Jerusalem on Mount Moriah . . .' (2 Chr. 3:1).

Second Samuel 7 (= 1 Chr. 17) closely links the need to build a temple (7:2–13) with the following aspects of Genesis 1:28: (1) ruling and subduing (7:9–16), and (2) a blessing on God's kingly vice-regent (7:29). It may also not be unexpected, therefore, that 2 Samuel 7:9, 'I will make you a great name', would allude to Genesis 12:2, 'I will . . . make your name great.' Accordingly, it is natural that the overall purpose is linked to God giving 'rest' to Israel's king from his enemies (7:1, 11). This prophecy is fulfilled only partially by Solomon, however, since 2 Samuel 7:10–16 says that the coming kingdom and temple will last for ever,[61] which was not true with Solomon's and his descendants' (Exod. 15:17–18 also affirms the same thing of the coming kingdom and, implicitly, of the temple, to which allusion is made in 2 Sam. 7:10, 12–13 cf. also 2 Chron. 8:16 [LXX]).

Post-exilic Israel

That Noah, the patriarchs, Moses and David were building nascent temple structures is further apparent from noticing that the same embryonic temple-building pattern occurs when the remnant of Israel returns from Babylon to reconstruct the temple. They (1) 'built the altar of the God of Israel' on the 'foundation' of the former temple at Mount Zion (Ezra 3:2–3); and (2) began 'to offer burnt offerings' (Ezra 3:2), and worshipped through the playing of music and by 'praising and giving thanks' (Ezra 3:10–11). (3) They also refer to the structure as 'a house to our God' (Ezra 4:3). In this situation,

---

[61] Sometimes the Hebrew word *'ôlām* may connote a long time or an 'eternal' period. Though there is debate, the word in 2 Sam. 7:13 best refers to an eternal epoch because of its links with the purposes of Eden that are developed with the patriarchs and because of the links with the eternal eschatological temple and kingdom later in the OT and NT (e.g., cf. Heb. 1:5; similarly Acts 2:30; 13:23).

however, there appear to be no clear references to Genesis 1:28 nor the Abrahamic promises. And even before the post-exilic temple was constructed, Ezekiel 11:16 says that though God had exiled Judah and Benjamin to Babylon, 'yet I [Yahweh] was a *sanctuary* for them a little while ...' This suggests that the presence of the Lord, which gave essential meaning to the temple, continued with the faithful remnant in exile to form a veritable invisible temple for them until they could return and begin building the second temple (Clowney 1972: 163).

Like Solomon's temple, Israel's second temple did not fulfil the prophecy of Exodus 15:17–18 and 2 Samuel 7:10–16.[62] Therefore, Exodus 15, 2 Samuel 7 and subsequent prophets foresaw an eschatological temple, the ideal descriptions of which both the first and second temples fell short (followed by 2 Maccabees 1:27–29; cf. 2 Maccabees 2:17–18).[63] Not only were these two temples not eternal, but we will see later that they could not fulfil the end-time expectations for other reasons.

End-time Israel

Israel's prophesied eschatological temple has the same associations as most of the preceding temple constructions. In Leviticus 26:6–12, allusion is made to Genesis 1:28 in direct connection to the erection of the tabernacle in Israel's midst: if Israel is faithful, they will defeat their enemies in the land, and 'I will turn toward you and *make you fruitful and multiply you*, and I will confirm My covenant with you ... Moreover, I will make My *tabernacle* among you ... I will also walk among you and be your God, and you will be My people.'[64]

Ezekiel 36 – 37 makes the same link: after promising that God would restore Israel and 'multiply men', and make them 'increase and be fruitful' (36:10–11), he also promises a 'multiplication' of fruitfulness (36:29–30), so that Israel's formerly desolated land will 'become like the garden of Eden' in which God 'will increase their men like a flock' (cf. 36:35–38). Then, in direct development of these preceding ideas and of Leviticus 26:6–12 (!),[65] Ezekiel 37:26–28 again refers to

---

[62] *Sirach* 47:13 and 49:12 show respectively that from Israel's vantage-point, Solomon's temple and the second temple were designed to last 'for ever' and for 'everlasting glory', neither of which materialized.

[63] Kerr (2002: 305–307) sees that John 14:2–3 applies Exod. 15:17 to Jesus and his community as the end-time temple.

[64] Philo understands Lev. 26:12 to refer to the human soul or mind as 'a holy temple' (*Som.* 1.148–149) or 'house of God' (*Som.* 1.148–149; *Praem.* 123).

[65] See Cohen 1989: 32–33 for fuller substantiation of the allusion to Lev. 26.

that aspect of the promise of 'multiplying them' and ties it to Israel's temple:[66] 'It will be an everlasting covenant ... And I will ... multiply them, and will set My sanctuary in their midst forever. My dwelling place [or 'tabernacle'] also will be over them; and I will be their God, and they will be My people. And the nations will know that I am the LORD who sanctifies Israel, when My sanctuary is in their midst forever.'[67]

Strikingly, there is also an association of an eschatological Eden with an end-time temple (Ezek. 36:35), which Ezekiel later identifies with the latter-day temple in chapters 40 – 48, and which is also depicted with imagery from Eden (e.g., see 43:7–12). While Leviticus 26 and Ezekiel 37 could be read as prophesying God's tabernacling presence in a temple structure, it is just as possible, if not preferable, to understand them as foretelling a time when the temple will be, not a physical handmade house, but God's manifest presence alone that will fill Israel (and the earth) as never before. Leviticus 26:11–12 could imply this: 'moreover, I will make My *tabernacle among you* ... I will also *walk among you* and be your God, and you will be my people.' God's tabernacling presence will abide with all his redeemed people. It would be hard for God freely to 'walk among' his people if his tabernacling presence were confined to a physical sanctuary, unless one were to think of it more figuratively as when God's tabernacle sojourned with Israel during her wilderness wanderings.[68] But, especially in light of its development in Ezekiel 37, the Leviticus promise of God's 'walking among' the people likely expresses a more ultimate personal and intense relationship than his present dwelling with them within an encased structure.

What indicates that this tabernacle is not to be like the former, smaller physical structures is the phrase in Ezekiel 37:27: 'My dwelling place also will be *over* [preposition '*al*] them.' Apparently, at the least, the new tabernacle will extend over all of God's people who have been 'multiplied' and 'shall live on the land', that is, living throughout the land of promise (on which see

---

[66] Woudstra 1970: 98, though he does not mention Leviticus.

[67] Note the further link between Ezek. 36:28–30 and 37:27 in the common phrase 'you will be My people, and I will be your God'; cf. Ezek. 11:16–20 which may also allude to Lev. 26.

[68] Indeed, 'walking' is used figuratively in Exodus, Numbers and Deuteronomy for God's presence with Israel (apparently in the tabernacle) during the wilderness wanderings (Deut. 23:14 [15]; 2 Sam. 7:6–7). The verb form in Lev. 26:12 is hithpael, the same form used for God 'walking back and forth' in the Eden sanctuary (Gen. 3:8).

37:24–28)![69] That the temple's worldwide goal is being achieved is alluded to in verse 28: 'the nations will know that I am the LORD' (both in judgment and in 'blessing' those who believe).

Along similar lines, Jeremiah 3:16–18 combines the commission found in Genesis 1:28[70] with the notion of a latter-day temple and makes explicit that God's tabernacling presence would not be restricted to an inner cultic room:

> [16]'And it shall be in those days when you *are multiplied and increased* in the land', declares the LORD, 'they shall say no more, "The ark of the covenant of the LORD." And it shall not come to mind, nor shall they remember it, nor shall they miss it, nor shall it be made again. [17]At that time they shall call Jerusalem "The Throne of the LORD", and all the nations will be gathered to it, for the name of the LORD in Jerusalem; nor shall they walk anymore after the stubbornness of their evil heart. [18]In those days the house of Judah will walk with the house of Israel, and they will come together from the land of the north to the land that I gave your fathers as an inheritance.'

Israel will finally fulfil the Genesis mandate 'to multiply and increase' at the time of her latter-day restoration (Jer. 3:16). The fact that Gentiles will stream in suggests that they also will play a role in fulfilling that commission. Though this fulfilment is coupled with a promise of a future temple, it is one that will not be like any earlier

[69] So Woudstra 1970: 98. We will see later that the NT understands Ezek. 3:26–28 to refer to the church as the gathered people of God wherever they may dwell on the earth (2 Cor. 6:16), in heaven (Rev. 7:15) or in the new cosmos (Rev. 21:3). See D. I. Block (1998: 421), who agrees that the preposition *'al* is to be translated *'over'* them' but sees this only as a possible reflection of the glory of the Lord that resided over the tent of meeting in the wilderness. The usual rendering of the preposition when not designating a logical function ('because, on the ground of, etc.') is 'upon, over, on' (see BDB, 752ff.). Notions of 'by, beside, together with' are less usual but certainly possible, depending on context. The context in the present passage may favour the usual use though it permits 'with' as well. The use of this preposition directly following the noun 'tabernacle' (*miškān*, connoting that it is 'over' something else) occurs only here. Elsewhere (approximately 36 times, almost exclusively in Exodus and Numbers) the noun always follows the preposition and almost always refers to something being 'over' the 'tabernacle', often the glorious presence of God. The unique use in Ezekiel appears to suggest that God's latter-day presence will become equated with the tabernacle and that it will extend not merely in the midst of but 'over' all his people.

[70] Cohen (1989: 31–32) has observed that the phrase 'when you are multiplied and increased in the land' in Jer. 3:16 alludes to Gen. 1:28.

structures. Not even the centrepiece of the old temple, the ark of the covenant, will exist in the renewed Jerusalem. Only God's presence will exist as the new sanctuary.

The ark represented the special manifestation of God's ruling presence that extended from heaven to earth. The ark is repeatedly called God's 'footstool' (1 Chr. 28:2; Pss. 99:5; 132:7). The Israelites pictured God to be sitting on a throne in heaven with his feet extending to the ark as his footstool in the earthly temple (Is. 66:1, 'Heaven is My throne, and the earth is My footstool'; 2 Kgs. 19:15; Lam. 2:1). Recall that a 'footstool' was attached to Solomon's 'throne' (2 Chr. 9:18), which was modelled after the notion that the ark was the footstool of God's heavenly throne.

Thus, the ark and God's heavenly throne were inextricably linked.[71] Jeremiah 3 says not that a future cultic structure in Jerusalem will be the place of God's presence but the entire future Jerusalem itself will be called 'the throne of the LORD'. The reason for this is that the essence of the old temple, God's ruling presence, will be expressed in an unfettered way at the end time.

As we will see, the reason that the ark in the temple will have waned in significance when the Genesis 1:28 commission is finally fulfilled is that there will be a greater temple with a greater glory than a mere physical one, not only expanding to encompass all of Jerusalem (thus the point of Jer. 3:17) but the entire earth, as other biblical texts will testify.[72]

The differences between the commission to Adam and that passed on to his descendants

Despite the many similarities between the original commission in Genesis 1 and that given to Abraham and his Israelite seed, some differences exist. Before Adam's disobedience, he would have fulfilled the 'subduing and ruling' part of the commission by demonstrating sovereignty through cultivating the earth and having mastery over all the creatures of the earth, including the satanic 'serpent' who existed outside the Garden and who would subsequently enter into it. After Adam's sin, the commission would be expanded to include renewed humanity's reign over unregenerate human forces arrayed against it. Hence, the language of 'possessing

---

[71] See Holladay (1986: 121), who says that some OT writers viewed the ark as God's throne itself, though more precisely it is better to see the ark as the 'footstool' of the throne.

[72] See beginning of ch. 4 for fuller argument.

the gate of their enemies' is included, which elsewhere is stated as 'subduing the land' (note here Num. 32:22, 'and the land is *subdued* before the LORD', where the same word [*kābaš*] is used for 'subdue' as in Gen. 1:28) (N. T. Wright 1992a: 23). The mention of 'all the nations of the earth' being 'blessed' by Abraham's 'seed' alludes to a renewed human community bearing God's image and 'filling the earth' with regenerated progeny who also reflect God's image and shine out its luminosity to others in the 'city of man' who do not rebel and also come to reflect God. Thus, these new converts are 'blessed' with the favour of God's presence and become a part of God's ever-increasing kingdom.

Another difference in the repetition of the Genesis 1 commission is that it is now stated formally as a *promise*,[73] with the commission being implied. That the aspect of the 'commission' is still retained is apparent from the imperatives introducing the commission in Genesis 12:1–3: 'Go forth from your country ... be a blessing.' The implication is that humanity cannot carry out this commission on its own, but God will enable them in some way to perform it (see also Gen. 17:1–7; 18:18–19).

God's assurance that 'I am with you' was not addressed to Adam or Noah, and is not formulated until the promise is repeated to Jacob. This assurance is the basis for God's promise and commission to spread out in order that his tabernacling presence would spread (see with respect to Isaac [Gen. 26:24], Jacob [Gen. 28:15] and Moses [Exod. 3:12]). The divine assurance 'I am with you' is central to the task of extending the 'temple' of God's presence, as is apparent from noticing that this forms part of God's promise and commission to Isaac, to Jacob and to Moses (again, see respectively Gen. 26:24; 28:15; Exod. 3:12). It was this very presence that provided enablement of the task and assured the fulfilment of the promise.[74] In response to God's presence, Israel was 'to walk in His ways and to keep His commandments' in order to fulfil the original Adamic commission: to 'live and multiply, and that the LORD your God may bless you in the land where you are entering to possess it' (Deut. 30:16). Ultimately, only if God 'circumcised their heart' would they be able to love and obey him, continue in his presence, and inherit the promise and truly 'live' (Deut. 30:5–6, 16).

---

[73] N. T. Wright (1992a: 22) sees only the aspect of 'becoming fruitful' being transformed into a promise.

[74] The same promise could be made to individual Israelites other than the patriarchs: e.g., see 1 Chr. 4:10.

Essentially the same formula is repeated to Solomon. David says to his son, 'the LORD be with you that you may be successful, and build the house of the LORD your God just as He has spoken . . . Only the LORD give you . . . understanding . . . so that you may keep the law of the LORD your God' (1 Chr. 22:11–12). The promise formula occurs in direct connection to Solomon building the temple.

God pronounces the same formula when he commissions Jeremiah and enables him to be a 'prophet to the nations' (1:5) and 'to destroy and to overthrow, to build and to plant' (1:10; for the formula, see 1:8, 19). God speaks the same formula to Israel when he tells them that his purpose in regathering them from exile was to renew their commission to be a 'witness' to the nations about his purpose in creating 'new things' (Is. 43:5–21).

It may not be coincidental that, after the return from Babylonian exile, this formula is also applied twice to the remnant in the land to encourage them to rebuild the temple (Hag. 1:13; 2:4). Haggai 2:5 elaborates the meaning of the formula: 'As for the promise which I made you when you came out of Egypt, My Spirit is abiding in your midst . . .' (likewise, it is 'My Spirit' that Zech. 4:6–9 says will empower King Zerubbabel to build the second temple). The promise referred to is likely that made in Exodus 33:14–17:

> [14]And He said, 'My presence shall go [with you], and I will give you rest.' [15]Then he [Moses] said to Him, [16]'. . . how then can it be known that I have found favor in Thy sight, I and Thy people? Is it not by Thy going with us, so that we . . . may be distinguished from all the [other] people who are upon the face of the earth?'
> [17]And the LORD said to Moses, 'I will also do this thing of which you have spoken . . .' (cf. also Exod. 34:9).

Perhaps Haggai 2 also alludes to Exodus 19:5–6: 'you shall be My own possession among all the peoples . . . you shall be to Me a kingdom of priests . . .' The entire nation was to live in the midst of God's presence, and were all to become like priests standing in the presence of God in his temple and reflecting his glorious light, being intermediaries for the nations living in darkness and apart from God.

Thus, Haggai 2 refers to a time when God will enable his people to build his temple through the power of his Spirit, which is to be a fulfilment of the promise in Exodus 33 and the promissory commission in Exodus 19. In other words, Haggai 2 interprets the promise in the two Exodus passages to be that of building God's end-time temple among his people. Haggai's description of the temple to be built goes well beyond the second temple that was eventually constructed. Though the building project might look insignificant in comparison to the earlier Solomonic temple, nevertheless, God promises to make 'the latter glory of this house ... greater than the former' (Hag. 2:3–9). Since the building of the second temple did not excel the glory of the Solomonic temple nor fulfil the expectation of Ezekiel's prophesied, eschatological temple (see Ezek. 40 – 48), 'intertestamental' Judaism naturally awaited a future eschatological time when this would finally happen. Not only was the second temple initially smaller than Solomon's but it did not last for ever, having been destroyed in AD 70, thus causing a crisis in the way Jews thought about the temple from then on.

Certainly Adam's obedience within the garden sanctuary was key to carrying out his mandate by means of God's presence with him (recall 'God walking back and forth in the garden' [Gen. 3:8]). But there is no scriptural record that God promised to him that his presence would always be with him in carrying out his mandate. Indeed, God withdrew his presence from Adam. As a result of sin, Adam was cast out of the sanctuary of God's glorious presence and was not able to fulfil the divine commission.

Just as in the case of Adam, Israel's obedience within their 'garden of Eden' to the laws regulating the temple was a part of carrying out their renewed commission as a corporate Adam. Israel's land is explicitly compared to the Garden of Eden (see Gen. 13:10; Is. 51:3; Ezek. 36:35; 47:12; Joel 2:3) and is portrayed as very fruitful in order to heighten the correspondence to Eden (cf. Deut. 8:7–10; 11:8–17; Ezek. 47:1–12) (see Dumbrell 2002: 58–59). The Promised Land itself is called God's 'holy land' (Ps. 78:54; Zech. 2:12) because it was to be a Garden of Eden on a grander scale (Dumbrell 2002: 58–61). The commission to have dominion (Gen. 1:26–28), first expressed through Adam's role in Eden, is expressed in Israel's temple that also represented God's cosmic rule (Clements 1965: 67–73).[75]

---

[75] Later midrashic exegesis on the temple may have been partly inspired by Gen. 1:26–28 in its understanding that the temple brought the blessing of fertility, even, for example, of children. Likewise, the existence of the temple and the rites performed therein procured blessing and fruitfulness for Israel (and implicitly the earth in general; so Patai [1967: 122–128], who cites, e.g., *The Fathers According to Rabbi Nathan* 4). For expansion of the above ideas and sources for them in Judaism, see fn. 30, p. 97.

This commission is expressed well in Exodus 19:6, a text alluded to earlier, which says of the whole nation, 'you shall be to Me a kingdom of priests and a holy nation'. They were to be mediators in spreading the light of God's tabernacling presence to the rest of the dark world. Such a connection of Genesis 1:28 to Eden and the temple may have sparked off the following thought in the *Hymn Scroll* of Qumran: 'my dominion shall be over the sons [of the ear]th ... I will shine with a seven-fold li[ght] in the E[den which][76] Thou hast [m]ade for Thy glory' (1QH 7.23–24, where the temple lampstand with seven lamps is probably behind the image of the 'seven-fold light').

Nevertheless, like Adam, Israel sinned and was cast away from God's presence and out of the land. At the same time God withdrew his presence from their temple (Ezek. 9:3; 10:4, 18–19; 11:22–23). The same thing happened to restored Israel in AD 70, when the Romans destroyed Jerusalem and the temple, though God's presence had long since left that temple.[77] Thus, the promise of divine accompaniment to enable fulfilment of the Genesis 1 mandate was not ultimately fulfilled in Abraham or any of the physical descendants nor in Israel's temple but remained yet to be realized.

The commission as a mandate to witness

We briefly observed above that Abraham's descendants were to be a renewed humanity. They were to bear God's image and 'fill the earth' with children who also bore that image, being beacons of light to others living in spiritual darkness. They were to be God's instruments through whom God caused the light of his presence to shine in dark hearts of people in order that they too might become part of the increasing expansion of the temple's sacred space and of the kingdom. This is none other than performing the role of 'witness' to God throughout the earth.

In fact, we can speak of Genesis 1:28 as the first 'Great Commission' that was repeatedly applied to humanity. The commission was to bless the earth, and part of the essence of this blessing was God's salvific presence. Before the fall, Adam and Eve were to produce progeny who would fill the earth with God's glory being

---

[76] This follows the translation of Dupont-Sommer, though his is the only translation that fills the lacunae with 'Eden'. For further elaboration concerning this debated translation see p. 79.

[77] God's presence had left the temple at least by the time of Christ's coming, since he himself became the place of the special divine presence in the midst of the nation instead of the temple, as we will see, in ultimate fulfilment of Hag. 2:5. It is quite possible that the divine presence never returned to the post-exilic temple.

reflected from each of them in the image of God. After the fall, a remnant, created by God in his restored image, were to go out and spread God's glorious presence among the rest of darkened humanity. This 'witness' was to continue until the entire world would be filled with divine glory.

Israel's 'witness' as a corporate Adam was especially significant. In this connection, the question of why the tabernacle was sometimes called the 'tabernacle of testimony' (5 times: e.g., Exod. 38:21) or 'tent of testimony' (5 times: e.g., Num. 9:15) needs addressing.[78] The most obvious answer is that the tabernacle housed the 'ark of the testimony' (so 14 times: e.g., Exod. 25:22; 26:33–34). But why is the ark referred to in this way? The reason is that the ten commandments are sometimes called the 'testimony'.[79] God gave the commandments to Moses at Sinai, and Moses placed them in the ark. The ten commandments were called the 'testimony' because they were written 'by the finger of God' (Exod. 31:18) and were the visible evidence of God's truth and will. The Law was God's 'testimony because it is his own affirmation relative to his very person and purpose' (Schultz 1980: 650). Moreover, this 'testimony' functioned for the nation as a 'witness' of God's saving acts (van Leeuwen 1997: 844). This latter point is apparent by recalling that the ark was not only the depository of the ten commandments (Exod. 25:16–22) but also directly in front of the ark were placed items that recalled God's great acts on behalf of Israel: the jar of manna (Exod. 16:31–36), a portion of Moses' incense (Exod. 30:36) and Aaron's rod that budded (Num. 17).

Thus, the ten commandments reminded Israel not only of God's moral will for them but of their deliverance from Egypt (Exod. 20:2), God's creation of the world (Exod. 20:11), and of his presence with and providential care of them in the wilderness. All of these items were an evidential, legal 'testimony' of God's saving and preserving presence as it had been manifested in various ways to Israel.[80] The emphasis on the divine presence with respect to the ark or tabernacle of 'testimony' is underscored by repeated statements that each of the four holy items located at the place of the ark were in God's very

---

[78] The Hebrew word '$\bar{e}d\hat{u}t$ used in these texts can mean 'testimony', and not only has overtones of 'witness' but can sometimes mean 'witness'. Accordingly, see van Leeuwen 1997: 844; '$\bar{e}d\hat{u}t$ is closely related to '$\bar{e}d$, which means 'witness'.

[79] So 6 times in Exodus: e.g., Exod. 25:16, 21; the word is used to refer to God's Law in the Psalms (so approximately 12 times: e.g., Pss. 78:5; 119).

[80] E.g., Num. 17:10 says, 'Put back the rod of Aaron before the *testimony* to be kept as a *sign* against the rebels.'

presence.[81] In this respect, the Hebrew of Exodus 30:36 refers to 'the testimony in the tent of meeting, where I shall meet with you' (so also Num. 17:4). The Hebrew expression 'tent of meeting' referred to 'the appointed place where Yahweh will meet with Moses'.[82] The Greek Old Testament's substitution of 'testimony' for 'meeting' indicates that the point of God's presence with Moses was that he would 'testify' to Moses about himself, his Law, and his redemptive deeds for Israel, all of which have demonstrated his presence with the entire nation.[83]

The legal nature of the 'testimony' is evident from observing that the cognate noun '$\bar{e}d$ is almost always translated as 'witness' and occurs typically in legal contexts (e.g., to find someone guilty of a crime in Israel requires 'two witnesses'). A 'witness' (*martys*) 'testifies' (*martyreō*) in court to confirm the truth of something (e.g., see the LXX of Num. 35:30). Accordingly, when Israel would disobey God's Law, 'the book of the law ... beside the ark of the covenant' would be 'a witness against' Israel (Deut. 31:26). Therefore, the two tablets of the Law served as a daily reminder of the covenant between Yahweh and Israel.

Presumably, part of the point of the repeated reference to the 'tabernacle of testimony' and the 'ark of testimony' is that Israel herself was to accept God's 'testimony' and then bear witness to God's saving presence with her in the past and present by declaring God's own 'testimony' to his Law and to the various redemptive acts performed on their behalf.[84] In addition, the nation was to be a 'testimony' by obeying the Law. All of this would bear witness to the truth of God's presence.[85]

Consequently, the way God's presence was to spread out from the holy of holies was for his people to pay heed to his testimony deposited there by giving testimony in word and obedient deed before the

---

[81] Cf. Exod. 25:22 and 30:6 where the ten commandments, incense and rod are all located at the place where 'I [God] will meet with you [Moses]'; the manna is also to be placed 'before the LORD' in Exod. 16:33. The particular accent on the presence of God is expressed by the Greek OT in its rendering of the Hebrew 'tent of meeting' by 'tent [or tabernacle] of the testimony' (*skēnē* + *martyrion*; so approximately 160 times, the majority of which occur in the Pentateuch).

[82] Strathmann, '*martys ktl.*', *TDNT* 4:482.

[83] Ibid., 484.

[84] *Tanhuma Yelammedenu Exodus* 11:2 says the tabernacle was called the 'Tabernacle of testimony' because 'it bears testimony to all people that the Holy One ... would be reconciled with Israel despite the episode of the calf'.

[85] Which is similar to the 'altar' later built by the tribes of Reuben and Gad that functioned as 'a witness ... that the LORD is God' (Josh. 22:34).

nations to God's truth. If Israel did this, it would show that God's presence was with them as the enabler of their faithfulness. Deuteronomy 4:5–7 expresses this purpose well, especially in linking Israel's understanding and obeying of God's law with his presence, and thus implicitly with the role of witness:

> [5]"See, I [Moses] have taught you statutes and judgments just as the LORD my God commanded me, that you should do thus in the land where you are entering to possess it. [6]"So keep and do them, for that is your wisdom and your understanding in the sight of the peoples who will hear all these statutes and say, "Surely this great nation is a wise and understanding people." [7]"For what great nation is there that *has a god so near to it as is the LORD our God whenever we call on Him?*'

This is likewise closely linked with Exodus 33:14–17, where God tells Moses that 'My presence shall go [with you]' and Moses responds by saying that 'Thy going with us' will result in Israel being 'distinguished from all the people who are upon the face of the earth'. After the restoration from Babylon, God commands Israel to be 'witnesses'[86] to their 'knowledge' and 'belief' that God was the only true God, and that he will express his divine omnipotence by again delivering Israel out of a second bondage and performing a second exodus to the promised land (Is. 43:10–12; 44:6–8).

That Israel was to be a 'witness' to the nations is implied at various points (cf. Is. 43:9) but made explicit in Isaiah 55:4, where God says that he had made David 'a witness to the peoples', a commission that Israel should share. Israel's kings were to be leaders in bearing this 'testimony'.[87] This commission was Israel's task to 'call' the nations to God (Is. 55:5). In order to accomplish this mission Israel was first to 'seek the LORD while He may be found' and 'call upon Him while He may be near' (Is. 55:6).

However, just as Adam 'hid ... from the presence of the LORD' (Gen. 3:8), thus ensuring failure to accomplish his mission, Israel, as representative of God's true humanity, also separated themselves from the divine presence and failed to carry out the commission. Thus, it is not an overstatement to say that Israel was conceived of

---

[86] Cf. again the use here of the cognate *'ēd*, and the Greek OT's *martys*.

[87] E.g., 2 Chr. 23:11 says that when Joash was crowned king, they placed the 'testimony' in his hands, indicating that he was to uphold the Law and all it stood for; cf. also 2 Chr. 34:29–33.

as a 'corporate Adam'. The nation's task was to do what Adam had first been commissioned to do. Israel failed even as had Adam. And like Adam, Israel was also cast out of their 'garden land' into exile. Though a remnant of Israel returned from exile, her failure to carry out the Adamic task continued until the beginning of the first century AD.

Chapter Four

The expanding end-time purpose of temples in the Old Testament

There are indications elsewhere in the Old Testament, which are developed later by Jewish commentators, that Eden and the temple signified a divine mandate to enlarge the boundaries of the temple until they formed the borders around the whole earth. Sometimes the thought may be that the entire land of Israel, conceived as a large Garden of Eden, was to be expanded. The subject matter in the present chapter is one of the strongest pieces of evidence substantiating our contention in the preceding chapter that the boundaries of the Eden garden-sanctuary and of Israel's temples were meant to be extended to encircle the entire world. While the eschatological goal of the Old Testament was discussed in the preceding chapter, here we will focus more explicitly on that goal.

We will first survey a number of Old Testament passages where an expanding end-time garden or temple is found, some of which should be seen as the precursors, together with Genesis 1 – 2, inspiring later portrayals by Jewish writers, which we will survey toward the end of this chapter.

The view of the Old Testament

Numbers 24:5–9

This passage has an abbreviated portrayal of an expanding garden, which has affinities with our intial explanation of the original purpose of Eden[1] sketched out at the beginning of the preceding chapter:

---

[1] Brown (1999: 212–215) understands the community of Israel in Num. 24:5–9 to be depicted metaphorically as another Garden of Eden.

[5]'How fair are your *tents*, O Jacob,[2]
Your *dwellings*, O Israel!
[6]'Like palm trees that stretch out,
Like gardens beside the river,
Like aloes planted by the LORD,[3]
Like cedars beside the waters.
[7]'Water shall flow from his buckets,
And his seed shall be by many waters,
And his king shall be higher than Agag,
And his kingdom shall be exalted.
[8]'God brings him out of Egypt . . .
He shall devour the nations who are his adversaries . . .
[9]'Blessed is everyone who blesses you,
And cursed is everyone who curses you.'

On analogy with later Old Testament texts referring to the temple in the plural, the same may well be the case in verse 5.[4] Furthermore, when these two Hebrew words for 'tent' and 'dwelling' occur together everywhere else in the Pentateuch (so 25 times up to Num. 24), only once (Num. 16:27, in the plural) do they refer generally to Israel's dwellings around the tabernacle, and twenty-four times they refer to the 'tabernacle'.[5] If 'tents' and 'dwellings' in Numbers 24:5 is a plural reference to the tabernacle, this is another passage explaining Israel's

---

[2] *Tg. Neofiti* and *Tg. Pseudo-Jonathon* render the Hebrew of this line partly as 'How beautiful is *the tent of meeting*', thus clearly identifying the 'tents' as Israel's tabernacle.

[3] The LXX reads here 'as *tabernacles* [or tents] pitched by the Lord', on which see further below.

[4] So Pss. 43:3; 46:4; 84:1–4; 132:5, 7; so also Lev. 21:23; Ezek. 7:24; Jer. 51:51; e.g., Ps. 84:1–4 equates God's 'dwelling places' with his 'courts' and his 'house'; following Stordalen (2000: 443), who concludes that the plural in Num. 24:5 refers to 'the tabernacle and its surrounding camp', and would later have been identified as 'the dwellings of Israel around the House of YHWH in Zion' (especially, in light of the same two plurals in Jer. 30:18 which refer to Jerusalem). See also *Judith* 4:12; 16:20; 1 Maccabees 3:43, 58–59 for *ta hagia* ('the holies') as a reference to the one sanctuary (following Ellingworth 1993: 400). Note also that Philo sometimes refers to 'the Holy of Holies' as 'the Holies of Holies' (*Leg. All.* 2.56; *Mut. Nom.* 192) or 'the innermost places of the Holies' (*Som.* 1.216). The Hebrew words rendered 'tents' and 'dwellings' in Num. 24:5 are respectively '*ōhel* and *miškān*, the typical words referring to Israel's tabernacle. 1 Chr. 17:5 refers to God during the pre-Solomonic period as having 'gone from tent to tent and from one dwelling place to another'. Job 21:28 refers to the 'tent, the dwelling places of the wicked'.

[5] Though each of these occurrences is in the singular; likewise, four times elsewhere in the singular (2 Sam. 7:6; Ps. 78:60; 1 Chr. 6:32; 17:5); cf. 'tent . . . dwellings' in Is. 54:2, which we identify below as Israel's eschatological tabernacle.

task by linking a portrayal of her as a tabernacle[6] with the picture of vegetation and waters spreading out over the earth. Israel's 'tabernacle' is like 'palm trees that stretch out, like gardens' that expand abundantly along river banks.

Strikingly, the Greek Old Testament translates the Hebrew of verse 6, 'like *aloes* planted by the LORD', by 'as *tabernacles* [or tents] pitched by the LORD'. The Greek translation appears interpretatively to identify the 'trees that stretch out like gardens' (v. 6a) to form a veritable 'tabernacle[s]' (v. 6b). Is it too speculative to say that part of the reason for the close association of garden imagery with that of the tabernacle is due to the inextricable link between the same images in Genesis 2, especially in view of the echoes to the Adamic commission and Abrahamic promise in the following verses?[7]

In this respect, it may not be inappropriate to jump ahead and take a very brief glance at a relevant New Testament passage. The continued reference to 'tabernacles' in the Greek Bible of Numbers 24:6 is important to observe because the New Testament book of Hebrews (8:2) alludes to this Greek Old Testament rendering of Numbers 24:6 to describe 'the true tabernacle' in heaven, which it equates also with the heavenly 'sanctuaries', also a plural reference to the one sanctuary, just like that in Numbers 24:5, though the one in Hebrews refers to the heavenly dimension:[8] the Messiah is 'a minister in the sanctuaries, and in the true tabernacle, which the LORD pitched, not man'. Thus, as we will see in our later study of Hebrews, in addition to the Greek Old Testament, we have a clear interpretation by the New Testament of the garden language of Numbers 24:6 to be a reference to the 'tabernacle'.

The depiction of Numbers 24:5–8 is also associated with the Abrahamic promise (cf. an increase of 'seed' in v. 7, and the 'blessing and cursing' in v. 9 repeats Gen. 12:3b). There may also be an echo of the original Adamic commission here (note 'king' and 'kingdom' in v. 7 and 'dominion' in v. 19).

The Aramaic Bibles of Judaism treat Numbers 24:6 along the same lines as the Greek Old Testament. Remarkably, one Aramaic Bible

---

[6] Late Jewish tradition understood Num. 24:5 to include reference to Israel's later temple: *Tg. Pseudo-Jonathon* and *Neofiti 1 Numbers* 24:5; *Midrash Rabbah Exodus* 31:10; *Midrash Rabbah Numbers* 12:14 (exclusively so).

[7] Such echoes of Genesis may be confirmed further by noticing the clear allusions to other Genesis passages: e.g., the prophecy of Judah's kingship from Gen. 49:9 in Num. 24:9 (cf. also Gen. 49:10 in Num. 24:17).

[8] Another difference is that the plural reference in Num. 24:5 is *skēnai* and in Hebrews it is *hagiōn*.

(*Tg. Neofiti*) understands the botanical phrase 'like aloes planted by the LORD' to refer to the tabernacle: 'like the heavens which God has spread out as the house of his Shekinah [glorious dwelling], so shall Israel live and endure for ever beautiful ... and exalted among his creatures'.[9] Here we have the astonishing picture of Israel's commission to spread out over the earth being like the extension of the tabernacle of the heavens that God spread out to house his glory. Another Aramaic Bible (*Pseudo-Jonathon*) interprets the last phrase of verse 6 ('like cedars beside the waters') in the following manner: 'They are exalted and raised up over all the nations as the cedars of Lebanon which are planted by the springs of water.'

Ezekiel

The emerging domination of ungodly kingdoms over the world is sometimes described with the imagery of the outgrowth of Eden's trees as a kind of parody. Though the dominance of such kingdoms is a perversion of humanity's commission to subdue the earth, they are portrayed with the language of the growing primeval garden to underscore that they have failed in executing the eschatological Adamic commission. Such unbelieving empires plant gardens to 'enjoy the aesthetic without the ethic'; they 'collectivize themselves ... to seek a community without a covenant' (Gage 1984: 60–61). Ezekiel's parody of the sinful Assyrian world kingdom (Ezek. 31:3–16) is one of the best examples of this:

> [3]'Behold, Assyria was a cedar in Lebanon
> With beautiful branches and forest shade,
> And very high;
> And its top was among the clouds.
> [4]'The waters made it grow, the deep made it high.
> With its rivers it continually extended all around its planting
>   place,

[9] This rendering is the result of reading the Hebrew *'ăhālîm* ('aloes') as *'ōhālîm* ('tents') either unintentionally or, more probably, consciously under the influence of 'tents' in verse 5 (cf. McNamara 1995: 137). Almost identically, as we saw above, the LXX reads here 'as *tabernacles* [or tents = *skēnē*] pitched by the LORD'. The similarity of the Hebrew word for 'aloes' and 'tents' facilitated an interpretation by the Greek and Aramaic translator by which 'tents' representing the whole garden (recalling the Eden equation with tabernacle) is substituted by synecdoche for 'aloes' as part of a garden (note reference to 'tents' and 'gardens' in the directly preceding phrases). In contrast to *Tg. Neofiti*, cf. Etheridge, who cites the somewhat different rendering of the Palestinian Fragment Targum: 'as the heavens which the Memra spread forth for the dwelling of His Shekinah, so shall Israel live . . .' (1968: 428–429).

And it sent out its channels to all the trees of the field.
⁵"Therefore its height was loftier than all the trees of the
    field,
And its boughs became many and its branches long
Because of many waters as it spread them out.
⁶"All the birds of the heavens nested in its boughs,
And under its branches all the beasts of the field gave birth,
And all great nations lived under its shade.
⁷"So it was beautiful in its greatness, in the length of its
    branches;
For its roots extended to many waters.
⁸"The cedars in God's garden could not match it;
The cypresses could not compare with its boughs,
And the plane trees could not match its branches.
No tree in God's garden could compare with it in its beauty.
⁹"I made it beautiful with the multitude of its branches,
And all the trees of Eden, which were in the garden of God,
    were jealous of it.
¹⁰"Therefore, thus says the Lord God, "Because it is high in
stature, and it has set its top among the clouds, and its heart is
haughty in its loftiness, ¹¹therefore, I will give it into the hand
of a despot of the nations; he will thoroughly deal with it.
According to its wickedness I have driven it away. ¹²And alien
tyrants of the nations have cut it down and left it; on the
mountains and in all the valleys its branches have fallen, and
its boughs have been broken in all the ravines of the land. And
all the peoples of the earth have gone down from its shade and
left it. ¹³On its ruin all the birds of the heavens will dwell. And
all the beasts of the field will be on its fallen branches ¹⁴in
order that all the trees by the waters may not be exalted in
their stature, nor set their top among the clouds, nor their
well-watered mighty ones stand erect in their height. For they
have all been given over to death, to the earth beneath, among
the sons of men, with those who go down to the pit . . . ¹⁶ I
made the nations quake at the sound of its fall when I made
it go down to Sheol with those who go down to the pit; and
all the well-watered trees of Eden, the choicest and best of
Lebanon, were comforted in the earth beneath."'

Assyria is presented in the passage as growing to envelop the
earth in the way that Eden should have done (hence, Eden's trees are

portrayed as being envious of Assyria's arboreal growth). However, the way Assyria accomplished the growth was unjust and sinful. Therefore, her world-encompassing tree had to be cut down in judgment, just as was Eden's. Daniel 4:10–12 depicts virtually the same though more abbreviated picture of Babylon's world dominance. She is portrayed as a huge tree in which 'was food for all'. The tree was 'visible to the end of the whole earth' and the branches spanned the earth, so that all 'the beasts of the field found shade under it, and the birds of the sky dwelt in its branches'. Like Assyria, the tree is cut down in judgment because of pride and sinful disobedience to God.

The point of Ezekiel's portrayal about Assyria is to apply it to the Egyptian kingdom and to foretell its same doom (Ezek. 31:2, 18). The application of this world-expanding garden picture to Egypt is intriguing in light of a fascinating feature of Egyptian religion that we discovered in chapter 2. The Egyptians themselves believed that the first hill of creation (i.e., their version of Eden) had been located in Egypt and that all of creation had expanded out from their country. Accordingly, their temples, which contained a profusion of garden-like scenes, symbolized such a cosmic expansion. They believed that their kingdom should dominate and cover the world in imitation of the original creation. The Egyptian temple was emblematic not only of past creation's expansion but of the mandate to expand Egypt's kingdom under the leadership of Pharaoh.

Ezekiel 17 and 19 depict Israel with the same image of the cosmic tree that had begun to grow high from a garden but then was cut down. Unlike Assyria, Babylon and Egypt, Israel had been directly commissioned by God to perform the task of Genesis 1:28 by expanding their new Garden of Eden, which, as we have seen, the Promised Land was sometimes called. Unlike the optimistic outlook on the temple by some intertestamental Jewish writers (e.g., *Sirach*),[10] Ezekiel gives the divine 'bird's eye' view that Israel also had failed in carrying out Adam's renewed commission. They had become as idolatrous as the nations around them:

> [22]Thus says the Lord GOD, 'I shall also take a sprig from the lofty top of the cedar and set it out; I shall pluck from the topmost of its young twigs a tender one, and I shall plant it on a high and lofty mountain. [23] On the high mountain of Israel I shall plant it, that it may bring forth boughs and bear fruit,

---

[10] On which we will elaborate at the end of this chapter.

and become a stately cedar. And birds of every kind will nest under it; they will nest in the shade of its branches'. (Ezek. 17:22–23)

[10]'Your mother was like a vine in your vineyard,
Planted by the waters;
It was fruitful and full of branches
Because of abundant waters.
[11]'And it had strong branches fit for scepters of rulers,
And its height was raised above the clouds
So that it was seen in its height with the mass of its branches.
[12]'But it was plucked up in fury;
It was cast down to the ground;
And the east wind dried up its fruit.
Its strong branch was torn off
So that it withered;
The fire consumed it.
[13]'And now it is planted in the wilderness,
In a dry and thirsty land.
[14]'And fire has gone out from its branch;
It has consumed its shoots and fruit,
So that there is not in it a strong branch,
A scepter to rule.' (Ezek. 19:10–14)

In this light, and in view of our prior study of the patriarchal altar-building activities, it is possible that Israel's repeated tendency to build idolatrous altars on 'every high hill and [under] every leafy tree' (Ezek. 20:28; so likewise 1 Kgs. 14:23; 2 Kgs. 17:10; Jer. 2:20; 3:6) was a sinful and perverted attempt to replicate the conditions of Eden for which only judgment could come. Pre-exilic Israel had failed to carry out the divine commission, and it remained for post-exilic Israel to execute the mandate. Interestingly, Isaiah depicts eschatological Israel as recovering the arboreal and floral features of the Garden of Eden, so that it comes to be portrayed as a veritable 'temple grove'.[11]

Isaiah 54

One of the greatest promises that restored Israel would finally obey God and perform his will for the benefit of the world occurs in Isaiah 54. This chapter sees that after the Babylonian exile Israel will be

---

[11] Brown 1999: 241–248.

restored and will complete the mission designed for God's true humanity. Isaiah 54:2–3 says to the barren woman, Jerusalem, 'Enlarge the place of *your tent* [*'ohŏlēk*];/Stretch out the curtains of *your tabernacles* [dwellings] . . ./Lengthen your cords,/And strengthen your pegs./For you will spread abroad to the right and to the left./And your seed will possess [LXX = inherit] nations.' This passage appears to develop the earlier mentioned Abrahamic promise ('I blessed him and multiplied him', itself an allusion to Gen. 1:28) in Isaiah 51:2, where God promises to restore and create Israel 'like Eden . . . like the garden of the LORD' (Is. 51:3, alluding to Gen. 2). That Isaiah 51:2–3 combines references to the Abrahamic promise (echoing Gen. 1:28)[12] and the Garden from Genesis 2 may be a reflection of the same link inherent originally between Genesis 1:28 and Genesis 2, for which we argued at the beginning of chapter 3.

In addition to the possible links with Genesis 1 – 2 via Isaiah 51, further echoes to Genesis may also be present in Isaiah 54. Among all the patriarchal promises, Isaiah 54:3 is a further elaboration specifically on Genesis 28, since it is the only promise that contains the precise wording that Abraham's 'seed' will 'spread out' to affect the nations:[13]

Genesis 28:14	Isaiah 54:3
Your *seed* [*zera'*] . . . shall spread out [*paraṣ*] to the west and to the east and to the north and to the south . . . And in your seed [*zera'*] all the families of the nations will be blessed.	For you will spread out [*paraṣ*] to the right and to the left. And your seed [*zera'*] will possess nations . . .

In addition, Genesis 28 introduces the Bethel episode (28:10–22) with the promise to Jacob that God would bless his 'seed', so 'that you may possess the land of your sojournings' (Gen. 28:4), which confirms further the allusion to Genesis 28:14 in Isaiah 54:3 (that concludes with 'and your seed will possess nations').[14] The specific

[12] The echo of Gen. 1:28 may be apparent from the directly following reference to Gen. 2 in Is. 51:3.

[13] This particular connection has been hinted at by Hartopo 2002: 58.

[14] The only other OT passages with the precise wording that the 'seed' of Jacob would 'possess' the land are Gen. 22:17; 24:60, Num. 14:24; Is. 65:9; and Ps. 25:13. Perhaps Gen. 22:17 and 24:60 are echoed secondarily, since they speak of expansion through the multiplication of seed. Other possible parallels are Exod. 34:24, which speaks of 'enlarging your [Israel's] borders' (cf. Is. 53:2), while Ps. 44:2 refers to God

allusion to Genesis 28:14 points to the possibility that the Isaiah passage is concerned with expanding the borders of the temple, since we have seen that, of all the patriarchal accounts, the Bethel episode in Genesis 28 was the clearest example of embryonic temple building with a view to further expansion. Since we have already seen connections between Isaiah 51:2–3 (Abrahamic blessing, multiplication, Garden of Eden) and 54:2–3,[15] it is tempting to suggest that 51:1, which refers to God being 'the rock from which you [Israel] were hewn, and ... the excavation pit from which you were dug', is an apt metaphor for the foundation-laying activities of a temple.[16]

Isaiah 54:1–3 also develops Isaiah 49:19–22. Both texts picture Jerusalem as a 'barren' mother in exile, where she is given an abundance of children, thus indicating her restoration and the ingathering of the nations. Also, the influx of restored Israelites together with the nations means that Jerusalem must be radically expanded. This growth is explicit in 49:20, where the restored inhabitants proclaim, 'The place is too cramped for me; make room for me that I may live here.' Isaiah 54:2–3 gives the prophetic response to this complaint: 'enlarge the place of your tent; stretch out the curtains of your tabernacles ... For you will spread abroad to the right and to the left.'[17]

The 'cramped place' in Isaiah 49:20 is either Jerusalem or perhaps the land of Israel. On the other hand, the reference to Israel's 'tent' (*skēnē* in LXX) in Isaiah 54:2 may connote more particularly the 'tabernacle' (since that is its usual translation elsewhere) and its eschatological expansion, which may well be tantamount to an expanding latter-day Garden of Eden, which expands throughout Israel's land. Indeed, the land itself comes to be explicitly identified

---

'spreading them [Israel] abroad', though the latter text employs a different Hebrew word than found in Gen. 28:14 and Is. 54:3.

[15] The image of 'barren women' bearing children (cf. Is. 54:1).

[16] 1 Kgs. 6:7 says that Solomon's temple 'was built of stone prepared at the quarry'. Perhaps not coincidentally, the 1 Kings verse goes on to say that no tool, not even a 'hammer' (*maqqebet*) was used to prepare the stones on site. Literally, the Hebrew for 'hammer' could be rendered a 'piercing instrument' or 'piercing tool', the very same word found in Is. 51:1: literally, 'the excavation [or 'piercing' or 'hammering'] pit from which you were dug' (though BDB, 666, categorizes the noun in Is. 51:1 as a different noun from 'hammer', there appear to be no ultimate grounds for doing so). It may merely be that in Is. 51:1 there is a metonymy of the cause for the effect: piercing with a hammer is substituted for the usual Hebrew word for 'excavation' in order to highlight the element of construction. The word occurs elsewhere only at Is. 44:12 and Jer. 10:4, both referring to a 'hammer'.

[17] I have followed the cue of *Tanhuma Leviticus* 2:16 in making the connection between Is. 49 and 54.

as Eden in Isaiah 51:3, probably because of the widening scope of the tabernacle (the Greek Old Testament of Is. 54:2 has only *skēnē* instead of the Hebrew text's 'tent' and 'tabernacles', thus identifying the two as the same reality). That a latter-day tabernacle could be in mind in Isaiah 54:2 is further pointed to by recalling that the plural 'tabernacles' (read by MT of Is. 54:2) elsewhere in the Old Testament can refer to Israel's one tabernacle or temple (see above discussion of Num. 24:5).

The connections between tent, Jerusalem and Eden find confirmation in Isaiah 33:20–21 (LXX), where latter-day 'Jerusalem' is 'a rich city, *tabernacles* which shall not be shaken, *neither shall the pins of her tabernacle* [plausibly = Israel's future temple] *be moved for ever, neither shall her cords be at all broken*: for the name of the Lord is great to you: you shall have a *place* [*topos*], even rivers and wide and spacious channels'. Just as the tent of Isaiah 54:2–3 is associated with a garden-like place (51:2–3) and a rich city (54:11–12), so Isaiah 33 (LXX) presents the same picture.

That Isaiah 54:2–3 alludes to the temple is suggested further by the observation that the majority of the ten times *topos* ('place') occurs in direct connection to *skēnē* ('tabernacle') in the Old Testament (Greek), the two are equated and refer to the tabernacle or temple: Leviticus 6:9, 19; 8:31; 2 Samuel 6:17; 1 Chronicles 15:1; Psalm 41:5 (e.g., cf. 1 Chr. 15:1, 'David ... prepared a *place* for the ark of God, and made a *tent* for it'). Even two other references in Genesis equate the word-pair in association with a sacred place of worship, since the patriarchs set up altars at the 'place' where they erect a 'tent' (Gen. 13:3; 33:17–20). The other reference combining the two is Jeremiah 10:20, which again equates the two and appears to refer to the destruction of the temple (the LXX is clearer about this than the MT).[18]

The image of end-time Jerusalem as a woman who has just married the Lord (Is. 54:1, 4) and as a city with gates, foundations and walls made of precious stones (54:11–13) enhances the possibility that Isaiah 54:2–3 alludes to an eschatological tabernacle-like temple and provided stimulus for the expanded dimensions of John's city-temple

---

[18] It is likely not coincidental that *topos* either by itself or together with adjectives (e.g., '*holy*' place) in the OT often refers to the temple (*topos* as a rendering of *māqôm* occurs in the LXX over 350 times, and of these approximately 40 times there is reference to the temple, approximately 10 times to the promised land and 20 times to the promised land in some connection with the sanctuary. About 20 times in 2, 3 and 4 Maccabees *topos* occurs with and without the qualifying adjective in reference to the temple (for similar conclusions of the LXX material see also Koester, '*topos*', *TDNT*, 8:195–199, 204–205).

in Revelation 21. Thus, Revelation understands Isaiah 54, partly at least, to be a prophecy of a grand end-time city-temple.[19] Likewise, later Jewish tradition understood Isaiah 54:1–3 to be referring, at least in part, to Israel's temple.[20] On the basis of Isaiah 54:2 and Ezekiel 41:7 (both of which contexts are alluded to in Rev. 21), some Jewish traditions expected a new Jerusalem with radically escalated dimensions in order to hold all the redeemed (e.g., by way of reference to Is. 54:2).[21] Other expectations of a radically enlarged end-time Jerusalem can be found in later Judaism.[22]

The expansion of the tabernacle in Isaiah 54:2–3 because of a population increase is in line with our earlier discussion at the beginning of chapter 3 that the garden sanctuary of Eden was to be expanded by an increase in Adam's multitudinous progeny.

Isaiah 66

Isaiah 66:1 states, 'Thus says the LORD,/"Heaven is My throne, and the earth is My footstool./Where then is a house you could build for Me?/And where is a place that I may rest?"' The implied but unstated answer is that *no* human structure can be adequate for God to reside in. This passage appears to be an allusion to Solomon's prayer reported in 2 Chronicles 6:18.[23] It is, therefore, necessary first to review the Chronicles' passage that records the entire account of the prayer. Solomon prays in 2 Chronicles 6:18, 'But will God indeed dwell with mankind on the earth? Behold, heaven and the highest heaven cannot contain Thee;[24] how much less this house which I have

---

[19] On which see further Beale 1999a: 1082–1087; cf. also 1109–1111.

[20] *Pesikta de-rab Kahana*, Piska 20 says the 'desolate' woman Jerusalem of Is. 54:1 is the desolated temple. *Midrash Rabbah Genesis* 59:5 combines Is. 54:3 with Ezek. 48 in describing the eschatological divisions of Israel's land, the latter text in direct connection with the end-time temple of Ezek. 40 – 47. Similarly, the same Isaiah text is combined with Ezek. 47:7 (describing the expanding 'width of the temple . . . as it went higher') in depicting the supernatural expansion of Jerusalem (so *Midrash Rabbah Song of Songs* 7:5 §3; so also *Pesikta de-rab Kahana*, Piska 20).

[21] Cf. *Midrash Rabbah Genesis* 5:7; *Midrash Rabbah Leviticus* 10:9; *Pesikta de-rab Kahana*, Piska 12.22 and Piska 20.7; *Tanhuma Leviticus* 2:16; and likewise but with reference to Ezek. 41:7, cf. *Sifre on Deuteronomy*, Piska 1; *Pesikta Rabbati*, Piska 41.2; *Midrash Rabbah Song of Songs* 7:5 §3.

[22] *Midrash Psalms* 36:6; 48:4; *Pesikta Rabbati* 1.3; 21.8; *Pesikta de-rab Kahana*, Suppl. 5.4; cf. *Pesikta de-rab Kahana*, Piska 21.4. An escalated new temple is also anticipated in earlier Judaism (*1 Enoch* 90:28–29 [on which see below]; *Tobit* 13:13–18 and 14:5).

[23] Though the composition of 2 Chronicles took place after Isaiah, it is likely that Isaiah had access to oral tradition that preserved the content of Solomon's prayer later written down by the chronicler.

[24] Likewise, cf. *Baruch* 2:16 with 3:24–25; Josephus, *War* 5.458.

built.' This prayer may imply that the earthly temple was not designed to be an eternal structure but one which was only a temporary dwelling for God during the Israelite theocracy. This could also be suggested from observing that verses 32–33 say that Israel's temple had a universal design: it was for 'foreigners' to 'pray toward this house ... in order that all the peoples of the earth may know your name, and reverence you'.

This purpose of the temple may be formalized in Isaiah 56:7 that calls the end-time temple 'a house of prayer for all the peoples', a passage Jesus also will subsequently quote in highlighting the shortcomings of Israel's second temple. We will have to wait until later to see that this universal purpose for the nations will make the localized temple obsolete, though we have already seen indications in Genesis 1 – 2 and elsewhere that the temple was meant to be expanded worldwide.

Isaiah 63:15 reinforces the notion that God's present true temple is only in heaven: 'Look down from heaven, and see from your *lofty dwelling place* [*zĕbûl*] of holiness and glory' (i.e., the temple in heaven) (Koehler and Baumgartner 1994: 263). The holy of holies represented the invisible, heavenly temple and throne of God (= Is. 66:1a), and it was the actual place where the heavenly dimension extended down to earth, that is, in Isaiah's language, it was God's 'footstool', which referred precisely to the ark of the covenant.[25]

The desire that God's heavenly temple would descend and encompass the earth may be expressed in Isaiah 64:1–2 (especially in the light of 63:15): 'O that Thou wouldst rend the heavens and come down, that the mountains might quake at Thy presence [cf. Exod. 19:18!] ... to make Thy name known to Thine adversaries that the nations may tremble at Thy presence!' This is a plea that there would be a new revelatory descent of God's presence on analogy with his revelation at Sinai (which we have argued was a mountain temple) and at the subsequent tabernacle at the first Exodus to accomplish finally the divine intentions inherent in that initial Exodus (Kissane 1943: 299). Part of these divine intentions was that God's special revelatory presence would not be limited to the tabernacle (and to Moses) but be extended to all of God's true people. The universal goal of this revelation may be alluded to in Isaiah 66:18–21, where, apparently, God will make Gentiles into 'priests' and 'Levites'

---

[25] The same use of 'footstool' occurs also in 1 Chr. 28:2; Pss. 99:5; 132:7; Lam. 2:1. See further Haran 1978: 255–257.

(Young 1996: 535) who would serve in the new, expanded temple. A similar prophecy that foreigners will be priests in the temple appears in Isaiah 56:3–8.

Therefore, the future-oriented redemptive-historical 'new Exodus' context of Isaiah 63 – 66 (indeed, of chs. 40 – 66) points strongly to Isaiah 66:1 not being merely a reference to the fact that the *entire present* cosmos is God's temple in which he dwells (*pace* Levenson 1984: 296), but that there will be a future new cosmos and temple that God will create and in which he will dwell for ever, and which will be an extension of the present *heavenly* temple. Additional analysis of Isaiah 66 points further in this direction. Specifically, Isaiah 66:1–2 appears to develop 57:15:

Isaiah 57:15	Isaiah 66:1–2
For thus says the high and exalted One Who lives forever, whose name is Holy, 'I dwell on a high and holy place, And [I will dwell] also with the crushed and fallen of spirit In order to make alive the spirit of the fallen and to make alive the heart of the crushed.	[1]Thus says the LORD, 'Heaven is My throne, and the earth is My footstool. Where then is a house you could build for Me? And where is a place that I may rest? [2]'For My hand made all these things, Thus all these things came into being,' declares the LORD. 'But to this one I will look, To him who is afflicted and smitten of spirit, and who trembles at My word.'

Isaiah 57 is part of an eschatological prophecy about the temple (developing 56:3–8). The passage appears to affirm that God will come from his heavenly sanctuary and extend it to encompass humble saints. Thus, Isaiah 66:1–2 is not a general theological statement detached from redemptive history but is amplifying 57:15. In the time to come, God will cause his heavenly temple to descend and to include 'the afflicted and smitten'.[26] Consequently, Isaiah 66:2

[26] See Bruce (1990: 212–213), who has drawn this parallelism between the two Isaiah texts in connection with Acts 7:48–50 and Heb. 9:11, but not Acts 7:55–56. 'Look' in Is. 66:2 refers to God's favour of blessing the afflicted from his heavenly tabernacling

gives two reasons for the implied negative answer to the preceding question in 66:1 (asked in two different ways) about whether or not any human-made structure or any part of the old creation could be an enduring dwelling for the eternal God. The first reason is: 'for My hand made all these things,/Thus all these things came into being [by Me]'. That is, since God is the Creator, no particular part of his creation is big enough to contain his presence, and certainly no part of the sin-tainted old creation.[27]

This disjunction between the old, idolatrous world and God's coming new world and temple is underscored by contrasting his 'humble and contrite' people (66:2) with those who prefer to dwell with idols (66:3–5). These idolaters profess faith but hate the true people of God, and they will be judged by God from his heavenly temple (66:5–6). All idolatry must be removed before the new creation is ushered in. The old 'sky will vanish', 'the earth will wear out like a garment' (Is. 51:6), and 'all the host of heaven will wear away' (Is. 34:4) because of sin (cf. 51:6–8, as well as 13:9–13 and 34:1–6). In contrast, God's eternal saving presence will dwell openly again in the new 'Garden of Eden' (Is. 51:3 + 51:6–8).[28] Only an *entire new* creation can adequately house the Creator's presence, which is why Isaiah 66:1–2 is sandwiched between two of the most well-known new creation texts in all of the Old Testament: Isaiah 65:17 and 66:22. In fact, verses 1 and 2 are a continuation in some manner of the new-creation prophecy that began back in 65:16.[29]

The second reason for the implied negative answer to the question of 66:1 must be seen in the light of the parallel to 57:15: in the new creation God will enable 'the afflicted and smitten' to become part of his new order by 'making them alive' (the Aramaic interprets this as

---

presence ('look' [*nābaṭ*] can refer elsewhere to God issuing blessings from his heavenly temple: Is. 63:15; 64:9; Pss. 33:13; 80:14; 102:19; see Is. 18:4, where it refers to cursings from the heavenly temple).

[27] Note the interspersed disparagement of the old creation conditions throughout 65:16–23 and the association of idolatry with the old world in 65:2–12; 66:3–5!

[28] We are not so interested to discuss whether the cosmic conflagration language is literal or not, but are content to understand these texts affirming, at least, a renovated and purified new world system in contrast to the old, sinful world epoch. Our ultimate judgment on the issue is that the Isaiah prophecies begin fulfilment in the NT age in a 'non-physical' manner and have consummate fulfilment physically as well. For further discussion of the nature of this language, see the subsequent section on Acts below (pp. 211–216) and Beale 1999a: *in loc.* on Rev. 6:12–14 and 21:1, 4.

[29] In this light it is hardly coincidental that Is. 65:22 [LXX, Tg.] refers to part of the 'new' conditions being 'like the days of the tree of life', recapitulating the image of latter-day Eden from Is. 51:3.

resurrected people in 57:16). Accordingly, God also 'will dwell' with them, as he extends his heavenly temple to include the new creation and those humans living in it. That is, not only is everything in the old created order an inadequate container for God's residence, but those from the old world who will be able to dwell with him must be created anew and be made a part of the new creation. Anticipating the events of the New Testament, one can see how suitable it is to see 'the afflicted and smitten' Jesus as a good example of the beginning fulfilment of this prophecy at his resurrection, as well as his suffering servant Stephen.

That Isaiah 66:1–2 refers to an end-time temple is supported further by Stephen's speech in Acts 7. Not coincidentally, Stephen quotes Isaiah 66:1 (Acts 7:49) as part of his answer to the charge that he had spoken 'against this holy place, and the Law' by saying that 'Jesus will destroy this place and alter the customs which Moses handed down ...' (Acts 6:13–14). This charge parallels the charge against Jesus in Mark 14:58: 'We heard Him say, "I will destroy this sanctuary made with hands, and in three days I will build another made without hands."' Hence, Stephen's comments relate to Jesus' building of the eschatological temple that began with his earthly ministry and especially his resurrection (so John 2:19–22), which in turn was an escalated inauguration of the restoration promises to Israel, which had begun only on a small scale with the return of a tiny remnant from Babylon.[30]

Stephen proclaims that since Israel's physical temples were 'hand-made' (Acts 7:44–47), they could never be a permanent dwelling place for God. His point of citing Isaiah 66:1 is to demonstrate that, just as God's own hand created the first cosmos that had become tainted with idolatry (cf. Acts 7:44–47 with 7:41–43 in contrast to 7:50), so God would create a new, eternal creation and Jerusalem, not by human hands but by his own hand (so Is. 65:17–19 and 66:22). And, Levenson has argued[31] that the new creation and Jerusalem in Isaiah 65:17–19 are likely equivalent to the new temple, which may be correct. Levenson's conclusion is pointed to further by Isaiah 66:21–23, where the coming 'new heavens and the new earth' (v. 22) are given as the reason that God will 'take' Gentiles 'for priests and for Levites' (v. 21). In other words, the reason that Gentiles will be included as priests is because now the place of true worship and temple service is not geographically located in the old, temporal

[30] On which see further, e.g., the various works of N. T. Wright (e.g. N. T. Wright 1992b), as well as Watts 1997.

[31] See the Introduction above.

Jerusalem but throughout the entire earth, where 'all mankind will come to bow down before Me' for ever (Is. 66:23).[32] This is part of the reason inplied in Isaiah 66:2b that no earthly structure could contain God's presence, since his presence is designed to be in the midst of multitudes who could not fit into any human-made dwelling.

As discussed earlier, we may assume that God created the cosmos to be his great temple in which he rested after his creative work. Nevertheless, his special revelatory presence does not fill the entire earth yet, since it was his intention that this goal be achieved by his human vice-regent, whom he installed in the garden sanctuary to extend the garden boundaries of God's presence worldwide. Adam, of course, disobeyed this mandate, so that humanity no longer enjoyed God's presence in the Garden, and the entire earth became infected with sin and idolatry in a way it had not been previously, even while yet in its still imperfected state.

Therefore, the statements about God's inability to dwell in any structure on earth not only refers to the Creator's transcendence but plausibly includes reference to the necessity for purification and re-creation before God's Shekinah presence, formerly restricted to heaven and the earthly holy of holies, can dwell universally throughout creation together with his multitudes of worshippers.

Jeremiah 3 and related passages

We have seen in an earlier chapter that Jeremiah 3:16–18 combines the Genesis 1:28 commission with the notion of an eschatological temple, making plain that God's tabernacling presence would no longer be restricted to an inner cultic room. It is instructive to cite this passage again:

> [16]'And it shall be in those days when you *are multiplied and increased* in the land,' declares the LORD, 'they shall say no more, "The ark of the covenant of the LORD." And it shall not come to mind, nor shall they remember it, nor shall they miss it, nor shall it be made again.
> [17]'At that time they shall call Jerusalem "The Throne of the LORD," and all the nations will be gathered to it, for the name of the LORD in Jerusalem; nor shall they walk any more after the stubbornness of their evil heart.

---

[32] Which is part of the point in John 4:20–24: e.g., 'an hour is coming when neither in this mountain nor in Jerusalem, shall you worship the Father' (4:23).

[18]'In those days the house of Judah will walk with the house of Israel, and they will come together from the land of the north to the land that I gave your fathers as an inheritance.'

At the time of her end-time restoration, Israel will finally fulfil the Genesis mandate 'to multiply and increase' (Jer. 3:16). The observation that 'all the nations will be gathered to ... Jerusalem' suggests that they also will play a role in fulfilling that commission. This fulfilment is combined with a promise of a future temple, but one that will not be like Israel's prior temples. Not even the centrepiece of the old temple, the ark of the covenant, will exist in the renovated Jerusalem. Rather, the Lord's presence alone will be the new temple. The ark represented the special manifestation of God's sovereign presence that stretched to earth from heaven. The ark is repeatedly called God's 'footstool' (1 Chr. 28:2; Pss. 99:5; 132:7). Various Old Testament passages picture God to be sitting on a throne in heaven with his feet resting on the ark as his footstool in the earthly temple: Isaiah 66:1, 'heaven is My throne, and the earth is My footstool' (also 2 Kgs. 19:15; Lam. 2:1). A 'footstool' was attached to Solomon's 'throne' (2 Chr. 9:18), which was modelled after the idea that the ark was the footstool of God's throne in heaven.

Thus, the ark and God's heavenly throne were inseparably bound together.[33] Jeremiah does not say that a sacred structure *in* Jerusalem will be built but that the future Jerusalem in its entirety will be called 'the throne of the LORD' because the essence of the old temple, the divine rule, will be expressed in an unfettered way at the end time. '*All* the city will have become throne, and hence there will be no further need for a *separate throne*' (i.e., an 'ark' representing the throne) (Woudstra 1970: 97, my emphasis). The same reality is probably indicated in Ezekiel 40 – 48, where the ark is absent from the temple and the vision climaxes with the statement that the new Jerusalem will be called 'the LORD is there' (48:35). This finds a parallel in the Ancient Near East, where description of a Sumerian 'temple' is referred to twice as 'indeed, it is a city, who knows its interior?' (*Keš Temple Hymn*, lines 58–59 in Sjöberg et al. 1969: 170–171).

Almost identically, Isaiah 4:5 states that at the end-time the whole area of Zion will become a sanctuary: 'the LORD will create over the whole area of Mount Zion and over her assemblies a cloud by day,

---

[33] Holladay (1986: 121) says that some OT writers viewed the ark as God's throne itself, though more precisely it is better to see the ark as the 'footstool' of the throne.

even smoke, and the brightness of a flaming fire by night; for over all the glory will be a canopy'. That Isaiah 4 refers to the entire area of Jerusalem becoming a tabernacle[34] is apparent from recalling that the 'fire' and 'cloud' were expressions of God's presence both at Sinai (which we have seen was a mountain temple) and in the tabernacle (Num. 9:15–16), and 'canopy' is an apt synonym for 'tabernacle' (Woudstra 1970: 98–99). Isaiah 4:6 further points to this connection by referring to the 'canopy' as a *sukkâ* ('booth'), which can be a synonym for 'tabernacle' (2 Sam. 11:11; cf. Ps. 31:20; Acts 15:16–18, quoting Amos 9:11–12).

The early Jewish apocalypse of *2 Baruch* also foresees a similar reality: God showed to Moses 'the end of time . . . and then further, also the likeness of Zion with its measurements which was to be made after the likeness of the present sanctuary' (*2 Baruch* 59:4). Latter-day Zion[35] was to be constructed according to the pattern of the tabernacle, which is close to the idea expressed in Jeremiah 3. Comparably, Ezekiel 37:24–28 suggests, as we have observed in the previous chapter, that the eschatological 'sanctuary' will not only extend over Jerusalem but all of Israel's land of promise (as 37:24–25 implies; cf. esp. 37:27: 'My dwelling place also shall be over [preposition *'al*] them') (Woudstra 1970: 98). Ezekiel 37:28 even mentions a worldwide effect of the temple, since as a result of the establishment of the temple 'the nations will know that I am the LORD'.

The reason the ark in the temple will have waned in significance when the Genesis 1:28 commission is finally fulfilled is that there will be a greater temple than a mere physical one, not only expanding to encompass all of Jerusalem (thus the point of Jer. 3:17) but the whole world, as texts analysed throughout this segment testify. This future temple will be so incomparably greater than the former that God's people will not even 'remember it nor shall they miss it' (Jer. 3:16). Furthermore, a physical ark within a small localized temple 'shall not be made again' because everything to which it pointed has been realized. Haggai 2:9 describes this same reality by saying 'the latter glory of this house' will be 'greater than the former'. In this light, Jeremiah 3 is affirming that once the greater glory of the eschatological temple

---

[34] See *Midrash Rabbah Numbers* 21:22, which says that the brightness of this canopy 'will shine from one end of the world to the other'.

[35] That the renewed Zion is the subject in *2 Baruch* 59 is apparent from the clear parallel in *2 Baruch* 4:1–7, which calls old Zion 'a building' and closely relates end-time Zion to 'the likeness of the tabernacle' shown to Moses.

comes, one will not focus on the lesser glory of the earlier temple, much less should one ever desire to rebuild it.[36]

The phrase found in Jeremiah 3:16 'and it shall not come to mind, nor shall they remember it' (with minor variants) is a way elsewhere of saying that the greatness of the coming new creation will diminish the memory of the former temple, Jerusalem, and old creation to a distant memory, an afterthought. For example, after Isaiah 54:1–3 speaks of the worldwide expansion of the tabernacle, in verse 4 it adds, 'but *you will forget* the shame of your youth, and the reproach of your widowhood *you will remember no more*'! That is, Israel's time of captivity would be incomparable to the coming restoration of her new temple (54:1–3) and new city (54:11–12) and of her own new creation (cf. 54:5 with 54:9–10). Isaiah 65:17–18 affirms the same reality: '*For behold, I create new heavens and a new earth;*/And the former things *shall not be remembered or come to mind.*/But be glad and rejoice forever in what I create;/*For behold, I create Jerusalem* for rejoicing,/And her people for gladness.'

The same wording of 'not remembering or coming to mind' occurs as in Jeremiah 3:16, and it is applied to the coming new creation. The future new world will be so incomparable to the old world and its captivity that God's people will no longer focus on the 'former things'. Strikingly, these verses in Isaiah 65 do not appear to be speaking of a new Jerusalem to be created in one geographical area of the new creation. Rather, the prophesied 'new heavens and a new earth' of verse 17 may even be equated with the creation of the new Jerusalem in verse 18 (note the parallelism: 'For behold, I create' in both verses 17a and 18a).[37] Our earlier analysis of Isaiah 54:1–3 confirms such an expansive understanding of the future Jerusalem in 65:17–18. Isaiah 43:18–19a also uses a similar negation to contrast the former creation with the new: '*Do not call to mind the former things,*/Or ponder things *of the past.*/Behold, I will do something new,/Now it will spring forth;/Will you not be aware of it?/I will even make a roadway in the wilderness/Rivers in the desert.'

Therefore, when this emphatic negation of not remembering former realities occurs in restoration contexts, it refers to the contrast between the greatness of the coming new creation (especially the

---

[36] In contrast to sectors of Judaism that believed the ark had been hidden and would be returned to the end-time temple: 2 Maccabees 2:1–18; *2 Baruch* 6:6–9; cf. *Mishnah Sheqalim* 6.2).

[37] As we have seen, this equation is argued most eloquently by Levenson 1988: 89–90; 1984: 294–295.

expanded new Jerusalem) and Israel's former city or temple. That such an expanded Jerusalem may be implied by Jeremiah 3:16–17 is suggested not only by its links to Isaiah's new creation texts but also by realizing that a new Jerusalem the size of the old one would not be large enough to contain 'all the nations' who 'will be gathered' to it in the last days.[38]

We will observe toward the end of this chapter the same irresistible implication in the early Jewish work of *1 Enoch* 90 and its portrayal of an expanded end-time temple. The same universal implication arises from recalling that Jeremiah 3:16–17 also promises that the Genesis 1:28 commission will finally come to pass when Israelites and 'all the nations' will 'be multiplied and increased' (so cf. v. 16 with v. 17) to accomplish the goal of 'filling the earth' (Gen. 1:28) and 'ruling ... over all the earth' (Gen. 1:26). Just as a significant increase in population would have necessitated an expansion of the first temple in Eden following upon the first couple's obedience, so it is that when God's people at last do what Adam and Eve should have done, an expansion of the temple and Jerusalem will be required. This conclusion coalesces with our assessment about Isaiah 4:5, Ezekiel 37:26–28 and Isaiah 54:2–3, which respectively refer to the tabernacle extending over Jerusalem, the land of promise and the entire earth. The last two passages even develop the original Genesis 1:28 commission.

Zechariah 1 and 2

Zechariah 1:16 predicts that God 'will return to Jerusalem' and that his 'house will be built in it ... and a measuring line will be stretched over Jerusalem'. The stretching out of the 'measuring line' after mention of building the temple refers most likely to the construction of the temple on a grander scale than formerly; that is, over the entire site of latter-day Jerusalem. This fits well with Ezekiel 40 – 46, where an angelic figure repeatedly 'measures' the dimensions of the temple that the prophet sees in a vision.[39] Zechariah 2 begins with a vision of 'a man with a measuring line in his hand'. His purpose is 'to measure Jerusalem, to see how wide it is and how long it is' (2:2). The point of this vision is explained in verse 4: 'Jerusalem will be inhabited without

---

[38] Similarly, later Judaism understood that the Jeremiah text together with Is. 54:2 predicted an expanded Jerusalem because of a population explosion: *Midrash Rabbah Genesis* 5:7; *Midrash Rabbah Leviticus* 10:9; *Pesikta de-rab Kahana*, Piska 20.7; similarly, cf. *Pesikta Rabbati*, Piska 21.8.

[39] E.g., Ezek. 40:5; 42:20; and, as we will see, the temple is 'measured' in Rev. 11 and 21.

walls, because of the multitude of men and cattle within it'. Apparently, the borders of old Jerusalem will be expanded to make room for the many people and their possessions that will dwell in it in the future.

The reason there will be no walls is that the Lord 'will be a wall of fire around her, and ... be the glory in her midst' (2:5). Thus, Zechariah speaks not merely about the enlargement of Jerusalem but refers to its entirety as a holy sanctuary in which God's flaming glory will reside. Quite like Jeremiah 3:16–17, the Shekinah presence of God, formerly sequestered in the old holy of holies, will burst forth from the heavenly sanctuary and encompass the entire future new Jerusalem. Zechariah 14:20–21 also suggests that the holiness, which was formerly restricted to the temple, will spread throughout the future new Jerusalem and Judah. 'God's fiery presence fills the eternal city to its unwalled limits . . . it is in its entirety a temple, hence has no temple within it' (Kline 2001: 76).

In response to this prophetic vision, captive Israel is exhorted to come out of captivity (2:6–7) because God has determined that they return to Zion and from there to 'spread them out as the four winds of the heavens' (Kline 2001: 79). These commands again echo the commission that Israel, as a corporate Adam, must spread out to subdue the earth and fill it with his glory. God will judge Israel's captors, which implicitly means their deliverance (2:8–9). Israel is to rejoice because God 'will dwell in' Israel's 'midst' when they return (2:10). The 'multitude of men' that will necessitate Jerusalem's enlargement in 2:4 is now defined in 2:11 as 'many nations' who 'will join themselves to the LORD ... and will become *My people*'.[40] In addition, 2:11 repeats the theme from 2:10 that God 'will dwell in your [Israel's] midst'. The repeated Hebrew verb 'dwell' (*šākan*) is the typical word used for God's 'dwelling' in the tabernacle, and the noun form of the verb is rendered 'tabernacle' throughout the Old Testament.

The point is that Zechariah 2:11 has come full circle back to the introductory note about the temple in 1:16. God will construct his future temple on a huge scale, and his tabernacling presence will reside with both Jews and Gentiles who trust in him.[41] The last phrase

---

[40] A name reserved in the OT for ethnic Israel but now applicable to all who trust in him in the latter days; see also Zech. 8:22–23; Hos. 1:8 – 2:1; Rom. 9:25–26; 1 Pet. 2:10.

[41] For a more in-depth analysis of Zech. 1 – 2 along the lines just given, see Kline (2001: 71–94), who refers to the future Jerusalem as a 'cosmic temple-city' that is a renewed 'Eden' (76–78).

of Zechariah 2 ('for he is aroused from his holy habitation') suggests that his coming judgment has begun or is imminent, and his heavenly tabernacling presence will descend once again and fill Israel in a greater way than ever before.

Daniel 2: an expanding worldwide kingdom

Also relevant for consideration is Daniel 2:34–35, 44–45, though there is no apparent explicit reference to a temple but only God's kingdom. King Nebuchadnezzar had a dream that no-one save Daniel could interpret. In his dream the king saw a giant statue of a man consisting of four sections. Daniel explained that this represented four kingdoms on the earth, the last of which would be destroyed:

> 34'You continued looking until a stone was cut out without hands, and it struck the statue on its feet of iron and clay, and crushed them.
> 35'Then the iron, the clay, the bronze, the silver and the gold were crushed all at the same time, and became like chaff from the summer threshing floors; and the wind carried them away so that not a trace of them was found. But the stone that struck the statue became a great mountain and filled the whole earth.'

Daniel interprets the climax of the king's vision to mean that God would destroy the last evil kingdom of world history and would establish his own kingdom for ever: 'And in the days of those kings God will set up a kingdom which will never be destroyed, and that kingdom will not be left for another people; it will crush and put an end to all these kingdoms, but it will itself endure forever' (Dan. 2:44).

Daniel 2 sees that God's kingdom will permeate the entire earth: the 'stone' that became a 'great mountain ... filled the whole earth'. The notion of God's kingdom 'filling the whole earth' appears to echo Genesis 1:26, 28, where God commissions Adam to 'fill the earth' and to 'rule ... over all the earth'. Further evidence of a Daniel 2 allusion to Genesis 1:28 appears in Daniel 2:38, where Daniel says that God has given the Babylonian king rule over 'the birds of the sky and the fish of the sea', almost verbatim with the Greek Old Testament of Genesis 1:28.[42] (We have also seen the warped

---

[42] Following Lacocque 1979: 50, who notes also the same parallel with Ps. 8:8; similarly, in line with the Greek OT of Gen. 1:28 is mention that the second kingdom 'will have dominion over all the earth' (Dan. 2:39).

universal kingdoms of Assyria and Egypt portrayed by Ezekiel with language from Genesis 1 and 2.)[43]

Daniel 2 in the light of other Old Testament passages: an expanding worldwide temple

André Lacocque has made the tantalizing suggestion that the 'stone ... cut out without hands' of Daniel 2 'represents Mount Zion, the Temple not built by human hands' (Lacocque 1979: 124; see also 49). Other than offering parallels where 'the symbolism of a mountain is applied to Israel' (e.g., Is. 2:2–3; Ezek. 40:2), Lacocque does not adduce any substantial evidence supporting his proposal (1979: 49). Nevertheless, there are some indications that Daniel's stone-mountain may, indeed, be closely associated with a gigantic temple.

First, not only does Isaiah 2:2–3 utilize a 'mountain' to symbolize Israel, but the image is integrally connected to the temple, 'the mountain of the house of the Lord'.

Second, such a close link between mountain and temple is made throughout the Old Testament, so that Mount Zion is sometimes merely referred to as 'mountain', 'hill' or other like image. These ways of speaking about Mount Zion either closely associate it or virtually equate it with the temple as a synecdoche of the whole for the part[44] (the entire mountain is substituted for the top part where the temple is located). For example, repeatedly such phrases occur as 'mountain of the house' (Jer. 26:18; Mic. 4:1), 'holy mountain' (about 16 times), 'holy hill' (Pss. 15:1; 43:3; 99:9; Jer. 31:23) and 'temple hill' (1 Maccabees 13:52; 16:20). Sometimes these references are equated with the temple in the following context: e.g., in Isaiah 66: 20 'holy mountain' = 'house of the LORD'; in Psalm 15:1 'holy hill' = 'your tent'; in Psalm 24:3 'hill of the LORD' = 'His holy place' (cf. also Ps. 43:3).

Thus, 'mountain', when referring to Zion, often includes reference

---

[43] The link between Dan. 2 and Gen. 1 may be pointed to further by recognizing the parallel between the four sections of the statue that are demolished and replaced by God's eternal kingdom and the four beastly kingdoms that are judged and replaced by God's eternal kingdom in Dan. 7. In this respect, a number of commentators note that the portrayal in Dan. 7 alludes to the remnant of Israel as God's true humanity, a kind of corporate Adam figure, who has been given dominion over 'beasts' that had formerly persecuted them (so, e.g., N. T. Wright 1992: 23; Lacocque 1979: 128–129, 132–133). In both Dan. 2 and 7 God's kingdom replaces the ungodly kingdoms who had abused the rule over creation that God had placed into their hands.

[44] A synecdoche is a figure of speech wherein the whole represents the part or the part represents the whole.

to the temple.[45] Among the best illustrations of this is Isaiah 2:2–3 and Micah 4:1–2 which equate 'the mountain of the house of the LORD' with 'the mountain of the LORD ... the house of the God of Jacob' (Mic. 4:1–2 is identical). The description of the mountain in Daniel 2 rings with the same intonations of these descriptions in Isaiah and Micah.

Enhancing this point is the observation that every temple associated with God's people in the Old Testament is on a 'mountain': Ezekiel 28:13–14, 16, and 18 refers to 'Eden, the garden of God ... the holy mountain of God', and also refers to it as containing 'sanctuaries'![46] As we have seen, the patriarchal small-scale temples were all on mountains, and Mount Sinai appears to have been conceived of as a temple. Furthermore, the pattern of the tabernacle was given to Moses on Sinai (Exod. 25:9, 40), and the impermanent tabernacle pointed to the final temple on Mount Zion.[47] Additionally, it is clear that the eschatological temple was to be situated on a mountain (Ezek. 40:2; Rev. 21:10). In line with these precedents, Daniel also portrays a mountain to be created at the end of time.

Third, what is further attractive about linking Daniel 2 and Isaiah 2:2–3 (= Mic. 4:1–2) as temple texts is that both are introduced as containing events that are to occur 'in the last days' (Dan. 2:28 [so also Dan. 2:29, LXX] and Is. 2:2; Mic. 4:1). Micah even

---

[45] *4 Ezra* 13:6–7, 35–36, equate the Dan. 2 mountain with 'Mount Zion' and 'Zion', on which, see further S. M. Bryan (2002: 194–195, 230), who argues that 'Mount Zion' in *4 Ezra* 13 implies the presence of the temple.

[46] For the plural 'sanctuaries' being a reference to the temple, see the above discussion of Num. 24:5. In addition, see further Van Dijk (1968: 122) for the notion that the plural 'sanctuaries' in Ezek. 28:18 refers to 'a single temple and denotes a single sanctuary with its precincts'. Especially see Stordalen (2000: 352), who also notes the plural use of 'sanctuaries' (*miqdāš*) in application to Israel's one tabernacle (Lev. 21:23) or temple in Jerusalem (Ezek. 7:24), one of the best examples being Jer. 51:51: 'For aliens have entered the holy places of the LORD's house.' This is significant, since Ezek. 28:18 says, 'You profaned your sanctuaries', especially since whenever the OT refers to the 'sanctuary' (*miqdāš*) being 'profaned' (*ḥālal*), it refers always either to Israel's tabernacle or temple in Jerusalem (so seven times outside of Ezek. 28, two of which, as we saw above, are plural, on which see Stordalen 2000: 352). The use in Ezek. 28:18 may be like that in Jer. 51, conceiving of the temple as containing multiple 'holy spaces' or 'sanctuaries', which would be, at least, the outer court, the inner holy place, and the innermost holy of holies (accordingly Is. 62:9 mentions 'courts of My sanctuary'; likewise, virtually identically, see Ps. 65:4, where 'Thy courts' equals 'Thy house' and 'Thy holy temple'; similarly, see Pss. 84:3; 96:8, following Van Dijk 1968: 122). Alternatively, the plural in Ezek. 28:18 may be an emphatic plural 'used because the subject was a scandalous profanation of the most important temple' (Stordalen 1968: 352). Cf. also John 14:2: 'In my Father's house are *many dwelling-places* (*monai pollai*)'.

[47] E.g., cf. Exod. 25:9, 40 with 1 Chr. 28:19 and 2 Sam. 7:1–13; the equivalence of the tabernacle and temple was also made by early Judaism: so *Wisdom of Solomon* 9:8.

equates 'the mountain of the house of the LORD' (4:1) with God's eternal kingdom, the latter an explicit element of the mountain in Daniel 2: 'the LORD will reign over them in Mount Zion . . . forever' (Mic. 4:7). Exodus 15:17–18 also equates 'the mountain of Thine inheritance' with 'the place, O LORD, which Thou hast made for thy dwelling . . . the sanctuary', from where 'the Lord will reign forever and ever'.

Fourth, both Isaiah 2:2–3 and Micah 4:1–2 portray the mountain on which the temple sits as growing: it 'will be raised above the hills'. While this is not as explicit as Daniel's rock that becomes a mountain and fills the earth, neither is it far from that picture. Both the Daniel and Isaiah-Micah passages reverberate with echoes of new creation, since they are so eschatologically oriented. The image of an emerging new creation may be perceived in the depiction of a growing holy mountain, since the emergence of mountains was certainly a feature of the original creation.

In this regard, the paradisal garden imagery of Micah 4:4 is not unexpected in a passage that has just pictured a latter-day temple-mountain, especially since Eden was a garden on a mountain (as we have just seen in Ezek. 28:14, 16, 18, which is to be compared with Mic. 4:4: 'And each of them will sit under his vine and under his fig tree, with no one to make them afraid') (Stordalen 2000: 426–428). Thus, primal history is repeated in eschatological history (*Barnabas* 6:13 says, 'Behold, I make the last things as the first'). Neither is Isaiah unfamiliar with an eschatological arbor-like temple atmosphere: 'The glory of Lebanon will come to you,/The juniper, the box tree, and the cypress together,/To beautify the place of My sanctuary,/And I shall make the place of My feet [the ark of the covenant] glorious' (Is. 60:13).

Fifth, one final observation points to the Daniel 2 stone being the foundation of a mountain-temple. Could the reference to a mountain growing out of the place of a 'threshing floor' (Dan. 2:35) be a subtle allusion to the episode narrated in 2 Chronicles 3:1?[48] The Chronicles text reads, 'Then Solomon began to build the house of the LORD in Jerusalem on Mount Moriah, where the LORD had appeared to his father David . . . on the *threshing floor* of Ornan the Jebusite.' This 'threshing floor' is referred to four times in 1 Chronicles 24:16–24 and

---

[48] As in the case of the relationship of Is. 66:1 to 2 Chr. 6:18 discussed above, so likewise the date of Daniel's composition (according to a conservative perspective) precedes that of 1 Chronicles, so that our proposal, if correct, would mean that Daniel was aware of a tradition written down later by the chronicler.

five times in the parallel of 1 Chronicles 21:15–28.[49] There David saw 'the angel of the LORD standing between earth and heaven' (1 Chr. 21:16), and at that site 'David built an altar to the LORD ... and offered burnt offerings ... And he called to the LORD' (1 Chr. 21:26). In addition, David calls the place 'the house of the LORD God' (1 Chr. 22:1). As we discussed, these are all the same elements found with the small-scale temple-building activities of Abraham, Isaac and Jacob. This Davidic episode mirrors the account of Jacob in particular, where also God and angels appear to him and a link between 'earth' and 'heaven' is highlighted.

The reason that David performed priestly activities in an informal sanctuary was twofold, as we saw in the preceding chapter. First, because from that very site the temple of Israel was to be built, and, second, because the 1 Chronicles 21 passage goes on to say that 'the tabernacle ... which Moses had made ... and the altar of burnt offering were in ... Gibeon at that time' (21:29). This second observation suggests not only that, because of the immediacy of the situation, he was unable to go to Gibeon to offer sacrifices at the properly designated cultic place, but that a transition from the tabernacle to the temple was occurring. Mount Moriah was being designated as the new place for sacrifice because the temple would imminently be constructed there.

Perhaps, it is not coincidental, keeping in mind the stone-mountain of Daniel 2:34–35, that during this same episode David begins preparations for construction of the temple by arranging that 'stonecutters ... hew out stones to build the house of God' (1 Chr. 22:2).

Daniel 2 in the light of the Ancient Near East and Judaism: an expanding worldwide temple and new creation
Daniel's picture of an expanding mountain is compatible with Ancient Near Eastern cosmogonies that sometimes portray a hillock arising amidst the chaos seas as the bridgehead of a new creation, as we have already observed in Egyptian mythology.[50] For instance, the

---

[49] I was first made aware of this possibility by my former student, C. Thompson, who also anticipated the above points about the features of a growing eschatological temple-mount in common between Dan. 2 and Is. 2. Some commentators see Is. 2 (and Mic. 4) as a close parallel (Collins 1993: 165 and Porteous 1965: 50), though Russell 1981: 53 sees the Daniel passage as 'recalling' Is. 2.

[50] See above (p. 93) and James (1969: 100–101), on the similar Hermopolitan and Heliopolitan forms of this mythic emerging hillock; likewise, Clifford (1994: 105–110) also notes similar notions of primordial hills in Sumerian and Mesopotamian cosmogonies (1994: 45–46, 62–64).

beginning of the Egyptian Sun god's (Re's) rule at the beginning of creation is identified with the emergence of a 'primeval hillock': 'Re began to appear as king ... when he was on the [primeval] hill which is in Hermopolis.'[51] Egyptian pyramids were analogues of such primeval hillocks (Pritchard 1969: 3). We need to remember that just as the primordial hillock was thought to have expanded to form the entire earth, so temples were constructed to memorialize symbolically this initial creation: hillocks were depicted in the back of temples and the temple structure from that point was built in an ever-widening, expansive design. That successive Pharaohs actually expanded the borders of the temples' sacred space also symbolically memorialized the expansion of the original creation. We also saw at the beginning of chapter 3 a somewhat similar phenomenon in Babylonian temple mythology.

We have already argued that Adam was to extend the hospitable part of new creation in Mount Eden into the inhospitable world (for the location of Eden on a mountain, see Ezek. 28:13–16). The same principle may be reflected in the second creation episode, where the first land that emerges from the waters is the tip of a mountain, on which Noah's ark comes to rest,[52] and from where Noah and his family were to repopulate the earth. Judaism also held that the 'world was [started] created from Zion ... the world was created from its centre' when God 'cast a stone into the ocean, from which the world then was founded' (b. Yoma 54b). This stone became 'the foundation stone with which the Lord of the world sealed the mouth of the great deep from the beginning' (Tg. Pseudo-Jonathon Exodus 28:29), from which new land emerged and spread out until the main land-mass of the creation was formed.[53] While it is unlikely historically true that Zion was the place from which the land of the original creation expanded, this Jewish reference probably reflects the notion that the building of Israel's temple marked the beginning of a new creation. In this new creation Israel was to function as a kind of corporate

---

[51] See Pritchard (1969: 3–4), who also cites there a similar passage about the beginning of creation: 'O [divine] Atum-Kheprer, thou wast on high on the (primeval) hill; thou didst arise as the ben-bird of the ben-stone in the ben-House [temple] in Heliopolis.'

[52] See Levenson 1988: 74–75; for the idea, intriguingly, that Noah's ark was a temple, see Holloway 1991: 328–354; Haywood 1999: 37.

[53] Interestingly, the stone supporting the holy of holies was thought by later Judaism to be that upon which 'all the world was based, since God had begun to create the world from that point in the beginning (Midrash Rabbah Song of Songs 3:10 §4; Pirke de Rabbi Eliezer 35; Midrash Tanhuma Yelammedenu, Exodus 11:3; so also Midrash Tanhuma Qedoshim 10 [on which see Branham 1995: 325]).

Adam in their renewed Garden of Eden and spread out from there, reflecting God's glory in obedience to the commission of Genesis 1:28. History was starting over again, and Israel was the crown even of the human creation.

The Ancient Near East sometimes pictured the construction of a temple as the growing of a mountain from a stone and linked it with the dominion of the kingdom in which the temple started its growth. This is well illustrated by the Sumerian Cylinders of Gudea that commemorate king Gudea's building and dedication of a temple for the god Ningirsu in Lagash, which we have had occasion already briefly to discuss in chapter 2:

> The day will build the temple for you ...
> From the mountain of stone, the great stone of the mountain range
> I [the god Ningirsu] will have cut blocks for you.
>
> (Cyl. A 12.1–9)

> Gudea put the clay into the brick-mold ...
> the [foundation] brick of the temple he set forth in splendid appearance.
>
> (Cyl. A 18.24–25)

> He lifted the brick out of the box of the brick-mold.
> (Like) a holy crown lifted up to heaven ...
>
> (Cyl. A 19.13–14)

> being (like) that brick lifting its head toward heaven ...
> He placed the brick (and) walked about in the temple ...
> Gudea was laying out the plan of the temple.
>
> (Cyl. A 19.17–20)

> They were making the temple grow (high) like a mountain range ... making it raise (its) head high in the mountains ... making the temple raise (its) head high in heaven and earth like a mountain range.
>
> (Cyl. A 21.19–23)

> the lord [god] Ningirsu,
> made [king] Gudea firm upon his throne.
>
> (Cyl. B 23.25)

The temple, mooring pole of the land,
which grows (high) between heaven and earth ...
the beautiful mountain range, which stands out as a marvel,
(and) which towers above the mountains;
the temple, being a big mountain, reached up to heaven;
... it filled heaven's midst ...
The people were set firm there.

(Cyl. B 1.1–10)

Here, with almost identical language, we have all the elements of Daniel 2 and Isaiah 2. This depiction was not unique among the Sumerian temple portrayals. Another temple hymn says that the temple was a 'mountain' that 'has grown high, (uniting) heaven and earth' (Janowski 2001: 236). Still another Sumerian temple portrayal (the *Keš Temple Hymn*) describes the 'Keš temple' as a 'foundation' that was 'growing up like a mountain, embracing the sky' and as a 'great temple, reaching the sky' (Sjöberg et al. 1969: 167, 169). This Sumerian account shows that it would have been natural for the ancient mind to associate the mention of a foundation 'stone [or brick of a temple] cut out of a mountain' and a mountain that is a temple which grows and 'fills' the cosmos, indicating the sovereign dominion of a king and his people.[54]

As in the depiction of King Gudea's temple, mention of 'cutting out stones from a mountain' for Israel's temple also occurs repeatedly: 1 Kings 5:15–17 says that from 'the mountains ... they quarried great stones, costly stones, to lay the foundation of the house with cut stones' (see also 1 Chr. 22:2; 2 Chr. 2:18). Israel's second temple also commenced with the laying of a foundational 'top stone' (Zech. 4:7). Not only can 'mountain' be a reference to Israel's temple but so can 'stone' or 'rock'.[55] Since mountains were also associated with temples specifically in Babylon (note the ziggurats), it is appropriate that such a cultic mountain would be revealed in vision to the king of Babylon in Daniel 2,[56] portraying to him the true divine

[54] Averbeck (2000: 428) compares this Sumerian passage to Mount Sinai, Exod. 15:17; Is. 2 and Mic. 4.

[55] E.g., Ps. 27:5, 'For in the day of trouble He will conceal me in His *tabernacle*; in the secret place of His *tent* He will hide me; He will lift me up on a *rock*'; cf. also Ps. 71:3; sometimes 'mountain' and 'stone' are used synonymously: 'go to the mountain of the LORD, to the Rock of Israel' (Is. 30:29). Judaism identified the foundation stone of the prophesied temple in Zech. 4:7 with the stone of Dan. 2:34–35 (*Midrash Tanhuma Genesis* 6:20).

[56] Cf. Showers 1982: 21.

temple mount in contrast to the false Babylonian pretenders, as well as to similar Egyptian pretenders that would likely have been known in Babylon.

Daniel 2 in the light of a glimpse forward to the New Testament: an end-time temple

Further indication that the 'stone' of Daniel 2 is associated with a temple-like image comes from the gospels which allude to this Old Testament passage: 'The stone which the builders rejected, This became the chief corner stone [i.e., of the temple][57] ... Every one who falls on that stone will be broken to pieces; but on whomever it falls, it will scatter him like dust' (Luke 20:17–18 = Matt. 21:42, 44).[58]

Possibly also another link between the stone-mountain of Daniel 2 and the eschatological temple is that both are not made by human hands. Again, it is the New Testament that repeatedly refers to the new, end-time temple as 'not made with hands' (see Mark 14:58;[59] 2 Cor. 5:1; Heb. 9:11, 24; cf. Acts 7:48). The Old Testament image corresponding closest to this is Daniel's stone 'cut out without hands'.[60] For instance, Hebrews 9:11 says that Christ entered 'through the greater and more perfect tabernacle, not made with hands, that is to say, not of this creation'. Accordingly, Acts 17:24 affirms that 'the God who made the world and all things in it, since he is Lord of heaven and earth, does not dwell in temples made with hands'. Paul says this after the great redemptive–historical divide when Christ and his people had begun to replace Israel's 'handmade' temple. There could be no human-made structures separating God and his people in order that he dwell fully and unfettered with them. This is why no human can answer affirmatively God's question in Isaiah about his eschatological, eternal dwelling, 'Where then is a house you could build for me?' (Is. 66:1). Thus, God's perfect heavenly dwelling, which would eventually descend and encompass the entire earth, could never be altered or changed by human hands (*Odes of Solomon* 4:1–3).

God's intention as the Creator is one day to fill every part of his creation with his presence. God's holy presence could not dwell fully in the old creation because it was a sin-tainted and idolatrous world,

---

[57] For further discussion identifying the 'stone' here with a temple (see pp. 181–187 below).

[58] Is. 8:14 may also be combined with the Dan. 2 allusion.

[59] See Evans 2001: 445, who sees Christ's claim in Mark 14:58 to 'build another [temple] made without hands' to be an allusion to Dan. 2:44–45.

[60] Following a suggestion made by my student C. Thompson.

which we have also seen is an implication of Isaiah 66:1–2. Hence, his special revelatory presence dwelt in a limited and temporary manner in human-made structures. But when he would fully redeem the world and recreate it (so Rom. 8:18–25), he would dwell in it in a fuller way than ever before.

Even before the early Christian evidence, Daniel's stone 'not cut by human hands' (Dan. 2:34, 45) may have resonated with cultic implications because the only other places in the Old Testament where 'uncut stones' are mentioned is in Exodus, Deuteronomy and Joshua, where Israel was to build 'an altar of *uncut stones* [literally 'whole stones'], on which no man had wielded an iron tool', and 'they offered burnt offerings . . . and sacrificed peace offerings'.[61] Similarly, 1 Kings 6:7 says that Solomon's temple 'was built of stone *prepared at the quarry, and there was neither hammer nor axe nor any iron tool* heard in the house while it was being built'.

Interestingly, the *Sibylline Oracles*, a Jewish work (c. AD 80), affirms a similar notion to that of the above passages speaking of temples 'not made with hands' (likewise also cf. *4 Ezra* 13:6–7, 35–36, alluding to Dan. 2:34, 45 and *2 Enoch* 22:1). Perhaps as a result of contemplating the recent destruction of Jerusalem's temple in AD 70, this text asserts: 'the great God, whom no hands of men fashioned . . . does not have a house, a stone set up as a temple . . . but one which it is not possible to see from the earth nor to measure with mortal eyes, since it was not fashioned by mortal hand' (*Sibylline Oracles* 4:11). Consequently, God's true people 'will reject all temples when they see them; altars too, useless foundations of dumb stones' (*Sibylline Oracles* 4:27–28). Even pagans seemed to perceive this truth: 'What house built by craftsmen could enclose the form divine within enfolding walls?' (Euripides, *Fragment* 968).[62]

In the light of the evidence adduced so far in this section and the preceding three, Daniel 2 likely speaks of an eternal kingdom, which is also portrayed as a huge mountain-temple.

Psalm 72: an expanding worldwide kingdom

Finally, Psalm 72, though lacking any specific reference to the temple, speaks of an ideal eschatological Israelite king who defeats enemies (72:9–11) and establishes the borders of his rule around the earth:

---

[61] So Josh. 8:31 in fulfilment of Exod. 20:25; Deut. 27:6; Exodus and Daniel both use cognate forms of *temnō + lithos*.

[62] Bruce (1954: 357) first made me aware of this quotation. For convenient access to a version of this fragment, see Charlesworth 1983: 827.

'May he also rule from sea to sea, And from the river to the ends of the earth' (72:8; so likewise Ps. 2:6–9!). Verse 17 (71:17, LXX) alludes to Genesis 28:14 and 12:2–3 ('I will . . . make your name great and . . . I will bless those who bless you . . . and in you all the families of the earth shall be blessed'): 'May his name increase . . . And let men bless themselves by him; let all the nations call him blessed'.[63] The universal extension of the king's rule and blessing (72:8, 17) is also part of the allusion to Genesis 28:14: 'Your descendants shall also be like the dust of the earth, and you shall spread out to the west and to the east and to the north and to the south; and in you and in your seed shall all the families of the earth be blessed' (cf. also Gen. 13:15).

The statements of the king's worldwide rule and domination of enemies together with the divine blessing also echo Genesis 1:28.[64] Psalm 72:19 gives the ultimate goal of the king's rule and of the blessing 'may the whole earth be filled with His [God's] glory', which we have argued is the final goal of Genesis 1:28 and its reapplications to God's people throughout the Old Testament. Though the psalm does not mention the sanctuary, its development of Genesis 1:28, 12:2–3, and 28:14 fits admirably with our other findings concerning the worldwide nature of the eschatological sanctuary.

Views of early Jewish commentators

In addition to the above references in the Old Testament, early Jewish authors also elaborate explicitly and implicitly on how the borders of Eden and the temple were to be enlarged and to spread throughout the earth. We have alluded only to a few such writings in the preceding part of this chapter. The purpose in this section is to focus on them. The following Jewish writings represent interpretative insights and organic developments of some of the Old Testament passages and themes that we have discussed above.

The Dead Sea Scrolls (second century BC – first century AD)

First, consider an important text from column 6 of the early Jewish Qumran community's *Hymn Scroll*.

---

[63] So Bauckham 1993: 319–322; the LXX ties Ps. 72:17 even more closely to Gen. 12 and 28, since all three passages have the common phrase 'all the tribes of the earth' [*pasai hai phylai tēs gēs*].

[64] So likewise Dan. 7:13–14, 27, following N. T. Wright 1992a: 23.

[12] ... And all the nations shall know Thy truth
And all the peoples, Thy glory ...
[14] ... And Thou hast sent out
[15]a sprouting
as a flower that shall bloom for ever,
that the Shoot may grow into the branches of the eternal
   planting.
And its shade shall spread over all [the earth]
[and] its [top]
[16]reach up to the hea[vens]
[and] its roots go down to the Abyss.[65]
And all the rivers of Eden [shall water] its [bou]ghs and it shall
   become a [mi]ghty
[17]forest,
[and the glory of] its [fo]rest shall spread over the world
   without end,
as far as Sheol [for ever].
[And] it shall be a well-spring of light as an
[18]eternal unfailing fountain.
In its brilliant flames
All the son[s of darkness] shall be consumed ...
[19] ... And they that participated in my testimony ...
[... have not held fast] to the service of righteousness.

This passge (1QH 6.12–19) compares the Qumran saints to an Edenic tree with a 'well-spring of light' and 'brilliant flames', which is directly linked to the 'testimony' (!) of the Teacher of Righteousness (1QS 8.5–6 speaks likewise of the DSS community as 'an everlasting planting ... the House of holiness for Israel and the Council of the Holy of Holies', who are to be *witnesses of truth*'). A few sections later the *Hymn Scroll* identifies the Qumran community as the place where 'salvation' will 'flower' and the 'Shoot ... grow' (1QH 7.19) and as 'the fruitful planting' and 'the glorious Eden', which 'shall bear fr[uit for ever]' (1QH 8.20, though cf. all of 8.4–23, which contains many allusions to Eden's fertility).

Accordingly, another Qumran writing (4QFlor 1.6) says that 'a sanctuary of Adam [or mankind]' (*miqdaš 'ādām*) will be built in the

---

[65] Pseudo-Philo, *Biblical Antiquities* 12.8, depicts Israel at Mount Sinai in similar fashion as 1QH 6.14–16.

midst of the community.[66] In this respect, we have already observed that the seven lamps on the temple lampstand may well have inspired the hymnist's affirmation in 1QH 7.24, 'I will shine with a *seven-fold li*[*ght*] in the *E*[*den*[67] which] Thou has [m]ade for Thy glory' (my italics). This 'shining' is an expression of establishing 'dominion … over the sons [of the ear]th' (1QH 7.23), which alludes to the theme of universality, again in conjunction with the garden. Thus, the end-time temple of Eden had been established among the Qumran covenanters, to which another Dead Sea Scroll document attests in fulfilment of the Ezekiel 40–48 temple prophecy: God 'built for them a sure House in Israel such as did not exist from former times till now. They who cling to it' will have 'all the glory of Adam' (CD 3.19–20).[68]

Of special note in the *Hymn Scroll* text just quoted (1QH 6.15–17) is that not only does it compare the Essene community to the tree of Eden that God has planted in the past but that the tree's 'shade shall spread over all [the earth] [and] its [top] reach up to the hea[vens] … And all the rivers of Eden [shall water] its [bou]ghs and it shall become a [mi]ghty forest, [and the glory of] its [fo]rest shall spread over the world without end'. The new Eden's tree will grow its branches over the entire globe and its shade accordingly will spread until the earth is under a massive arboreal-like tabernacle, filled not with literal shade but with divine glory. The metaphorical outgrowth of the tree is not only associated with Qumran's 'testimony' and 'witness' but a picture of the previously stated notion that 'all the nations will know Thy truth and all the peoples, Thy glory' (1QH 6.12).

Similarly, 1QH 8.20–22 repeats, though not as explicitly, the portrait of 6.12–19:

[20]… But the fruitful planting [shall prosper],
[and it shall become an] everlasting [fount]ain for the glorious Eden

---

[66] See ch. 2 (p. 78) on the debated translation of *miqdaš 'ādām*, which could also be rendered 'sanctuary of man' or 'of humanity' or 'consisting of men'.

[67] Our translation follows Dupont-Sommer, who is the only translator who supplies the lacunae with 'Eden'. For fuller discussion of this problem, see ch. 2 (p. 79), where it is pointed out that Eden is in mind in both preceding and following contexts, so that our point is not dependent on this rendering.

[68] See discussion in Gärtner 1965: 81–84. 'Adam' could be rendered 'man' but the former makes better sense (which is also the rendering of the Vermes and Martínez–Tigchelaar translations) because of the historical sketch of great personages from Israel's past in CD 2.17 – 3.4. CD 3.21 – 4.2 quotes specifically Ezek. 44:15 with the introductory fulfilment formula 'just as God swore to them by Ezekiel the prophet'.

and shall bear fr[uit for ever].
[21]And Thou hast opened their fountain by my hand
among the [water] courses,
[and Thou hast disposed] ... the planting
[22]of their trees ... to stre[ngthen it and cause] a glorious
branch to [gro]w.

We see in these early Jewish hymnic texts an interpretation of the tree of life that understands Eden to have universal eschatological significance[69] similar, as we will see, to the depiction in the last vision of Revelation (cf. Rev. 22:1–5 with 21:1–27). The Qumran community extends its figurative arboreal borders by witnessing to the truth and spreading the light of that truth to the nations throughout the world.

One final text from the Dead Sea Scrolls is particularly noteworthy (4Q418, frag. 81 = 4Q423 8 + 24?). God is said to be 'your portion and your inheritance among the sons of Adam, [and over] his [in]heritance he has given them authority' (line 3). Thus, the members of the Qumran community are those who are the true 'sons of Adam' whom God has given authority over an 'inheritance'. Those who 'inherit the earth' will 'walk' in an 'eter[nal] plantation' (lines 13–14), likely referring to the whole earth as a large Eden.[70] They 'shall fill [apparently the earth] and ... and be satiated with the abundance of good' (line 19). So far, the description of the community echoes the commission of Genesis 1:26, 28. They are also to 'honour' God 'by consecrating yourself to him, in accordance to the fact that he has placed you as a holy of holies [over all][71] the earth, and over all the angels ...' (line 4).[72] Strikingly, the community is seen to be the eschatological 'holy of holies' extending over all the earth! As such, they are 'sons of Adam', finally doing what he should have done in his primeval garden sanctuary. Just as we have seen

[69] Cf. also the Qumran document 4Q433a (4QHodayot-like text B), frag. 2.
[70] A closely related passage in 4Q475 (4Q Renewed Earth) is apparently the most explicit Qumran text affirming that the earth will become Eden: after all sin has been extinguished from the earth, 'all the world will be like Eden, and all ... the earth will be at peace for ever, and ... a beloved son ... will ... inherit it all'.
[71] The Martínez–Tigchelaar Hebrew–English edition rightly supplies the lacunae with 'over all' because of the following parallelism with 'over all the angels' [literally 'gods'], though in Martínez's earlier English edition he did not do so and gave an otherwise quite different translation, which does not reflect the Hebrew as well as the later translation.
[72] Similarly, 4Q511 (frag. 35) says 'God makes (some) hol[y] for himself like an everlasting sanctuary ... And they shall be priests ...' (lines 3–4). As such, their task is to 'spread the fear of God in the ages' (line 6).

earlier that the commission of Genesis 1:26–28 was to have begun in the garden sanctuary of Genesis 2,[73] so this Qumran passage reflects the same kind of linkage between the first two chapters of Genesis.

This last passage from Qumran is amazing, since as we saw in our introductory chapter, and will again in the conclusion to the book, John pictures the new creation in Revelation 21 to be one enormous holy of holies. As a worldwide holy of holies, God 'has multiplied your glory exceedingly' (line 5a). Thus, the divine glory is no longer cordoned off in a back room in Israel's physical temple but extends into the world through his end-time image bearers. God 'has placed' them 'for him as a first-born' (line 5b), another reference to them as the true communal Adam who are extending out and reflecting his glory because they reflect his image (line 5b). They are priest-kings who carry out the eschatological purpose that we have seen to be inherent in Genesis 1 – 2.

Though it may appear out of place here in a section on Judaism, we must mention *Odes of Solomon* 11 – 12, an early Jewish-Christian writing (c. AD 100), because it has more unique similarities to the preceding Qumran descriptions than any other extant work of the time:

[11:1]My heart was pruned and its flower appeared ...
and it produced fruits for the Lord ...
[5]And I was established on the rock of truth ...
[6]And speaking waters touched my lips
from the spring of the Lord ...
[7] And so I drank ...
from the living water that does not die.
[11]And the Lord ... possessed me by his light.
[12]And from above he gave me immortal rest;
and I became like the land which blossoms and rejoices in its
    fruits.
[13]And the Lord [is] like the sun
upon the face of the land ...
[16]And he took me to his Paradise ...
[16a](I contemplated blooming and fruit-bearing trees ...
[16b]Their branches were flourishing
and their fruits were shining;
their roots [were] from an immortal land.

---

[73] See ch. 3 (pp. 81–87). For analysis of the garden and temple metaphors in DSS and their theological complementarity, see the unpublished dissertation by P. N. W. Swarup (2002), the abstract of which I have only had opportunity to consult.

[16c]And a river of gladness was irrigating them,
and the region round about them in the land of eternal
    life.) . . .
[18]And I said, blessed, O Lord, are they
who are planted in your land,
and who have a place in your Paradise;
[19]And who grow in the growth of your trees, and have passed
    from darkness into light.
[20]Behold, all your laborers are fair,
they who work good works . . .
[21] . . . they were planted in your land . . .
[22] . . . [Blessed are the workers of your water,] . . .
[23]Indeed, there is much room in your Paradise . . .
everything is filled with fruit.
[24]Praise be to you, O God, the delight of Paradise for ever.
[12:1]He has filled me with words of truth,
that I may proclaim him.
[2]And like the flowing of waters, truth flows from my mouth,
and my lips declare his fruits . . .
[12]For the dwelling place of the Word is man,
and his truth is love.

This passage combines themes seen in Qumran with some earlier ideas that we have seen are associated with the Eden sanctuary: (1) repeated descriptions of the Garden of Eden, especially its growing trees, as well as mention of the garden's expansiveness (11:23); (2) people are established in the garden on 'a rock' (11:5); (3) the image of the tabernacle (12:2) and notions of witnessing (12:1–2); (4) those in the garden are exposed to divine light (11:13, 19); (5) those in the garden labour in it, which is interpreted as 'good works' (11:20–22); (6) people receive 'rest' in the garden (11:12) and (7) benefit from life-giving waters. The 'paradise' has expanded and 'there is much room' in it (11:23) because it contains a multitude of believers, who throughout this passage are said to be part of the garden (11:18–23).

Another passage from chapter 38 of the *Odes* is similar:

[38:16]But I have been made wise so as not to fall into the hands
    of the deceivers,
and I myself rejoiced because the Truth had gone with me.
[17]For I was established and . . . my foundations were laid on
    account of the Lord's hand;

because he has planted me.
[18]For he set the root, and watered it and ... blessed it,
and its fruits will be forever.
[19] It penetrated deeply and sprang up and spread out,
and it was full and was enlarged.
[20] And the Lord alone was praised,
in his planting and in his cultivation ...

This text also combines temple-building language together with that of expanding garden imagery. The speaker says that he was not deceived but remained in the truth *because* God had established him as a well-planted garden. This is very comparable to the Qumran *Hymn Scroll* (1QH 6.15–17), which we saw above combined the same images of temple, expanding garden, and truth.

Sirach (second century BC)

An intriguing passage from *Sirach* 24 contains imagery much like the Qumran *Hymn Scroll*. Just as the preceding discussion revealed that Qumran was primarily dependent on Genesis 2 for its depictions, so also the preceding *Sirach* passage may be based partly on Numbers 24:5–7, which, as we saw at the commencement of this chapter, has a similar though more abbreviated portrayal of an expanding garden. The *Sirach* text personifies 'wisdom' as 'set over the created order' and as the model for true humanity, 'corresponding to the place intended for Adam'.[74] Adam should have possessed this wisdom to be a wise ruler, but he did not. *Sirach* 24:28 says, 'the first man knew her [wisdom] not perfectly'. What is startling about this for our purposes is that 'wisdom's' role is explained primarily through the language of the temple and the Garden of Eden. 'Wisdom' is first portrayed as 'seeking rest' somewhere on the created earth (24:7), and

> [8]so the Creator of all things gave me a commandment, and he that made me caused my tabernacle to rest, and said, Let thy dwelling be in Jacob, and thine inheritance in Israel ...
> [10]In the holy tabernacle I served before him; and so was I established in Zion.
> [11]Likewise, in the beloved city he gave me rest, and in Jerusalem was my power.

[74] So N. T. Wright 1992a: 25–26, who also adduces other texts in *Sirach* and *2 Baruch* for support.

[12]And I took root in an honorable people, even in the portion of the Lord's inheritance.
[13]I was exalted like a cedar in Libanus, and as a cypress tree upon the mountains of Hermon.
[14]I was exalted like a palm tree on the sea shore, and as a rose plant in Jericho, as a fair olive tree in a plain, and grew up as a plane tree.
[15]I gave a sweet smell like cinnamon and aspalathus, and I yielded a pleasant odor like the best myrrh, as galbanum, and onyx, and sweet storax, and as the fume of frankincense in the tabernacle.
[16]As the turpentine trees I stretched out my branches, and my branches are the branches of glory and grace.
[17]As the vine brought I forth pleasant savour and my flowers are the fruit of glory and riches ... [19]Come unto me all you that are desirous of me, and fill yourselves with my fruits ...
[23]All these things are the book of the covenant of the most high God, even the law which Moses commanded ...
[25]He [God] fills all things with his wisdom, as Pishon, and as Tigris in the time of the new fruits.
[26]He makes the understanding abound like the Euphrates, and as Jordan in the time of the harvest. [27]He makes the doctrine of knowledge appear as the light, as Gihon in the time of vintage.
[28]The first man knew her [wisdom] not perfectly ... [30]I [wisdom] also came out as a brook from a river, and as a conduit into a garden.
[31]I said, I will water my garden bed: and, lo, my brook became a river, and my river became a sea. [32]I will yet make instruction to shine as the morning, and will send forth her light afar off.
[33]I will yet pour out teaching as prophecy and leave it to all ages forever.
[34]Behold that I have not labored for myself only, but for all them that seek wisdom.

This is either an idealization of what divine 'wisdom' should have done in Israel or, more probably, it is an assertion of the task 'wisdom' was conceived of performing in Israel but had not yet completed. The approximate first half of the passage (24:7–19) portrays 'wisdom' as dwelling in the temple and as itself being fertile and garden-like (compared to trees and vines and their fruits). The combination of these two images is natural in the light of our earlier assessment that Genesis 2 has in view Eden as a garden sanctuary. In particular, Numbers 24:5–7, itself possibly a development of Eden, appears to be part of the inspiration for *Sirach*'s imagery:

> [5]How fair are your *tents*, O Jacob,
> Your *dwellings*, O Israel!
> [6]Like palm trees that stretch out,
> Like gardens beside the river,
> Like aloes planted by the Lord,
> Like cedars beside the waters.
> [7]Water shall flow from his buckets,
> And his seed shall be by many waters,
> And his king shall be higher than Agag,
> And his kingdom shall be exalted.

As we saw earlier, the Numbers passage is quite suggestive of an expanding tabernacle-like garden, and was interpreted to be a reference to Israel's tabernacle by the Greek Old Testament, the Aramaic Bible, and by the author of Hebrews. Strikingly, the *Sirach* passage (24:8–17), like the Greek and Aramaic Old Testament renderings, also understand the garden imagery of Numbers 24:6 (growing 'palm trees' and 'cedars' and other garden descriptions) to be part of tabernacle and temple portrayals. In fact, just as in Numbers 24:5–6, *Sirach* 24:8–17 first explicitly mentions the 'tabernacle' and 'dwelling' (though in the singular) followed by the garden language, as well as by descriptions of abundant waters (cf. Num. 24:6–7 with *Sirach* 24:25–31).

The second half of the passage (24:25–32) explicitly equates 'wisdom' to God's Law and likens her to water as the source of fertility and concludes by comparing her to 'light'. The point is that 'wisdom' was to be the source of Israel's faithful obedience to God that would bear spiritual fruit (e.g., 'glory and grace', 'understanding', and 'knowledge'), which would not only fill the land of Israel but the entire earth.

Accordingly, the goal is that God 'fill all things with his wisdom' (24:25). Just as water came from Eden to water the garden and then branched out into the four rivers and watered the earth, so 'wisdom' is like that water: the earth is not merely to be filled with all kinds of material fecundity but spiritual fruitfulness. It is well known that physical fruitfulness often symbolizes spiritual faithfulness by God's people, Israel's experience in the land being the prime example. This connection is probably also the case here. This portrayal, especially the description of 'wisdom' as a 'brook . . . as a conduit into a garden', likely is based on our earlier observation that the water source in Eden was identified with the very presence of God dwelling in an arboreal inner sanctum and extending out to the adjoining garden-like 'holy place'. This description now applies to the temple in Jerusalem.

Furthermore, the description of 'wisdom' 'filling all things' and growing from a 'brook' into a 'river' and becoming a 'sea' is an image of 'wisdom' expanding to fill the entire earth, and may itself be an allusion to Habakkuk 2:14: 'For the earth will be filled with the knowledge of the glory of the LORD, as the waters cover the sea'[75] (on which see further below).

The pictorial expansion of the Edenic brook of wisdom into a sea coalesces well with our earlier conclusion that Adam's original task was to enlarge the borders of the garden sanctuary until they included the whole earth. Then God's presence would permeate the earth as never before. The conclusion of the *Sirach* passage interprets the picture of worldwide deluge as 'wisdom' 'making instruction shine as the morning', 'sending forth her light afar off', and 'pouring out teaching . . . to all ages forever'. The goal is that divine wisdom in Israel's temple should fill the whole earth, a goal not 'yet' achieved (note 'yet' ['etî] introducing each of the statements in 24:32 and 24:33).

Significantly, the last line of the passage shows that 'wisdom', as it should have done through Adam, now is to spread out by means of humans 'that seek wisdom' (24:34). In such people 'wisdom' will 'take root' (24:12), will 'stretch out her branches . . . of glory' (24:16) and 'send forth her light afar off' (24:32). 'They that work by me ['wisdom'] will not sin' (24:22) but shine divine light into every nook and cranny of the creation until it becomes a holy auditorium filled with God's tabernacling being.

It is again appropriate to look ahead to the early Jewish-Christian work of the *Odes of Solomon* (ch. 6) for a remarkably similar portrayal to part of *Sirach*'s description of 'understanding' and 'wisdom' proceeding out from the temple and progressing from a brook to a river (24:30–31; cf. 24:25–27).

---

[75] So also Is. 11:9; *Sirach* 39:22 appears to reflect the same reality: 'His [God's] blessing covered the dry land as a river, and watered it as a flood.'

[6]The Lord has multiplied his knowledge ...
[8]For there went forth a stream,
and it became a great river and broad;
indeed it carried away everything, and it shattered
and brought (it) to the Temple.
[9]And the restraints of men were not able to restrain it ...
[10]For it [the water] spread over the face of all the earth,
and it filled everything.
[11]Then all the thirsty on the earth drank,
and thirst was relieved and quenched;
[12]For from the Most High the drink was given.[76]

The *Odes* passage may even be an allusion to *Sirach*. The picture differs only in that the water flows out to the earth and back to the temple again, apparently indicating that God's knowledge conquered people on the earth and brought them into relation to his temple.

1 Enoch (second century BC)

1 Enoch 90:28–36 envisions Israel's old temple 'folded up, dismantled, and carried off', only to be replaced by a new house 'greater and loftier than that first' and all redeemed humanity 'assembled in that house' because it was 'large and broad and very full'. This may imply that the extent of this temple structure is worldwide,[77] especially since the eschatological temple is also portrayed as housing the redeemed who are described as '*all* the beasts of the field, and *all* the birds of the heaven' who 'assembled in that house'.

Philo (first century AD)

The evidence of Philo with respect to the theme of temple expansion is certainly not explicit, but he does assert that the temple rituals have an efficacious effect for the whole world, which may point further to the universal end-time significance of the temple. Philo says that the offering at the altar of the first-fruit from the land of Israel serves an efficacious purpose 'both to the nation ... and for the whole human race ... The reason for this is that the Jewish nation is to the whole inhabited world what the priest is to the State' (*Spec. Leg.* 2.162–163). This may be an implicit corroboration also that what the temple was to Israel, Israel was to be to the whole world. For Philo the cosmic

---

[76] I am grateful to my student Kevin Cawley for bringing this text to my attention.
[77] See Spatafora 1997: 64, who sees the temple in *1 Enoch* 90:28–36 expanding only over the new Jerusalem.

symbolism of the priest's vesture means that the priest not only prays for Israel but also 'on behalf of the whole human race' and 'for the parts of nature, earth, water, air, fire'. The ultimate purpose of these prayers is to petition God 'to make His creature a partaker of His own kindly and merciful nature'.[78]

The Sibylline Oracles *(c. AD 100)*

Sibylline Oracles 5:414–432 portrays a mammoth temple not unlike some of the others encountered in the preceding Jewish texts:

> For there has come from the plains of heaven a blessed man with the sceptre in his hand which God has committed to his clasp: and he has won fair dominion over all ... and the city [Jerusalem] ... he set ... as the jewel of the world, and made a temple exceeding fair in its fair sanctuary, and fashioned it in size of many furlongs,[79] with a giant tower touching the very clouds and seen of all, so that all the faithful and all the righteous may see the glory of the invisible God ... It is the last time of the saints when God accomplishes these things ... God [is] ... the Creator of the great temple.[80]

As in the case of *1 Enoch* 90, again we have a huge latter-day temple that is, at least, many miles in diameter, and it is so high that all the righteous inhabitants of the world can see its tower. Not unexpectedly, we also detect an echo of the Genesis 1:26–28 commission in direct connection with the building of the temple: a 'man' who is 'blessed' gains 'dominion over all' (cf. Dan. 7:13–14). We found the same connection between the Adamic commission and the garden sanctuary in Genesis 2 and the same link in the case of the patriarchs, pre-exilic Israel and post-exilic, latter-day Israel. The commission to rule and subdue typically involves building a temple and expanding its boundaries. The base of the temple in the Oracle is so many miles in diameter and its tower so high that all saints throughout the world are able to see it.

---

[78] *Spec. Leg.* 2.97; cf. similarly *Som.* 1.215 and possibly *Rer. Div. Her.* 205; I am grateful to Barker (1991: 113–116) for first attracting my notice to these Philo references. Similarly *Wisdom of Solomon* 18:24 understands the high priest's garment and jewels to be symbolic of the entire cosmos: 'in the long garment was the whole world, and in the four rows of the stones was the glory of the fathers'. The reference to the 'glory of the fathers' is also a cosmic allusion to the blessing upon Abraham's seed which would result in blessing to the whole world (so also 18:22).

[79] One furlong is an eighth of a mile.

[80] Here we are following the translation in Charles 1977: 405.

The Testament of Benjamin *(second century BC with subsequent Christian interpolations)*

Testament of Benjamin 9:3 (likely a Christian interpolation) says, 'And the veil of the temple shall be rent, and the Spirit of God shall pass on to the Gentiles as fire poured forth.' Here the 'veil' symbolizes God's limited special revelatory dwelling with Israel that will be removed for the sake of the world at the end of history.

Concluding thoughts on the Old Testament and Jewish views about an expanding garden or temple

The thesis of the all-consuming nature of the latter-day temple is consistent with Numbers 14:21 ('indeed, as I live, all the earth will be filled with the glory of the LORD') and Habakkuk 2:14 ('For the earth will be filled with the knowledge of the glory of the LORD, as the waters cover the sea' = Is. 11:9). Since the temple was the symbolic repository of the Law, the epitome of Israel's wisdom, its universal extension would entail the permeation of the cosmos with divine wisdom and knowledge in line with *Sirach*, which was discussed towards the conclusion of this chapter.

The various builders and planners of Israel's temples may have expressed some awareness of the need for an expanding temple on Mount Zion, since each successive temple became bigger and bigger, particularly with respect to their outer court area: tabernacle → Solomon's temple[81] → second temple and its expansions of an additional outer 'court of the women' and a further outer 'court of the Gentiles'[82] → the Ezekiel 40 – 48 temple (containing an inner and outer court)[83] = the temple of the Qumran *Temple Scroll*, which had

---

[81] The length and width of Solomon's temple was approximately twice that of the tabernacle, and there was an even greater difference in height (e.g., see Homan 2000: 24–26).

[82] On which, e.g., see Wightman 1995: 277, 282–283. See Josephus (*War* 1.401), who says that 'in the fifteenth year' of Herod's reign 'he restored the temple' and 'enlarged the surrounding area to double its former extent . . .' Note also S. M. Bryan (2002: 199–206), who contends the allocation of a space for the Gentiles in an outer section of the outer court was due to the influence of Is. 56:6–7 (i.e., that the purposes of the temple would be expanded to include Gentile worship).

[83] There is debate about the size of Ezekiel's temple (see ch. 5 on Ezek. 40 – 48). Some see its dimensions to be comparable to those of the temple in the Qumran *Temple Scroll*.

an inner court and an outer court; both the latter two temples encompassed the whole populated area of Jerusalem.[84] Such expanding building projects may point to an instinct based on the original intention that Eden's garden-temple was to expand, an intuition we have seen that appears to have motivated the Pharaohs to engage in similar temple-projects.

[84] The dimensions envisioned in the Qumran *Temple Scroll* are the largest in comparison to earlier temple boundaries, except probably for Ezekiel, on which see Broshi 1987: 36–37, and Shiffman 1989: 267–284.

Chapter Five

The 'already and not yet' fulfilment of the end-time temple in Christ and his people: the Gospels

Introduction

The New Testament pictures Christ and the church as finally having done what Adam, Noah, and Israel had failed to do in extending the temple of God's presence throughout the world. Luke 2:32 and Acts 26:23 picture Christ as fulfilling this commission to be a 'light' to the end of the earth (an allusion to the Servant Israel's commission in Is. 49:6). This is why Matthew 28:18 portrays Jesus as the Son of Man saying, 'All authority has been given to Me in heaven and on earth.' This is an allusion to the prophecy of Daniel 7:13–14, where it is said of the 'Son of Man', 'authority was given to him, and all the nations of the earth ... [were] serving him' (so LXX). On the basis of this authority, Jesus then gives the well-known commission 'therefore, as you go, disciple all the nations, baptizing them ... teaching them to keep all things whichsoever I commanded you; and, behold, *I am with you* all the days until the end of the age'. Notice that Christ uses the same accompaniment formula as God used with the commissioning of his people in the Old Testament to subdue and rule over the earth. His presence will enable them to fulfil 'the great commission' to rule over and fill the earth with God's presence, which Adam, Noah and Israel had failed to carry out.

In this respect, as we will see more clearly in the following section of this chapter, Jesus is a Last Adam figure, and this is partly why he implicitly identifies himself with Daniel's 'Son of Man' in issuing the universal commission to his followers: he is the 'son of Adam', the equivalent to Daniel's 'Son of Man', finally accomplishing what the first Adam should have and what Daniel predicts the messianic end-time Adam would do.

The Edenic imagery describing the city-temple in Revelation 22:1–3 also reflects an intention to show that the building of the temple that began in Genesis 2 but was abandoned will be commenced again and completed in Christ and his people, and will encompass the whole new creation. The cosmic reflection of the broad tripartite structure of the temple implicitly suggested that its purpose was to point to a future time when it would engulf the whole world. Accordingly, Israel's temple functioned much like an architect's model of a newly planned building. It was but a small replica of what was to be built on a much larger scale. Ideally, when the Israelites looked at and thought of their temple they were not to think of it as an end in itself, only a sign of their election as a nation. Rather, they were to be reminded of the great goal of spreading the light of God's presence throughout the earth until the entire world was under God's tabernacling presence. Since the Old Testament temple was the localized dwelling of God's special revelatory presence on earth, the temple's symbolic correspondence with the cosmos pointed to an eschatological goal of God's presence tabernacling throughout the earth, an eschatological goal which Revelation 21:1 – 22:5 appears to be developing (cf. Rev. 21:3).

Few have come close to elaborating the redemptive-historical significance of the temple's expanding cosmic symbolism either in the Old or New Testament in the manner this book has attempted to so far.[1] We are now in a position to ask: why is the description of Christ as a 'temple' particularly apt? How does this description relate to the Old Testament background of the temple as symbolic of creation or like a sacred organic structure growing to fill creation? The answer, in brief, is that the New Testament refers to Christ appropriately as a temple because he was the beginning of the new creation. His resurrection was the first, great act of new creation, as testified to explicitly by Paul: 'he died and rose again ... so that if anyone is in Christ, that one is a new creation ... (2 Cor. 5:15, 17; so likewise Gal. 6:15–16;

---

[1] Though see J. D. Levenson's perspective, which has affinities with my own (Levenson 1986: 32–61; 1984: 296–298; 1985: 182–184). W. Dumbrell draws some of the same conclusions as I have drawn, especially with regard to Adam being placed as a 'king-priest' in Eden as a sanctuary in order to expand the sanctuary worldwide (2002: 53–65). In so doing, he expresses dependence partly on my earlier commentary excursus (Beale 1999a: 1109–1111), as well as on some of the sources upon which I was originally dependent (e.g., Wenham 1987; 1994). Here Dumbrell actually develops similar thoughts from his earlier work (1985: 37–38, 41–42). Likewise, Kline 1989: 55–56, 62–63, briefly anticipated my thesis, and it is quite possible that years ago my reading of Kline and Dumbrell's earlier work planted the seed of this idea in my mind.

Col. 1:18; Rev. 3:14, though the concept occurs throughout the New Testament). This is the best explanation, for example, of why the Gospels repeatedly refer to Christ as 'destroying the [old] temple, and in three days raising it up' (Matt. 26:61; 27:40; Mark 14:58; 15:29; John 2:20–21; cf. Acts 6:14). As we will see, Jesus' followers carry the same description of the 'temple of God' because they are corporately represented by the resurrected Lord of the new creation.

The majority of the remainder of this book will survey those parts of the New Testament that portray Christ and his people either composing the beginning form of God's end-time temple or being a part of its consummate fulfilment. We will also try to see how the themes of Eden, Adam's commission and Israel's temple observed in the preceding chapters shed further light on the New Testament conception of the temple, especially with respect to its expanding nature.

Jesus as the Last Adam and the temple of the new creation in the Synoptic Gospels

Jesus as the Last Adam and inaugurator of a new creation

The Gospels portray Jesus as an Adam figure who is inaugurating a new creation. Matthew's genealogy begins with the Greek expression *biblos geneseōs*, which can be translated the 'book of the genealogy' or the 'book of beginning' or even the 'book of genesis'. This appears to be an allusion to Genesis 2:4 which also has *biblos geneseōs*: 'This is the book of the generation (or 'genesis') of heaven and earth, when they came about, in the day in which the Lord God made the heaven and the earth.' Likewise, Genesis 5:1–2 has, 'This is the book of the generation (*biblos geneseōs*; some render it 'genealogy') of man [Adam] in the day in which God made Adam, according to the image of God He made him. Male and female He made them, and blessed them; and He called his name Adam in the day in which He made them.' Then, just as in Matthew 1, there follows a genealogy (the first in the Bible), beginning with Adam and ending with Noah. That Matthew is, indeed, alluding to Genesis 2 and 5 is enhanced by observing that these are the only two places in the entire Greek Old Testament where the phrase *biblos geneseōs* occurs. Matthew's point in using this phrase is to make clear that he is narrating the record of the new age, the new creation, launched by the coming, death and resurrection of Jesus Christ.

Perhaps, also mention of the Holy Spirit in conceiving Jesus

(1:18–20) points further to him as the beginning of the new creation, just as the Spirit was mentioned in Genesis 1:2 as forming the first creation. Matthew 1:18, 20 says, 'now the generation (the genesis) of Jesus Christ was in this manner . . . that which is begotten (*gennēthen*) in her is from the Holy Spirit'.

Instead of beginning with David and Abraham and working down towards the time of Jesus like Matthew, Luke's genealogy begins with the time of Jesus and works back to Adam, with which it ends: 'the son of Adam, the son of God' (Luke 3:38). The purpose is to identify Jesus as the Last Adam (Glickman 1980: 55–58). For his part, Mark's Gospel begins with 'the beginning (*archē*) of the Gospel of Jesus Christ' (cf. *en archē*, Gen. 1:1).

The 'forty days and forty nights' of Jesus' temptation in the wilderness echo Israel's forty years in the wilderness. Jesus, as true Israel, is the micro-Israel who has replaced the macro-national Israel. Hence, years are reduced figuratively down to days. Each response by Jesus to Satan is taken from a response by Moses to Israel's failure in the wilderness (Deut. 8:3 in Matt. 4:4; Deut. 6:16 in Matt. 4:7; Deut. 6:13 in Matt. 4:10). Jesus succeeds in facing the same temptations to which Israel succumbed.

The reason, however, that Luke's genealogy ends with 'Adam the son of God' (Luke 3:38) is to identify Jesus as an end-time Adam, the true Son of God, resisting the temptations to which Adam and Eve succumbed. That Eden's temptations are in mind is apparent from Mark's comments that after Jesus successfully endured the temptations in the wilderness, 'he was with the wild beasts, and the angels were ministering to him' (which shows that he, in fact, was the promised one of Ps. 91:11–12, and compare 91:13).

The defeat of the devil in the wilderness may also be viewed secondarily to be Jesus' first act of conquering the latter-day 'Canaanites in the promised land' as true Israel. One might question whether or not this idea is present in the temptation account, since the major theme, as we noted above, is that of Jesus resisting temptations to sin to which Israel surrendered. The theme of temptation is certainly highlighted by noticing that each of the three Old Testament citations from Deuteronomy refers to the manner that Israel should have responded to their temptations but did not. Closer inspection of each of the Deuteronomy contexts, however, reveals the goal of what would happen if Israel did respond faithfully to their temptations: they would 'go in and possess the good land which the LORD swore' to give 'by driving out all your enemies from before you' (Deut.

6:18–19).[2] Plausibly, Jesus may well have had in mind this common purpose of each of the three contexts.

Consequently, Jesus' victory over temptation appears to have prepared him to conquer the one who was the ultimate satanic prince of the Canaanites and of all wicked nations[3] and to conquer the land in a way that Israel had not been able to. His very resistance to these satanic allurements was the very beginning of his defeat of the devil. Jesus' ministry of casting out demons continues this holy warfare of the true Israel, Jesus. Christ's casting out of demons was an expression of his beginning, though decisive, defeat of Satan, who had brought creation into captivity through his deception of Adam and Eve. This is the significance of the parable of the binding of the strong man (Matt. 12:29). By casting out the devil and his forces, Jesus was accomplishing the latter-day defeat of Satan that Adam should have accomplished in the first garden.[4] The devil tries to tempt Christ by quoting Scripture, 'If you are the Son of God throw Yourself down [from the pinnacle of the temple]; for it is written, "He will give His angels charge concerning You"; and "On their hands they will bear You up, Lest You strike Your foot against a stone"' (Matt. 4:6). This is a quotation of Psalm 91:11–12. Psalm 91:13, however, goes on to say that the righteous man cared for by the angels 'will tread upon the lion and the cobra, the young lion and the serpent you will trample down'. Psalm 91:13 may allude to the great Genesis 3:15 promise 'He shall bruise you on the head, and you shall bruise

---

[2] Likewise, Deut. 6:13 is directly followed by what will happen if Israel follows other gods in the land: God 'will wipe you off the face of the land'; i.e., they will not possess it. Part of the introduction to Deut. 8:3 is, 'be careful to do [the law], that you may live and multiply, and go in and possess the land which the LORD swore to give to your fore-fathers' (Deut. 8:1).

[3] This idea may be enhanced by recalling that the devil is elsewhere referred to in the Gospels as 'Beelzebul' (Matt. 10:25) or 'Beelzebub', variant names for deities associated with 'Baal' in Canaan (e.g., see 'Baalzebub' in 2 Kgs. 1:2–3, 6, 16, referring to the Philistine god, apparently translated as 'lord of the flies'). See further Lewis 1992: 638–640.

[4] McCartney 1994: 10. McCartney also mentions that Jesus' proclamations of the kingdom are expressions that the vicegerency lost with the first Adam was now being announced and his power over nature was another example of exercising the dominion over the earth as God's vice-regent, which the first Adam should have exercised (1994: 10). Cf. also Kline (1989: 65–67), who makes the suggestive observation that 'the tree of the discernment of good and evil' in Gen. 2 refers to Adam's duty to discern between good and evil, so that when the serpent entered the Garden, he was to judge the serpent as an evildoer. Kline supports this partly by adducing other texts which refer to a discerning between 'good and evil' as the exercise of 'a legal-judicial kind of discrimination' (Is. 5:20, 23; Mal. 2:17), such as 'a king engaged in rendering judicial decisions' (2 Sam. 14:17; 1 Kgs. 3:9, 28).

him on the heel.' Christ's refusal to follow Satan's advice during the wilderness temptations was the beginning victory over Satan prophesied in the psalm. Matthew likely intends that the reader be aware of this broader context of the psalm, to some degree at least, which together with the three Deuteronomy contexts above, further reveals the theme of Jesus' victory over opposition.

After defeating the devil in the promised land, Jesus again is seen as beginning to fulfil Isaiah's promises of Israel's restoration (Matt. 4:12–16). Consequently, in 4:18–22 Jesus begins to regather the tribes of Israel by beginning to call his twelve apostles. The twelve represent the microcosmic true Israel under their leader Jesus (i.e., Yahweh), though Jesus is also portrayed as a latter-day Moses (Allison 1993). This restoration involves various kinds of healings, which were prophesied to occur when Israel would undergo her true end-time restoration to God (Matt. 4:23–25; 11:4–6; Is. 32:3–4; 35:5–6; 42:7, 16).

Such healings also represented the restoration of creation from the fallen condition of the world. The physical (and spiritual) curses of the fall are beginning to be removed by Jesus, as he is re-establishing the new creation and kingdom, which Adam should have established. Seen within the framework of the new creation, Christ's miracles of healing not only inaugurated the end-time kingdom but signalled the beginning of the new creation, since the healings were a beginning reversal of the curse of the old fallen world. The miracles were a sign of the inbreaking new creation, where people would be completely healed. Those he healed, and especially raised from the dead, foreshadowed his own resurrection. Christ's resurrection was the first-fruits of all believers. They, like him, would be raised with perfected, restored bodies at the very end of the age, when the new world would be ushered in. The repeated and dominating notion of the kingdom in the Gospels is one of the main ways by which the Evangelists express ideas about the new creation which is consistent with the inextricable link between the kingship of Adam and new creation in Genesis 1 – 2.

The reason that Jesus reflects both the Old Testament figures of Adam and Israel is because, as we have seen earlier, Israel and her patriarchs were given the same commission as was Adam in Genesis 1:26–28. Consequently, it is not an overstatement to understand Israel as a corporate Adam who had failed in their 'Garden of Eden',[5] in much the same way as their primal father had failed in the first

---

[5] Note, again, OT texts where Israel's promised land is called the 'Garden of Eden' (Gen. 13:10; Is. 51:3; Ezek. 36:35; Joel 2:3).

garden. For these reasons, it is understandable that Jesus is called 'Son of God' partly because that was a name for the first Adam (Luke 3:38; cf. Gen. 5:1–3) and for Israel (Exod. 4:22; Hos. 11:1). Likewise, the expression 'son of man' from Daniel 7:13 refers to end-time Israel and her representative king as the son of Adam who is sovereign over beasts (recall that the 'son of man' takes over the kingdoms of former evil empires portrayed as beasts). Understandably, against this background, it is natural that 'Son of Man' became one of Jesus' favourite ways of referring to himself.

The resurrection of Jesus is a further development of the new creation (e.g., Matt. 27:57 – 28:15). Resurrection is a full-blown new creation notion, since the way the righteous were to enter in and become a part of the new heavens and earth is through God recreating their bodies. Jesus' claim that 'all authority has been given to Me in heaven and on earth' (Matt. 28:18) alludes to Daniel 7:13–14, which prophesied that the 'son of man' would be 'given authority, glory and sovereignty' for ever.[6] Then, as we noted at the introduction of this chapter, he immediately gives the disciples the so-called 'Great Commission': 'Go therefore and make disciples of all the nations ... teaching them ... and lo, I am with you always' (Matt. 28:19–20). This edict not only continues the allusion to the Daniel 7 prophecy (v. 14, 'that all the peoples, nations, and men of every language might serve him'), but is itself a renewal of the Genesis 1:26–28 commission to Adam.

As we also observed earlier, even the divine accompaniment formula ('I am with you') occurs in Matthew 28:20 to indicate how the disciples will be empowered to carry out the commission, just as we saw in the later applications of Adam's commission to the patriarchs and Israel. In fact, the reference to 'all the nations' (*panta ta ethnē*) is an echo of Genesis 22:18 (likewise, Gen. 18:18), which, as we have seen, is one of the inchoate sanctuary-building narratives. The reminiscence of the Abrahamic promise returns to the theme found in the first verse of Matthew's Gospel (1:1): 'that the blessings promised to Abraham and through him to all peoples of the earth (Gen. 12:3) are now to be fulfilled in Jesus the Messiah'.[7]

Thus, Christ is the Son of Adam, or 'the Son of Man', who has begun to do what the first Adam should have done and to inherit what the first Adam should have, including the glory reflected in God's image. That Jesus' baptism was part of his work 'to fulfil all righteousness' (Matt.

---

[6] See also France (1971: 142–143), who also sees the allusion to Dan. 7.
[7] See Carson 1995: 596. Gen. 12:3 (LXX) has 'all the tribes of the earth'.

3:13–17) likely alludes to the fact that he was coming to set right what Israel and Adam had done wrong; he was coming to obey successfully in contrast to Israel's former disobedience.

Jesus as the new temple

Part of Jesus' doing what Adam should have done included establishing the new temple and extending it obediently. In reality, he himself was that temple because he was the beginning of the new creation, especially in his resurrection. To call Christ the 'temple' is merely another way of referring to him as the new creation, since the temple was symbolic of creation (which we took great pains to demonstrate in ch. 2)!

We have seen in our discussion of Genesis that Adam's commission in Genesis 1 was to be carried out by his serving in the Edenic temple, managing it in an orderly manner, and expanding its boundaries. In fact, we have seen that the reapplication of Adam's commission to Noah, the patriarchs, Israel and end-time Israel also was inextricably linked to the beginning of building temples and expanding them. Therefore, it should be no surprise that Christ also initiates the building of a new temple, once again performing the duties that the first Adam and Israel failed in executing. At various points in the Gospels, Christ indicates that the old temple is becoming obsolete and that he is replacing it with a new one.

The first place to start is to pick up on our preceding discussion of Matthew 28, with which we concluded the last section. In addition to Daniel 7:13–14, Jesus' 'Great Commission' to his disciples appears also to allude to 2 Chronicles 36:23: 'Thus says Cyrus king of Persia, "The LORD, the God of heaven, has given me all the kingdoms of the earth, and He has appointed me to build Him a house in Jerusalem, which is in Judah. Whoever there is among you of all His people, may the LORD his God be with him, and let him go up!"' This passage has three things in common with Matthew 28:18–20: (1) both Cyrus and Jesus assert authority over all the earth; (2) the commission to 'go'; and (3) the assurance of the divine presence to fulfil the commission. Jesus' commission, however, escalates that of Cyrus's in that Jesus' also has authority over 'heaven' as well as 'earth', and he speaks of his own presence going with the people being addressed. In addition, Jesus' commission is not aimed at old Jerusalem but 'nations' throughout the whole earth. Furthermore, if the temple construction of 2 Chronicles is in mind, then this is an implicit commission for the disciples to fulfil the Genesis 1:26–28 mandate by rebuilding the new temple, composed of worshippers throughout the earth.

Three further observations point to an allusion to 2 Chronicles in Matthew 28. First, 2 Chronicles in the Hebrew canon of Scripture was the last book of the Old Testament. Accordingly, 2 Chronicles 36:23 becomes the last verse of the entire Old Testament, which now ends with the commission to rebuild the temple, so that it serves as a nice canonical transition to an even more escalated commission to build the temple in Matthew's Gospel. Second, Matthew's Gospel portrays Jesus' genealogy partly on the basis of that in 1 Chronicles 1 – 3. Third, Isaiah refers to Cyrus as a 'messiah' (Is. 44:28 – 45:1) because he had the task of enabling Israel to rebuild her temple.

With these facts in mind and recalling that Jesus' reference to 'all the nations' in Matthew 28:19 harks back to Matthew 1:1, it is attractive to suggest that, like 1 and 2 Chronicles, Matthew constructs his Gospel partly to reflect the beginning and ending of Chronicles but applies the goal of the genealogy to Jesus. Thus, the concluding commission is not spoken by a pagan king to theocratic Israel but spoken by the true, divine king Jesus to the beginning remnant of true Israel, 'the Twelve'. In this respect, the 2 Chronicles passage would be viewed as a historical event to commission a temple that foreshadowed typologically the much greater event of Jesus' 'Great Commission' to build a greater temple.[8]

In addition to the temple-building implicit in the Great Commission, Jesus' various statements that he can forgive sin could also suggest that he is beginning to replace the temple (Luke 7:49–50). Jesus' Jewish audience recognized that his claim to forgive sin also was a unique divine prerogative, and they accused him of blasphemy (Matt. 9:3), which underscores that the major point of this passage is the divine function of Jesus in forgiving sin. Perhaps also echoes of the function of the temple are implicit in this narrative. The temple was the divinely instituted place where sacrifices were offered for the forgiveness of sins, but now Jesus has become the divinely instituted location where forgiveness is to be found, since he himself is also the sin offering. Matthew 9:2–6 (= Mark 2:1–12; Luke 5:18–26) says that 'the Son of Man has authority on earth to forgive sins', which may

---

[8] This discussion of 2 Chr. 36:23 is based on Vance 1992. In this light, it may be more understandable that later Judaism identified Is. 41:25 (Cyrus's efforts to restore Jerusalem and the temple, in view of Is. 44:28; 45:1) with the Messiah who would rebuild the temple (so *Midrash Rabbah Numbers* 13:2; *Midrash Rabbah Leviticus* 9:6; *Midrash Rabbah Song of Songs* 4:16, §1).

suggest that his pardoning of sins, formerly obtained at the temple, is part of his work as the priestly last Adam. Hence, again, we have the close association of a temple function (albeit echoed) with the Adamic commission to have authority over the earth.[9] Consequently, Jesus could send out his disciples to announce this new basis of forgiveness (Matt. 16:19; John 20:23).

Jesus' self-identification with the temple is underscored in Matthew 12:6, where he says about himself, 'something greater than the temple is here'. Jesus 'is greater than Jonah' as a prophet and his deliverance will be greater because he will *actually* die for three days and rise (Matt. 12:39–41). Jesus is 'greater than Solomon' because he is a greater king and has more wisdom (Matt. 12:42). Similarly, Jesus is greater than the temple now because 'God's presence is more manifest in Him than in the Temple. On him, not on the Temple, rests the "Shekinah" glory' (Cole 1950:12) in an even greater way than previously in the temple (echoing perhaps the prophecy in Hag. 2:9, 'the latter glory of this house will be greater than the former'). Therefore, not only is Jesus identified with the temple because he is assuming the role of the sacrificial system, but he is also now, instead of the temple, the unique place on earth where God's revelatory presence is located. God is manifesting his glorious presence in Jesus in a greater way than it was ever manifested in a physical temple structure.

This statement about Jesus' superiority over the temple occurs in a context where he is offering eschatological Sabbath rest to people (Matt. 11:28–30) (Laansma 1997: 159–251) which was forfeited by Adam and his fallen progeny. In fact, Matthew 12:7 quotes from Hosea 6:6 ('I desire compassion and not a sacrifice'), and the very next statement in Hosea says, 'But like Adam they have transgressed the covenant' (Hos. 6:7).[10] Thus, it may not be coincidental that Christ alludes to this context in Hosea, nor that he refers to himself as 'the Son of Man [Adam]' who 'is Lord of the Sabbath' only two verses after comparing himself to the temple (Matt. 12:8). We have seen that the temple was the place where God was to 'rest', after he had given Israel 'rest' from her enemies.[11] What we have then in Matthew 11:28 – 12:8 is the confluence of notions concerning eschatological rest, Adam and the Son of Adam, and the temple, which

---

[9] This paragraph was inspired by N. T. Wright 1996: 406–412.

[10] Possibly, 'Adam' could be rendered generally as 'men' or 'mankind' (referring to past generations of Israel or to humanity in general) or to a place-name where a grievous sin was committed. See Andersen and Freedman 1980: 435–439.

[11] On which, see pp. 60–66. See also Laansma 1997: 58–76.

should not be surprising given the association of Christ elsewhere with Adamic and temple themes.

Jesus' so-called 'cleansing' of the temple may also point to his task of replacing the old temple with a new one (Matt. 21:12–13 and parallels).[12] The Jews had made the temple into an economic enterprise instead of a place of worship. Christ's radical act in the temple was a parable of judgment against the temple, not only because of its misuse, but because it represented Israel's rejection of God's word and commandments and ultimately of Jesus himself (so N. T. Wright 1996: 413–427). Jesus quotes Isaiah 56:7 ('My house will be called a house of prayer'), which is a prophecy that the temple would become a 'rallying place' and location of prayer for the Gentiles in the latter days (see Is. 56:3–8). Jesus' point is that the temple must be replaced because it 'was not fulfilling its God-ordained role as witness to the nations but had become, like the first temple, the premier symbol of a superstitious belief that God would protect and rally his people irrespective of their conformity to his will' (Carson 1995: 442).[13] The second temple had failed to achieve the end-time purpose for which it had been designed (see further, S. M. Bryan 2002: 199–225).

Though not mentioned in this passage, Jesus' violent act in the temple would briefly have stopped the offering of sacrifices by shutting down the procedure by which animals were bought and sacrificed. If the temporary ceasing of sacrifices is to be inferred to any degree from the passage, then in performing this action, Jesus would have been indicating that the temple's purpose in offering sacrifices for forgiveness was passing away and that the temple was awaiting judgment.[14] Directly after this episode, those who were forbidden to enter the temple because of their deformity were now accepted by Jesus: the 'blind and the lame came to Him in the temple, and He healed them' (21:14). This suggests further that he is beginning to clear the way for the eschatological temple, since the Old Testament prophesied that in the future sanctuary eunuchs and other outcasts could worship even together with Gentiles. That which was formerly unclean will be considered clean for worship in the true temple (Is. 56:3–8).

The healing in the temple is yet another reflection of Jesus taking

[12] The discussion here is against that of Fitzmyer 1985: 1266–1267, who sees that Jesus' 'cleansing' did not entail any notion of judgment of the temple nor of its rebuilding.

[13] Cf. also Hooker 1991: 268.

[14] See N. T. Wright 1996: 423, though Wright's proposal needs further exegetical substantiation, since mention of the shutting down of the sacrifices is omitted in Matthew and the other Synoptic parallels.

over the true role of the temple, since we have seen that his healings demonstrated that he could heal spiritual disease through offering forgiveness himself (e.g., the lame man in Mark 2:1–12) and that he had become the source of forgiveness instead of Israel's temple. His death and resurrection is the climax of this role of temple-building: 'he builds the new temple by fulfilling the function of the temple eschatologically, i.e., by offering his life for all as the atoning and covenant-establishing sacrifice'.[15] The old temple dies (his body; the sacrificial system), and a new temple arises (his body, which becomes a corporate house of prayer for all nations).[16]

Excursus: an early patristic text linking the Adamic commission to Christ and the church as a temple under construction

One early Christian non-canonical text linking the Adamic commission to Christ and the church to the building of the temple is the *Epistle of Barnabas* (written around AD 95):

> [11]So ... he renewed us [Christians] by the forgiveness of sins ... as if he were creating us all over again.
>
> [12]For the Scripture speaks about us when he says ... 'Let us make man according to our image and likeness, and let them rule over the beasts of the earth and the birds of the air and the fish of the sea.' And when he saw that our [new] creation was good, the Lord said: 'Increase and multiply and fill the earth' ...
>
> [13]He made a second creation in the last days. And the Lord says: 'Behold, I make the last things as the first.' It was with reference to this, therefore, that the prophet proclaimed: 'Enter into a land flowing with milk and honey, and rule over it.'
>
> [14]Observe, then, that we have been created anew, just as he says ... 'I will take away from these ... their stony hearts, and put in hearts of flesh,' because he was about to be manifested in the flesh and to dwell in us.
>
> [15]For the dwelling-place of our heart, my brothers, is a holy temple dedicated to the Lord.

---

[15] Kim 1987: 143, though the entire article supports this notion.
[16] Following especially Heil 1997: 76–100, though his comments are focused on Mark and not Matthew.

[16]... 'I will confess you in the congregation of my brothers'...
Therefore we are the ones whom he brought into the good
land.

[17]... we too, being nourished by faith in the promise and by the
word, will live and rule over the earth.

[18]Now we have already said above: 'And let them increase and
multiply and rule over the fish.' But who is presently able to
rule over beasts or fish or birds of the air?...

[19]If, however, this is not now the case, then he has told us when
it will be: when we ourselves have been made perfect, and so
become heirs of the Lord's covenant. (*Barnabas* 6:11–19)

This passage applies Adam's commission, and the same commission
renewed to Israel in the land, to Christ and the church as a new creation and temple. Christ and the church have begun to fulfil this commission (*Barnabas* 6:11–17) and it will be fulfilled consummately in the
future (6:18–19) when the church has 'been made perfect'. The passage
is introduced in 6:3 by Christ being called a 'stone that crushes [Dan.
2:34–35, 45]... a precious stone, especially chosen, a cornerstone' (Is.
28:16).[17] Likely this is an implicit reference to Christ as the cornerstone
or beginning of the temple, which is developed in 6:14–15, where
Christ is said to 'dwell in us... a holy temple dedicated to the Lord'.
The epistle later understands that the eschatological temple continues
throughout the church age to grow out from Christ (perhaps still with
Christ as the initial foundation stone in the background of thought):
'there is in fact a temple of God... [that] he is building and completing', and at the 'end God's temple will be built gloriously' (16:6). The
remainder of the chapter (16:7–10) explains how the temple 'is being
built for the Lord' by God 'dwelling in our dwelling place' by means of
people believing in 'the forgiveness of sins', 'setting their hope' on
Christ, and trusting in 'his righteous decrees' and 'commandments'.

Barnabas 6:15 identifies the 'dwelling-place of our heart' (i.e., of
the believer) as 'a holy temple dedicated to the Lord', which appears
to focus on an individual, small-scope conception of the temple and
not on the large-scale latter-day temple-theme discussed so far in this
book. Nevertheless, in the context, wider redemptive-historical concerns are evident, especially in 16:7–10, in particular the mention of
the growing process of the temple construction and its glorious end-
time culmination.

[17] Christ as the 'cornerstone' is repeated in 6:4 by allusion to Ps. 118:22.

The allusion to Ezekiel 11:19 in *Barnabas* 6:14 may also be significant in this respect: '"I will take away from these ... their stony hearts, and put in hearts of flesh," because he was about to be manifested in the flesh and to dwell in us.' The phraseology is also fraught with notions of God's larger-scale, corporate tabernacling presence during the exile and the post-exilic eschatological period, which the immediate context of the Ezekiel quotation highlights.[18] Possibly, for Barnabas, the other side of the coin of Christ dwelling in believers and creating them into individual temples is that of Christ himself being a temple (*Barnabas* 6:3), so that when one believes in Christ one becomes identified with Christ as the temple, a temple which grows as more and more people become built into it.

That a wider perspective on the temple is included in Barnabas's discussion is also apparent from recalling that the temple discussion is put in the context of God 'creating' believers to carry out the worldwide Adamic commission of Genesis 1:26–28 (*Barnabas* 6:11–12). One could conceive of the portrayal of Jesus in the Gospels as a temple to be an individualistic perspective about the temple, which is partly true, since there the very beginning establishment of the temple is in mind (i.e., Christ is the individual cornerstone of the temple). Yet the testimony of the Gospels and the apostolic reflections about Christ as a temple combine this individualistic messianic notion with his role as a representative figure. For example, 1 Peter 2:4–9 depicts Christ as the living cornerstone upon which believers as living stones 'are being built up as a spiritual house' (likewise Eph. 2:19–22).[19] The reference to Christ as 'a precious stone, especially chosen, a cornerstone' (Is. 28:16) in *Barnabas* 6:3, the same wording and allusion found in 1 Peter, fits in to this idea of a corporate temple that is growing.

Jesus as the destroyer of the old temple and the rebuilder of a new temple

Jesus not only begins to take over the role of the old temple but he forecasts its imminent doom. He prophesies that God will destroy the temple (Matt. 24 and parallels), not only because it was becoming obsolete but because of its flawed use and Israel's rejection of Jesus. Immediately after the cleansing of the temple, an acted-out parable provides further indication of Jesus' symbolic rejection of the temple. Jesus sees a fig tree without any fruit, and says '"No longer shall there

---

[18] On which see Ezek. 11:16–20 in comparison with Ezek. 36:27 and 37:26–28, as well as my discussion of these texts in my chapter below on Ezekiel.

[19] We will examine both of these passages again at a later point in the book.

ever be any fruit from you." And at once the fig tree withered' (Matt. 21:19). The fig tree without fruit symbolizes Israel's spiritual destitution, and the withering indicated the temple's and nation's rejection and judgment by God (just as it did in Jer. 8:11–13, to which allusion is made here) (N. T. Wright 1996: 421–422).[20] The following statement about 'this mountain' and 'casting' it 'into the sea' may not merely be a teaching on prayer. It may also be about judgment on the temple,[21] since, as we have seen in the preceding chapter, the temple sometimes became synonymous with the mount on which it sat.

The significance of the parable of the vineyard in relation to Jesus as the 'cornerstone'

Matthew 21:33–46 (and parallels) continues the theme of Israel's rejection through the telling of the parable of the wicked tenant farmers. A landowner planted a vineyard and rented it to some vine-growers. But when the time came to collect rent, the vine-growers mistreated the landowner's rent collectors, even killing some, including the landowner's own son. Jesus concludes by saying that the landowner 'will bring those wretches to a wretched end, and will rent out the vineyard to other vine-growers, who will pay the proceeds at the proper seasons' (Matt. 21:41). Jesus alludes to Isaiah 5:1–6, which compares Israel to a vineyard that God had planted and which he would tear down because of unfaithfulness. The Aramaic Bible of early Judaism (the Targum) identified the 'vineyard' in Isaiah 5:2 primarily as Israel's 'sanctuary': with reference to the 'vineyard', this version asserts 'I built my sanctuary in their midst, and I even gave my altar to atone for their sins.' Other sectors of Judaism made the same identification.[22] As a result of Israel's sin, the Isaiah Targum says that God would remove his glorious presence from the temple and 'break down the place of their *sanctuaries*' (*Tg. Isaiah* 5:5).[23] This

---

[20] See pp. 186–187 for further rationale that the fig tree incident has negative connotations for Israel's temple.

[21] So N. T. Wright (1996: 422), who underscores that 'this mountain' could have no other probable referent in the context than the temple mount.

[22] Davies and Allison (1991: 176, 180) suggest that the vineyard 'tower' in Matt. 21:33 is equated with the temple, especially on the basis of the following Jewish sources: *b. Sukkah* 49a interprets the 'choicest vine' of Is. 5:2 to be the temple; *1 Enoch* 89:41–77 identifies the 'tower' of the 'house' (= Jerusalem) to be the temple (on which, e.g., see Black 1985: 269, 273); 4Q500 seems to locate the 'winepress' of Is. 5:2 at the gate of the temple on Mount Zion (so Baumgarten 1989: 1–6), who suggests that the location of Eden is combined with that of Jerusalem's temple mount).

[23] 'Sanctuaries' sometimes, as we have seen earlier, being a way of referring to the multiple sacred spaces within the temple: e.g., Jer. 51:51; Ezek. 28:18.

background points to the possibility that Jesus and the Gospel writers understood the 'vineyard' in Jesus' parable to be closely associated with the temple, if not identified with it. What directly follows the parable provides even further intimation of this.

Jesus interprets the parable to mean that Israel's rejection of him would lead to their destruction (implicitly including their temple), and the erection of a new temple. In so doing, he appears to be identifying himself with the 'cornerstone' of a new temple that is being laid in their midst: 'the stone which the builders rejected, this became the chief cornerstone'. This quotation from Psalm 118:22 refers to a righteous sufferer whom God delivered from oppressors. As a result of his deliverance, he enters through the 'gate of the Lord', which is likely the gate of the temple courtyard, in light of the following references in the psalm to the figure being blessed 'from the house of the LORD' (v. 26) and to binding 'the festival sacrifice with cords to the horns of the altar' (v. 27).

Thus, the mention of the 'cornerstone' in Psalm 118:22 probably refers to part of the foundation of the temple as a metaphor for the righteous sufferer who has been oppressed not only by the nations (v. 10) but also by those within the covenant community (metaphorically portrayed as temple 'builders' who 'rejected' him as the 'chief cornerstone'). This pious victim then is likely a kingly figure in Israel's history, perhaps David himself, who had been oppressed both by the nations round about, as well as by those within Israel.

Jesus applies the psalm's temple 'cornerstone' image to himself. That he has in mind such a self-identification is pointed to by noticing that Matthew 21 is also set in the context of the temple: (1) he cleanses the temple (21:12–13); (2) the physically handicapped come to him in the temple to be healed (21:14); (3) he is praised in the temple for his healings (21:15); (4) he speaks the parable of the tenants after he had 'come into the temple' (21:23ff.). Therefore, the implication is that rejection of Jesus as the 'cornerstone' of the temple ('the stone which the builders rejected') is equivalent to rejection of Jesus as the true temple ('this became the chief cornerstone'), which is in the process of being built. While the cornerstone in the psalm was metaphorical for a king, here it is likely more than merely figurative but an actual reference to Jesus, the King of Israel, becoming the foundation stone of the new temple.[24]

---

[24] Davies and Allison (1991: 185–186), who also identify the 'cornerstone' with the new temple, citing in partial support *Testament of Solomon* 22 – 23, which refers to the stone of Ps. 118 as the one that completed Solomon's temple.

That, in fact, Jesus is identifying himself with the temple becomes clear from Paul's and Peter's later explicit identification of Jesus with the 'cornerstone' upon which the rest of the 'temple' of the church is being built and from which it will grow (Eph. 2:20–22; 1 Pet. 2:4–8, the latter also quoting Ps. 118:22). Outside the New Testament, the *Epistle of Barnabas* 6:14–15, as we have seen, also appears to identify Christ as the temple together with his followers, which also plausibly develops earlier references to him as the stone of Psalm 118 (*Barnabas* 6:3–4).

That Jesus is portraying himself as the beginning of a new sanctuary is enhanced by the following statement in Matthew 21:44: 'he who falls on this stone will be broken to pieces; but on whomever it falls, it will scatter him like dust'. Some commentators have rightly noticed that this second statement about a stone also has an Old Testament background, this time from Daniel 2:34–35:[25] 'a stone was cut out without hands, and it struck the statue ... and crushed [it]' and it 'became like chaff from the summer threshing floors; and the wind carried them away ...'

Recall from our earlier discussion of Daniel 2 that the statue represented the evil world empires that oppress God's people, and the stone symbolized God's kingdom of Israel that would destroy and judge these unbelieving kingdoms. Now, unbelieving Israel has become identified with pagan kingdoms and is portrayed as being judged along with them. Remember also that the 'stone' of Daniel's statue, after smashing the colossus, the evil kingdoms, 'became a great mountain and filled the whole earth'. I argued in some depth earlier[26] that this statement appeared to describe the 'stone' as a foundation stone of a temple that would expand to fill the entire earth. If this assertion is correct, then it makes sense why Jesus would follow up his reference to the temple 'cornerstone' of Psalm 118 with the same temple 'stone' of Daniel 2.[27] The temple images from Psalm 118 and Daniel 2 are fitting portrayals of the victorious act of new creation brought about in Christ's resurrection, since the Old Testament

---

[25] E.g., Fitzmyer 1985: 1282, 1286; Nolland 1993: 953, 955; Bock 1996: 1604–1605; see also Evans (2001: 445), who sees Christ's claim in Mark 14:58 to 'build another [temple] made without hands' to be an allusion to Dan. 2:44–45. Some manuscripts omit Matt. 21:44, though it is probably original; but even if not, Luke 20:18 includes it without any manuscript variants to the contrary.

[26] See the preceding chapter.

[27] Kim (1987: 134–148) argues that Jesus understood these OT passages, together with others like Zech. 4 and 6, to be fulfilled in the temple-building activity of his sacrificial death.

temple was symbolic of the old creation, and Daniel's stone depiction is associated with the primeval hillock from which the original creation spread (and from which the land mass spread after Noah's flood in the so-called 'second creation').

Commentators have noted that there appears to be no logical connection between the architectural and agricultural imagery in Matthew 21:33–44.[28] It would seem, however, that the connection lies in the common temple imagery. Is it mere coincidence that the cultic stone passages of Psalm 118 and Daniel 2 would be attached as an explanation of the Isaiah vineyard parable, in light of the fact that Israel's vineyard in Isaiah 5 was viewed by early Judaism to represent the temple? Such a 'vineyard' image also flows naturally into the following stone passages about the temple, since we have seen already that both the Old Testament and early Judaism viewed the Garden of Eden as a temple, and that the interiors of Israel's tabernacle and temple were constructed on the inside to remind one of a garden. We are not saying that the Old Testament notions of a temple being like a garden were at the top of Jesus' mind but that this may have facilitated to some degree the transition from the picture of the vineyard to the image of a temple.

Accordingly, Jesus says in Matthew 21:43 that 'the kingdom of God will be taken away from you, and be given to a nation producing the fruit of it'. In the context of the preceding vineyard parable, his pronouncement combines the notions of kingdom and cultic vineyard, which are two sides of the same coin, just as the 'stone' in Daniel explicitly symbolizes the 'kingdom' (Dan. 2:44–45) and implicitly also represents the temple.[29] This may also be the reason that the image of the withered 'fig tree' precedes the vineyard parable, since it was a common arboreal image typically found in botanical descriptions for Israel's prosperous land throughout the Old Testament,[30] its first occurrence being in Genesis 3:7. In particular, since Israel's land was viewed sometimes as 'the Garden of Eden' with connotations of the first primal sanctuary, the fig tree would have been a suitable

---

[28] E.g., see Snodgrass 1998: 203, who cites others in support.

[29] See Fitzmyer (1985: 1282, 1286), who identifies Jesus as 'the chief stone of the heavenly sanctuary' in Luke 20:17–18 and sees that allusion to Dan. 2:34–35, 44–45 stands partly behind the stone image.

[30] Such descriptions occur four times in the OT. In addition, the stock phrase 'each man sitting under his vine and his fig tree' occurs five times, referring to prosperity in the land (two of which pertain to eschatological conditions: Mic. 4:4; Zech. 3:10; cf. Joel 2:22). Conversely, destroying vines and fig trees connote judgment on Israel (about 8 times).

feature to include together with the vineyard and temple imagery in Matthew 21.

The Old Testament temple represented God's presence on earth, and Jesus now represents that presence in the midst of his followers. Jesus makes it abundantly clear in Matthew 24 (and parallels) that Israel's temple will be destroyed. Nevertheless, another temple would arise instead in the form of Jesus and his followers.

Perhaps the 'stone' texts of Matthew 21 are anticipated by Jesus' mention of the 'rock' in chapter 16: 'And I also say to you that you are Peter, and upon this rock I will build My church; and the gates of Hades shall not overpower it' (16:18). Though there is debate about to whom the 'rock' refers, it is certainly possible that it is Jesus.[31] More likely, however, the 'rock' is a reference either to Peter's confession that Jesus is 'the Christ, the Son of the living God' (v. 16) or preferably to Peter himself.[32] Though Jesus is not here the foundation stone, he is certainly the builder of the new temple.[33] He builds his church on the foundation stone of the apostles' teaching (as Paul later asserts in Eph. 2:19–22), which, of course, is about himself. In view of the entire Gospel of Matthew, Jesus builds both on the foundation stone of himself and the disciples. In this light, it is natural that the place of forgiveness of sins in the next verse (v. 19) would be transferred from Israel's old temple to the new temple of the church, where forgiveness in Jesus is proclaimed to the world.[34] In verse 19, Jesus introduces the means of forgiveness in the new age by saying, 'I will give you the keys of the kingdom of heaven,' showing that the authoritative basis for dealing with sins has passed from the old temple to the new ecclesiological community, which may here be conceived to be a new temple.[35]

If Matthew 16:19 is an allusion to Isaiah 22, it might enhance the

---

[31] This receives early attestation from the *Odes of Solomon* 22:12 (AD 100), which identifies the 'rock' of Matt. 16:18 as the foundation of the new temple: 'and the foundation of everything is your rock. And upon it you have built your kingdom, and became the dwelling place of the holy ones'.

[32] On the debate about the identification of the 'rock' see Caragounis (1990), who himself prefers that Peter's confession about Christ is the 'rock'. Alternatively, see also Carson 1995: 367–370 and Hagner 1995: 470–472, who identify Peter with the 'rock'.

[33] Davies and Allison (1991: 626–627) also understand the 'stone' of Matt. 16:18 to be the foundation of a temple.

[34] On which see further Matt. 18:15–18, where the church authoritatively proclaims forgiveness or lack thereof, based on one's life as a consistent expression of faith in Christ; so likewise see John 20:23: 'if you forgive the sins of any, their sins have been forgiven them; if you retain the sins of any, they have been retained'.

[35] See Carson 1995: 367–374 for fuller elaboration of the meaning of Matt. 16:18–19.

possibility that Jesus is speaking about the temple. Isaiah 22:22 portrays Eliakim, prime minister to king Hezekiah, as having 'the key of the house of David on his shoulder' because he controlled who could enter into the king's presence and service. There were priestly connotations associated with Eliakim's kingly administration, since Isaiah 22:21 portrays him clothed with a 'tunic' and a 'sash securely about him'. The Aramaic translation of Isaiah 22:22 says that God 'will place the key of the sanctuary and the authority of the house of David in his hand'. And then Isaiah 22:24 (of the Aramaic version) says that even Eliakim's relatives will be 'priests wearing the ephod'. Like Eliakim, Christ establishes himself as having an authoritative position in the new temple in Matthew 16:18, and then extends his priestly authority to his disciples, who also have priestly authority. Matthew 16:19, in the light of 18:15–18 and John 20:23, says they express what would appear to be their priestly task by declaring who is forgiven and who is not. Revelation 3:7 portrays Christ as having the 'keys' of Isaiah 22:22 and relates these 'keys' to his followers being able eventually to become 'a pillar in the temple of My God' (cf. Rev. 3:8–9 with Rev. 3:12). 'Keys of the temple' are also said to be in the possession of priests in 1 Chronicles 9:27 and 2 Baruch 10:18. In both Isaiah 22 and 2 Baruch, the keys are being taken away from unworthy keepers in Israel and transferred elsewhere, which appears to be the case here in Matthew 16: could the idea be that the keys to the true temple are being taken from old Israel and transferred to true Israel, Jesus and his followers?[36]

In light of the evidence above, it should not be surprising to observe that in the context directly preceding and following Matthew 16:18–19 Jesus identifies himself as 'Son of Man' three times (16:13, 27–28), and Peter identifies him as 'Son of God' (16:16). These names, as we have already seen, show that Jesus is doing what Adam and Israel should have done. He is the 'Son of Adam' who does what his human father failed to do. He is the 'Son of God', which not only was a name for Adam but also for the corporate Adam, Israel, who was disobedient to their divine father.

The significance of the tearing of the temple veil at the time of Christ's death

This discussion of Jesus as the beginning of the new temple in replacement of the old in Matthew 21 may also be the best context

---

[36] The texts of 1 Chronicles and 2 Baruch and their significance were brought to my attention by my colleague S. J. Hafemann in an as yet unpublished article.

within which to understand Matthew 27:40, where, in virtual repetition of 26:61, those mocking Jesus say, 'You who are going to destroy
the temple and rebuild it in three days, save Yourself! If You are the
Son of God, come down from the cross' (see the parallels in Mark
14:58 and 15:29).[37] Then, after Jesus 'yielded up his spirit' on the
cross, Matthew discloses that 'the veil of the temple was torn in two
from top to bottom, and the earth shook; and the rocks were split,
and the tombs were opened; and many bodies of the saints who had
fallen asleep were raised' (Matt. 27:50–52).

Irony is neatly woven throughout this passage. Jesus is mocked
because he said that he would tear down the temple and rebuild it in
three days, and at virtually the same time Matthew tells us that Jesus
actually was in the process of destroying the temple when he died.
That the 'veil of the temple was torn in two' in verse 51 is a direct
result of his death in verse 50. The temple veil was a part of the
temple, so that its tearing symbolically represented the destruction of
the temple. Commentators have never successfully explained why the
mention of the torn temple veil is part of language describing the
breakup of the world in the phrases of Matthew 27 that follow
directly.

When, however, it is remembered from the Old Testament and early
Judaism that on the veil was embroidery of the starry heavens, its
tearing would be an apt symbol of the beginning destruction, not only
of the temple (which itself even as a whole symbolized the cosmos) but
of the very cosmos itself. Consequently, though the text does not
explicitly point out to readers the cosmic embroidery on the veil, this
implicit reality suggests that the veil's destruction is compatible and
admirably fits with the mention of darkening of the sun (so Luke
23:44–45), earthquake, splitting of rocks, and raising of believers (vv.
51–53).[38] Luke 23:44–45 adds that 'darkness fell over the whole land',
and 'the sun failed' at the time 'the veil of the temple was torn in two',
adding further to the language of cosmic conflagration. These were not
signs of the final destruction of the cosmos but signs that it had begun
in Jesus' death, and that his resurrection (v. 53) was the beginning of a

---

[37] Commentators tend to see these passages affirming Jesus as the builder of the new
temple and the temple itself as the new Christian community (on which see Juel 1977:
145 for a representative list of commentators on the Markan statements).

[38] In the light of Mark 15:30–39, the tearing of the veil happened immediately after
Christ's death, and three days later the earthquake at the end of v. 51 occurred together
with the event of Christ and the saints' resurrection (vv. 52–53; Matt. 27:54 appears to
identify the breakup of the earth in v. 51 with the 'earthquake' that occurred when
Christ rose from the dead).

new creation.[39] Jesus' statement in Luke 23:43, that he and the believing criminal would be together 'in Paradise [or the Garden]' immediately after their death, suggests further that Jesus' death was in fact a pathway leading to a new creational Eden, apparently beginning to fulfil the intention of the primeval garden sanctuary.[40] His subsequent resurrection as new creation was the formal rebuilding of the temple.

Also likely in mind is the more traditional interpretation of the tearing of the veil, whereby immediate access into God's holy presence is signified. Nevertheless, like the embroidery on the veil, this idea is not mentioned in any of the passion contexts of the Gospels. This association with the veil, however, is clearly and repeatedly found in the Old Testament, and, therefore, it is probably implied in the Gospels' narrative. Thus, the rending of the veil indicates both a cosmic and cultic reality: the inbreaking destruction of the old creation and inauguration of the new creation, which introduces access for all believers to God's holy presence in a way that was not available in the old creation.

It is difficult to know whether the veil was the outer veil covering the entrance to the holy place or the veil separating the holy place from the holy of holies, but both contained heavenly symbolism.[41] Nevertheless, several considerations may point to the latter as more likely. Part of our argument throughout the book so far has been that the goal of the old temple was that God's presence would break out of the holy of holies and encompass the rest of the visible cosmos, as represented by the outer two sections of the temple. Some argue that the outer veil is in view, since Jewish and Jewish-Christian sources allude to an amazing event that occurred at the outer door of the Herodian temple before its destruction.[42] On the other hand, though the word 'veil' (*katapetasma*) can refer in the Greek Old Testament to

---

[39] Since this was not the consummate end of the world and the final new creation, the saints who did come out of their tombs (vv. 52–53) presumably, like Lazurus, died again at some subsequent point, only to be raised again at the very end of history.

[40] The Greek word 'paradise' in the OT refers to the 'Garden' of Eden 21 times out of 33. The word occurs only two times elsewhere in the NT: 2 Cor. 12:4, which appears to refer to the same heavenly 'paradise' of Luke 23:43, and Rev. 2:7, which explicitly alludes to the Garden of Eden.

[41] See p. 46 above for references in Josephus and Philo for the heavenly symbolism of all the curtains in the temple. However, see Ulansey (2001: 123–125), who builds on earlier studies arguing that the tearing of the heavens in Mark 1:10 is linked to the tearing of the veil in 15:38, as an inclusio designating the beginning and ending of Jesus' ministry. He then contends that the veil is the outer veil, since Josephus (*War* 5.212–215) says on the outer veil was embroidery 'that typified the universe' and that 'portrayed a panorama of the heavens'.

[42] See Michel, '*naos*', *TDNT*, 4:885, n. 21. There was also an outer curtain (*katapetasma*) at the outermost entrance to the tabernacle (Num. 3:26).

either the outer or inner veil, the latter is more likely, since its tearing would connote that Jesus' death 'opened up access to the holy of holies', which carries more apparent theological significance than a reference to the outer curtain.[43]

That the inner veil had more theological importance is supported by recalling that there was both a *door* and curtain at the entrance to the temple, but only a veil separated the holy place and holy of holies, the latter where God's presence dwelt. Only the high priest could pass through that inner veil, and even then he could do that only once a year (so Hooker 1991: 377). Thus, the tearing of the innermost veil would provide a clearer symbol that the barrier between God and mankind had been removed. The obvious point, therefore, is that the inner veil was next to the holiest place in the entire temple, the holy of holies, and, hence, carried more significance. The only other uses of 'veil' (*katapetasma*) in relation to Christ's death in early Christian writings refer to the inner veil (Heb. 6:19; 9:3; 10:20), which also suggests that the same notion is being discussed in the Synoptics (the Coptic *Gospel of Phillip* 85 also refers to the inner veil). However, which veil was torn does not ultimately affect our larger argument, since both the inner and outer veils contained symbols of the cosmos.

In this respect, the fact that centurions both witnessed the opening of Christ's tomb and confessed him as 'the Son of God' shows that Jesus was finally confessed to be whom the mockers sarcastically said he was. The confession shows further that the ultimate design of the temple was beginning to be fulfilled in Jesus' resurrection: Yahweh's revelatory presence was extending out beyond the boundaries of ethnic Israel to include Gentiles.[44] The centurion's confession was the beginning of the prophetic fulfilment that the eschatological temple

---

[43] See Schneider, '*katapetasma*', *TDNT*, 3:628–630. Gurtner (2003) has advanced Schneider's argument further by elaborating on three theological aspects of the innermost veil's separating function, which are not functions of the outer veils: (1) a distinction between the *most* holy and less holy; (2) an impediment to the atoning effect of the blood of the sin offering (cf. Lev. 4:6, 17), so that its sprinkling would not progress to the 'mercy seat'; (3) a barrier to the physical and visible accessibility of God's most holy presence. Matthew's context shows that these three functions ceased with the death of Christ. According to Gurtner, also in favour of a reference to the innermost veil is the observation that of the 34 times *katapetasma* is used in the LXX, 32 are translations of *pārōket*, which refers to the inmost curtain.

[44] This was anticipated by the centurion at the foot of the cross who, immediately after the temple veil was rent, also confessed Jesus to be 'the Son of God' (Mark 15:38–39). Perhaps this was the same centurion who later proclaimed the same thing in the Matthean account.

would be the place to which God 'will bring' foreigners (Is. 56:7) and 'the nations would stream' (Is. 2:2–3; Mic. 4:1–3).

Early Judaism understood that when 'the curtain of the temple will be torn' it would signify Israel's disobedience (*Testament of Levi* 10:3; cf. *Lives of the Prophets* 12:12) and early Christian tradition believed that at the time 'the temple curtain will be torn ... the Spirit of God will move on to all the nations as fire is poured out' (Christian interpolation in *Testament of Benjamin* 9:3).[45] These references understand the tearing of the temple curtain to indicate either Israel's disobedience or the entrance of Gentiles into the true faith. It is the case also with the Gospels' episode. Christ was recreating the temple in himself so that it would finally fulfil its world-encompassing purpose.[46]

Jesus as the temple of the new creation in John

Like Matthew 26 – 27, John 2 confirms the analysis in Matthew 21 that the 'vineyard' and 'stone' convey the notion of an old temple being replaced by a new one. John 2:14–22 also begins with the cleansing of the temple episode (vv. 14–17). The Jews ask Jesus in verse 18 'what sign do you show to us' to demonstrate by what authority he had cleansed the temple. He responds by saying, 'Destroy this temple, and in three days I will raise it up' (v. 19). The Jews respond, 'It took forty-six years to build this temple, and You will raise it up in three days?' (v. 20). John concludes by saying that 'He was speaking of the temple of His body' (v. 21) and that, after Christ had been resurrected, they identified his resurrection with his promise of raising the temple (v. 22).

It is possible that Christ is not referring to the old Israelite temple

---

[45] Likewise, the ancient Jewish work *Joseph and Aseneth* (early second century AD) narrates a story about Joseph's wife, and says that before they were married, she lived in a pagan temple. When she was converted to belief in Yahweh, she 'took down . . . the skin (which hung there for a) curtain' (10:2). Note also the temple features of the outer court in *Joseph and Aseneth* 2:10 (17)–12 (20). See Bohak 1997: 1–71, esp. 67–74 for the context of the pagan temple in which Aseneth lived, and who compares the curtain tearing to Mark 15:38.

[46] This purpose is explained in *Sibylline Oracles* 8:303, 305 [c. AD 175] in the following manner: Christ 'will stretch out his hands [at the cross] and measure the entire world . . . The veil of the temple will be rent'). Note that throughout this section, I have focused more on segments in Matthew in tracing the theme of the temple. See Heil 1997 for a brilliant analysis of Mark 11:1 – 15:41, showing how the denunciation, destruction or replacement of the temple in Jesus and his followers is the key to the narrative strategy at every point! There is not space to summarize the argument, but a number of his points lend further confirmation to conclusions reached above.

at all when he speaks of 'destroying' the temple. He may well be referring to his own person that had begun to replace the temple and that would be destroyed by death and then be rebuilt again by resurrection. If so, his resurrection would be an escalated form of the new temple that had begun to exist in Jesus during his pre-crucifixion ministry. More likely, Jesus' statement about destroying and raising up the temple was a double entendre: on one level he was speaking of the old temple that he would tear down and raise up in new form, though he also had in mind the destruction of his own body as a temple that would be raised up again.[47] The spiritual destruction of Israel's temple occurred decisively at Jesus' death and resurrection, and its physical demise came finally in AD 70.

That Jesus had in mind both the destruction of Israel's old temple and his body as the temple and the replacement of it with his resurrection body as the new temple may also be suggested by Mark 14:58, where Mark gives prominence to a revealing but false testimony concerning Jesus: 'We heard Him say, "I will destroy this temple made with hands, and in three days I will build another made without hands."' A chiasm could be apparent in Mark 15:23–38, which develops the theme of Jesus as the new temple by means of a five-fold chiasm. One of the five self-interpreting parallel pairs is the following:

Wine is offered	Vinegar is offered
Crucifixion	Christ dies from crucifixion
Christ's garments divided	The curtain of the temple is
(vv. 23–27)	torn in two
	(vv. 36–38)

If this chiasm is present, then Mark interprets the 'unveiling' of Jesus (stripping him) to be the 'unveiling' of the temple. Accordingly, the crucifixion would be the destruction, not only of Christ's body as a temple, but the demise of the old temple itself and the release of the divine presence from the holy of holies, which has its first effect in the conversion of the centurion (v. 39) (though God's presence had probably already left Israel's sanctuary much earlier).[48] Thus, even before the formal rebuilding of the new temple by resurrection, we might

---

[47] See Marshall (1989: 211), who sees the destruction of the Jerusalem temple to be the primary meaning and Jesus' body the secondary meaning. Likewise, Walker 1996: 165–166.

[48] So see Bailey 1990–91: 102–105 for the observation of the chiasm and the interpretative implications, though his proposal is debatable.

venture to say that the crucifixion was the destruction of the old temple in the midst of which the new holy of holies had already begun to emerge invisibly in the very face of the Roman soldier,[49] whom John himself later has in mind in his account of the two centurions who were present at Jesus' crucifixion (see John 19:32–37).[50]

It is the resurrection that marks the first visible act of temple rebuilding. Acts 6:13–14 together with Acts 7:47–50 also points to the Synoptic and Johannine interpretation that Jesus' resurrection was the rebuilding of the new temple in replacement of the old (as does *Barnabas* 16).[51] The Mark and Acts texts shed the same light on the shorter statements in Matt. 26:61, 27:40 and Mark 15:29, which are parallels to John 2:19.[52]

Jesus' 'building' of the new temple through his resurrection was, broadly speaking, a fulfilment of Zechariah 6:12–13, even though that Old Testament passage is not expressly cited anywhere in the New Testament. In the Zechariah text, the messianic 'Branch' is prophesied to 'build the temple' and rule in glory.[53] Even the earlier promise in 2 Samuel 7:12–13 'that God's house would be built by the Son of David naturally pointed to the final building of the temple as the task of the Messiah', David's son (so Clowney 1972: 171). Strikingly, the Aramaic rendering of Isaiah 53:5 says that the Messiah 'will build the sanctuary which was profaned for our sins' (likewise, *Sibylline Oracles*

---

[49] Along these same lines, see Chronis 1982: 108–114, though he denies that Jesus predicted the destruction of the physical temple.

[50] On which see further Michaels 1967: 102–109.

[51] See further below on the discussion of Acts 7.

[52] Gundry (1993: 885–907) views the wording of Mark 14:58 to be purely false testimony, and that Jesus never made a claim to destroy the temple and rebuild it. But, following Carson (1995: 554) and France (1985: 378–379), the testimony was false, not because Jesus did not make the statement but because of the evil intent and the disregard of the true meaning of Jesus' saying recorded in John 2:19 (which Gundry does not believe is authentic to Jesus). From another perspective, see Juel (1977: 124, 169, 205–206) and Chronis (1982: 108, 112), who say that within the overall narrative structure of Mark the false testimony ironically becomes fulfilled prophecy at Jesus' death and resurrection.

[53] So Clowney 1972: 171. The Targum of the Zechariah passage identifies the 'Branch' as the Messiah who will build the temple. For the Messiah as a temple-builder, see also *Tg. Isaiah* 53:5; *Midrash Rabbah Numbers* 13:2; 18:21; *Midrash Rabbah Leviticus* 9:6; *Midrash Rabbah Lamentations* 1:16 §51; *Midrash Rabbah Song of Songs* 4:16 §1; *Pirke de Rabbi Eliezer* 48. See further S. M. Bryan 2002: 193–199 for discussion of most of these Jewish texts, where he also contends that 4Q174, 1.3–7 and *4 Ezra* 13:6–7, 35–36 affirm that the messiah would build the end-time temple, the latter of which is supported by our earlier extended analysis of the Dan. 2 stone-mountain being an end-time temple (see ch. 4). Following Clowney, see Pusey 1885: 374–375 for the messianic associations with 'branch' in Zech. 6:12, including Jewish identifications of Zech. 6:12 as messianic.

5:415–424). The initial fulfilment shows that Jesus' resurrection body itself is the material for the beginning phase of that building project. Consequently, it would be wrong to conclude, as some do, that Jesus was merely like a temple. It is true enough that he, indeed, is 'like' a temple, but that is because he *is* the beginning fulfilment of these end-time prophecies concerning the building of the temple.

The reference to Jesus as a temple in John 2 is presumably a development of John 1:14: 'And the Word became flesh, and *tabernacled* among us, and we beheld His glory.' The special revelatory presence of God, formerly contained in the holy of holies of the tabernacle and temple, has now burst forth into the world in the form of the incarnate God, Jesus Christ. Then, Jesus says in John 1:51: 'you shall see the heavens opened, and the angels of God ascending and descending upon the Son of Man'. This is an allusion to Genesis 28:12, where God appeared to Jacob at Bethel, and, in response, Jacob established a small sanctuary. There Jacob saw steps ascending to heaven and angels going up and down on them. The point of that vision was that this was a temporary sanctuary, where there was a link between heaven and earth. This little temple at Bethel was a precursor of the large temple to be built in Jerusalem, which became the permanent place in Israel, and the ancient world, where God's presence in heaven was linked to the earth (for the fuller discussion, see ch. 3 above).

Jesus' identification of himself with the temple stairway of Genesis 28 is thus another way of claiming that he, not the Jerusalem temple, is the primary link between heaven and earth.[54] Therefore, Jacob's small sanctuary in Genesis 28 did not point merely to the temporary Jerusalem temple but ultimately to the permanent temple built by Christ. One need not go to the Jerusalem temple to be near God's revelatory presence but only need trust in Jesus to experience that presence. This is why Jesus says that the time was dawning when true worship would not occur at the Jerusalem temple, nor any other holy site, but would be directed toward the Father (and, by implication, through the Messiah) in the sphere of the coming eschatological Spirit of Jesus (John 4:21–26). A link with heaven would be created by the Spirit wherever there was trust in Christ, and those so trusting would come within the sphere of the true temple consisting of Christ and his Spirit.

[54] I have subsequently found that Marshall (1989: 211–212) has made the same observation; likewise, Spatafora (1997: 111–112), though see Kerr (2002: 136–166), who sees a reference to the temple in this passage to be unlikely, with which I respectfully disagree.

That Jesus identifies himself as 'the Son of Man' who is the stairway between heaven and earth appears to be a way of indicating that he is finally doing what Adam and Israel should have done: he is building a permanent temple that has begun to link heaven to earth. Our earlier study of Noah, the patriarchs and Israel showed that interwoven with their inchoate temple-building activities was the reapplied commission to Adam to multiply, fill the earth, subdue it, rule over it and be a blessing. We saw the way this commission was to be carried out was by building temples and then expanding their borders until, ideally, they would circumscribe the whole earth. This recommission was a central feature of the sanctuary-building episode in Genesis 28 (see 28:13–15). Christ is affirming that he is the true Adam ('Son of Man [Adam]') and true Israel (i.e., Jacob's seed), and, along with this, he may also be affirming that he has finally begun to fulfil successfully the commission of Genesis 1:26–28 and to complete Jacob's earlier small-scale building activity by establishing the true temple and increasing its borders throughout the earth. With the coming of Jesus the foundation stone of the new temple has been moved into place and nothing can thwart its building process.

Temple imagery may also be expressed when Jesus tells the Samaritan woman at Jacob's well that he is the source of 'living water' which will 'spring up to eternal life' for those drinking from him (John 4:10–14). Just as water had its source in the first sanctuary in Eden and flowed down and became a life-giving element, likewise Ezekiel, alluding to the Garden of Eden, prophesied that the same thing would be the case with the end-time temple to be built in the new Jerusalem (Ezek. 47:1–12): 'Then he brought me back to the door of the house [the holy of holies]; and behold, water was flowing from under the threshold of the house toward the east' (v. 1); 'so everything will live where the river goes' (v. 9b; so also v. 12).[55] Joel 3:18 ('a spring will go out from the house of the LORD') and Zechariah 14:8 ('living waters will flow out of Jerusalem') prophesy the same reality. John's Apocalypse sees the consummate future fulfilment of Ezekiel's, Joel's and Zechariah's prophecies and restoration of an escalated Eden, in which 'a river of the water of life, clear as crystal', comes 'from the throne of God and of the Lamb' (Rev. 22:1), who just a few verses earlier have been identified as the 'sanctuary' (Rev. 21:22).

In light of this background and of the discussion so far about Jesus

---

[55] A spring was also identified as having its source under the holy of holies in Israel's temple and flowing out from there: see pp. 72–73.

as the new temple in John's Gospel, Jesus' offer of 'living water' to the Samaritan woman should be viewed as another reference to him being the beginning form of the true temple from which true life in God's presence proceeds. John 7:37–39 confirms this connection. Teaching in the temple on the last day of the Feast of Tabernacles, Jesus says, 'If any man is thirsty, let him come to Me and drink. He who believes in Me, as the Scripture said, 'From his innermost being shall flow rivers of living water.' But this He spoke of the Spirit, whom those who believed in Him were to receive, for the Spirit was not yet given, because Jesus was not yet glorified.'

In verse 38 Jesus alludes to the prophecy of water flowing from the temple in Ezekiel, Joel and Zechariah.[56] The 'innermost being' from which 'flow rivers of living water' is Jesus himself as the new 'holy of holies' and not the one who believes in Jesus.[57] This is apparent, first, from recalling that the Old Testament prophecies identify the source of the water to be from the innermost part of the temple (i.e., the holy of holies) where Yahweh's presence had dwelt in the past and would dwell again in the latter-day temple. Jesus was that presence on earth. Secondly, John 7:39 interprets the 'living water' to be the Spirit poured out at Pentecost by Jesus himself to all those who would believe in him (see Acts 2:32–38).

John 7:37 tells us that Jesus spoke the words of John 7:37–39 'on the last day, the great day of the feast' of Tabernacles, at which time was a special water drawing and pouring ritual (*m. Sukkah* 4.9–10).[58]

---

[56] Commentators generally acknowledge these OT allusions here, especially that of Ezekiel (recently, see Spatafora 1997: 114, 292).

[57] Whether the 'innermost being' refers to Jesus or to the believer is not necessarily a crucial issue to solve, since v. 37 clearly posits Jesus as the ultimate source of the water and v. 39 implicitly sees Jesus as the source of the Spirit, of which the water is a symbol (especially in light of 20:22 Jesus is the source of the Spirit). Even if the 'innermost being' refers to the believer in v. 38, Jesus is still the implied ultimate source of the water who causes an abundant flow from the believer's heart. Nevertheless, I prefer that Jesus is explicitly the one from whom living waters flow in v. 38. On the debate see Carson (1991: 322–329), who prefers that the 'innermost being' refers to the believer.

[58] On which see further Edersheim 1994: 220–227. Likewise, on the last day of the feast there was a great bonfire in one of the outer temple courts, so that 'there was not a courtyard in Jerusalem that did not reflect the light' of that fire (*m. Sukkah* 5.2–3). Early the next morning after the bonfire, Jesus proclaims in the temple, 'I am the light of the world; he who follows Me shall not walk in the darkness, but shall have the light of life' (John 8:12). Again, he appears to be identifying himself with the temple by representing himself as the light of the temple. See similarly Walker (1996: 167–170), who also notes that John portrays Jesus to be fulfilling the theological ideas associated with the feast of Passover (see John 13:1; 18:28; 19:14, 26).

The timing of Jesus' pronouncement may have enhanced further his identification with the water of the new temple.

That Jesus is the source of the end-time temple's water (= the Spirit) may find further confirmation from John 20:22, which is anticipatory of Pentecost, where the resurrected Christ 'breathed on them [the disciples] and said to them, "Receive the Holy Spirit."' It is no coincidence that some commentators have observed that this act of 'breathing' echoes Genesis 2:7, where God 'breathed' (the same Greek word as in John 20) into Adam 'the breath of life, and Adam became a living being'. In the preceding verse (v. 21), Christ says, 'as the Father has sent Me, I also send you'. This is another episode like the 'Great Commission' given in Matthew 28:18–20, which we have seen is plausibly to be understood as a renewal of the commission given to Adam. In this sense, this event is different from the subsequent event of Pentecost, when many more received the Spirit.

Therefore, the allusion to Genesis 2:7 takes on more significance: Jesus is empowering his followers not with physical life, as with Adam, but with spiritual empowerment to do what Adam and others had failed to do (note the parallel empowerment formula in Matt. 28:20, 'I am with you always'). The Twelve are commissioned as the representative bridgehead of the new humanity, the new Israel.[59] Pentecost shows this bridgehead expanding further with a greater outpouring of the Spirit.

Could John 20:22 be a development of the promise of the Spirit from John 7, which we have argued is associated with the new temple in Jesus (John 7:39)? A positive answer to this question may be pointed to by observing that this is the first time the language of 'receiving the Spirit' in application to Jesus' followers has occurred since John 7:39 ('but this He spoke of *the Spirit*, whom *those who believed in Him were to receive*'). The link with John 7 is suggested further by noticing that John 7:39 affirmed that the Spirit would not be given until Jesus had been glorified ('for the Spirit was not yet given, because Jesus was not yet glorified'). One might be able to say that Jesus' glorification had begun with the resurrection,[60] even

---

[59] This is indicated further if the 'in-breathing' is an allusion also to Ezek. 37:7, where the same Greek verb, *emphysaō* ('breathe into') as in Gen. 2:7 is used in portraying the creation of end-time Israel.

[60] That the resurrection was an inaugurated reality of the promise of Jesus' glorification in John 7:39 may be further pointed to by recalling that God 'glorifies' Jesus at his crucifixion (12:23, 28; 13:31; 17:1, 5; though these texts might even implicitly have in mind the resurrection).

though his full glorification at his ascension had not yet happened (or alternatively, the resurrection, at least, was the beginning of a process inextricably linked to the glorification at the ascension). If this link with John 7 can be maintained, then Jesus' breathing the Spirit on the disciples could be considered a part of a commission of and an enablement for them to be part of the new temple and to expand its borders, so that others in the world may be included (on which see John 17:18–23).[61] The primary message they are to announce in their mission is the forgiveness of sins (v. 23), which, as we have seen in the Synoptic Gospels, became the function of Jesus instead of Jerusalem's temple. In fact, we saw that the announcement of forgiveness in Matthew 16:19 may have been the equivalent message given to Jesus' followers as a result of their identification with him as the 'foundation rock of the new temple'. Now, similarly, the followers of Jesus have authority to announce the same message for the same reason: 'If you forgive the sins of any, their sins have been forgiven them; if you retain the sins of any, they have been retained.'[62] Just as God's breathing into Adam made him part of the first creation and resulted in his being placed into the garden-temple, so Jesus' breathing into the disciples might well be considered to incorporate them into the new creation[63] and temple. They are part of the temple, and they announce the life-giving forgiveness that can come only from Christ, the centre and foundation of the temple and, hence, also of the new creation of which the old temples were emblematic.

Thus, though the mention of the 'temple' does not occur in John 20, it has some unique language and ideas there in common with the prophecy of John 7, so that Jesus' address to the disciples would appear to be linked to John 7. Not only this, but the John 20

---

[61] It is certainly possible that Jesus' breathing on the apostles is an acted out parable of the Spirit they were to receive shortly afterwards at Pentecost (so Carson 1991: 649–655). If so, they did not receive the Spirit at that point in John 20:22 but were guaranteed to receive him. In either case, our point still stands.

[62] The Matthean equivalent reads, 'I will give you the keys of the kingdom of heaven; and whatever you shall bind on earth shall have been bound in heaven, and whatever you shall loose on earth shall have been loosed in heaven.'

[63] See Beasley-Murray (1987: 380–381), who has recognized the new creation significance of this passage on the basis of allusion not only to Gen. 2:7 but Ezek. 37:9–10, which prophesies Israel's eschatological resurrection at the time of their restoration (and which develops earlier reference to an end-time 'Garden of Eden' for Israel from Ezek. 36:35). See also the use of Gen. 2:7 in connection with the 'First Adam' and Christ, 'the last Adam', in relation to his resurrection and the Spirit in 1 Cor. 15:45.

passage would seem also to be associated to some degree with the new temple, since the earlier promise of John 7 itself was formulated by allusions to Old Testament end-time prophecies about the temple.[64]

[64] Another passge in John that may refer to the end-time temple is 14:2–3, on which, see Beale (1999a: 648–649) and S. M. Bryan (forthcoming), the latter especially for the argument that the plural 'dwelling places' reflects early Jewish expectations that all saints would have a dwelling place in the future temple.

See also Kerr (2002), not only for discussion of 14:1–2 (pp. 293–313), but also for a thorough analysis of the temple-theme throughout John, including discussion of a number of passages not addressed in this section (and relevant bibliography not included in this present work), and which contains numerous conclusions with which I agree.

Chapter Six

The inauguration of a new temple in the book of Acts

The descent of the new temple in the form of the Spirit at Pentecost[1]

If the anticipation of Pentecost in John 20 is linked to Jesus and his followers as the beginning form of a new temple, it might not be unexpected to find that the actual event of Pentecost is likewise associated. A few observations point in this direction.

The relationship between the tongues of Babel and Pentecost

The speaking in tongues at Pentecost is best seen first within its redemptive-historical context of the whole Bible. The 'tongues' result in people from different parts of the ancient world with different languages hearing 'each ... speak in his own language' (Acts 2:8). The list of the different nations represented by Diaspora Jews at Pentecost in Acts 2:9–11 alludes in abbreviated manner to 'the Table of Nations' in Genesis 10: 'Parthians and Medes and Elamites, and residents of Mesopotamia, Judea and Cappadocia, Pontus and Asia, Phrygia and Pamphylia, Egypt and the districts of Libya around Cyrene, and visitors from Rome, both Jews and proselytes, Cretans and Arabs ...'[2]

The allusion to Genesis 10 has been anticipated in Luke 10:1–12. There, after Luke 9:1–6 narrates the sending out of the twelve disciples (representing the tribes of Israel, Luke 22:30), Jesus sends out seventy (or seventy-two) witnesses. They represent the nations of the world to be evangelized, since seventy (or seventy-two) nations was the traditional number associated with the number of nations listed in Genesis 10 (Scott 1995: 162–163).[3] These were the nations who had

---

[1] For a fuller discussion of this section, see my forthcoming 2004 Tyndale Biblical Theology Lecture by the same title (which I hope to publish subsequently).

[2] See Scott (1995: 162–180), who argues this on the basis of similarities not only to Gen. 10 but also to early Jewish lists that are linked to Gen. 10.

[3] Metzger (1971: 150) notes that the problem of the textual reading of 'seventy' or 'seventy-two' in Luke 10:1 is difficult to solve because the Hebrew text of Genesis has a total of seventy nations while the LXX has a total of seventy-two.

been disobedient to the commission of 'multiplying', 'swarming in the earth' and 'filling' it (see Gen. 9:1, 6–7, which develops Genesis 1:28).[4] They had united at Babel in an attempt to force God to come down to them. In response, God did come down at Babel, but in judgment by 'confusing' their 'tongues' (*Sibylline Oracles* 3:105; Josephus, *Ant.* 1.117, 120), so that they could not understand one another. The judgment also entailed them being 'scattered ... over the face of the whole earth' (Gen. 11:1–9). They were forced to do what they should have done in submission to Genesis 1:28 and 9:1, 6–7 but which they had refused to do.[5] Although they did not spread out voluntarily to fulfil the Adamic commission,[6] a remnant did begin to obey – Abraham and his seed.

The mention of representatives of these nations being in Jerusalem together with the presence of 'tongues' (Acts 2:3) and different 'dialects' (Acts 2:6–8) strengthens an intended link to Genesis 10 – 11, since there also different languages played such a crucial part in what happened.[7] The theophany at Babel, like that in Acts 2:2, also was thought to have manifested itself in a strong 'wind' (Josephus, *Ant.* 1.118; *Sibylline Oracles* 3:101–102) and 'various sounds' (*Sibylline Oracles* 3:106). Why does Luke want readers to see the link to Genesis 10 – 11? Babel's sin of uniting and consequent judgment of confused languages and of people being scattered throughout the earth is reversed at Pentecost: God causes representatives from the same scattered nations to unite in Jerusalem in order that they might receive the blessing of understanding different languages as if all these languages were one.

The reversal of Babel may be indicated even by the common

---

[4] Despite the plausible protestations of Walton (1995: 166), who does not see disobedience to the Genesis mandate at Babel. My view of Babel in relation to Gen. 1:28 follows the majority of commentators, which I still find most convincing, especially in the light of the development of Gen. 1:28 throughout the OT and humanity's disobedience to it, both before and after Babel.

[5] See Cohen (1989: 61–63) and Ross (1981: 119) for an essentially identical view of the significance of Babel in relation to Gen. 1:26–28. Among the earliest such interpretations of the Babel episode, Josephus, *Ant.* 1.110–112, is certainly to be included.

[6] Josephus (*Ant.* 1.110–112) says that the people at Babel had refused God's 'command to send out colonies that they might . . . cultivate much of the earth and enjoy an abundance of its fruits'; they, however, 'refused to obey'.

[7] Cf. the almost identical language of Acts 2 with Josephus's interpretative paraphrase of Gen. 11: 'they began to speak *with other tongues* [*heterais glōssais*], as the Spirit was giving them utterance' (Acts 2:4) and 'we hear *each in our own dialect* [*hekastos tē idia dialektō*]' (Acts 2:8; likewise, 2:6); they spoke with 'different tongues [*alloglōssous*]' (*Ant.* 1.117; so also *Ant.* 1.120); God 'gave *to each his own language* [*idian hekastō phōnēn*]' (*Ant.* 1.118).

element of tongues causing 'confusion' (cf. Acts 2:6, 'they were confused'): whereas unintelligible tongues caused confusion at Babel, at Pentecost intelligible tongues are so startling and unexpected that confusion of amazement resulted.[8] The purpose of having a unified understanding is to demonstrate the power of the eschatological Spirit in attesting to Jesus' death, resurrection and ascension to the heavenly throne to reign as cosmic king. Under the kingship of Jesus and through the power of his Spirit the representatives of these nations were to 'scatter' again and subdue the powers of evil by filling the earth with God's presence, just as Jesus' smaller band of seventy witnesses had begun to do during his earthly ministry. The precise manner by which they were to do this was by 'witnessing' through the power of the Spirit in word and deed on behalf of Jesus Christ (see Acts 1:8).

That the events of Pentecost likely took place in the Jerusalem temple is appropriate (cf. Acts 2:1–2, 46). The judgment at Babel occurred as a result of the people uniting to build a temple tower in order to force God to come down from heaven in blessing. Such cultic towers were typical of the time in ancient Mesopotamia. Their purpose was to serve as a gateway between heaven and earth whereby the god could come down and even refresh himself on the way to the earthly temple.[9] Like Babel's temple tower, the Jerusalem temple was intended to be the link between heaven and earth. Because of Israel's sin, however, their earthly temple was about to be judged, as we have already seen prophesied by Jesus in the Gospels. Israel believed their temple to be the emblem that they were God's chosen people. In fact, however, God's presence had long since appeared to have departed from the temple because of their rebellion, idolatry and apostasy (Ezek. 11:22–25, *Tg. Isaiah* 5:5; *Midrash Rabbah Numbers* 15:10; *Midrash Rabbah Lamentations*, Proem 24; and *b. Yoma* 21b may point to this, though Matt. 23:21; *Sirach* 24:8–34; Josephus, *War* 6.299, *m. Sukkah* 5:4, and *Midrash Rabbah Exodus* 2:2 could point in the other direction; on which, see Davies 1991: 32–36). As we will see, Stephen reiterates this judgment, and like Jesus, he is also killed for it (Acts 6:11–15; 7:48–50). The Gospels also affirm that Jesus himself began to replace the old temple during his ministry and more climactically at his resurrection (John 2:19–22; Matt. 26:61; 27:40; Mark 14:58; 15:29).

---

[8] So Witherington 1998: 136, following a suggestion by Barrett 1994: 119.
[9] See Walton (1995: 155–175), who gives ample evidence that the 'tower of Babel' was part of a temple complex.

Pentecost as a fulfilment of Jesus' prophecy of the temple

Hints of a *new* spiritual temple may also be discernible in Acts 2. Such hints should not be surprising, if we have been correct to identify the anticipatory Pentecost of John 20:21–23 with the Holy Spirit as an expression of the new temple in fulfilment of Jesus' own prophecy of the temple in John 7:37–39. Just as in John 20, the coming of the Spirit indicates a shift in redemptive history whereby forgiveness of sins derives from Jesus instead of the physical temple and is announced by Jesus' priestly followers instead of Israel's temple priests (e.g., Acts 2:38: 'Repent, and let each of you be baptized in the name of Jesus Christ for the forgiveness of your sins, and you shall receive the gift of the Holy Spirit').

Tongues of Pentecost as a theophany of a latter-day Sinai sanctuary

The appearance of 'tongues as of fire' is an expression of the coming Spirit that reflects a theophany, which appears to be associated with the heavenly temple. A number of considerations point to this. First, the mention that 'there came from heaven a noise like a violent, rushing wind' and that there appeared 'tongues as of fire' calls to mind the typical theophanies of the Old Testament. God appeared in these theophanies with a thunderous noise and in the form of fire. The first great theophany of the Old Testament was at Sinai, where God appeared in the midst of loud 'voices and torches and a thick cloud' and 'fire' (e.g., Exod. 19:16–20; 20:18). This was the model theophany for most later similar divine appearances in the Old Testament, and to some degree God's coming at Sinai stands in the background of the Spirit's coming at Pentecost.[10] The fact that Pentecost celebrated not only the firstfruits of harvest but also, beginning in the second century BC, commemoration of God's giving of the Law to Moses at Sinai points further to the presence of that background in Acts 2.[11]

If our earlier analysis of Sinai as a sanctuary is correct, then the theophany at Pentecost also may be understood as the irrupting of a newly emerging temple in the midst of the old Jerusalem temple that was passing away. This description, and the way it was developed in

---

[10] So Niehaus, 1995: *passim*, and in particular, 371; Niehaus's work traces the biblical-theological development of the Sinai theophany throughout the OT and NT.

[11] On which, e.g., see Lincoln (1990: 243–244), who also points out that Exod. 19 – 20 and Num. 17 – 18 were read during Pentecost in the synagogue liturgy.

early Judaism, is similar to that at Pentecost, where people saw 'tongues of fire being distributed' (Acts 2:3).[12] In fact, while Luke's account of Pentecost contains no direct reference to the Sinai theophany,[13] there are links and even more 'indirect allusions' than we have shown here to indicate that Luke was aware of the background of Sinai in his depiction of Pentecost.[14]

'Tongues of fire' in the Old Testament as a theophany from a heavenly sanctuary

Sinai is not the only background that portrays the image of speech in the midst of fire. The actual phrase 'tongues as of fire' occurs in two Old Testament passages. Isaiah 30:27–30 refers to God 'descending' from his temple ('a remote place' and 'the mountain of the Lord') appearing in 'dense ... smoke ... His *tongue like a consuming fire* [Theodotion reads: *hē glōssa autou hōs pur esthion*] ... in the flame of a consuming fire', and 'the Lord will cause His voice of authority to be heard'. This itself alludes to the prototypical Sinai theophany (likewise a 'tongue of fire' [Aquila, Symmachus and Theodotion read *glōssa puros*] occurs as an emblem of judgment in Isaiah 5:24–25 with allusion to the Sinai theophany).[15] The 'tongue like a consuming fire' connotes God's judgment and could be different from the same image in Acts 2 (*glōssai hōsei puros*), since there it appears to be a sign only of blessing. That the same flaming image even in Acts, however, may also allude both to blessing and judgment is apparent from the Sinai backdrop, where the fiery theophany was associated with both blessing (the giving of the Law) and judgment (for those entering too close to the theophany or rebelling: cf. Exod. 19:12–24; 32:25–29). We will see below that the background of the Joel 2 quotation in Acts 2 confirms a dual blessing–cursing theme. Consequently, Isaiah's linking of

---

[12] In this regard, Philo's first-century description of God's appearance at Sinai may not be a haphazard parallel: God's revelation came 'from heaven' being like a 'flame' (*pyr* and *phlox*) that became 'a dialect' (*dialektos*) which caused 'amazement' (Philo, *Decal.* 46, a parallel noted by several commentators; note the identical wording in Acts 2:3 and 2:6). Philo's rendering is not that far removed from the account in the book of Exodus, where 'voices' is closely linked to 'torches' of fire: 'all the people saw the voices and the torches' (Exod. 20:18; 'torches' of fire also describe a heavenly temple scene in Ezek. 1:13).

[13] Though Acts 2:3 may be an exception.

[14] So Fitzmyer 1998: 234.

[15] Niehaus 1995: 307–308. The heavenly temple scene in Is. 6 involves fiery images of God's presence resulting both in blessing (6:6) and in judgment (6:13). Note also, the combined use in Is. 5:24 and 6:6–7 of 'fire' (on which, see Ziegler 1983: 143 for Is. 6) and terms associated with the mouth (respectively 'tongue' and 'mouth'/'lips'). In this light, Is. 5:24–25 may be associated with a divine judgment coming from the heavenly temple.

'tongues of fire' to God's theophanic presence in a temple points even further to the same link in Acts 2.

Tongues in Judaism as a theophany from a heavenly sanctuary

There are some early Jewish writings that could show some awareness of or be inspired by the Old Testament image of 'tongues of fire' being associated with a divine theophany in a heavenly or earthly temple. The phrase 'tongues of fire' also occurs in these Jewish passages. Perhaps a parallel to the fiery 'tongues' of Acts 2:3 is *1 Enoch* 14:8–25.[16] There Enoch ascends in a vision to the heavenly temple. Enoch comes to the wall of the outer court that was 'surrounded by tongues of fire', and he 'entered into the tongues of fire' (14:9–10). He then enters through the holy place and is able to peer into the holy of holies, which was 'built with tongues of fire' (14:15). Likewise, in *1 Enoch* 71:5 Enoch sees a temple-like 'structure built of crystals; and between those crystals tongues of living fire'. Thus, the 'tongues of fire' form part of the heavenly temple and contribute to the overall effect of the burning theophany in the holy of holies, where 'the flaming fire was around about him, and a great fire stood before him' (14:22).

What could such a heavenly scene have to do with the earthly scene of Pentecost depicted in Acts 2? It is possible that the wording 'tongues of fire' in *Enoch* is a mere coincidental parallel to Acts 2. On the other hand, the contextual usage of the wording there may have some overlap with the use of the same phrase in Acts 2. The *Enoch* passage may possibly be a creative development of the above Exodus and Isaiah texts, which themselves appear to be developments of imagery from the Sinai theophany. In the light of this *Enoch* text, could it be that the descent of the Holy Spirit at Pentecost 'from heaven' in the form of 'tongues of fire' is to be conceived as the descent of God's tabernacling presence from his heavenly temple?[17] Since the heavenly temple is partly pictured by 'tongues of fire', it might be appropriate that the descent of that temple would be pictured with the same thing. Thus, it may be perceivable that, just as the heavenly temple was constructed of 'tongues of fire', the new temple on earth (God's people

---

[16] For the Qumran version of this portion of *1 Enoch*, see 4Q204 6.19–29, where also the phrase 'tongues of fire' occurs similarly (though in reconstruction of lacunae; see the Martínez–Tigchelaar DSS Study Edition).

[17] The Greek *glōssais pyros* ('tongues of fire') from *1 Enoch* 14:9 and 15 (as well as the almost identical 14:10) is virtually the same as *glōssai hōsei pyros* ('tongues as of fire') in Acts 2:3.

vivified by the Spirit) that had descended from heaven was beginning to be built with the same fiery image. This suggestion may gain more force when seen in the light of the other observations throughout this section which point from different angles to Pentecost as a phenomenon expressing the divine theophanic presence *in the temple*.

In addition, the Dead Sea Scrolls interpret the Urim and Thummim stones to have shone gloriously with 'tongues of fire' (1Q29). The Urim and Thummim were two stones placed in a pouch in the high priest's breastplate (Exod. 28:30; Lev. 8:8). He was to carry them 'when he enters the holy place ... before the LORD continually' (Exod. 28:29–30). Likely, these stones were one of the means by which God's prophetic revelation came. They apparently would be cast by the priest or drawn out of the pouch ceremonially, and the way they came out revealed a 'yes' or 'no' answer to the question at hand.[18] Qumran (1Q29; 4Q376) understands the Urim and Thummim to have shone with 'tongues of fire', when God gave the prophetic answer in the midst of his theophanic cloud to the high priest's question about whether a prophet is true or false.[19]

Therefore, once more we have the 'tongues of fire' as a phenomenon occurring within the 'holy of holies' or, more probably, the 'holy place' of the temple as an expression of God's revelatory presence (it might be recalled from an earlier chapter that the pouch containing the Urim and Thumim symbolized the holy of holies). This time, however, it is the earthly and not the heavenly temple that is the focus. Even more striking is that the 'tongues' is an occurrence not merely of God's revelatory presence but of his prophetic communication. This is, of course, what happens at Pentecost: not only are the 'tongues as of fire' a manifestation of God's presence in the Spirit, but that presence causes the people to 'prophesy' (as Acts 2:17–18 later makes clear). And the location from which God's Spirit descends at Pentecost must not be only generally 'from heaven' but from the heavenly holy of holies or temple, particularly when seen in the light of the descriptions in the Sinai theophany, Isaiah 5 and 30, and the later possible developments of these images in

---

[18] See Motyer (1996: 1219) for a concise explanation of the function of the Urim and Thummim in the OT. For the prophetic function of the Urim and Thummim, see, e.g., 1 Sam. 28:6: 'When Saul inquired of the LORD, the LORD did not answer him, either by dreams or by Urim or by prophets.'

[19] The Qumran text envisions the high priest discovering the prophetic revelation of the Urim and Thummim in the temple (presumably the innermost sanctuary or the holy place) and then revealing the prophetic answer to the congregation of Israel in the courtyard.

1 Enoch 14 and 71, and Qumran. Thus, all of these passages together collectively contribute from various vantage points to a picture that resembles something like God's heavenly temple descending upon his people and making them a part of it.

Two texts, both in Revelation, paint a picture similar to Pentecost, although they do not contain the phrase 'tongues of fire'. Revelation 4:5 pictures 'seven lamps of fire burning before the throne', which is interpreted to be 'the seven spirits of God' (i.e., the Spirit of God). This vision occurs within an overall scene of the heavenly temple where God sits on his throne.[20] The 'lamps of fire' themselves are conceived of as burning on the temple lampstands, which Revelation has already identified as the churches.[21] This is probably John's way of portraying the similar reality of Pentecost: the divine Spirit from the heavenly temple has descended and rested on God's people who become part of the heavenly temple on earth; that is, the lampstands. Revelation 11:3–5 even says that the purpose of the church becoming lampstands on earth is that they would 'stand before the Lord of the earth' and be 'witnesses' who 'will prophesy', and their prophetic utterance is portrayed as 'fire proceeding out of their mouth'! This is surprisingly close to Acts 2, where the Spirit from the heavenly temple descends in fire and rests upon God's people in order that they be empowered to 'witness' (Acts 1:8; 2:40) and 'prophesy' (Acts 2:17–18).

What would appear to be the building of the new spiritual temple at Pentecost included symbolic representatives of all the nations because this temple will not fail to fulfil the intention of Eden's and Israel's temples to expand its borders until the entire earth comes under its roof.

Pentecost as a fulfilment of John the Baptist's prophecy of the Spirit

Matthew 3:11 records John the Baptist proclaiming that while he 'baptizes in water', one will come after him who 'will baptize you with the Holy Spirit and fire'. Then he baptizes Jesus, after which 'the heavens were opened, and he saw the Spirit of God descending as a dove and coming upon him' (Matt. 3:16). This was Jesus' individual

---

[20] Note, e.g., the presence of the 'sea' (= the molten sea in the temple courtyard) and the cherubic-like seraphim who guard God's throne in the heavenly temple (by allusion to Ezek. 1 and 10 and Is. 6:1–4).

[21] That Rev. 4 – 5 is a temple scene becomes even more evident as the following visions expand on that initial scene (e.g., 8:3–5; 11:19; 15:5–8).

Pentecost, whereby the Spirit empowered him for his prophetic ministry. The same pattern for the latter corporate Pentecost occurs for the same purpose of prophetic empowerment. We can assume that at Pentecost the 'heavens were opened' as the Spirit descended in fire in fulfilment of Matthew 3:11.

Judaism employed the same language as Matthew 3:16 in its expectation of a priestly Messiah: 'the heavens will be opened, and *from the temple of glory* sanctification will come upon him ... And the spirit of understanding ... shall rest upon him [in the water]' (*Testament of Levi* 18:6–7). The source of the Spirit in Matthew 3 may likewise be the heavenly temple. The implicit association of the heavenly sanctuary with Jesus' reception of the Spirit in Matthew 3 is perhaps not coincidental in the light of our argument that the Spirit at Pentecost also descended from the heavenly holy of holies.

Pentecost as a fulfilment of Joel's prophecy of the Spirit

Peter explains the theophanic episode of tongues in Acts 2:1–12 to be an initial fulfilment of Joel's prophecy that God would 'pour out' his 'Spirit upon all flesh' and all classes of people in the covenant community would 'prophesy' (Joel 2:28–29). At the beginning of the Joel 2:28 quotation, Peter substitutes the phrase 'in the latter days' (*en tais eschatais hēmerais*) in place of Joel's 'after these things' (*meta tauta*). The substitution comes from Isaiah 2:2 (on which, see Pao 2000: 156–159): 'In the last days,/The mountain of the house of the Lord/Will be established as the chief of the mountains/And will be raised above the hills;/And all the nations will stream to it.' Thus, Peter appears to interpret the Spirit's coming in fulfilment of Joel to be also the beginning fulfilment of Isaiah's prophecy of the end-time temple, under the influence of which the nations would come, as we will see the book of Acts narrates.

In the Mosaic era, only prophets, priests and kings were bestowed with the gifting function of the Spirit to serve usually in the temple (i.e., priests) or in conjunction with the temple (i.e., kings and prophets). Joel and Acts do not have in mind primarily the regenerating function of the Spirit but that function which would enable people to serve in various capacities. Joel foresaw a time, however, when everyone in Israel would be given this gift. That Joel 2 and Acts may have in mind gifting for service in the new temple is apparent from recognizing that Joel's prophecy is also developing the earlier text of Numbers 11.[22]

---

[22] Dillard (2000: 87–93), who demonstrates that Joel develops Num. 11:1 – 12:8.

Moses desires that God give him help to 'bear the burden of the people' he was leading (Num. 11:11, 17; Exod. 18:13–27). God responds by telling Moses to gather 'seventy men from the elders' and to 'bring them to *the tent of meeting*, and let them take their stand there with you. Then I will come down and . . . will take of the Spirit who is upon you, and will put Him upon them' (11:16–17). Moses obeys God: 'he gathered seventy men of the elders . . . and stationed them *around the tent*. Then the LORD came down in the cloud . . . and He took of the Spirit who was upon him and placed Him upon the seventy elders. And it came about when the Spirit rested upon them, they prophesied . . .' (11:24–25). They then stopped prophesying, but two elders at another location continued to prophesy. When Joshua reports this development to Moses, demanding that he stop them, Moses declines to do so, replying: 'Would that all the LORD's people were prophets, that the LORD would put His Spirit upon them' (11:26–29).

Accordingly, Joel 2 transforms Moses' prophetic wish into a formal prophecy. Peter quotes Joel's prophecy to show that in his day it was finally being fulfilled in Pentecost. The Spirit's gifts, formerly limited to prophets, kings and priests, usually for service in connection with the temple, are universalized to all of God's people from every race, young and old, male and female. That the Spirit's gifting in Acts 2 was for service in relation to the temple is intimated by Numbers 11, which notes twice that the 'seventy elders' received the Spirit as they were gathered around the 'tent' (i.e., the tabernacle). In fact, that 'tongues of fire . . . rested on each one' and 'they were all filled with the Holy Spirit and began to speak with other tongues' (explained to be 'prophesying' in 2:17–18) may be an allusion to Numbers 11:25: 'when the Spirit rested upon them, they prophesied'.[23] Furthermore, Numbers 11:25 says that God 'took of the Spirit who was upon him [Moses] and placed Him upon the seventy elders'. Likewise, Acts 2:33 refers to Jesus as first 'having received from the Father the promise of the Holy Spirit' and then having 'poured forth' the Spirit upon those at Pentecost. In this respect, Jesus may be a second Moses figure.

Even the prophesying of the 'seventy' in Numbers 11 has links with

---

[23] See, similarly, Num. 11:29, which NA[27] cites as an allusion to Acts 2:18b. Acts 2:3b–4a also may allude to Num. 12:25–26, 29, where the 'Spirit rested upon' the elders, (cf. also 12:17). The occurrence of the 'Spirit' coming and causing 'prophesying' appears also in 1 Sam. 10:6, 10; 19:20, 23; Luke 1:67; and 2 Pet. 1:21. The preceding verses refer respectively to the gifting of a king of Israel and his official servants, to a priest in the temple and to OT prophets, thus showing the association of the Spirit's gifts in the OT only with these three classes of people.

the people prophesying in Acts 2. We have seen that the list of nations represented at Pentecost (Acts 2:9–11) are an abbreviated allusion to the seventy nations of the earth in Genesis 10, and that the Acts narrative is a further development of Luke's earlier narration of Jesus' sending of the 'seventy' to symbolize a beginning witness to the world (Luke 10:1–12). Thus the links between the seventy nations represented in Acts 2 and the 'seventy' of Numbers 11 may not be coincidental.

The manner in which God's presence comes to fill the tabernacle, temple and church enhances the plausibility that Luke is describing Pentecost as the temple for this new age. When Moses finished constructing the tabernacle, 'the cloud covered the tent of meeting, and the glory of the LORD filled the tabernacle' (Exod. 40:34),[24] and when Solomon finished building his temple, '*the cloud filled the house of the LORD* ... [and] the glory of the LORD *filled the house of the LORD*' (1 Kgs. 8:6–13). In the light of what we have said so far about Acts 2 narrating an inauguration of a new heavenly temple on earth, Acts 2:2–3 may include the Exodus 40 and 1 Kings texts in its quarry of Old Testament allusions: 'there came from heaven a noise like a violent, rushing wind, and *it filled the whole house* ... and there appeared to them tongues as of fire distributing themselves ...'[25] The Solomonic episode is particularly interesting, since the parallel in 2 Chronicles 7:1 describes the theophany as, '*fire came down from heaven* ... and the glory of the LORD filled the house ... and they gave ... praise to the LORD'. Both texts also conclude with a response of praise by the onlookers (2 Chr. 7:3, 'they gave ... praise to the LORD'; cf. Acts 2:11, 'we hear them speaking ... of the mighty deeds of God').

One additional item of relevance is the last part of the Joel 2 quotation in Acts 2:19–21:

And I will grant wonders in the sky above,
And signs on the earth beneath,
Blood, and fire, and vapor of smoke.
The sun shall be turned into darkness,
And the moon into blood,
Before the great and glorious day of the LORD shall come.
And it shall be, that everyone who calls on the name of the
LORD shall be saved.

---

[24] Exod. 40:35 repeats the wording of v. 34 nearly identically.
[25] I follow here Niehaus (1995: 202–203, 243–244) in his contention that the Exod. 40 and 1 Kgs. 8 passages are anticipations of God's descent at Pentecost and filling of his new people.

Some commentators view this part of the quotation not to have begun fulfilment at Pentecost but still yet to occur at the very end of history. Nevertheless, the language probably indicates that even this part of the prophecy started fulfilment, since Peter says 'this' (i.e., the preceding events of Pentecost in Acts 2:1–13) 'is what was spoken of through the prophet Joel' (2:16). Thus, the entire quotation should be understood as inaugurated at Pentecost. If not, then the burden of proof otherwise must be provided.[26]

That this last segment of the quotation is equally applicable to the events of Pentecost as that of the first part is apparent by observing that the very last line of the Joel quotation in Acts 2:21 ('everyone who calls on the name of the LORD shall be saved') is likely a description of those who began to be 'saved' at Pentecost (Peter says 'be saved' [2:40] and a significant group responded: 'the Lord was adding to their number day by day those who were being saved' [2:47]). Also, the concluding phrase of Acts 2:39 ('as many as the Lord our God shall call to Himself') is based on the very last phrase of Joel 2:32 ('Even among the survivors *whom the LORD calls*') which Peter stops short of quoting in Acts 2:21. This allusion to Joel in Acts 2:39 shows that the end of that prophecy did, indeed, begin at Pentecost. Finally, the allusion to Joel's 'wonders in the sky above and signs on the earth beneath' together with 'fire' (Acts 2:19) plausibly describes in part the 'noise like a violent, rushing wind' that came 'from heaven' and the 'tongues of fire' (Acts 2:2–3).

Pentecost as a fulfilment of Joel's prophecy of the destruction of the old world and emergence of a new order

One further observation about the concluding part of Joel's prophecy is that it is stock-in-trade Old Testament cosmic dissolution language. The portrayal in Joel is part of a group of similar texts: Isaiah 13:10–13; 24:1–6, 19–23; 34:4; Ezekiel 32:6–8; Joel 2:10; 2:30–31; 3:15–16; and Habakkuk 3:6–11 (possibly also Amos 8:8–9; Jer. 4:23–28; and Ps. 68:7–8). The same Old Testament texts are also influential for the portrayals of Matthew 24:29 and Mark 13:24–25, which themselves likewise formed a part of the apocalyptic quarry of passages influencing the dramatic portrayal of Revelation 6:12–14.[27] All of these references include at least four of the following elements found in Joel 2 and Acts 2: the shaking of the earth (including

---

[26] In the next section, we will see how this apocalyptic language is to be understood.

[27] *Testament of Moses* 10:3–6 and *4 Ezra* 5:4–8 (cf. 7:39–40) stand in the same OT tradition.

mountains), the darkening or shaking of the moon, stars, sun and heaven, and the pouring out of blood.

The language of these passages describes the destruction of the cosmos. Typically, the language is figurative to refer to the historical end of a sinful nation's existence through divine judgment and the emerging dominance of a victorious kingdom. God executes the judgment by employing one nation to defeat another in war. Though the tone of judgment is dominant, sometimes there is a positive aspect resulting in the deliverance or refinement of a faithful remnant (especially when Israel is the object of the judgment). Such figurative language occurred because prophets had a literal conception of the end of history, and they applied this metaphorically to the ends of various epochs or kingdoms during the Old Testament era.[28]

The uses of these same Old Testament passages in Matthew 24:29 and Mark 13:24–25 may also be figurative to indicate the end of Israel, since some of the Old Testament portrayals also indicated the same figurative end (Is. 2:19–21; 5:25; Jer. 4:23–28; Amos 8:7–10). Just as Babylon had earlier destroyed Israel, so Rome would do so again.[29] For example, Jeremiah 4:23–28 describes Israel's destruction by Babylon to be comparable to the earth becoming 'formless and void', to the heavens having 'no light' and being 'dark', and to the 'mountains . . . quaking'. It would be a 'cloudy and gloomy day' when Israel would suffer defeat (Ezek. 34:12) because God would 'make the sun go down at noon and make the earth dark in broad daylight' (Amos 8:9; cf. Jer. 15:9). Even when these texts are predominantly figurative, likely included is a literal notion of a person being destroyed,

---

[28] E.g., note the defeat of Babylon (Is. 13:10–13), Edom (Is. 34:4), Egypt (Ezek. 32:6–8), enemy nations of Israel (Hab. 3:6–11), of Israel herself (Joel 2:10, 30–31; cf. *Sibylline Oracles* 3:75–90). Other examples in the OT of figurative cosmic disruption language are: above all, 2 Sam. 22:8–16 (= Ps. 18:7–15), figuratively referring to David's victory over his enemies; Eccles. 12:1–2, referring to human death; Is. 2:19–21; 5:25, 30; Ezek. 30:3–4, 18; Amos 8:7–10; Jer. 4:23–28; Mic. 1:4–6. There are also passages where the same language could possibly be understood literally: Is. 24:1–6, 19–23; 51:6; 64:1; Ps. 102:25–26; Ezek. 38:19–20; Hag. 2:6–7; in addition, this language describes the past theophanic events at Mount Sinai (Exod. 19:18; Deut. 4:11; Pss. 68:7–8; 77:18). Interestingly, *Midrash Psalms* 104:25 says, 'Wherever the term "earthquake" occurs in Scripture it denotes the chaos between [the fall of] one kingdom and [the rise of] another.'

[29] Both Synoptic texts signal judgment on Israel in AD 70, though it is possible that they refer to the very end of history at Christ's second coming; on the synoptic passages see France (1971: 227–239), who contends for an AD 70 application, and see Carson (1995: 488–509), who opts for a second-coming reference, though he admits the cosmic destruction language could be metaphorical for the end of a political kingdom. Possibly, both are true: the events of AD 70 point typologically to the events at the very end of the world. Space does not allow discussion of this thorny problem.

whereby for such people the lights of the cosmos can no longer be seen (on which, e.g., see Eccles. 12:1–2). These destructive ends of earthly kingdoms were microcosmic examples of and pointers to the macrocosmic end.

Consequently, Peter probably understands the language of Joel 2:30–31 to have begun fulfilment figuratively at Pentecost, though part of it could literally depict the theophany described in Acts 2:2–3. If the Old Testament usage of this kind of language is determinative for Peter, then here also the wording connotes the end of one kingdom and the emergence of another. The kingdom ending is, of course, Israel, but this time it is her definitive end. Rome would destroy Jerusalem and her temple in AD 70. Joel's language of the earth's destruction in Acts 2 is also appropriate as a figurative portrayal of the temple's destruction, since, as we have seen so often earlier, the temple itself and its parts symbolized the cosmos.[30] We observed that when the temple veil, with embroidered work of the starry heavens, was torn, it was symbolic of the beginning destruction of the old creation. Acts 2 may continue a similar symbolic portrayal of destruction of the old temple, but also appears to depict believers as part of the new, descending and emerging temple because they are identified with the resurrected Christ. If they are part of the new temple, then they are part of the new creation, since the two notions are synonymous, as our Old Testament analysis in chapter 2 has demonstrated.

The destruction of Israel and her temple, however, was the mere outward expression of the judgment that had already taken place at Christ's death, resurrection and at Pentecost. Israel's rejection of Jesus sealed their fate as a nation (as elaborated already in Matt. 23:29–38). What underscores the picture in Joel 2:30–31 as figurative for Israel's final demise is the observation that the very same language was used earlier in Joel 2:10b to signify clearly the imminent destruction of Israel in the Old Testament epoch itself ('the sun and the moon grow dark'; cf. the full cosmic conflagration imagery in Joel 2:1–5, 10a, c). Rather than saying that the Joel language is used symbolically in Acts 2, it may be better to say that it indicates the real beginning destruction of the old world, represented by Israel and her temple, which begins in the spiritual realm. That is, unbelieving Israel and the temple were judged to be spiritually condemned at the time

---

[30] See Fletcher-Louis (1997: 156–164), who makes the same conclusion about the virtually identical language of Mark 13:24–25, 31!

of Jesus (e.g., Matt. 23:29–39) and Pentecost, and a generation later the destruction of her temple occurred as an expression of the earlier spiritual judgment. The consummated fulfilment of Joel 2 will express itself in the destruction of the entire physical cosmos, which the temple symbolized.

The same expression found in Joel 2:10 occurs again in Joel 3:15a ('The sun and moon grow dark') that likewise probably refers to the same reality as in Joel 2:30–31. There the appearance of the Lord comes from 'Zion', the 'holy mountain', and 'the house of the LORD'[31] (Joel 3:16–18). Joel 3 clarifies what Joel 2 may already have implied twice about the origin of revelatory cosmic destruction, since there it occurs in connection with 'Zion ... my holy mountain' (cf. 2:1–11; likewise, 2:31–32). Again, we have one more indication that theophanic revelation connected with Joel 2:30–31 comes from the heavenly temple, suggesting further that the theophany in Acts 2 also comes from the heavenly sanctuary.

Joel 2:30–32 also indicates that not only judgment but blessing results from the theophanic revelation. As we have seen, the cosmic destruction language means that judgment comes, but also often that a faithful remnant survives the judgment. Joel 2:32 says that 'whoever calls on the name of the LORD will be delivered ... There will be those who escape ... even among the survivors whom the LORD calls.' And, as we have seen, some in Acts 2 respond in faith in Christ and are 'saved'. This faithful remnant is the beginning of the new people of God, the continuation of true Israel, and, what we have argued, the initial corporate form of the new spiritual temple. On the other hand, the phenomenon of 'tongues', though a sign of blessing (as we have seen), is also a harbinger of judgment, as is the cosmic conflagration language of Joel. The association of judgment is apparent from 1 Corinthians 14:21–25, which asserts that uninterpreted tongues are a sign of judgment, as Isaiah 28:9–13 makes clear. The Isaiah text says that the 'tongues' of foreigners (i.e., the Assyrians) being heard in Israel would indicate that judgment on the nation was commencing, as the foreigners were invading to desolate the nation.[32] Likewise, the same sign of judgment is apparent with the tongues at Pentecost, though this time it indicates Israel's definitive destruction together with her temple. The voices Israel hears are not those of Assyrian

---

[31] The Targum here (= Joel 4:16–18) reads 'sanctuary of the LORD'.
[32] Robertson (1975–76: 43–53) and Grudem (1982: 194–199) see 'tongues', at least in part, to be indicating judgment in 1 Cor. 14:20–25 because of the Isaiah background.

soldiers preparing to destroy their land, but Galileans (Acts 2:7) proclaiming that the establishment of a new temple had begun.

Christ as the cornerstone of the new temple

Acts 4:11 is the most direct identification of Christ as the beginning of the new temple in the entire book of Acts: Christ is 'the stone which was rejected by you, the builders, which became the very cornerstone'. As we have noted earlier in our discussion of Matthew 21:42 and Mark 12:10, this wording is an allusion to Psalm 118, which in its original context and in the synoptics refers to the chief stone of the temple. Christ is now the cornerstone of the true temple. Acts 4:10 identifies Christ's death as the epitome of him being 'the stone which was rejected' and his resurrection as him becoming 'the chief cornerstone'. Just a few verses earlier, Luke has identified Jesus' resurrection with the beginning fulfilment of the 'blessing' promised to the 'fathers' by quoting Genesis 22:18: God says, 'to Abraham, "And in your seed all the families of the earth shall be blessed"' (Acts 3:25–26 citing Gen. 22:18). We have seen earlier the combination of the Adamic–patriarchal promise with temple building throughout Genesis, of which Genesis 22 was one of the main examples. That we find the combination again in connection with Christ is natural, since he is the commencement of the true fulfilment of that repeated promise.

Christ as the emerging new temple: Stephen's testimony

The next significant mention of the temple is in Acts 6:13–14, where the Jews bring Stephen into the court of the 'Sanhedrin', and witnesses testify that he spoke 'against this holy place ... for we have heard him say that this Nazarene, Jesus, will destroy this place and alter the customs which Moses handed down to us'.

Stephen's defence of Christ as the true temple in contrast to the old temple

Stephen begins his defence by appealing to God's appearance to Abraham, including that in Genesis 12:7a: God 'promised that He would give it [the land] to him as a possession, and to his seed after him' (Acts 7:5; see also Gen. 17:8). This was part of the Adamic commission that was reissued to Abraham in Genesis 12:1–3. Genesis 12:7 is also the first occurrence of small-scale sanctuary building by the patriarchs in combination with the Adamic promissory commission! Genesis 12:7b concludes with, 'So he [Abraham] built an altar there to the LORD who had appeared to him.' Thus, the promise to Abraham was that his seed would eventually extend the work of his own sanctuary-building activity.

But how does the introductory discussion of Abraham (Acts 7:1–7) relate to the conclusion about the rejection of Israel's temple (Acts 7:48–50)? In this respect the work of John Kilgallen on Acts 7 is helpful, for he asserts that Stephen mentions Abraham because he believed God's promise to the patriarch was essentially about the temple! Kilgallen observes that Stephen's concern about Abraham in relation to the tabernacle is apparent from the goal of the exodus and of God's promise of giving the land to Abraham's seed noted in Acts 7:7: Abraham's seed 'will come out [of Egypt] and *worship* Me in this place'! Indeed, 'worship of God in the Temple was the final reason why Abraham (and through him the Israelite nation) was ever called at all. In short, this worship was to be the fundamental reason for, and the essential quality of, the very nation itself' (Kilgallen 1976: 94). The role then of Abraham in Stephen's speech is to demonstrate 'that the temple, where Israel works out its national purpose, is a contradiction of that very nature and purpose' (1976: 94) because of its idolatry and disobedience.

After Abraham, Stephen summarizes Israel's rejection of Joseph and Moses. Israel was rebellious towards God not only during Egyptian captivity, but they became idolatrous during their wilderness sojourn. The establishment of the tabernacle and its entrance into the promised land led to David's desire to make God's dwelling in Israel permanent. This found fruition in Solomon's building of the temple. Thus the statement that 'Solomon ... built a house for Him' is the conclusion and climax of Stephen's historical narration (Acts 7:47).

In response to the climax of Solomon's building a temple for God, Stephen says, 'however, the Most High does not dwell in handmade things', and in support he quotes Isaiah 66:1–2: 'Heaven is My throne, and the earth is My footstool./Where then is a house that you could build for Me?/And where is a place that I may rest?/For My hand made all these things ...' The reference to Isaiah indicates that Stephen did not believe that Solomon's building of the temple was a sufficient fulfilment of the divine promise that a son of David would build God a temple (as announced in 2 Sam. 7:12–13, 26).[33] This is,

---

[33] Following Bruce 1954: 158.

of course, a natural corollary to the even more obvious assumption of Acts 2:29–33 that Solomon was not the ultimate fulfilment of the promise that God 'will raise up' David's 'seed ... who will come forth', and God 'will establish his kingdom' (2 Sam. 7:12).

Christ was the long-range fulfilment of this promise to David. Acts 13:22–36 will repeat this affirmation from Acts 2 (cf. Acts 13:23, 'From the seed of this man [David] according to promise God has brought to Israel a Savior, Jesus.' This same notion has been anticipated by Luke 1:32–33 (in partial allusion to 2 Sam. 7:12–16). Christ is the one who began to build the true temple composed of himself and his people.[34] Christ likewise fulfils Zechariah 6:12–13, which repeats that the messianic 'branch ... will build the temple of the LORD', and then says he 'will ... rule on His throne' and 'be a priest'.[35]

The purpose of Acts 7:46–52 is to conclude that 'as *Moses* was rejected and the people's worship became blasphemous thereby [7:20–43], so with *Christ* rejected, the *Temple worship* becomes a blasphemy' (Kilgallen 1976: 94). But there is more. Discernible in these verses also is the hope of a new temple that has arisen in place of the old.

Stephen's appeal to Isaiah 66 in defence of Christ as the true temple

The broader context of Isaiah needs some study in order to understand Stephen's use of Isaiah 66:1–2 better.[36] Isaiah 63:15 reinforces the notion that God's present true temple is only in heaven: 'Look down from heaven, and see from your *lofty dwelling place* of holiness and glory' (i.e., the temple in heaven) (Koehler and Baumgartner 1994: 263). The holy of holies represented the invisible, heavenly temple and throne of God (= Is. 66:1a), and it was the actual place where this heavenly dimension extended down to earth. In Isaiah's language, it was God's 'footstool', which precisely referred to the ark of the covenant.[37] The desire that God's heavenly temple would come

---

[34] See the similar conclusion by Bruce (1954: 158–159), though Witherington (1998: 273) does not see Stephen suggesting Jesus or the church as the new temple in Acts 7, citing Marshall in agreement; however, Marshall in a forthcoming work (c. 2006) has subsequently developed a position in time with Bruce.

[35] Similarly, *Tg. Isaiah* 53:5 says the suffering servant 'will build the sanctuary which was profaned for our sins'.

[36] The following paragraphs in this and the following section are a summarization and reapplication of earlier discussions of Is. 66:1 and Dan. 2 (see respectively pp. 133–138 and 144–153).

[37] See further Haran 1978: 255–257. The same use of 'footstool' occurs also in 1 Chr. 28:2; Pss. 99:5; 132:7; Lam. 2:1.

down and spread throughout the earth may be expressed in Isaiah 64:1–2 (esp. in the light of 63:15): 'O that Thou wouldst rend the heavens and come down, that the mountains might quake at Thy presence [cf. Exod. 19:18] ... to make Thy name known to Thy adversaries, that the nations may tremble at Thy presence.' This is a plea for a new descent of God's presence, on analogy with his revelation at Sinai and in the tabernacle at the first Exodus, to accomplish finally the divine intentions inherent in that first Exodus (so Kissane 1943: 299). The primary divine intention was that God's glorious presence would not be limited to the tabernacle (and to Moses), but be extended to all of God's true people (cf. Num. 11:24–30 discussed earlier).

We have seen that Pentecost was a Sinai-like theophany of a descending heavenly temple. Thus, the latter-day Siniatic theophany prophesied by Isaiah began fulfilment at Pentecost. The universal goal of this revelation may be alluded to in Isaiah 66:18–21, where God will make Gentiles into 'priests' and 'Levites' (so, e.g., Young 1996: 535) who will serve in the new, expanded temple. Likewise, a similar prophecy that foreigners will be priests in the temple appears in Isaiah 56:3–8.

Therefore, the future-oriented, redemptive-historical 'new Exodus' context of Isaiah 63 – 66 (indeed, of Is. 40 – 66) points strongly to Isaiah 66:1 not merely as a reference to the *entire present* cosmos being God's temple in which he dwells (*pace* Levenson 1984: 296), but that there will be a future new cosmos and temple that God will create and in which he will dwell for ever, which will be an extension of the present *heavenly* temple.

Stephen's speech in Acts 7 further supports this line of thought. Not coincidentally, he quotes Isaiah 66:1 (in Acts 7:49) as part of the climax of his answer to the charge that he had spoken 'against this holy place, and the Law' by saying that 'Jesus will destroy this place and alter the customs which Moses handed down ...' (Acts 6:13–14). This itself is an allusion to the charge against Jesus in Mark 14:58: 'We heard Him say, "I will destroy this temple made with hands, and in three days I will build another made without hands."' Hence, Stephen's comments relate to Jesus' building of the eschatological temple that began with his earthly ministry and especially his resurrection (so John 2:19–22).[38]

Stephen catches a glimpse of the new heavenly temple directly

---

[38] These events were an escalated inauguration of the restoration promises to Israel, which had begun only on a small scale with the return of a tiny remnant from Babylon; see the works of N. T. Wright (e.g., 1992b), as well as Watts 1997.

before he is stoned: 'he gazed intently into heaven and saw *the glory of God* . . . and he said, "Behold, I see *the heavens opened up* and the Son of Man standing at the right hand of God"' (Acts 7:55–56). In view of our above discussion about Isaiah 63, perhaps the prophet's plea from Isaiah 64:1 is answered for Stephen: 'if you would open the heaven' (so LXX), which we saw in Isaiah referred to the heavenly temple. Elsewhere in the Bible, the expression 'heavens were opened' together with the mention of the 'glory' of God always introduces a vision of the heavenly temple where the 'glory' of God abides.[39]

Our earlier discussion of Isaiah 57 and 66 may be relevant here (see pp. 135–137). We saw that Isaiah 66:1–2 appears to develop 57:15:

Isaiah 57:15	Isaiah 66:1–2
[15a]For thus says the high and exalted One who dwells forever, whose name is Holy, 'I dwell on a high and holy place,	[1]Thus says the LORD, 'Heaven is My throne, and the earth is My footstool. Where then is a house you could build for Me? And where is a place that I may rest? [2a]'For My hand made all these things, thus all these things came into being,' declares the LORD.
[15b]'and [I will dwell] also with the crushed and fallen of spirit in order to make alive the spirit of the fallen and to make alive the heart of the crushed.'	[2b]'But to this one I will look, to him who is afflicted and smitten of spirit, and who trembles at My word.'

[39] E.g., Rev. 15:5, 8, 'After these things I looked, and the temple of the tabernacle of testimony in heaven was opened . . . And the temple was filled with smoke from the glory of God'; so also Rev. 11:19 (cf. with 11:13); Ezek. 1:1 (cf. with 1:2–28, esp. v. 28); see almost identically Rev. 4:1 (cf. with 4:3, 11); see likewise John 1:51, which we have seen to be associated closely with the temple (cf. with John 1:14 where Christ 'tabernacled' and his 'glory' was beheld). See also *Testament of Levi* 18:6–7, a close parallel to Matt. 3:13 ('the heavens were opened, and he saw the Spirit of God descending as a dove coming upon him'): 'the heavens were opened, and from the temple of glory sanctification will come upon him . . .' Similarly, *Testament of Levi* 2:6–10 portrays Levi saying, 'And behold, the heavens were opened' directly before he enters a three-tiered heaven, which probably was a heavenly temple, since in the last tier Levi was to 'stand near the Lord' and 'be his priest'. Dumbrell (1985: 68) also understands that Stephen sees Christ in the heavenly temple.

Though the Isaiah 57 passage is probably not alluded to in Acts 7:48 ('however, the Most High does not dwell in handmade things, as the prophet says'),[40] the passage may have served as the underlying transition to Stephen's quotation of chapter 66 in verses 49–50. Isaiah 57 has importance for how Stephen's quotation of 66:1–2 relates to his vision of 'heavens [being] opened'. It is part of an eschatological prophecy about the temple (developing 56:3–8). Apparently, God will come from his heavenly sanctuary and extend it to encompass humble saints. Isaiah 66:1–2 is not some general theological or Platonic statement detached from redemptive history, but it develops 57:15. In the time to come, God will cause his heavenly temple to descend and will include 'the afflicted and smitten'.[41]

Isaiah 66:2 gives two reasons for the implied negative answer to the question of Isaiah 66:1: (1) no part of the creation can adequately house God, especially an old, sin-affected creation (Is. 66:2a); (2) in light of Isaiah 57, God will dwell only in a new creation by extending his heavenly temple to it and extend it by making multitudes of the 'afflicted and humble' participate in it through 'making them alive' (Is. 66:2b). As Stephen was being 'afflicted and smitten', he was beginning to experience the latter-day tabernacling presence of God expressed in Isaiah 57 and 66 in his midst. Perhaps, neither he nor Luke quotes the last part of Isaiah 66:2, because his experience in Acts 7:54–60 is the fulfilment of it!

Thus, not only Acts 7 but Acts 2 and 4 are better understood against the background of the later chapters of Isaiah. Levenson has shown (see pp. 25, 141, above) that the new creation and Jerusalem in Isaiah 65:17–19 are likely equivalent to the new temple. His conclusion is pointed to further by Isaiah 66:21–23, where the coming 'new heavens and the new earth' (v. 22) are given as the reason that God will 'take' Gentiles 'for priests and for Levites' (v. 21). In other words, the reason that Gentiles will be included as priests is because now the place of true worship and temple service is not geographically located in a man-made temple in the old, temporal Jerusalem, but in the entire new, eternal earth, where 'all mankind will come to bow down before Me' for ever (v. 23, which is part of the point in John 4:20–24).

---

[40] Though Richard (1978: 133) posits that Acts 7:48 alludes to Is. 57:15.

[41] See Wiens 1995: 80 for an almost identical assessment. See also the earlier discussion of Is. 66:1–2 for further analysis, including the notion that 'look' of 66:2 concerns God's issuing of blessing from his heavenly temple (in development of Bruce 1990: 212–213).

It is passages such as Isaiah 57:15 and 66:1–24 that lie behind the beginning democratization of the Spirit in Acts 2, remembering that the recipients of the Spirit at Pentecost represented the people groups of the known earth. Though those first baptized with the Spirit in fulfilment of Joel 2 were Palestinian and Diaspora Jews, as well as Gentile proselytes, the Spirit's gifting work later enveloped Samaritans (Acts 8:14–17) and other Gentiles (Acts 10:44–48; 19:1–7). It is important to recognize that Joel 2:28–32 was a prophecy of the pouring out of the Spirit *on all in Israel*, which the pronouns ('you, your') in Joel 2:28–32 demonstrate, since they are referring to the same pronouns used for Israel in Joel 2:18–27. This suggests that, based on Peter's identification of Pentecost as fulfilling Joel 2:28–32, not only ethnic Jewish Christians but also Gentile Christians are the beginning fulfilment of Spirit-filled latter-day Israel. The reason that both are identified as end-time Israel is because of their identification with and representation by Jesus Christ, the true Israel and representative of the remnant prophesied by Joel 2:32. He was, after all, the epitome of the first 'Spirit-filled' Israelite who initially fulfilled the Joel prophecy, since he received the end-time Spirit before anyone else and then passed him on to his followers (so Acts 2:33; as well as Matt. 3:16 and parallels).

Stephen's contention that God's eternal end-time temple cannot be 'handmade'

Stephen's appeal to Isaiah 66:1 is also appropriate, since that Old Testament passage itself appears to be an allusion to 1 Kings 8:27, where at the dedication of the temple, Solomon proclaims, 'heaven and the highest heaven cannot contain Thee, how much less this house which I have built'. This verse probably provided part of the transition from speaking about Solomon building the temple in Acts 7:47–48 to the quotation of Isaiah 66:1 in Acts 7:49–50. From the inception of the temple there was an unsolved paradox of God's simultaneous inability and ability to live within an earthly temple. Stephen's narrative explains that this paradox is resolved by realizing that Solomon's temple was a mere pointer to a time when God's dwelling on earth would not be limited to a 'handmade' house. Israel's physical temples were 'handmade' (Acts 7:44–47) and could never be a permanent dwelling place for God. Stephen's point in citing Isaiah 66:1 is to demonstrate that, just as God's own hand created the first cosmos that had become tainted with idolatry (cf. Acts 7:44–47 with 7:41–43 in contrast to 7:50), so God would create a new, eternal creation and Jerusalem, not by human hands but by his own hand (so Is. 65:17–19 and 66:22). This is why even Solomon's temple was not the ultimate fulfilment of the promise that David's son would build God a temple – because Solomon's temple was 'handmade'.

Isaiah 66:3–6 makes clearer that Isaiah's (and Stephen's) point is about the inadequacy of human temples *both* because of God's transcendence and their inherent association with sin. The disjunction between the old idolatrous world and God's coming new world and temple is underscored by contrasting his 'humble and contrite' people (66:2) who will dwell in the future temple with those who prefer to dwell with idols (66:3–5). These idolaters profess faith but hate the true people of God, and they will be judged by God from his heavenly temple (66:5–6). All idolatry must be removed before the new creation is ushered in. It appears that Acts 7:51–52 echoes Isaiah 66:4–5: Stephen calls the unrepentant Jews those who are 'uncircumcised in heart and ears [and] ... always resisting the Holy Spirit' and who have become 'persecutors' like their fathers of God's true 'prophets' (especially of Jesus). Likewise, Isaiah refers to Israelites who 'did not listen' when 'God called'[42] and who professed covenant loyalty but who 'hated' and 'exclude' the true people of God. If Isaiah 66:4–5 is echoed, then Stephen's Jewish enemies are also to be identified with the idolaters in Isaiah 66:3, which would fit with Stephen's earlier depiction of Israel as idolatrous (Acts 7:42–43) and his identification of the present generation with their sinful fathers (7:52).

Stephen's terminology is in line with the rest of the New Testament, where 'handmade' refers to the old creation and 'made without hands' refers to the new creation, most specifically to the resurrection state as the beginning of the new creation. The clearest expression of this is in Mark 14:58. The narrative of Stephen's speech is launched (6:14) on the basis of this saying, which later came to be written down in Mark's Gospel: 'I will destroy this temple made with hands, and *in three days I will build* another made without hands.' Likewise, Hebrews 9:11 refers to the resurrected Christ entering into the 'tabernacle, not made with hands, that is to say, not of this creation' but of the new creation; virtually identically Hebrews 9:24 asserts, 'Christ did not enter a holy place made with hands'. In Acts

---

[42] Amazingly, the Targum renders the Hebrew, 'because I called, but no one answered; I spoke but they did not listen', as 'because, when I sent my prophets, they did not repent, when they prophesied they did not attend'. This is strikingly close to Acts 7:51–52, as both serve to summarize Israel's rebellious history.

17 Paul cites the ultimate contrast being between idols that 'dwell in temples made with hands' (17:24) and Christ who was 'raised ... from the dead' (17:31). The believer who is identified with Christ also begins to exist in the new creation state: 'we have a building from God, a house not made with hands, eternal in the heavens' (2 Cor. 5:1).

The only other New Testament use of this terminology occurs in Ephesians and Colossians, where unbelieving Jews are referred to as the 'circumcision made by hand', in contrast to being God's 'workmanship, created in [the resurrected] Christ Jesus' (Eph. 2:10–11; cf. 2:5–6, 15). Conversely, believers have been 'circumcised with a circumcision made without hands ... by the circumcision of Christ; having been buried with Him in baptism, in which you were also raised up with Him through faith ...' (Col. 2:11–12).[43] This distinction finds further confirmation from Daniel's stone 'cut out without hands' (Dan. 2:34, 45) and the *Epistle of Barnabas* 16, which contrasts people in the old creation as an old 'temple built by human hands' with those who have become 'new, created again' through God's powerful dwelling presence[44] (on both Daniel and *Barnabas* see further below).

The latter part of Stephen's speech served to criticize those who did not even perceive the paradox of God's simultaneous inability and ability to exist in an earthly temple. Such people believed that God's earthly dwelling was restricted to the temple in Jerusalem. This one-sided perspective was, in fact, idolatry. The word 'handmade' (Acts 7:48) always refers to idols in the Greek Old Testament and is without exception a negative reference in the New Testament.[45] In fact, the

---

[43] This paragraph was inspired by Ellis 1994: 201. Likewise, see Juel 1977: 154–155 for the difference between 'made with hands' and 'not made with hands' being a reference to two different kinds of realities or different orders, especially as this pertains to the temple in Mark 14.

[44] Cf. also *Midrash Psalms* 90:19, which says that the 'temple having been built by the hands of mortals was destroyed ... but in the time-to-come I [God] myself shall build it ... and it will never again be destroyed'.

[45] The word *cheiropoiētos* ('handmade') occurs 14 times in the Greek OT and always refers to idols! Outside Acts 7:48, the word in the NT occurs five times, once with respect to pagan temples (Acts 17:24), three times to the Jerusalem temple that was passing away (Mark 14:58; Heb. 9:11, 24), and once with regard to physical circumcision that was not true circumcision (Eph. 2:11). The wording 'the work of men's hands' in the Greek OT refers without exception to idols (these observations follow Moule, 1950: 34). Among the approximately 54 times the Hebrew phrase 'work of the hands' (*ma'āseh* + *yād*) occurs, almost half refer to idolatrous works: Deut. 4:28; 27:15; 31:29; 2 Kgs. 19:18; 22:17; 2 Chr. 32:19; 34:25; Pss. 115:4; 135:15; Is. 2:8; 17:8; 37:19; Jer. 1:16; 10:3; 25:6–7, 14; 32:30; Hos. 14:3; Mic. 5:13; Rev. 9:20; cf. Is. 44:9–10.

only other use in Acts refers to an idolatrous pagan temple: 'the Lord of heaven and earth does not dwell in temples made with hands' (Acts 17:24)![46] Further, Acts 19:26 uses a synonymous expression in quoting Paul as 'saying that gods being manufactured with hands are no gods', which includes a condemnation of small 'temples' (*naous*) for idols (Acts 19:24). Stephen's reference to the idolatrous golden calf being the result of 'the works of their hands' only a few verses earlier (Acts 7:41) makes it probable that Stephen has idolatry in mind in verse 48 (Kilgallen 1976: 90).

As in the Old Testament uses of 'handmade', Stephen's use serves to belittle that which is idolatrous.[47] This takes on significance when it is remembered that even the priests 'defiled' Solomon's temple with the idols of the nations (2 Chr. 36:14). This notion is enhanced by a Jewish tradition that understood Isaiah 66:1 to be a response by Isaiah to King Manasseh's erecting of an idol in the temple.[48] In addition to the fact that human-created structures inherently could not serve as a permanent residence for God, when these structures become defiled with 'handmade' idols, not only can God not live in them, but they must eventually be destroyed (on which cf., e.g., 2 Kgs. 22:17; Is. 2:5–22; Jer. 25:6–14; Mic. 5:13).[49]

---

[46] Cf. also Kilgallen (1976: 93), who contends that Acts 17:24ff. 'may be the closest area of thought that we can offer as background for Chapter 7'.

[47] See Walker (1996: 10, 66–67), whose discussion of the significance of 1 Kgs. 8:27 in relation to Is. 66:1 for the most part I have followed.

[48] Thornton (1974: 432–434) cites a late Aramaic midrash on Is. 66:1 to this effect, which also says that Manasseh killed Isaiah for announcing this prophecy. Thornton thinks that if the midrashic tradition existed in the first century, it may have provided the transition between the tabernacle and temple in Acts 7:44–50 and the topic of the prophets' being persecuted in v. 52.

[49] Sylva (1987) argues that Acts 7:45–46 is only an affirmation 'of God's transcendence over the temple' rather than a denunciation of the temple or replacement of the temple by Christ. My argument, on the other hand, is that all three of these are in mind. The high points of my disagreement with Sylva's argument rests on: (1) his understanding of the use of 1 Kgs. 8:27 (= 2 Chr. 6:18b) in Acts 7:49–50 to the exclusion of any attempt to understand the Is. 66:1–2 citation there and (2) his belief that the use of Mark 14:58 in Acts 6:14 carries with it no implicit reference to Christ's resurrection from Mark 14:58 (which is difficult to accept, especially because of the allusion to Christ's resurrection saying from Mark 14:62 and 16:19 [cf. also Matt. 16:64; Luke 22:69] in Acts 7:55–56); (3) the redemptive-historical connotations in the NT of 'handmade' vs. 'made without hands'; (4) the organic links with Acts 15:16–18 and 17:24–25, on which see below. On the other hand, Simon (1951: 127–142) goes too far the other way and believes that Stephen held that the very existence of the temple was not God-ordained, but idolatrous from the very beginning of its construction by Solomon. Marshall (forthcoming, c. 2006) grants the possibility of Sylva's view but does not see how it could constitute a plausible answer to the charge against Stephen that Christ would destroy the temple (Acts 6:14); he sees that a better answer is the contention that there would be a new temple to replace the old.

We discovered earlier that the stone-mountain of Daniel 2 and the prophesied eschatological temple are linked in that both are not made by human hands. As we have also seen, the New Testament repeatedly refers to the new, end-time temple as 'not made with hands' (in addition to Acts 7:48, see Mark 14:58; 2 Cor. 5:1; Heb. 9:11, 24). The image in the Old Testament corresponding closest to this is Daniel's stone 'cut out without hands' (Dan. 2:34, 45). We have already found that it is not surprising that Christ identifies himself with the stone of Daniel, the true temple (Luke 20:17–18 = Matt. 21:42). Accordingly, Paul affirms that 'The God who made the world and all things in it, since He is Lord of heaven and earth, does not dwell in temples made with hands' (Acts 17:24). Paul says this after the great redemptive-historical divide when Christ and his people had begun to replace Israel's idolatrous 'handmade' temple. There could be no human-made structures separating God and his people in order that he dwell fully and unfettered with them. This is why no human can answer affirmatively God's question about his eschatological, eternal dwelling, 'Where then is a house you could build for Me?' (Is. 66:1).

Even before the early Christian evidence, Daniel's stone 'not cut by human hands' (Dan. 2:34, 45) may have resonated with cultic implications because the only other references to 'uncut stones' are in Exodus, Deuteronomy and Joshua, where Israel was to build 'an altar of *uncut stones* [literally 'whole stones'], on which no man had wielded an iron tool', and 'they offered burnt offerings ... and sacrificed peace offerings' (so Josh. 8:31 in fulfilment of Exod. 20:25).[50] Similarly, 1 Kings 6:7 says that Solomon's temple 'was built of stone prepared at the quarry, and there was neither hammer nor axe nor any iron tool heard in the house while it was being built'. This description of the silence of human tools during the construction of Solomon's temple may be a subtle pointer to the ultimate temple which would be made completely without human hands.

The Daniel stone may also have represented a sacred antithesis of the image that it smashed. The stone smashes the statue which is repeatedly said to be made of 'gold, silver, bronze, iron, and clay' (Dan. 2:31–45) and which symbolized the ungodly nations. The only other times the same combination of four metals are listed together are in Daniel 5:4, 23, where they refer to Babylonian idols! We have argued directly above and in an earlier chapter that the stone 'not cut by human hands' is the beginning form of the new temple. If that identifi-

---

[50] Deut. 27:6, Exodus and Daniel all use cognate forms of *temnō* + *lithos*.

cation is correct, then what we have in Daniel 2 is the divine undefiled temple replacing the world-system's impure worship of idols.

Interestingly, the *Sibylline Oracles*, a Jewish work (c. AD 80), affirms a similar notion, perhaps as a result of contemplating the recent destruction of Jerusalem's temple in AD 70: 'the great God, whom no hands of men fashioned ... does not have a house, a stone set up as a temple ... but one which it is not possible to see from the earth nor to measure with mortal eyes, since it was not fashioned by mortal hand' (*Sibylline Oracles* 4:6–11). Consequently, God's true people 'will reject all temples when they see them; altars too, useless foundations of dumb stones' (*Sibylline Oracles* 4:27–28). Philo likewise affirms the inability of created structures to house the divine presence: 'What house shall be prepared for God ...? Shall it be of stone or timber?' (*Cherub.* 100). Even pagans seemed to perceive this truth: 'What house built by craftsmen could enclose the form divine within enfolding walls?' (Euripides, *Fragment* 968).[51]

To sum up the point of this section so far, we may say that God's intention is one day to fill every part of his creation with his presence because he is the Creator. God's holy presence could not fully dwell in human-made structures of the old creation both because of his transcendence and because it was a sin-tainted world. Hence, his special revelatory presence dwelt in a limited manner in human-made structures. But when he fully redeems the world and recreates it (so Rom. 8:18–25), he will fill the entire creation with his presence and dwell in it in a fuller way than ever before.[52]

As discussed earlier, we may assume that God created the cosmos to be his great temple in which he rested after the creative work. Nevertheless, his unique revelatory glory did not fill the entire earth yet, since it was his intention that this goal be achieved by his human vice-regent whom he installed in the garden sanctuary to extend the cultic boundaries of God's presence worldwide. Adam, of course, disobeyed this mandate, so humanity no longer enjoyed God's presence, as they had in Eden. In addition, the entire earth became infected with sin and idolatry in a way it had not been previously even during its still imperfected, newly created state. Israel's failure not to expand

---

[51] See Bruce 1954: 357 for the quotation. For convenient access to a version of this fragment, see Charlesworth 1983: 827.

[52] Pagans also partially perceived this truth: 'the universe is a most holy temple and most worthy of a god' (Plutarch, *Ethical Essays* 477:C); 'the whole world is the temple of the gods, and, indeed, the only one worthy of their majesty and grandeur' (Seneca, *On Benefits* 7.7.3). Cf. similarly Cicero, *On the Nature of the Gods* 3:26.

the borders of the temple and the light of God's presence throughout the world (cf. Is. 42:6; 49:6) was a failure in falling short in fulfilling the original divine intention of the temple, and this disobedience became bound up with their idolatrous rebellion. Therefore, in the light of Adam's and Israel's failures, the statements about God's inability to dwell in any structure on earth plausibly include reference to the old creation and temple, not only being tainted with idolatry but also requiring divine purification and recreation. Such a purgation would prepare the way for God's glorious presence, formerly limited to heaven and the holy of holies, to dwell universally throughout creation,[53] by means of a divinely made temple.

Early Christian evidence confirming the above interpretation of Isaiah 66 in Stephen's speech

The *Epistle of Barnabas* also cites Isaiah 66:1 in connection with the notion of 'handmade things' and gives an interpretation along the lines given by Stephen, though even more explicitly:

> I will also speak to you about the temple, and how those wretched men went astray and set their hope on the building, as though it were God's house, and not on their God who created them. For they, almost like the heathen, consecrated him by means of the temple. But what does the Lord say in abolishing it? Learn! 'Who measured heaven with the span of his hand, or the earth with his palm? [Is. 40:12] Was it not I, says the Lord? Heaven is my throne, and the earth is a footstool for my feet. What kind of house will you build for me, or what place for me to rest?' [Is. 66:1] You now know that their hope was in vain. Furthermore, again he says: 'Behold, those who tore down this temple will build it themselves'. This is happening now. (*Barnabas* 16:1–3)

The author is explicit that Isaiah 66 indicates that Israel's old temple had become idolatrous and had to be abolished. He even paraphrases Jesus' own words 'destroy this temple and in three days I will raise it up' (e.g., John 2:19) by interpreting it of the Gentiles who tore down the temple in AD 70, and also are rebuilding the church in

---

[53] This perspective is not far from that of Michel, '*naos*', *TDNT*, 4:886, who cites and follows Schlatter in affirming that it is impossible that a handmade temple could ever be the eschatological temple (especially in the light of Mark 14:58; Acts 7:48; Rev. 21:22).

Christ. It is likely this thought that leads directly to the next section of the epistle:

> But let us inquire whether there is in fact a temple of God. There is – where he himself says he is building and completing it! . . . I discover, therefore, that there is in fact a temple. How, then will it be built in the name of the Lord? Learn! Before we believed in God, our heart's dwelling-place was corrupt and weak, truly a temple built by human hands, because it was full of idolatry and was the home of demons, for we did whatever was contrary to God. 'But it will be built in the name of the Lord' . . . How? Learn! By receiving the forgiveness of sins and setting our hope on the Name, we became new, created again from the beginning. Consequently God truly dwells in our dwelling-place – that is, in us. How? The word of faith . . . opening to us who had been in bondage to death the door of the temple . . . he leads us into the incorruptible temple (*Barnabas* 16:6–9).

After speaking of Israel's temple as idolatrous and doomed to destruction, the passage asserts that those who are not truly God's people are as idolatrous as (presumably) Israel's or any pagan 'temple built by human hands', since they are unbelieving, disobedient, and a part of the 'corrupt and weak' old creation. Such people may become part of the new temple being built by God through believing in the Lord and 'receiving the forgiveness of sins'. Then they become 'created again' and part of God's 'incorruptible temple'.

The *Barnabas* passage seems to be an expanded interpretation of Acts 7:48–51, as the author even alludes to the 'destruction of the temple' (*Barnabas* 16:2–3) in Acts 6:14. Barnabas does not develop so much the idea that God's transcendence prohibits his dwelling in human structures, but focuses on that part of Stephen's argument concerning the old temple as an unfit place for God's dwelling because of its idolatrous nature. If this epistle is not reflecting directly on Acts 7, it is remarkably similar to its concepts and, especially, to that part which disavows the continuing validity of the temple because of its idolatrous taint. Barnabas too quotes Isaiah 66 to indicate that Israel's temple had to be jettisoned because it was 'handmade' and had become idolatrous and the people disobedient, and in its place Christ and his people formed a new temple.

Paul's contention that a permanent temple for God's presence cannot be 'handmade'

Brief reference has been made above to Paul's speech in Athens, which is relevant for further elaboration. Acts 17:24–25 explains that in the present age people are not to fulfil the commission of Genesis by building material temple structures and finding God there: 'The God who made the world and all things in it, since He is Lord of heaven and earth, does not dwell in temples made with hands; neither is He served by human hands, as though He needed anything, since He Himself gives to all life and breath and all things.'

Not only are man-made temples inadequate to house the divine presence permanently (v. 24) but also such structures imply that God needs to be 'served by human hands'. This is an impossibility, since God is the self-sufficient Creator of everything (v. 25). Furthermore, one would be quite mistaken to think that God's presence is to be found behind idols of 'gold or silver or stone, an image formed by the art and thought of man' (v. 29). The reason for this is that humans were created to be God's sons (i.e., 'the offspring of God'). Just as children reflect the image of their parents, so God's children should reflect him, which they do by reflecting the glorious attributes of his 'divine nature' (cf. Gen. 1:27) and not by not reflecting the unspiritual nature of handmade idols. Paul's logic is simple: 'if like begets like, it is illogical to suppose that the divine nature that created living human beings is like an image made of an inanimate substance' (Larkin 1995: 259).

Acts 17:26–31 is a fitting summary of how humanity is to fulfil their Adamic commission in a post-fall world[54] in relation to temple building (though here it is pagan temple construction that is negatively assessed [v. 24] to make the point):

> and He made from one, every nation of mankind to live on all the face of the earth, having determined their appointed times, and the boundaries of their habitation, that they should seek God, if perhaps they might grope for Him and find Him, though He is not far from each one of us . . . 'Therefore having overlooked the times of ignorance, God is now declaring to men that all everywhere should repent, because He has fixed a

---

[54] Larkin (1995: 257) sees Acts 17:26 to be alluding to 'God's design . . . for various cultures . . . to cover the face of the earth . . .' (citing Gen. 1:28; 9:1, 7; 10:5, 20, 31–32).

day in which He will judge the world in righteousness through a Man whom He has appointed, having furnished proof to all men by raising Him from the dead.'

Paul says that God has caused humanity to spread out (presumably from Babel)[55] in order 'that they should seek God', and that since the coming of Christ they may 'seek' and 'find' him by repenting and trusting in the resurrected Christ. If they do this, he will not judge them.

If 'all men everywhere should repent', then the Adamic commission would finally be fulfilled. That the Genesis 1:28 commission is in the background receives confirmation from noticing that Acts 17:25 alludes to Genesis 1:29 and 2:7 (see Greek OT): 'I [God] have given to you every seed-bearing herb' (Gen. 1:29), and God 'breathed upon his face the breath of life' (Gen. 2:7).[56] Both of these Genesis passages are elaborations of Genesis 1:28.

The phrase 'For we also are his offspring' (Acts 17:28) is a quotation from the Greek poet Aratus (*Phenomena* 5), the immediate context of which is amazingly similar to the goal of Adam's commission, that God's presence would fill the entire cosmos: 'all ways are full of Zeus and all meeting-places of men; the sea and the harbours are full of him. In every direction we all have to do with Zeus.'[57] Paul has taken a pagan affirmation about a false god and applied it to the true God, whom it truly describes, and possibly to his original universal intentions.[58] Thus, biblical writers often 'plunder the Egyptians'[59] in this manner.

It is thus remarkable to find the Acts 17 passage combining

[55] Witherington (1998: 527) sees the second part of Acts 17:26 as an echo of the tower of Babel event and an allusion to Deut. 32:8 ('When the Most High gave the nations their inheritance,/When He separated the sons of man,/He set the boundaries of the peoples/According to the number of the sons of Israel'). Deut. 32:8 of the Palestinian Targum (Etheridge 1968) explicitly alludes to the Babel episode.

[56] The allusion of Acts 17:25 may include Gen. 9:3, where the restatement of Adam's commission to Noah in Gen. 9:1–7 includes the expression 'I have given all things to you,' and occurs as part of the means by which the commission is to be carried out (9:3), being introduced (9:1) and concluded (9:7) by 'be fruitful and multiply, and fill [populate] the earth'! Larkin (1995: 257) cites Gen. 1:29; 2:7; and 9:3 as parallels. Witherington (1998: 526) also sees allusion to Gen. 1:27–28 and 2:7 in Acts 17:26.

[57] Citing Bruce's translation (1954: 360) instead of Loeb.

[58] The Aratus quotation probably pertains to the divine omnipresence of Zeus, but, in the light of the Gen. 1 allusions in the immediate context of Acts 17, Paul may well also have transformed the universal descriptions about Zeus in terms of God's ultimate intentions to fill the earth with his glorious rule.

[59] This phrase has become proverbial in referring to those times when Christians benefit from the unbelieving world's labours, which are accomplished under the beneficent hand of God.

allusions to the Genesis commission and to temple themes, a combination we have found often elsewhere in the Old Testament and Gospels. Also noteworthy in this regard is that this text has unique connections with Acts 7:46–50 and 15:16–17, passages that discuss Israel's outmoded temple and the eschatological temple.[60] Acts 17 then appears to develop further the theme of these earlier passages. Though we have not yet directly addressed the Acts 15 passage, we now turn our attention to it in the next section.

Christ as the emerging new temple: James's testimony

Another possible reference to a new temple in Acts is the quotation of Amos 9:11–12 in Acts 15:16–17: 'After these things I will return, and I will rebuild the tabernacle of David which has fallen, and I will rebuild its ruins, and I will restore it, in order that the rest of mankind may seek the LORD, and all the Gentiles who are called by My name.'[61] Amos prophesied concerning what God would do after Israel's captivity, when he would restore them. While this is a hope to rebuild Jerusalem, it also pertains to the rebuilding of Israel's 'tabernacle' or temple. James's quotation of Amos supports the earlier testimony of Peter, Paul and Barnabas that Gentiles are 'saved through the grace of the Lord Jesus' (v. 11) and by God 'cleansing their hearts by faith' (v. 9) and not by the old Law (v. 10). Moreover, the 'signs and wonders ... among the Gentiles' (v. 12) were evidence that God was 'giving them the Holy Spirit, just as He did to' believing Jews because their faith also made them 'clean' (v. 8). That obedience to the Mosaic laws of cleanness and uncleanness could no longer 'cleanse' people had been shown to Peter in a vision (Acts 10:11–16) and demonstrated in the experience with Cornelius, the Roman (Acts 10:17–48).

James interprets Peter's witness (15:7–11) to be an explanation of 'how God first concerned Himself about taking from among the Gentiles a people for His name' (15:14). Gentiles could become 'clean' and become true end-time Israelites by receiving Joel's prophesied

---

[60] Hemer (1990: 190) notes that Stephen's critique of God dwelling in 'temples made with hands' (Acts 7:48) influenced Paul's virtually identical critique of pagan temples (Acts 17:24). In addition, the combination of 'men' and 'all nations' who 'seek God [or the Lord]' (and Greek equivalents) occurs only in Acts 15:17 and 17:26–27.

[61] See below for discussion of why Acts follows the LXX here instead of the Hebrew text, though no solution is without problems.

Spirit by faith without having to keep the Law (vv. 5, 10). Thus, while the whole Law is in mind, it is the laws of cleanness and uncleanness that are uppermost in mind. When James says that Gentiles must 'abstain from things contaminated by idols and from fornication and from what is strangled and from blood' (v. 20; see v. 29), he is not imposing Mosaic food laws on them, but telling them to abstain from idolatry in order to be spiritually 'clean' in the new age. Each of the four things Gentiles are to stay away from are connected to the worship of idols, the first, third and fourth referring to the animal sacrifices offered to idols ('fornication' may refer to cult prostitution or merely to immorality, in which all Christians must not participate).

But how does James's quotation of Amos 9 support the earlier contention that Gentiles' hearts are 'cleansed by faith' and not by obedience to the Old Testament laws of uncleanness? The laws about uncleanness were primarily aimed at revealing who was not clean to dwell within the perimeter of Israel's camp and who could come into the outer court of the tabernacle to worship God. James's quotation demonstrates that Gentiles are now to be considered clean for entrance into and worship in the 'tabernacle' without keeping the Mosaic uncleanness laws, which Peter notes is 'a yoke that neither we nor our fathers have been able to bear' (v. 10). The reason is that their 'hearts are cleansed by faith' in Christ. He took the penalty of their sinful uncleanness upon himself: through Christ 'forgiveness of sins is proclaimed ... and through Him everyone who believes is declared righteous from all things, from which you could not be declared righteous through the Law of Moses' (Acts 13:38–39). Therefore, because believers have 'died with Christ' and have become clean in him, they no longer have to worry about 'submitting ... to decrees, such as, "Do not handle, do not taste, do not touch!"' (Col. 2:20–21).

Christ's resurrection as the rebuilding of Israel's fallen temple

Christ's resurrection is most likely to be seen as the beginning fulfilment of the Amos 9:11–12 prophecy that God would 'rebuild the tabernacle of David which has fallen ... in order that the rest of mankind may seek the LORD'. Jesus is the latter-day cosmic tabernacle in which not only believing Jews but also Gentiles throughout the cosmos may worship. Since all are 'cleansed' in him and not by Mosaic laws of uncleanness, they also are considered clean for worship in him as the temple. Likewise, physical circumcision is no longer necessary for membership in true Israel nor for entrance to the temple not made 'by human hands' (Acts 7:48) because believers have been 'circumcised with a circumcision made without hands, in the removal of the body of the flesh *by the circumcision of Christ* [i.e., his death]' (Col. 2:11).

That Christ's resurrection is the realization of the prophecy that God would 'rebuild the tabernacle of David' is apparent from several observations. Luke's reference to 'David' elsewhere in Acts is always linked to the prophetic expectation of the Messiah's coming, especially the resurrection fulfilled in Jesus. Acts 13:22–23 says that 'from the seed' of David 'according to promise, God has brought to Israel a Savior, Jesus', thus showing that the promise of 2 Samuel 7:12–13 had a more ultimate fulfilment than Solomon: 'I will raise up your seed after you . . . and I will establish his kingdom . . . forever.' Only a few verses later in Acts 13:34, the fulfilment of the Davidic 'promise' focuses on Jesus' resurrection: 'that He [God] raised Him up from the dead, no more to return to decay, He has spoken in this way: "I will give you the holy and sure blessings of David"' (quoting the prophecy of Is. 55:3). Psalm 16:10, a Davidic psalm, is then quoted in support (already cited by Peter to make the same point in Acts 2:27), which foresaw Christ's resurrection: 'Thou wilt not allow Thy Holy One to undergo decay' (Acts 13:35). Likewise the allusions to David in Acts 2 refer to Jesus fulfilling David's prophecy that his seed would rule, after having been raised from the dead (Acts 2:24–36, where Luke explicitly mentions 'David' three times in this connection).[62]

Hence, in the passages of Acts in the preceding paragraph, the name 'David' is primarily associated with Jesus' resurrection as a fulfilment of prophecy, though events surrounding Jesus' death are likewise found. The last mention of David outside of Acts 15 is in 7:45–47, which we discussed briefly above and now draw out further implications in the light of Acts 13 and 15. We have seen that Solomon's building of the temple is the climax of Stephen's survey of Old Testament history (Acts 7:47). Stephen does not see, however, that Solomon's temple was the final fulfilment of God's promise that David's 'seed' would 'build a house for My name' (2 Sam. 7:12–13, 26). No human-built structure could contain the manifestation of God's presence in his eschatological temple (Acts 7:48). To confirm this Stephen appeals to Isaiah 66:1–2, where the rhetorical question

---

[62] Two other places in Acts where David's name occurs are Acts 1:16 and 4:25–28, which respectively mention David's prophecy that one of the Messiah's associates would betray him and that opposition to him would come from both the nations and the covenant community of Israel.

'Where then is a house you could build for Me?' must be answered negatively, since no sinful human could ever construct a dwelling that could properly house the Creator's presence in the eternal new creation.

Just as Christ's resurrection was the long-range fulfilment that God would 'establish the kingdom' of the Davidic 'seed ... who will come forth' (2 Sam. 7:12), so the promise in the same verse of 2 Samuel 7 about this descendant building a temple likewise discovers its distant realization in Christ's resurrection. The reason that Solomon's kingdom and temple also could not be the completion of the prophecy is that the prediction says that the fulfilment would last 'forever' (2 Sam. 7:13)[63] and that the temple would be made by God himself without human involvement (2 Sam. 7:11b: '*the LORD will make a house* for you'). Solomon's kingdom and temple, on the other hand, were made by human hands and did not last 'forever', even though early Jewish thought believed that it would![64] 2 Samuel 7:10–13 is itself developing Exodus 15:17–18, which also prophesies concerning 'the sanctuary' that God's 'hands have established' and predicts that 'the LORD shall reign [there] forever and ever'.[65] Note, again, the emphasis on the temple being made by divine 'hands' and not human hands, and God's rule being there for ever. God's construction of the temple without human help in the new creation will last for ever.[66] What humans build is by nature temporary.

Given Luke's prior association of 'David' primarily with Christ's resurrection, James's quotation of the prophecy that God would 'rebuild the tabernacle of David' (Acts 15:16) also refers to Christ's resurrection, which opened the gates 'that the rest of mankind may seek the Lord' (Acts 15:17). The use of the Amos citation is probably a direct development of Acts 13, where 'David' is referred to four times, especially with a view to fulfilment of David's prophecies in Jesus' resurrection. The events of Christ's resurrection and ascent

[63] I have noted already the possibility that the Hebrew word '*ôlām* could refer to a limited temporal period, however long or short, though it is more likely that in this passage 'eternal' is the better rendering (see p. 109).

[64] *Sirach* 47:13; *Tobit* 1:4; even as some believed the second temple would endure for eternity (*Sirach* 49:12).

[65] Likewise, 1 Sam. 2:35 is echoed: 'I [God] will raise up for Myself a faithful priest ... and I will build him an enduring house, and he will walk before My anointed always.'

[66] Judaism highlighted this by saying that God would 'build the temple [of Exod. 15:17] ... with his two hands' (*Mekilta de-Rabbi Ishmael*, *Tractate Shirata* 10.40–42). *Midrash Psalms* 90 says that 'the temple having been built by the hands of mortals was destroyed ... but in the time to come I Myself shall build it ... and it will never again be destroyed'.

inaugurated his heavenly reign, as well as his establishment of the new temple, of which his Jewish and Gentile followers are able to become a part. The statement about 'rebuilding the tabernacle of David' appears to be the answer about 'what kind of a house will you build for me?' from Acts 7:49 (and Is. 66:1). No human can build an adequate structure to house God's presence in the eternal new order; only God can do so, which he began to do when he raised Jesus from the dead and inaugurated the new cosmos. Again, we see in Acts 15:16 the equation of Jesus' resurrection, which is new creation, with 'building a temple'. The best rationale for the equation is remembering that the Old Testament tabernacle and temple were symbolic of the new cosmos to come in which God could dwell fully.

It becomes further apparent that the '*tabernacle* of David' in Acts 15:16 is the new temple when one recalls that the only other uses of 'tabernacle' (*skēnē/skēnōma*) in Acts refer to one of three things: Israel's tabernacle in the wilderness (Acts 7:44), the more permanent subsequent temple (Acts 7:46) or to idolatrous tabernacles of worship (Acts 7:43). Particularly interesting is that Acts 7:46 says that David 'asked [God] that he might find a *dwelling place* [*skēnōma*] for the God of Jacob'. Hence, David's request was not granted him but was first given to Solomon, yet his temple fell. Ultimately, David's request to build a permanent temple for God is granted, not to Solomon, but to the greatest son of David, Jesus, who erects a permanent temple.[67] This organic connection between Acts 7:46–50 and Acts 15:16 is indicated by the similar conceptual discussions and the telltale use of the words 'build' and 'tabernacle' together with 'David' in both passages.[68] The word *skēnē* also is the technical term for 'tabernacle' in the Greek Old Testament, especially in the Pentateuch where it occurs often with this sense.[69]

Similarly, the same word *skēnē* in Hebrews alludes either to Israel's tabernacle (Heb. 8:5; 9:2–3, 6, 8, 21) or to the new, heavenly tabernacle associated with Christ, of which the physical tabernacle was but

---

[67] See Cole 1950: 46–50. That Jesus also participated in the rebuilding together with God is apparent from, among other texts, John 10:18, where he says with regard to his resurrection, 'I have authority to lay it [his life] down, and I have authority to take it up again'. Yet, the Father also raised Jesus from the dead.

[68] Though *skēnōma* occurs in Acts 7, while *skēnē* appears in Acts 15, even in the LXX the two words can be synonymous in referring to the tabernacle of God (so 1 [3] Kgs. 2:28; 8:4). In addition, note the use of *oikodomeō* twice in Acts 7:47–49 and the use of *anoikodomeō* twice in 15:16.

[69] The Hebrew word *sukkâ*, rendered 'hut' or 'tabernacle' in Amos 9, can also refer to God's earthly tabernacle (2 Sam. 11:11) or heavenly tabernacle (Is. 4:5–6; perhaps also 2 Sam. 22:12 in comparison to verse 7).

'a copy and shadow' (Heb. 8:2; 9:11; 13:10; so also Rev. 13:6). In striking affinity with our interpretation of Acts 7 and 15, Hebrews 8:1–2 directly links Christ's having 'taken His seat at the right hand of the throne ... in the heavens' with 'the true tabernacle, *which the Lord pitched, not man*'! The Hebrews passage likely understands Jesus' resurrection and ascent to heaven as the establishing of the temple in which he also ministers as a priest. The phrase 'which the Lord pitched, not man' underscores that the new temple is 'the greater and more perfect tabernacle, not made with hands, that is to say, not of this creation' (Heb. 9:11) but built by God in the inaugurated new creation. The discussion in Hebrews fits admirably into the analysis of Acts 7 and 15, where the Solomonic temple was an imperfect human-made realization of the prophecy that a descendant of David would build a temple, and which has found fulfilment on a grander scale in Christ's resurrection.

Qumran also apparently understood that the prophecy of Amos 9:11 was about the building of the end-time temple: 'This is the Branch of David who will arise with the Seeker of the Law and who will sit on the throne of Zion at the end of days; as it is written, *I will raise up the tabernacle of David which is fallen*. This *tabernacle of David which is fallen* (is) he who will arise to save Israel' (4QFlor 1, 11b–13). Amazingly, the writer appears to identify the Messiah with the new eschatological temple.[70] What is especially striking is that this same Qumran document[71] equates the future fulfilment of the Amos 9 prophecy with the fulfilment of the temple prophecies of respectively Exodus 15:17 and 2 Samuel 7:11–13, both of which we have also seen to be connected to the Amos quotation in Acts:

> this is the house [will be built at the e]nd of days; as it is written
> in the Book of [Moses, *In the sanctuary, O Adonai,*] *which thy
> hands have established, Yah*[*w*]*eh will reign forever and ever.*
> (4QFlor 1.2)

> '[*And*] *Yahweh* [*de*]*clares to thee that He will build thee a house;*

---

[70] The Qumran *Damascus Document* (CD 7.15–16) also quotes Amos 9:11 and identifies 'the hut of David which is fallen' as the law that will be re-established in Israel. This might not be so unrelated to the identification in 4QFlorilegium as might first appear, since, as discussed in an earlier section, the 'wisdom' of the law was understood to reside in the temple, from which all ethical life was to be ordered. Further connection between the two passages is that the erection of the temple in 4QFlorilegium occurs when the 'Seeker' or 'Interpreter of the Law' also arises.

[71] 4QFlor 1.2, 10–11.

*and I will raise up thy seed after thee, and I will establish his royal
throne [forev]er'*. (4QFlor 1.10–11)

As did Luke, Qumran understood these two prophecies,[72] like
Amos 9:11, to look forward not merely to Solomon's temple but to
the more distant latter-day temple.[73] Later Judaism also interpreted
Amos 9:11 to be the eschatological temple.[74]

The Old Testament background for the Gentiles' relationship to Christ's rebuilt temple

It is important to point out that James introduces the quotation of
Amos 9:11 by saying, 'with this the words of the *Prophets* agree, just
as it is written' (Acts 15:15). This indicates that James has in mind
more than merely one Old Testament passage. In fact, it is apparent
that he weaves into the Amos citation, at least, two other Old
Testament texts: Hosea 3:5 (LXX) and Jeremiah 12:15–16 (LXX):

And *after these things* the children of Israel shall *return* and
shall seek the Lord their God and *David* their king. (LXX of
Hosea 3:5)

And it shall be that, *after* I have cast them [the Gentiles] out, *I
will return* and have mercy on them, and will cause them to
dwell, each in his inheritance and each in his land. And it shall
be that, if they will indeed learn the way of my people, to swear
by my name, 'The Lord lives', as they taught my people to
swear by Baal, then also they *shall be built* in the midst of my
people. (LXX of Jer. 12:15–16)

Hosea 3:5 promises the restoration of Israel and her king, which
implicitly includes the rebuilding of the temple, since verse 4 has said
that Israel would be 'without' the temple during the exile which is rem-
edied by the promise of return in verse 5. This points further to the
'rebuilding' of 'the tabernacle of David' in Acts being, not merely the
re-establishment of a new Davidic dynasty, but the reconstruction of
the new temple. Jeremiah is intriguing because he speaks of the

---

[72] Though Luke does not explicitly have in mind Exod. 15.
[73] One major difference, however, is that Qumran believed that even the end-time
temple would be 'a sanctuary (made by hands) of man' (4QFlor 1.6). See likewise the
Qumran *Temple Scroll*.
[74] *Midrash Psalms* 76:3; *Pesikta Rabbati*, Piska 29/30B.

Gentiles being '*built* in the midst of my people' at the time of the future restoration. The language is especially conducive to understanding Gentiles becoming part of true Israel by means of being built as the true temple. This understanding of Acts 15:14–18 is consistent with several Old Testament prophecies that affirm that Gentiles will come into the divine presence in the temple of the messianic epoch (Ps. 96:7–8; Is. 2:2–3; 25:6; 56:6–7; 66:23; Jer. 3:17; Mic. 4:1–2; Zech. 14:16).[75]

We remarked above that the mandate to Gentiles to 'abstain from things contaminated by idols and from fornication and from what is strangled and from blood' (v. 20; see v. 29) did not entail the imposing of Old Testament food laws, but was a command that they abstain from idolatry. Each of the four things Gentiles are to keep away from are associated with idol worship.

This perspective may now be refined. Commentators generally acknowledge that the four prohibitions are based specifically on Leviticus 17 – 18. Part of the reason that Leviticus has been drawn in is because of the catchphrase 'in the midst of my people' (*en mesō tou laou mou*, and its Hebrew equivalent) that occurs in Jeremiah 12:16 (one of the references woven in with Amos 9:11 in Acts 15:16–17)[76] and in Leviticus 17 – 18, where the expression appears five times (Lev. 17:8, 10, 12, 13; 18:26). The phrases are part of four commandments that not only Israelites but also 'the alien who sojourns in your/their midst' must keep. These four prohibitions correspond to the same four in the apostolic decree of Acts and in the same order:[77]

1. 'Things sacrificed to idols' (= Lev. 17:8–9) concern both burnt offerings and sacrifices that could be eaten by the worshipper, which are not brought to the proper place to be 'sacrificed to the LORD' because they are illicitly offered to idols (in light of Lev. 17:7 [LXX], 'they shall no longer offer their sacrifices to vain gods').

2. The reference to 'blood' (= Lev. 17:10, 12) involves a prohibition of the eating of 'blood', no doubt because this was part of pagan idolatrous worship.

3. 'Things strangled' (= Lev. 17:13–14) refers to a law that anything killed for an offering to be eaten must have its blood poured out first

---

[75] As far as I am aware, Bauckham is the first to have pointed out the presence and the significance of these other OT texts together with Amos 9 (1995: 452–462).

[76] Another closely related prophecy is Zech. 2:11a (LXX): 'And many nations shall flee for refuge to the Lord in that day, and they shall be for a people to him, and they shall dwell in the midst of thee.' Zech. 2:10 likely refers to the temple where God 'will dwell in your midst', so that the same cultic setting is in view for v. 11 (as argued on pp. 142–144).

[77] So Acts 15:29, though Acts 15:20 exhibits a different order.

(hence, that which does not have its blood poured out is 'choked by its blood' or 'strangled'). Again, the reason for the precept is likely because the protocol of pagan idolatrous offerings was not to pour out the blood of the sacrifices before eating them.

4. The reference to 'sexual immorality' (*porneia*) (= Lev. 18:26) summarizes varieties of sexually immoral relationships described in Leviticus 18:6–25 (e.g., incest, adultery, homosexual relations, bestiality).[78]

One reason that these immoral relationships are prohibited in the context of Leviticus is because they are connected with idolatrous customs, which confirms our earlier identification of the four prohibitions in Acts 15:20, 29 as a collective prohibition from idol worship. Sexual immorality was intertwined with Egyptian and Canaanite idol worship. In this regard, Leviticus 17:7 appears to be a general introductory statement fleshed out by verses 8–16, which give the particulars associated with idolatrous worship. Likewise, Leviticus 18:1–5 and 18:24–30 form literary bookends, introducing and summarizing verses 6–29 in the same way: Israel is exhorted not to practise the idolatrous ways of the nations. For example, the last verse of chapter 18 concludes by saying, 'Thus you are to keep My charge, that you do not practice any of the *abominable* customs which have been practiced before you, so as not to defile yourselves with them; I am the LORD.'[79] There is little doubt that '*abominable* customs' and 'abominations' (in Lev. 18:22, 26, 27, 29) refer to idolatrous customs, since the word *tôʿēbâ* ('abomination') predominantly refers in the Old Testament and especially in the Pentateuch to idolatry.[80]

Why then does Acts 15:20, 29 allude to Leviticus 17 – 18? It is to show that one of the ultimate purposes of the Law for Gentile proselytes or Israelites was to guard them against idolatry.[81] Now, though the specificities of the Mosaic Law no longer apply to God's people, they are still expected to stay away from idolatry and the immoral sexual practices associated with it. In other words, that part of the

[78] So far the discussion of the significance of Leviticus 17 – 19 is based on Bauckham 1995: 458–459.

[79] Only four verses later, 'I am the LORD your God' is given as the reason that Israel should 'not turn to idols or make for yourselves molten gods' (19:4).

[80] Outside of Lev. 18:22, 26, 27, 29, 30, approximately 60 uses in the OT refer to idolatry and only about 20 (not including the generic uses in Proverbs) are *possibly* used generally without reference to idolatry. Deut. 20:17–18 says, 'you shall utterly destroy them . . . in order that they may not teach you to do according to all their abominable things which they have done for their gods . . .' (likewise, see 2 Kgs. 21:2–9; Deut. 18:9–11).

[81] Other passages also attest to this as one of the main purposes of the Law (e.g., 2 Kgs. 17:34–41).

Law prohibiting idolatry continues to apply generally to God's people in the new age even as it did in the Mosaic age. Leviticus 17 also explains the reason that idolatry was not to be practised: worship and sacrifice were to be given only to the true God whom the resident 'alien' in Israel and Israelites professed.[82] And the true God's presence manifested itself at the tabernacle, to the door of which Leviticus 17 says the 'alien' and the Israelite were to bring their sacrifices. Failure to do so meant that idolatrous sacrifices were being offered, since the tabernacle was the only place to offer legitimate sacrifice. Four times Leviticus 17 repeats that such sacrifices were to be brought to 'the doorway of *the tent* of meeting' (vv. 4, 5, 6, 9), where 'tent' is translated by the Greek Old Testament as *skēnē*, another element in common with Acts 15 (v. 16).

Therefore, just as Gentile 'aliens' in Israel were to worship at the tabernacle while abstaining from idolatry, so Gentile worshippers in the church were to worship at the new tabernacle (*skēnē*) while keeping away from idolatry. Just as God's presence at the tabernacle was the reason to stay away from idol worship, so Christ's end-time presence as the true tabernacle is the reason for not participating in idol worship. 'True worshippers shall worship the Father in [the] Spirit and truth' (John 4:23). It is Christ's Spirit, no longer rituals of Mosaic Law, that now cleanses from idolatry and all uncleanness (Acts 15:8–9) and, indeed, protects from idolatry.[83] Such cleansing qualifies both ethnic Jews and Gentiles to participate in worship in the true tabernacle of Jesus Christ, so that there is no longer a 'distinction' of people groups in Christ (Acts 15:8–9). This is why 'it seemed good to the Holy Spirit and to us [the Council at Jerusalem] to lay upon you [Gentiles] no greater burden than these essentials [i.e., the essentials of abstaining from idolatry]' (Acts 15:28).

An important concluding observation about the Old Testament background of Acts 15 and the relation of Gentiles to the restored temple remains to be made. After mention of God returning and rebuilding 'the fallen tabernacle of David' in Acts 15:16, the second half of the quotation from Amos 9 is different from the Hebrew text

---

[82] Note this reason is stated at the beginning and ending of Lev. 18: 'I am the LORD your God' (18:2, 30).

[83] A textual variant (D and Irenaeus) at the end of Acts 15:29 reads, 'if you keep yourselves free from such things [idolatrous practices], *you do* well, *being borne along by the Holy Spirit*', a scribal insertion thus affirming the Spirit as the sphere of protection from idolatry.

but in basic agreement with the Greek Old Testament version:

Amos 9:12 (Hebrew)	Acts 15:17 and Amos 9:12 (Greek)
'That they may possess the remnant of Edom and all the nations who are called by my name ...'	*Acts*: 'in order that the rest of mankind may seek the Lord, and all the Gentiles who are called by my name'. *Amos*: 'in order that the remnant of mankind and all the nations, upon whom my name has been called, should seek [the Lord] ...'

This is a very complex textual problem, and the limits of the present study do not allow for a thorough analysis. Some scholars too quickly assume, however, that the Greek text of Amos and (or) Acts is an erroneous translation of the Old Testament. More probably, either the Hebrew text is corrupt and the Greek Old Testament and Acts preserve the original Hebrew; or, alternatively and perhaps more likely, the Hebrew text is original, and the Greek Old Testament and Acts is an interpretation of the Hebrew.[84] It would be difficult to prove which is the case.

If the Hebrew is original, then it is developing the earlier promises to the patriarchs and Israel that they would 'possess' the land of enemy 'nations' (Deut. 7:1; 9:4–5; Is. 54:3; cf. also Gen. 15:7–8; 22:17; 24:60; Deut. 8:1). More precisely, Amos 9:12 may be alluding to Numbers 24:17–19:

Numbers 24:17–19	Amos 9:11–12
'And a scepter *shall rise* from Israel ... And *Edom shall be a possession* ... One from Jacob shall have dominion, and shall destroy *the remnant ...*'	'I *will raise up* the fallen tabernacle of David ... that they may *possess the remnant of Edom* and all the nations who are called by My name ...'

---

[84] For discussion of the textual complexities, see Braun (1997: 114–117), and the nuanced analysis by Bauckham (1995: 455–456), who contends that a Christian exegete familiar with the Hebrew text would have been attracted to the interpretative potential of the Greek text of Amos 9:12 'as a legitimate way of reading the Hebrew text of that verse'.

The Numbers passage is the continuation of a discourse only a few verses earlier, where Israel's domination of other nations is expressed through the language of the Abrahamic promise: note the increase of 'seed' (24:7) and the near verbatim repetition of Genesis 12:3b in Numbers 24:9b: 'Blessed is everyone who blesses you, and cursed is everyone who curses you.' In addition, Numbers 24 also depicts Israel's supremacy through the metaphor of her 'tabernacle' being like 'palm trees that stretch out, like gardens' that expand abundantly along river banks, echoing the Garden of Eden as the primal tabernacle.[85] Is it accidental then that Amos also begins his restoration prophecy with a reference to Israel's tabernacle? Likely not. Furthermore, the continuation of Amos's prophecy about the 'raising up of the tabernacle of David' pictures 'the rebuilding' of Israel's ruins together with repeated horticultural language (Amos 9:13–15). This is also in keeping with the Numbers' prophecy, where the same combination of images occurs, as the conclusion of the Amos passage demonstrates:

> When the plowman will overtake the reaper
> And the treader of grapes him who sows seed;
> When the mountains will drip with sweet wine . . .
> They will also plant vineyards and drink their wine,
> And make gardens and eat their fruit.
> I will also plant them on their land,
> And they will not again be rooted out from their land.
>
> (Amos 9:13–15)

Therefore, the Greek version of Amos and, especially, Acts would be interpreting the prophecy of Israel's militaristic domination to be partially fulfilled, at least, through the nations 'seeking the Lord' and voluntarily submitting themselves to him in faith and participating in worship in the latter-day temple.[86] At the same time, this is an explanation of the fulfilment of the Abrahamic promise. Ultimately, this fulfils the original intention of Adam in the garden tabernacle, who

---

[85] See above, pp. 123–126, for fuller analysis of Num. 24:5–7.

[86] This interpretation was likely fuelled by reflection on the phrase 'Gentiles who are called by My name', since, without exception this phrase 'called by My name [or the name of the Lord]' is positive throughout the OT, always referring to Israel as God's people (see Deut. 28:10; 2 Chr. 7:14; Is. 43:7; Jer. 14:9; cf. Is. 63:19). The implication of the phrase in Amos 9:12 is that the Gentiles will become God's people, so that the notion in the Hebrew text of Israel 'possessing' the Gentiles takes on a more positive note of spiritual conversion.

was to expand it by multiplying his seed and filling the earth with godly progeny. Consequently, Acts 15 is a part of the New Testament testimony to the new temple of Christ expanding by opening its gates and enlarging its borders to include people from all the nations.[87]

Conclusion

The book of Acts has elaborated further on what the Gospels have affirmed about Christ, the Spirit, and earliest Christians as forming the beginning of the end-time temple. It remains to be seen what Paul and other New Testament writers say on this topic.

---

[87] See also Van Aarde (1991: 60–61), who refers to the notion of 'the broadening of the temple' in Luke-Acts and defines it as Gentiles and other socially despised people who could now experience God's 'temple presence' outside the temple structure and its associated laws by believing in Jesus.

Chapter Seven

The inauguration of a new temple in the epistles of Paul

Paul further develops what the Gospels and Acts assert about Christ, the Spirit and believers being the inaugurated form of the latter-day temple.

1 Corinthians 3

The issue in the first part of this chapter is how the leaders of the church relate to its members. Paul explains this through the use of two pictures. In the first (3:5–9a), Paul portrays the leaders of the church as agricultural workers in a field, and the church he depicts as the field. It is God alone who gives the 'increase', as a result of the leaders' labour. Thus, the Corinthians should not be forming divisive parties in the church that are in extreme allegiance to particular leaders like Paul or Apollos. Such allegiance should be focused instead on God and Christ. In the second image (3:5b–15), the workers are architects and builders who construct a building on a foundation. The 'building' is the church, the 'work' of the architects or builders, and the foundation they build on is Christ.

Paul then shows explicit awareness that the church is the 'temple of God, and that the Spirit of God dwells in' the church (1 Cor. 3:16; so also 1 Cor. 3:17: 'the temple of God is holy, and that is what you are'). Believers are a temple because of their identification with Christ's Spirit (3:16) and with Christ himself (3:23), though the latter identification is not explicit in the Corinthian epistles. It may be discernible that the subject of the temple has been anticipated in the preceding context.

The church as a garden-temple?

Paul refers to himself as having 'planted' the Corinthian church and to Apollos as having 'watered, but God was causing the growth' (3:6; likewise, 3:7). The 'planter' and the 'waterer' (i.e., the one who establishes and the one who pastorally leads the church) 'will receive his own reward according to his own labor' (3:8). The reason that such people will receive a 'reward' is because they 'labor' for their divine master in his field, and he will give a reward to the faithful laborers: 'for we are fellow-workers [with one another] under God; you are God's field' or 'vineyard' (3:9a).[1] After speaking of the Corinthians as 'God's cultivated field/vineyard', Paul abruptly says they are 'God's building' (3:9b).

Is this one of Paul's purportedly strange, sudden metaphorical shifts?[2] What does a 'cultivated field' have to do with a 'building'? Upon closer analysis, as we will see, Paul is not speaking of a generic 'building' but of the temple as a 'building'. If so, the shift from the agricultural metaphor of a 'cultivated field' or 'vineyard' to a temple may be viewed to be more natural in the light of our prior study in the Old Testament and Gospels. There we discovered that the Garden of Eden, Israel's garden-like promised land, and Israel's future restoration in a garden-like land were either equated or associated with a temple.[3] We are not suggesting that Paul is explicitly equating the 'cultivated field' with the following portrayal of the church as a temple. Rather, the close association of 'garden' and 'temple' in the Old Testament and Judaism would plausibly have influenced a similar link in Paul's mind at some level. If so, this link, whether conscious or unconscious, is a better possible explanation than heretofore offered for inspiring the combination of the same images in 1 Corinthians 3.

That Paul compares God's people to a temple in verses 10–15 is apparent from the specific description of the structure. Paul 'laid a foundation ... which is Jesus Christ', 'and another is building upon it'. If anyone 'builds upon the foundation with gold, silver, precious stones, wood, hay, straw', the fire of the day of judgment will reveal

---

[1] The word *geōrgion* can plausibly be rendered 'cultivated field' or 'vineyard' (e.g., see the LXX of Gen. 26:14; Prov. 6:7; 9:12; 24:5; though in Prov. 24:30 [Rahlfs 1971] and 31:16 it is equated with a 'vineyard'. Interestingly, the word *geōrgos* occurs repeatedly in the Synoptic Gospels with reference to those who take care of a 'vineyard' (often translated 'vinedressers' or 'vine growers': e.g., Luke 20:9–16). BDAG, 196 defines *geōrgos* as 'one who is occupied in agriculture or gardening'.

[2] E.g., see Gal. 4:19: 'My children, with whom *I am again in labor* until *Christ is formed in you.*'

[3] The closest parallel is the early Christian *Odes of Solomon* 38:17–21, which says the saint was 'established' on 'foundations [that] were laid' and that he was 'planted' and 'watered' by God and was God's 'cultivation'. This text is probably a development of the OT or early Judaism rather than of 1 Cor. 3. Later Judaism could also speak of Solomon's temple as a 'field': *Tg. Pseudo-Jonathon Genesis* 27:27 and *Pesikta Rabbati*, Piska 39.

the quality of each builder's work. The costly stones will survive and the 'wood, hay, straw' will be 'burned up'.

The only other place in Scripture where a 'foundation' of a building is laid and 'gold', 'silver' and 'precious stones' are 'built'[4] upon the foundation is Solomon's temple: 'They quarried great stones, costly stones, to lay the foundation of the house' (1 Kgs. 5:17); 'and the inner sanctuary ... he overlaid ... with pure gold ... So Solomon overlaid the inside of the house with pure gold' (1 Kgs. 6:20–21). He also covered with gold the altar (1 Kgs. 6:20), the cherubim around the ark (1 Kgs. 6:28), the floor of the temple (1 Kgs. 6:30) and the engraved work on the temple doors (1 Kgs. 6:35; see similarly 2 Chr. 3 – 4). Indeed, '100,000 talents of gold and 1,000,000 talents of silver' were 'prepared' for the construction of the entire temple (1 Chr. 22:14; likewise, 1 Chr. 22:16; 29:2–7). First Chronicles 29:1–7 repeatedly refers to 'gold ... silver ... [precious] stones' (vv. 2, 7–8) to be used for all the various parts, pieces of furniture and utensils of the temple.[5] Verse two of that chapter is likely the precise passage to which Paul alludes:

1 Chronicles 29:2 (esp. LXX)	1 Corinthians 3:12
'I have provided for the house of my God the gold ... silver ... wood ... precious stones ...'	'if any man builds on the foundation with gold, silver, precious stones, wood ...'

Paul also calls himself a 'wise master builder' (*sophos architektōn*) in laying the foundation, which echoes the use of the same word applied to those who helped build Israel's tabernacle. For example, Exodus 35:31–32 refers to a skilled workman of the tabernacle as 'filled with a divine spirit of *wisdom* [*sophias*] ... to be a master builder [*architektonein*][6] in all works of a master builder [*architektonias*] in order to form gold and silver ... and works in stone'.[7]

Remember also that Solomon's temple, like the new Corinthian

---

[4] The word 'build' (*oikodomeō*) is used repeatedly in describing the construction of Solomon's temple (see 1 Kgs. 6 and 2 Chr. 2 – 3 of the LXX); Paul uses *epoikodomeō* three times in 1 Cor. 3:10–12.

[5] See 2 Chr. 3:6 also for 'precious stones and the gold'.

[6] Jon Laansma drew my attention to the use of this word in Exodus and its noun form in 1 Cor. 3.

[7] So identically Exod. 31:4, though 'master builder' occurs only once! Similarly, Exod. 35:35, where 'master builder' of the 'sanctuary' also appears. Cf. Lanci (1997: 59–60), who argues that Paul's usage in 1 Cor. 3:10 was influenced by the early extrabiblical use of *architeknôn* with respect to those helping in the construction of big buildings, even of building temples.

temple of believers, was also described, not only as containing precious metals but also full of garden-like items: wood-carved 'gourds and open flowers' (1 Kgs. 6:18), 'palm trees and open flowers' (1 Kgs. 6:29, 32 [twice mentioned]), 'pomegranates numbered two hundred in rows around both capitals' on the two doorway pillars (1 Kgs. 7:18–20 ['pomegranates' occurs twice]), on the top of which was a 'lily design' (1 Kgs. 7:22). The bronze sea in the courtyard had two rows of 'gourds' under its brim, which was 'made . . . as a lily blossom' (1 Kgs. 7:24–26); 'four-hundred pomegranates' around the two capitals of the pillars (1 Kgs. 7:42); ten (!) lampstands that were configured like trees with blossoms (1 Kgs. 7:49–50), thus resembling a little grove. We have seen that the purpose of the garden descriptions was to reflect the primeval sanctuary of the Garden of Eden. This combination of precious metals with botanical depictions in Israel's temple would have been sufficient itself to facilitate a swift move on Paul's part from a 'cultivated field/vineyard' image to that of a temple.[8]

Paul identifies the 'foundation' of the new temple to be Jesus Christ. Paul 'laid' this foundation among the Corinthians when they first believed, and now Apollos and others are 'building upon it' by teaching and pastoring the congregation on the basis of God's word, as understood through the redemptive work of Jesus. Hence, to 'build on the foundation' with precious metals is not to build up the Corinthians in their faith by 'worldly wisdom' (1:18–21; 2:1, 4–5; 3:18–23) but in Christ, by instructing them in God's wisdom from the Scriptures and how those Scriptures relate to the new community of faith (so 1 Cor. 10:11; Rom. 15:4–13). In this instruction, the church leaders were 'not to exceed what is written' in the Old Testament in the light of how it has been understood in the new age (so 1 Cor. 4:6). The Old Testament compared God's word to 'gold and silver' in the sense that these most valuable of earth's commodities are surpassed by the value of God's wisdom (Ps. 119:72; Prov. 3:14; 8:10; 16:16). The ultimate precious possession in all the cosmos is God's word because it is permanently true and will never pass away (Is. 40:6–8). Those who are truly saved and built up in their faith are constructed

---

[8] We noted in ch. 4 that Ezek. 17 (LXX) speaks of Israel through the imagery of the Garden of Eden, which has affinities with Paul's 'cultivating' language in 1 Cor. 3: 'And he took of the seed of the land, and sowed it in a cultivated field planted by much water' (17:5), and this field needed to be 'watered' for 'the growth of her plantation' (17:7; the words 'planted', 'plantation' and 'watered' are the same as in 1 Cor. 3, though 'cultivated field' (*pedion*) and 'growth' (*bōlos*) in Ezekiel are synonyms respectively of *geōrgion* and *auxanō* in Paul.

by God's word and become a permanent part of his temple; accordingly 1 Peter 1:23 – 2:7 states:

> [23]you have been born again not of seed which is perishable but imperishable, that is, through the living and abiding word of God.
> [24]For, 'All flesh is like grass, and all its glory like the flower of the grass. The grass withers, and the flower falls off, but the word of the Lord abides forever.'
> [25]And this was the word which was preached to you. [2:1]Therefore ...
> [2]long for the pure milk of the word, that by it you may grow in respect to salvation ...
> [4]And coming to him as to a living stone ... choice and precious in the sight of God,
> [5]you also as living stones, are being built up as a spiritual house ...
> [6]For this is contained in Scripture: 'Behold I lay in Zion a choice stone, a precious cornerstone, and he who believes in Him will not be disappointed.'
> [7]This precious value, then, is for you who believe ...

Consequently, Paul, like Peter, is saying that faithful ministers who build up their flock in the wisdom of God's word will cause them to become part of God's temple, firmly secured to the foundation of Christ. Peter's and Paul's text bears striking resemblance to Psalm 92:12–15, where the temple is equated with a garden and believers are perceived as trees 'planted' and growing on a rock foundation:

> [12]The righteous man will flourish like the palm tree, he will grow like a cedar in Lebanon.
> [13]Planted in the house of the LORD, they will flourish in the courts of our God.
> [14]They will still yield fruit in old age; they shall be full of sap and very green,
> [15]To declare that the LORD is upright; He is my rock, and there is no unrighteousness in Him.

The psalm shows that the notion of saints being part of a garden-like temple and resting on a rock comes from the Old Testament, and thus the similar picture in 1 Corinthians 3 may not

be surprising.[9] The rough parallel between the agricultural metaphor and architectural metaphor does not provide justification for
this book's large-scale thesis about Eden and the temple. Rather, the
suggestion is that the reason why the portrayal of the 'temple' arises
in Paul's mind at this point in 1 Corinthians 3:9b–17 is because the
thesis, found elsewhere in the Old Testament and developed by
early Jewish writers, was plausibly known to some degree by Paul,
and may have sparked his linking of the two apparently disparate
images. Therefore, this may not be such a radical change of pictures
as is often thought.

The Malachi background of the temple

The fire of the last judgment will 'test the quality of each man's [min-
ister's] work' in building on the temple foundation. That is, God will
examine the 'true metal' of the flock (1 Cor. 3:13). 'If any man's [min-
ister's] work which he has built upon it remains, he [the minister] shall
receive a reward' (1 Cor. 3:14). In other words, if his flock passes successfully through the fires of judgment, then their pastoral leader will
receive their saved souls as a reward.[10] 'If any man's [minister's] work
is burned up, he shall suffer loss' of his congregation (part or whole;
1 Cor. 3:15a). In such a case, the Christian leader 'himself shall be
saved, yet so as through fire' (1 Cor. 3:15b).

That Paul has been talking about construction of the church in
Corinth as the temple becomes explicit in 3:16–17, where three times
he calls the Corinthians 'the temple of God'. In addition to the background of Solomon's temple, the Old Testament background of

---

[9] Similarly, Ps. 52:8 says, 'But as for me, I am like a green olive tree in the house
of God'; similarly, recall that Israel's 'tabernacles' were like 'gardens beside the river,
like aloes planted by the LORD' (Num. 24:5–7; cf. also LXX; Hos. 14:5–8). Gärtner
(1965: 65) notes that the Qumran depictions of the community as a temple and plantation influenced Paul's description here. He has not seen that these combinations
occur in the OT and Judaism and that the garden imagery is another way of speaking of the temple, and that Paul shows familiarity with it. For the most relevant passages in Qumran, see 1QS 8.5–8; 11.4–5, 7–8 and 1QH 6.15–19, 26–27. Note also
that after Levi sees a heavenly temple with the Lord in it, an angel says to him, 'your
life will be from the Lord's portion', which in context refers, at least partly, to Levi's
close priestly position to God in the holy of holies. The angel then goes on to say
that God 'shall be to you as a field, vineyard, fruits, silver, gold' (my translation of
the Greek version of the *Testament of Levi* 2:12; cf. also 3:1–10), almost identical to
Paul's combination of agricultural and precious metal metaphors.

[10] Likewise, in Rev. 3:10 those who have faithfully 'kept my [Christ's] word' (cf. 3:3,
8) will pass 'victoriously' through the coming 'testing' (3:10, 12) and receive the reward
of Christ 'making him a pillar in the temple of My God, and he will not go out from
it any more' (3:12).

Malachi 3 – 4 appears to be behind 1 Corinthians 3:10–17. The Malachi text suggests that Paul thinks the faithful Corinthians are part of the final end-time temple that will withstand the fiery storm winds of the last judgment:

> [3:1]Behold, I am going to send My messenger ... And the Lord, whom you seek, will suddenly come to His temple ... [2]But who can endure the day of His coming? And who can stand when He appears? For He is like a refiner's fire[11] ... [3]And He will sit as a smelter and purifier of silver [LXX adds 'gold'], and he will purify the sons of Levi and refine them like gold and silver, so that they may present to the LORD offerings in righteousness ... [4:1]For behold, the day is coming, burning like a furnace ... and every evildoer will be chaff; and the day that is coming will set them ablaze ... so that it will leave them neither root nor branch.

In language very close to Paul's, Malachi predicts that the Lord will 'come to his temple' in the latter days and will 'refine' the priests[12] in the temple with 'fire ... like silver and gold', 'burning' up every evildoer like 'stubble' and the wood of branches (cf. Prov. 17:3). That Paul would have Malachi in mind is perhaps not unexpected because Christ had already applied Malachi 3:1 to himself (Matt. 11:10; as does also Mark 1:2). Though Malachi portrays the refining of priests in the temple, Paul transforms the imagery by seeing that believers who are part of the temple are refined like precious metal. That Paul would draw from a prophecy concerning the end-time temple is understandable in light of his preoccupation with the temple in verses 9–17. Paul believes the time is coming for the fulfilment of Malachi, when God will test the 'metal' of the temple, the church, in order to 'distinguish between the righteous and the wicked' (Mal. 3:18), the former being preserved and the latter judged. Those who are preserved will endure as the true, eschatological temple composed of Christ and his people, which is well pictured in Revelation 21:1 – 22:5.

Three times Paul speaks of 'building upon' the foundation (3:10, 12,

---

[11] The LXX of Mal. 3:2 portrays the Lord as 'entering in [presumably to the temple] as fire'.
[12] See Rom. 12:1 for Paul's conception of believers as priests (so also Heb. 13:15; 1 Pet. 2:5, 9; Rev. 1:6; 5:10; 20:6). Paul also views himself as performing priestly functions (Rom. 15:16; Phil. 2:17; 2 Tim. 4:6).

14), clearly implying the notion of a structure that grows over time. This fits with the concept of the growth of the Edenic and patriarchal sanctuaries, and the Solomonic and second temples, all of which were intended to be expanded from their original borders or measurements to encompass the cosmos. Not only is there the concept of growth but now there is the implicit notion of the temple being expanded beyond the bounds of geographical Israel to include Gentiles who are being built on Christ, the true foundation-stone of the temple and the authentic Israel.

Perhaps not coincidentally, the word 'growth' in verses 6–7 occurs typically in the Greek Old Testament as part of the commission to Adam, that was then passed on to Noah and the patriarchs and was combined with small-scale temple building episodes.[13] Despite the fact that a temple of God's people is being built, Paul wants the church's ministers to realize that what appears to be the growing construction of the visible temple may well not be the true temple. After God's refining judgment, only those who are constructed with permanent construction materials will remain as the true temple.

A few chapters later, Paul resumes his argument that the church is the 'temple of the Holy Spirit' (6:19). Paul underscores this point to remind the Corinthians about why they are to avoid immorality: they are part of the latter-day temple, and just as the Old Testament temple was to be kept clean from defilement, how much more so are they to keep their bodies clean and separate from immorality (6:18). In line with the purpose of the Old Testament temple, which was to house and show forth God's glory, Paul commands them to 'glorify God in your body' (6:20). Just as God's glory uniquely dwelt in Israel's old temple, so the glorious attributes of God are to be manifested in the Corinthians both individually and corporately, since they are the new temple. Similarly, the consummated temple in the new creation will perfectly reflect 'the glory of God' (Rev. 21:11), and 'nothing unclean ... shall ever come into it' (Rev. 21:27).

---

[13] E.g., Gen. 9:7, 'And as for you, *be fruitful* [grow] and multiply; populate the earth abundantly and multiply in it.' Approximately 20 out of 39 uses of the verb occur in connection with the formulaic commission. Interestingly, 1 Chr. 17:10–12 (LXX) says God 'will *plant*' and cause Israel '*to grow*', and David's seed would '*build* me [God] a house [i.e., temple]' (all three italicized words in Greek also occurring in 1 Cor. 3:6–10).

2 Corinthians

Some commentators speak of the temple in 1 Corinthians only as a metaphor: the church is merely 'like' a temple, but it is not part of the beginning fulfilment of the eschatological temple prophecies from the Old Testament.[14] Our contention that Malachi 3:1–2 and 4:1 are alluded to in 1 Corinthians 3 points to the church being the actual beginning fulfilment of the end-time temple prophesied in the Old Testament. Paul's continued discussion of the temple in 2 Corinthians suggests further that he compares the church to a temple because he understands it to be the inaugurated fulfilment of the expected latter-day temple.

One of the most theologically pregnant statements in all of Paul's writings occurs in 2 Corinthians 1:20a: 'For as many as may be the promises of God, in Him [Christ] they are yes.' The 'promises' most certainly refer to Old Testament promises that began fulfilment in Christ. But which promises are in mind? Perhaps all of God's prophetic promises are implied, but the ones uppermost in Paul's mind are those that he addresses in the following context of the epistle, particularly from 1:21 – 7:1. The observation that 1:20 and 7:1 both refer to 'promises' (the latter introduced with 'therefore') is one of the signposts that it is this section, at least, within which he expounds prophetic fulfilment. Certainly, Paul is thinking partly about the promises of a 'new covenant' with Israel (3:1–18), her resurrection (5:14–15), new creation (5:16–17) and restoration from captivity (5:18 – 6:18). As we have seen in an earlier chapter, the establishment of a new temple was to be part of Israel's restoration (e.g., see Ezek. 37:26–28; 40 – 48). Accordingly, Paul lists the temple among the initial fulfilments of Old Testament prophecy.

The church as the end-time temple in 2 Corinthians 6:16–18

Paul's most explicit reference to believers forming an end-time temple is 2 Corinthians 6:16a, which Paul identifies as part of the dawning restoration promises: 'For we are the temple of the living God; just as God said'. Paul cites several texts from the Old Testament to support this declaration, the first of which is a prophecy of the future temple.

---

[14] Fee (1987: 147) expresses a perhaps not atypical tentativeness: the notion that the eschatological temple is in mind in 1 Cor. 3 'is possible, though by no means certain', yet says in a footnote that such an end-time view 'is *probably* correct' (my italics).

Leviticus 26:11–12 and Ezekiel 37:26–27	2 Corinthians 6:16b
Lev.: 'I will make My dwelling among you ... I will also walk among you and be your God, and you shall be My people.' *Ezek.*: 'I will ... set My sanctuary in their midst forever. My dwelling place also will be with them; and I will be their God, and they will be My people' (cf. Exod. 29:45).	'I will dwell in them and walk among them; and I shall be their God, and they shall be My people.'

That this Old Testament allusion is a prediction of a coming temple indicates that Paul is not merely making an analogy between a temple idea and that of Christians, but that Christians *are* the beginning fulfilment of the actual prophecy of the end-time temple.[15]

Paul appends to this prophecy two additional allusions to the Old Testament promise that a temple would be rebuilt when Israel would return from Babylonian captivity. The first is from Isaiah 52.

Isaiah 52:11; Ezekiel 11:17; 20:34, 41	2 Corinthians 6:16b
Is.: 'Depart, depart, go out from there, touch nothing unclean; go out of the midst of her, purify yourselves, you who carry the vessels of the LORD.' *Ezek.*: 'I will welcome you'[16] (LXX).[17]	'Therefore, come out from their midst and be separate,' says the Lord. 'And do not touch what is unclean; and I will welcome you.'

Isaiah does not exhort Israelites in general to 'depart' from Babylon, but specifically priests who carry the holy 'vessels' of the temple that Nebuchadnezzar had taken from Solomon's temple and had kept in Babylon during the captivity. They are to return the 'vessels' to the temple when it is rebuilt. When Ezekiel repeatedly speaks of God 'welcoming' Israel back from captivity, the restoration

[15] See also Clowney (1972: 185–186), who has made a similar point about 2 Cor. 6:16.

[16] Ezek. 11:17 (MT) has 'you', while LXX has 'them'.

[17] Perhaps also echoed are the following passages that also refer to God 'welcoming' Israel back from restoration: Mic. 4:6; Zeph. 3:19–20; Zech. 10:8, 10; Jer. 23:3; the first two of which have in mind also a return to the temple (cf. Mic. 4:1–3, 7–8; Zeph. 3:10–11).

of the temple is in mind: e.g., Ezekiel 20:40–41 (LXX) says, 'For on my holy mountain, on my high mountain ... will I accept you, and there will I have respect to your first-fruits, and the first-fruits of your offerings, in all your holy things. I will accept you with a sweet-smelling savor ... and I will welcome you from the countries wherein you have been dispersed.' When God will 'welcome' Israel back, she will bring offerings to the temple on Mount Zion.

Intriguingly, Ezekiel 11:16 says that when Israel was in captivity God 'was a sanctuary for them a little while in the countries where they had gone'! This assertion is made in direct connection with Ezekiel 10:18, in which 'the glory of the LORD departed from the threshold of the temple' in Jerusalem (Ezek. 10:18; similarly, Ezek. 11:23). It is likely not coincidental that God's glorious presence departed from the temple and then is said to be with the remnant, who have gone into captivity. His presence would return with the restored people and would once again take up residence in another temple. It is likely that this did not occur in the second temple that was built after Israel's return. God's tabernacling presence expressed itself in the coming of Christ, who 'tabernacled among' Israel, and they 'beheld his glory' (John 1:14). Those who identify with Christ become like the Corinthians, part of the true temple.

Paul's last allusion supporting his contention that the Corinthians are 'the temple of the living God' is from 2 Samuel 7:14.)

2 Samuel 7:14	2 Corinthians 6:18
'I will be a father to him and he will be a son to Me.'	'And I will be a father to you, and you shall be sons and daughters to Me,' says the Lord Almighty.

While 2 Samuel is the primary text, 'son' has been expanded into 'sons and daughters' under the influence of three passages in Isaiah that foretell the restoration of Israel's 'sons and daughters' (Is. 43:6; 49:22; 60:4), the last of which includes in its context the promise that Israel will again worship at a restored temple (Is. 60:7, 13). The 2 Samuel prophecy is concerned with the future king and temple: 'He [the coming king] shall build a house for My name, and I will establish the throne of his kingdom forever' (2 Sam. 7:13).[18] Our discussion of Acts has demonstrated that this prophecy in 2 Samuel

[18] See Beale 1989: 235–239 for a more detailed analysis of the allusions in 2 Cor. 6:16–18.

was not finally fulfilled in Solomon and his temple, but climactically in Christ's kingship and his resurrection as the inaugurated creation of the ultimate temple. Here, as in Acts 15, we find that the church also forms part of the temple foretold in 2 Samuel. As also in Acts, the new temple is widened to include nations living around Israel, in this case Corinthian Greeks. As also in the Gospels and Acts, the new temple is another way of speaking about the new creation that has resulted from Christ's resurrection. In this respect, 2 Corinthians 6:16–18 continues the line of argument begun at least at 5:15–17:[19] Christ 'died and rose again on their behalf . . . Therefore if anyone is in Christ, there is *a new creation*; the old things passed away; behold, *new things have come.*' Christ and his people have become what the microcosmic symbolism of the old temple foreshadowed.

Thus, 'as many as may be the promises of God, in Him [Christ]' they have begun fulfilment; that is, 'they are yes' (2 Cor. 1:20); including the prophecies of the final temple. Second Corinthians 7:1a underscores that foremost among these promises is that of the temple prophecy, since it appears in the directly preceding context (2 Cor. 6:16–18): 'Therefore, having these promises'. Christ initially fulfilled the temple promise (cf. 1:20), and the readers participate in that fulfilment also, as they are ones 'having these promises' (7:1). The reason they and Paul fulfil the same promise that Christ does is because God 'establishes us with you in Christ' by 'sealing' believers and giving the 'Spirit in our hearts as a down payment' (1:21–22). While they have only begun to fulfil the eschatological expectation of the temple, a time will come when they will perfectly realize that hope. And since the Corinthians form part of the new temple along with Paul, he exhorts them to keep the new sanctuary pure, as was God's command to priests in the Old Testament temple: 'let us cleanse ourselves from all defilement of flesh and spirit, completing holiness in the fear of God' (2 Cor. 7:1b).

The church as the inaugurated and consummated end-time temple in 2 Corinthians 4:16 – 5:5

Paul anticipates in 5:1–5 his explicit discussion of the Corinthians as a temple in chapter 6:

> [5:1]For we know that if the earthly tent which is our house is torn down, we have a building from God, a house not made with hands, eternal in the heavens.

[19] For the tracing of the organic thread connecting 5:17 to 6:16–18, see Beale 1989.

[2]For indeed in this house we groan, longing to be clothed with our dwelling from heaven;
[3]inasmuch as we, when we are clothed, shall not be found naked.
[4]For indeed while we are in this tent, we groan, being burdened, because we do not want to be unclothed, but to be clothed, in order that what is mortal may be swallowed up by life.
[5]Now He who prepared us for this very purpose is God, who gave to us the Spirit as a pledge.

The 'earthly tent' (v. 1) refers to the believer's mortal body that will eventually suffer corruption (be 'torn down'). After death, however, the Christian will 'have a building from God, a house not made with hands, eternal in the heavens' (v. 1). This refers to their future resurrection and transformation into becoming part of the new 'heavens' and earth, which, as we have seen and will see, is equated with becoming part of the temple of God. The notion of the 'clothing' being the final resurrection is clear from verse 4. That Paul has a temple image in view[20] is apparent from the phrase 'not made with hands', which virtually everywhere else is a technical way of speaking about the new eschatological temple.[21] In addition, the references to 'building', 'house' (v. 1), and 'dwelling' (v. 2) occur in Paul elsewhere with respect to Israel's temple or the church as the temple.[22]

Though 5:1–5 pictures the future consummate form of the temple, its reality has been inaugurated, as 2 Corinthians 6:16–18 has shown. This is also apparent from the preceding context of 4:16–18, the thought of which is continued in 5:1ff:[23]

[4:16]Therefore we do not lose heart, but though our outer man is decaying, yet our inner man is being renewed day by day.

---

[20] Ellis (1959–60: 217–218) is a leading proponent of the view that Paul has in mind the church as a temple here, though his notion that the temple is a present reality in 5:1–4 is questionable.

[21] See above discussion of this phrase and like expressions (pp. 222–227); accordingly, the relevant citations are Exod. 15:17; Is. 66:1–2; Dan. 2:34, 35 (LXX); Mark 14:58; Acts 7:48–49; 17:24; Heb. 9:11, 24; *Sibylline Oracles* 4:11; Euripides, *Fragment* 968 (on which see Bruce 1954: 357). Col. 2:11 refers to 'circumcision made without hands'.

[22] 'Building' (*oikodomē*) refers to Israel's temple (Matt. 24:1; Mark 13:1–2) or to the church as the temple (1 Cor. 3:9; Eph. 2:21); Paul does not use 'house' (*oikos*) anywhere else to refer to the temple, though the word has this reference elsewhere in the OT (e.g., 2 Sam. 7:6–7, 13) and NT (e.g., Luke 19:46; 1 Pet. 2:5); 'dwelling' (*oikētērion*) appears only outside of 2 Corinthians in Jude without reference to the temple, but its synonym (*katoikētērion*), used by Paul only once, refers to the church as the temple in Eph. 2:22.

[23] On which, e.g., see Hafemann 2000: 206–207.

[17]For momentary, light affliction is producing for us an eternal weight of glory far beyond all comparison,

[18]while we look not at the things which are seen, but at the things which are not seen; for the things which are seen are temporal, but the things which are not seen are eternal.

Verses 16–17 explain that this ongoing inner renewal is equivalent to a present increasing 'eternal weight of glory' that will finally eventuate in a 'glory far beyond all comparison', no doubt at the time of the final resurrection spoken of in 5:1–4. Though the readers will be 'swallowed up by [resurrection] life' at the end of the age (2 Cor. 5:4), such 'life' was already at 'work' in them (2 Cor. 4:12). Just as the Spirit is linked to the origin of the resurrection life of faith in 4:12–13, so the Spirit is the 'down payment' for the future consummation of resurrection life (5:5) (Hafemann 2000: 186–187).

The Spirit himself is the beginning evidence of the new creation, wherein is resurrection existence and the abode of the cosmic temple.[24] Second Corinthians 5:5 says that God 'who prepared us for this very purpose' of receiving resurrection life and becoming a part of the eternal temple 'gave to us the Spirit as a down payment' of these realities. The Spirit is not merely an anticipation or promise of these realities but is the beginning form of them. Second Corinthians 1:20–22 makes this clearer: 'the promises of God [from the Old Testament] in Him [Christ] ... are yes', which mean they have begun fulfilment in Christ's first coming. Paul then says that God 'establishes us with you in Christ ... and gave us the Spirit in our hearts as a down payment'.[25] That is, the Spirit is the beginning evidence that the latter-day promises have begun to be realized in Christ and his people. The Spirit is 'the first-fruits' of the future 'redemption of our body' (Rom. 8:23). Likewise, Ephesians 1:13–14 asserts that believers have been 'sealed with the promised Holy Spirit who is the down payment' of the full 'inheritance' to come at the end of the age.

It is appropriate that the process of resurrection 'renewal' (2 Cor. 4:16) is equated with a process of building up glory (4:17), since the temple was the proper place throughout history for the abode of divine glory. Now, God's glory appropriately resides among those in

---

[24] See Eph. 1:14 and Rom. 8:23 for similar statements concerning the Spirit.

[25] In Hellenistic Greek the word *arrabōn* can refer to 'an "earnest", or a part given in advance of what will be bestowed fully afterwards' (Moulton and Milligan 1972: 79): e.g., the word can refer to a down payment to someone to perform a commercial task, and after the task is accomplished the remainder of the promised money is paid.

Christ, the new Adam and the new temple. Paul says as much in 1 Corinthians 6:19–20: 'Or do you not know that your body is a temple of the Holy Spirit ... therefore glorify God in your body', a glory that would perfectly be reflected in the temple of the new creation throughout eternity (e.g., Rev. 21:11; cf. Rev. 15:8). Since the new temple that has already sprung into existence is 'not made with hands' like the old one, likewise neither can it be seen as the old temple could: 'the things which are seen are temporal, but the things which are not seen are eternal' (4:18).

The manner by which glory grows in the temple is rather ironic: it is as the believer perseveres through suffering. God's glorious 'power is perfected in weakness' (2 Cor. 12:9). In fact, this increasing glory through the weakness of the true, visible church is the growth of the temple itself. As Christians trust God in the midst of trial and their own weaknesses, God makes his glory shine in us. God has designed that 'we have this treasure' of his glory 'in earthen [weak] vessels in order that the surpassing greatness of the power may be of God and not from ourselves' (2 Cor. 4:6b–7).

Ephesians

Ephesians 2:19–22 is one of the most explicit descriptions of the church as the temple in all of the New Testament:

> [19]So then you are no longer strangers and aliens, but you are fellow citizens with the saints, and are of God's household,
> [20]having been built upon the foundation of the apostles and prophets, Christ Jesus Himself being the cornerstone,
> [21]in whom the whole building, being fitted together is growing into a holy temple in the Lord;
> [22]in whom you also are being built together into a dwelling of God in the Spirit.

Argument is not needed to demonstrate that Paul is portraying the church as a temple, since it is obvious. Nevertheless, the question still needs to be asked whether Paul merely conceives of the church as being analogous to the temple, or whether he actually thinks the church is the inaugurated fulfilment of the Old Testament expectations of the end-time temple. On the basis of our investigation so far of the Gospels and Acts, as well as particularly 1 and 2 Corinthians, the answer to the question is most probably that Paul, indeed, believes not merely that the church is 'like' the temple but that it is the actual beginning fulfilment of the latter-day temple prophecies from the Old Testament.

The immediate context of the Ephesians 2 passage also suggests an affirmative answer. Verse 17 quotes a restoration prophecy from Isaiah 57:19: 'And He came and preached peace to you who were far away, and peace to those who were near.' The quotation supports Paul's preceding point, that Christ's death and resurrection reconciled Jews and Gentiles to God and, thus, to one another. If Jews and Gentiles are reconciled to God because they are in the one Christ, then they are also reconciled to and have peace with one another because their identity as 'one new man' in Christ surpasses any nationalistic identities that formerly alienated themselves from one another (2:15–16). And if they are part of Christ and a new creation in him, they are also part of the 'one Spirit' and have open 'access' to the Father (2:18). This open access in the Spirit is interpreted in verses 19–22 to be the temple of God and of the Spirit, the 'cornerstone' being Christ.

Christ set himself as the 'cornerstone' of the temple through his ministry, death and resurrection.[26] On this 'cornerstone' together with the 'foundation of the apostles and prophets', the church began to be built. Thus, the images of being 'in Christ' (i.e., 'in him', 2:15), 'in one new man' (2:15), 'in one Spirit' (2:18), and 'into a holy temple' (2:21) are all equated with one another. They refer to the one reality of dwelling in the presence of God in the commencement of the new creation. The inclusion of 'temple' in these parallel descriptions of new creation is now natural to understand when it is recalled that the Old Testament temple was a small model of the entire universe.

The Isaiah 57 quotation is a prophecy of Israel's return from captivity, which Paul understands to have begun fulfilment in Jews and Gentiles turning in faith to Christ, the true Israelite inheritance.[27] It is no coincidence that the verses preceding Isaiah 57:19 also speak of Israel's restoration in terms of them returning to dwell in God's temple as a new resurrected creation:

---

[26] So see Matt. 21:42 and parallels, on which see discussion above (pp. 181–187).

[27] So Eph. 3:6 says that 'Gentiles are fellow-inheritors [together with Jewish Christians] and fellow-members of the body, and fellow-partakers of the promise *in Messiah Jesus* through the gospel.' People participate in the end-time promises to Israel only by being identified with Messiah Jesus, the corporate representative head of true Israel. On the interpretation of this passage along these lines, see further Beale 1998: 242–246.

[13b]'But he who takes refuge in Me shall inherit the land,
And shall possess My holy mountain.'
[14]And it shall be said,
'Build up, build up, prepare the way,
Remove every obstacle out of the way of My people.'
[15]For thus says the high and exalted One
Who lives forever, whose name is Holy,
'I dwell on a high and holy place, and [I will dwell] also with
the crushed and fallen of spirit in order to make alive the
spirit of the fallen and to make alive the heart of the
crushed.'

It is not surprising that Paul refers to Isaiah 57 in relation to the
temple, since we have observed that the same chapter was developed
by Isaiah 66:2, which was quoted by Stephen in his discussion of the
temple.[28] The promise of the return to dwell in God's restored temple
in 57:13–15 picks up the same promise from chapter 56:3–8.

[3]Let not the foreigner who has joined himself to the LORD say,
'The LORD will surely separate me from His people.' Neither
let the eunuch say, 'Behold, I am a dry tree.'
[4]For thus says the LORD, 'To the eunuchs who keep My
Sabbaths, and choose what pleases Me, and hold fast My covenant,
[5]To them I will give in My house and within My walls a
memorial, And a name better than that of sons and daughters;
I will give them an everlasting name which will not be cut off.
[6]'Also the foreigners who join themselves to the LORD, to minister to Him, and to love the name of the LORD, to be His servants, every one who keeps from profaning the Sabbath, and
holds fast My covenant;
[7]Even those I will bring to My holy mountain, and make them
joyful in My house of prayer. Their burnt offerings and their
sacrifices will be acceptable on My altar; for My house will be
called a house of prayer for all the peoples.'
[8]The Lord GOD, who gathers the dispersed of Israel, declares,
'Yet others I will gather to them, to those already gathered.'

This passage makes clear that both redeemed Jews and Gentiles will
worship together in God's temple in the new age, the same point Paul

---

[28] For discussion of Stephen's quotation of Is. 66, see pp. 218–222.

makes in Ephesians 2. Isaiah even says that the 'foreigner' who 'has joined himself to the LORD' will not be 'separated from his [God's] people' Israel (56:3). Pre-Christian Jewish readers would have understood this to mean that Gentiles would become part of eschatological Israel in the same way as formerly (i.e., through moving to Israel, being circumcised, worshipping at a temple structure and following Israel's Law). Part of the point in Ephesians is that Jews and Gentiles fulfil the Isaiah prophecy by 'moving', not to geographical Israel but to Christ, the true Israel, the true temple, the zenith of the Law, and the true circumcision (see Heb. 12:18–24). This was part of the 'mystery of Christ, which in other generations was not made known to the sons of men, as it has now been revealed' (Eph. 3:4–5). In particular, Gentiles no longer need to adopt the customs and outward signs associated with national Israel's Law in order to become true Israelites and worship in the true temple. Their identification with Christ means that they are part of the true Israel and authentic latter-day temple.[29] It was not so clear in the Old Testament that when the Messiah would come the theocracy of Israel would be reconstituted, so that it would continue only as the new organism of the Messiah. Part of the revealed 'mystery' is that in the Messiah Jews and Gentiles would be fused together, on a footing of complete equality, through corporate identification in the one Christ (Beale 1998: 242–244).

The background of Isaiah 57 shows that Paul has in mind not merely the temple as a metaphor for the church,[30] but that the church is the initial phase of the building of the final temple that will appear at the end of the age. Why does Paul mention that Gentiles formerly were separated from Israel's 'promise' (Eph. 2:12) but 'now' are fellow-sharers in that 'promise' (3:6)? The reason, in part, is to under-

---

[29] Is. 56:6 even says that Gentiles will 'minister' to the Lord in the temple as priests, which Is. 66:18–21 makes clearer. How OT readers could have conceived of this happening is hard to know, since Israel's Law affirmed that only those from the tribe of Levi could serve as priests in the temple. Possibly, the thought may have been that some Gentiles could have been conceived of as converting to Israel's faith and Law and joining the tribe of Levi.

[30] So Feinberg (1971: 99), who sees here only 'that the church is presented under the figure of a temple'. Ironically, Feinberg insists that where the NT refers to eschatological prophecies about the temple, they must be taken 'literally'. If he were aware that Ephesians was referring to an eschatological prophecy about the temple, one wonders if he would change his figurative view of Eph. 2. Perhaps he would say that Paul does not have in mind the eschatological-prophetic element of the temple but only wants to take the image of the temple and apply it analogically. The problem with this is that Paul would not be paying attention to the main contextual idea of the OT text, but neutering its prophetic and redemptive-historical significance.

score that Gentiles are identified in Ephesians 2:19–22 with the long-awaited temple promised in Isaiah and the other prophets.

Finally, one other feature of Ephesians 2 worth noting is the emphasis on the ongoing nature of the new temple's construction: in Christ 'the whole building, *being fitted together is growing* into a holy temple in the Lord; in whom you also *are being built together into* a dwelling of God in the Spirit' (vv. 21–22).[31] We saw a similar notion of the building or growth of the temple in 1 Corinthians 3 (vv. 6–7, 10, 12, 14). This notion of a temple gradually increasing in size is one we have previously observed. The borders of Eden and all subsequent temples were to be expanded until they circumscribed the globe with God's all-pervasive presence. Yet this purpose was never successfully pursued until it began to be accomplished in Christ. Here, as we have also seen in 1 Corinthians 3, the temple's expansion is beginning to be executed, in that its boundaries are expanding to include Gentiles from around the world. The temple will continue to expand to include more and more people until God's presence will pervade the entire earth at the end of the age (cf. Eph. 4:13).

The concept continued to influence early Christian writers, such as the author of the *Epistle of Barnabas*, who sees God 'building and completing' the 'incorruptible temple' in Christ (see *Barnabas* 16:6; see also 16:7–10). As we saw earlier in this chapter, 1 Peter 2 portrays the same image (see p. 249). Both Paul and Peter likely got the picture from Christ himself, since they both allude to him as the 'cornerstone' of the temple, which is based on Psalm 118 and also, as we have seen, applied to Christ in the Gospel accounts (e.g., Matt. 21:42).

That at times Christ can be referred to as the 'cornerstone' of the temple and, at other times, the temple itself is not inconsistent. The former picture underscores that he is the foundation of the eschatological temple, while the latter affirms that he is the fulfilment of the prophecies of the temple, and he is the substance which the Old Testament temples foreshadowed.

Colossians[32]

After his greeting in verses 1–2, Paul launches off into his typical introductory thanksgiving (vv. 3–8). The first Old Testament allusion

---

[31] An almost identical image of growth is continued in Eph. 4:13–16.

[32] For much fuller elaboration and analysis of the allusions in this section, see Beale, (forthcoming).

in the epistle occurs in 1:6, 10, the former a part of the thanksgiving. and the latter a part of a prayer based on the thanksgiving.

Genesis 1:28	Colossians 1:6, 10
'increase [auxanō] and multiply and fill the earth … and rule over *all the earth'.*	'in *all the world* also it ['the word of truth, the gospel'] is *bearing fruit and increasing [auxanō]'* (v. 6); 'in every good work *bearing fruit and increasing [auxanō]* …' (v. 10).

Several commentators have noticed that verses 6 and 10 are an allusion to Genesis 1:28 (and perhaps 1:22). It appears that the Hebrew text may be the focus, since the Greek Old Testament renders the Hebrew *pārâ* ('bear fruit') by *auxanō* ('increase') and *rābâ* ('to multiply') by *plēthunō* ('to multiply'). Paul appears to give perhaps a bit more of a literal rendering than the Greek Old Testament by translating *pārâ* by *karpophoreō* ('bear fruit').

One might doubt that such an allusion exists in Colossians 1 because, whereas Genesis 1 refers to the increase of humans on 'all the earth' and their dominion over it, Colossians 1:6 refers to the word of the gospel 'bearing fruit and increasing' 'in all the world' and 1:10 refers to good works as 'bearing fruit' and Christians' growth 'in the knowledge of God [i.e., in God's word].'

There does appear, nevertheless, to be sufficient linguistic evidence to posit a probable and conscious allusion to Genesis 1:28. Furthermore, the repetition of the wording in Colossians 1:10 highlights the earlier identical phrase and points further to Paul's conscious awareness of alluding to Genesis 1:28.

Even already in Genesis 1 – 3, as we have seen, it is apparent that obedience to God's word was crucial to carrying out the task of Genesis 1:26, 28 (and disobedience to it led to their failure: cf. Gen. 2:16–17 and 3:3–4, where there are three examples of misquotation or intentional twisting of the divine word in Gen. 2). Carrying out the mandate included defeating and ruling over the evil serpent partly by remembering and trusting in God's word of command in 2:16–17 (note the emphasis on God 'said' or 'saying' with reference to 2:16–17 in 2:15; 3:1a, 1b, 3). Nevertheless, the serpent ended up ruling over Adam and Eve by deceiving them with his deceptive word.

Being 'fruitful and multiplying' in Genesis 1:28 refers to the increase of Adam and Eve's progeny, who were also to reflect God's glorious image and be part of the vanguard movement, spreading out over the earth with the goal of filling it with divine glory. This assumes that essential to Adam and Eve's raising of their children was spiritual instruction in God's word that the parents themselves were to remember and pass on.

Paul has tapped into one of the most important veins of the redemptive-historical story-line of Scripture. In fact, as noted in chapter 3, the mandate of Genesis 1:28 is repeated throughout the Old Testament (usually in the form of a promise), for example, Genesis 9:1, 6–7; 12:2; 17:2, 6, 8; 22:17–18; 26:3, 4, 24; 28:3–4; 35:11–12; 47:27; Exodus 1:7; Leviticus 26:9; Psalm 107:38; Isaiah 51:2; Jeremiah 3:16; 23:3; Ezekiel 36:10–11, 29–30; most of these contain the actual dual terminology of 'increase and multiply' (cf. also 1 Chr. 29:10–12).

In the repetition of the commission to the patriarchs, the mention of 'all the nations of the earth' being 'blessed' by Abraham's 'seed' alludes to a renewed human community bearing God's image and 'filling the earth' with regenerated progeny who also reflect God's image. Thus, these new converts are 'blessed' with the favour of God's glorious presence and become a part of God's ever-increasing kingdom and rule which the first Adam had forfeited. Hence, the 'ruling and subduing' of Genesis 1:28 now includes spiritually overcoming the influence of evil in the hearts of unregenerate humanity which has multiplied upon the earth. By implication, the notion of physical new-born children 'increasing and multiplying' in the original Genesis 1:28 commission now includes people who have left their old way of life and have become spiritually new-born and have come to reflect the image of God's glorious presence and participate in the expanding nature of the Genesis 1:26–28 commission (a similar notion is expressed in Col. 1).

The presupposition underlying such a use is likely the notion of the 'Last, Eschatological Adam', Jesus Christ, who first came as the true 'image of the invisible God' (Col. 1:15) and who initially carried out the commission, so that his people could walk after his steps in continuing to obey the mandate (cf. Rev. 14:4).

Such an interpretation of Genesis 1:28 which we have seen in Colossians 1, especially with the emphasis on God's word, has apparently not been acknowledged as present in early or late Judaism. Indeed, there are a number of examples which indicate that Jewish commentators understood Genesis 1:28 'literally' in terms only of human reproduction (e.g., *Jubilees* 6:5; 10:4; 32:17b–19; *Sibylline*

Oracles 1:55–58, 272–274; *1 Enoch* 67:1–3; 89:49; *2 Esdras* 3:12–14a; *Sirach* 44:21; *Testament of Isaac* 3:7–8; *Barnabas* 2:34).

Nevertheless, the interpretation of Genesis 1:28 that we have discovered in Colossians becomes more plausible by observing that it has some precedents in Judaism and is attested elsewhere in early Christianity, especially through a combination of the language of Genesis 1:28 together with garden imagery (often with pictures of growth) from Genesis 2. Some Jewish texts are quite close to Colossians in affirming that the 'increasing' of Genesis 1:28 is a growth specifically in God's 'word' (Col. 1:5–6) or in regenerate 'knowledge' (Col. 1:10). In the eschaton, 'the nations will be multiplied in knowledge on the earth', and 'saints' will possess immortal 'life', and 'be clothed with righteousness' (*Testament of Levi* 18:9–10, 14). Particularly striking is a Qumran document (4Q158 [frags. 1–2] 7–8) which interprets God's 'blessing' to Jacob in Genesis 32:29b as follows: 'may Yah[weh] make you fruitful and [make] you [numerous ... may he fill you with] [know]lege and understanding' (note Col. 1:9–10: 'that you should be filled with knowledge ... in all wisdom and understanding ... growing in the knowledge of God'; relevant also is a passage from the Qumran *Hymn Scroll* [1QH 6.12–19 and 8.20–22]; so also 4Q433a [frags. 1–2]; 4Q418 [frags. 81 = 4Q423 8 + 24?]; and in early Christian literature, see *Barnabas* 6:11–19).

The book of Acts refers four times to Genesis 1:28, and, like Colossians 1:6–10 and early Judaism, may refer collectively to the repeated commission and promise later in Genesis and elsewhere together with an interpretative focus on the 'word': 'And *the word of God continued to increase,* and the number of the disciples *continued to multiply* greatly in Jerusalem, and a great many of the priests were becoming obedient to the faith' (Acts 6:7); 'But *the word of the Lord continued to grow and to be multiplied*' (Acts 12:24); and 'So *the word of the Lord was growing mightily and prevailing*' (Acts 19:20).

That the repeated promisory commission is most likely in mind in these three verses is evident from noticing that Acts 7:17 actually quotes one of the repeated commissions from Exodus 1:7, 20 (see Pao 2000: 167–169). The two verbs for 'increase and multiply' are identical to Genesis 1:28 (LXX, except for 'prevail' in 19:20, which uses *ischuō* instead of *plēthunō*, though the former verb occurs in Exod. 1:20 and the prefixed form in Exod. 1:7). These passages are virtually identical in sense to Colossians 1:6, they all view the literal commission about progeny to be interpreted in the new age as the increase of the reception of God's word in new believers and the multiplication

266

of believers. And, as we have seen, the notion in Colossians 1:10 is very similar.

What is striking is that Christ is identified as the eschatological Adam in Colossians 1:15 ('the image of the invisible God') and in 3:10 those believing in Christ also are said to 'have put on the new man' (i.e., they are in Christ, the new Man, Adam) and are being 'renewed to a true knowledge according to ... [God's] image ...' This identification shows the rationale behind Paul's application of the Genesis 1:28 commission to believers in 1:6, 10, who are identified with the Last Adam and his commission. Even more striking is Colossians 1:9: 'we have not ceased to pray for you and to ask that you may be filled with the knowledge of his [God's] will *in all wisdom and spiritual understanding*'. The last phrase is based partly on Exodus 31:3 (35:31 is virtually identical): 'I have filled him with a divine Spirit [*pneuma*] of wisdom [*sophia*] and understanding [*synesis*] and knowledge [*epistēmē*]'. The Exodus passage describes the ability to build the tabernacle. Such an allusion here fits admirably between two references to Genesis 1:28, since our thesis throughout the book so far has been that Genesis 1:28 is carried out by expanding the temple of God. In fact, the same conception is likely expressed by the Acts 6:7 allusion to Genesis 1:28 and the reference in 6:3 to people 'full of the Spirit and wisdom' (from Exod. 31:3; 35:31; cf. also Is. 11:2) who were to perform tasks helping the apostles to spread the 'word'. Stephen was one such person (so 6:10). All of this is a suitable introduction to Stephen's defence that Christ would destroy the temple and pave the way for a new one (6:13 – 7:60, on which see the discussion in ch. 6).

Furthermore, Colossians 1:19 refers to Christ as the end-time temple.

Psalm 67(68):16–17 (LXX)	Colossians 1:19
'God was well-pleased [*eudokeō*] to dwell [*katoikoō*] in it [*en autō* (Zion)] ... the Lord will dwell [there] forever ... in the holy place.'	'in him [*en autō*] all the fulness of deity was well-pleased [*eudokeō*] to dwell [*katoikoō*]'. (Alternatively, 'in him he was well-pleased for all the fulness to dwell'.)

Paul applies the psalmist's reference to God dwelling in Israel's temple to God now dwelling in his son, apparently as the expression of the latter-day temple in which God's presence fully resides.

Therefore, the identification of believers with temple-building in verse 9 becomes more understandable (they are building on Christ, the foundation of the temple). Some of the earlier Jewish references that understood Genesis 1:28 in terms of including an expansion of God's word by saints also compared the Qumran saints to an expanding temple (4Q158 [frags. 1–2] 7–8; 1QH 6.12–19 and 8.20–22; 4Q433a [frags. 1–2]; 4Q418, frag. 81 = 4Q423 8 + 24?; so also *Barnabas* 6:11–19)! Hence, both Paul and Qumran have interpreted Genesis 1:28 in connection with the temple in similar ways.

Chapter Eight

The temple in
2 Thessalonians 2

This chapter[1] will be a more in-depth study of one passage than other chapters of the book, since 2 Thessalonians 2:4 is considered by many commentators and many in the church to be one of the clearest passages in the New Testament affirming that a future temple will be built in Israel directly prior to Christ's second coming.

Second Thessalonians 2:4 refers to the Antichrist 'who opposes and exalts himself above every so-called god or object of worship, so that he takes his seat in the temple of God'. Does this refer to a future physical temple to be built in Israel during the period of a great tribulation? Does it refer to the Roman emperor who led his armies in destroying Israel's temple in AD 70? Is it a mere vague apocalyptic reference without a precise historical identification? The circumstances that lead up to this reference first need brief summary in order for us to understand its specific meaning better.

The content of the false teaching in Thessalonica

Paul highlights in 2:1–12 that false teaching will not deceive God's people, if they stand firm in the truth. He opens this chapter by referring to the subject of Christ's final 'coming' (*parousia*). It is Paul's response to a misguided understanding of both the nature and the timing of Christ's glorious coming. There were several forms of false teaching about Christ's final advent in the early church, which points to the fact that erroneous doctrine in general had run rampant in the first Christian communities.

It is unlikely that the errant teaching was about incorrectly set timetables concerning Christ's imminent return. Rather, the erroneous instruction claimed that eschatological events *had already happened*. This is apparent from observing that Paul's use of *enistēmi*

---

[1] See Beale (2003: *in loc.*) for amplified discussion of the following analysis of 2 Thess. 2:1–7.

('to be present', 'come') in his other epistles, in line with the typical contemporary Hellenistic usage (Moulton and Milligan 1972: 215), alludes to the present time in contrast to the future (e.g., Rom. 8:38; 1 Cor. 3:22; 7:26).[2] Therefore, the use of the perfect tense verb in 2 Thessalonians 2:2 likely has the classic 'perfect nuance' of an event occurring in the past, the effects of which continue into the present: the false claim is that Christ's coming and the final resurrection have already happened, so that there should be no present expectation of any further future occurrence of either of these events.

This deceptive teaching in Thessalonica has analogy with a false teaching in Corinth that denied there was to be a final, *physical* resurrection of the dead (1 Cor. 15:12–24). The false teachers apparently believed that spiritual resurrection from the dead, which Paul would affirm happens to all at conversion as an inaugurated end-time event,[3] is the only resurrection there would ever be. This may have entailed a belief that there would be no final coming of Christ at all. Paul combats such a notion by contending that all dead believers will be physically resurrected at the end-time, when Christ comes to conclude history (cf. 1 Cor. 15:20–58). There was also a similar problem in other early Christian churches (2 Tim. 2:18; Ignatius, *Letter to the Philadelphians* 7:1; 2 Pet. 3:3–13; *Gospel of Thomas* 52 [51]).

Apparently in Thessalonica, as elsewhere, false teachers were claiming that Jesus' future advent had already happened in some spiritual manner: either by his coming in the person of his Spirit (perhaps at Pentecost) or in conjunction with the final (spiritual!) resurrection of the saints. That both Christ's coming and the saint's resurrection are in mind in verse 1 and are the content of the 'day of the Lord' in verse 2 is discernible respectively from the wording of verse 1: 'the coming of our Lord Jesus Christ, and our gathering together to Him', which alludes to Christ's coming in the first epistle to gather saints at the final resurrection (so 1 Thess. 4:14, 'God will bring with Him [Jesus] those who have fallen asleep in Jesus'). The common wording and theme show that 2:1ff. is a further unpacking of 1 Thessalonians 4:14–17 and that the false teaching was an over-realized distortion of that part of Paul's first epistle.

When Christians become 'shaken' and uncertain about the verities of their faith, they become 'disturbed' (*throeō*). Paul writes to keep them fastened to the solid rock of truth. Paul's own authentic divinely

---

[2] So Best (1972: 276), who highlights Rom. 8:38 and 1 Cor. 3:22, and secondarily mentions Gal. 1:4 and 1 Cor. 7:26, though these have ultimately the same contrastive sense, as does Heb. 9:9.

[3] E.g., Rom. 6:1–9; Col. 2:12; 3:1; also John 5:25.

inspired 'word' or 'letter' is the cure-all to any pseudo-'prophecy, report or letter' (NIV) allegedly coming from him.

The prophesied sign of the final future apostasy

Paul summarizes in verse 3 what he has just said in verses 1–2: 'Let no one in any way deceive you' (v. 3a). True saints are to respond positively to this command in the face of the false teaching of verse 2. Why should they not be misled by such instruction? The first reason is that Christ will not come back finally until there has 'first' come a 'falling-away' (*apostasia*) from the faith. Though the word *apostasia* can refer to a political or a religious crisis,[4] the latter is the only use in the Greek Old Testament[5] and New Testament,[6] and it is the meaning here (so also Frame 1912: 251). Such a meaning is apparent because of the immediate context of false teaching (vv. 1–2 and vv. 9–12) and the clear allusions to Daniel's prediction of an end-time opponent who will bring about a large-scale compromise of faith among God's people.[7] That the apostasy will not occur primarily in the non-Christian world, as thought by Frame (1912: 251), but within the covenant community is clear from four observations:

1. 'a falling away' assumes some sort of 'prior turning to God';[8]
2. the above-noted usage of *apostasia* in the Old Testament;
3. the immediate context of deception within the church;
4. the closest verbal parallel in *Martyrdom of Isaiah* 2:4–5, where 'the angel of iniquity' empowers evil Manasseh 'in causing apostasy [*apostasia*], and in the lawlessness [*anomia*] which was disseminated in Jerusalem'.[9]

Apostasia in the Greek Old and New Testaments always refers to a 'departure from faith' and never to a 'bodily resurrection', as some want to argue who see the word referring to a pre-tribulation 'rapture'.[10] A negatively religious nuance of 'departure' is also

---

[4] See Schlier, '*apostasia*', *TDNT*, 1:513–514, for the former.
[5] Josh. 22:22; 2 Chr. 29:19; Jer. 2:19; 1 Maccabees 2:15.
[6] Acts 21:21; cf. verbal form in 1 Tim. 4:1; Heb. 3:12.
[7] On the Daniel background see further below.
[8] Schlier, '*apostasia*', *TDNT*, 1:513.
[9] Some commentators think the following served as models for 2 Thess. 2:4: *Psalms of Solomon* 17:11–22; Josephus's account of the Roman emperor Gaius Caligula (*War* 2.184–185); the *Sibylline Oracles'* summary of the emperor Nero's self-deifying career (*Sibylline Oracles* 5:29–34, 150).
[10] A conclusion corroborated by Feinberg 1995: 310. Indeed, as far as I am aware, such a use of the noun referring to 'physical removal' occurs nowhere in the ancient Greek world.

probable, since in verse 3 it is conjoined with the 'man of lawlessness', and in verses 8–12 deception and departing from the faith also appear in conjunction with 'the lawless one'.

The prophesied sign of the future Antichrist in the temple

In addition to the sign of 'apostasy', a second reason why the readers should not be misled into believing that Christ has already come is because the eschatological appearance of the Antichrist must also precede the Messiah's last advent. Therefore, Christ cannot have come back yet, since these two signs have not yet come about in their full form. Possibly, 'first' means the 'apostasy' will come before 'the man of lawlessness', but commentators are probably correct in generally agreeing that 'first' formally applies to both events merely happening before Jesus' final coming.

Therefore, it may be that at the same general time there is a 'falling away' from the faith, the Antichrist himself will make his appearance in history, especially in a future temple. On the other hand, despite the formal meaning of 'first', the 'falling away' could occur initially, and then the Antichrist could appear and take advantage of the 'falling away',[11] or, more probably, as in Daniel 8 and 11, his coming could instigate the 'apostasy'. This is supported by recalling that Antiochus Epiphanes instigated 'apostasy' (*apostasia*) in Israel (e.g., 1 Maccabees 2:15 and context), which is significant since many believe his activity to be the first fulfilment of the Daniel 11:31ff. prophecy.

A major question posed by verses 3–4 is whether this refers to a future apostasy in the land of Israel and the coming of the Antichrist to defile a yet future rebuilt temple in Israel or to the Roman emperor's defiling of Israel's temple in AD 70. In contrast to these alternative views, the following analysis will contend that these verses refer to a future apostasy throughout the worldwide church and the Antichrist's influence in the church, which is itself the inaugurated end-time temple of God. Of course, this discussion has significant implications for the main topic of this book, the relation of the Old Testament temple to the inter-advent age and its culmination.

---

[11] So see Schlier, 'apostasia', *TDNT*, 1:513, who proposes the apostasy could come first, setting up the fertile situation from which the Antichrist could arise, followed by an intensification of the apostasy through Antichrist's deception.

Paul's allusion to the Old Testament prophecy of the Antichrist

In verse 4, Paul is developing the prophecy about the Antichrist from Daniel 11.[12]

Daniel 11:31, 36	2 Thessalonians 2:3–4
[31]'forces from him will arise, desecrate the *sanctuary* fortress, and do away with the regular sacrifice. And they will set up the abomination of desolation' (so also Dan. 9:27; 12:11); [36]'he will exalt and magnify himself *above every god*, and will speak monstrous things against the God of gods ...'	[3]'the man of lawlessness ... [4]who opposes and exalts himself *above every* so-called *god* or object of worship, so that he sits in the *temple* of God, proclaiming himself to be God'.[13]

In addition, the expression 'man of lawlessness' (*anthrōpos tēs anomias*) echoes Daniel 12:10–11 (Theodotion), which is strikingly similar to Daniel 11:29–34, and refers to the end-time trial as a period when 'the *lawless ones* [*anomoi*] will do *lawlessness* [*anomēsōsin*], and all the *lawless ones* [*anomoi*] will not understand' (i.e., they will mislead or be misled, or both). This doing of lawlessness in Daniel is directly linked to, if not partly explained by, 'the time that the regular sacrifice is abolished and the abomination of desolation is set up' (Dan. 12:11; cf. 11:31) by the end-time enemy *in the temple*.[14]

According to the prophecy of Daniel 11:30–45, a final enemy of God will attack the covenant community. The attack is to take two forms. First, a subtle attack of deception by influencing with 'smooth words' some within the community 'who forsake the holy covenant' (v. 30) and 'who act wickedly toward the covenant' (v. 32), all of which stands behind Paul's reference to 'the apostasy' in verse 3 (Vos 1979: 111). The Antichrist will influence these people to become 'godless' themselves (v. 32), to compromise and to foster deception

[12] Among those who discern some degree of Daniel influence in verse 4, see Betz 1963: 282–284; Bruce 1982: 168; Marshall 1983: 190–191; Wanamaker 1990: 246–247; Hartman 1966: 198–205.

[13] See Frame 1912: 255 for verbal parallels.

[14] So also Dan. 7:25 speaks of Israel's persecutor as opposing God's 'law' (so Hendriksen 1979: 176).

and further compromise among others. Daniel says that 'many will join with them [the faithful] in *hypocrisy*', claiming to be faithful but in fact are not (v. 34). Second, the end-time foe will persecute those who remain loyal to God's covenant (vv. 33–35, 44). This end-time antagonist will appear openly before the community, 'exalt and magnify himself above every god' (v. 36), and then meet his final end under God's judicial hand (v. 45). Hence, Paul is developing the Daniel 11 – 12 prophecy in verses 3–4 and following.

What does it mean that the end-time adversary of God's people will 'take his seat in the temple of God', where he will do his deceiving work? Does Paul believe that Daniel prophesies the desecration of a literal, physical temple? Many believe this refers to the rebuilding of a material temple structure for Israel in Jerusalem at the end of time and the setting up of the Antichrist himself in that temple to deceive and be an object of worship.

Problems with understanding the temple as a material structure in light of the issue of the 'apostasy'

The problem with a 'material' view of a future temple building is manifold. First, 2 Thessalonians 2:3 appears not to be talking about an 'apostasy' from the faith in a geographically conceived Israel. The majority of Israel was always 'apostate' and unbelieving throughout the Old Testament era and at the time of Christ, and has been throughout history since that time. Even according to a futurist perspective, it may be difficult to view this passage as referring to a falling away of ethnic Israel, since the majority of Israel will have continued to be unbelieving up to and during the time the Anitchrist will appear (according to the futurist view, it is only at the very end of history that the majority of Israel will believe).[15] It is also difficult to conceive of verse 3 as alluding to an apostasy of unbelievers among the nations who are not part of the visible church, since the majority of them will have been unbelieving throughout the interadvent age.[16] Verse 3 instead appears to be alluding to a yet future massive 'falling away' in the community of faith, the church, throughout the world that has not happened hitherto.

It is certainly possible to opt for some kind of apostasy among ethnic

[15] Alternatively, it could be possible to conceive of an apostasy among ethnic Israelites in the sense that the remnant of true Israel existing throughout her history would be reduced to an even more radically smaller number at the eschaton right before her mass conversion, but this would be a pedantically strange viewpoint.

[16] On analogy with the view that the majority of Israel will be saved at the end, some believe the majority of the nations will be saved at Christ's final coming (so Bauckham 1993: 238–337).

Israelites and reject the alternative adopted here (Best 1972: 282–283). A reason for preferring this view could be that it was too early in the Christian movement for Paul to conceive of such widespread unbelief in the earliest churches, and nowhere else in the so-called 'genuine' letters does Paul suggest any such widespread apostasy. This objection is deflected, however, by recalling that Paul understood the Christian community as the continuation of true Israel in the midst of which pseudo-covenant keepers could exist. This is why Paul can apply prophecies about Israel to the church throughout his writings,[17] including the Daniel 11 prophecy about Israel's eschatological falling away.[18]

Problems with understanding the temple as a physical structure in the light of the gospels

Furthermore, that verse 3 is about a massive apostate movement towards the end of history in the church and not in Israel is apparent from the phrase 'the temple of God' in verse 4. This reference to 'the temple' also shows that the church community is the place where end-time prophecies about Israel and its temple will take place. The actual phrase 'temple of God' is found ten other times in the New Testament outside of 2 Thessalonians, and, except once, it always refers to the church.[19] Only one time does it refer to a literal temple in Israel of the past or future. In Matthew 26:61 Jesus is quoted as saying, 'I am able to destroy *the temple of God* and to rebuild it in three days.' This use is significant because it provides a transitional perspective between the Old Testament prophecies of a future, eschatological temple and the way Jesus began to view those prophecies as beginning to be fulfilled.[20] The physical temple is mentioned in order to indicate a redemptive-historical shift to the end-time temple. Matthew sees the material temple being destroyed[21] and rebuilt in Jesus' resurrection body.

---

[17] E.g., see Beale 1989a: 89–96; 1989b: 550–581; 1999b: 1–26.

[18] Early Christians would also have viewed through a similar redemptive-historical transmutative lens Jewish traditions expecting a similar apostasy in Israel (e.g., cf. *Jubilees* 23:14–23; *b. Sanhedrin* 97).

[19] Matt. 26:61; 1 Cor. 3:16, 17a, 17b; 2 Cor. 6:16a, 16b; Rev. 3:12; 7:15 ('his [God's] temple'); 11:1, 19. Seven of these appear with the article ('the') and three without. See almost identically 1 Cor. 6:19 ('a temple of the Holy Spirit'); Rev. 15:8 ('the [heavenly] temple was filled with smoke from the glory of God'); 21:22 ('and I saw no [physical] temple in it [the new Jerusalem] because the Lord God almighty is its temple and the Lamb').

[20] Such passages as 2 Sam. 7:13, Zech. 6:12–13 and *Tg. Isaiah* 53:5 prophesy that the coming Messiah will build the future temple.

[21] Though, as we will see below, even the reference to destroying the temple may have included allusion to Jesus' own body that had begun already to replace Israel's structural temple (likewise, see above, pp. 192–194).

That Jesus' resurrection represented the initial rebuilding of the temple is even clearer in John 2, where Jesus says essentially the same thing as in Matthew 26:61 (2:19–22), and there the evangelist adds that when Jesus referred to rebuilding or 'raising up' the temple, 'he was speaking of the temple of his body' and of his own resurrection. Jesus' resurrection was the beginning of the rebuilding of the latter-day 'temple of God'.[22] Israel's former, physical temple was but a physical foreshadowing of Christ and his people as the temple. For, remember, the primary point of the temple was that it was the place where God's glorious presence was manifested on earth to his people. Now that Jesus has come as God incarnate, he is now the place where God's presence is manifested in the world. In this respect, even preceding the John 2 statement, John 1:14 says, 'and the word became flesh, and tabernacled [or 'became a temple'] among us, and we beheld his glory, glory as an only-begotten from the Father, full of grace and truth'.

Problems with understanding the temple as a physical structure in the light of Paul's writings elsewhere

As we have seen in the preceding chapter, Paul elsewhere refers to believers as 'the temple of God' because they have believed in Jesus, who is the temple, and are identified with him as such and are a part of his body. Paul says twice in 1 Corinthians 3:16–17 that believers are a temple of God. Similarly, 2 Corinthians 6:16 affirms twice that believers 'are the temple of God'. Second Corinthians 1:20 says that the 'many promises God has made [in the OT] . . . are "Yes" in Christ' (NIV), which means they have begun to be fulfilled in the Corinthians who are 'in Christ'. Among the prophecies beginning fulfilment are those about the eschatological temple, as 2 Corinthians 7:1 says in further explanation of 6:16–18: 'we are the temple . . . Since we have these promises . . . let us purify ourselves' (NIV; likewise, cf. Eph. 2:19–21; 1 Pet. 2:4–7; Rev. 3:12, etc.).[23]

That the 'temple of God' in 2 Thessalonians is the church is pointed to further by recalling Paul's earlier depiction of the

---

[22] As we saw in an earlier chapter, Jesus' statement 'Destroy this temple, and in three days I will raise it up' (John 2:19) is probably like other of his double entendres in the Gospel of John. On one level, he refers to the destruction of the old temple that will be replaced by the true, eschatological temple of his resurrection body; on another level 'destroy this temple' could well refer to Jesus himself as the emerging new temple, who had already begun to replace the old one. If they attempted to destroy the new temple, it would only be raised again in the form of his resurrection body.

[23] See the extended discussion on 2 Cor. 6 and Eph. 2 (pp. 253–256, 259–263).

Thessalonian church by imagery and wording in 1 Thessalonians 4:8 ('God who gives His Holy Spirit to you') that parallels the cultic imagery in 1 Corinthians 6:19: 'Or do you not know that your *body is a temple of the Holy Spirit who is in you, whom you have received from God?*'[24] Such an understanding is consistent with Paul's penchant to refer to the church with the Old Testament names of Israel: e.g., 'the Israel of God' (Gal. 6:16),[25] 'the elect of God' (Col. 3:12), 'saints', 'the circumcision . . . who worship in the Spirit of God' (Phil. 3:3), etc. (so Findlay 1904: 170).

Problems with understanding the temple as a physical structure in the light of the book of Revelation

Particularly striking in comparison with 2 Thessalonians 2:4 is the apocalyptic text of Revelation 13:6, which even portrays the Antichrist attacking believers who are depicted as a 'tabernacle' (*skēnē* in Greek) and who live in the midst of deception all around them (cf. Rev. 13:3–8). I will argue in the following chapter that Revelation 11:1–7 contains the same picture. In Revelation 13:6, the phrase 'his tabernacle' is immediately followed by 'the ones tabernacling in heaven', which is a recollection respectively of the 'sanctuary' and heavenly 'host' in Daniel 8:10–13: the end-time tyrant 'caused some of the host [of heaven] and some of the stars to fall to the earth', and 'magnified himself to be equal with the Prince of the host and . . . the place of His sanctuary was thrown down' (Dan. 8:11). That is, in Revelation 13:6, 'his tabernacle' blasphemed by the beast is immediately clarified, even without a conjunction, to be 'the ones tabernacling in heaven'. In Daniel 8:10–11, the action is directed both against heavenly saints[26] and saints on earth, though in 2 Thessalonians the focus is only on an earthly attack, which is also the focus in Revelation 11:1–7 (though there the attack is against saints who are pictured as a 'sanctuary' and 'lampstands' in it).

What brings the 2 Thessalonians and Revelation passages close together for comparison is the fact that both are apocalyptic in nature and allude to and interpret Daniel's eschatological opponent prophecies. Furthermore, as we will argue below (on 2 Thess. 2:6), the

---

[24] Likewise, in both cases, the point is that the readers are to keep away from 'immorality' (*porneia*): cf. 'flee from *porneia*' (1 Cor. 6:18) and 'abstain from *porneia*' (1 Thess. 4:3). The upshot is that Paul wants the 'temple' to be 'holy' (so cf. 2 Cor. 6:16 – 7:1 with 1 Thess. 4:3–7, where both use the *hagios* ['holy'] word-group with reference to the readers).

[25] On which, see Beale 1999c: 204–223.

[26] Cf. Eph. 2:6 and Col. 3:1, which views the whole church as seated in heaven.

fulfilment of the Daniel 11 prophecy has begun unexpectedly (from an Old Testament reader's vantage point) within the church and thus further identifies the church with the temple, since Daniel foresees these events as inextricably linked to the temple.[27]

Objections to understanding the church as the temple and responses

Some conclude that the Christian church is not the temple in 2 Thessalonians 2:4, since 'in the present context ... no mention is made of the believer and the indwelling of the Spirit of God as in 1 Corinthians'.[28] But neither in the context is there a hint of any other kind of temple, so that the next best context within which to interpret 2:4 is the other epistolary references to God's new temple, which is the church. This discussion so far of the preceding context also favours the church on earth being the temple. The identification of the temple as being 'God's holy temple in heaven' is secondarily right.[29] The temple of God is Jesus and all who identify with him, so that the cultic eschatological centre of gravity has shifted to heaven where Jesus is, and his glorified saints, but with Pentecost that heavenly temple extends to earth wherever God's Spirit indwells people. The greater focus in 2 Thessalonians, however, is on Antichrist's attack on the earthly form of this temple, though in most of the relevant passages in the Apocalypse the heavenly form of the temple is pictured.[30]

F. F. Bruce is a likely representative of others in his objection to identifying 'the temple of God' with the church because such a conception 'is inapplicable at this early stage, when there was no united church organization which could provide such a power base' (Bruce 1982: 168–169). Bruce's contention, however, is weakened because it does not take into consideration the following important issues:

1. The locus of true Israel had already shifted from the theocratic nation to Christ and his followers (if we are to rely on the testimony of the Gospels).

2. Similarly, as we have seen in the first Thessalonian epistle (2:16),

---

[27] On the Rev. 11 and 13 texts, see Beale 1999a: *in loc.*

[28] As argued by Wanamaker 1990: 246.

[29] Frame 1912: 256, followed also by Richard 1995: 328–329, though Frame's focus is not on the temple as consisting of the people of God.

[30] On which, see Beale 1999a: *in loc* at 7:15; 11:19; 14:15, 17; 15:5–6, 8; 16:1, 17; for the earthly focus, see at 11:1–2; cf. as well as the mention of 'lampstands' at 1:12–13, 20 and 11:4, and for the location of the temple in the new creation, see at 3:12 and 21:22.

Paul believed that national Israel as the chosen people of God had come to its end. Presumably, the end of Israel's temple also would have been included in Paul's understanding, since Christ had predicted its destruction (e.g., Luke 21:6, 32). This means that Paul could not have viewed Israel's temple as 'the [true] temple of God' *even before* its actual destruction in AD 70, and it is unlikely that he uses this phrase in verse 4 to refer to 'the temple of God' as the same kind of Israelite temple directly preceding the lawless one's entrance into it (following Findlay 1982: 170). Such an unlikelihood is supported by realizing that an Antichrist would not be very effective at trying to deceive the true people of God (Christians), if he made the centre of his religious activities a temple controlled by unfaithful Israelites. In addition, it is not merely the ungodly nature of the temple's management that renders it improper as a reference to the true temple, but Christ's coming as the true temple, priest and sacrifice (so Heb. 7:11 – 10:22) made the first-century temple obsolete in a redemptive-historical sense: e.g., see especially Hebrews 9:11, 24, 'when Christ appeared as a high priest ... He went through the greater and more perfect tabernacle, not made with hands ... the true one ... heaven itself'. Likewise, Hebrews 10:19–21 asserts that believers 'have confidence to enter the holy place by the blood of Jesus, by a new and living way which He inaugurated for us through the veil [of the temple], that is, His flesh . .. since we have a great priest over the house of God ...'

3. The point of 2 Thessalonians 2:3–4 is that whatever the temple is to be identified with, it pertains to the visible covenant community in which true believers dwell and into which the lawless one is to make his entrance. In this respect, the small fledgling church throughout Palestine, Greece and Asia Minor is as good a candidate for an identification of the 'temple' as is a localized physical temple in only one small nation of the world.

4. This point is bolstered by recognizing that the pseudo-Christ figure of verses 3–4 is paralleled with Christ. This makes it more probable that his false messianic claims aimed at deceiving Christians would be made primarily in the new covenant community, where Christians exist, and not in the cultic centre of the old covenant community in Jerusalem (Hamann 1953: 428), or in a future revival of such a cultic place. Furthermore, the lawless one's activities summarized in verse 4 are amplified in verses 8–12, where among the people deceived are likely those who considered themselves part of the church community (e.g., those deceived are people who 'did not receive the love of the truth so as to be saved').

Unlikely also is the objection that the temple cannot be the church since 'the scope of the lawless one's actions seem much broader than just the church' (Martin 1995: 236). Only if the 'temple' were to be construed as the entire world of believers *and unbelievers* could this objection be sustained. From one perspective, it is correct that the end-time opponent's activities will occur throughout the world, since the church as the temple is to be found scattered throughout the world. It is also true that, in the light of other New Testament texts (Rev. 16:12–16; 19:19–20; 20:7–10), the scope of some of Antichrist's deceiving activities goes beyond the church, but the only place where the end-time adversary's activity occurs in 2 Thessalonians 2:4 is the 'temple', which I have argued is the church. And, though the Antichrist may deceive many outside the church, it is only within the worldwide church where his deception leads to 'apostasy', since those outside the church never professed faith in the first place.

Leon Morris also objects to the church being the 'temple' for two additional reasons (1959: 223). First, for the final antagonist to be able to establish himself in a position of authority in the church and call himself God would preclude the church from being considered a Christian church. True enough, but the same could be said about Israel's physical temple (an identification Morris prefers). Such a temple would not function according to its true purpose if the Antichrist were allowed to establish himself in it and arrogate to himself divine authority. Furthermore, the point Paul appears to be making is that the visible church community, within which true saints exist, will become so apostate that it will be dominantly filled with people who profess to be Christian but really are not.[31] The church will continue to profess to be Christian but most in it will actually not be true believers.

Second, Morris believes that, while the New Testament does refer to a falling away in the end times, it does not view the church as becoming apostate. But Jesus himself says that 'many will fall away . . . and many false prophets will arise, and will mislead many. And because lawlessness is increased, most people's [covenantal] love [for God] will grow cold' (Matt. 24:10–12). Global unbelief like that in the 'days of Noah' will occur directly before Jesus' final coming (Matt. 24:38–39; Luke 17:26–27). Jesus warns those in the community of faith to be ready for the apostasy and his return, acknowledging that

---

[31] In fulfilment of Dan. 11:30–34, which predicts an increase of those who 'forsake the holy covenant', are 'turned to godlessness' and who are 'hypocrites'.

some will not be vigilant and will be judged (Matt. 24:40 – 25:46; Luke 17:28–37). This points to the likelihood that both those outside the church and many, if not most, within the church will be unbelieving. Revelation 11:7–13 and 20:7–10 also prophesy a great, universal deception at the end, which likely means both an intensification of unbelief among already hardened people outside the church and especially 'apostasy' within the church.[32]

It needs to be remembered that the universal 'apostasy' is to occur only within the covenant community spread throughout the world and that unbelievers outside the church will be further hardened and deceived, leading to their attempt to annihilate any true believers remaining. As already noted, the 'falling away' spoken of in 2 Thessalonians precisely and predominantly takes place, not in the unbelieving world, but in the church because it involves a 'falling away' from an earlier condition of 'being close' to God (i.e., at least, a profession of such). If Paul leaves apostasy open as a possibility for the Thessalonians, why could he not have considered the same as a possibility for the entire church at the end of the age (Martin 1995: 234)? If Paul can say even before his death that 'everyone in [the churches of] the province of Asia has deserted me' (2 Tim. 1:15, NIV), how much more could this be true at the end of the age? Thus, just as Christians in the church of Sardis were known to 'live' though they were really spiritually 'dead' (Rev. 3:1; cf. also Matt. 7:21–23!), so it will be the case for the worldwide professing church at the very end. Such an expectation comports well with early Jewish beliefs of large-scale apostasy within the community of faith in the latter days.[33] Just as 'many' in Israel were apostate at the time of the first phase of fulfilment of Daniel 11:31ff. (1 Maccabees 1:11, 15, 43; 2:15), and the majority likewise were unbelieving during the second phase of fulfilment (AD 30–70), even more so will it be the case in the new covenant community at the final phase of fulfilment immediately before Jesus' final coming (Hendriksen 1979: 169).

The question of whether the Antichrist's 'sitting' is literal or figurative

What does it mean that the Antichrist will 'take his seat in the temple of God' in 1 Thessalonians 2:4? We have contended so far that some future temple in Israel is not in mind. Nor is it likely to refer to

[32] On which, see Beale 1999a: *in loc.*

[33] *Jubilees* 23:14–23; *2 Baruch* 41:3; *b. Sanhedrin* 97; cf. also *1 Enoch* 91:4–11; *4 Ezra* 1–2, which view unbelief as global and apparently extending beyond Israel.

a particular past desecration of the temple in Jerusalem, ineptly or otherwise prophesied by Paul (which some identify with the Roman overthrow in AD 70).[34] No temple desecration in the first century could be in mind, since verses 3–4 speak of an escalated 'falling away' that had not yet happened in Paul's time and probably did not occur only twenty years later in AD 70.[35] Furthermore, the final coming of Antichrist is still expected in the nineties by John.[36]

I. H. Marshall takes an opposite stance by concluding that no particular temple is in mind. Instead, he argues that verse 4 is speaking metaphorically only 'to express the opposition of evil to God'.[37] While possible, it is more probable that the temple is a more specific reference to the church as the continuation of the true temple because of the arguments set forth so far above, which we summarize here:

1. The use of the phrase 'the temple of God' elsewhere in Paul without exception refers to the church, and 'temple' in Revelation can refer to both true believers on earth or in heaven.

2. The Daniel 11:30ff. prophecy and its initial fulfilments (with Antiochus Epiphanes and then the Romans) take place within the covenant community and revolve around the temple in that community. Futhermore, if Antiochus Epiphanes in the second century BC was an initial fulfilment of Daniel 11:31–36, then that fulfilment could be considered an event concerning Israel's second architectural temple that became a typological foreshadowing of the church as the eschatological spiritual temple.

3. The 'apostasy' and its uses elsewhere in biblical literature all have to do with a 'falling away' by those within the covenant community from a former confession of loyalty to God.

Accordingly, 'to take his seat in the temple of God' is likely not a reference to the Antichrist's literal positioning of himself in a chair in the physical temple. Rather, a figurative 'sitting' is in view, in line with other metaphorical uses in the New Testament. For example, Matthew 23:2 says, 'the scribes and the Pharisees have seated themselves in the seat of Moses' (expressing a class of authoritative inter-

---

[34] Though Wanamaker (1990: 246–249) sees Paul mistakenly prophesying some such event like that of the AD 70 desolation of the temple.

[35] Israel was just as apostate in Paul's time as later in AD 70, and such a universal apostasy does not appear to describe anything that took place in the early church.

[36] As evident in 1 John 2:18–22; 3:4; and 4:16, a passage which is organically related to 2 Thess. 2:3–7 and also to the Antichrist prophecy of Daniel (see, e.g., Brown 1982: 400 as the link to 1 John).

[37] Marshall 1983: 192, followed by Stott 1991: 160; similarly, Hoekema 1979: 160; cf. likewise, Giblin 1990: 462.

preters), and there are repeated references to 'Christ sitting at the right hand of God' in heaven, which is figurative for his 'rule',[38] since it is unlikely that there is literal furniture in heaven.[39]

A non-literal notion of 'sitting in the temple' is supported further by the observation of many commentators that 2 Thessalonians 2 is apocalyptic in nature. '*Sit* on a throne' (with *kathizō* or *kathēmai*) in the Apocalypse is used often (approximately 15 times) figuratively for God, Jesus or saints being in a position of authority, which is enhanced by the obviously metaphorical picture of Jesus '*sitting* on a cloud' in heaven (in Rev. 14:14–15). Perhaps most comparable to 2 Thessalonians 2:4, however, is the negative picture of Babylon the Whore 'who *sits* on many waters' (Rev. 17:1) and is dressed as a priest (17:4; 18:16), which is interpreted as ruling over 'peoples and multitudes and nations and tongues' (Rev. 17:15, 18; 18:7).[40] This conclusion is consistent with the apocalyptic imagery of 2 Thessalonians 2:8 that is based on the same Isaiah 11:4 text as in Revelation 19:15, both of which portray Jesus judging the final enemy. The Revelation passage portrays Jesus defeating the corporate foe and their leader, while 2 Thessalonians pictures Christ 'slaying' the eschatological fiend 'with the breath of his mouth'. The depiction in both apocalyptic passages underscores Jesus' convicting and punishing the enemy by means of God's Law that has been disobeyed (on which see below at v. 8). The figurative nature of 2 Thessalonians 2:4 is also in keeping with 2:15, where Paul does not command the Thessalonians literally to 'stand' like soldiers on parade rest or to 'hold' on to something with their hands but to continue to believe the truth (Callow 1982: 81–82)!

Consequently, verses 3–4 mean that the latter-day assailant will come into the midst of the church, 'the temple of God', and cause it to become predominantly apostate and unbelieving. He will then try to take control of the church by spreading deception in it. That the end-time antagonist will 'display himself as being God' could mean that he makes himself out to be God, which is the epitome of blasphemy. Such blasphemy is most comparable to the Greek and Roman rulers who conquered Israel and the temple and set up idols of themselves in the temple to be worshipped as gods.

On the other hand, the idea may be that the Antichrist assumes so much influence and religious authority in the global community of

---

[38] Following Callow 1982: 63.

[39] For a heavenly throne, where Christ sits at God's right hand, see Matt. 26:64; Mark 16:19; Acts 2:30–36; Eph. 1:20; Col. 3:1; Heb. 1:3; 8:1; 10:12; 12:2; Rev. 3:21.

[40] On all of which, see Beale 1999a: *in loc.*

faith that he might as well be calling himself God. This is more consistent with the description of the eschatological adversary in Daniel 11, where it says that he will 'magnify himself above every god' and will honour a false god himself (so Dan. 11:36–39a). Therefore, he must not be claiming that he is an actual god, since he still worships some false god or idol. The point is that there are some ways that he sins so intensely that he is putting himself in the place of God. For example, he changes God's laws in Scripture and teaches other laws that contradict divinely revealed truth (Dan. 7:25; 8:11–12, 25; 11:30–32 affirm this). This is one reason that he is called 'the man of lawlessness'. In doing so he is acting like God. In essence, the Antichrist claims to be the ultimate Lawgiver, and the laws he gives contradict the God of the Bible's laws.[41]

The beginning fulfilment of Antichrist's prophesied defilement of the temple in the Thessalonian church

Paul has said in verses 3–4 that the readers should not be led astray in thinking that Christ's coming has already happened because the two signs of the final apostasy in the church and the final appearance of Antichrist have not yet occurred.[42] He states emphatically in verse 5 that a third reason they should not be deceived about this is because what Paul has just told them is not new information. Paul has repeatedly told them about the coming apostasy and Antichrist: 'Do you not remember that when I was still with you I was telling you these things?' Verses 3–4 were a reminder of what they already knew. The implication of the reminder is that Paul has perceived that the readers were becoming vulnerable to false teaching because they were in process of forgetting the truth he had already taught them.

---

[41] The earliest source in line with the understanding that the 'man of lawlessness' will deceptively infiltrate the church as the 'temple of God' is the *Epistle of Barnabas* 4 (mid-nineties AD), which appeals to the Dan. 7 prophecy of the end-time tyrant and associates him with 'the works of lawlessness' and 'the age of lawlessness', and equates the church with the temple (see also *Barnabas* 6 and 16 for the church as the temple)! Similarly, Rev. 11 and 13 develop the same prophecies of Dan. 7, 8, and 11 – 12, and also equate persecuted saints with the temple (see Beale 1999a: *in loc* on 11:1–2, 7, and on 13:1–7).

[42] There is a theological problem of relating 2 Thess. 2:1–4 to 1 Thess. 5:1ff., the former affirming that there are signs presaging Christ's coming and the latter saying there are no signs but that Christ's coming will occur unexpectedly for all. Though the scope of the present discussion does not allow further elaboration, see Beale 2003: *in loc.* for possible resolution of the problem.

Though Paul has underscored that the final manifestation of the Antichrist is yet future, in verses 6–7 he warns them that they cannot relax and let down their guard against his deceptive powers in the present. In fact, Paul makes the radical statement that they are not any safer from deception now than when Antichrist will actually come! Consequently, saints must not suppose that because the Antichrist has not yet come he cannot mislead them now.

We saw in verses 3–4 that Daniel 11:30–45 prophesied that a final foe of God would attack the covenant community in the latter days. The attack was to take three forms: persecution, desecration of the temple and deception through the subversion of divine truth. Paul first says in verse 6 that this antagonist has not yet come in full consummate form because something 'is restraining him now, so that in his time he may be revealed'. The purpose of the restraining force is to hold back the manifestation of the lawless one until it is the right time for his appearance. This also they should know because it is part of the instruction he had given them during previous visits (so v. 5).

The 'restrainer' who temporarily prevents Antichrist's final appearance

Commentators are greatly divided about the identification in verses 6–7 of 'the one who now holds ... back' (NIV's rendering of *ho katechōn* in v. 7, though also possible is the translation of 'the one who restrains'). Any identification faces the problem of explaining the change from referring to the 'restrainer' with the neuter gender in verse 6 (*to katechon*) to the masculine gender in verse 7 (*ho katechōn*). Most of the proposed solutions attempt to isolate an impersonal force in verse 6 and then link it with a personal one in verse 7. There are, at least, seven different identifications of the 'restrainer'.[43]

It is difficult to determine with probability the precise identification of the 'restrainer' ('possessor' is also a possible translation). Nevertheless, what is likely is that it/he is good and not evil, since a contest or tension between two inimical powers appears to make the most sense of the passage.[44] Additionally, it is clear that God is the ultimate power behind whatever historically particular agent is in mind.[45] This

[43] See the excellent summary and evaluation of Marshall 1983: 196–200; see Beale 2004: *in loc.* for the view that the 'restrainer' is the angel Michael.

[44] Marshall 1983: 199; despite the valiant proposal by Giblin.

[45] See Wanamaker 1990: 251–252 for other alternative identifications in addition to the ones listed above.

is explicit from the observation that the 'restrainer' will restrain until the revelation of the Antichrist 'at the proper time' (NIV, literally 'in his [the restrainer's or the Antichrist's or God's] own time') (see Best 1972: 276 for these three options). This 'time' is certainly set by God, since the whole segment (vv. 6–12) is placed within a prophecy-fulfilment framework.[46] God will bring history to a conclusion in his own timing. Verse 9 may suggest that Satan determines the timing of the lawless one's appearance (so Wanamaker 1990: 254). The verse, however, focuses more on the force which 'energizes' the activities of the final tyrant (in line generally with Rev. 13:2, 4) (so Bruce 1982: 173) rather than on the time when he will be revealed. The closest Pauline parallel is 1 Timothy 6:14–15: 'until the appearing of our Lord Jesus Christ, which He [God] will bring about in His own time (*kairois idiois*)'. This passage in 1 Timothy points further to Paul's thought being upon God as the sovereign disposer of historical events (cf. *heautou kairō* of 2 Thess. 2:6 with *kairois idiois* in 1 Tim. 6:15).

In the meantime, the 'restrainer' will continue to hold back the appearance of the final opponent 'until he [the restrainer] is taken out of the way', when it is finally time for Antichrist to be manifested (v. 7b).[47]

The 'mystery' of how Daniel's prophecy of the Antichrist in the temple has already begun fulfilment

Though Paul says the prophesied 'man of lawlessness' has not yet come in full incarnate form, he nevertheless claims there is a sense in which he has come: 'the mystery [*mystērion*] of lawlessness is *already* at work'. What does Paul mean by this? As with the majority of New Testament uses of 'mystery' (*mystērion*), this one also is placed in close connection with an Old Testament reference, this time to Daniel 11 in 2 Thessalonians 2:4. The word elsewhere, when so linked to Old Testament allusions, is used to indicate that prophecy is beginning fulfilment but in an unexpected manner in comparison to the way Old Testament readers might have expected these prophecies to be fulfilled (see Beale 1998: 215–272).

The reason Paul uses the word 'mystery' in verse 7 is that he understands the Antichrist prophecy from Daniel as beginning to be ful-

---

[46] This is consistent with the earlier affirmation that God 'destines' saints for 'trials' (1 Thess. 3:3), 'destines' them for 'salvation' (1 Thess. 5:9) and 'chooses' people 'for salvation' (2 Thess. 2:13).

[47] Verse 7b literally reads as an incomplete sentence: 'but the one who now holds it back till he is taken out of the way'. See Beale 2004: *in loc.* for further discussion of v. 7b, especially with respect to other possible translations.

filled in the Thessalonian church in an enigmatic manner not clearly foreseen by Daniel. Daniel says that the final Antichrist would appear in full force and openly to all eyes ('to exalt and magnify himself'), when he would attempt to deceive and persecute. Paul sees that, though this fiend has not yet come so visibly as he will at the final end of history, he is *nevertheless* 'already at work' in the covenant community through his deceivers, the false teachers. We would expect from Daniel's prophecy that when this fiend's deceivers are visibly on the scene, he would be visibly present as well. The revealed 'mystery' in the church at Thessalonica is that the prophecy of Daniel 11 is starting to be fulfilled unexpectedly, since the devilish foe has not come in bodily form, but he is already inspiring his 'lawless' works of deception through false teachers!

There is another unexpected element of the way Daniel is fulfilled. Daniel predicts that the end-time tyrant will desecrate the physical temple in the Israelite city of Jerusalem. This prophecy, however, begins fulfilment through false prophets, the corporate 'body of the Antichrist', who infiltrate the church, not only as the new covenant community but also as the new temple in a Gentile city! First John 2:18, 22 also says the Antichrist was already present in the church to which John was writing: 'it is the last hour; and just as you heard [from Daniel and Jesus] that antichrist is coming, even now many antichrists have arisen; from this we know that it is the last hour. . . the one who denies that Jesus is the Christ . . . is *the antichrist*' (so also 1 John 4:3; 2 John 7!). Therefore, the Thessalonian Christians, and we, must not think that the Antichrist's deception will come only when he appears in final fleshly form, but we must be on our guard *now* in order not to be deceived by his unusual invisible coming into the new covenant temple through his corporate emissaries, the false teachers!

Jesus also refers to the same prophecy from Daniel to which Paul is referring (see Matt. 24:4–5, 10–13, 23–26). Just as the main point in 2 Thessalonians 2:1–7 is on 'do not let anyone deceive you' (v. 3), the main point of the Matthew 24 passage is that no-one mislead Jesus' followers about his second coming (vv. 3–4). Jesus predicts that before he comes, many antichrist's will, indeed, come. He is focusing not on the final arrival of one Antichrist but on the coming into the church of many antichrist's who are the semi-fulfilments and forerunners of the final predicted opponent of God (Matt. 24:5, 10–15, 24). These are the same false prophets to which 1 John 2:18 and 2 Thessalonians are referring. Jesus even says in Matthew 7:21–23 that those who were regarded as teachers of the church will be judged as false teachers at the final judgment. Note that Jesus refers to them as those who practised 'lawlessness' (*anomia*), the same word used in 2 Thessalonians 2:7 in the phrase 'the mystery of lawlessness'.

Paul is saying that even now the false teachers that have been prophesied by Daniel and Jesus (cf. Matt. 24:4–5, 23–24, etc.) are with us. This means that the end-time 'great tribulation' has begun in part! The prophecy of the 'apostasy' and coming of 'the man of lawlessness' into the temple of the new covenant church has started fulfilment!

Indeed, the sign of Jesus' death together with what 1 John 2:18 and 2 Thessalonians 2:6–7 have said makes it clear that the great tribulation, when Antichrist would come, has already begun to take place. The prophesied latter-day temple has also started to appear in the form of the church community (see on v. 4) into which verse 7 says the Antichrist has already begun to enter and defile. Daniel predicted that there would be three telltale marks of the great tribulation: persecution, desecration of the temple and deception through false teachers within the temple and in the covenant community. It is clear that persecution and deception in the ecclesiological sanctuary started in the first century and has continued ever since. The desecration of the temple is the entry of the unclean and deceptive spirit of the Antichrist into the sacred community of faith, which attempts to alter God's laws. Therefore, the tribulation has been going on throughout the age of the church (for persecutions in Thessalonica see Acts 17:5–8; 1 Thess. 1:6; 2:14; 3:3–4). To be sure, this tribulation has not yet reached its climax. There will be an escalation of the present tribulation when *the* incarnate Antichrist appears at the end of history. At that time, persecution and deception, which have formerly affected only part of the church throughout history, will be present throughout the worldwide church, the temple, at which point Christ will return (see Rev. 11:1–13; 20:1–10). In this light, the expression the 'temple of God' in 2 Thessalonians 2:4 is not an exception to but naturally falls in line with all of the New Testament's (including Paul's) nine other applications of the same expression to the church elsewhere.

Conclusion: does Paul spiritualize Daniel's temple prophecy? A 'literal' versus a 'redemptive-historical' approach

Some will surely object to the preceding discussion on the grounds that it 'spiritualizes' Daniel's prophecy about the Antichrist and especially the temple. Many affirm that the prophet Daniel surely had in mind a physical temple that will exist in latter-day Israel. Accordingly, to say that this prophecy is fulfilled in Christ and the church is to violate 'a literal hermeneutical' principle by which all Scripture is to be interpreted.

A number of responses are in order, some of which have already been anticipated in earlier discussions, and more will be given in a concluding chapter on 'Theological conclusions'. First, a 'literal hermeneutic' is not the best way to describe a biblical hermeneutic. Perhaps a 'literate hermeneutic' that aspires to the broad literary meaning in the canonical context is a better way to put it (see Vanhoozer 2001: 312–314). We should want to follow an interpretative method that aims to unravel the original intention of biblical authors, realizing that that intention may be multi-layered, without any of the layers contradicting the others. Such original intentions may have meaning more correspondent to physical reality (hence so-called 'literal interpretation') while others may refer to 'literal' spiritual realities.

Second, the progress of revelation certainly reveals expanded meanings of earlier biblical texts. Later biblical writers further interpret earlier biblical writings in ways that amplify earlier texts. These subsequent interpretations may formulate meanings that earlier authors may not have had in mind but which do not contravene their original, essential, organic meaning. This is to say that original meanings have 'thick' content and that original authors likely were not exhaustively aware of the full extent of that content. In this regard, fulfilment often 'fleshes out' prophecy with details of which even the prophet may not have been fully cognizant.

Third, our interpretation of 2 Thessalonians 2:1–7 indicates that Paul understood the Daniel 11 prophecy about the end-time opponent desecrating the temple as beginning fulfilment in his own time. Possibly, my interpretation is wrong. To say it is wrong, however, primarily on the basis that it does not 'literally' interpret the book of Daniel is not enough to overturn my analysis. Or, one could say Paul illegitimately 'spiritualizes', though this is not an attractive option for those with a high view of Scripture. Such a conclusion could also reveal an over-confidence in the standards of modern interpretative methods as the ultimate arbiter of the correctness of ancient interpretative methods.

If my analysis of 2 Thessalonians is on the right track, then Paul is developing the interpretation of Daniel 11 – 12 in the light of progressive revelation: the beginning fulfilment of Daniel's prophecy in Christ and the church. We have observed in the preceding chapters and in this chapter that Christ is the true end-time temple, and all who identify with him by faith become part of that temple. There are pseudo-believers who claim to be part of the true temple. It is into the midst of that temple of a mixed multitude of loyal and disloyal covenant-keepers that the incarnate Antichrist steps during the very last days of history.

God promised to dwell in a temple among his eschatological people. The main purpose of the temple in the Old Testament and the purpose of the expected end-time temple was to house God's glory before which his people were to worship. Many Israelites may well have understood the prophecy in Daniel 11 to refer to a physical temple in which the Antichrist would appear, and, following his demise, God's glory would be manifested in such a temple to a greater extent than ever before. We have discovered in preceding chapters, however, that some of the Old Testament's explicit end-time prophecies of the temple foresee a non-structural, non-human-made reality (e.g., Is. 4:5–6; 57:15; 66:1–2; Dan. 2; Zech. 1 – 2). In addition, similar observations have been made about the Garden of Eden (Gen. 2; Ezek. 28:18), the small-scale sanctuaries of the Patriarchs, Mount Sinai and God's dwelling with Israelite exiles (Ezek. 11:16; cf. also Is. 8:14.) How does one put together the passages like Daniel 11:30–39 that appear to predict a structural eschatological temple[48] and those prophesying a non-structural one? Do the former serve as the interpretative key for the latter or vice versa? Or, are these two sets of prophecies contradictory or impossible to harmonize from the human interpreter's perspective?

We believe the non-structual prophecies should interpret the apparent structural ones because this best fits the New Testament's interpretation of the Old Testament prophecies about the temple. We have endeavoured, not only in this chapter, but in preceding chapters, to show that the New Testament explains that the temple prophecies have begun fulfilment through Christ's glory in the land of Israel, and views the consummated fulfilment to be God and Christ's glory manifested throughout the entire cosmos. The precise physical form in which the temple promise may have been conceived has been surpassed in the fulfilment of a greater literal reality of God's expansive presence. It should certainly not be a surprise that the New Testament

---

[48] See also Dan. 8:11–14; 12:11.

could conceive of the new temple as non-structural in the light of the numerous Old Testament precedents of such a phenomenon!

This is to say that progressive revelation has clarified those prophecies that appeared to be predicting a structural temple. The prophecy and the fulfilment of Daniel are comparable to a father's promise to his young son in 1900 that he will give his son a horse and buggy when he grows up and gets married. When the son marries thirty years later, the father gives him a car, which has since been invented and mass-produced. Does the father not literally fulfil his promise to the son? It is true that the precise form in which the promise of a mode of transportation was given has changed, but the essence of the promise has not changed: a convenient mode of personal transportation. Indeed, the progress of technology has made the fulfilment of the promise even greater than initially conceived.[49]

The substantial essence of the new temple is still the glory of God, however that glory is no longer confined within a material building but revealed openly to the world in Christ and his subsequent dwelling through the Spirit in the worldwide church as the temple.[50] The progress of God's revelation has made the fulfilment of apparent prophecies of an architectural temple even greater than originally conceived by finite minds. This is what Haggai 2:9 appears to express: 'The latter glory of this house will be greater than the former.'

The practical relevance of this discussion for the contemporary church, the temple, is that the spirit of the Antichrist may already be found hovering in its midst when its leaders change God's word and contradict its meaning. For example, many church leaders today say that we need to be accepting of other faiths, contending that sincerity in any kind of faith may be a legitimate path to God. 'Who are we to say that *we* have the only truth?' To many, the exclusive claim of Christianity sounds narrow and harsh. Yet Jesus himself said, 'I am the way, and the truth, and the life; no one comes to the Father, but through Me.' His follower Peter said, 'there is salvation in no one else; for there is no other name under heaven that has been given among men by which we must be saved' (Acts 4:12). Such teachings represent

---

[49] This illustration was inspired by Satterthwaite 2000: 43–51.

[50] After coming to the conclusion that the 'temple of God' in 2 Thess. 2:4 is equivalent to the church, I have found that Findlay 1982: 170–174 is apparently the first among modern commentators consulted who held the same view, followed by, e.g., Lenski 1934: 414–415; Hamann 1953: 178; Giblin 1967: 76–80 (though Giblin subsequently rejected this view in a 1990 article); and LaRondelle 1989: 345–354; so also Calvin 1984: 330–331; and even earlier Chrysostom and other Antiochene Fathers (on which, see Milligan 1908: 100–101).

'the lawlessness' of the Antichrist prophesied by Daniel to pollute the end-time temple. True believers need to be on the alert not to be deceived by such eschatological corruption, in order to keep 'the temple of God' doctrinally and ethically pure.

Indeed, it should not be assumed that the 'spirit of the Antichrist' (1 John 4:1–3) influences only unbelieving false teachers. Leaders who are true Christians and those under their guidance are susceptible to this influence and can be caught up in worldly ways of thinking. All in the church to one degree or another are confronted and tempted by this worldly influence. This is why we need continually to be alert to resisting it.

Chapter Nine

The inauguration of a new temple in Hebrews

The book of Hebrews discusses the tabernacle or temple more than any other New Testament book, except perhaps for John's Apocalypse, which gives prolonged descriptions of the heavenly temple. The author speaks more of the 'tabernacle' than the 'temple', but what he says of the former also applies to the latter. We have seen that the temple in Jerusalem was the permanent form of the mobile tabernacle and that the two are so closely related that, for all intents and purposes, they are functionally identical.[1] Hebrews may focus more on the tabernacle than the temple because its overall shape and the furniture in it are described in more detail in the Old Testament (in Exodus) and are more explicitly related in the Old Testament to a heavenly 'pattern' than is the temple (see Exod. 25:9, 40). This focus presumably makes it easier for the author to draw parallels from the earthly tabernacle to his conception of the present heavenly tabernacle and sanctuary.

Before focusing on the temple, however, it is important to recall the main points of Hebrews within which discussion of the temple occurs as a subordinate topic to the overriding concern of the book: who is Jesus in relation to the Old Testament epoch? The book begins by underscoring the absolute supremacy of Jesus over angels and humans (1:3 – 2:16). He is also greater than Moses (3:1–6), partly because Moses' leadership did not result in the ultimate 'rest' for God's people (3:7–19); likewise, Christ is greater than Joshua for the same reason (4:6–11). Jesus is the high priest par excellance (4:14 – 5:10), and as such he is a priest in the line of Melchizedek, a priestly order superior to that of the Levitical priesthood, offering up a superior sacrifice in comparison to the sacrifices of the old covenant (7:1–28). In fact, the Levitical priesthood, their temporary sacrifices, and the sanctuary in which the priests served are but old covenantal shadows of the new covenant in which Christ is the eternal high priest as well as the abiding sacrifice in an everlasting tabernacle (8:1 – 10:22).

---

[1] E.g., see p. 32.

Throughout the epistle there are paraenetic sections exhorting the readers to press forward in their profession of Christ and not drift back to the old covenantal forms of worship. The purpose of the writer is to exhort the readers to maintain their faith in Christ, his priestly work and his sacrifice for them, from which they are in danger of falling away and thus committing apostasy.

Having briefly surveyed the main themes of Hebrews[2] and how the tabernacle is a part of those themes, we now want to attempt to determine in the following discussion how the view of the tabernacle in Hebrews fits in or contributes to the overall biblical perspective of the temple that we have so far been studying in this book.

The temple in Hebrews 8

The first substantial discussion of the temple in Hebrews occurs in 8:1–5 in conjunction with the subject of the role of the priesthood. In particular, verses 1–2 affirm the following:

> [1]Now the main point in what has been said is this: we have such a high priest, who has taken His seat at the right hand of the throne of the Majesty in the heavens,
> [2]a minister in the sanctuary, and in the true tabernacle, which the Lord pitched, not man.

Christ is a new high priest who, as a result of his resurrection and ascension, has sat down at the right hand of God's heavenly throne. This heavenly place of rule is, however, not merely a king's palace. It is also a 'sanctuary . . . and true tabernacle' (v. 2). 'Sanctuary' is a rendering of the Greek plural of *hagios*, which literally means 'holies' or 'holy places' (*hagiōn*). We have seen that this plural form is an Old Testament way of speaking about the earthly temple complex with its various holy precincts (e.g., Lev. 21:23; Ezek. 7:24; Jer. 51:51).[3] Thus, this is probably a specific reference to the 'holy of holies' since the next mention of plural 'holies' in 9:3 has this in mind: 'And behind the second veil, there was a tabernacle which is called the Holy *of Holies.*' Likewise, this abbreviated form 'holies' clearly refers to the holy of holies in 9:8; 10:19; and 13:11 (following Ellingworth

---

[2] See Carson, Moo and Morris 1992: 391–394, 401–404 for an overview of the development of thought and major themes in Hebrews, upon which this discussion has been partly dependent.

[3] On which, see further above, pp. 75, 124.

1993: 400).[4] Instead of the earthly sanctuary, the focus in 8:2 is on the sanctuary in heaven, which the author also calls 'the true tabernacle'.

Does Hebrews spiritualize the tabernacle? A 'literal architectural' versus a 'redemptive-historical' approach

The heavenly sanctuary of Hebrews 8 is called the 'true tabernacle' because the earthly one was but a 'copy and shadow of the heavenly' one (8:5a). The gist of verse 5b confirms this: 'just as Moses was warned by God when he was about to erect the tabernacle; for, "See ... that you make all things according to the pattern which was shown you on the mountain"' (quoting Exod. 25:40). Hebrews informs us of something that was not clear in Exodus: the pattern that Moses saw on Sinai was apparently of the true heavenly tabernacle that was to come later with Christ and descend and eventually fill the whole earth. It was this eschatological sanctuary of which Moses was to make a small earthly model. This was the 'true tabernacle' because it was the 'genuine article', the 'literal' and real one. In contrast, the earthly tent was but 'a copy and shadow', a figurative portrayal of the literal heavenly one (so also Heb. 9:24) that was 'the greater and more perfect tabernacle' (Heb. 9:11). Heaven is viewed 'axiologically ... as the "place" of God's presence, [that] transcends earth as the source of all reality and value' (Lane 1991: 210–211).

It is important to underscore the 'true' nature of the new tabernacle in which Christ now dwells and the 'figurative' tabernacle that God dwelt in during Israel's wilderness wanderings. Some Christian interpreters believe that what is literal can only be physical and what is non-literal must be non-physical. The author of Hebrews, however, gives precisely the opposite definition: the literal sanctuary is the heavenly one and the figurative sanctuary is the earthly. Hebrews 9:8–9 even refers to the old 'tabernacle' (precisely, the holy place) as a 'symbol' or 'parable' of the end-time tabernacle (e.g., in 9:11) in order to underscore that the former tabernacle was not ultimately the real one (Walker 1996: 204). Part of the reason for this resides in the meaning of the author's use of 'true' (*alēthinos*). The reference to the tabernacle as 'true' in Hebrews 8:2 and 9:24 connotes both (1) that which is 'genuine' or represents 'the real state of affairs'[5] of reality and (2) prophetic typological fulfilment.

---

[4] Philo occasionally refers to 'the Holy of Holies' as 'the Holies of Holies' (*Leg. All.* 2.56; *Mut. Nom.* 192) or 'the innermost places of the Holies' (*Som.* 1.216).
[5] On which see Bultmann, '*alētheia, alēthinos, ktl.*', *TDNT*, 1:238–251.

One of the best illustrations of a similar use of 'true' occurs in Revelation 3:14, where Christ calls himself the 'faithful and *true* witness', and designates himself as the genuine or authentic witness in contrast to fleshly Israel as false witnesses.[6] The word 'true' likely includes more than mere moral and cognitive truth, but also the idea of 'authentic' in the redemptive-historical sense of Jesus being *true* Israel by fulfilling the Isaiah 43:10–19 prophecy about God and Israel's witness to the new creation. In contrast to unfaithful Israel, he fulfilled the prophecy by perfectly testifying to the new creation both before and after his resurrection. Jesus' witness was about himself, since he was the centrepiece of the new creation. In this manner, he demonstrated himself to be the true end-time Israel prophesied by Isaiah. This attribute of authenticity in Revelation 3 may also be viewed against the Isaiah background of God saying that Israel should be a faithful witness, in contrast to the nations as false witnesses to their idols or their idols themselves being false witnesses, which the nations mistakenly believe to be the 'truth' (*alēthē*; Is. 43:9). Therefore, Christ is the 'true witness' after which all other faithful witnesses are modelled (cf. Rev. 2:13).[7]

Likewise, Hebrews refers to the heavenly tabernacle as 'true' because it is the fulfilment, not only of direct prophecies of the eschatological temple, but of everything the Old Testament tabernacle and temples foreshadowed. They were all intended to be imperfect models and temporary 'copies' of the coming true, eternal temple (see again Heb. 8:5). As we will see in our study of the use of Haggai 2 in Hebrews 12:26–28 below, the end-time temple is 'greater and more complete' (Heb. 9:11) than the old one because it is 'unshakeable', permanent, and eternal. It cannot be changed, nor can it ever pass away, because it is made not by imperfect human hands, but by God's hand as a new creation.

Thus, we may say that the eschatological temple is 'true' not only in the sense of fulfilment but also in that, unlike the previous temples, it is the ultimate one that will remain for ever. The former temple was not the 'true one', not only because it was a mere shadow of the one to come

---

[6] Cf. Jesus as 'true', without the addition of 'faithful', in Rev. 3:7 in contrast to those in 3:9 'who call themselves Jews, and they are not, but they lie'.

[7] Likewise, the manna in the wilderness was but a foreshadowing of Jesus, 'the true bread out of heaven' (John 6:32), and Israel's description as a 'vine' was but an imperfect foreshadowing of Jesus, 'the true vine' (John 15:1; for similar such uses of 'truth', see John 1:9, 17; 4:23–24).

but because it would cease to exist.[8] To believe that a physical temple will be built after the eschatological one has been inaugurated would be to return to the former 'shadowy' stage of temple existence. Once the end-time, eternal temple that corresponds to the reality of the heavenly one comes, it would be a strange reversal for God to commend a return to the shadows. To believe that Israel's temple or one rebuilt by human hands would last for ever is a false view because it mistakes the symbolic temple (Heb. 9:8–10) for the real one (Heb. 9:11).

Edmund Clowney has underscored how crucial it is to comprehend that this perspective of the temple

> is not spiritualization in our usual sense of the word, but the very opposite. In Christ is realization. It is not so much that Christ fulfils what the temple means; rather Christ is the meaning for which the temple existed ...
>
> Our reflection on the claims of Christ has already shown us that his use of the Old Testament is far from figurative. The situation is completely reversed. In the wisdom of God's purpose the earlier revelation points forward to the climax, when, in the fullness of time, God sent his own Son into the world.
>
> Christ is the true temple, the true light, the true manna, the true vine. The coming of the true supersedes the figurative. The veil of the temple made with hands is destroyed, for its symbolism is fulfilled.
>
> At the cross the actualization of the symbolism of sacrifice is particularly clear. It is not a figurative use of Old Testament language to say that Christ is the Lamb of God offered to make atonement for sin. The sin-offering at the temple altar is not being 'spiritualized' when we say it is fulfilled in Christ. Neither is the temple being 'spiritualized' when we say that in the resurrection the true temple was raised up. No earthly temple made with hands can ever again become the place of God's dwelling. (Clowney 1972: 177, 182–183)

These notions are certainly part of what is behind Christ's self-assertion that his presence on earth meant that 'something greater

---

[8] A further reason for the eternal existence of the new temple in the new creation is that it will exist in the midst of God's unfettered glory, whereas God's special presence in the old cosmos was cordoned off in a back room of the old temple. In this respect, see Cody (1960: 81–84, 154–155), who focuses on 'God's dynamic presence' in heaven as defining 'true' but does so more in a Platonic sense.

than the temple is here' (Matt. 12:6). All of the things that pointed towards Christ in the Old Testament (sacrifices, temple, manna, kings, priests, etc.) find their most 'literal' or 'true' meaning in him.

There may be additional reasons that can be inferred from other biblical writings which could lie behind Hebrews' assertion that the literal temple is not the physical but the heavenly one: (1) the perspective of the Old Testament and Acts with respect to why the end-time temple cannot be 'handmade' and (2) Revelation's view that God's presence in Israel's temple was to be extended throughout the new creation, which becomes equivalent to a latter-day temple. Though these reasons are not explicitly mentioned by the author of Hebrews, they may have contributed to the background of his thinking. (See the excursus at the end of this chapter.)

The Old Testament background of Hebrews 8:2

Hebrews 8:2 highlights further the fact that the eternal 'true tabernacle' could only be the one 'the Lord pitched, not man'. Not coincidentally, as we briefly noted in chapter 4, Hebrews 8:2 alludes to Numbers 24:6 (Greek OT):[9]

Numbers 24:5–6	Hebrews 8:2
'How good are ... your tabernacles, Israel ... tabernacles which God pitched.'	'the holy places ... and the tabernacle which the Lord pitched'.

There was a sense in which God was responsible for constructing Israel's tabernacle in that he commanded Moses to make it. But Hebrews 8:5 emphasizes that the tabernacle Moses was to make was to be done 'according to the pattern which was shown you on the mountain'. That is, that tabernacle was only a copy and small model of the yet-future end-time tabernacle to be made only by God by incorruptible materials, not of this creation but of the coming new creation. Thus, 'the Lord pitched' the new tabernacle and 'not man'. What is significant about the reference to Numbers 24 is that it is one of the Old Testament passages we have proposed to be a part of Israel's Adamic mandate as a corporate Adam to enlarge the boundaries of her garden-like tabernacle until they circumscribed the entire earth.[10]

---

[9] Note even the common plural reference to the temple.
[10] Indeed, the LXX is an interpretative rendering of the botanical Hebrew phrase 'like aloes planted by the Lord'.

In like manner, an Aramaic version (*Tg. Neofiti*) of Numbers 24:6 understands the botanical expression 'like aloes planted by the Lord', originally part of the expanding garden depiction in the Hebrew text, to refer to the tabernacle: 'like the heavens which God has spread out as the house of his Shekinah, so shall Israel live and endure for ever beautiful . . . and exalted among his creatures'.[11] Thus, we have in this Aramaic interpretation of Numbers 24:6 the picture of Israel's commission to spread out over the earth being compared to the extension of the cosmic tabernacle of the heavens that God spread out in his first creation to house his glory.[12]

The connection of Hebrews 8:2 with the similar Greek and Aramaic biblical traditions of Numbers 24:6 is enhanced by noticing that it also is a 'tabernacle' that is 'in the heavens' (Heb. 8:1–2; so also 8:5; 9:24), in which Christ the 'high priest . . . has taken His seat at the right hand of the throne of the Majesty'. This notion of kingship, like that echoed in Numbers 24, is possibly related to the epistle's earlier portrayal of Christ as the inaugural fulfilment of everything Adam should have been as a human vice-regent over creation (Heb. 2:6–9). This portrayal is based on the ideal Adam passage of Psalm 8. This connection to Hebrews 2 may be enhanced by noticing that the earlier Adamic depiction leads directly into the first discussion in the epistle of Christ as a 'high priest' (2:10–17). Could this echo the pattern that we have seen in Genesis 1 – 2, where Adam is first portrayed as a 'king' (1:26–28) and then as a priestly figure, ruling and worshipping in a temple (Gen. 2:15)?[13] Furthermore, the earlier discussion in Hebrews 2 also identifies him not only as a priest but as ruling over evil (2:14) and as having God as his Father, implying his sonship (cf. 2:11 with 7:28 – 8:2).

Consequently, Christ is the priest-king whose resurrection was the beginning of the latter-day temple and whose ascent into heaven meant that the temple's centre of gravity had shifted from earth to heaven, and would remain there during the present age. Christ as a priest-king continues reigning and ministering within the heavenly temple-palace.

---

[11] See pp. 125–126 above for fuller discussion of the relationship of the Hebrew, Greek and Aramaic texts of Num. 24:6.

[12] Furthermore, this extension is conceived of as led by a 'king' widening his 'kingdom' (Num. 24:7).

[13] On which see the concluding section of ch. 2 and the beginning of ch. 3.

Christ as the veil of the heavenly end-time tabernacle

Interestingly, the author of Hebrews also identifies Christ with the veil of the temple: believers can 'enter the holy place by the blood of Jesus' that is 'a new and living way which He inaugurated for us *through the veil, that is, His flesh ...*' (Heb. 10:19–20). As a 'great priest over the house of God' (Heb. 10:21), Jesus has cleared the way for his people to enter into and dwell in the true, heavenly 'Holy of Holies' (cf. also Heb. 9:11, 24). Might this be comparable to Mark 15:29 and 38–39? While debatable, if the analysis of the chiasm there was correct, the crucifixion of Jesus' body was interpreted to be the 'rending of the temple veil', and resulted in a Gentile being ushered into God's presence, formerly limited to the holy of holies.[14] Could this also be a metaphorical equivalent of referring to Christ as the beginning of the new creation (the 'new and living way'), as Paul and John explicitly state (so 2 Cor. 5:14–17; Gal. 6:15–16; Col. 1:18; Rev. 3:14)?[15] Together with 'new', the word 'living' (*zōsan*) refers to resurrection life in the age to come, both words underscoring the notion of new creation.

Indeed, the next mention after 10:19 of Jesus' sacrificial 'blood' is in Hebrews 13:12, which is inextricably linked to the way to the 'lasting city ... to come' (13:14) and to the new creation by resurrection: 'God ... who brought up from the dead' Christ 'through the blood of the eternal covenant' (13:20). The Old Testament's and early Jewish tradition's view of the veil as representing the heavenly cosmos may have sparked the thought of comparing Christ's work of new creation to entering through the veil of his own flesh. Believers who identify with the resurrected Jesus as an inaugurated new creation enter into God's holy of holies' presence, which can dwell only in a perfected new creation. Their only access to the new creation, and hence the divine presence, is through Jesus.

That Christ was a priest in performing this work may merely be a mixed metaphor (Heb. 10:20–22 portrays Christ as sacrifice, veil and priest). Alternatively, it may reflect the earlier notion implicit in the Old Testament and developed explicitly in Judaism that, just as the temple symbolized the world, so the priest was an even more miniature symbol of the cosmos, representing at the same time the

[14] On which see ch. 5 (pp. 193–194).
[15] For the texts on new creation in Paul and Revelation, see Beale 1989b: 550–581; 1996: 133–152; 1999c: 204–223.

temple.[16] This earlier tradition was possibly responsible for the later midrashic idea that 'the temple corresponds to the whole world and to the creation of man who is a small world'.[17] Perhaps, the unspoken rationale bridging the portrayal of Christ as a 'veil' and 'priest' may be the fact that both were symbols of the cosmos; accordingly, Christ is the inauguration of the new cosmos, providing 'a *new* and *living* way'. Though the main point of these verses is the new access into God's presence through the priestly work of Jesus, the association of his work with the new inbreaking creation may not be out of sight. Thus, Christ's priestly work of sacrifice is so closely tied to his resurrection as new life, that they are almost two sides of one coin.

In fact, this preceding discussion is consistent with the idea that Christ as the last Adam, king and high priest represents true humanity (Heb. 2:6–17), implying that, as a new Adam figure, he has inaugurated a new world. In this respect, we have seen above that the conception of Christ as the ultimate Adam and priest-king from Hebrews 2:6–17 may lie behind Hebrews 8:1, where Christ is referred to as a 'high priest' and king ruling 'at the right hand of the throne'.

Christ as the heavenly end-time tabernacle itself

Similar to Hebrews 10:19–20, Hebrews 9:11 asserts that Christ as a priest entered 'through the greater and more complete tabernacle, not made with hands, that is to say not of this creation'. Verse 12 adds that he entered 'through his own blood', thus equating the 'tabernacle' with Jesus' 'blood'. Here again we have an identification of the tabernacle of the new creation with Christ himself (here 'his blood').[18]

'Mount Zion' and the 'Heavenly Jerusalem' as equivalent to the end-time temple

The theme of the temple in Hebrews appears to undergo further development in chapters 12 and 13. The author contrasts God's visible revelation at Mount Sinai that caused fear (12:18–21) with

---

[16] So, e.g., in this respect, see ch. 2, pp. 47–48 and the references in that chapter to Philo and Josephus, which indicate that in his role the high priest was representative, not merely for the tribes of Israel, but for all humanity. (For the priest's attire representing the temple and the cosmos, see pp. 39–45).

[17] *Midrash Tanhuma*, Pequde, §3, cited from Patai 1967: 116.

[18] So Cody 1960: 158–165 on Heb. 9:11–12, with minor qualifications.

his new revelation at 'Mount Zion' and 'the heavenly Jerusalem' (12:22–29):

> [22]But you have come to Mount Zion and to the city of the living God, the heavenly Jerusalem, and to myriads of angels, [23]to the general assembly and church of the first-born who are enrolled in heaven, and to God, the Judge of all, and to the spirits of righteous men made perfect,
> [24]and to Jesus the mediator of a new covenant and to the sprinkled blood, which speaks better than the blood of Abel.
> [25]See to it that you do not refuse Him who is speaking. For if those did not escape when they refused him who warned them on earth, much less shall we escape who turn away from Him who warns from heaven.
> [26]And His voice shook the earth then, but now He has promised, saying, 'Yet once more I will shake not only the earth, but also the heaven.'
> [27]And this expression, 'Yet once more,' denotes the removing of those things which can be shaken, as of created things, in order that those things which cannot be shaken may remain.
> [28]Therefore, since we receive a kingdom which cannot be shaken, let us show gratitude, by which we may offer to God an acceptable service with reverence and awe;
> [29]for our God is a consuming fire.

Though there is no explicit mention of 'temple' or 'sanctuary', the concept is implied, as the passage uses an Old Testament phrase sometimes synonymous for Israel's temple, 'Mount Zion'. Verses 18–21 contrast Mount Sinai with the heavenly Mount Zion. We saw in chapter 3 that Mount Sinai was conceived of as a mountain temple, so that Hebrews 12 may serve to contrast the earthly and heavenly temples. Believers need to utilize their 'faith eyes' to realize that they have begun to come to the heavenly temple on Mount Zion, regardless of where they may be located on the old physical earth. 'Mount Zion' appears to be roughly equivalent to the 'kingdom which cannot be shaken' that believers 'receive', in verse 28. The closest Old Testament parallel to verse 28 is Daniel 7:17, where the saints 'will receive the kingdom' (Ellingworth 1993: 689), and is itself a further development of Daniel 2:44: 'the God of heaven will set up a kingdom which will never be destroyed ... it will itself endure forever'. This eternal kingdom in Daniel 2 is pictured in verse 45 as the 'stone' that 'became a great mountain and filled the whole earth' (2:35), and is contrasted with ungodly kingdoms that are pictured as a statue that has been smashed to dust (2:31–35). Since we have already observed associations of the Daniel 2 mountain with the eschatological temple,[19] Hebrews 12:22–29 may well be alluding to this Daniel background.

Furthermore, verse 22 equates 'Mount Zion' with 'the heavenly Jerusalem', which itself must surely be associated with the 'heavenly tabernacle' elsewhere in Hebrews (Heb. 8:1–2, 5; 9:24). Indeed, we will see that in Revelation 21:2–3 the heavenly Jerusalem – a metaphor for God's redeemed people – is equated with God's end-time 'tabernacle'. Similarly, here we have the heavenly Jerusalem directly associated with the redeemed from all ages (Heb. 12:23).

The prophecy of the latter-day temple from Haggai 2 as the background for Hebrews 12:26–27

Another reference to the temple in the concluding portion of Hebrews 12 comes in verses 26–27, which quotes from Haggai 2:6, and suggests further that the idea of an end-time temple has already been in mind in the preceding verses. The passage from Haggai is part of a prophecy about the glory of the latter-day temple (Hag. 2:3–9):

> [3]'Who is left among you who saw this temple in its former glory? And how do you see it now? Does it not seem to you like nothing in comparison?
> [4]'But now take courage, Zerubbabel,' declares the LORD, 'take courage also, Joshua son of Jehozadak, the high priest, and all you people of the land take courage,' declares the LORD, 'and work; for I am with you,' says the LORD of hosts.
> [5]'As for the promise which I made you when you came out of Egypt, My Spirit is abiding in your midst; do not fear!'
> [6]'For thus says the LORD of hosts, 'Once more in a little while, I am going to shake the heavens and the earth, the sea also and the dry land.
> [7]'And I will shake all the nations; and they will come with the wealth of all nations; and I will fill this house with glory,' says the LORD of hosts.
> [8]'The silver is Mine, and the gold is Mine,' declares the LORD of hosts.
> [9]'The latter glory of this house will be greater than the former,'

---

[19] See pp. 144–153.

says the LORD of hosts, 'and in this place I shall give peace,' declares the LORD of hosts.

We have had occasion to comment on Haggai 2 in an earlier chapter,[20] and it will be helpful here to revisit that discussion. The 'promise' referred to in Haggai 2:5 is likely that made in Exodus 33:14–17:

> [14]And He said, 'My presence shall go [with you], and I will give you rest.' [15]Then he [Moses] said to Him, [16]'. . . how then can it be known that I have found favor in Thy sight, I and Thy people? Is it not by Thy going with us, so that we . . . may be distinguished from all the [other] people who are upon the face of the earth?' [17]And the LORD said to Moses, 'I will also do this thing of which you have spoken . . .' (so also Exod. 34:9)

Haggai may also have in mind Exodus 19:5–6: 'you shall be My own possession among all the peoples . . . you shall be to Me a kingdom of priests . . .' In any case, the entire nation was to live in the midst of God's presence, so that they all would become like priests before God in his temple, being intermediaries between God and the unbelieving nations.

Therefore, Haggai 2 refers to a future time when God will enable his people to build his temple through the power of his Spirit,[21] which is to be a fulfilment of the promises in Exodus 33 and the promissory commission in Exodus 19. In other words, Haggai 2 interprets the promises in the two Exodus texts to be that of building God's eschatological temple among his people. Though the temple rebuilding project looked insignificant in comparison to the earlier Solomonic temple, nevertheless God promises to make 'the latter glory of this house . . . greater than the former' (Hag. 2:3–9). Since the actual, subsequent rebuilding and expansion of the second temple did not excel the glory of the Solomonic temple or fulfil the expectation of Ezekiel's prophesied, eschatological temple (see Ezek. 40 – 48) because of Israel's disobedience (e.g., Zech. 6:15), intertestamental Judaism naturally and rightly waited for the time when this would happen.

According to Haggai 2:6, the fulfilment of this promise would be in the new creation, when 'once more in a little while' God will 'shake

---

[20] See pp. 115–116.
[21] Likewise, it is 'My Spirit' that Zech. 4:6–9 says will empower Zerubbabel, the governor, to build the second temple.

the heavens and the earth, the sea also and the dry land'. Though this language of cosmic upheaval is often figurative in the Old Testament for destruction of particular nations, here it probably refers to the actual breakup of the old creation. This is likely how Hebrews understands the verse 'And this expression, "Yet once more", denotes the removing of those things which can be shaken, as of created things, in order that those things which cannot be shaken may remain' (Heb. 12:27). At the least, some kind of radical transformation of the old world-system will occur to make way for the establishment of an eternal, unchanging and new order. This fits well with the theme that the true tabernacle was 'not made with [human] hands, that is to say, not of this [old] creation' (Heb. 9:11).

That Haggai 2:9 concludes by saying that 'the latter glory of this house will be greater than the former' also dovetails with the notion in Hebrews that the 'new' and 'true' tabernacle is 'greater and more perfect' than the first one (cf. Heb. 9:1–11, 24; cf. 10:20). God has 'taken away the first' system of temple sacrifices and offerings (and hence has removed the temple along with them) 'in order to establish the second' eschatological institution of Christ's once-for-all-sacrifice in the newly inaugurated temple (Heb. 10:9). The reason for this is that the new temple reality is a part of the 'new covenant', which is 'a better covenant' because it 'has been enacted on better promises' than the 'first' (Heb. 8:6–7, 13), Mosaic covenant. The new covenant temple is likewise 'better and greater' than the old one because the former is 'unshakeable', permanent and eternal. It is unchangeable and never fading because it is made by God's immutable hand as a new creation.

That the author of Hebrews has in mind the latter-day temple in the context of Haggai 2 is evident from noticing that another Old Testament temple allusion appears to lead from the Haggai quotation in Hebrews 12:26–27 to the mention in verse 28 of 'receiving a kingdom which cannot be shaken', wherein people 'offer to God an acceptable service'.

> Worship the Lord in his holy court, let all the earth be shaken before him. Say to the nations, 'The Lord has inaugurated his reign,' for he will complete the [heavenly] world, which will not be shaken. (LXX of Psalm 95 [96]:9–10; cf. also vv. 6–7 on the temple context)[22]

---

[22] See Lane 1991b: 485 for this insight on and translation of Ps. 95 [96], following an article by A. Vanhoye.

Therefore, Hebrews 12:22–28 says that believers have begun to participate in an unshakeable mountain, temple and kingdom, which are different images for the same one reality of God's glorious kingship in a new creation.

Those identified with the end-time temple will perform priestly service and be at peace

In response to their inclusion in God's unshakeable kingdom and temple, Christians are to 'show gratitude' by performing the priestly duty of 'offering to God an acceptable service with reverence and awe' (12:28). Hebrews 13:15–16 observes that the believer's priestly service also includes 'offering up a sacrifice of praise to God, that is, the fruit of the lips', and 'doing good and sharing; for with such sacrifices God is pleased'. Such a priestly manner of living is appropriate for those who 'do not have a lasting city' on this old earth but 'are seeking the [consummated form of the] city which is to come', in which they have begun to share in its inaugurated form (Heb. 13:14).

The entire concluding section of chapter 12 (vv. 18–29) serves as a basis for verses 14–17, the main point of which is 'Pursue after peace with all men, and the sanctification without which no one will see the Lord' (v. 14), and 'that no one comes short of the grace of God' (v. 15). The main point of verses 18–29 is 'offering to God an acceptable service' (v. 28) because believers 'receive a kingdom [and temple] which cannot be shaken', which is based primarily on Haggai 2:6–7. Just as the temple prophecy of Haggai 2 concludes with its main point ('in this place [the end-time temple] I shall give peace', v. 9b), Hebrews directs believers to 'offer to God an acceptable [priestly] service' (v. 28) by 'pursuing peace ... and ... sanctification' (v. 14) because they serve in the end-time heavenly temple that extends to earth (vv. 26–28a).

Verse 15 expands the exhortation of 'pursuing peace' (v. 14) by stating, 'See to it that ... no root of bitterness springing up causes trouble'. Verses 16–17 then adduce Esau as an example of someone who was characterized by just such bitterness. Esau is faulted because he lived by sight and not faith; he could not wait for and trust in the blessing of the coming Abrahamic inheritance. Instead, he 'sold his own birthright for a single meal' because he wanted to possess what he could see and enjoy in the present, and could not believe and wait for his unseen future inheritance.

In contrast, God's true people, like Abraham and Jacob, live by faith in the future, unseen Zion, temple and kingdom (Heb. 11:13–16).

They will 'pursue peace' and not be bitter when they do not experience material blessings in the present, even when what they own in this world is wrongly taken away from them. The author of Hebrews comforted his readers with the knowledge that they had 'accepted joyfully the seizure of your property, knowing that you have for yourselves a better possession and an abiding one' (Heb. 10:34). Their 'way of life' is to be 'free from the love of money, being content with what' they have because God has promised them, 'I will never desert you, nor will I ever forsake you' (Heb. 13:5). What can one possess that is more valuable than God's presence? The climax of that promise is their possession of Zion and the new creation, wherein they will live in God's presence eternally (Heb. 12:22–29; Rev. 21:4–5).

Consequently, believers can 'confidently say, "The Lord is my helper, I will not be afraid. What shall man do to me?"' (Heb. 13:6). Wanting to have a strong grasp on things in the old creation is ultimately vain, since these things are 'shakeable' and will eventually perish. The focus should be on the invisible Zion, Jerusalem, temple and new creation, which have broken in from the future into this old age. Christians have begun to share in this inaugurated reality that will be consummated at Christ's final coming in the future (Heb. 9:28). It is this in which we are to have faith.

Such an uncovetous lifestyle will free believers to 'pursue peace' and not be 'bitter' when their rights in the old world are trampled on. The outcome of such living will be 'sanctification' (Heb. 12:14) and not being 'defiled' (Heb. 12:15). These, indeed, are requirements for holiness to qualify one for priestly service, which point towards the following section on the believers' beginning participation in Zion, Jerusalem and the temple (Heb. 12:22–28). These priestly qualifications are expanded, as we have seen, in 12:28 and 13:10–15, where the priestly activities of all God's people are elaborated. In the light of the notion of 'peace' mentioned so far, it is not accidental that Hebrews concludes with a prayer to the 'God of peace' (Heb. 13:20–21).

Peace was to be the main mark of the expected new creation that was foreseen by the Old Testament prophets. Isaiah's well-known prophecy of the new heavens and earth include the image of antagonistic animals of the old creation lying peacefully with one another (Is. 65:17–25; see also Is. 11:6–9). The point of Isaiah's depiction is to underscore that the crown of creation, formerly alienated as Jews and Gentiles, will be at peace with one another (Is. 11:9–12). In fact, Gentiles even will become Levitical priests (Is. 66:18–22; so also Is. 56:3–8)!

The Isaiah background is relevant since Isaiah 66:22 ('the new heavens and the new earth which I make will endure') is echoed in Hebrews 12:26–27, 'I will shake not only the earth, but also the heaven ... as of created things, in order that those things which cannot be shaken may remain.' This earlier echo may anticipate the clear allusion to Isaiah 63:11 here in 13:20:

Isaiah 63:11 (LXX)	Hebrews 13:20
'Where is he that brought up from the sea the shepherd [Moses] of the sheep [Israel]?'[23]	'God ... who brought up from the dead the great Shepherd of the sheep.'

Now, Jesus is the greater Moses whom God has delivered from death at the greater exodus, along with his people.[24] And just as the exodus was thought of as a new creation,[25] so it is followed by the even more monumental new exodus and creation of Jesus' resurrection. Just as the first exodus was to lead to the establishment of the temporary temple (e.g., Exod. 15:17 and Is. 63:18), so Isaiah 63:15 ('Look down from heaven, and see from Thy holy ... habitation') and 64:1 ('Oh, that Thou wouldst rend the heavens and come down') prophesy that the second, end-time exodus (Is. 63:11) will also lead to God's heavenly sanctuary descending to earth and residing permanently. As Hebrews has recounted in earlier chapters, Jesus has led his people to that heavenly mountain-tabernacle (cf. Heb. 6:19–20; 9:11–12, 23–24; 10:19–22; 12:22–24). Hence, the quotation of Isaiah 63:11 in Hebrews 13:20 may not be too distant in theme from the heavenly temple themes that we have discussed in the previous pages.

Only the 'God of peace' can give to his people the ability 'to do his will' by 'pursuing peace' and thus 'pleasing' him. But he gives this ability only to 'sheep' who are identified with the resurrected 'great Shepherd' and have begun to experience the resurrection power of

[23] Some Greek OT mss. have 'the great shepherd'; see mss. 564 Bohairic Version and Eusebius, *Ecologae Propheticae*.

[24] Even the phrase 'the eternal covenant' at the end of Heb. 13:20 occurs approximately six times in the OT to refer to the new, eternal relationship God will have with his eschatological people at the end-time exodus and final restoration out of sin's captivity (so Is. 55:3; 61:8; Jer. 32:40; 50:5; Ezek. 16:60; 37:26). Perhaps the reference in Is. 61:8 is uppermost in mind because it, like the Is. 63:11 allusion, is part of a second exodus prophecy (see Is. 61:1–3).

[25] See further Beale 1997: 47. E.g., see *Wisdom of Solomon* 19:6: 'For the whole creation was again renewed in its own kind anew.'

their Lord in 'the eternal covenant'. In fact, resurrection in the New Testament is the beginning act of new creation, so that it is natural that it would be mentioned here together with 'the eternal covenant'. An unshakeable relationship with God can be attained only within the sphere of this 'eternal covenant' and new creation, wherein also is 'Mount Zion', 'the heavenly Jerusalem', the 'true tabernacle' and the 'kingdom'. All of these are equivalent realities, which are aimed at achieving God's 'glory forever and ever' (Heb. 13:21b).

Excursus: further biblical-theological reflections related to Hebrews' contention that the eternal end-time temple cannot be 'handmade'

It was noted earlier in this chapter that there may have been possible additional reasons from other biblical books that could have formed part of the background for the author of Hebrews' thinking about the temple. To some extent, these notions could have shaped the author's belief about the latter-day, literal temple not being like Israel's old physical one but being the heavenly one.

We have stated most of these ideas at various points in earlier chapters but they bear repeating here in one place. Even if Hebrews does not have these ideas explicitly in mind, they nevertheless form the broader biblical conception of why the eschatological temple could not be human-made.

The essential meaning of Israel's temple was that it represented the glorious presence of God that was revealed more fully in the holy of holies than anywhere else on earth. God's glorious presence, however, could be only incompletely expressed because it was contained within a human-made structure. This, as we have seen, is part of Stephen's point in Acts 7:48–49: 'the Most High does not dwell in houses made by human hands; as the prophet says,/"Heaven is My throne/ And earth is the footstool of My feet;/What kind of house will you build for Me?" says the Lord;/"Or what place is there for My repose?/Was it not My hand which made all these things?"'

Israel's physical temples were 'handmade' (Acts 7:44–47) and could never be a permanent dwelling place for God. We have seen that Stephen's point in citing Isaiah 66:1 appears to demonstrate that, just as God's own hand created the first cosmos that had become tainted with idolatry,[26] so God would create a new, eternal creation and

---

[26] Cf. Acts 7:44–47 with 7:41–43 in contrast to 7:50.

Jerusalem, not by human hands but by his own hand (so Is. 65:17–19 and 66:22). This is why even Solomon's temple was not the ultimate fulfilment of the promise that David's son would build God a temple – because Solomon's temple was 'handmade'. Not only was a human-made structure an inappropriate container for God's presence, but Israel made her temples objects of idolatry. Just as Israel had constructed 'the tabernacle of Moloch' during their wilderness sojourn, so also Israel set up idolatrous images in the later Solomonic temple (2 Kgs. 16:10–16; 21:4–9; 23:4–12). Likewise, the second temple had become idolatrous, since Israel had supplanted their tradition for God himself. The temple became the central focus of their idolatry (cf. Rom. 2:22).

As we saw earlier in our discussion of the Gospels, Jesus' so-called 'cleansing' of the temple possibly points further to his task of replacing the old temple with a new one (Matt. 21:12–13 and parallels). The reason for this was that the Jews had made the temple into an economic enterprise instead of a place of worship. Jesus' radical act in the temple was an acted-out parable of judgment on the temple, not only because of its misuse but because of Israel's rejection of God's word and commandments and of Jesus himself (N. T. Wright 1996:413–427). The religious establishment superstitiously viewed the temple as a guarantee that God would guard and prosper the nation despite their disobedience to his will. They did not understand that God had designed the temple to be a rallying point and witness for the Gentiles.[27] Such rejection was tantamount to idolatry (see Mark 7:1–13). As a result, Israel's temples had to be destroyed since this was the divine judgment on other idolatrous objects (e.g., Exod. 34:14; Deut. 7:5; 2 Kgs. 23:14; 2 Chr. 31:1; 34:4).

We have also proposed earlier that the end-time stone-mountain of Daniel 2 was a temple image. The main reasons suggesting this identification were twofold: that Daniel's image contained descriptions similar to Solomon's temple and the latter-day temple, and that both Daniel's mountain and the eschatological temple are said not to be made by human hands.[28] The New Testament repeatedly refers to the new, end-time temple as 'not made with hands' (in addition to Acts 7:48, see Mark 14:58; 2 Cor. 5:1; Heb. 9:11, 24). The image in the Old Testament corresponding closest to this is Daniel's stone 'cut out without hands'. We have found that it may not be surprising that

---

[27] E.g., see discussion of the allusion to Is. 56:7 in Matt. 21:13 and Mark 11:17 (p. 179).

[28] See pp. 144–153 for the full discussion.

Christ identifies himself with the stone of Daniel, which is an apparent attempt to designate himself to be the true temple (Luke 20:17–18 = Matt. 21:42). Furthermore, Hebrews 9:11 says that Christ entered 'through the greater and more perfect tabernacle, not made with hands, that is say, not of this creation' (so also Heb. 9:24).[29]

Accordingly, Acts 17:24 affirms that 'The God who made the world and all things in it, since He is Lord of heaven and earth, does not dwell in temples made with hands'. Paul says this after the great redemptive-historical divide when Christ and his people had begun to replace Israel's 'handmade' temple. There could be no human-made structures separating God and his people in order that he might dwell with them in a full and unrestricted manner. This would appear to be the reason that no human can answer affirmatively God's question in Isaiah 66:1 about his latter-day, eternal dwelling, 'Where then is a house you could build for Me?'

God's intention is one day to fill every part of his creation with his presence because he is the Creator. God's holy presence could not dwell universally in any handmade localized structure nor, indeed, could he dwell fully in any part of the sin-tainted old creation. Hence, his special tabernacling presence dwelt in a limited manner within human-made structures. However, when he would fully redeem the world and recreate it (so Rom. 8:18–25), he would dwell in it more fully than ever before. Consequently, the new temple would be an eternal and perfect abode for God's universal presence because it would not be 'made with hands, that is to say, not of this [old] creation' (Heb. 9:11), and without moral blemish. This is why John says in Revelation 21:22, 'I saw no [structural] temple' in the new cosmos because 'the Lord God, the Almighty, and the Lamb, are its temple'. The former temples that were imperfect dwellings for God's presence 'are replaced by God and the Lamb in person, so that unrestricted dealings with God are possible'.[30]

As discussed earlier, we may assume that God created the cosmos to be his great temple, in which he rested after his creative work. Nevertheless, his special revelatory presence did not fill the entire earth yet, since it was his intention that his human vice-regent, whom he installed in the garden sanctuary, would extend worldwide the

---

[29] Similarly, cf. *Sibylline Oracles* 4:11: 'the great God, whom no hands of men fashioned . . . does not have a house, a stone set up as a temple . . . but one which it is not possible to see from the earth nor to measure with mortal eyes, since it was not fashioned by mortal hand'.

[30] Michel, *'naos'*, *TDNT*, 4:889.

boundaries of that sanctuary and of God's presence. Adam, of course, disobeyed this mandate, so that humanity no longer enjoyed God's presence in the little localized garden. Consequently, the entire earth became infected with sin and idolatry in a way it had not been previously before the fall, while yet in its still imperfect newly created state. Therefore, the various expressions about God being unable to inhabit earthly structures are best understood, at least in part, by realizing that the old order and sanctuary have been tainted with sin and must be cleansed and recreated before God's Shekinah presence, formerly limited to heaven and the holy of holies, can dwell universally throughout creation.

Chapter Ten

The world-encompassing temple in Revelation

The preceding study so far has contended that the various forms of the temple in the Old Testament were intended to point to the final eschatological goal of God's presence filling the entire creation in the way it had formerly filled only the holy of holies. While I believe that this thesis about the ultimate redemptive-historical significance of the temple is plausible, I am sure that there are some, perhaps many, who would doubt the probability of it. When, however, we come to the New Testament, there are passages that fit admirably into such a scheme. I have tried to show in preceding chapters how this is so. Some of the clearest evidence for the thesis, however, is in John's Apocalypse, particularly, for our purposes, Revelation 11:1–4 and Revelation 21:1 – 22:5, though the entire book is filled with the theme of the temple.[1] Likewise, 1 Peter 2 testifies to the same reality, which will confirm our conclusions about Revelation. First, I give an analysis of 11:1–4, then I briefly discuss 1 Peter 2 together with a couple of other passages in Revelation, and, finally, I relate both more intentionally to the concluding vision of the Apocalypse.[2]

The church as the eschatological temple in Revelation 11:1–4

Revelation 11:1–2 is a minefield of problems:

> And there was given me a measuring rod like a staff; and someone said, 'Rise and measure the temple of God, and the altar, and those who worship in it. And leave out the court which is outside the temple, and do not measure it, for it has

---

[1] See Stephanovic 2002: 32–37 (and literature cited therein), who, e.g., concurs with earlier studies arguing that there is a sevenfold structure of Revelation, which is based on a temple setting, especially in a heavenly context.

[2] Beale 1999a addresses how the temple in Rev. 11:1–4 related to the vision of the temple in chapters 21 – 22. Here I attempt to elaborate further on that discussion.

been given to the nations; and they will tread under foot the holy city for forty-two months.'

Space allows only a brief review of the alternative interpretations and my preference, support of which can be found elsewhere (e.g. Beale 1999a: *in loc.*). Some believe the reference is to a physical temple structure to be built in the eschatological future, while others see a similar temple building of the past that was destroyed in AD 70. There are also those, however, who see a non-structural temple composed of believing (= the inner court) and unbelieving (= outer court) ethnic Israelites that will exist in the future, directly preceding Christ's coming. Still others understand the image similarly but see it as a reality existing throughout the church age. Accordingly, the inner court represents true believers and the outer court pseudo-Christians.

I prefer a variant of this last view. I would contend, however, that this is not a 'figurative' view but that, whereas God's unique tabernacling presence in Israel was manifested in the physical temple, this same unique presence manifests itself in the midst of God's true people, the church. God's literal presence as the essence of Israel's physical temple now abides in the midst of the church as the true temple.

The inner court stands for true, spiritual Israel, while the outer court represents the physical bodies of God's true people, which are susceptible to harm. This is consistent with the notion that the outer court of the Old Testament temple represented the physical aspect of creation. This view of Revelation 11:1–2 is linguistically allowable because the language of 'casting outside' can also have the nuance of God's true people who are rejected and persecuted by the unbelieving world.[3] The significance of the measuring means that their salvation is secured, despite physical harm. This is a further development of the 'sealing' of 7:2–8 and is consistent with *1 Enoch* 61:1–5, where the angelic 'measuring' of the righteous elect ensures that their faith will be strengthened and not demolished, despite the fact that their bodies will be destroyed. In the Old Testament generally, 'measuring' was metaphorical for a decree of protection.[4]

---

[3] Cf. Matt. 21:39; Mark 12:8; Luke 4:29; 20:15; John 9:34–35; Acts 7:58; cf. 1 Maccabees 7:16–17; Josephus, *War* 4.316–317; Heb. 13:11–12.

[4] E.g., with reference to protection, see 2 Sam. 8:2; Is. 28:16–17; Jer. 31:38–40; Zech. 1:16, though sometimes 'measuring' refers to judgment (e.g., 2 Sam. 8:2; 2 Kgs. 21:13; Lam. 2:8; Amos 7:7–9).

The church as the eschatological temple in Revelation 11:1–4 against the background of Ezekiel 40 – 48

The 'measuring' is best understood against the background, not of the first-century Herodian temple, but the prophecy of the temple in Ezekiel 40 – 48.[5] We will summarize how we see John utilizing Ezekiel's temple prophecy in this section, but we will wait until the next chapter to give an in-depth study of Ezekiel itself, where we will also elaborate further on John's use in Revelation 21 and 22.

An angel measuring various features of the temple complex in Ezekiel 40 – 48 metaphorically pictures the sure establishment and subsequent protection of the temple.[6] In Revelation 21:15–17 an angel, also in dependence on the same Ezekiel text, 'measures with a reed' (*metreō* + *kalamos*, as in 11:1) 'the city and its gates and its wall'. There the measuring of the city and its parts pictures the security of its inhabitants against the harm and contamination of unclean and deceptive people (so 21:27). This cordoning off of the city guarantees protection of God's latter-day community. Jewish and Gentile Christians will compose this temple community (as is evident from 3:12; 21:12–14, 24–26; 22:2). What is figuratively established by the measuring in Ezekiel and Revelation 21 is the infallible promise of God's future presence, which will dwell for ever in the midst of 'a purified cult and purified community' (Wevers 1969: 295–296).

In Revelation 11, the 'measuring' connotes God's presence which is guaranteed to be with the temple community living on earth before the consummation of history. This means that the faith of God's people will be upheld by his presence, since without faith there can be no divine presence. No outside aberrant theological or ethical influences will be able to spoil or contaminate the true faith or worship of God's true people. In Revelation 11 this means that the fulfilment of the promise about God's end-time presence begins with the establishment of the Christian community in the first century. The command to measure is to be viewed from God's perspective as representing a decree already enacted prior to the issuing of the command. Even before the church age began, God made a decree, which secured the salvation of all people who would become genuine members of the church. The same conclusion is applicable to the meaning of the

---

[5] So also Lohmeyer 1970: 89–91; Ernst 1967: 130; Kraft 1974: 152; Prigent 1981: 159.

[6] Where in the Greek OT the verb 'measure' (*diametreō*) occurs approximately 30 times and the noun (*metron*) 30 times.

'sealing' in 7:3–8 (see Beale 1999a: *in loc.*). Therefore, the two metaphors of 'measuring' and 'sealing' connote synonymous theological concepts.[7]

The fact that the temple prophesied in Ezekiel 40 – 48 includes a sacrificial system should not be understood to be physically literal but interpreted in the light of Hebrews 10:1–12 (see below). The reason that the Ezekiel expectation is interpreted as beginning fulfilment in a perhaps somewhat unexpected way is because of Christ's death, which has caused the redemptive-historical turn of the ages. Christ's work is now the dominant interpretative lens through which to understand Old Testament expectations. In Revelation 11:1–2 the temple of the church is being patterned after Christ, who is the true temple.[8] Just as Christ, so the church will suffer and appear defeated. Nevertheless, through it all, God's presence will abide with them and protect them from any contamination leading to eternal death. God's abiding presence also guarantees them ultimate victory. On the other hand, this is not that surprising of a fulfilment when we remember that the Old Testament temple's tripartite structure ultimately indicated that God's presence in the inner sanctuary would eventually invade and take over the entire earth. Christ is that divine presence which has begun to invade the space–time creation.

Though *naos* ('sanctuary') can sometimes refer to the whole temple complex (Matt. 26:61; 27:5; John 2:20), here it has reference to the inner sanctuary or inside house, where only the priests were allowed (which appears to be its meaning in the other approximately 13 uses in the book). Some commentators think the 'temple' to be metaphorical for Christians, and another way of speaking of them as true Israel. This is generally correct. The phrase 'temple of God' in the Old Testament referred to that place where God's presence uniquely dwelt on earth.[9] In the prophecy of the new temple in Ezekiel 40 – 48 (especially 43:1–12; 37:26–28), God promised that his presence would be re-established for ever. In Revelation 11:1 the focus is now on the whole covenant community forming a spiritual temple in which God's presence dwells.[10] This is not so much a figurative perspective nor merely a spiritual interpretation of Ezekiel's temple prophecy.[11] It is also a redemptive-historical understanding. There is a literal

---

[7] Likewise, Lohmeyer 1970: 89; Ernst 1967: 130.
[8] So Krodel 1989: 220; see further Beale 1999a: *passim*, on Rev. 11.
[9] Perhaps a genitive of possession or content.
[10] So also 1 Cor. 3:16–17; 6:19; 2 Cor. 6:16; Eph. 2:21–22; 1 Pet. 2:5.
[11] The latter of which Lohmeyer 1970: 89 and Ernst 1967: 130 highlight.

spiritual realm and a literal physical realm. What Ezekiel prophesied has begun to find its real, true fulfilment on a literal spiritual level, which will be consummated in fuller form physically and spiritually in a new creation (see on Rev. 21:1 – 22:5).

Already in John 2:19–22 Christ has identified his resurrection body as the true temple and this is developed in Revelation 21:22 (likewise Mark 12:10–11 and par.). There John says he 'saw no temple' in the new Jerusalem 'for the Lord God ... and the Lamb, are its temple'. There is no reason to limit this identification to the future new Jerusalem, since the identification began to be made when Christ was resurrected, and the resurrected Christ is the central feature of the heavenly temple scene in 1:12–20 (likewise, Eph. 2:20 pictures Christ as the cornerstone of the temple).

Therefore, Christians who are identified with Christ are also presently identified with the temple. The New Testament elsewhere also portrays the church as the new spiritual temple, as we have seen.[12] Without exception *naos* elsewhere in Revelation refers to the heavenly temple of the present[13] or the temple of God's presence that dominates the cosmos of the future.[14] This usage points to the same identification of a heavenly temple in 11:1–2: the people of God who are members of God's temple in heaven are referred to in their existence on earth as 'the temple of God'. Indeed, the only other use of the phrase 'temple of God' in the book appears in 11:19 with reference to the end-time *heavenly* temple, which is the same reality having protected believers during their sojourn on earth.

Not coincidentally, the temple of the Old Testament was conceived of as providing a link between heaven and earth.[15] Revelation 11:1–2 depicts the temple of the age to come as having broken into the present age. If one insists on identifying the sanctuary in 11:1–2 as the earthly temple structure instead of the invisible and heavenly, then one must assume that this is a completely unique employment of that concept within the book (Bachmann 1994: 478). It would also be a unique use of the word *naos* ('sanctuary') within the book and in the New Testament outside the Gospels and Acts. Even when *naos* occurs in the Gospels and Acts almost always it is in the context of

[12] 1 Cor. 3:16–17; 6:19; 2 Cor. 6:16; Eph. 2:21–22; 1 Pet. 2:5.

[13] So 3:12; 7:15; 14:15, 17; 15:5–6, 8; 16:1, 17; though 3:12 and 7:15 could include reference to the future temple, and some would even say are exclusive references to the future (for further discussion, see Beale 1999a: *in loc.*).

[14] So 11:19 and 21:22, as well as possibly 3:12 and 7:15 (on which, see the previous note).

[15] Terrien 1970: 317–318, 323, and bibliography therein.

the inadequacy of the physical temple and its replacement by Christ or God's universal presence.

The specific precedent of understanding Ezekiel's prophesied temple not to be a structural building, as in Revelation 11:1–2, is also found in the Qumran community. Qumran declared the Jerusalem temple apostate.[16] They believed themselves to represent the true, spiritual temple.[17] The presence of God in the Qumran temple would ensure the invincibility of it against the deceptive designs of Belial (4QFlor 1.7–9; CD 3.19).[18] This spiritual invincibility is seen as a fulfilment of the prophecy of the temple in Ezekiel 44![19] Metaphors of measurement are even used to express the inviolable security of this temple.[20]

As with the two witnesses in Revelation 11:3–7, so in Qumran, worship in the spiritual temple consisted not of physical offerings, but of proclaiming God's word and obedience out of a sincere heart (1QS 9.3–5; 4QFlor 1.6). After the destruction of the temple and its altar of atonement, sincere commitment to the Lord and consecration of one's own table by words of the Law were able to make atonement. This spiritualization of the altar in the temple was based on analogy with the temple altar in Ezekiel 41:22.[21] To engage continually in the study of the Law was equivalent to building the temple prophesied in Ezekiel 40 – 47 (*Midrash Rabbah Leviticus* 7:3). Repentance could be 'accounted unto a person as if he had … built the Temple and the altar, and offered thereon all the sacrifices' (*Midrash Rabbah Leviticus* 7:2). Part of the precedent for Qumran and John conceptualizing Ezekiel's temple in a non-structural manner and applying it to a remnant of Israel or to the church may have been given by the prophet Ezekiel himself! Immediately after God's presence departed from Israel's physical temple (see Ezek. 11:22–23), he tells exiled Judah and Benjamin that this presence would be uniquely among them, despite the fact there was no physical Israelite temple in the exile: he would be 'a *sanctuary* for them a little while …' (Ezek.

[16] See the references in Ford 1975: 174–175.

[17] Cf. 1QS 5.5–6; 8.4–10; 9.3–6; 11.7ff.; CD 3.19 – 4.6; 4QFlor 1.2–9; so Gärtner 1965: 16–44, and McKelvey 1969: 45–53; Morray-Jones 1998: 400–431, who, for example, discusses the community's identification with a present heavenly form of the Ezek. 40 – 48 temple in the *Sabbath Songs* (4Q405).

[18] Gärtner 1965: 34–35; though in 4QFlor Dupont-Sommer sees the emphasis on an assurance against persecution (1961: 312).

[19] Cf. CD 3.19 – 4.6; cf. 4QFlor 1.15–17.

[20] Cf. 'cord of righteousness' and 'plumbline of truth' in 1QH 6.26; cf. McKelvey 1969: 52.

[21] *M. Aboth* 3.2, 6; *b. Berakot* 55a; *b. Menahot* 97a.

11:16). He continued to be such an invisible sanctuary for the remnant after the return from Babylon, since the second temple clearly did not fulfil the grand prophecies of Israel's restoration, which included a greater temple than even Solomon's. This invisible sanctuary became transmuted into Christ and the church at the time of the escalated restoration at Christ's first coming which would be consummated at his last coming.

Literally, *to thysiastērion* in Revelation 11:1 can be translated 'the place of sacrifice',[22] which here would be the suffering covenant community. The 'altar' refers to the way God's people now worship in the community. In line with 6:9–10 the altar connotes the sacrificial calling, which entails suffering for their faithful witness (as affirmed by vv. 3–9; see on 6:9–10). The close proximity of believers to the altar in 6:9–10 implies that they are not only worshippers but also priests who have brought themselves to be sacrificed on the altar of the gospel to which they have been called to testify. The unusual picture of Christians simultaneously portrayed as a temple and as priests worshipping in the temple is found also in 1 Peter 2:5. Indeed, Revelation 1:6 and 5:10 allude to the same Old Testament text as 1 Peter 2:5 in identifying Christians as priests (likewise, as we have seen, Christ himself is portrayed as a priest, sacrifice and veil of the temple [Heb. 10:19–21]). How this living temple on earth in 11:1–2 relates to the other references in the book to the heavenly temple must be clarified by later chapters of the Apocalypse. In brief, however, the saints depicted in Revelation 11:1–2 are members of a heavenly community who dwell on earth.

This view of *thysiastērion* is corroborated by its contextual use elsewhere. As we saw in the preceding chapter, Hebrews 13:9–16 says that believers have an altar (i.e., Christ) through which they offer up sacrifices to God. Christians are exhorted not to be deceived by false doctrine and not to place their hope in the impermanent 'city' of Jerusalem, but to 'seek the city which is to come' and is already here (cf. Heb. 12:22 and 13:14). They are to heed this exhortation by focusing on the spiritual altar and by being willing to 'go out to Him outside the camp (= temple and Jerusalem), bearing His reproach' (so Heb. 8:1ff. and 10:19–20 speak of Christ being in the true temple and that believers presently enter it through him).[23]

---

[22] Cf. BAGD, 366.

[23] The above analysis of the 'altar' corresponds to early Christian interpretation. In Ignatius's *Letter to the Ephesians* (5:2), 'the place of the altar' is the authoritative unity of 'the whole church' (so also Ignatius, *Letter to the Trallians* 7:2; cf. Ignatius, *Letter*

'The ones worshipping in it [the temple]' in Revelation 11:1b refers to believers worshipping together in the temple community.[24] Possibly the 'worshippers' in Revelation 11:1 are to be identified as members of the heavenly court, though still living on earth, since *proskuneō* ('worship') refers elsewhere in the book to the 'elders' in heaven worshipping God: cf. 4:10; 5:14; 7:11; 11:16; 19:4 (cf. also Heb. 12:22–23) (Giblin 1984: 455). An earthly location of the 'worshippers' is favoured by the immediate context of verses 1–2 and broader context of verses 3–10, where the community of faith is pictured on earth. Alternatively, the focus may be on people who have been qualified to worship in heaven because of the measuring. This focus is suggested in the near context (11:11–12) by three observations: (1) the ultimate, heavenly destiny of the earthly community of believers, (2) usage of 'worship' (*proskuneō*) elsewhere, and (3) Rev. 13:6, 'His tabernacle, [which are] those who dwell in heaven.' Certainly, the measuring of the 'worshippers' guarantees their membership in the heavenly spiritual temple, despite what happens to them on earth.[25]

The view of the eschatological temple in Revelation 11:4 against the background of Zechariah 4

Revelation 11:3–6 explains the primary purpose of 'measuring the sanctuary' in verses 1–2. That is, God's establishment of his presence among his latter-day community as his sanctuary is aimed to ensure the effectiveness of their prophetic witness. Noting that the two witnesses bear their testimony not only in earthly courts but also in an unseen courtroom, as they are 'standing before the Lord of the earth', intensifies the legal nature of the witness in verses 3–4. The Lord is the earth's omniscient judge because his 'eyes . . . range to and

---

to the Philadelphians 4). The exhortation to maintain such unity is based on 'the one temple [*naos*], even God . . . [and] the one altar . . . the one Jesus Christ' to whom all should come (Ignatius, *Letter to the Magnesians* 7:2). This altar is later equated with believers being 'stones of a temple [*naos*]', which is a 'temple shrine [*naophoroi*]' carried by all in the church (so Ignatius, *Letter to the Ephesians* 9; likewise, ibid. 15). Cf. also Rom. 12:1, where believers are exhorted to offer their bodies 'as a living, holy sacrifice, acceptable to God, [which is] their reasonable service of worship'. See Beale 1999a: *in loc.* on 6:9 with regard to whether the altar in 11:1 refers specifically to the altar of incense or the altar of burnt offering.

[24] In *1 Enoch* 61:3–4, which may shed light on the meaning of Rev. 11:1, the measuring of saints results in them first being 'strengthened in righteousness' and faith, which has the further result that 'the elect begin to dwell with the elect'.

[25] Likewise, the Qumran saints were identified with the heavenly community in their worship: e.g., 1QS 11.7ff.; 1QH 3.21ff.; 6.12ff. (so McKelvey 1969: 37–38).

fro throughout the earth' (cf. Zech. 4:10, 14; Rev. 5:6). The expression of the witnesses' close proximity to the Lord also emphasizes their close relation to and commission by the Lord (cf. Kraft 1974:157). This likewise means that, though the prophetic witnesses live in a world of danger, they are never far from their Lord's sovereign presence and nothing can separate them from their secure relationship with him (cf. Prigent 1981:156–167). This idea appears to be part of a larger conception, since in Judaism the notion of 'standing before the Lord' connoted an eternally secure relationship of the faithful with God.[26] The phrase was also commonly used in the Old Testament to refer to people being in God's presence. Among these uses are numerous references in Exodus and Leviticus to priests standing 'before the Lord' in the tabernacle (Exod. 27:21; 30:8; Lev. 24:3). Together with Zechariah 4:14 (on which see below), Revelation 11:4b may also allude to Leviticus 24:4, where 'the pure gold lampstand [is] before the Lord continually'.

The witnesses are identified as 'the two olive trees and the two lampstands'. The 'lampstands' refer to the church, since that was the repeated meaning of the 'lampstands' in chapters 1 – 2. It would be 'a defiance of common sense to use the same distinctive symbol for two different ideas, within the compass of one book' (Kiddle 1940: 181).

The lampstand in the tabernacle and temple was in the presence of God, and the light that emanated from it apparently represented the presence of God.[27] Similarly, the lamps on the lampstand in Zechariah 4:2–5 are interpreted in 4:6 as representing God's presence or Spirit, which was to empower Israel (= 'the lampstand') to finish rebuilding the temple, despite resistance (cf. Zech. 4:6–9). So new Israel, the church, as God's spiritual temple on earth is to draw its power from the Spirit, the divine presence, before God's throne in its drive to stand against the resistance of the world. This continues the theme from verses 1–3 of God's establishment of his presence among

---

[26] E.g., *Jubilees* 30:18–20; 1QH 4.21; 18.24–29.

[27] See Num. 8:1–4; in Exod. 25:30–31 the lampstand is mentioned directly after the 'bread of Presence'; likewise, 40:4; 1 Kgs. 7:48–49. We observed in ch. 2 that Gen. 1:14–16 uses the unusual word 'lights' (*mĕ'ōrōt*, 5 times) to refer to the 'sun' and 'moon', a word that is used throughout the remainder of the Pentateuch (10 times) only for the 'lights' on the tabernacle lampstand. Among the three other uses elsewhere in the OT, two also refer to the 'lights' of the heaven, and the remaining use refers to God's presence (Ps. 90:8, 'the light of your presence'). Could this suggest that the lampstand 'lights' also symbolized the light of God's glorious presence, just as the stars were held to reflect God's glory?

his end-time community as his sanctuary, which is aimed to ensure the effectiveness of its prophetic witness![28]

The two pictures of olive trees and lampstands together with the concluding clause of verse 4 come from Zechariah 4:14 (cf. 4:2–3, 11–14). In Zechariah's vision, the lampstand represented the second temple[29] for which Zerubbabel had laid the foundation (see Beale 1999a: *in loc.* on 1:13–15). On either side was an olive tree, which provided the oil to light the lamps. The olive trees are interpreted as 'the two anointed ones, who are standing by the Lord of the whole earth' (v. 14). In context, 'the anointed ones' likely refer to Joshua the high priest and Zerubbabel the king.

The meaning of the entire vision of Zechariah 4 is summarized in 4:6–10. Though the temple building had begun, there was opposition from hostile powers halting the completion of the construction ('the mountain' of v. 7 probably represents forces hostile to the building of the temple). The main point of Zechariah 4 is a divine assurance that the opposition will be overcome and the temple completed: 'Not by [fleshly] might nor by power, but by My Spirit' and manifold grace (vv. 6–9). This would be true even though the initial construction appeared inauspicious and the possibility of completion improbable in view of the opposition (v. 10a). God would provide his fruitful Spirit (the oil) and cause it to issue forth from the priest and king (the olive trees) to lead the process of successfully completing the temple. It is notable that the 'stone' of Zechariah 3:9 is associated with 'seven eyes', which are to be identified with the 'seven eyes of the LORD' in Zechariah 4:10. In both cases the eyes are providentially watching over the foundation stone of the temple and figuratively indicate that the laying of that stone was a divine assurance that the temple will be completed.

This background shows the appropriateness of choosing Zechariah 4:14 at this point in John's Apocalypse. Despite the fact that John creatively uses Zechariah, it is a creative development that

[28] *Midrash Rabbah Numbers* 15 (on Num. 8:2–3) affirms that the reward for Israel continually lighting the seven lamps on the lampstand would be that God would preserve their 'souls from all evil things' (15:4) and that their blessings would 'never be abolished' (15:6). It was in the light of these seven lamps that God's presence dwelt (15:9). The Aramaic Bible (*Tg. Jerusalem*) of Lev. 24:2–4 directly links the dwelling of God's glory in Israel to the continued burning of the seven lamps on the lampstand. God's presence in the burning bush (or 'tree') at 'Sinai' points further to the divine presence being associated with tree images; likewise, deities were identified with trees in the ANE (so Yarden 1971: 39).
[29] By a figure of speech called 'synecdoche', whereby a part of something comes to represent the whole.

does not violate the meaning in its original context.[30] The establishing and preservation of the true temple despite opposition has been introduced in Revelation 11:1–2, and Zechariah 4:14 is a climax to a section concerning the very same topic. Just as the priest and king were the key vessels used by the Spirit for the establishment of the temple against opposition, so here the two witnesses are likewise empowered by the Spirit to perform the same role in relation to 11:1–2. Similar to the situation of the temple in Zechariah 4, the spiritual temple of God appears insignificant, perhaps especially since it is invisible, and its destiny seems questionable because it is opposed by worldly powers. The Aramaic Bible interprets the antagonistic 'mountain' of the Hebrew text as Rome, which is one of the opponents John had in view.[31] Despite resistance, the Christian community's successful establishment as God's temple throughout the church age is assured by means of the Spirit's empowerment of the church's faithful, prophetic witness (see on 1:13–15; 19:10).

The allusion to Zechariah enforces the thought of the prophets' empowerment by the Spirit, since the lamps of Zechariah 4 have already been identified in 4:5 and 5:6 with God's Spirit.[32] Revelation 11:4 is a symbolic picture of the church's commission in Acts 1:8. In contrast with Zechariah, the priestly and kingly figures are not individuals but represent the church universal, the eschatological continuation of true Israel. Indeed, the dual kingly–priestly role of the corporate church has already been explicitly affirmed (1:6; 5:10) and will be again (20:6). Similarly, Judaism interpreted Zechariah 4:3, 11–14 as referring generally to priestly and royal figures,[33] as well as to all of the righteous in Israel.[34]

---

[30] Though cf. Court 1979: 91–92.

[31] See Zech. 4:7 of *Tg. Pseudo-Jonathan* (codex f) in Sperber 1962: 482; see Beale 1999a: *in loc.* on 11:8.

[32] Prigent 1981: 166–167.

[33] Cf. *Midrash Rabbah Numbers* 18:16–17; *Midrash Rabbah Lamentations* 1:16, 51; *Pesikta Rabbati*, Piska 8.4]); sometimes, sectors of Judaism understood the same Zechariah verses as referring to priestly and kingly figures with specific messianic connotations (cf. CD 9.10–11; *Midrash Rabbah Numbers* 14:13; *'Aboth de Rabbi Nathan* 30b; and perhaps *Testament of Simeon* 7:1–2 and *Testament of Levi* 2:10–11); in the Kairaite tradition the two figures of Zech. 4:14 are identified with a messianic Elijah and a Messiah ben David (see Wieder 1955: 15–25).

[34] *Midrash Psalms* 16:12, *Midrash Rabbah Leviticus* 32:8, *Midrash Rabbah Ecclesiastes* 4:1 §1, *Sifre on Deuteronomy*, Piska 10, and *Pesikta Rabbati*, Piska 51.4, compare the lampstand of Zech. 4:2–3 to Israelites from all epochs gathered at the end of time; *Midrash Rabbah Leviticus* 30:2, *Midrash Rabbah Numbers* 13:8, *Midrash Rabbah Songs* 4:7 §1, *Pesikta de-rab Kahana*, Piska 27.2, *Pesikta Rabbati*, Piska 7.7 and Piska 8.4, interpret the lampstand of Zech. 4:2 to represent Israel.

Of course, as observed above in the analysis of 11:1–2, the church is a temple because of its identification with Christ, who is the true temple. The Spirit himself is evidence of Christ's victory through the resurrection. The Aramaic Old Testament of Zechariah 4:7 (*Tg. Zechariah*) similarly identifies the cornerstone of the temple as the Messiah, who will ensure the completion of the temple by defeating the evil kingdoms who oppose God's people. In particular, the Aramaic interprets the 'top stone' of the temple of Zechariah 4:7 as God's royal 'Anointed', who 'shall rule over all kingdoms'. Zechariah 6:12–13 calls a messianic-like figure 'Branch', and repeats twice that 'He will build the temple ... and rule ... [and] be a priest on His throne' (the Aramaic Targum substitutes 'Anointed' for 'Branch').[35]

This means that already in Zechariah the kingly and priestly roles of chapter 4 were to be performed by two people, but in chapter 6 the dual roles were to be combined into one messianic figure. In view of Zechariah 6, Jewish interpretative tradition on Zechariah 4:7, and the New Testament, especially Revelation, the building programme of chapter 4 may be better understood: it refers respectively to Joshua's and Zerubbabel's priestly and kingly functions of beginning the building of the second temple, which never reached its goal because of Israel's disobedience (cf. Zech. 6:15). Their incomplete building activities were continued but superseded by the Messiah's coming as the priest-king to establish the beginning of the eschatological temple only foreshadowed by the second temple.[36]

The broader context of Zechariah 4 shows the richness of the connection to the present context: (1) in Zechariah 1:16–17 and 2:1–5 an angel 'measures' Jerusalem to signify that it will surely be re-established in order that God's 'house will be built in it', and that God would be present there (cf. Rev. 11:1–2). Indeed, as we have seen, Zechariah 1 – 2 pictures future Jerusalem being measured in order to become the entire temple itself, with God's glory radiating throughout it: God would 'be a wall of fire around her and ... the glory in her midst' (Zech. 2:5).[37] (2) However, Satan, together with the world

---

[35] Likewise, the Aramaic *Tg. of Isaiah* 53:5 affirms that the Servant 'will build the sanctuary'.

[36] *Midrash Tanhuma Genesis*, Parasha 6, Toledoth §20 and Qumran also saw in Zech. 4:1–14 a messianic prophecy (cf. 1QS 9.10–11 and Dupont-Sommer 1961: 317); in development of Zech. 4:9, *Midrash Rabbah Genesis* 97 says the Messiah would be descended from Zerubbabel and would rebuild the temple; '*Aboth de Rabbi Nathan* 30b identifies one of the figures of Zech. 4:14 as the Messiah.

[37] See ch. 4 (pp. 142–144) for discussion of Zech. 1 – 2 and its depiction of God's presence as an expanding temple.

powers, opposed the re-establishment of God's temple in Jerusalem (Zech. 3:1–2; 4:7), as the beast and the world oppose the witnesses (Rev. 11:5–10).

In this respect, the image of the church as a lampstand in Revelation 2:5 has important bearing. It is appropriate that if the Ephesian Christians overcome by being God's faithful lampstand of witness (2:5) and identify now with his presence, then God will cause them to be identified consummately with 'the tree of life' (2:7). Both the 'the tree of life' and the lampstand are partly symbolic of God's presence. In particular, as we have seen in the analysis of Revelation 11:4, the light which emanated from the lampstand represented God's presence that Israel was to mediate to the world.[38] This notion of the lampstand connoting divine presence with the church is confirmed more clearly from 11:4, where the 'lampstands ... stand *before* the Lord of the earth'. Recognizing that the lampstand in the temple represented the tree of life in Eden (as we have argued) enhances the identification of the two images. The two metaphors are virtually identical or, at least, two versions of the same picture and reality.

As observed earlier, the lampstand's 'stylized tree shape and vocabulary of botanical terms that describe it suggest that the cultic lampstand symbolized the fructifying powers of the eternal, unseen God'.[39] As we have already likewise seen, even the decorative palm trees, carvings of flowers, and cherubim portrayed as part of the Solomonic temple and of the end-time temple of Ezekiel were probably allusions to the garden setting of Eden.[40] The Dead Sea Scrolls (1QH 6.14–19) compare the Qumran saints to Eden's tree with a 'well-spring of light' and 'brilliant flames', which is directly linked to the 'testimony' (!) of the Teacher of Righteousness. In this respect, could the seven lamps on the lampstand be related to the hymnist's affirmation in the *Hymn Scroll* (1QH 7. 24), 'I will shine with a *sevenfold li[ght]* in the E[den[41] which] Thou hast [m]ade for Thy glory'? The

[38] See also Beale 1999a: *in loc.* on 1:12.

[39] Meyers 1985b: 1094; see also Meyers 1985a: 546; for the botanical descriptions, see especially Exod. 25:31–40; 37:17–24.

[40] Furthermore, just as the lampstand was composed of gold (see Exod. 25), so Judaism conceived of Eden's tree of life as gold (*2 Enoch* 8:3–4 [J]). And just as the seven lamps of Zech. 4 were fed oil by olive trees, so *2 Enoch* thinks of the tree of life in the same way (*2 Enoch* 8:5 [A]). Philo also appears to have associated the tree of life and the lampstand of the later temple, since he compared both with the planetary lights (cf. *Quaest. Gen.* 1.10 with, e.g., *Quaest. Exod.* 2.73–81). For these references to Judaism with respect to the tree of life, see Barker 1991: 90–95

[41] On the proposed reading of 'Eden' here, see the earlier discussions above of 1QH 7.24.

Qumran *Hymn Scroll* (1QS 8.5–6) also speaks of the Essene community as 'the House of holiness' and 'an everlasting planting', who are to be '*witnesses* of truth'!

Similarly, not accidental is Irenaeus's understanding that Isaiah 11:1–2 pictures 'the Spirit of God' resting 'in seven forms on the Son of God' and that Moses had 'revealed the pattern of this in the seven-branched candlestick'[42] (likewise, Clement of Alexandria, *Stromata*, 5.6). This identification reflects the scriptural truth that the Spirit was first given to God's Son as a representative of his people, to whom he subsequently gave the Spirit (e.g., see Acts 2:33).[43] Intriguingly, in this connection the Old Testament 'tree of life' could be associated with notions of witnessing (Prov. 11:30: 'the fruit of the righteous is a tree of life, and he who is wise wins souls'). The observation that the five churches who are accused of sin in Revelation 2 – 3 all have problems with being faithful witnesses (see Beale 1999a: *in loc.*) further enhances the association of the temple with witness and the spread of God's presence outward to the world!

This link between Revelation 2 and 11 provides an additional connection with the final vision of the temple where it is also pictured as a garden whose prominent feature is a giant 'tree of life' (22:2) and the Lord whose 'face' will be in the midst of his people (22:4) and who will be their eternal 'lamp' (21:23; 22:5). In the light of the discussion so far, it is perhaps not coincidence that the same Qumran text noted above (1QH 6.14–17) compares the Essene community to the tree of Eden which God has planted in the past and which will provide shade for the whole earth in the future![44] We see here an early Jewish interpretation of the tree of life in Eden, which understands it to have eschatogically universal significance similar to that in the last vision of Revelation.

These preceding paragraphs on the lampstand and Eden confirm further that humanity's original purpose in the first garden sanctuary was to expand outward and spread the light of God's presence throughout the earth. After the fall, the commission to spread this presence entailed 'witnessing', since now unbelievers exist who need to be enlightened by God's glorious presence through his evangelical priest-king image bearers (e.g., cf. Exod. 19:6). Therefore, the church's

---

[42] Irenaeus, *The Preaching of the Apostles*, ch. 9, on which see J. N. Sparks' edition (1987: 31–32).

[43] And see further on ch. 6 above for our discussion of the Spirit at Pentecost as a descent of the heavenly temple to encompass God's people.

[44] On which, see further at ch. 4, pp. 154–156.

role as an arboreal lampstand of witness begins at the commencement of the church age and is consummated when Christ returns.[45]

Concluding reflections on the eschatological lampstand in Revelation 11:1–4

The church symbolized as a 'lampstand' in Revelation 11 represents God's temple-presence that is given power by 'the seven lamps' (= the Spirit, as in Rev. 1:4; 4:5) on it. This is a power primarily to witness as a light uncompromisingly to the world so that the gates of hell (cf. 2:9–11, 13) would not prevail against the building of God's temple, the true Israel, which is identified with the heavenly temple and the divine presence (see Beale 1999a: *in loc.* on 1:16). This reiterates the mission of true Israel as expressed by the use of Exodus 19:6 in Revelation 1:6, both of which have their ultimate roots in the first 'Great Commission' in Genesis 1:26–28. The end-time temple has been inaugurated in the church.[46] Revelation 11:1–13 confirms that the lampstands represent the church as the true temple and the totality of the people of God witnessing between the period of Christ's resurrection and his final coming. The Aramaic version of Zechariah 4:7 (*Tg. Zechariah*) foresees that the successful building of the temple in the midst of the world's opposition will be achieved ultimately by 'the Anointed One' who 'shall rule over all kingdoms'. In the light of Revelation 1:5–6, Christ's death and resurrection have laid the foundation for the new temple, which he will build through the Spirit (the lamps on the lampstand).

The shift from one lampstand in Zechariah to seven in Revelation stresses not only that the book is intended for the church universal of the escalated end times, but also the idea that true Israel is no longer limited to a nation but encompasses all peoples. The escalation of lampstands already had a precedent in Solomon's temple which had ten lampstands (1 Kgs. 7:49) in comparison to the tabernacle's one, and which probably was a foreshadowing of the escalation to occur

[45] For the church's beginning identification with the 'tree of life' see: *Barnabas* 11:10–11, where the image of eating from the trees of the new creation (so. Ezek. 47:1–12; cf. Rev. 22:2) is used to describe the *present* experience of baptism; *Odes of Solomon* 11:16–24 refers to those who are presently identified with the blessing of the trees of paradise (so likewise 20:7); *Psalms of Solomon* 14:2 affirms that 'the Lord's paradise, the trees of life, *are* his devout ones', and yet this is also seen as a future hope in 14:10; also see Daniélou (1964: 30–35), who shows that the earliest fathers predominantly understood the symbols of the tree of life and paradise as referring to inaugurated realities of which Christians already partook.

[46] The later Jewish *Midrash Rabbah Numbers* 15:10 expresses the hope that when God restores the end-time temple, he will also restore the 'candlestick'.

in the end times. The observation that the effect of the two witnesses extends to 'some from the peoples and tribes and tongues and nations' (11:9) and to 'the ones dwelling on the earth' (11:10) also indicates the progressive and inaugurated advancement of God's end-time temple that was beginning to be extended throughout the earth.

Other texts in the Apocalypse that further contribute to understanding the end-time temple in Revelation 11 and 21 – 22

The mention in Revelation 3:12a of believers becoming identified eternally with the 'temple' (*naos*) by being made a permanent 'pillar' (*stylos*) in it emphasizes the above-mentioned theme of divine presence even more. This is evident from 21:22 – 22:5, which explains that there is no physical 'temple' (*naos*) in the heavenly Jerusalem but that 'the Lord God almighty is its temple [*naos*] and the Lamb' (21:22; so also 7:15–17), and those in the city walk by their light (21:23–25; 22:5) and dwell in their immediate presence (22:3–4).

Christ's statement that he would write upon the overcomer who becomes permanently identified with the temple 'the name of My God, and the name of the city of My God' (Rev. 3:12) recalls Ezekiel 48:35 (cf. 1 Maccabees 14:26ff.). There the 'name of the city' of the new Jerusalem is 'the Lord is there' because he has established his latter-day temple in its midst, where his glory will reside for ever.[47] Likewise, the verbatim language of Revelation 3:12 is repeated again in Revelation 21:2 to introduce a vision of the end-time temple of God, where God will dwell for ever with his people, and which is modelled on the Ezekiel 40 – 48 temple (see on 21:10 – 22:5). This further emphasizes the theme of divine presence in 3:12. Identification with Jesus' 'name' (3:12b) is tantamount to being identified with Jesus as the temple (21:22), so that the believer becomes permanently associated with the tabernacling presence of God in Jesus.

This line of thought in which Jesus' followers persevere through tribulation and then are rewarded with the presence of God and Christ in the 'temple' (*naos*) is also developed in 7:14–17, which indicates inaugurated, or possibly consummated, fulfilment of the prophecy in

---

[47] So Ezek. 40 – 47; 48:10, 21; *Tg. Ezekiel* 48:35; *b. Baba Batri* 75b renders Ezek. 48:35 by 'the Lord is its name' by changing the Hebrew pointing (see Epstein 1948: *in loc.*).

Ezekiel 37:25–27 that God's 'dwelling place' and 'sanctuary' would be with his people. The temple promise of the Ezekiel 37 passage is a part of the promise of the future temple in Ezekiel 40 – 48. That both passages are part of the same promise is apparent from noticing that twice in 37:25–28 and twice in 43:7, 9 occurs the phrase 'I will dwell among the sons of Israel forever'.[48]

The believer's permanent identification with the 'sanctuary' in Revelation 3:12 includes in its purview the consummation of the process which began with Christ unlocking the doors of the invisible sanctuary of salvation to them, as expressed in Revelation 3:7b–8a: '. . . I have put before you an open door which no one can shut'.[49] This true sanctuary is placed in clear contrast with the false synagogue of the Jews who now give ultimate allegiance to Satan (so 3:9). A link with 3:7–8 is borne out further by noticing that the closest parallels to 3:8 and 3:12 are found in chapter 21 (respectively 21:25 and 21:2, 10): Christ begins to 'open' the doors of the heavenly Jerusalem and temple for the faithful here on earth, which no-one can shut, and this is consummated when his people enter through 'the gates' of the new Jerusalem and temple, which 'by no means will they shut'. That the promise of a place in the Ezekiel 40 – 48 end-time temple has been inaugurated is suggested by the above parallel with Revelation 11:2, and the fact that 11:2 pictures the community of faith on earth as already identified with the latter-day temple of Ezekiel (see on 11:1–2).

The permanent establishment of the overcomer as a pillar in the temple may also continue the imagery of Isaiah 22:22ff. from Revelation 3:7, where Eliakim's relatives achieve glory by 'hanging on him as a *peg* firmly attached to a wall'. Some Greek Old Testament witnesses even refer to Eliakim as being set up as a 'pillar' in Isaiah 22:23.[50] The Aramaic translation of Isaiah 22:23–25 also views Eliakim as a priest in the temple and that other priests depend on him for their service in the temple.[51] Eliakim eventually loses his place as a firm peg, but the latter-day Eliakim, Jesus, is immovable as a 'peg'

---

[48] With minor variations in wording.

[49] Note the Aramaic OT's interpretative paraphrase of Is. 22:22, the Hebrew of which is quoted in 3:7: 'I will place the key of the *sanctuary* and the authority of the house of David in his hand . . .'

[50] Vaticanus, Origen and Q read, *stēlō*, 'I will set up as a pillar' or 'I will inscribe on a pillar'; following Kraft 1974: 82; cf. Fekkes 1994: 130–133, though sceptical about LXX influence.

[51] Likewise, the Jewish commentary of the *Midrash Rabbah Exodus* 37.1 understands Eliakim in Is. 22:23 to be a 'high priest'.

or 'pillar' of the temple, with which his followers become permanently identified, even during the church age.

Intriguing again is the observation that, assuming the validity of the association of Isaiah 22:22 with the temple in Revelation 3:7, the portrayal of the temple is explained by witnessing to the world of unbelief (cf. Rev. 3:8–9), as is the case in Revelation 11 and 1 Peter 2 – 3! That the letter to Philadelphia begins and ends with a reference to the temple is supported by the other letters where Christ introduces himself from part of chapter 1's description of him that is uniquely appropriate to each particular church's situation and which has some essential identification with the kind of reward given to that church. For example, we noted above that the 'lampstand' in Revelation 2:1, 5 is an inaugurated reality of the 'tree of life' with which true saints begin to be identified in the present and are consummately identified on the Last Day (2:7). Or, the present ruling 'Son of God', an allusion to Psalm 2:7, is introduced in 2:18 in the letter to Thyatira; then at the end of the epistle (2:26–28), he says he has begun to fulfil the Psalm 2 prophecy of the Son of God's rule over the earth. Or, again, Christ's eternal resurrection life (2:8) will be imparted to the overcomers (2:10–11).

These texts from Revelation 7 and especially Revelation 3 alluding to Ezekiel's eschatological temple have a biblical-theologically organic connection to the conceptions of the same Ezekiel temple in Revelation 11 and 21 – 22! Both also underscore the spiritual nature of the new temple notion, as well as its already and not yet end-time nature. That Revelation 3:12 in particular pictures believers having begun to become part of the latter-day temple is further apparent from noticing that some of the other promises to the 'overcomers' in the other letters have also likely begun fulfilment during the church age. For example, the reward of 'white garments', becoming identified with Christ's 'name' and sitting on a throne with Christ begins to be given even during the course of the Christian age.[52]

The word 'sanctuary' or 'temple' (*naos*) occurs ten more times between Revelation 11:2 and 21:22. All refer to the heavenly temple. All these uses likely refer to various facets of the same inaugurated end-time temple as spoken of in the passages examined in Revelation so far.[53] The focus in these remaining texts is on the heavenly location

[52] For the beginning realization of the promise of 'white garments', see 3:18; 4:4; 7:13; likewise, for identification with Christ's 'name' in the present, see 2:13; 3:8; and for the same perspective on the 'throne', cf. 4:4, as well as 1:6 and 5:10.

[53] On these uses see Beale 1999a: *in loc.*

of the temple. It extends in part to encompass saints on the earth during the church age. In addition to Revelation 11:1–4, Revelation 13:6 probably also portrays the extension of the heavenly sanctuary to surround Christians living on earth: the forces of evil 'blaspheme' God's 'tabernacle, that is, those who [spiritually] tabernacle in heaven' but who physically live on earth (especially in light of Rev. 13:7: 'it was given to him [the beast] to make war with the saints [on earth]') (on 13:6 see Beale 1999a: *in loc.*). This heavenly temple comes down completely to envelop the entire cosmos at the end of the age. Revelation 21 portrays this consummated reality of the temple.

The church as the eschatological temple in 1 Peter 2 and its relationship to Revelation's temple

First Peter 2:4–9 confirms the analysis of Revelation 11 that in sectors of early Christianity the church was conceived of both as a 'royal priesthood' (in allusion to Exod. 19:6, as in Rev. 1:6; 5:10) and as a temple in the process of being built and expanded from Christ, the foundation stone of the new temple. The purpose of the church as a temple and priests is that they 'may proclaim the excellencies of Him who has called you out of darkness into His marvelous light' (1 Pet. 2:9). We observed earlier that Psalm 92:12–15 had close parallels both with 1 Corinthians 3, as well as 1 Peter 2. The psalm pictures the 'righteous' as trees planted and growing in 'the house of God' on a 'rock' foundation. The goal of believers being identified with the temple was 'that they might declare that the Lord ... God is right-eous'. First Peter's statement of the virtually identical goal may be echoing the psalm passage. Regardless, the psalmist's conception of the 'evangelical' goal of the living temple finally finds much greater redemptive-historical fulfilment in Christ and his people. They are the true latter-day temple, who finally are able to fulfil the commis-sion of extending God's glory from the sanctuary.

The cultic goal of 'proclaiming the excellencies' of God in 1 Peter 2:9 is developed further in 1 Peter 3:14–15 where Peter cites Isaiah 8:12–13 in affirming that Christians are not to fear unbelieving opposition but are 'to make a defense to everyone who asks you to give an account for the hope that is in you ...' Indeed, Isaiah 8:14 was part of the earlier description of the church as a temple in 1 Peter 2, and this Isaiah back-ground is appropriate to express this notion: Isaiah 8:13–14 says, '[God] shall be your fear ... Then He shall become a sanctuary' (the Greek OT paraphrases, 'If you shall trust in him, he will be for you a sanctuary').

This is all comparable to Revelation 11, since both contexts refer to God's people as a spiritually inviolable temple who spread God's presence and word but whose physical being can be harmed.

What we have in Revelation 11 and 1 Peter 2 then is the conception of God's saints being the true temple of God's presence in initial fulfilment of the Ezekiel 40 – 48 temple prophecy (though 1 Peter quotes other OT temple texts) and extending that presence throughout the earth by means of their witness. The new temple begins with Christ as the foundation 'stone' and continues to be 'built up as a spiritual house' (1 Pet. 2:4–6) until it is completed on the last day of history.[54] Ephesians 2:20–22 also highlights the same point:[55] Christ is 'the corner stone, in whom the whole building, being fitted together is growing into a holy temple in the Lord; in whom you also are being built together into a dwelling of God in the Spirit'![56] During the present age, the very being of the church as witnesses of an invisible temple conveys the presence of God to others, either in blessing or judgment (the latter being the focus of Revelation 11).

Our earlier discussion of a passage in the early Christian *Epistle of Barnabas*[57] merits review at this point. The text applies the commission of Adam (Gen. 1:28), and the same commission renewed to Israel in the land, to Christ and the church as a new creation. Jesus and his people are the beginning true fulfilment of the commission (*Barnabas* 6:11–17), which will be completed in the future (6:18–19). Christ is called a 'stone that crushes [Dan. 2:34–35, 45] ... a precious stone, especially chosen, a cornerstone [Is. 28:16]' (*Barnabas* 6:3).[58] Christ is referred to as the centre of the new temple in 6:14–15, which seems to develop the allusion to him as a 'cornerstone' at the beginning of the same chapter (6:3–4). The end-time sanctuary grows out from Christ (the initial foundation stone) during the church age:

---

[54] Cf. likewise, Ignatius, *Letter to the Ephesians* 9: 'you are stones of a temple, prepared beforehand for the building of God the Father'. Similarly, *Barnabas* 4:11 says, 'Let us become spiritual; let us become a perfect temple for God.' Note the reference to *Barnabas* 16:6, 10 directly below.

[55] As does Matt. 21:42–44; Mark 12:10; Luke 20:17–18; Acts 4:11.

[56] Cf. Morray-Jones 1998, who compares Qumran's identification of itself as the embodiment of the heavenly temple with Eph. 2:21–22, though he is not focusing on the aspect of the cosmic expansion of God's presence in the temple, as here. Similar to our observation in Eph. 2 is *Barnabas* 16:6 and 10, which says respectively that 'there is in fact a temple of God ... he is building and completing it', and that 'the spiritual temple ... is being built for the Lord'.

[57] On which see at the beginning of ch. 4.

[58] *Barnabas* 6:4 refers again to Christ as the 'cornerstone' by way of allusion to Ps. 118:22.

'there is in fact a temple of God ... [that] he is building and completing', and at the 'end God's temple will be built gloriously' (16:6). The remainder of *Barnabas* 16 (16:7–10) explains that the way the temple 'is being built for the Lord' is by God 'dwelling in our dwelling place' by means of people believing in Christ for forgiveness of sin, setting their hope on him, and trusting in his righteous precepts.

Excursus on Christ as the foundation stone of the temple, and, hence, of the new creation in the light of the Ancient Near East, the Old Testament and Judaism

Ancient Near Eastern mythologies sometimes portray a hillock arising amidst the chaotic seas as the bridgehead of creation, as we have seen, for example, in the Egyptian cosmogonies.[59] The same thing may be reflected in the second biblical creation episode, where the first item that emerges from the waters is the tip of a mountain on which Noah's Ark comes to rest (see Levenson 1988: 74–75). Intriguingly, the stone supporting the holy of holies was thought by later Judaism to be that upon which 'all the world was based', since, it was believed, God had begun to create the world from that point in the beginning.[60] The 'world was started [created] from Zion ... the world was created from its centre' when God 'cast a stone into the ocean, from which the world then was founded' (*b. Yoma* 54b). The light God made in Genesis 1 'was created from the place of the Temple' (*Midrash Rabbah Genesis* 3:4).[61]

It is this background that likely gave rise to the notion that Israel was the 'middle (or navel) of the earth'.[62] The reason that Israel and her temple were likely also considered to be the centre of the earth is because it was the place where divine wisdom resided.[63] The wisdom

---

[59] See ch. 3 (p. 93), as well as ch. 4 and the discussion of the Dan. 2 stone image.

[60] See the Jewish commentary of *Midrash Rabbah Song of Songs* 3:10 §4; so also *Midrash Tanhuma Qedoshim* 10; on which see Branham 1995: 325; see also *Tanhuma Yelammedenu, Exodus* 11:3.

[61] See Levenson 1985: 118, for additional similar references in Judaism. For literature supporting the presence of this notion in the OT, see Terrien 1970: 317–322. Perhaps the closest the OT comes to this idea is Job 38:6 in relation to Ps. 87:1 (on which see Keel 1985: 113–115, 181).

[62] So Ezek. 5:5; 38:12; *Jubilees* 8:12, 19; *1 Enoch* 26:1–4; the latter two referring to Israel's temple; cf. similarly, Josephus, *War* 3.52.

[63] E.g., the ten commandments in the ark represented such wisdom and the priests carrying out their cultic duties exemplified God's wisdom; see Hayward 1999: 31–46, for these notions in *Sirach*.

needed to maintain ethical order emanated from the temple, and when humanity violated the ethical cosmic order, the physical world order began to break up. Hence, Israel's temple was the theological centre of the earth. It is likely against this background that the following saying arose: 'Upon three things the universe stands: upon Torah, and upon the Temple service, and upon deeds of loving-kindness' (*m. Aboth* 1.2).[64]

The New Testament contends that Christ is the stone upon which the new world is based and from which it proceeds; likewise, Christ is the source from which true cosmic wisdom proceeds (so, e.g., Col. 2:2–3).

---

[64] For the translation and discussion, see Hayward 1991: 31–32.

Chapter Eleven

The temple in Ezekiel 40 – 48 and its relationship to the New Testament

Though the preceding chapter discussed the use of Ezekiel 40 – 48 in Revelation 3, 7 and 19, more clarification of this vision in its Old Testament context is needed. Indeed, it would be remiss in a book on a biblical theology of the temple not to include a chapter on the well-known temple vision of Ezekiel 40 – 48. Though the constraints of the present book do not allow a thorough investigation of Ezekiel's temple vision, it is still important to give a broad sketch of what we think is the best approach. The main lines of interpretation are, at least, fourfold. First, the vision is prophetic of a literal physical temple to be built in Israel.[1] Second, the vision is figurative of an ideal heavenly temple that was never intended to be built or established on the earth (Tuell 1996: 649–664). Third, the portrayal is a figurative vision of an ideal temple. Fourth, the depiction is of a real heavenly temple that would descend and be established on earth in non-structural form in the latter days.

The primary argument for the first view is that a 'literal historical-grammatical hermeneutic' dictates that the vision be understood as referring to a future physical structure, quite comparable to the Solomonic temple. According to this interpretative principle, one interprets 'literally' (which usually means interpreting in a way corresponding to physical reality) unless the context demands a figurative analysis. This is supported further by appeal to the extensive descriptions of the temple in chapters 40 – 46. As we shall see, however, there are indications from the context of the vision that point to the second, third or fourth interpretations as more likely. A combination of the last two might even be possible: Ezekiel 40 – 48 foresees an ideal heavenly temple that already has existence and that will descend to earth at the end of history.[2] The purpose of this analysis is also to

[1] Judaism believed this would occur in the eschatological future, while some recent conservative commentators view the fulfilment to be during a 'millennial period'.

[2] So also Eichrodt 1970: 542.

335

show how Ezekiel's vision fits into the biblical-theological patterns of temple establishment and expansion discussed thus far.

The contextual connections of chapters 40 – 48 within the book of Ezekiel that point to a non-structural end-time temple

The first hints that the vision is not about a conventional architectural structure occur at its inception (40:1–2), where God sets the prophet on 'a very high mountain' in Israel, and where on the south part of the mountain he sees 'a structure like a city'. All commentators agree that the location is Jerusalem, but there is no 'very high mountain' in Jerusalem.[3] This lack of a referent indicates that we are entering into the realm of symbolic geography of heaven or earth that pertains to eschatological conditions.[4] That this is so finds confirmation in Revelation 21:10, where John similarly finds himself 'carried ... away in the Spirit to a great and high mountain', and an angel showed him 'the holy city, Jerusalem, coming down out of heaven from God'. That Ezekiel then sees 'a structure like a city' on the mountain shows that the mountain is not only high but of extraordinary enough size to contain the entire city of Jerusalem. It is true that even the old temple on Mount Zion could be referred to as situated on a very high place but when such descriptions occurred they were figurative to emphasize the link of the old temple with the heavenly temple (e.g., see 1 Kgs. 8:13,[5] as well as Exod. 15:17 and possibly Jer. 17:12). At such points the focus was on the heavenly sanctuary 'high' in heaven, which the earthly holy of holies symbolized. While there are similarities, the depiction of the mountain in Ezekiel 40 is different from figurative language applied to Israel's earthly temple, since even 'the city' is seen to be situated on the 'very high

---

[3] The ridge on which Jerusalem sits is only 2,500 feet above sea level (on which, see Block 1998: 501). Some commentators believe that the high mountain is a literal future reality, when the topography of the earth will be radically altered at the commencement of a final period of millennial bliss.

[4] 'High mountain' in Ezek. 17:22–23 and 20:40 refers to the place of Israel's end-time restoration. So also 'the mountain of the house of the LORD' is equated with 'the chief of the mountains' in Is. 2:2 and Mic. 4:1, which will exist 'in the last days' (cf. Block 1998: 501, who cites these texts, but nevertheless concludes that the 'high mountain' in Ezek. 40:2 is not an eschatological but ideal reality). The similarity of the huge end-time mountain of Dan. 2:35 to that of Ezek. 40:2 also points to the eschatological nature of the latter.

[5] On which, e.g., see above in ch. 1 (pp. 36–38).

mountain', thus pointing to a focus on a temple set only in a symbolic geographical world of another dimension.

The geographical symbolism is enhanced from noticing that the threefold introductory vision phraseology of Ezekiel 40:1–4 occurs in the book only at chapter 1 (1:1–3) and chapter 8 (8:1–3):[6] (1) an initial comment about the specific date on which the experience occurred; (2) 'the hand of Yahweh came upon him'; (3) and Ezekiel 'saw . . . visions'. Two additional common elements are that the visions occur by 'the river Chebar' (1:1, 3; 10:15, 22; 43:3) and that 'the glory of God' is an essential component of all three vision episodes (1:28; 8:4; 9:3; 10:4, 18–19; 11:22–23; 43:2, 5). What is unique about the uses in Ezekiel 1 and 8 is that each introduces a vision in which the prophet receives a glimpse of part of a heavenly temple. This is quite clear in chapter 1, where Ezekiel says 'the heavens were opened', and he saw the four cherubim guarding God's heavenly throne. The theophany was coming from the 'north' (*ṣāpôn*) which reflects the great cosmic heavenly mountain where God's true throne was thought to reside. The heavenly dimension of the temple comes to Ezekiel in Babylon, so that the earthly Jerusalem temple is not the subject. Furthermore, this theophany of Yahweh in his heavenly temple was intended to reassure the prophet that the faithful among the exiles were still related to the true heavenly temple, though the old one had been decimated.[7] Thus, chapter 1 focuses only on the temple's heavenly dimension.

Chapters 8 – 9 are a vision of the heavenly dimension of the sanctuary dwelling in the midst of the physical temple, while chapter 10 describes that heavenly dwelling[8] as beginning to depart from the earthly complex, and 11:22–23 pictures the final departure of God's glory from the dwelling. The climax of these chapters is in 11:22–23, where the presence of God's heavenly sanctuary, formerly having extended down to the earthly holy of holies, finally departs back to heaven. Then this presence returns to earth, not to inhabit a structural temple but to be an invisible 'sanctuary for them [remnant Israel] a little while' in exile (11:16). This was a heavenly sanctuary that had its corresponding earthly sanctuary in the faithful remnant of exiles in Babylon. As remarked above, the chapter 1 vision probably represents the same reality, since it occurs in Babylon to

---

[6] These commonalities have been recognized most clearly by Tuell 1996: 654–656; cf. also Block 1998: 496.

[7] See Block 1998: 505, who makes virtually the identical point.

[8] That this chapter describes the heavenly dimension of God's temple is clear from the abundant parallels throughout with 1:5–28.

Ezekiel, a prophetic representative of the faithful (as Ezek. 11:25 suggests).

The unique introductory formulae that chapters 1 and 8 share in common with chapter 40 bind them all together. Since chapters 40 – 48 also pertain to a temple, the question is whether it refers to the purely heavenly temple dimension that descends in the midst of the faithful saints on earth (as in chapters 1 and 11), or the heavenly dimension in the midst of another (new) earthly temple in structural form, as in chapters 8 – 9. Whichever is the case, the focus is on the heavenly temple. The pressing question then is: what is the earthly reality to which the heavenly temple of Ezekiel 40 – 48 corresponds? The answer to this all-important question is that the vision likely pertains to the heavenly temple corresponding to God's dwelling in the midst of his people, and not in a physical temple. The reason for favouring this comes from the following cumulative evidence presented in the remainder of this chapter, both from within the book of Ezekiel, as well as from elsewhere in the Old Testament.

As we have said, the initial mention of Ezekiel being on a mountain (40:2) focuses the vision on heavenly geography, not earthly. We have seen earlier that Israel's earthly temple was a reflection or copy of the heavenly temple.[9] Most clearly, we have observed in a preceding chapter that the holy of holies represented the invisible dimension of God's heavenly dwelling.[10] Since the heavenly temple did not descend through Israel's earthly temple to fill the earth (so Ezek. 8 – 11), Ezekiel 40 – 48 pictures the ongoing existence of the heavenly temple in the future when it will descend, but, we would argue, not through a handmade structure. Such an interpretation receives early attestation in the Qumran *Songs of Sabbath Sacrifice* (4Q400–407), where images and terms from Ezekiel 40 – 48 are applied to a heavenly eschatological temple that the Dead Sea community believed to have been inaugurated, and to which they were spiritually related.[11]

The thematic link with the heavenly temple descending among the faithful and not into an earthly structure (11:16) is enhanced by noticing that the vision there ends with God's tabernacling presence remaining 'over the mountain which is east of the city' (11:23). Likewise, 40:2 begins with God carrying Ezekiel to 'a very high mountain; and on it to the south was a structure like a city'. These

---

[9] Exod. 25:8–9, 40; Ps. 78:69a; *1 Enoch* 14:8–25; *Tg. 2 Chronicles* 6:2; likewise, *Tg. Exodus* 15:17; Heb. 8:5; 9:23–24; cf. 1 Chr. 28:11–19.

[10] See ch. 2, pp. 34–60.

[11] So Tuell 1996: 659–660; Davila 2002: 5–6; Martínez 1988: 441–452.

are probably the same symbolic mountains, but if not, they are very similar. If the former, then chapter 40 begins where chapter 11 left off: describing God's heavenly presence that had departed from the physical temple and had taken up invisible residence with the remnant of Israel in exile (11:16, 23–25).[12] It is, therefore, quite viable that Ezekiel's final vision of the temple describes the heavenly sanctuary to which the remnant on earth are related (Tuell 1996). The formal and thematic parallels between chapters 1, 8 – 11, and 40 – 48 'require that the same hermeneutical principles [of symbolism] employed in the interpretation of the previous prophecies apply here, and that one interpret this block [chs. 40 – 48] in the light of the previous visions of God' (Block 1998: 496–497).

More plausibly, therefore, the vision describes the heavenly temple that will relate to the eschatological people of God. This is borne out also from a key phrase in 11:20, in which God says that Israel 'will be My people, and I shall be their God' at the time of the end-time restoration, when he gives them a 'new spirit' and 'heart' (11:19 = 36:26). This phrase is interpreted in Ezekiel 37:26–28 to be a promise that God would establish his eschatological 'sanctuary' in Israel.[13]

In an earlier chapter (ch. 3), we concluded for two reasons that this sanctuary in Ezekiel 37 was not a building but God's tabernacling presence. First, this passage is a clear allusion to Leviticus 26:11–12: 'moreover, I will make My *tabernacle among you* ... I will also *walk among you* and be your God, and you will be my people'. A 'literal' reading of Leviticus could well suggest that the promise of God's eschatological 'walking among' the people will express itself more intensely and personally than would his dwelling with them in an encased structure during the wilderness wandering.[14]

Second, Ezekiel 37:27 says, 'My dwelling place also will be *over* [preposition *'al*] them'. If this is also taken straightforwardly, it refers to God's spiritual presence being over *all Israelites*, which means that it would extend over not only the city but the entire promised land. Hence, as with the 'sanctuary' in 11:16, a small cultic building does not appear to be in mind. Twice in this passage God says that 'My

---

[12] Zimmerli 1983: 547, who notes that God, who had left the temple because of Israel's idolatry (chs. 8 – 11), 'will once again be with his people' (chs. 40 – 48).

[13] Note the further link between Ezek. 36:28–30 and 37:27 in the common phrase (with minor variations) 'you will be My people, and I will be your God'; cf. Ezek. 11:16–20, which may also allude to Lev. 26:12.

[14] Though it is true that 'walking' is used figuratively in Exodus, Numbers and Deuteronomy for God's presence with Israel (presumably in the tabernacle) during the wilderness journeying.

sanctuary is in their midst forever' (vv. 26, 28; note 'dwelling place' in v. 27). Ezekiel 43:7, 9 also says virtually the same thing twice in the course of describing the extended vision of the temple: 'I will dwell in the midst of the sons of Israel forever.' It is possible that these synonymous expressions refer to different sanctuaries, but when it is recalled that they pertain to the same period of the end-time, it is probable that Ezekiel 43 is developing the prophecy of the sanctuary in Ezekiel 37.[15] What further unites the sanctuaries of Ezekiel 37 and 43 is their common Garden of Eden imagery: cf. Ezek. 36:35 and 37:5, 26–28 with 47:1–12. These observations bolster our conclusion that Ezekiel 40 – 48 refers to a heavenly temple linked to a non-architectural earthly reality, in development of Ezekiel 37.[16]

The descriptions within chapters 40 – 48 that point to a non-structural end-time temple

Not only the broad context of Ezekiel 40 – 48 but the text of the temple vision itself provide evidence suggesting that this is not a vision of a traditionally conceived handmade temple.

Unusual features that point beyond a localized temple

That Ezekiel sees a much bigger reality than one localized temple structure is evident from the vision's introduction (40:2), where he summarizes the temple vision that follows by saying that he saw on the top of the mountain 'a structure like a city'. That is, he saw a temple structured like a city, or perhaps a city structured like a temple. The very end of the vision (48:35) says that 'the name of the city from that day shall be, "The Lord is there."' In other words, what formerly was true of the holy of holies will one day be true of the entire city of Jerusalem. Thus, Ezekiel 40:2 and 48:35 form the boundaries of the whole temple vision, and plausibly provide the vision's interpretative summary: the temple is equivalent to the city because the whole city will be filled with God's presence that was formerly limited to the innermost sanctuary of Israel's temple. In chapter 4, we saw a similar prophecy in Jeremiah 3:16–17. There the ark of the

---

[15] So also Duguid 1999: 489, and likewise, Zimmerli 1983: 327. Zimmeli also says that in both 37:26–28 and 43:7, 9 'there is nothing about Yahweh's dwelling in his temple, but of his dwelling in the midst of Israel' (Zimmerli 1983: 416).

[16] See also C. J. H. Wright 2001: 334–335. Wright sees the phrase 'I will live among them forever' in Ezek. 43:7–9 summarizing the hopes of chs. 34 – 37; so likewise, Block 1998: 421–422.

Lord was to be remembered no more in the end-time restoration because God's throne will expand from the holy of holies to cover, at minimum, the whole city of Jerusalem: 'At that time they shall call Jerusalem "The Throne of the LORD," and all the nations will be gathered to it for the name of the LORD in Jerusalem ...' (Ezek. 43:7 uses the language of 'the place of My throne').

The boundaries of Ezekiel's temple are particularly striking in that they are approximately the same size (a little over one mile) as the boundaries of ancient Jerusalem (during the second temple era).[17] The massive expansion of the temple is a quite similar picture to that in Jeremiah 3:17. This magnification of the tabernacling glory is apparent from observing that God's glory not merely filled the temple (43:4–5), as it had at the consecration of Solomon's temple (1 Kgs. 8:10–11), but even 'the earth [or land] shone with His glory' (43:2) (Duguid 1999:489). The water that flowed from the temple also affected the territory throughout Israel. The trickling waters from the temple quickly became a deep river and 'healed' all life in it, as well as feeding into and 'healing' the Dead Sea. Such magnified perspectives of the temple and the divine glory, together with the widening effects of the temple river may have supplied the impetus for later Judaism to assert that those waters affected the entire earth.[18] At least one recent Old Testament commentator has made a similar conclusion: 'The return of paradise [in Ezek. 47:1–12], apparently at present limited to Palestine, is of its very nature a universal event embracing the whole world ... Palestine is a part that stands for the whole' (Eichrodt 1970:585).

This conclusion is supported from observing that the expanding features of the vision fit admirably into the numerous other Old Testament, Jewish and early Christian accounts of an expanding temple or garden of Eden (or both) that we have examined earlier,

[17] Fairbairn 1863b: 438 contends that the boundaries of Ezekiel's temple are almost twice the size of ancient Jerusalem. The basis of Fairbairn's calculations are not clear, and, indeed, appear to be incorrect. Ezek. 42:20 says the length and width of the temple was 'five hundred' reeds (cf. also 42:15–19). Our calculation of the temple's size is based on the pre-Babylonian measuring reed (which is the one relevant for Ezekiel's time), which was approximately 6.2 cubits long: 500 reeds × 6.2 cubits = 3,100 cubits (the Babylonian reed was 7 cubits, so that the size of the temple would be bigger, using it as the basis of calculation, but not nearly as large as Fairbairn's estimate). Then 3,100 cubits × 0.52 metres = 1,612 metres, which equals between one and one and a quarter miles (based on one cubit being equal to 0.52 metres). The Qumran *Temple Scroll* drew up a plan for a temple based also on Ezekiel, which was about the same size as Ezekiel's temple. I am grateful to my archaeology colleague, John Monson, who has helped me with the calculations of Ezekiel's temple.

[18] At least as implied by *Pirke de Rabbi Eliezer* 51; *Midrash Rabbah Exodus* 15:21; *Midrash Rabbah Numbers* 21:22.

especially eschatological prophecies of non-structural temples (e.g., Is. 4:5–6; 57:15; 66:1–2; and Zech. 1 – 2; cf. also Is. 8:14). Therefore, the fact that Ezekiel 47:1–12 portrays the water flowing from the temple and causing widespread fertility should be no surprise.[19] Allusions to Eden are seen in the temple-city's river and trees, and the fact that it is located on 'a very high mountain'.[20] Waters that go out from Eden and cause the garden's trees to grow and envelop the earth in Ezekiel 31 is one of the expanding garden scenes we have observed earlier. However, the image of chapter 31 describes a pagan nation that failed, as Adam had, in expanding their garden-like empire. Ezekiel 17:1–10 and 19:10–14 describe Israel's rise and demise through the very same Edenic arboreal imagery. What Adam and subsequent ungodly kingdoms had failed to do, Ezekiel 47 represents as finally being accomplished at some future point,[21] a link which confirms further the universal scope of the scene in Ezekiel 47. Similarly, the 'high mountain' of 40:2, on which the temple and city sit, develops Ezekiel 28's reflection on 'the holy mountain of God' (28:14; cf. 28:16), upon which was 'Eden, the garden of God' (28:13) (cf. Levenson 1976: 25–26). Whereas Ezekiel 28 recounts the corruption of the garden, the mountain of God with its pure garden in Ezekiel 40 – 48 provides a sharp contrast.

Additional details of Ezekiel's vision are so strange that they would seem to require a symbolic understanding. The city is perfectly square (Ezek. 48:16); the territorial allotments for each Israelite tribe are 'divided by dead straight lines running east and west and ignoring all the facts of geography (48:1–29)' (Ellison 1956: 139). The dimensions of the city and temple are described with multiples of five, with twenty-five being particularly repeated (Block 1998: 502). Further, horizontal measurements are the only recorded dimensions, with no apparent regard for vertical distances that are necessary for an architectural plan (Block 1998: 510–511). Equally unusual is the water that flows out of the temple (47:1–2). A little over a half-mile to the east the waters deepen into an ankle-deep brook (v. 3). Within another half a mile, the

[19] So, e.g., Levenson 1976: 25–36.

[20] If Levenson 1976: 41–44 is correct that Ezekiel's mountain also typologically corresponds to Sinai, then the whole mountain may have cultic connotations, since we have seen that Sinai was a mountain temple.

[21] See Levenson 1976: 29–30 for the intimation of the connection between Ezek. 31 and 47. The phrase 'very many trees' (or 'a very great forest') on each side of the river in Ezek. 47:7 could easily be translated 'the great tree', so that two trees could be in mind, both recalling the two specific trees mentioned in Gen. 2, as well as the 'very high tree' in Ezek. 31:3 (as well as 31:5, 7; following Levenson 1976: 30–31).

water deepens to the knees, and eventually to the waist (v. 4). About another quarter of a mile further on, the river deepens to such a degree that it can be crossed only by swimming (v. 5). The problem with a literal understanding of the river is that there are no tributaries mentioned that feed into the river to make it deeper. And, if there are unmentioned tributaries, then 'common' water would be mixed with the pure water of life. If the picture were of an actual river, then it would have to be supernaturally produced and its purity supernaturally maintained (which some might dare to believe describes a condition in a coming millennium).[22] That this river requires supernatural maintenance is underscored by realizing that the salinity of the Dead Sea does not affect the fresh water's purity, but rather the reverse (C. J. H. Wright 2001: 356).

Thus, the overall impression one gets from the various descriptions in Ezekiel 40 – 48 is that they are 'highly contrived, casting doubt on any interpretation that expects a literal fulfilment' (Block 1998: 502).

Features that point beyond a localized temple, especially in the light of the fuller revelation of the New Testament

The notorious problem of what to make of the sacrifices in Ezekiel's temple may be solved by seeing them beginning fulfilment in Christians who offer themselves to God by suffering for their faith, as we discussed in the preceding chapter. Implicitly, Christ's great sacrifice is the ultimate fulfilment of Ezekiel's temple vision, since Revelation 11 portrays the career of the church according to the outline of Christ's career.[23] Hence, it is not incorrect to say that Ezekiel speaks in the language and images familiar to his audience in portraying sacrifices in a temple to prophesy about the escalated redemptive-historical realities of Christ's sacrifice and the church's imitation of that sacrifice. Both of these 'sacrifices' of the new epoch are linked exegetically by allusions to the Ezekiel temple in Revelation 11:1–2 and the Lamb of 21:22.

Those who see a literal temple structure as the fulfilment of Ezekiel's prophecy usually interpret the sacrifices there to be 'memorial sacrifices' that commemorate Christ's death. In response, numerous commentators have pointed out that this would violate the principle of Hebrews: the Old Testament sacrifices pointed to Christ's 'once for all' sacrifice (Heb. 9:12, 26, 28; 10:10–18), so that to go back to those sacrifices would indicate the insufficiency of Christ's sacrifice for sin (cf., e.g., Heb. 10:18: 'Now where there is forgiveness of these

---

[22] See again Ellison 1956: 139–140, for this discussion.
[23] On which, see Beale 1999a: 567–568.

things, there is no longer any offering for sin'). This would appear to amount to a reversal of redemptive history and, more importantly, a denial of the efficacy of Christ's sacrifice.

The Scofield Bible, espousing the standard literalist dispensational approach, gives a surprising response to what appears to be a vexing problem for those arguing for the future revival of the sacrificial system. In addition to saying that the sacrifices might be memorials, Scofield also offers the following possibility: 'The reference to sacrifices [in Ezekiel's temple prophecy] is not to be taken literally, in view of the putting away of such offerings [according to Hebrews], but is rather to be regarded as a presentation of the worship of redeemed Israel, in her own land and in the millennial temple, using the terms with which the Jews were familiar in Ezekiel's day' (Scofield 1967: 888).

More than one commentator has recognized the inconsistency in this quotation from the Scofield Bible: 'These words convey a far-reaching concession on the part of dispensationalists. If the sacrifices are not to be taken literally, why should we take the temple literally? It would seem that the dispensational principle of the literal interpretation of Old Testament prophecy is here abandoned, and that a crucial foundation stone for the entire dispensationalist system has been set aside!' (Hoekema 1979: 204). Therefore, 'make the sacrifices symbolic and the temple becomes symbolic too' (Ellison 1956: 140). Even to entertain the possibility that the sacrifices are memorials contravenes a literal interpretation of prophecy because of the Hebrew word that Ezekiel uses to explain the purpose of the sacrifices: 'to make atonement' (45:15, 17, 20). The verb is *kipper* (in the Piel verb form), which is the exact word (and verb form) employed in the Pentateuch to describe sacrifices that have an atoning purpose (Lev. 6:30 [23]; 8:15; 16:6, 11, 24, 30, 32, 33, 34; Num. 5:8; 15:28; 29:5) (following Hoekema 1979: 204). Of course, the atoning purpose in the Old Testament accomplished only a temporary 'covering' (which is the meaning of *kipper*) of Israel's sin, which pointed typologically to Christ's 'once for all atonement'. The point is that Ezekiel does not call these sacrifices 'memorials', but puts them on a par with the Levitical typological sacrifices of atonement. From a New Testament perspective, the Lord's Supper is the only memorial instituted by Christ to 'memorialize' his redemptive work. To suggest that this memorial will cease in a coming millennium, to be replaced by the 'old' Old Testament sacrifices,[24] not

---

[24] A suggestion made by Schmitt and Laney 1997: 118–119, and more adamantly stated by Feinberg 1971: 108.

only is at variance with the book of Hebrews, but abrogates Christ's command to remember him in the Lord's Supper (Ellison 1956: 142).[25] Thus, in light of the evidence, it does not seem likely that Ezekiel's sacrifices will be literally fulfilled in a future temple.[26]

A related issue is whether or not to take literally Ezekiel's apparent portrait of Jerusalem as the centre of the world to which Gentiles must come in order to be related to God (Ezek. 47). If taken in a narrowly literal manner, then the redemptive-historical principle of John 4:21, 23 would be radically violated: 'an hour is coming when neither in this mountain, nor in Jerusalem, shall you worship the Father ... but an hour is coming, and now is, when the true worshipers will worship the Father in [the Holy] Spirit and truth'.[27] This principle is related in Jesus' mind to Ezekiel's vision. Jesus alludes to the water flowing from Ezekiel's end-time temple in John 7:38 and interprets it of himself and of the Spirit in relation to believers, a passage that further develops the 'living water' theme of John 4.[28] One could say, therefore, that just as the picture in Ezekiel 47 of Jerusalem as the centre for world worship is meant to be taken figuratively on the basis of Jesus' teaching, so also is all of Ezekiel 40 – 48 to be taken.

One does not need, however, to resort to a figurative approach to be consistent with Jesus' teaching, if one of our main lines of argument so far in the book is correct: that in the end time an Eden-temple will be established as a new Jerusalem that will extend throughout the whole earth. That the Ezekiel 40 – 48 vision is a part of this universally expanding pattern observed elsewhere in the Old Testament is likely, given the hints of widening in the vision that we have observed earlier in this chapter (e.g., see Ezek. 48:35 in light of Jer. 3:17, and note the implicit universal effect of the temple's waters upon the fertility of the entire earth).

---

[25] Though, one could attempt to resist the force of this point about the Eucharist by arguing that, since Christ commands that the Lord's Supper be practised 'until He comes' (1 Cor. 11:26), the Supper would not be in force during the millennial kingdom, after his coming.

[26] Feinberg (1971: 101–103) has missed the essence of the preceding argument, responding to criticisms of his 'literal' view that are clearly erroneous and not representative of the thrust of our present argument. See Duguid 1999: 521 for negative evaluation of another variant of a literal approach to the sacrifices. Schmitt and Laney (1997: 118–119) also propose that, in addition to commemorative 'atonement' sacrifices, some of the offerings will be 'peace offerings' for worship, which would not be as inconsistent with Hebrews, though these were still part of the overall sacrificial system linked to the old temple.

[27] Cf. similarly, Ellison 1956: 142. See also Heb. 12:18–24.

[28] On which see the discussion on the temple in John's Gospel in chapter 5.

Is the temple-city in Revelation 21 the fulfilment of Ezekiel's vision?

Some commentators do not see an eschatological focus in Ezekiel 40 – 48, which would mean that no prophetic fulfilment of the vision is to be expected. For example, Daniel Block argues that Ezekiel's vision is primarily 'a lofty spiritual ideal' and de-emphasizes any specific end-time fulfilment of it (1998: 506).[29] His argument for an idealized temple is acceptable, but why is this incompatible with an end-time fulfilment? He contends that the Ezekiel narrative is *not eschatological* for three primary reasons: (1) there are no explicit latterday expressions; (2) the word 'eternal' (or 'forever') in 43:7, 9 should not be viewed eschatologically; and (3) the blueprint of the temple is not presented as something to be built with human hands (e.g., there is no command that it be built, as there is with the tabernacle) (1998: 504–505). Regarding the first point, expression of eschatological 'concepts' does not always depend on the use of technical eschatological 'terms'. Second, that 'eternal' in 43:7, 9 is, indeed, eschatological is apparent from seeing these verses as a development of 'eternal' in 37:26, 28, where it clearly describes the end of history, as Block himself acknowledges (1998: 419–423).[30] Third, that no-one is commanded to build the temple does not necessitate that it will never be built, only that no human will do so – only God himself will, as we have argued throughout (see, e.g., discussion of Acts 7). Finally, the clear links between the prophesied end-time restoration in Ezekiel 20:33–44 and 40 – 48 demonstrates also the latter's eschatological nature.[31]

Despite some minor disagreements with Block's view, we believe that his view of an ideal temple could be combined with an eschatological approach. Ezekiel portrays what Israelites at that point in redemptive history could have considered an ideal blueprint or perfect prototype of the temple. The temple was expressed in ideal concrete terms 'and yet these were merely the forms in which the

---

[29] Block alludes to only a secondary and nebulous notion of fulfilment, explaining that the essence of the 'ideal' vision is that 'where God is, there is Zion . . . order and the fulfilment of all his promises', which he does not view as eschatological (1998: 503–504), and does not identify with the consummated fulfilment in Rev. 21:1ff. (on which see below).

[30] Block refers to the 'eternal covenant' in Ezek. 37:26–28 as part of the 'eschatological' restoration promises (most explicitly that of Deut. 4:30 ['in the latter days you will return']) that will be fulfilled in Israel's future. Block even says that the brief prophecy about God's sanctuary in Israel's midst is 'the tip of the iceberg' that 'receives extended treatment in his final vision (chs. 40 – 48)' (1998: 421–422).

[31] See Block 1998: 496–497, who himself acknowledges these links.

general principles of God's activity were enshrined' (Taylor 1969: 253).[32] The vision represented what God stood for, what he required and, therefore, what could additionally find more concrete realization in the dawning eschatological age: e.g., (1) God's eternal presence with his restored people; (2) the centrality of worship (expressed in the detailed observance of rites); (3) the protection of God's people from fatal contamination from impurity (this is the significance of the focus on measuring sacred space); (4) the blessings of God's presence that will go out to give life to the entire earth ('the river of life').[33]

Somewhat differently than Block, Steven Tuell sees Ezekiel 40 – 42 as an amplification of Ezekiel 11:16b ('I [God] was a sanctuary for them [exiled Israel] a little while'): through the prophet's communication of the vision to the exiles they are given access to this heavenly reality (Tuell 1996: 664). This is close to my view, but, like Block's, it falls short in taking seriously enough the eschatological interrelationships within the book and elsewhere in prophetic literature. Nevertheless, one could see Ezekiel 40 – 48 as a subsequent, latter-day phase of the earlier heavenly sanctuary which had been described in Ezekiel 11:16 to be in the midst of the exiles. As a result of Ezekiel 11:16, a precedent has now been set within the book of Ezekiel that God's 'temple presence' can be experienced apart from the physical temple complex of Israel.[34] In addition, one other passage preceding that of chapters 40 – 48 contains a similar notion. Ezekiel 28:12–18 depicts the Garden of Eden as a 'sanctuary' (v. 18), despite the fact there was no structural building there![35] It was God's presence that made the Garden the first temple. Chapters 11 and 28 are especially significant as precedents for a non-material temple in Ezekiel 40 – 48, since we have seen earlier in this chapter that these two prior segments are explicitly developed in the book's last vision!

In addition to denying that Ezekiel's temple is eschatological, Block also does not believe that Revelation 21 is its fulfilment because of several differences between the two (Block 1998: 503). Though

[32] We will argue in a following excursus, however, that Ezekiel's portrait is actually not quite 'ideal'.

[33] Following Taylor 1969: 253, though with minor adjustments.

[34] Spatafora (1997: 238) says that this is the first time that such a concept occurs in the Old Testament. On the other hand, this entire study has contended that such a 'cultic' presence could be experienced in other ways than in a building (whether it be a garden or in some other 'spiritual' manner). See below in this chapter for further references outside of Ezekiel to a past or future temple that does not take the form of a physical temple complex.

[35] See pp. 75–76 for analysis of the plural 'sanctuaries' in 28:18 as a typical way of referring to Israel's temple.

Block may be correct, the differences do not appear to be substantial enough to deny that Revelation 21 fulfils Ezekiel. First, the two cities are given different names ('Yahweh is there' versus the 'new Jerusalem'). But the concepts of both names are true of both cities. In fact, Revelation 21:2 develops 3:12: 'I will write on him [the 'overcomer'] the name of My God, and the name of the city of My God, the new Jerusalem, which comes down out of heaven ...' This actually recalls Ezekiel 48:35, where the 'name of the city' of the new Jerusalem is called 'the Lord is there' because he has established his latter-day temple in its midst in which his glory will reside eternally.[36]

A second difference Block notes between the cities is that Ezekiel's is square in shape and John's cubic. However, fulfilments do not have to be photographic reproductions of Old Testament prophecy. Furthermore, a square and a cube *are* similar in shape. In fact, Revelation 21:16 uses the word 'four-square' (*tetragōnos*) to describe the temple-city in dependence on Ezekiel.[37] The reason that John's picture of the new Jerusalem is four-square is because he combines Ezekiel's vision with an allusion to the cubic shape of the holy of holies from Solomon's temple (1 Kgs. 6:20 [esp. LXX]) (see Caird 1966: 272–273).

Third, Block says that Ezekiel's temple is composed of common stones, whereas the temple in Revelation is made up of precious stones. In fact, Ezekiel does not comment about the precise kind of stones making up the foundation and walls of the temple. They may well contain precious stones.

Block's fourth objection is that Ezekiel's temple is at the centre of everything, whereas the temple's existence is denied in Revelation 21:22. But only the physical temple's existence is denied. The true temple, that is, God and the Lamb, is now central: 'And I saw no [physical] temple in it [the new Jerusalem] because the Lord God, the Almighty, and the Lamb are its temple' (21:22). The equation of God and the Lamb with the temple approaches closely the essence of the Ezekiel vision, which is God's glorious presence itself (e.g., 48:35, 'the name of the city' is 'the Lord is there'). All that Israel's old temple pointed to, the expanding presence of God, has been fulfilled in Revelation 21:1 – 22:5, and such a fulfilment has been anticipated within Ezekiel 40 – 48 itself.

---

[36] *b. Baba Batri* 75b renders Ezek. 48:35 by 'the Lord is its name' through changing the Hebrew pointing (see Epstein 1948: *in loc.*).

[37] The Greek OT of Ezek. 45:1–5 and 41:21 uses the same word for the entire temple complex.

Fifth, Block notes that Ezekiel portrays a parochially Israelite city and Revelation 21 a cosmopolitan place of Jews and Gentiles. The former, however, does picture Gentiles in the new Jerusalem (47:22–23), though this probably would have been understood as Gentiles who convert to the faith of Israel and who adopt the corresponding national badges. In reality, Revelation 21 depicts believing Jews and Gentiles as true Israel.[38]

Sixth, Block contrasts the sacrificial animals that are at the heart of Ezekiel's temple with the living Lamb at the heart of John's temple. This may not be so much of a contrast, but only a difference in prophetic perspective. We have already proposed that Ezekiel may have chosen to employ the language and imagery of the temple familiar to his readers to prophesy a far off and not so clearly seen eschatological reality. The preceding point about Israelite parochialism is relevant here: Ezekiel's readers likely understood that Gentiles would become part of Israel by trusting in Yahweh and demonstrating that trust through moving to Jerusalem, being circumcised, obeying the Law, worshipping at the temple, submitting to dietary laws of clean and uncleanness, and so on. The New Testament, including Revelation, declares that Gentiles become true Israelites by believing in Jesus (e.g., Eph. 3:6), identifying with and moving to him as true Israel (e.g., Heb. 12:22–24), being circumcised in him (Col. 2:11), worshipping in him as the true temple (1 Pet. 2:4–9) and becoming 'clean' only in him.[39]

Finally, Block observes that in the Ezekiel temple there is still a need to distinguish between the clean and unclean, but there is no longer any such distinction within Revelation's temple. This is not just a problem in comparison to Revelation; it also does not fit with Block's alternative notion of Ezekiel 40 – 48 as an 'ideal' temple. Furthermore, we will argue in a following excursus that while Ezekiel's temple portrays end-time conditions, these conditions are part of an inaugurated, but not a consummated, eschatology. If this is the case, then the problem of distinguishing pure from impure in Ezekiel's temple can be explained as characterizing a new but still imperfect temple. Indeed, Paul's understanding of the *beginning* fulfilment of the temple described in Ezekiel 37:26–28 involves an ongoing need to 'not touch what is unclean' (2 Cor. 6:17) and to 'cleanse' oneself 'from all defilement of flesh and spirit' (2 Cor. 7:1;

---

[38] E.g., see Beale 1999a: *in loc.* on 21:3 and 22:4, as well as 7:14–17.
[39] See further Beale 1998: 215–272.

so also 1 Cor. 6:18–19). Perhaps, Ezekiel's enigmatic sacrifices also could be understood along these lines. We have found that John also alludes to the Ezekiel 40 – 48 temple and applies it both to an inaugurated stage of fulfilment (Rev. 11:1–4) and to a consummated stage (Rev. 21:1 – 22:5). In fact, Revelation 11:1–4 pictures believers as priests making sacrifices in the 'outer court' through suffering for their faith (Beale 1999a: *in loc.* on 11:1–2).

In light of these considerations, Block's objections to Revelation 21 being the final fulfilment of the Ezekiel vision are possible but not decisive. Consequently, the picture of Ezekiel's temple that is integrated into Revelation 21:1 – 22:5 probably indicates its *consummated* fulfilment. The new heavens and earth are the holy of holies, as well as the new Jerusalem and new Eden, all of which are anticipated to varying degrees in the last segment of the book of Ezekiel.

The broad structure of the city from 21:12 – 22:5 is based on the vision of Ezekiel 40 – 48. Ezekiel 40 – 44 prophesies the pattern of the final temple, and Ezekiel 45 – 48 primarily depicts the future arrangement of the eschatological city and the divisions of the land around the temple compound. Revelation 21:12 – 22:5 further interprets the yet-future fulfilment of Ezekiel by collapsing temple, city and land into one end-time picture portraying the one reality of God's communion with his people. This identification is apparently based on Ezekiel's own identification of temple, city and land as representing the same truth, though Ezekiel never collapses the three explicitly in the manner that Revelation 21:9 – 22:5 does. Ezekiel explains the inheritance of land and the final sanctuary to be indications of God's 'everlasting covenant of peace', in which his 'dwelling place also will be with' Israel (Ezek. 37:25–28; so also 43:7, 9 with respect to the significance of the temple). The concluding statement of the Ezekiel 40 – 48 vision likewise interprets the ultimate meaning of the renovated city to be God's presence with his people: cf. 48:35, 'the name of the city from that day [will be], "the LORD is there."'

Our present purposes do not necessitate a detailed listing and discussion of all the various allusions to Ezekiel and their specific uses in John's final vision, since this has been done elsewhere (see Beale 1999a: 1030–1117 *passim*). Nevertheless, a brief overview is in order.[40]

---

[40] The following is based on Beale 1999a: 1030–1117 (*passim*), on which see for further discussion of each allusion.

Revelation 21:1 – 22:5	Ezekiel
God's tabernacling (21:3)	43:7 (+ 37:27 and Lev. 26:11–12)
prophetic commission formula (21:10)	40:1–2 and 43:5 (+ 2:2; 3:12, 14, 24; 11:1)
God's glory (21:11)	43:2ff.
twelve city gates at four points of the compass (21:12–13)	48:31–34 (+ 42:15–19)
Measuring of parts of the temple-city (21:15)	40:3–5 (and throughout chs. 40 – 48)
'Four-cornered' shape of the city, measured by 'length and width' (21:16)[41]	45:1–5 (+ 40:5; 41:21; 48:8–13 + Zech. 2:6 [2]; 1 Kgs. 6:20)
Illuminating glory of God (21:23)	43:2, 5 (+ Is. 60:19)
Living waters flowing from the temple (22:1–2a)	47:1–9 (+ Gen. 2:10; Zech. 14:8 and possibly Joel 3:18)
A tree with 'fruit' and 'leaves for healing' on either side of a river (22:2b)	47:12

Given the many parallels between the Revelation and Ezekiel passages, the only logical way to contend that Revelation 21 does not prophetically fulfil Ezekiel is to argue that John uses the numerous allusions to Ezekiel merely in an analogical manner. We have contended, on the other hand, that John's temple is like Ezekiel's because *it is*, in fact, what Ezekiel prophesied. This judgment is based not only on the many similarities between the two, but also on our assessment that Ezekiel 40 – 48 itself was a prophecy of an eschatological temple (with which most OT commentators would agree), and John's temple depicts the eschatological temple. If John's vision does not show the fulfilment of Ezekiel, then there is no other Old or New Testament passage recording such a fulfilment. If Revelation 21 – 22 is the fulfilment, then Ezekiel's temple is not to be established in a temporary 'millennial' period, but in the

---

[41] Though Revelation's city-temple is more precisely 'cubic' and Ezekiel's temple is square, the terminology in describing the dimensions of both is even identical in some cases (on which see further Beale 1999a: 1073–1076).

eternal new heavens and earth, which is the setting of John's final vision.

In conclusion, it is best not to formulate the debate about Ezekiel's temple in a 'literal versus non-literal' framework. The question of whether or not the future literal temple will take the basic material and architectural form of Israel's first two temples is a better way to address the issue. Our contention has been that the presence of God filling the whole new creation is the 'literal' reality to which Israel's first two temples pointed. Indeed, all along, these architectural temples were but copies or reflections of the heavenly temple.[42] I have attempted to show that Ezekiel's portrayal already anticipated such a heavenly temple established on earth. We have seen that other Old Testament texts prophesied more explicitly than Ezekiel a non-material and non-localized latter-day temple.[43] Similar observations have been made about the Garden of Eden as a non-structural temple (Gen. 2; Ezek. 28:18), as well as the informal small-scale sanctuaries of the patriarchs and Mount Sinai itself.

But even if Ezekiel's eschatological temple were best read from an Old Testament reader's perspective according to the general pattern of Israel's earlier temples, then the progressive revelation of the New Testament would indicate that its fulfilment was not in a localized physical temple. Nevertheless, such an apparently different fulfilment in 'form' is essentially the same in 'content'.

The earlier illustration of a father's promise in 1900 to a young son is relevant again. The father promises to give the son a horse and buggy when he grows up and marries. During the early years of expectation, the son reflects on the particular size of the buggy, its contours and style, its beautiful leather seat and the size and breed of horse that would draw the buggy. Perhaps the father had knowledge from early experimentation elsewhere that the invention of the automobile was on the horizon, but coined the promise to his son in terms that his son would understand. Years later, when the son marries, the father gives the couple an automobile, which has since been invented and mass-produced. Is the son disappointed in receiving a car instead of a horse and buggy? Is this not a 'literal' fulfilment of the promise? In fact, the essence of the father's word has remained the same: a convenient mode

---

[42] E.g., Exod. 25:8–9, 40; Ps. 78:69a; *1 Enoch* 14:8–25; *Tg. 2 Chronicles* 6:2; likewise, *Tg. Exodus* 15:17; Heb. 8:5; 9:23–24; cf. 1 Chr. 28:11–19.

[43] Is. 4:5–6; 8:13–14 (cf. the use in 1 Pet. 2:8 and 3:14–15); 57:15 in relation to 66:2; Jer. 3:16–17; Ezek. 37:26–28; cf. Ezek. 11:16, which refers to an immaterial temple for Israelite exiles.

of transportation. What has changed is the precise form of transportation promised. The progress of technology has escalated the fulfilment of the pledge in a way that could not have been conceived of when the son was young. Nevertheless, in the light of the later development of technology, the promise is viewed as 'literally' and faithfully carried out in a greater way than earlier apprehended.

Likewise, the purpose of the temple in the Old Testament and the purpose of the expected end-time temple was to house God's glory, before which his people were to worship. Some prophecies may have been conceived of as referring to a small-scale structure that would encase the divine glory. However, their fulfilment revealed that the entire recreated cosmos and not a manmade building would be the physical temple housing God's glory instead of a little building in a small part of the earth. Both the Old Testament and eschatological temples are 'physical', and hence 'literal', but the 'form' of the sacred containers of the divine glory is quite different. In both cases, God's glory inhabits a temple, but in the former its expression is limited, while in the latter it shines forth in unfettered manner.

The preceding illustration also serves as probably the best conceptual model for understanding the sacrifices in Ezekiel's temple. The 'essential content' of the prophesied sacrifices are fulfilled but the 'form' is expressed differently. What appears in Ezekiel to be animal sacrifices, which formerly could give only incomplete and temporary covering for sin, find escalated realization in Christ's sacrifice, which provides eternal 'covering' for sin. Therefore, to say that Christ actualizes Ezekiel's sacrifices as the Lamb sacrificed for sin is not a figurative or spiritualizing use of the Old Testament, but the eschatological reality to which the animal sacrifices foreshadowed (following Clowney 1972: 177, 182–183). John himself elsewhere draws such a connection between the Passover sacrifice (Exod. 12:46; Num. 11:12) and Christ's sacrificial death (John 19:36)!

Conclusion

On the basis of cumulative evidence, we have reached the conclusion that Ezekiel 40 – 48 is a figurative vision of a real heavenly temple that would descend and be established on earth in non-structural form in the latter days. This conclusion is based on cumulative evidence from inside and outside the book of Ezekiel. The conclusion also 'fits' well with the biblical-theological patterns of the Garden of Eden and of the temple explored in the preceding chapters of the book. Though the constraints of the present project have not allowed thorough analysis, I have outlined the approach towards Ezekiel's temple which I think is most viable.

Excursus: further reflections on the nature of Ezekiel's vision of the temple

This excursus contains tentative proposals that I have not found argued hitherto, but which need more exploration and substantiation than the limits of this study allow. Nevertheless, they are included here because I think they may well be on the right track, and they fit well into the overall argument of this chapter and book.

Omitted features of Ezekiel's temple that point beyond a localized earthly temple

There are still yet more features of Ezekiel's temple vision that appear to correspond better to a non-material building than to a physical one. An initial impression of an unusual temple portrayal is that it lacks the following significant elements that were in the Solomonic and second temples: (1) the large bronze basin (called the 'bronze sea') in the courtyard; (2) a golden lampstand; (3) the table of show-bread; (4) the altar of incense in the holy place;[44] (5) the veil separating the holy of holies; (6) the high priest to serve either in the holy place or in the holy of holies; (7) the anointing oil; (8) the ark of the covenant in the holy of holies; (9) covering cherubim in the holy of holies.[45] In addition, though the altar of sacrifice is present, its description has changed: it is to be approached by steps from the east instead of by its former approach on a ramp from the south.[46] Also

[44] In Ezek. 41:22, the prophet sees an 'altar of wood' that is then called 'the table that is before the LORD'. This is different, however, from the table of showbread in the old temple because that one was composed of acacia wood and overlaid with gold, and its proportions were different. Perhaps this represents an adjusted form of that table or it represents an adjusted altar of incense, though wooden altars would be burned with what was burned on them (so Block 1998: 559), or it is some other piece of furniture. The latter option is enhanced in light of the observation, among others, of Mitchell (1980: 36), who says that 'no incense altar is mentioned' anywhere in Ezekiel's temple vision. Also present in the gates to the inner court, though lacking in the descriptions of the tabernacle and Solomon's temple, are tables for slaughtering animals and for implements of slaughtering.

[45] Note that in 1 Kgs. 6 – 7 two cherubim were made of wood. The extent of their wings touched each of the opposite walls (6:23–28) and then the ark was placed into 'the most holy place, under the wings of the cherubim' (8:3–7).

[46] See Schmitt and Laney 1997: 141–152 for discussion of most of these changes and the observation that also missing was the 'court of the women' and the wall of

lacking is any mention of an evening sacrifice and a Day of Atonement, the latter of which was central to the Levitical sacrificial system (C. L. Feinberg 1971: 103).

It is certainly possible that the missing items are simply not mentioned, but are assumed to be in the temple. Accordingly, Ezekiel may be focusing on defining sacred space and not the rituals carried out in that space, since they would be tangential to the point of the discussion. Thus, the accoutrements of ritual would be omitted only because of focusing on something else. It seems improbable, however, that these absent items are merely not noted because of a different focus, and are assumed to be in the temple. I have so far come across no persuasive reasons proposed for such a highlighting of sacred space in which the objects of ritual are assumed to remain. But whatever view one holds about the missing items, it involves an argument from silence. Arguments from silence are difficult to prove or disprove. Therefore, whatever position is finally taken on this issue will be difficult to substantiate.

Nevertheless, I believe reasons other than a change in focus can be offered for why the ritualistic items are not mentioned. More than likely, they are not mentioned because, indeed, they are not present. One reason for this may be that the repeated focus on both sacred space *and* the 'measuring' of that space probably connotes, at least, the notion of the security of worshippers in the temple and of protection of the worshippers from the fatal contamination of impurity or idolatry.[47] This does not rule out the possibility of sacred furniture also being present, but it makes the importance of such items less weighty.

Another reason for considering the items to be absent is that Ezekiel's description of the temple is in fact longer than the depiction of the interior of Solomon's temple, which included the articles not found in Ezekiel. Likewise, the account of the tabernacle's design in Exodus includes all the sacred furniture mentioned in Solomon's temple. Further, it would be speculative to attach much significance to

---

partition, cordoning off the inner court from the outer court, where only Gentiles could be. Both these latter features were added in the Herodian temple but were not present in the Solomonic temple. See also C. L. Feinberg 1971: 103, 105 for a list of missing items similar to that of Schmitt and Laney, though he adds the Levitical priesthood. Cf. Block 1998: 544, who notes the striking differences with Solomon's temple, the most obvious of which 'is the absence of detail', in order to highlight merely sacred space (so also p. 568).

[47] On which see Beale 1999a: 559–561, for this idea in Ezekiel and its use in Revelation.

only one or two lacking elements. When, however, at least, *nine* major features of Israel's traditional temple complex are missing in the description, the cumulative effect of their absence points to the need of some other explanation than simply positing that they were present but not important to mention merely because of a different focus.

In addition, as we have seen earlier, Jeremiah 3:16–17, states that there would be no 'ark of the covenant of the LORD' in the future temple but that God's ruling presence would extend over all of Jerusalem and not be contained within the confines of the old holy of holies.[48] This confirms that Ezekiel's omission of the ark is not due to a different literary focus, but because the ark is really absent! Thus, if the most crucial piece of the temple's furniture was missing, it should not be surprising that other less significant appurtenances should also be absent.[49] We will suggest below that the 'bronze sea' and the 'lampstand' are missing because, like the ark (symbolic of the divine presence), the realities they represented have also moved out of their former temple boundaries.

Some 'literalist' interpreters acknowledge that most of these items are truly absent, the reason being that Christ has fulfilled them.[50] For example, the 'bronze sea' laver is no longer present because Christ's blood has washed sins away.[51] The absence of the table of showbread indicates that Christ is the true bread. The missing lampstand is due to Christ's coming as the light of the world. The veil is lacking because Christ has shown himself to be the entrance to God's presence. The holy of holies without an ark indicates that Christ himself will sit on a throne and rule in that inner sanctum.

In the light of the New Testament, this analysis could be the right approach, since it is as viable an attempt to account for the absent items as the explanation that claims the items are not mentioned only because of a focus on sacred space. Nevertheless, even though the explanations of these fulfilments could be theologically correct as far as they go, there is nothing in either testament that would support

---

[48] C. J. H. Wright (2001: 334) contends that Ezekiel's not mentioning the ark is 'in agreement with Jeremiah's prediction of the relegation of that particular sacred object in favour of Jerusalem itself as the throne of God in an international eschatological setting'.

[49] 2 Maccabees 2:4–8 adds that Jeremiah took away the tabernacle, ark and altar of incense and hid them on Mount Sinai, though they would be revealed again in the latter days. The garbled legend may reflect the notion that Jer. 3's prophecy of the absent ark may have included more absent items, including a missing altar of incense.

[50] E.g., Schmitt and Laney 1997: 141–152.

[51] There is, however, no recognition by these commentators of any cosmic symbolism in the laver.

many of these links exegetically.[52] Furthermore, these proposed fulfilments do not attempt to recognize the cosmic symbolism of the various items in the temple and then how these could be linked to New Testament fulfilment.

Nevertheless, even some interpreters who recognize the fulfilment of these temple items in Christ still affirm that everything else in Ezekiel's depiction of the temple will be built in a strictly physical and structural manner (Schmitt and Laney 1997: 141–152). The threefold broad structure of outer courts, holy place and holy of holies will be built as portrayed.[53] But, with regard to the missing temple items, something more radical seems to be afoot.

The missing items formed the symbolic heart of the old temple. Any future temple structure would be rather empty and useless without them, especially without the ark of the covenant, which was inextricably linked to God's presence. Our study in chapter 2 of the cosmic symbolism of these items suggests here that their absence could signal to the reader that this is no vision of a material structure. Recall that the three main parts of the temple symbolized the three parts of the cosmos: visible earth and sea (= outer court), visible heavens (= holy place) and invisible heavenly dimension (= holy of holies). To have some of the symbolic items in each of these sections missing suggests a significant alteration in the way the future temple was to be conceived. Is this change a mere alteration of furniture or a greater transformation in the essence of the temple that signifies a change in the cosmos itself? Could it be that a missing symbolic item in each section of the temple indicates that the corresponding cosmic reality which that section represented has been altered in some way? The cumulative effect of having nine items absent throughout the three sections of the temple suggests that this may, in fact, be the case.

If our symbolic understanding throughout this study so far is correct, then the essential parts of the cosmos symbolized by the items from the old temple are no longer symbolized in Ezekiel's temple. This means that the altered features in the new temple symbolize some kind of alteration in the future cosmos. What is the nature of that alteration? We have noted that some commentators

[52] Except Heb. 10:19–20, which identifies Christ as the eschatological veil of the heavenly tabernacle, though no allusion to Ezekiel is made. Of course, Heb. 8 – 10 explains that Christ fulfils everything towards which the high priest pointed.

[53] See Block 1998: 541 for a diagram of the bipartite temple building surrounded by the courtyard (the vestibule should be considered as an introductory part of the holy place). There was actually an inner and outer court around the holy place and holy of holies in Ezekiel's portrayal of the temple (Schmitt and Laney 1997: 82).

have seen that the change is due to Christ fulfilling some aspects of the temple. But in fact, this fulfilment needs to be understood as more radical in nature than only pertaining to an individual believer's spiritual salvation.

The result of our overall study so far indicates that Christ is not merely fulfilling the various absent holy items by providing individual 'salvation', but his first coming would even begin to alter the very shape and composition of the cosmos. The reason is that his resurrection was the beginning of a new creation, which we have seen is also spoken of in terms of a temple (e.g., John 2:19–22). A new world has begun to emerge in Christ, as has a new temple. The complete alteration of the cosmos will be consummated at Christ's final coming. Even without considering New Testament data, the changes in Ezekiel could well have represented to the Old Testament reader some future alteration in the cosmos.

Therefore, the lack of these items in Ezekiel's temple seems to point to a metamorphosis of the temple and thus of the creation that the temple symbolizes. Put another way, because there will be a significant transformation of the cosmos in the eschatological future, the temple that symbolizes that altered cosmos also must be changed. Just as if a child were to pick up a small doll's house and shake it and some of the furniture were to fall out, so God's shaking of his cosmic house in the eschatological future may be symbolized by Ezekiel's altered temple with missing pieces. For example, the absence of the sea (= absence of the bronze laver) and the heavenly light sources (= absence of the lampstand and the starry needlework of the veil) may indicate such a cosmic shake-up. The absence of the veil (dividing the holy place from the inner sanctuary), and especially the ark, may indicate that there has also been a change in the invisible dimension of the cosmos: God's heavenly holy of holies presence has begun to break out into the visible world, which the New Testament indicates begins with the coming of Christ. The lack of a mediatorial human high priest and an altar of incense[54] also signifies virtually the same reality.

If one acknowledges that these items are absent because Christ has fulfilled them, then is it not likely that the overall structure itself has been completely surpassed in Christ because the New Testament also makes it abundantly clear that Christ's resurrection was the rebuilding of the temple? In fact, the New Testament, as we have observed,

---

[54] Representing, in part, the saints' prayers meditated to God by the priest. For the 'incense' symbolizing the saints' prayers in the NT, see Rev. 5:8; 8:4.

is just as clear about Christ being the fulfilment of the entire temple as it is about him fulfilling some of its parts.[55]

There is, however, a problem with the preceding analysis because it affirms only a partial shake-up of the cosmos and not a complete, definitive one. If Ezekiel pictures an ideal temple in the eternal new creation, then our interpretation of a provisionally adjusted temple appears inadequate to describe an eternal condition. Our approach is even more inadequate, of course, if Ezekiel's picture is of a physically ideal temple. Perhaps this last difficulty is partly solved by understanding that prophets typically 'depict the future in terms which make sense to its present' and 'clothe the purposes of God' in the thought-forms of the contemporary culture and learned tradition (so Bauckham 1993: 450–451). Accordingly, Ezekiel may well have prophesied the end-time temple through the traditional symbols of a material temple that Israelites at the time would have understood. In this regard, he portrays an altered temple to highlight in part that this will be a different kind of temple. The progressive revelation of the New Testament makes clearer just how different the eschatological temple was to be: it was not, in fact, to be a building but it was to be fulfilled by the divine Messiah dwelling in the midst of his people. This approach of seeing a provisionally altered temple would also solve the problem that there is still a need to maintain a distinction between clean and unclean in Ezekiel's temple. This distinction would only confirm our proposal of the provisional nature of the prophesied new temple.

The perspective of progressive revelation may well solve how what appears to be incomplete or temporary is ultimately fulfilled in something that is perfect. This may well be the correct perspective. In fact, however, the solution may lie in a somewhat different direction. We have contended at the outset of this discussion that Ezekiel 40 – 48 foresees a figurative vision of a heavenly temple that will descend to earth at the eschaton. This does not mean that what he sees is the 'ideal' or 'perfect' view of the future temple. The observation that a temple structure is still seen with a visible court and inner holy place suggests that the redemptive-historical purpose of the temple has not yet been reached. The adjusted arrangement of the heavenly temple is, nevertheless, plausibly a result of the inauguration, but not necessarily consummation, of the eschatological age. The prophet does not see the consummated form of the temple, since we have noted

---

[55] E.g., Hebrews says Christ is not only the 'veil', the ultimate sacrifice, and the definitive high priest, but John 2:19–22 also views Christ as the entire new temple.

throughout that the completed stage of the temple will be so extensive that it will be equated with the cosmos itself.[56] The consummation will occur when the heavenly temple descends completely to fill the earth and transform it. The heavenly temple's former extension to the holy of holies will be widened to include the whole earth. Thus, Ezekiel's depiction of a provisionally adjusted temple may well describe the inaugurated form of the latter-day temple.

Another indication that Ezekiel 40 – 48 depicts an eschatological temple (at least in inaugurated form) is the relationship of the absent lampstand and bronze sea to two items in chapter 47.[57] First, the original 'tree of life' in Genesis has become multiplied into 'trees for food', and having 'leaves for healing' (47:12).[58] Quite possibly the lampstand is no longer in the holy place because its redemptive-historical symbolism has begun to be fulfilled. Recall that the lampstand signified the tree of life from Eden. If the two are, indeed, to be equated, then the absence of this symbol from the holy place and its placement outside of the temple may signify that its expanding latter-day goal is commencing. God's presence, partially symbolized by the lampstand, is going out into the world. Similarly, Revelation 22:2 pictures 'the tree of life' as a giant tree or as a grove 'on either side of the river', bringing healing, and only two verses later John says, 'they shall not have need of the light of a lamp' (22:5a). Hence, no lampstand is depicted in the Revelation 21 – 22 vision. The ultimate reason for this is that 'the Lord God shall illumine them' (22:5b), and it is his presence that brings the healing symbolized by the 'tree of life'.

Likewise, recall that the 'bronze sea' symbolized part of the visible earth that would be engulfed by God's presence in the end-time. Could it be that this item is absent from the courtyard because the water from this temple now flows and becomes a massive river that feeds into 'the Great Sea' and 'heals'[59] its waters (47:9–10)? Again, could it be that another cultic eschatological cosmic symbol has passed away because God's end-time healing presence has moved beyond the temple and

---

[56] Tuell (1996) argues that the vision is not even about an eschatological temple but the heavenly temple to which the Israelite exiles are related in some invisible spiritual manner while still in Babylon.

[57] See Alexander 1986: 945–946. He similarly sees Ezek. 40 – 48 to be portraying a sort of firstfruits or beginning of the consummated state in Rev. 21, but he views this initial stage being a 'millennium' after the church age and Christ's second coming.

[58] Rev. 22:2 alludes to Ezek. 47:12 and explicitly identifies these trees as a kind of corporate 'tree of life'.

[59] Ezek. 47:12 uses the noun form for 'healing' and the verb form of the same root is used in 47:9.

invaded the world and is renewing it? Revelation 21:1 may correspond to the missing 'sea' in the courtyard of Ezekiel's temple: when the 'new heaven and a new earth' appear, 'there is no longer any sea'. Therefore, the missing lampstand and sea in Revelation 21 – 22 is due to the cosmic shake-up of the old world and the creation of a new world; thus, confirming our same conclusion about the same missing objects in Ezekiel's temple. If this is a correct reading of Ezekiel and Revelation, then we may deduce without too much speculation that the other unmentioned items in Ezekiel's temple are missing in order to indicate a radical change in the future cosmos.

The viability of reading Ezekiel's temple in this way is suggested by John's interpretation of it in Revelation 11:1–4. As we argued above in chapter 10 and will elaborate on further in chapter 12, John portrays the church as the inaugurated but not yet consummated end-time temple. Believers are identified spiritually as being priests serving in the temple holy place, and part of their service is to function as a 'lampstand' of witness, shining the light of God's presence out to the world. Furthermore, John identifies the physical side of the church as the 'outer court', where it offers itself in sacrifice to the Lord by suffering for its witness in the world. It is obvious that this is not formally the same description as Ezekiel's, but both prophets speak of an inaugurated latter-day temple that is significantly different from the old temple. Accordingly, Revelation 11 depicts part of the inaugurated fulfilment of Ezekiel 40 – 48 and Revelation 21:1ff. the consummated fulfilment.

Omitted features in other heavenly temple visions and their bearing on Ezekiel's vision

Like the account just given about the reason for the missing cultic furniture, the following discussion must be considered provisional until further research is carried out, which the limits of the present work cannot allow. As a supplement or alternative to the directly preceding analysis, our earlier conclusion that understanding Ezekiel 40 – 48 as a vision of a *heavenly* temple explains the absent items omitted in its narration. As in Ezekiel's vision, visions of heavenly temples in the Old Testament, in early Judaism and in the New Testament do not describe furniture in the temple with the exception of the divine throne, which was never a piece of furniture in the earthly temple anyway.[60] Old

---

[60] We will see below that there is a further exception in Revelation, where a few more items of temple furniture or holy vessels are portrayed in the heavenly temple. We will argue that these exceptions prove the 'rule' being contended for here.

Testament visions of the heavenly temple also depict only a throne and live cherubim or other heavenly beings around it (Ezek. 1; Is. 6:1–6; Dan. 7:9–10, 13–14; 1 Kgs. 22:19–23).

One of the most extensive depictions of a heavenly temple is *1 Enoch* 14:8–25, which, we observed earlier, portrays Enoch touring through a heavenly outer court, holy place and then peering into the holy of holies. Not one piece of traditional furniture is mentioned, and no cultic appurtenances are described in the outer court. As Enoch enters the holy place, he says explicitly that 'there was nothing inside' (14:13). Then he describes the inner sanctum, which has only a 'lofty throne' with God sitting on it, which is a partial allusion to Ezekiel 1:15–21, 26. Other similar visions in Judaism likewise describe only a throne or God's presence surrounded by angels. One of the most striking among these is the Qumran (Dead Sea Scrolls) *Songs of Sabbath Sacrifice* (4Q400–407). Again, no sacred furniture is described, only heavenly beings surrounding God, although it is interesting that the heavenly beings themselves are sometimes portrayed as forming the structure of the temple itself. This is a pertinent reference because the portrayal makes much allusion to Ezekiel 40 – 48 (as observed earlier in this chapter). Other similar passages in Judaism also picture no traditional furniture in the heavenly temple (*1 Enoch* 71:5–10; *Prayer of Azariah* 1:31–38; *3 Enoch* 1:1–12; 7).

The most extended heavenly temple vision in the New Testament is that in John's Apocalypse. Throughout Revelation 4 – 21 the throne of God or the Lamb, usually surrounded by heavenly beings, is portrayed in various ways. The vision in Revelation 4 – 5 is greatly indebted to the prior visions of Ezekiel 1, Daniel 7 and Isaiah 6, and the chapter 21 temple vision is heavily dependent on Ezekiel 40 – 48. Significantly, neither of these two extended visions in Revelation contains any furniture, except a throne! Most other temple visions in the book have no descriptions of heavenly 'furniture'.

There are, however, some furniture and sacred vessels mentioned in a few of the temple visions of Revelation. Intriguingly, one of the two items repeatedly mentioned is also found in Ezekiel's vision: an altar (Rev. 6:9; 8:3–5; 9:13; 11:1). Even more interestingly, there is lack of clarity about the identity and purpose of this altar in chapter 6 and 11 (see Beale 1999a: *in loc.*), just as we have seen that there is lack of clarity in Ezekiel. There is virtual unanimous acknowledgment among scholars that these depictions of an altar are figurative for some heavenly reality. We will argue in a following chapter that, at least in part (especially in 6:9 and 11:1), the altar symbolizes the suffering destiny of God's people who follow the Lamb by laying down their lives as sacrifices to God. Revelation 11:1 is especially relevant since it alludes to the 'measuring' of Ezekiel's temple! The figurative nature of the incense altar in 8:3–5 is apparent from noticing that the 'bowls' from which the incense comes have been explicitly identified to be figurative: the 'golden bowls of incense, which are the prayers of the saints' (cf. 5:8 with 8:4).

One of the few other mentions of pieces of furniture in Revelation is in 11:19, where John sees that at the end of the age 'the temple of God which is in heaven was opened; and the ark of His covenant appeared in his temple ...' A 'throne' is also sometimes pictured in these visions. The word 'throne' occurs about thirty-five times in the book (up to ch. 20), where it refers to God's or the Lamb's sovereign dwelling in the heavenly temple.[61] Since this is a vision of a heavenly temple, the 'ark' is likely figurative for God's rule, as are the many references to the 'throne'. We have already noted that the 'ark' in Israel's temple was symbolic itself for God's ruling presence.[62]

The upshot of this discussion is that, *as a rule*, visions of heavenly temples do not contain cultic furniture, and the exceptions to the rule involve symbolic representations of such furniture. The Ezekiel temple vision with its missing cultic features fits most naturally into this genre of heavenly temple visions (Ezek. 1 and 40 – 48, Is. 6 and 1 Kgs. 22 would represent the earliest forms of this genre). This evidence points further to the viability of our overall argument that Ezekiel's vision is of a heavenly temple and not a future earthly temple. It is the heavenly form of the temple to which the faithful remnant was spiritually related at the time Ezekiel himself was writing (see Ezek. 11:16),[63] and it will be this heavenly temple that will begin to descend to earth in the latter days.

More likely, however, as we have argued from a number of angles, Ezekiel's temple is the heavenly temple of the latter days that is on the verge of descending or, more preferably, has begun to come down. The reason that heavenly temples do not contain the furniture of the earthly temple is that, as we have found throughout our study, the earthly temple was but a copy and reflection of the heavenly temple's reality, and when an occasional item is seen in a heavenly temple, it is

---

[61] It occurs in this manner 4 more times in 21:1 – 22:3 but with reference to the new creation.

[62] 2 Chr. 28:2, Ps. 132:7 and Is. 66:1 picture God sitting on his heavenly throne with his feet extending down to the ark and resting on it; cf. 2 Chr. 9:18 and Jer. 3:16–17.

[63] For which, as we have seen above, Tuell argues.

obviously symbolic. In addition to this difference in heavenly temples, Ezekiel's vision also is missing some items possibly because the symbolic realities to which the old furniture pointed have begun in some way to find their end-time realization.

Chapter Twelve

Theological conclusions: the physical temple as a foreshadowing of God's and Christ's presence as the true temple

A not unusual method of argumentation throughout this entire study has been to present several lines of evidence in support of an inter-pretation. Some lines have been more compelling than others, but the strategy has been that when all of the pertinent data is considered together, the less convincing material becomes more significant than when seen by itself. Consequently, it has, no doubt, sometimes been discernible that some of the explanations in favour of a viewpoint have not stood on their own, but it needs to be remembered that these weaker points are aimed to take on more persuasive power when viewed in light of the other lines of analysis. And, even when this may not be granted, the broader design is that the overall weight of the cumulative arguments point to the plausibility or probability for the main idea being argued.

We now attempt to pull together the major biblical-theological points made throughout our study. We will also suggest some further insights that grow out of some of these concepts observed earlier.

The consummate eschatological stage of the world-encompassing temple in Revelation 21:1 – 22:5

We return now to the question posed at the beginning of the book: why does John see 'a new heavens and earth' in Revelation 21:1, while in Revelation 21:2, 10–21 he sees a city that is garden-like, in the shape of a temple? This is an interpretative and theological problem. John does not describe all the contours and details of the new creation; he portrays only an arboreal city-temple. Recall that the dimensions and architectural features of the city in these verses are drawn to a significant extent from Ezekiel 40 – 48, which we have seen is a prophecy of a future temple (cf., Rev. 3; 7; 11; 21:27 – 22:2; also ch. 11 on Ezek. 40 – 48). The precious stones forming the foundation (vv.18–21) clearly allude to the description of Solomon's temple which also was overlaid with gold and whose foundation was composed of precious stones.[1]

How can we explain the apparent discrepancy that he saw a new heaven and earth in verse 1 and then saw only a city in the shape and structure of a temple in the remainder of the vision? It is possible, of course, that he merely first sees the new world and then sees a city-temple *in* that world. But this is not likely the solution because he seems to equate the 'new heavens and earth' with the following description of the 'city-temple'. The following two paragraphs rehearse the evidence adduced in the opening chapter in favour of this equation.

The equation becomes clearer, for example, when one reflects on Revelation 21:27 that 'nothing unclean ... shall ever come into' the city-temple. Recall that in the Old Testament uncleanness was to be kept out of the tabernacle or temple precincts (e.g., Num. 19:13, 20; 2 Chr. 23:19; 29:16). That the perimeters of the new city-temple of chapter 21 will finally encompass the whole of the new creation is suggested by Revelation 21:27, which says that no uncleanness was allowed into the urban temple, probably meaning that no uncleanness will be allowed into the new world. This conclusion is further evident, since 22:15 says that the unclean will be excluded from the city, so they will also be excluded from dwelling in the new creation, since they will be in the lake of fire for ever (see on 21:8; 22:15; cf. 21:27), and that lake is certainly outside the bounds of the new creation.

Another observation that we have made points further to the equation of the new cosmos with the city-temple. The 'seeing–hearing' pattern elsewhere in Revelation, where what John sees is interpreted by what he then hears (or vice versa), suggests that 21:1–3 refers to the same reality. A classic example is Revelation 5:5 (John hears about a 'lion from the tribe of Judah' who 'conquered'), and 5:6 interprets how the messianic lamb has done so (he won victory ironically by dying as a 'slain lamb'). Revelation 21:1 commences, as we have seen, with

---

[1] Cf. respectively, 1 Kgs. 6:20–22 (and 5:17) and 7:9–10, and note that the dimensions of Rev. 21:16 ('its length and width and height are equal') are based on the dimensions of the 'holy of holies' in 1 Kgs. 6:20 (LXX, where the 'length . . . and the breadth . . . and the height' of the holy of holies were equal in measurement).

John's vision of a 'new heaven and new earth', followed by his vision of the 'new Jerusalem descending from heaven' (v. 2). He then hears a 'great voice' (v. 3) proclaiming that 'the tabernacle of God is with men, and he will tabernacle with them . . .' It is likely that the second vision (v. 2) interprets the first and that what is heard about the tabernacle (v. 3) more explicitly interprets both verses. This is to say that the new creation of verse 1 is identical to the 'new Jerusalem' of verse 2, and both represent the same reality as the 'tabernacle' of verse 3.

A number of conclusions made throughout the preceding chapters further support Revelation 21:1, 2 and 3 referring to equivalent realities. For example, what substantiates John's equation of the new Jerusalem (v. 2) with 'the tabernacle of God with men' and his 'dwelling with them' (v. 3) is that verse 3 is a combined allusion to Leviticus 26:11–12 and Ezekiel 37:27. We have observed that the Ezekiel passage alludes to Leviticus and clarifies its prophecy that God would make his 'dwelling among you' to be God's tabernacling over the entire promised land of Israel ('My dwelling place also will be *over* them'). The temple vision of Ezekiel 40 – 48, which expands on the prophecy of 37:26–28,[2] concludes with a summary of its significance: 'the name of the city from that day shall be, "The LORD is there"' (48:35). The capital city of Israel especially will be covered by God's sacred presence, as we have discovered also in Isaiah 4:5–6[3] and Jeremiah 3:16–17 (especially cf. Jer. 3:17 with Ezek. 48:35). We saw in the previous chapter that the dimensions of Ezekiel's new temple were to be the size of ancient Jerusalem itself. Ezekiel 40:2 also spoke of a temple 'structure like a city' on top of 'a very high mountain'[4] (see also Rev. 21:10). Hence, Ezekiel predicts an enlargement of the tabernacle to include Jerusalem and even the land of Israel. This has already been hinted at by the use of Ezekiel 37:27 in Revelation 7:15, where it had fulfilment in uncountable multitudes (cf. Rev. 7:9ff.) of Jews and Gentiles.[5] What points to the tabernacle of Revelation 21:3 as also being equivalent to the new earth of 21:1 is the

---

[2] That Ezek. 40 – 48 elaborates on the same temple prophecy as 37:26–28 is apparent from noticing that the common expression 'I will dwell among them forever' (with minor variants) is found twice in both passages (Ezek. 37:26, 28 and 43:7, 9).

[3] That the Is. 4 prophecy of God's tabernacle widening over all Jerusalem is also in mind is deducible later in Rev. 21:27, where 'nothing unclean . . . will ever come into it [new Jerusalem], but only those whose names are written in the Lamb's book of life'. Likewise, those who inhabit the broadened tabernacle over 'Jerusalem will be called holy – everyone who is recorded for life in Jerusalem' (Is. 4:3). Recall that this is another passage in Rev. 21 that implies the equivalence of the new creation with the new Jerusalem, since nothing unclean also will ever enter the new creation.

[4] See Duguid 1999: 472 for this identification in Ezekiel.

[5] So likewise, 2 Cor. 6:16, where both Lev. 26:12 and Ezek. 37:27 are combined.

fact that both Leviticus 26 and Ezekiel 37 view their temple prophecies as developments of the Genesis 1:28 commission 'to be fruitful and multiply, and fill the earth' (cf. Lev. 26:9; Ezek. 36:35–38).

That the 'new heaven and new earth' of 21:1 is defined by and equated with the paradisal city-temple of 21:2 and 21:9 – 22:5 is also pointed to further, as we have seen, by J. D. Levenson's observation that 'heaven and earth' in the Old Testament may sometimes be a way of referring to Jerusalem or its temple (1988: 89–90; 1984: 294–295). He quotes Isaiah 65:17–18 as one of the texts most illustrative of this: '*For behold, I create new heavens and a new earth*; and the former things shall not be remembered or come to mind [65:17]. But be glad and rejoice forever in what I create; *for behold, I create Jerusalem* for rejoicing [65:18].' Revelation 21:1–2 follows the pattern of Isaiah 65:17–18. Since Isaiah 65:17 is clearly alluded to in Revelation 21:1, it is most natural to understand that the new Jerusalem of 21:2 also echoes Isaiah 65:18 and is equated with the 'new heaven and earth' of Revelation 21:1! In the light of the evidence even only of this chapter so far, that the new creation in verse 1 and new Jerusalem in verse 2 are interpreted in verse 3 to be 'the tabernacle of God' among all humanity would also be a natural equation,[6] a conclusion also borne out by earlier chapters of our study.

Consequently, the new creation and Jerusalem are none other than God's tabernacle, the true temple of God's special presence portrayed throughout chapter 21. It was this divine presence that was formerly limited to Israel's temple and has began to expand through the church, and which will fill the whole earth and heaven, becoming co-equal with it. Then the eschatological goal of the temple of the Garden of Eden dominating the entire creation will be finally fulfilled (so Rev. 22:1–3). Hence, eschatology not only recapitulates the protology of Eden but escalates it (see further Beale 1997: 11–52).

John, indeed, is equating the new cosmos with the arboreal city-temple. But why does he make such an equation? Why does John not see a full panorama of the new heavens and earth? It seems problematic at a first or even second glance. Some might attribute the apparent discrepancy to the irrational nature that visions and dreams can have, though this would be hard to accept for a vision that John claims has its origin in God (e.g., cf. 21:9 with Rev. 1:1 and 22:6).[7]

---

[6] In fact, later Judaism (*Pirke de Rabbi Eliezer* 51) could even say that 'in the future the temple will be raised up and renewed' in fulfilment of the new creation prophecy in Is. 43:19 ('Behold, I will create a new thing').

[7] Though some with a high view of Scripture might want to posit that the apparent discrepancy is due to a transrational aspect of the vision.

In order to solve this problem, we have investigated throughout this book the meaning and role of the temple in the Old Testament in order to discover its purpose, and then see how such a purpose relates to the New Testament conception of the temple. It has become evident in pursuing this task that the first tabernacle and temple existed long before Israel became a nation. Indeed, it is apparent that the first sanctuary is discernible from the very beginning of human history. Adam's purpose in that first garden-temple was to expand its boundaries until it circumscribed the earth, so that the earth would be completely filled with God's glorious presence. Adam's failure led, in time, to the re-establishment of the tabernacle and temple in Israel. Both were patterned after the model of Eden and were constructed to symbolize the entire cosmos in order to signify that Israel's purpose as a corporate Adam was to extend its borders by faithfully obeying God and spreading his glorious presence throughout the earth.

The entire discussion of our study up to this point confirms the conclusion that the temple in Revelation 21 – 22 symbolically represents the entire new cosmos because that was the goal of God's temple-building process throughout sacred history. Chapters 21 – 22 form the consummation of the prophetic hope of an end-time universal temple, which Revelation 11 (as well as Rev. 1 – 2, Eph. 2, 1 Pet. 2 and others) portrays as having begun fulfilment and as advancing to fill the entire earth during this age in Christ and his church. Both Revelation 11 and 21 – 22 indicate various facets of the fulfilment of the Ezekiel 40 – 48 prophecy of the temple. These Revelation passages also make reference to other Old Testament passages to explain how Christ and the church are the realization of the end-time temple.

Therefore, the mystery of how John can see a new heavens and earth in Revelation 21:1, but then see only a city in the form of a garden-like temple (21:2–3, 9 – 22:5), is solved by discovering the purpose of the temple throughout biblical history. His equation of the new cosmos with the temple-city becomes natural, not strange. The new heavens and earth are described as a temple because God's goal of universally expanding the temple of his glorious presence will have come to pass. Everything of which Old Testament temples were typologically symbolic, a recapitulated and escalated Garden of Eden and whole cosmos, will have finally been materialized. The holy of holies stood for the invisible heavenly dimension of the cosmos where God dwelt; the holy place represented the visible heavens; the outer court symbolized the visible earth (land, sea, the place of human habitation). God's special presence that was formerly confined to the holy of holies, which was the essence of temple reality, will at last encompass the whole new earth and heaven because of the work of Christ. At the very end of time, the true temple will come down from heaven and fill the whole creation, as Revelation 21:1–3, 10 and 22 affirm.

Why does Revelation 21:18 say the city-temple will be pure gold? The reason is that the entire 'holy of holies' of Israel's temple, which was paved with gold on the walls, floor and ceiling (so 1 Kgs. 6:20–22; 2 Chr. 3:4–8), has been expanded to cover the whole earth. This is why the three sections of Israel's old temple (holy of holies, the holy place and then the outer courtyard) are no longer found in the Revelation 21 temple – because God's special presence, formerly limited to the holy of holies, has now burst forth to encompass the whole earth. This is also why Revelation 21:16 says the whole city was 'square' or cubic – because the holy of holies was such a shape (1 Kgs. 6:20). In addition, that the entire creation has become the holy of holies is evident from 22:4. Whereas the high priest, who wore God's name on his forehead, was the only person in Israel who could enter the holy of holies once a year and be in God's presence, in the future all of God's people will become high priests with God's 'name on their foreheads' and standing, not one day a year, but for ever in God's presence.

This last point is enhanced by observing that God's 'throne' is now in the midst of God's people (see 22:1, 3) throughout the new creation, whereas in the previous chapters of Revelation God's throne was only in the heavenly temple.[8] Furthermore, the ark of the covenant in Israel's holy of holies was viewed as Yahweh's 'footstool', to where his feet extended while sitting on his heavenly throne (cf. Is. 66:1 with 2 Chr. 9:18; 1 Chr. 28:2; Ps. 99:5; 110:1; 132:7; Acts 7:49).[9] Only the high priest could enter once a year into the space where the 'footstool' was. In the new creation, all of God's people living throughout the new world will be high priests always in the presence of God because the dimensions of the heavenly holy of holies and God's ruling presence, symbolized by his throne, have broken in and expanded to include the entire new cosmos.[10]

Towards the end of my research on this book, I found that M. H.

---

[8] E.g., the word 'throne' occurs approximately 37 times in Revelation outside 21:3, 5 and 22:1–3 with reference either to God or Christ's throne *in heaven*.

[9] A 'footstool' was also attached to Solomon's 'throne' (2 Chr. 9:18), which likely was modelled after the notion that the ark of the covenant was the footstool of God's heavenly throne.

[10] Intriguingly, in Egypt the determinative used before one of the words for 'throne' 'in the case of the gods . . . indicates that the "throne" is the whole temple' (Wilson 1997: 547).

Woudstra has come close to making the same conclusion about the gigantic widening of the end-time temple. He noticed, as we have seen, that Isaiah 4:5, Jeremiah 3:16–17 and Ezekiel 37:26–28 all refer to a future time when the blessings of paradise return and the tabernacle will be extended over Jerusalem (though we have seen that in Ezekiel 37 the tabernacle extends over the entire promised land). The old temple 'will cease to be, simply because God always intended the cultus to extend its categories on to the life of the ordinary citizen' (Woudstra 1970: 99). Consequently, this is not so much a fading away of the former temple institution but a fulfilment of all to which it pointed and 'an accomplishment in becoming the city-wide refuge that it was intended to be' (1970: 99). He further notes, 'the purpose of the cultus, prior to that point in time, is therefore to bring this great reality into being. Far from being a "withering away" of the cultic institution ... the opposite actually is the case. The cultic establishment makes itself superfluous as a separate institution by extending itself over the whole city area (1970: 98).

Woudstra then applies his Old Testament conclusions to Revelation 21 – 22:

> The tabernacle's highest realization is depicted in Revelation 21:3, which describes the eschatological stage of the history of redemption ... the area of the temple is widened so as to become coextensive with the entire city of Jerusalem. The very form of the sacred city, with its length and breadth and height equal (Rev. 21:16), suggests that the new Jerusalem will become one giant holy of holies. At the same time the city symbolizes the shalom of paradise, with its river, and with the tree of life. (1970: 100–101)[11]

Woudstra stopped short of affirming that the temple is coextensive with the entire cosmos since he stresses its equivalence only with the new Jerusalem.[12] Nevertheless, his notion that Ezekiel 37:26–28

[11] Others seeing that the New Jerusalem is equivalent to the end-time sanctuary are Caird 1966: 273, 279; Hughes 1990: 229; Walker 1996: 245; and Duguid 1991: 483; though, unlike Woudstra, they do not see this equivalence to be anticipated prophetically in the OT.

[12] As noted in ch. 5 and warranting repetition here, just prior to publication, I found that Kline (1989: 55–56, 62–63) has briefly made the same point that the OT indicates a temple-building process beginning in Eden that culminates in the new creation of Rev. 21, which is equivalent to the new temple and new Jerusalem. Likewise, after writing most of the rough draft of the book, I discovered that Dumbrell had made the same point (2002: 53–65). In so doing, he expresses dependence partly on my earlier

points to a future time when the new Jerusalem 'will be all church' and 'coextensive with the life of the restored people of God' (Woudstra 1970: 98–99) certainly leaves the way open for the conclusion that I have made in equating the new cosmos with the city in the form of the holy of holies.[13]

As a result, the two outer sections of the temple (the holy place and outer court representing respectively the visible sky and the earth) have fallen away like a cocoon from which God's holy of holies presence has emerged to dominate all creation. This is why Hebrews 9:8 says, 'that the way into the [Holy of] Holies *has not yet been manifested* [i.e., it has been blocked] while the outer tabernacle [the holy place] is still standing'.[14] The way was not blocked for Christ when he entered into the heavenly holy of holies, and it will not be blocked for his people when they consummately enter at the very end of the age. There is nothing in the final new creation barricading the all-glorious presence of God from all of his people. To expect the restoration of a physical temple after the inaugurated new creation in Christ 'would be to offer new reason for confidence in the flesh, to build again the wall of partition and to destroy the unity of the people of God' (Clowney 1972: 177).

While I believe that the thesis about the ultimate redemptive-historical and cosmic significance of the temple in relation to Revela-

commentary excursus (Beale 1999a: 1109–1111), as well as some of the sources upon which I was originally dependent (e.g., Wenham 1987; 1994). Here Dumbrell actually also develops similar thoughts from an earlier work (1985: 37–38, 41–42). Caird sees that that the holy of holies 'has expanded . . . so that it not only fills the whole temple-less city, but embraces heaven and earth', though he sees no precedent in the OT for such an expansion (1966: 273). Spatafora similarly affirms that the church will be transformed into the new Jerusalem and that 'God's presence will fill completely the Church that will encompass the totality of the new creation' (1997: 246, 264). Though he briefly acknowledges the cosmic aspect of temples in the OT, he likewise does not argue for any OT precedent for the cosmic expansion, except to say, similarly to Woudstra, that John is close to the thought of Zech. 14:20–21, which 'announces for endtime [*sic*] an enlargement [out over the land of Israel] of the domain of the sacred' that was associated with the temple (Spatafora 1997: 273; so also pp. 50–51).

[13] See Cody 1960: 44 for a similar implication; Duguid calls the 'entire city' that has 'become a giant Most Holy Place' a 'new world', but he elaborates no further (1999: 483, 524). So, likewise, Congar 1962: 79, 95, 129, 200, 222, 234, 243–245, though only partly in relation to Revelation 21 (e.g., p. 222). Congar views the universalization in individual terms (e.g., 'every soul has become Jerusalem, a Temple of God . . .' [p. 79]), as well as corporate (e.g., pp. 157–171). See also Kline who views the new Jerusalem of Rev. 21:10ff. to be 'of cosmic dimensions' (2001: 88).

[14] For this interpretation of Heb. 9:8, see Attridge 1989: 240, who suggests similar implications for Heb. 10:19–20 (1989: 286–287), where Jesus is said to have become the 'veil' for his people in order that they may pass through to God's presence.

tion 21 – 22 is correct, I am sure that there are some who would doubt it, as no-one, to my knowledge, has developed this view in the way or to the degree in which this study has attempted to do.[15] I remain content to let the evidence of this book stand in the face of such doubts. Therefore, it is no understatement to say that the symbolism of the temple in both testaments is a highly significant strand of biblical theology.[16]

Hermeneutical reflections on the theological relationship of the Old Testament temple to the temple in the New Testament

In this section, I will continue to attempt to draw together some of my more important hermeneutical observations and conclusions made so far throughout the study, especially as these bear upon the theology of the temple.

Further reflections on the book of Hebrews

We have seen in Hebrews that the heavenly sanctuary is called the 'true tabernacle' because the earthly one was only a 'copy and shadow of the heavenly' one (8:5a). Verse 5b confirms this: 'just as Moses is warned when he was about to erect the tabernacle: for, "See ... that you make all things according to the pattern which was shown you on the mountain"'. The pattern seen by Moses on Sinai was a copy of the true heavenly tabernacle that was to appear at the end of history. It was this eschatological sanctuary of which Moses was to make a small earthly model. This was the 'true tabernacle' because it was the 'genuine article', the 'literal' and real one. In contrast, the earthly tent was but 'a copy and shadow' or figurative portrayal of the literal heavenly one (so also Heb. 9:24), 'the greater and more perfect tabernacle' (Heb. 9:11).

Some Christian interpreters maintain that what is literal can be only physical and what is non-literal is non-physical. The book of Hebrews, however, gives an opposite definition: the 'figurative' sanctuary is the earthly one, and the 'literal' sanctuary the heavenly one. Part of the reason for this lies in the meaning of 'true' (*alēthinos*). The reference to the tabernacle as 'true' in Hebrews 8:2 and 9:24 connotes

---

[15] Though, as I have remarked, Meredith Kline and William Dumbrell earlier alluded briefly to the notion.

[16] Barker also concludes that the temple is crucial to biblical theology (1991: 181), but she reaches this conclusion on different grounds.

both (1) that which is 'genuine' or represents 'the real state of affairs'[17] and (2) prophetic fulfilment.

One of the best illustrations of such usage occurs in Revelation 3:14, where Christ calls himself the 'faithful and *true* witness'. This means that he is the 'perfect substance and model' of everything that imperfect witnesses in the Old Testament should have been but failed to be, yet who were still a foreshadowing of Christ.[18] The word 'true' in the Old Testament refers to that which really exists and corresponds to reality (1 Sam. 9:6; 15:17; 1 Kgs. 10:6; 2 Chr. 9:5) and 'false' describes the opposite. Typically, a false witness or prophet does not speak that which corresponds to reality, whereas the true witness and prophet does (e.g., Num. 11:23; Deut. 13:2, 14; 17:4; 18:22).

Likewise, Hebrews refers to the heavenly tabernacle as 'true' because it is the fulfilment not only of direct prophecies of the eschatological temple but of everything the imperfect and temporary Old Testament tabernacle and temples foreshadowed. All of these physical temples were intended to be but models and copies of the coming true, eternal temple (see again Heb. 8:5). That consummate temple cannot be changed nor can it ever pass away, because it is not made by imperfect human hands but by God's hand, as a new creation. Thus, we may say that the eschatological temple is 'true' not only in the sense of fulfilment but in that it will remain a reality for ever.

The former temple was not the 'true one', not only because it was a mere shadow of the one to come but also because it would cease to exist. A further reason for the eternal existence of the new temple in the new creation is that it will exist in the midst of God's unfettered presence, whereas God's special presence in the old cosmos was cordoned off in a back room of the old temple. To believe that a physical temple will be built after the eschatological one has been inaugurated would be to return to the 'shadowy' stage of temple existence. Once the end-time, eternal temple that corresponds to the reality of the heavenly one comes, it would be bizarre for God to commend a return to the shadows.

To see Christ and the church as the true end-time temple is neither an allegorical spiritualization of the Old Testament temple nor of prophecies of an eschatological temple, but is an identification of the temple's real meaning. While it is true that Christ fulfils what the temple stands for, it is better to say, 'Christ is the meaning for which

---

[17] On which see Bultmann, '*alētheia, alēthinos, ktl.*', *TDNT*, 1:238–251.
[18] See the fuller discussion above on pp. 295–297.

the temple existed' (Clowney 1972: 177). This is well expressed by Jesus himself when he says, 'something greater than the temple is here' (Matt. 12:6).

Another reason why Hebrews says the literal temple is not the physical but the heavenly one is because God's luminous presence could only be imperfectly expressed there, as it was a human-made building. This, as we have seen, is part of Stephen's point in Acts 7:48–49: 'the Most High does not dwell in houses made by human hands, as the prophet says, "Heaven is My throne, and the earth is the footstool of My feet;/What kind of house will you build for Me?" says the Lord;/"Or what place is there for My repose?/Was it not My hand which made all these things?"'

Further reflections on the significance of 'handmade' versus 'made without hands'

Israel's physical sanctuaries had been 'handmade' (Acts 7:44–47) and could never be a permanent dwelling for God. Stephen's intent in quoting Isaiah 66:1 is to show that, as God's own hand had created the first world that had become tainted with idolatry (cf. Acts 7:44–47 with 7:41–43 in contrast to 7:50), so God would make a new, everlasting cosmos, not by human hands but by his own hand (so Is. 65:17–19 and 66:22). This explains the reason that Solomon's temple was not the ultimate fulfilment of the promise about David's son who would construct for God a temple: Solomon's temple was 'handmade'. In addition to the problem that a human-made structure was an inappropriate home for God's presence, Israel compounded the problem by making her temples places of idolatry. Since the divine judgment demanded the destruction of idolatrous places and objects (e.g., Exod. 34:14; Deut. 7:5; 2 Kgs. 23:14; 2 Chr. 31:1; 34:4), Israel's holy places had to be destroyed.

We have also found in our study that the stone-mountain of Daniel 2 and the eschatological temple are linked in that both are not made by human hands. Again, it is the New Testament that repeatedly refers to the new, end-time temple as 'not made with hands'. The picture in the Old Testament corresponding closest to this is Daniel's stone 'cut out without hands', referring to a new creational temple.[19] In this light, it is not surprising that Christ, the true temple, identifies himself with the stone of Daniel (Luke 20:17–18 = Matt. 21:42). Hebrews 9:11 says that Christ entered 'through the greater and more

---

[19] In addition to Acts 7:48, see Mark 14:58; 2 Cor. 5:1; Heb. 9:11, 24; *Barnabas* 16.

perfect tabernacle, not made with hands, that is to say, not of this creation' (so also Heb. 9:24).

In this regard, Acts 17:24 states that 'the God who made the world and all things in it, since He is Lord of heaven and earth, does not dwell in temples made with hands'. Paul says this after the great redemptive-historical divide, when Christ and his people had begun to replace Israel's 'handmade' temple. From this point on there could be no human-made structures separating God and his people, in order that he would dwell fully and unfettered with them. This is the reason that no human can answer affirmatively God's question in Isaiah 66:1 about his eschatological, eternal dwelling (quoted in Acts 7:49–50), 'Where then is a house you could build for Me?' In this respect, it is natural that in the New Testament 'handmade' refers to the old creation and 'made without hands' alludes to the new creation, most specifically to the resurrection state as the beginning of the new creation.

God's ultimate goal is to fill every part of his creation with his presence because he is its creator. God's glorious presence could not dwell completely in the old creation because it was a sin-sullied world. Thus, his special revelatory presence dwelt in a limited way in buildings made by humans. But, when he would fully redeem the world and recreate it, he would dwell in the world in a fuller way than ever before (so Rom. 8:18–25). Therefore, the new temple would be an everlasting and perfect container for God's ubiquitous presence because it would be without moral stain and would not be 'made with hands, that is to say, not of this [old] creation' (Heb. 9:11). It is for this reason that Revelation 21:22 says, 'I saw no [structural] temple' in the new cosmos because 'the Lord God, the Almighty, and the Lamb, are its temple'. The earlier sanctuaries that were flawed vessels for holding the divine presence 'are replaced by God and the Lamb in person, so that unrestricted dealings with God are [now] possible'.[20]

The importance of the notion of 'extended meaning'

Reflection on the nature of how people, especially authors, communicate will help us better perceive the nature of how biblical authors communicate and how God communicates through them. This, of course, will have important bearing on how the temple is to be understood throughout various segments of biblical revelation.

The act of 'literal' communication, whether of biblical writers or any human author, involves three aspects: (1) the content of the

---

[20] O. Michel, '*naos*', *TDNT*, 4:889.

utterance; (2) the manner in which the utterance is made; (3) the intended effect of the utterance.[21] It is this second step, the various ways God communicates content through human authors, that is the focus in this section. The ways Scripture conveys content is through such literary forms as poetry, parable, historical narrative, visionary apocalyptic, praise, mocking, satire, irony, prophecy, wisdom sayings, and so on. Some literary forms may only be discerned not from sentences or paragraphs but from considering the completed literary work as a whole. In our case, some of the divine forms of communication can only be discerned from considering the completed canon as a whole (Vanhoozer 2001: 34–37). One such form would be typology (on which see the example of John 19 below).

The biblical canon has similarities with other literary works which 'can grow in meaning' as a result of original authors sensing a fuller, potential meaning than they can express. This means that sometimes authors consciously intend that their literary acts, their 'literal sense', be open-ended or indeterminate, and other times such indeterminateness is unconscious or implied. This may be called 'transhistorical intentions' or 'open-ended authorial intentions', whereby an intended original meaning may go beyond the original content spoken (Hirsch 1967: 125; 1984: 202–244). Authors may wish to include a potential in what they say to extend meaning into the indefinite future by espousing principles intended for an indefinite number of applications. Or, alternatively, authors may be aware that their original meaning has the potential to be recontextualized by subsequent interpreters who ascertain creative applications of the meaning to new contexts. In such cases a provision is made for subsequent readers to interpret in a way that 'extends meaning'. Thus an original meaning is so designed to tolerate some revision in cognitive content and yet not be essentially altered.[22]

E. D. Hirsch helpfully distinguishes between what he calls 'meaning' and 'significance', which has relevance for the present discussion. The explanation of original, intentional, *verbal meaning* is distinct from the 'significance' of that meaning.[23] We can compare an author's original, unchanging meaning to an apple in its original context of an apple tree. When someone removes the apple and puts

---

[21] See Vanhoozer 1998: *passim* for elaboration of this concept, which is rooted in speech-act theory.

[22] This paragraph is based on Hirsch 1967: 125; 1984: *passim*; 1994: 558; and Vanhoozer 1998: 261–262 (following Hirsch), 313–314.

[23] See below for a further explanation of verbal meaning as a 'willed type'.

it into another setting (say, in a basket of various fruits in a dining room for decorative purposes), the apple does not lose its original identity as an apple, the fruit of a particular kind of tree, but the apple must now be understood, not in and of itself but *in relation to the new context* in which it has been placed.[24] Hirsch calls this new contextual relationship 'significance'. The new context does not annihilate the original identity of the apple, but now the apple must be understood in its relation to its new setting. It is the same with meaning and its significance: ' "Meaning" refers to the whole verbal meaning of a text, and "significance" to textual meaning in relation to a larger context' beyond itself (i.e., a context of 'another mind, another era, a wider subject matter, an alien system of values', etc. (Hirsch 1976: 2–3).[25] What Hirsch calls 'significance' may be divided into a concept of extended meaning or merely an application of an original unextended meaning (e.g., with respect to the latter, how does the message of a particular ancient biblical text apply to the lives of people living in the twentieth century?). Our focus here is on 'significance' as the organic extension of meaning (Hirsch 1967:49–50).[26]

[24] A more radical illustration could be taking the apple from the tree, cutting it up and making it part of a fruit salad, or making it into apple sauce or part of some other kind of sauce. Even in these 'new contexts' something is identifiable with the apple in its original setting, whether by sight or taste. An illustration we would disagree with is the taking of part of the apple and making it into something that can no longer be identified with anything in the original apple.

[25] The scope of the present work is unable adequately to discuss the hermeneutical debates between the more traditional and modern positions represented respectively: e.g., by Hirsch and Gadamer; these debates themselves have their roots in two alternative epistemological positions represented by Husserl and Heidegger; for discussion from Hirsch's perspective see Hirsch 1976: e.g., 4–6; 1967: 209–274; for an assessment from a similar perspective see Gruenler 1991: 74–86; N. T. Wright 1992b: 18–144 (*passim*); Carson 1996: 57–137, 163–174. Both Wright and Carson strike a good balance between the subjective and objective epistemological aspects involved in this debate.

[26] In this regard, Hirsch's notion of a 'willed type' as a further explanation of extended intentional, verbal meaning is worth trying to grasp. A 'willed type' is a meaning that has two characteristics: (1) a categorical concept with a boundary in which some specific ideas belong within a boundary and others are excluded, and which can be represented by only a single idea among the other similar ideas which belong within the legitimate boundary; (2) the categorical concept can be represented by more than only one of the ideas belonging to the category, as long as they fall within the boundary lines demarcating the categorical boundary. I have paraphrased Hirsch here. His actual twofold definition is more dense. He says a 'willed type' has two characteristics: (1) an entity with a boundary in which some things belong within the boundary and others are excluded, and it can be represented by only a single instance among the other things which belong within the legitimate boundary; (2) the type as an entity can be represented by more than a single instance, as long as the other representing instances fall within the boundary.

'Extended meaning' and its bearing on biblical interpretation in general and the temple in particular

The notion of 'extended meaning' is instructive for understanding and analysing the New Testament's use of the Old. I, along with others, believe that something like this is what is entailed in Old Testament literary forms of prophecy or visionary apocalyptic. Old Testament authors appear to have only dimly, implicitly or partly comprehended the things of which they were speaking.[27]

We may say that authorial intentions of Old Testament writers were not as comprehensive as the simultaneous divine intentions, which become progressively unpacked as the history of revelation progresses until they reach climax in Christ. The Old Testament writers prophesied events to occur not only distant in time from them but in another world, a new world, which Jesus inaugurated. These writers are comparable in a sense to people in a spaceship above the earth. They can see only the earth and its different shading, representing clouds, seas and land masses. When, however, they see magnified pictures of the earth from satellite cameras, they are able to make out mountains, rivers, forests, cities, buildings, houses and people. Both the distant and close-up views are 'literal'. The close-up picture reveals details that someone with a distant view could never have guessed were there. The close-up even 'looks' like a different reality from the distant. Nevertheless, both are 'literal' depictions of what is actually there. Similarly, the literal picture of Old Testament prophecy is magnified by the lens of New Testament progressive revelation, which enlarges the details of fulfilment in the beginning new world that will be completed at Christ's last advent.

With this illustration in mind, our contention is that Christ not only fulfils all that the Old Testament temple and its prophecies represent, but that he is the unpacked meaning for which the temple existed all along.[28] His establishment of the temple at his first coming is a magnified view of the new creational temple, and Revelation 21 is the most ultimate highly magnified picture we will have this side of the consummated new cosmos. Like the distant and close-up photographs, such a view of the temple should not be misconceived as diminishing a literal fulfilment of the Old Testament temple prophecies.

---

[27] This paragraph is based on Vanhoozer 1998: 313–314.
[28] To paraphrase Clowney 1972: 177.

We may also compare Israel's temple and prophecies of another to come to a small balloon with a map of the world stamped on it (indeed, we have argued that the OT temple was a symbolic model of the cosmos). The contour lines of the map are hardly discernible when no air is blown into the balloon. As the balloon begins to fill with a little air, the details of its map are a bit more discernible but still too close together to see it clearly. When the balloon is blown to full size, however, the details are expanded and become much clearer. The blown-up version is just as 'literal' as the smaller one, but its details are more understandable. In like manner, the fulfilment of the temple in the New Testament reveals that, far from a shrivelling up or fading away of the material temple complex, there is a material and spiritual expansion that begins with Christ and his people, and consummates with the entire new heavens and earth! Just as John the Baptist, the greatest prophet of the Old Testament era, said that he must decrease but Jesus had to increase (John 3:30), so Jesus says that with his coming the temple had to decrease and he had to increase (Matt. 12:6, 'something greater than the temple is here').

We have mentioned that in some cases the Old Testament predicts a non-material temple. In other cases, however, there *may be* prophecies describing what would seem to be a structural temple, which we have argued are fulfilled by an entirely literal, yet non-architectural temple; that is, Christ and the church fulfil them. To explain this hermeneutically, we have earlier used the illustration of a father's promise to a son of a horse and buggy in 1900 being fulfilled faithfully and on an escalated literal level by a car in 1930. This is, in fact, also an illustration of biblical typology in which 'Christ fulfils the Old Testament promises in ways that differ from the actual terms of the promises' (Goldsworthy 1991: 87). Typology is not mere analogy of something in the New Testament with something in the Old. Typology indicates fulfilment of the Old Testament's indirect prophetic foreshadowing of people, institutions and events in Christ, who is the ultimate climactic expression of everything God completely intended in the older revelation – whether it be the Law, temple and its rituals, various prophets, priests and kings, and so on.[29]

A classic example is John 19:36. There John says that Jesus' death on the cross, without broken bones, was a prophetic 'fulfilment' of the Passover lamb's sacrifice in Exodus (see Exod. 12:46; Num. 9:12; Ps. 34:20). Even though the Passover sacrifice was narrated only as a his-

---

[29] On which see Beale 1994: 396, and *passim*.

torical event and not as a formal prophecy in the Old Testament, in the light of Christ's coming, that event is seen as foreshadowing the divine Lamb's sacrifice on an escalated scale. Whether then we speak of going from a horse to a car, or from a sacrificial animal to the crucified God-man, the hermeneutical transition from Old to New is often that of going from the 'shadow' to the 'substance'.

The progress of revelation reveals enlarged meanings of earlier biblical texts, and later biblical writers further interpret prior canonical writings in ways that amplify earlier texts. These later interpretations may formulate meanings of which earlier authors may not have been conscious, but which do not contravene their original organic intention but may 'supervene'[30] on it. This is to say that original meanings have 'thick'[31] content and that original authors likely were not exhaustively aware (in the way God was) of the full extent of that content. In this regard, fulfilment often 'fleshes out' prophecy with details of which even the prophet may not have been fully cognizant.

Some final thoughts on 'extended meaning' and its bearing on interpretation of the temple

The lack of resolution in the discussion of whether some Old Testament prophecies (like the temple) are literally or non-literally fulfilled is partly cleared up by proper reflection on the notion of 'already and not yet' eschatology. The fulfilment of the final resurrection of saints is a good parallel to the nature of the end-time fulfilment of the temple. Daniel 12:2, for example, prophesies a resurrection of believers. John 5:25 says, 'an hour is coming and now is, when the dead shall hear the voice of the Son of God, and those who hear shall live'. The Daniel prophecy begins fulfilment in the first century, but only on a spiritual level. People are raised spiritually but not yet physically. Only a few verses later, however, Jesus refers to the consummate fulfilment physically of the same Daniel prophecy: 'an hour is coming, in which all who are in the tombs shall hear his voice, and shall come forth; those who did the good deeds, to a resurrection of life, those who committed the evil deeds to a resurrection of judgment' (John 5:28–29). Both fulfilments are literal. The 'spiritual' resurrection is just as 'literal' as the physical, since Daniel prophesied the resurrection of bodies *with resurrected spirits*! The prophecy is not fulfilled all at once, since first the spiritual resurrection occurs, followed

---

[30] This word comes from Vanhoozer 2001: 37.

[31] For further elaboration of this concept, see Vanhoozer 1998: e.g., 284–285, 291–292, 313–314, where he discusses 'thick description'. See further, Beale 1999b: 1–26.

later by the physical. Therefore, it is not the nature of fulfilment that has changed, but its timing. That is, the fulfilment of the spiritual and physical resurrections are not spiritualized nor allegorized but merely staggered.

There is another way in which the Old Testament prophecy of the resurrection was fulfilled in a twofold manner: Jesus' own resurrection was the beginning fulfilment ('the first fruits') and the subsequent physical resurrection of all saints at the end of history is the final fulfilment (1 Cor. 15:22–23). In light of both John 5 and 1 Corinthians 15, the predicted resurrection is actually fulfilled in three stages: (1) Christ's physical resurrection; (2) believers' spiritual resurrection; (3) believers' physical resurrection. Just as prophets like Daniel surely did not fully understand the staggered nature of the resurrection, neither did they understand the developmental fulfilment of the temple.

The fulfilment of the temple (and perhaps other kinds of fulfilment) follows a similar staggered realization. That is, Christ rises to become the cornerstone of the temple, and believers are first 'spiritually' part of the temple through spiritual resurrection, but later an actual physical part of the temple too at the time of the final physical resurrection (e.g., Rev. 3:12; 21:1–3), when the entire cosmos becomes the temple. The basis for comparing the resurrection with the temple lies in the New Testament's view of Jesus' resurrection body as the rebuilding of the new temple, so that in him the temple has also begun physically.[32] Therefore, the beginning form of the temple is not merely spiritual but also physical: it is composed of the spirits of saints with the physically resurrected Christ as its cornerstone.

We have seen that some prophecies of an end-temple foresee a non-architectural structure, while others are indefinite, merely referring to the establishment of a future temple.[33] These more indefinite prophecies could have been viewed by their original authors and readers to refer to a structure on the order of the prior Solomonic and second temples. Yet these contexts speak of the eschatological temple as being more glorious or greater than the prior ones (e.g., Is. 62:9; Ezek. 40 – 48; Zech. 6:12–13; 14:16; Hag. 2:1–9). It is theoretically possible that part of the inaugurated stage of these prophecies involves an actual larger building complex than ever before. If so,

---

[32] E.g., John 2:20–22; likewise, Mark 14:58; similarly, Heb. 9:11, 24; 1 Pet. 2:4–7; Rev. 21:22.

[33] Some of these include prophecies where no establishment of a temple is mentioned but the existence of a latter-day temple is noted (e.g., Dan. 8:11–13; 11:31).

that complex, like its Old Testament predecessors, would be symbolic of the cosmos and of the task to extend the essence of the temple and spread God's glory throughout the earth. This was the original purpose of the original Garden temple and of Israel's subsequent temples. Unlike its predecessors, Christ and his people associated with this temple would finally accomplish the task and extend the boundaries of God's holy of holies presence throughout the earth, the culmination of which is pictured in Revelation 21. Presumably, on such a reading, the beginning architectural form of the end-time temple would fade away once its symbolic task has been accomplished. Whatever precisely happens to it, the whole earth would finally be considered the consummate, eternal temple in which God's glory is present everywhere.

A better view, however, of these more indeterminate temple prophecies is that they are to be interpreted by the more explicit prophecies predicting an immaterial non-architectural structure.[34] Some prophecies understand that the temple was to extend over all of Jerusalem (Is. 4:5–6; Jer. 3:16–17) or even over all of the land of Israel (Ezek. 37:26–28; similarly, Lev. 26:10–13). We have seen in the preceding chapter that even Ezekiel 40 – 48 is not best interpreted as a prophecy of the building of an architectural temple.[35] We have reached comparable conclusions with respect to Eden as a non-architectural temple (Gen. 2; Ezek. 28:18), as well as the informal, small-scale sanctuaries of the patriarchs and the larger-scale one at Mount Sinai. Even in these cases, while not explicitly prophetic, we have argued that they contained a pattern in themselves of a temple expansion that was to pervade the world in fulfilment of the mandate of Genesis 1:28. We have seen that mandate was interwoven into many of the more explicitly prophetic texts about the temple, so that they also imply a sanctuary of universal dimensions.[36]

---

[34] Is. 8:13–14 (cf. the use in 1 Pet. 2:8 and 3:14–15); 57:15 in relation to 66:2; cf. Ps. 114:2 ('Judah became his sanctuary'); Ezek. 11:16, which refers to an immaterial temple for Israelite exiles.

[35] If the detailed prophecy of Ezek. 40 – 48 is jettisoned as such a prediction, then other much less descriptive prophecies usually placed in such a category wane in significance. However, see P. D. Feinberg, who sees Ezek. 40 – 48 as a reference to a physical structure and, because of its detail, as determinative in defining the other briefer prophecies about the temple as also foreseeing physical structures (1995: 109).

[36] So Lev. 26:10–13; Jer. 3:16–17; Ezek. 37:26–28; cf. Ezek. 40 – 48, where in ch. 47 allusion is made to Eden. Philo understands the prophecy of the tabernacle in Lev. 26 to be non-architectural in nature: he views Lev. 26:12 to refer to the human soul or mind as 'a holy temple' (*Som.* 1.148–149) or 'house of God' (*Som.* 1.148–149; *Praem.* 123).

Another reason these 'indeterminate temple prophecies' are better viewed as not including any traditional temple building has to do with the progression of redemptive history. Christ and his church clearly are the inaugurated form of the latter-day temple. To have a physical temple built towards the end of the church age, as a partial inaugurated fulfilment of the same Old Testament prophecies that Christ and the church had begun to fulfil, would be hermeneutically and theologically strange. It would be a redemptive-historical hiccup. Recalling the above summary of Hebrews enhances the unlikelihood of any future physical temple structure: physical temples were the 'shadows' and the inaugurated temple in Christ was the 'true substance' of the shadows. In conjunction with this, 'handmade' temples went out of theological style with the resurrection of Christ, which commenced the eschatological temple 'made without hands'. The early Christian community from the beginning reckoned that any humanly constructed temple was impossible in the eschatological era, since the old creation is referred to as 'handmade', and the temple of the new creation is alluded to as 'made without hands'[37] (as discussed earlier in this chapter). If this principle were violated, then redemptive history would take a retrograde step back from the new creation into the old; the inauguration of the new creation temple in Christ and the church would exist alongside an old-age temple. Certainly, when the old world is destroyed at the end of the age, and only the new, eternal creation remains, there is no room for such an antiquated structure.

Consequently, an approach of 'literal interpretation' that attempts to conform fulfilment of prophecies to physical realities as much as possible is probably not an ideal way to describe a biblical hermeneutic. Nevertheless, we have endeavoured to show that even someone guided by such an interpretative rule could see that our understanding of the end-time temple is not inconsistent with that approach. On the other hand, a 'literate canonical approach' that aspires to the broad literary meaning of the entire biblical context is a more felicitous way to summarize a single method of interpretation.[38] Such an interpretative approach aims to unravel the original intention of biblical authors, understanding that intention may be multi-layered,

---

[37] Cf. also Michel, 'naos', *TDNT*, 4:886. As earlier noted, Judaism (*Pirke de Rabbi Eliezer* 51) equated the coming temple with the new creation: 'in the future the temple will be raised up and renewed' in fulfilment of the new creation prophecy in Is. 43:19 ('Behold, I will create a new thing').

[38] On which see Vanhoozer 1998: e.g., 312–314.

without any of the layers contradicting the others. These original intentions may have meaning more correspondent to 'literal' physical reality, while others may allude to 'literal' spiritual realities. This is certainly true with respect to the temple. We have attempted to sail between the coast of 'literalism' on one side and that of 'spiritualiza-tion' on the other, and hope we have avoided the dangers of both.

We think that the approach we have taken avoids the criticism of mystical spiritualizing, since the end-time temple is physical but on a grander scale than former temples. Indeed, the entire new creation is what the localized temple pointed to and symbolized all along! Rather than a little structure, the new cosmos is the physical abode for the divine glory. This approach does not employ allegorical methods of interpretation or the reading in of symbols that have no controls. Rather, the controlling paradigm throughout this study has been Genesis 1:28 in relation to the Garden of Eden in Genesis 2. We have seen that later temples and prophecies of the end-time temple usually allude to one or both of these Genesis passages, so that these early Genesis texts provide the interpretative controls for understanding the progressive revelation of the temple in the Old and New Testaments. On the other hand, this ongoing biblical revelation itself sheds light on how these Genesis passages are developed, though this interpretative developmental growth cannot extend beyond the organic bounds of the first chapters of the Bible.[39] In fact, the image of God's glorious presence in a garden-like temple has formed an inclusio or kind of 'book-end' structure around the entire canon (Gen. 2 and Rev. 21:1 – 22:3), providing an interpretative key for understanding the material about the temple throughout Scripture. Another interpretative key has been the temple's cosmic symbolism, which pointed to the goal of its own extension to become co-equal with the cosmos itself.

Theological reflections on the relationship of the Old Testament temple to the temple in the New Testament

The primary words translated as 'temple' or 'sanctuary' in the New Testament are *hieron* (72 times) and *naos* (45 times), while 'house' (*oikos*, approximately 12 times), 'holy place' (*hagios*, approximately 11 times) and 'tabernacle' (*skēnē*, approximately 14 times) also occur.

---

[39] The potential criticism of allegorizing noted in this paragraph has been lodged by C. L. Feinberg 1971: 108–109.

All of these words can refer either to Israel's old tabernacle or temple structure in the Greek Old Testament (either to the holy of holies or the whole temple complex). In the New Testament, they refer either to the old tabernacle or temple *or*, with the exception of *hieron*, to the new temple inaugurated in Christ and the Spirit and those identified with Christ through the Spirit.[40]

Interestingly, *hieron* refers only to the old temple and never to the new temple in the New Testament. It occurs in this sense only in the Gospels, Acts and Paul. Perhaps the reason for this is mere stylistic preference, though there may be more behind the choice than at first meets the eye. The other words proliferate in the canonical Greek Old Testament with reference to Israel's temple, but *hieron* occurs only rarely with this sense.[41] Furthermore, *hieron* virtually never refers there to God's heavenly temple,[42] whereas the other words refer to it several times each.[43] It is possible that the reason the other words are used for the new temple is that they may have been deemed more suitable to refer to such a new temple because they had already referred to the heavenly temple in the Old Testament. The usage may have underscored continuity between God's prior holy dwelling in heaven and the beginning descent of that dwelling to earth in the form of Christ and the Spirit.

Regardless of whether or not the usage of these Greek words hints at this theological relationship, it is instructive to enquire about the relationship between the heavenly temple of the Old Testament age

---

[40] On *naos* see Matt. 26:61; 27:40; Mark 14:58; John 2:19–20; 1 Cor. 3:16–17; 6:19; 2 Cor. 6:16; Eph. 2:21; 2 Thess. 2:4; 15 times in Revelation; on *oikos* see Matt. 21:13 (and par.); John 2:17; Heb. 10:21; 1 Pet. 2:5; on *hagios* see Heb. 8:2; 9:12, 24–25; 10:19; on *skēnē* see Acts 15:16; Heb. 8:2; 9:11; Rev. 13:6; 15:5; 21:3.

[41] 1 Chr. 9:27; 29:4; 2 Chr. 6:13; Ezek. 28:18; 45:19 (though we have argued earlier that this last passage may refer to a heavenly temple, a number of commentators disagree).

[42] Though once the word refers to part of a description of the eschatological temple (Ezek. 45:19), as does *skēnē* (Is. 54:2; 9:11). Josephus uses *hieron* 'for the tabernacle, for Solomon's temple, for Zerubabbel's and for Herod's' (Schrenk, '*hieron*', *TDNT*, 3:234, 241), though, as we saw in the first chapter, he believes the earthly temple (*hieron*) was symbolic of various parts of the cosmos. Nevertheless, on the basis of Schrenk's overview, he apparently never used *hieron* for God's dwelling in heaven. Philo appears to use the word to refer to the 'whole cosmos' (*Spec. Leg.* 1.66) or the visible heavenly part of the cosmos (i.e., the visible heavens: *Opif. Mundi* 55; *Som.* 1.215) as a divine temple.

[43] On *naos* see 2 Sam. 22:7; Pss. 10(11):5; 17(18):6; 27(28):2; Hab. 2:20; on *oikos* see Gen. 28:17; Deut. 26:15 (and as an end-time temple see Is. 2:2–3; Mic. 4:2; Zech. 12:8); on *hagios* see Is. 63:15; Pss. 19(20):2 (cf. in relation to 19[20]:6); 11:4; 102:19; on *skēnē* see Exod. 25:9 (esp. in the light of Heb. 8:5; 9:11, 23–24); 2 Sam. 22:12; Ps. 18:11 (and as an end-time temple see Is. 54:2; Amos 9:11).

and the eschatological temple in heaven in the new age. Could it be that with the ascension of Christ and the giving of the Spirit a new redemptive-historical stage or instalment of the heavenly temple has developed? Comparing the developmental nature of the kingdom of God in the two testaments may be helpful in understanding the connection of the temple. God had always reigned as King, and with Christ's resurrection a new stage was reached in that now God rules through the Last Adam. God's kingdom has finally spread beyond Israel's geographical borders. Likewise, the new latter-day temple of Christ developed God's Old Testament heavenly temple. The incarnate Christ was God's presence descending to the earth from heaven in a way as never before. Christ's resurrection was an even greater expression of this end-time temple that descended to earth to a greater degree than previously. After Christ, who is the expression of the true temple ascended to heaven, the heavenly temple again began to descend in the form of the Spirit and expanded by growing through incorporating people into it. The expansion is consummated at the end of the age by the heavenly temple fully covering the entire earth, as we have discussed at the beginning of this chapter with respect to Revelation 21.

Thus, the first primary difference between the heavenly temple of the former era and that of the new is that Christ, the Last Adam, has been exalted to sit at God's right hand in the heavenly temple-palace. The latter-day goal all along of the heavenly temple was that it descend to earth and permeate every part of it. That did not happen during the epoch of Israel because of the nation's disobedience. Until the time of Christ, God's special revelatory presence extended only to the borders of the holy of holies. Then Christ came and did what Adam should have done, and in so doing he began to expand the temple even during his earthly ministry. When he ascended into the heavenly temple, he then sent his Spirit to create God's people as a part of that extending heavenly temple. But since the church represents only a remnant of the earth's inhabitants who accept the gospel, God's unique presence does not spread throughout the world, so that the universal extent of the temple has not yet been achieved, and will not during this age. Only when Jesus Christ returns a final time will he destroy the old cosmos and create a new one, wherein God's presence will dwell completely.

Therefore, while the latter-day temple of God's presence in Christ and the Spirit has irrupted into space-time history, it has not done so as completely as it will at the very end of history. In other words, the end-time temple has begun fulfilment among God's people through Christ and the Spirit, but that fulfilment has not been completed. This means saints imperfectly experience the 'holy of holies' presence of God in this age, but will experience his presence fully in the coming epoch of the consummated new creation (Rev. 22:4–5). In this connection, there is another instructive, though difficult, question to pose: what is the relationship of God's presence in the holy of holies of Israel's temple to his presence in the new temple? While it was true that God's presence filled the entire creation in the time before Christ (i.e., God was omnipresent), his presence was more immanent in the holy of holies than anywhere else on earth. We may call this his special revelatory presence, which extended from his heavenly throne down to the inner sanctum. This reality is pictured as God sitting on his heavenly throne with his 'feet' resting on the sacred 'footstool' of the ark of the covenant. Anyone, except the high priest, who would enter this inner room would die because of this holy presence. Even the high priest could not look directly on the divine glory, but had to offer incense, which clouded and shielded him from gazing directly at God.

God moved out of the holy of holies at the inception of the Babylonian exile (Ezek. 10:18; 11:22–23), and probably did not return to dwell in the second temple that was rebuilt after the return from Babylon. That unique presence returned to the heavenly sanctuary until the coming of Christ, when it returned to earth again, not to dwell in another handmade temple but in one made without hands: 'the Word became flesh and tabernacled among us, and we beheld his glory' (John 1:14). God's presence in the heavenly temple extended to earth, no longer into the old holy of holies but in Christ (John 1:51). After his resurrection and ascension, God's tabernacling presence descended in the form of the Spirit, making those identified with Christ into part of the temple. The Father and Son, however, still reside in the heavenly temple and not on earth. Therefore, the temple's centre of gravity during the church age is located in the heavenly realm, but it has begun to invade the earthly through the Spirit in the church. This is why the book of Revelation usually portrays the 'temple' (*naos*) in heaven (11 of 15 times),[44] though related to believ-

---

[44] Three of the four remaining uses (3:12; 11:1, 2) refer to the church on earth, though 3:12 is likely 'already and not yet', including the church's being on earth and its future existence in the new creation (cf. Rev. 21:1ff.). The fourth use refers to God and the Lamb as the temple in the new creation. The synonym 'tabernacle' (*skēnē*) occurs three times, twice referring to the heavenly sphere (13:6; 15:5) and once with respect to the new creation. 'Tabernacling' (*skēnoō*) is used twice of those who dwell in heaven (12:12; 13:6) and twice of God who dwells in the new creation (7:15; 21:3), though 7:15 could be 'already and not yet'.

ers on earth (e.g. 1:13; 11:1–4) through their identification with the Spirit existentially (cf. Rev. 1:4 and 4:5 with 1:13; 2:2; 11:4) and with Christ (cf. 3:12 with 21:22) and their representative angels positionally (cf. 1:13 and 1:16; 2:1).[45]

Though the three parts of Israel's old temple no longer exist, until the end of the age there may be a sense in which there are still three dimensions of the new temple. First, the holy of holies remains in heaven, the place of the temple's 'centre of gravity'. Second, the holy place is the spiritual dimension that extends to earth, where God's people function as a 'kingdom of priests' (Rev. 1:6; 5:10; cf. Exod. 19:6) and as 'lampstands' shining God's revelation to the world (Rev. 1:13, 20; 2:2; 11:1, 4). The Spirit is the lamp on these lampstands that enables the church to shine (cf. Rev. 1:4 with 4:6). Third, the 'outer court' represents the church's physical existence (Rev. 11:1–2), especially in its suffering, which is a part of the old earth.[46] Just as the outer courtyard was the place where animals were slain to be sacrificed, so believers sacrifice themselves in their willingness to suffer for their faith (cf. Rev. 6:9–11; Heb. 13:10–13).[47] As in the old temple, so in the new inaugurated one there is an increasing gradation in holiness beginning in the outer court and proceeding through the holy place into the holy of holies.

Priests in the old epoch had to be ritually clean in order to enter and minister in the holy place. If they tried to minister while unclean, they would be put to death. Believer priests minister in the spiritual 'holy place' even though they are unclean due to sin. Though believers are certainly existentially imperfect, they are not destroyed because of their 'blamelessness' in God's sight due to their corporate identification with Christ, the perfect Last Adam and great high priest, who represents them in two ways. First, he suffered the penalty of their sin through death on their behalf so that they are declared not guilty. Second, his righteousness vicariously becomes theirs. He has 'once for all' performed the priestly task that had originally been given to the first Adam.

Therefore, believers still do not yet *personally* enter into the heavenly holy of holies, but do so through their representative high priest,

---

[45] On all of these passages see further Beale 1999a: *in loc.*, including the additional 13:6.

[46] Spatafora believes that the outer court in Rev. 11:2 continues as an image for the church as the temple but that it refers to the sinful aspect of the church (1997: 168–173).

[47] Cf. also Rom. 12:1; Phil. 2:17; 2 Tim. 4:6.

Jesus Christ. He has entered in on their behalf (just as Israel's high priest entered in as a representative of the rest of the nation, and as a typological foreshadowing of Christ). There he 'obtained eternal redemption' (Heb. 9:11–12, 24–28; cf. 3:17). On the basis of Christ's priestly work of entering that heavenly sanctuary, believers 'have confidence' that they will 'enter the [most] holy place' themselves in the future (Heb. 10:19–21).[48] Believers have a 'hope' that 'enters within the veil, where Jesus has entered as a forerunner for us, having become a high priest' (Heb. 6:19–20).[49]

The temple curtain tore at Christ's death, and at his resurrection 'he entered through the veil' of the heavenly temple (Heb. 10:20). The removing of the veil of the heavenly temple will occur for believers when the church (the body of Christ) suffers death and resurrection at the end of the age, according to the principle that the church 'follows the Lamb wherever he goes' (Rev. 14:4). It is natural, therefore, that after Revelation 11:1–18 portrays the church's suffering, demise and vindication according to the model of Christ's career (on which see Beale 1999a: 567–568), 'the sanctuary [holy of holies] of God was opened in heaven, and the ark of His covenant [symbolic of the divine presence] in His sanctuary appeared' (Rev. 11:19; so similarly, Rev. 21:1 – 22:5). Perhaps this is what Isaiah 25:7–8a refers to: 'And on this mountain He will swallow up the face of the covering which is over all peoples, even the veil which is stretched over all nations. He will swallow up death for all time.'[50]

J. W. Mealy argues that this Isaiah passage is alluded to in Revelation 21:1 and 4 (the latter of which clearly alludes to Is. 25:8), where respectively 'there is no longer a sea' in the new creation nor any 'death' or sadness:

[48] Some contend that believers have progressed into the celestial holy of holies not merely in a redemptive-historical manner (positionally in Christ) but, in some way existentially. If so, the existential link with the holy of holies would be through the Spirit that bridges the two. Nevertheless, it is preferable to see the Spirit as having brought the church into the initial phase of the end-time temple, where their physical existence in the world is the outer court and their spiritual existence is in the heavenly dimension of the holy place that invisibly extends to earth.

[49] From one perspective, saints are like the OT high priest who could enter in and partially experience the holy of holies because he could not see the divine luminous presence, since the incense cloud shielded it. Otherwise, the priest would have been struck dead, since he was a sinful human. Likewise, Christians have partially entered the heavenly holy of holies: positionally in Jesus but not personally; otherwise they would be annihilated because they are still sinful.

[50] Note explicit reference to the final resurrection also in Is. 26:19.

Revelation 21.3–4, which says that the tabernacle of God has come to be among his people, must be understood in the context of its background in Revelation. Earlier in the text [of Revelation], heaven has been pictured as the present tabernacle of God's abode, and the expanse of the sky has been treated as corresponding sometimes ... to the veil that separated the holy of holies from the rest of the sanctuary, hiding the ark of God from human sight. Thus the parousia was described in terms of the parting or removal of that veil (6.14; 11:19), so that God's throne could be seen. Hand in hand with this conception ... went 21.3–4, which posited the establishment of a new sanctuary on earth, which has no such separating veil – God's people will corporately dwell in his immediate presence ... His presence will never again be hidden behind the separating veil of the sky, for in the new heaven and the new earth 'there is no longer any sea'.[51]

We think that, though this identification of the 'sea' may not be persuasive, Mealy's general line of thought is valid. Until that final day of unveiling, God's people 'draw near' to the heavenly holy of holies, which, we have argued, means they have begun to enter the outer court and holy place of the celestial temple (Heb. 10:22). They have *begun* to 'come to Mount Zion and to the city of the living God, the heavenly Jerusalem ...' (Heb. 12:22), which were seen earlier to be equivalent concepts to the eternal temple.[52] That the believers' 'coming to Mount Zion and to the [heavenly] city' is an inaugurated but not consummated reality is apparent from Hebrews 12:28 ('since we receive a kingdom that cannot be shaken')[53] and 13:14 ('for here we do not have a lasting city, but we are seeking the city which is to come').

During this present era, therefore, there still must be three sections even of the inaugurated latter-day temple because its purpose and fulfilment will not be completed until the destruction of the old order and establishment of the new. The consummate form of the new temple will appear at the end of time in the new creation, when the heavenly dimension fully breaks in and replaces the old earth, which has been

---

[51] Mealy 1992: 198–199 (though see also pp. 196–197, for the fuller argument). He also sees that Revelation portrays the visible sky as a veil that served as the door to the tent of witness (i.e., the heavenly holy place).

[52] See the discussion on Hebrews (pp. 301–309).

[53] On which see the earlier discussion of Heb. 12:26–28 (pp. 301–306).

destroyed (Rev. 21:1–3).[54] At this time there will be only one section of the temple: the holy of holies, the dimensions of which will cover the whole cosmos. Heaven will come down and not only perfectly fill the souls of God's people, but it will fill every part of the new creation because it will be the new creation. Then there will no longer be a need for the church's function as a lampstand, since their role of witnessing to God's light will be finished. They will no longer need to shine God's light in a dark world, since that world will be gone; instead, in the new creation, 'the glory of God' will have 'illumined it, and its lamp [will be] the Lamb' (21:23; so also 22:5). The shining function will have shifted to God and the Lamb, and the saints merely will be reflectors of that glorious light.

Conclusion

In view of the discussion so far in this book, we conclude that God created the cosmos to be his great temple, in which he rested after his creative work. His special revelatory presence, nevertheless, did not yet fill the entire earth because his human vice-regent was to achieve this purpose. God had installed this vice-regent in the garden sanctuary to extend the boundaries of God's presence there worldwide. Adam disobeyed this mandate, so that humanity no longer enjoyed God's presence in the small Garden. As a result, all humanity and all creation became contaminated with sin. Therefore, in view of the storyline of the Bible, the assertions about God's inability to exist in any building on earth include allusion to the old earth and temple not being an adequate abode for him because of being polluted with sin and the need for purification and restoration before God's Shekinah presence, limited to heaven and the holy of holies, could dwell everywhere throughout the cosmos. All human attempts to extend God's presence throughout a sinful earth met with, at best, limited success. The successful fulfilment of the Adamic commission awaited the presence – and obedience – of the last Adam, Jesus Christ.

Thus, the redemptive-historical development may be explained as proceeding from God's unique presence in the structural temple in the

---

[54] Spatafora gives partial confirmation of this idea (1997: 214): although the 'open [heavenly] temple' in Revelation signifies God's greater revelation to and his presence within the church, 'the full vision of divine glory is denied until this age is over'; the church as a 'temple . . . in the world' belongs to the heavenly sphere, but because it 'is still in the world . . . union with God is not total' (1997: 300).

Old Testament to the God-man, Christ, the true temple. As a result of Christ's resurrection, the Spirit continued building the end-time temple, the building materials of which are God's people, thus extending the temple into the new creation in the new age. This building process will culminate in the eternal new heavens and earth as a paradisal city-temple. Or, more briefly, the temple of God has been transformed into God, his people and the rest of the new creation as the temple.[55]

---

[55] This is a paraphrase of the book title of Spatafora 1997.

Chapter Thirteen

Practical reflections on Eden and the temple for the church in the twenty-first century

How does the vision of the worldwide temple in Revelation 21 – 22 relate to Christians and their role in fulfilling the mission of the church? We, as God's people, have already begun to be God's end-time temple where his presence is manifested to the world, and we are to extend the boundaries of the new garden-temple until Christ returns, when, finally, they will be expanded worldwide.

This is just what Ephesians 2:20–22 asserts: the church has 'been built upon the foundation of the apostles and prophets, Christ Jesus Himself being the cornerstone, in whom the whole building, being fitted together is growing into a holy temple in the Lord; in whom you are also being built together into a dwelling of God in the Spirit'. The church is growing and expanding in Christ throughout the present age (cf. also Eph. 4:13–16) in order that God's saving presence and 'the manifold wisdom of God might now be made known' even 'in the heavenly places' (Eph. 3:10). Likewise, quite comparably to Ephesians, after referring to Christ as a 'living stone' (1 Pet. 2:4), Peter alludes to Christians as 'living stones ... being built up as a spiritual house for a holy priesthood' (1 Pet. 2:5) in order to 'proclaim the excellencies' of God (1 Pet. 2:9). In both Ephesians and 1 Peter the church is an expanding, living temple of witness to God's saving presence.[1]

How do we first experience God's presence? By believing in Christ: that he died for our sin, he rose from the dead, and reigns as the Lord God. Then God's Spirit comes into us and dwells in us, in a similar manner as God dwelt in the temple of Eden and Israel's temple.

How do we increase the presence of God in our lives and our churches? How did Adam maintain God's presence in his life before

---

[1] Kline makes almost the same point but on the basis of Zech. 2:11–13 (2001: 91).

the fall? Certainly, remembering, believing and obeying God's word was crucial to a healthy relationship with God.[2] Remember that after God put him into the Garden in Genesis 2:15 'for serving [cultivating] and guarding', he gave Adam a threefold statement to remember by which he would be helped to 'serve and guard' the Garden-temple: in Genesis 2:16–17, God says, 'From any tree of the garden (1) you may eat freely; but (2) from the tree of the knowledge of good and evil you shall not eat, (3) for in the day that you eat from it you shall surely die.' When confronted by the satanic serpent, Eve either failed to remember God's word accurately or intentionally changed it for her own purposes. First, she minimized their privileges by saying merely 'we may eat', whereas God had said 'you may eat *freely*'. Second, Eve minimized the judgment by saying, 'lest you die', whereas God said, 'you shall *surely* die'. Third, she maximized the prohibition by affirming, 'you shall not ... touch it', becoming the first legalist in history (for God had originally said only that they 'shall not eat ... it').[3] Adam and Eve did not remember God's word, and they 'fell', and they failed to extend the boundaries of God's Edenic temple.

Jesus Christ, the Last Adam and true Israel, however, knew the word and, by obeying it, established himself as God's temple. Remember when the devil tried to tempt Christ, in Matthew 4? With each temptation Jesus responded to Satan by quoting from the Old Testament, from passages in Deuteronomy where Moses rebuked Israel for failing in their task. Christ succeeded in just those temptations where Adam and Israel failed because he remembered God's word and obeyed it. Therefore, Christ is the last Adam and true Israel who rules by his word as King over evil in the way Adam and corporate Adam, Israel, should have ruled.

Do we come by faith to God's word daily, as did Jesus, in order that we may be strengthened increasingly with God's presence in order to fulfil our task of spreading that presence to others who don't know Christ? Believers express their identification with Christ's Adamic

---

[2] Before his sin, Adam's trust and obedience either maintained his perfect relationship with God or caused him to grow in that relationship. The latter is more probable, since he was to receive an immortal and glorified body as a reward for his obedience, after his period of 'probation'. Presumably, part of this reward of consummation, among other things, was a fuller experience of God's presence than he had had earlier (for the escalated blessings Adam was to receive, see further, Beale 1997: 49). In this respect, though Adam had not yet sinned, there is overlap with the experience of believers, who grow in their relationship with God.

[3] See Ross 1988: 134–135. Ross has noticed these three changes in the original wording of Gen. 2:16–17.

kingship when they spread the presence of God by living for Christ and speaking his word and unbelievers accept it, and Satan's victorious hold on their heart is broken.

In addition to knowing and obeying God's word, Solomon's dedication of his temple underscores prayer as a crucial function in relation to the temple (1 Kgs. 8:23–53). Solomon repeatedly makes the point that, in response to various circumstances, Israel was to 'pray toward this place [the temple]', and he petitions God 'hear Thou in heaven, Thy dwelling place; hear and forgive' (1 Kgs. 8:30; so likewise 8:38–39, 42–43). In fact, the mention of 'prayer' or 'supplication' recurs constantly throughout the narrative (vv. 28, 29, 30, 33, 35, 38, 42, 44, 47, 48, 49, 52).[4] The reason prayers were to be directed specifically to the earthly temple and not directly to God in heaven was because, as we have often seen throughout the present study, God's presence in the heavenly temple extended to the holy of holies. This is what Solomon appeals to when he recalls that God had said, '"My name shall be there," to listen to the prayer which Thy servant shall pray toward this place' (1 Kgs. 8:29; so also 1 Maccabees 7:37). God's name represented his character and his presence. Thus, not merely were priests to offer up prayers in the temple precincts but certainly all Israelites, whether in the temple's outer court or elsewhere in the land or in territories outside Israel in exile, were to pray towards the earthly temple, where God's presence dwelt.

This role of prayer is enhanced for Christians who now are identified with Jesus through the Spirit as part of the end-time temple. From one perspective, all believers are priests and they function as priests by offering up prayers in the sphere of the spiritual temple. But saints are also true Israelites who are in exile because they still exist in the exile of this old, fallen world. At the end, this old world will be destroyed, and a new world will be created in which God's people will be resurrected, completely restored to God, and consummately delivered from exile. They will take their place as the crown of the eschatological creation in Christ, the Last Adam. They will all be high priests, dwelling eternally in the new creational holy of holies and in the midst of God's full latter-day presence. Until then, however, we pray as new covenant priests in the New Testament equivalent of the holy place, which is a spiritual sphere of our ministry and witness as a lampstand in the world. We also pray as exiled new Israelites, as we

---

[4] Levenson (1981: 164), who has drawn my attention to this particular focus on the temple.

live as pilgrims on the old, fallen earth. In both cases, our prayer is directed towards God in his heavenly holy of holies, until it descends to fill and encompass the new earth. Prayer as an activity inextricably linked to the temple is what is behind Jesus' words in Matthew 18:19–20:[5] 'Again I say to you, that if two of you agree on earth about anything that they may ask, it shall be done for them by My Father who is in heaven. For where two or three have gathered together in My name, there I am in their midst.'

Isaiah 56:7 says that the latter-day temple 'will be called a house of prayer for all the peoples'. Jesus rejects Israel's temple because it was not performing that role and because Jews believed the temple signified only their election from among all the nations of the earth (on which see the earlier discussion in ch. 5 of Matt. 21:13; Mark 11:17; Luke 19:46). Those who are a part of the temple today will demonstrate their participation in it by being continually prayerful.[6] If in the Old Testament prayer was considered 'like incense' and 'like an evening grain offering' (Ps. 141:2; cf. also Ps. 119:108),[7] how much more is that the case in the new age.

In summary, all Christians are now spiritual Levitical priests (in fulfilment of Is. 66:21). Our ongoing task is to serve God in his temple in which we always dwell and of which we are a part. Our continual priestly tasks are what the first Adam's were to be: to keep the order and peace of the spiritual sanctuary by learning and teaching God's word, by praying always, and by being vigilant in keeping out unclean moral and spiritual things.[8] We also continually offer sacrifices in order to keep the order of the spiritual temple's liturgy. The prayers of saints are now the 'incense' offerings given to God (Rev. 5:8; 8:3–5) that replace the old incense offerings made at the altar of burnt offering and the altar of incense in the holy place (e.g., 1 Chr. 6:49). As we saw above, already in Israel there was a sense in which 'prayer' was 'counted as incense before' God (Ps. 141:2). The Old Testament anticipated a time when incense offerings would be made to God 'in every place' (Mal. 1:11).

The essential sacrifice we offer is our own body, which is 'a living and holy sacrifice, well-pleasing to God', which is our 'spiritual

---

[5] Levenson (1981: 165), who makes almost the identical application to the Christian community; likewise, Marshall 1989: 211.

[6] See Heil 1997 for an excellent study of prayer being one of the key activities of those composing the end-time temple.

[7] See Haran (1988: 22), who brought these verses to my attention.

[8] For the latter idea, cf. 1 Cor. 6:18–19; 2 Cor. 6:14 – 7:1; note also *2 Clement* 9:3: 'We must, therefore, guard the flesh as a temple of God'; so likewise Ignatius, *Letter to the Philadelphians* 7:2; cf. *Barnabas* 4:11.

service of worship' (Rom. 12:1). In so doing, we follow our Saviour's example, who 'gave Himself up for us, an offering and a sacrifice to God as a fragrant aroma' (Eph. 5:2). As Jesus, when we are loyal to our covenantal relationship to God and suffer for our faith, we are offering ourselves as a sacrifice on an altar to God.[9] Hosea 6:6–7 says, 'I delight in loyalty rather than sacrifice, and in the knowledge of God rather than burnt offerings.[10] But like Adam[11] they have transgressed the covenant.' Possibly, pre-fall humanity was to offer such spiritual sacrifices, and Israel's offering of animal sacrifices in a post-fall world indicated not only their willingness to give themselves whole-heartedly to God but foreshadowed the return to spiritual sacrifices only, in the future Eden.[12] We even offer a well-pleasing sacrifice when we confess our sins and so humble ourselves before God: 'The sacrifices of God are a broken spirit;/A broken and a contrite heart, O God, Thou wilt not despise' (Ps. 51:17).[13]

The nature of our sacrifices as obedient Adamic-like priests is vitally linked to the idea of expanding the sacred sphere of God's presence in order that others would experience it and come into the sacred temple themselves. Believers are priests in that they serve as mediators between God and the unbelieving world. When unbelievers accept the church's mediating witness, they not only come into God's presence, but they begin to participate themselves as mediating priests who witness. As priests, we should make sure that we ourselves are growing in the experience of the divine presence. When we do not compromise our faith and relationship in God's presence and, consequently, suffer for our unswerving commitment, we are

[9] As we have seen above in Rev. 11:1–4, especially in light of Rev. 6:9–10; likewise, Heb. 13:10–13.

[10] See also 1QS 9.4–5, which is comparable to Hosea and explains that the members of the Qumran community did not offer animal sacrifices, but spiritual ones: 'they shall expiate guilty rebellion and sinful infidelity and (procure) loving-kindness upon earth without the flesh of burnt offering and the fat of sacrifice, but the offering of the lips in accordance with the law shall be an agreeable odour of righteousness, and perfection of way shall be as the voluntary gift of a delectable oblation'. Qumran did this because they had rejected the Jerusalem temple and its sacrifices as profane because of the unbelief and apostasy of the leaders and priests of Israel, believing that they were now the true faithful remnant of God's people.

[11] See ch. 5 ('The "already and not yet" fulfilment of the end-time temple in Christ and his people: the Gospels'), p. 178, for discussion of the translation 'Adam' here.

[12] *Pirke Rabbi Eliezer* 12 adduces Hos. 6:6 in saying that loyal love was a trait characteristic of the period before Adam's sin and that it was preferable to Israel's later sacrificial offerings.

[13] See also Ps. 40:6; Heb. 10:5–8. Cf. the similar idea in the Dead Sea Scrolls: *More Psalms of David* 154 (11Qps^a 154 = 11Q5 18.9–11).

sacrificing ourselves. It is this very sacrifice that God has designed in the new temple to be the means to move unbelievers to believe the church's testimony and to begin to experience God's presence themselves. The 'two witnesses' in Revelation 11 offer themselves as sacrifices by suffering for their faith *as they go throughout the world* and are rejected because of their testimony to Christ.

This is why whenever Paul speaks of being a sacrifice, without exception he is referring to his ministry of furthering his witness to unbelieving Gentiles. For example, Paul says he is 'a minister of Christ Jesus to the Gentiles, ministering as a priest the gospel of God, in order that my offering of the Gentiles might become acceptable' to God (Rom. 15:16). Paul and his fellow-workers are a sacrifice of a 'sweet aroma' and 'fragrance ... leading to God among those who are being saved', resulting in 'life'. That 'aroma' is none other ultimately than the glorious presence of God that Moses had experienced in the tabernacle (see 2 Cor. 3:12–18)! That divine presence is seen clearly in, among other things, the midst of suffering for the faith and not compromising (e.g., 2 Cor. 4:7–18; 12:9–10). No doubt, believers who have followed Paul's priestly lead have played their part in contributing to the church's effective mission throughout the ages, which is characterized by the saying 'the blood of the martyrs is the seed of the church'.

Furthermore, the church's support of others to go out and spread the gospel is also considered a 'sacrifice'. Paul said that the Philippians' financial support given to him during his 'first preaching of the gospel' in Thessalonica was 'a fragrant aroma, an acceptable sacrifice, well-pleasing to God' (Phil. 4:15–18). Even Paul's ministry of building up other believers in the faith, he believed, was 'pouring out' a 'drink offering on the sacrifice and service of' their faith (Phil. 2:17; so also 2 Tim. 4:6). He says elsewhere that persevering faithfulness in ministry for the upbuilding of the faith of others was tantamount to building up the temple on the foundation of Christ (1 Cor. 3:5–17).

Thus, extending the boundaries of the temple by witnessing and strengthening those receiving the witness is a priestly sacrifice and offering to God. God's presence grows among his priestly people by their knowing his word, believing it and by obeying it, and then they spread that presence to others by living their lives faithfully and prayerfully in the world. For example, a persevering and joyous faith in the midst of trial is an amazing priestly witness to the unbelieving world. It gets the world's attention. Such a witness either sparks more persecution or it influences some who persecute to join the church. This is what 'missions' is all about.

One summer my wife and I bought a 'Rose of Sharon' bush and planted it on the north side of our house. The bush was supposed to grow to about six feet high and four feet wide and bear flowers. After a few months, however, we noticed that our bush was not growing at all, though it had began to produce buds. The buds, however, never opened into full flowers. The problem was that our bush was not getting enough sunlight. If we did not transplant it, the bush would not grow to its normal size and it would not produce any flowers. Likewise, we as the church will not bear fruit and grow and extend across the earth in the way God intends unless we stay out of the shadows of the world and remain in the light of God's presence – in his word and prayer and in fellowship with other believers in the church, the temple of God. The mark of the true church is an expanding witness to the presence of God: first to our families, then to others in the church, then to our neighbourhood, then to our city, then the country and ultimately the whole earth.

May God give us grace to go out into the world as his extending temple and spread God's presence by reflecting it until it finally fills the entire earth, as it will according to Revelation 21 – 22. Jeremiah 3:16–17 says that in the end-time, people 'will no longer say "the ark of the … Lord [in Israel's old temple]." And it shall not come to mind, nor shall they remember it,' because the end-time temple that will encompass the new creation will be incomparable to the old temple.

I have heard it said that if you catch a small shark, it will stay a size proportionate to the aquarium that you put it in. Sharks can be six inches long yet fully matured at that size. But if you turn them loose in the ocean, they grow to their normal length of eight feet. We as individual Christians, as members of a local church and as part of Christ's church throughout the world must not merely share our lives and God's word with one another, but we need to get out of our own little fishbowls and manifest the presence of Christ through our words and lives, so that the boundaries of the temple, the church, will grow until the whole earth is encompassed with and manifests the presence of God.[14] Through us God will fulfil his promise in Habakkuk 2:14, 'For the earth will be filled/With the knowledge of the glory of the Lord,/As the waters cover the sea.' The mark of the true church is always to be outward-looking and expanding God's presence and not obsessively introspective.

---

[14] See Larson 1993: 93, from which the shark illustration was taken.

The main point of this book is that *our task as the covenant community, the church is to be God's temple, so filled with his glorious presence that we expand and fill the earth with that presence until God finally accomplishes the goal completely at the end of time!* This is our common mission. May the church of the twenty-first century unite in order to attain this goal. Then, may the church, the true Israel and true temple, experience the priestly blessing pronounced on Israel from the tabernacle, as it extends God's tabernacling presence:

> The LORD bless you, and keep you;
> The LORD make His face shine on you,
> And be gracious to you;
> The LORD lift up His countenance on you,
> And give you peace.
>
> (Num. 6:24–26)[15]

The psalmist understands this very blessing from the book of Numbers to have a worldwide goal:

> God be gracious to us and bless us,
> And cause His face to shine upon us
> Selah.
> That Thy way may be known on the earth,
> Thy salvation among all nations.
> Let the peoples praise Thee, O God;
> Let all the peoples praise Thee.
> Let the nations be glad and sing for joy;
> For Thou wilt judge the peoples with uprightness,
> And guide the nations on the earth.
> Selah.
> Let the peoples praise Thee, O God;
> Let all the peoples praise Thee.
> The earth has yielded its produce;
> God, our God, blesses us.
> God blesses us,
> That all the ends of the earth may fear Him.
>
> (Ps. 67:1–7)

---

[15] Not coincidentally, this blessing was apparently first pronounced 'on the day that Moses had finished setting up the tabernacle' (Num. 7:1), which further suggests that the blessing at that time was God's glorious presence that dwelt in the tabernacle. This presence now blesses those who are a part of 'the temple of God' in Christ and the Spirit.

Bibliography

Alexander, R. (1986), *Ezekiel*, EBC, Grand Rapids: Zondervan.

Allison, D. C. (1993), *The New Moses*, Minneapolis: Fortress.

Andersen, F. I. and D. N. Freedman (1980), *Hosea*, AB 24, New York: Doubleday.

Anderson, G. A. and M. E. Stone (eds.) (1994), *A Synopsis of the Books of Adam and Eve*, SBL Early Judaism and its Literature, 05, Atlanta: Scholars Press.

Attridge, H. W. (1989), *The Epistle to the Hebrews*, Philadelphia: Fortress.

Averbeck, R. E. (2000), 'The Cylinders of Gudea (2.155)', in W. W. Hallo and K. Lawson Younger (eds.), *The Context of Scripture* II, Leiden/Boston/Cologne: Brill, 418–433.

Bachmann, M. (1994), 'Himmlisch: der "Tempel Gottes von Apk 11.1"', *NTS* 40, 474–480.

Bailey, K. (1990–91), 'The Fall of Jerusalem and Mark's Account of the Cross', *ExpT* 102, 102–105.

Barker, M. (1991), *The Gate of Heaven*, London: SPCK.

Barrett, C. K. (1994), *A Critical and Exegetical Commentary on the Acts of the Apostles*, Vol. 1, ICC, Edinburgh: T. & T. Clark.

Barrois, G. A. (1980), *Jesus Christ and the Temple*, Crestwood, NY: St Vladimir's Seminary Press.

Bauckham, R. (1993), *The Climax of Prophecy*, Edinburgh: T. & T. Clark.

————(1995), 'James and the Jerusalem Church', in R. Bauckham (ed.), *The Book of Acts in Its Palestinian Setting*, The Book of Acts in Its First Century Setting 4, Grand Rapids: Eerdmans; Carlisle: Paternoster, 452–462.

Bauer, W., F. W. Gingrich, W. F. Arndt and F. W. Danker (1979), *A Greek-English Lexicon of the New Testament*, 2nd ed., Chicago: Chicago University Press.

Bauer, W., F. W. Danker, W. F. Arndt and F. W. Gingrich (2000), *A Greek-English Lexicon of the New Testament and Other Early Christian Literature*, 3rd ed., Chicago: Chicago University Press.

Baumgarten, J. M. (1989), '4Q500 and the Ancient Conception of the Lord's Vineyard', *JJS* 40, 1–6.

Beale, G. K. (1989a), 'Did Jesus and His Followers Preach the Right Doctrine From the Wrong Texts? An Examination of the Pre-suppositions of the Apostles' Exegetical Method', *Them* 14, 89–96.

——— (1989b), 'The Old Testament Background of Reconciliation in 2 Corinthians 5 – 7 and Its Bearing on the Literary Problem of 2 Corinthians 6:14–18', *NTS* 35, 550–581.

——— (1996), 'The Old Testament Background of Revelation 3:14', *NTS* 42, 133–152.

——— (1997), 'The Eschatological Conception of New Testament Theology', in K. E. Brower and M. W. Elliott (eds.), *'The Reader Must Understand': Eschatology in Bible and Theology*, Leicester: Apollos, 11–52.

——— (1998), *John's Use of the Old Testament in Revelation*, JSNTS 166, Sheffield: Sheffield Academic Press.

——— (1999a), *The Book of Revelation*, NIGTC, Grand Rapids: Eerdmans.

——— (1999b), 'Questions of Authorial Intent, Epistemology, and Presuppositions and Their Bearing on the Study of the Old Testament in the New: A Rejoinder to Steve Moyise', *IBS* 21, 1–26.

——— (1999c), 'Peace and Mercy Upon the Israel of God: The Old Testament Background of Galatians 6, 16b', *Bib* 81, 204–223.

——— (2003), *1 – 2 Thessalonians*, IVPNTC, Leicester: IVP; Downers Grove: IVP.

——— (2004), 'The Final Vision of the Apocalypse and its Implications for a Biblical Theology of the Temple', in S. Gathercole and T. D. Alexander (eds.), *Heaven on Earth*, Carlisle: Paternoster.

——— (forthcoming, c. 2006), 'The Old Testament in Colossians', in G. K. Beale and D. A. Carson (eds.), *Commentary on the Use of the Old Testament in the New*, Grand Rapids: Baker.

Beasley-Murray, G. R. (1987), *John*, WBC 36, Waco, TX: Word Books.

Beckerleg, C. (1999), 'The Creation, Animation and Installation of Adam in Genesis 2:7–25', SBLA, 310.

Best, E. (1972), *The First and Second Epistles to the Thessalonians*, Black's NT Commentary, Peabody, MA: Hendrickson.

Betz, O. (1963), 'Der Katechon', *NTS* 9, 282–284.

Black, M. (1985), *The Book of Enoch or 1 Enoch*, SVTP 7, Leiden: Brill, 38–39.

Blenkinsopp, J. (1992), *The Pentateuch*, New York: Doubleday.

Bloch-Smith, E. (1994), ' "Who is the King of Glory?" Solomon's Temple and Its Symbolism', in M. D. Coogan, J. C. Exum and L. E. Stager (eds.), *Scripture and Other Artifacts*, Louisville: Westminster John Knox, 183–194.

Block, D. I. (1998), *The Book of Ezekiel*, NICOT, Grand Rapids: Eerdmans.

Bock, D. L. (1996), *Luke 9:51 – 24:53*, BECNT, Grand Rapids: Baker.

Bohak, G. (1997), *Joseph and Aseneth and the Jewish Temple in Heliopolis*, SBLEJL 10, Atlanta: Scholars Press.

Botterweck, G. J. and H. Ringren (eds.) (1978), *Theological Dictionary of the Old Testament*, 4 vols., Grand Rapids: Eerdmans.

Branham, J. R. (1995), 'Vicarious Sacrality: Temple Space in Ancient Synagogues', in D. Urman and P. V. M. Flesher (eds.), *Ancient Synagogues*, Vol. 2, SPB 47, Leiden: Brill, 319–345.

Braude, W. G. (ed.) (1968), *Pesikta Rabbati*, Yale Judaica Series 18: 1 and 2, New Haven and London: Yale University Press.

———(1976), *The Midrash on Psalms*, Yale Judaica Series 13:1–2, New Haven: Yale University Press.

Braude, W. G. and I. J. Kapstein (eds.) (1975), *The Pesikta de-rab Kahana*, Philadelphia: Jewish Publication Society of America.

———(1981), *Tanna debe Eliyyahu*, Philadelphia: Jewish Publication Society of America.

Braun, M. A. (1977), 'James' Use of Amos at the Jerusalem Council: Steps Toward a Possible Solution of the Textual and Theological Problems', *JETS* 20, 113–121.

Breasted, J. H. (1906), *Ancient Records of Egypt*, 4 vols., New York: Russell & Russell.

———(1959), *Development of Religion and Thought in Ancient Egypt*, New York/Evanston: Harper & Row.

Brooke, G. J. (1999), 'Miqdash Adam, Eden, and the Qumran Community', in B. Ego, A. Lange and P. Pilhofer (eds.), *Gemeinde ohne Tempel/Community Without Temple*, WUNT 118, Tübingen, Mohr Siebeck.

Broshi, M. (1987), 'The Gigantic Dimensions of the Visionary Temple in the Temple Scroll', *BAR* 13.6, 36–37.

Brown, F., S. R. Driver and C. A. Briggs (1907), *A Hebrew and English Lexicon of the Old Testament*, Oxford: Clarendon.

Brown, R. E. (1982), *The Epistles of John*, AB, Garden City, NY: Doubleday.

Brown, William P. (1999), *The Ethos of the Cosmos*, Grand Rapids: Eerdmans.
Bruce, F. F. (1954), *The Book of Acts*, NICNT, Grand Rapids: Baker.
——— (1982), *1 & 2 Thessalonians*, WBC 45, Waco, TX: Word.
——— (1990), *The Epistle to the Hebrews*, NICNT, Grand Rapids: Eerdmans.
Bryan, B. M. (2002), '47 Pectoral of Psusennes I', in E. Hornung and B. M. Bryan (eds.), *The Quest for Immortality: Treasures of Ancient Egypt*, Washington, DC: National Gallery of Art and United Exhibits Group.
Bryan, S. M. (2002), *Jesus and Israel's Traditions of Judgment and Restoration*, SNTSMS 117, Cambridge: Cambridge University Press.
——— (forthcoming), 'The Eschatological Temple in John 14'.
Budge, E. A. (1951), *Book of the Dead*, New York: Barnes & Noble.
Bultmann, R. *'alētheia, alēthinos, ktl.'*, *TDNT*, 1:238–251.
Caird, G. B. (1966), *A Commentary of the Revelation of St. John the Divine*, London: A. C. Black; New York: Harper & Row.
Callender, D. (2000), *Adam in Myth and History*, Harvard Semitic Museum Publications, Winona Lake, IN: Eisenbrauns.
Callow, J. (1982), *A Semantic Structural Analysis of Second Thessalonians*, Dallas, TX: Summer Institute of Linguistics.
Calvin, J. (1984), *Commentaries on the Epistles of Paul the Apostle to the Galatians, Ephesians, Philippians, Colossians, and 1 & 2 Thessalonians, 1 & 2 Timothy, Titus, Philemon*, Grand Rapids: Baker.
Caragounis, C. C. (1990), *Peter and the Rock*, BZNW 58, Berlin: de Gruyter.
Carroll, R. (2000), 'Blessing the Nations: Toward a Biblical Theology of Mission from Genesis', *BBR* 10, 17–34.
Carson, D. A. (1991), *The Gospel According to John*, Grand Rapids: Eerdmans.
——— (1995), *Matthew*, EBC, Grand Rapids: Zondervan.
——— (1996), *The Gagging of God*, Grand Rapids, Zondervan.
Carson, D. A., Douglas J. Moo and Leon Morris (1992), *An Introduction to the New Testament*, Grand Rapids: Zondervan.
Cassuto, U. (1967), *A Commentary on the Book of Exodus*, Jerusalem: Magnes Press.
——— (1989), *A Commentary on the Book of Genesis*, 1, Jerusalem: Magnes Press.
——— (1992), *A Commentary on the Book of Genesis*, 2, Jerusalem: Magnes Press.

Charles, R. H. (ed.) (1977), *The Apocrypha and Pseudepigrapha of the Old Testament*, Vol. 2 (Pseudepigrapha), Oxford: Clarendon.

Charlesworth, J. H. (ed.) (1983), *The Old Testament Pseudepigrapha*, 2 vols., Garden City, NY: Doubleday.

Chronis, H. (1982), 'The Torn Veil: Cultus and Christology in Mark', *JBL* 101, 97–114.

Clements, R. E. (1965), *God and Temple*, Philadelphia: Fortress.

Clifford, R. J. (1984), 'The Temple and the Holy Mountain', in T. G. Madsen (ed.), *The Temple in Antiquity*, RSMS 9, Salt Lake City, UT: Brigham Young University Press, 112–115.

——— (1994), 'Creation Accounts in the Ancient Near East and in the Bible', CBQMS 26, Washington, DC: Catholic University Press of America.

Clowney, E. P. (1972), 'The Final Temple', *WTJ* 35, 156–189.

Cody, A. (1960), *Heavenly Sanctuary and Liturgy in the Epistle to the Hebrews*, St Meinrad, IN: Grail Publications (St Meinard Archabbey).

Cohen, A. (ed.) (1965), *The Minor Tractates of the Talmud*, 2 vols., London: Soncino.

Cohen, J. (1989), *Be Fertile and Increase, Fill the Earth and Master It*, Ithaca, NY, and London: Cornell University Press.

Cole, A. (1950), *The New Temple*, London: Tyndale.

Collins, J. J. (1993), *Daniel*, Minneapolis: Fortress.

Congar, Y. M.-J. (1962), *The Mystery of the Temple*, Westminster, MD: Newman Press.

Cornelius, I. (1997), '*gan*', in W. A. VanGemeren (ed.), *NIDOTTE*, Grand Rapids: Zondervan.

Court, J. M. (1979), *Myth and History in the Book of Revelation*, Atlanta: John Knox.

Cross, F. M. (1977), 'The Priestly Tabernacle in the Light of Recent Research', in A. Biran (ed.), *Temples and High Places*, Jerusalem: Nelson Glueck School of Biblical Archaeology of Hebrew Union College–Jewish Institute of Religion, 169–180.

Dalley, S. (1991), *Myths from Mesopotamia*, Oxford: Oxford University Press.

Danby, H. (ed.) (1980), *The Mishnah*, Oxford: Oxford University Press.

Daniélou, J. (1964), *Primitive Christian Symbols*, London: Burns & Oates.

Davidson, R. M. (2000), 'Cosmic Metanarrative for the Coming Millennium', *JATS* 11, 109–111.

Davies, G. I. (1991), 'The Presence of God in the Second Temple and

Rabbinic Doctrine', in W. Horbury (ed.), *Templum Amicitiae* JSNTS 48, Sheffield: Sheffield Academic Press.

Davies, W. D. and D. C. Allison (1991), *The Gospel According to Saint Matthew*, Vol. 2, ICC, Edinburgh: T. & T. Clark.

Davila, J. R. (2002), 'The Macrocosmic Temple, Scriptural Exegesis, and the Songs of the Sabbath Sacrifice', *DSD* 9, 5–6.

de Silva, A. A. (1994), 'A Comparison between the Three-Levelled World of the Old Testament Temple Building Narratives and the Three-Levelled World of the House Building Motif in the Ugaritic Texts KTU 1.3 and 1.4', in G. J. Brooke, A. H. W. Curites and J. F. Healey (eds.), *Ugarit and the Bible*, Münster: Ugarit-Verlag, 11–23.

de Vaux, R. (1965), *Ancient Israel*, New York: McGraw-Hill.

Dillard, R. B. (2000), 'Intrabiblical Exegesis and the Effusion of the Spirit in Joel', in H. Griffith and J. R. Muether (eds.), *Creator Redeemer Consummator, Festschrift for M. G. Kline*, Greenville, SC: Reformed Academic Press.

Dillmann, A. (1892), *Genesis: Critically and Exegetically Expounded*, Vols. 1–2, 6th ed., Edinburgh: T. & T. Clark.

Douglas, J. D. (ed.) (1980), *The Illustrated Bible Dictionary*, 3 vols., Leicester: IVP.

Douglas, M. (1999), *Leviticus as Literature*, Oxford: Oxford University Press.

Driver, S. R. (1904), *The Book of Genesis*, WC, London: Methuen.

Duguid, I. M. (1999), *Ezekiel*, NIVAC, Grand Rapids: Zondervan.

Dumbrell, William J. (1985), *The End of the Beginning*, Homebush West, Australia: Lancer.

——— (1994), *The Search for Order*, Grand Rapids: Baker.

——— (2002), 'Genesis 2:1–17: A Foreshadowing of the New Creation', in Scott J. Hafemann (ed.), *Biblical Theology: Retrospect and Prospect*, Downers Grove: IVP, 53–65.

Dupont-Sommer, Andre (1961), *The Essene Writings From Qumran*, Oxford: Blackwell.

Edersheim, A. (1994), *The Temple*, Peabody, MA: Hendrickson.

Ego, B. (1989), 'Im Himmel wie auf Erden', WUNT 2.34, Tübingen: Mohr Siebeck.

Eichrodt, W. (1970), *Ezekiel*, Philadelphia: Westminster.

Eliade, M. (1955), *The Myth of the Eternal Return*, London: Routledge.

Ellingworth, P. (1993), *Commentary on Hebrews*, NIGTC, Grand Rapids: Eerdmans.

Ellis, E. E. (1959–60), 'II Corinthians V.1–10 in Pauline Eschatology', *NTS* 6, 211–224.

———— (1994), 'Deity-Christology in Mark 14:58', in J. B. Green and M. Turner (eds.), *Jesus of Nazareth: Lord and Christ*, Grand Rapids: Eerdmans, 192–203.

Ellison, H. L. (1956), *Ezekiel: The Man and His Message*, London: Paternoster.

Epstein, I. (ed.) (1948), *The Babylonian Talmud*, London: Soncino.

Ernst, J. (1967), *Die eschatologischen Gegenspieler in den Schriften des Neuen Testaments*, Regensburg: Pustet.

Etheridge, J. W. (1968), *The Targums of Onkelos and Jonathan Ben Uzziel on the Pentateuch with Fragments of the Jerusalem Targum, on Genesis and Exodus*, New York: KTAV.

Evans, C. A. (2001), *Mark 8:27 – 16:20*, WBC 34B, Nashville, TN: Nelson.

Fairbairn, P. (1863a), *The Typology of Scripture*, New York: Tibbals.

———— (1863b), *Ezekiel*, Edinburgh: T. & T. Clark.

Fathers According to Rabbi Nathan, The (1955), translated by J. Goldin, New York: Schocken Books.

Faulkner, R. O. (1969), *The Ancient Egyptian Pyramid Texts*, Oxford: Oxford University Press.

Fee, G. D. (1987), *The First Epistle to the Corinthians*, NICNT, Grand Rapids: Eerdmans.

Feinberg, C. L. (1971), 'The Rebuilding of the Temple', in C. F. H. Henry (ed.), *Prophecy in the Making*, Carol Stream, IL: Creation House.

Feinberg, P. D. (1995), '2 Thessalonians 2 and the Rapture?', in T. Ice and T. Denny (eds.), *When the Trumpet Sounds*, Eugene, OR: Harvest House.

Fekkes, J. (1994), 'Isaiah and Prophetic Traditions in the Book of Revelation: Visionary Antecedents and their Development', JSNTS 93, Sheffield: JSOT Press, 130–133.

Findlay, G. G. (1982; 1904), *The Epistles of Paul the Apostle to the Thessalonians*, Grand Rapids: Baker.

Finnestad, R. B. (1997), 'Temples of the Ptolemaic and Roman Periods: Ancient Traditions in New Contexts', in B. E. Shafer (ed.), *Temples of Ancient Egypt*, Ithaca, NY: Cornell University Press, 185–237.

Fishbane, M. (1979), *Text and Texture*, New York: Schoken.

Fitzmyer, J. A. (1985), *The Gospel According to Luke (10–24)*, AB 28A, Garden City, NY: Doubleday.

———— (1998), *The Acts of the Apostles*, AB 31, New York: Doubleday.

Fletcher-Lewis, C. H. T. (1997), 'The Destruction of the Temple and Relativization of the Old Covenant: Mark 13:31 and Matthew 5:18', in K. E. Brower and M. W. Elliott (eds.), *The Reader Must Understand': Eschatology in Bible and Theology*, Leicester: Apollos, 156–162.

Ford, J. M. (1975), *Revelation*, AB 33, Garden City, NY: Doubleday.

Foster, B. (1995), *From Distant Days*, Bethesda: CDL Press.

———(1997), 'Epic of Creation (1.111)', in W. W. Hallo (ed.), *The Context of Scripture* 1, Leiden/Boston/Cologne: Brill.

Frame, J. E. (1912), *A Critical and Exegetical Commentary on the Epistles of St. Paul to the Thessalonians*, ICC, Edinburgh: T. & T. Clark.

France, R. T. (1971), *Jesus and the Old Testament*, Grand Rapids: Baker.

———(1985), *Matthew*, TNTC, Grand Rapids: Eerdmans; Leicester: IVP.

Frankfort, H. (1954), *The Art and Architecture of the Ancient Orient*, Harmondsworth, Middlesex: Penguin.

Freedman, H. and M. Simon (eds.) (1961), *Midrash Rabbah*, Vols. 1–10, London: Soncino.

Friedlander, G. (ed.) (1916), *Pirke de Rabbi Eliezer*, New York: Hermon.

Gage, W. Austin (1984), *The Gospel of Genesis*, Winona Lake, IN: Eisenbrauns.

Gamberoni, J. '*Māqôm*', *TDOT*, 8:532–544.

Gärtner, B. (1965), *The Temple and the Community in Qumran and the New Testament*, SNTS 1, Cambridge: Cambridge University Press.

Gaster, Theodor (1976), *The Dead Sea Scriptures*, Garden City, NY: Anchor Books.

Gaston, L. (1967), 'The Theology of the Temple', in F. Christ (ed.), *Oikonomia*, FS for Oscar Cullmann, Hamburg-Bergstadt: Herbert Reich Evang. Verlag GmbH.

George, A. R. (1993), *House Most High*, Winona Lake, IN: Eisenbrauns.

Gesenius, W., E. Kautzsch and A. E. Cowley (1970), *Hebrew Grammar*, Oxford: Clarendon.

Giblin, C. H. (1967), *The Threat to Faith*, An Bib 31, Rome: Pontifical Biblical Institute.

———(1984), 'Revelation 11.1–13: Its Form, Function, and Contextual Integration', *NTS* 30, 433–459.

———(1990), '2 Thessalonians 2 Re-read as Pseudepigraphical: A Revised Reaffirmation of *The Threat to Faith*', in R. F. Collins (ed.), *The Thessalonian Correspondence*, BETL 87, Leuven: University Press.

Gleason, K. (1997), 'Gardens in Preclassical Times', in E. Meyers (ed.), *Oxford Encyclopedia of Archaeology in the Near East*, New York: Oxford University Press.

Glickman, S. C. (1980), *Knowing Christ*, Chicago: Moody.

Goldsworthy, G. (1991), *According to Plan*, Leicester: IVP.

Goppelt, '*topos, ktl.*', *TDNT*, 8:246–259.

Gorman, F. (1990), *The Ideology of Ritual*, JSOTS 91, Sheffield: JSOT Press.

Grayson, A. K. (1976), *Assyrian Royal Inscriptions* 2, Wiesbaden: Otto Harrassowitz.

———(1987), *Assyrian Rulers of the Third and Second Millennia BC The Royal Inscriptions of Mesopotamia, Assyrian Periods* 1, Toronto: University of Toronto Press.

———(1996), *Assyrian Rulers of the Early First Millennium BC:* Toronto: University of Toronto Press.

Greenberg, M. (1997), *Ezekiel 21 – 37*, AB 22a, New York: Doubleday.

Grudem, W. A. (1982), *The Gift of Prophecy in 1 Corinthians*, Washington, DC: University Press of America.

Gruenler, R. G. (1991), *Meaning and Understanding*, Grand Rapids: Zondervan.

Gundry, R. H. (1993), *Mark*, Grand Rapids: Eerdmans.

Gunkel, H. (1997), *Genesis*, Macon, GA: Mercer University Press.

Gurtner, D. M. (2003), 'Functionality, Identity, and Interpretation: the Tearing of the Temple Curtain (Matt. 27:51 par) in Light of Pentateuchal Tabernacle Texts', a paper delivered at the 2003 Annual Meeting of the Evangelical Theological Society in Atlanta, GA.

Hafemann, S. J. (2000), *2 Corinthians*, NIVAC, Grand Rapids: Zondervan.

———(2001), *The God of Promise and the Life of Faith*, Wheaton: Crossway.

Hagner, D. A. (1995), *Matthew 14 – 28*, WBC 33b, Dallas, TX: Word.

Hallo, W. W. and K. Lawson Younger (eds.) (1997, 2000), *The Context of Scripture*, 2 vols., Leiden/Boston/Cologne: Brill.

Hamann, H. (1953), 'A Brief Exegesis of 2 Thess. 2:1–12 with Guideline for the Application of the Prophecy Contained Therein', *CTM* 24, 418–433.

Hammer, R. (ed.) (1986), *Sifre: A Tannaitic Commentary on the Book of Deuteronomy*, Yale Judaica Series, New Haven and London: Yale University Press.

Haran, M. (1978), *Temples and Temple Service in Ancient Israel*, Oxford: Clarendon.

——— (1988), 'Temple and Community in Ancient Israel', in M. V. Fox (ed.), *Temple in Society*, Winona Lake, IN: Eisenbrauns, 17–25.

Hartman, L. (1966), *Prophecy Interpreted*, CB, NT Series 1, Lund: Gleerup.

Hartopo, Y. A. (2002), 'The Marriage of the Lamb: The Background and Function of the Marriage Imagery in the Book of Revelation', PhD dissertation, Westminster Theological Seminary.

Hayward, C. T. R. (1991), 'Sacrifice and World Order: Some Observations on Ben Sira's Attitude to the Temple Service', in S. W. Sykes (ed.), *Sacrifice and Redemption*, Cambridge: Cambridge University Press, 22–34.

——— (1996), *The Jewish Temple*, London/New York: Routledge.

——— (1999), 'Sirach and Wisdom's Dwelling Place', in S. C. Barton (ed.), *Where Shall Wisdom Be Found?*, Edinburgh: T. & T. Clark, 31–46.

Heidel, A. (1942), *The Babylonian Genesis*, Chicago/London: University of Chicago.

Heil, J. P. (1997), 'The Narrative Strategy and Pragmatics of the Temple Theme in Mark', *CBQ* 59, 76–100.

Hemer, C. J. (1990), *The Book of Acts in the Setting of Hellenistic History*, Winona Lake, IN: Eisenbrauns.

Hendel, R. (1998), *The Text of Genesis 1 – 11*, New York: Oxford University Press.

Hendriksen, W. (1979), *Exposition of I and II Thessalonians*, Grand Rapids: Baker.

Henning von der Osten, H. (1934), *Ancient Oriental Seals in the Collection of Mr. E. T. Newell*, University of Chicago Oriental Institute Publications 22, Chicago: University of Chicago.

Himmelfarb, M. (1991), 'The Temple and the Garden of Eden in Ezekiel, the Book of Watchers, and the Wisdom of ben Sira', in J. Scott and P. Simpson-Housley (eds.), *Sacred Places and Profane Spaces*, Contributions to the Study of Religion 30, Westport, CT: Greenwood, 63–78.

Hirsch, E. D. (1967), *Validity in Interpretation*, New York: Yale University Press.

——— (1984), 'Meaning and Significance Reinterpreted', *CE* 11, 202–244.

——— (1994), 'Transhistorical Intentions and the Persistence of Allegory', *NLH* 25.

————(1976), *Aims of Interpretation*, Chicago: Chicago University Press.

Hoekema, A. A. (1979), *The Bible and the Future*, Grand Rapids: Eerdmans.

Hoffner, H. (1990), *Hittite Myths*, SBLWAW, Atlanta: Scholars Press.

Holladay, W. L. (1986), *Jeremiah*, Vol. 1, Hermeneia, Philadelphia: Fortress.

Holloway, S. W. (1991), 'What Ship Goes There: The Flood Narratives in the Gilgamesh Epic and Genesis Considered in Light of Ancient Near Eastern Temple Ideology', *ZAW* 103, 328–354.

Holmes, M. W. (ed.) (1992), *The Apostolic Fathers*, Grand Rapids: Baker.

Homan, H. (2000), 'The Divine Warrior in His Tent', *BRev* 16, No. 6, 22–33.

Hooker, M. D. (1991), *The Gospel According to Mark*, BNTC, Peabody, MA: Hendrickson.

Hornung, E. (1982), *Conceptions of God in Ancient Egypt*, Ithaca, NY: Cornell University Press.

————(1992), *Idea into Image*, Princeton: Timken.

Hornung, E. and B. M. Bryan (eds.) (2002), *The Quest for Immortality: Treasures of Ancient Egypt*, Washington, DC: National Gallery of Art and United Exhibits Group.

Horowitz, W. (1998), *Mesopotamian Cosmic Geography*, Winona Lake, IN: Eisenbrauns.

Hugenberger, G. P. (n.d.) 'Is Work the Result of the Fall?', an unpublished paper available at the website of Park Street Church, Boston, MA, USA.

————(1994), *Marriage as a Covenant*, VTSup 52, Leiden: Brill.

————(1997), 'A Neglected Symbolism for the Clothing of Adam and Eve (Genesis 3:21)', a paper read at the Triennial Meeting on Eschatology of the Tyndale Fellowship of Biblical Research in Swanwick, Derbyshire.

Hughes, P. E. (1990), *The Book of the Revelation*, Pillar Series, Grand Rapids: Eerdmans.

Hurowitz, V. [A.] (1992), *I Have Built You an Exalted House*, JSOTS 115, Sheffield: Sheffield Academic Press, 335–337.

Ismail, F. (2002), '73 Anthropoid Coffin of Paduamin, with inner board and lid', in Hornung and Bryan (eds.) (2002).

Jacobsen, T. (1976), *The Treasures of Darkness*, New Haven: Yale University Press.

————(1987), *The Harps That Once ... Sumerian Poetry in Translation*, New Haven: Yale University Press.

James, E. O. (1969), 'The Conception of Creation in Cosmology', in *Liber Amicorum, Studies in Honour of C. J. Bleeker*, SHR, NumSup, Leiden: Brill, 99–112.

Janowski, B. (1990), 'Tempel und Schöpfung. Schöpfungstheologische Aspeckte der priesterschriftlichen Heiligtumskonzeption', *Schöpfung und Neuschöpfung, Jahrbuch für Biblische Theologie* 5, 37–69.

————(2001), 'Der Himmel auf Erden', in B. Janowski and B. Ego (eds.), *Das biblische Weltbild und seine altorientalischen Kontexte*, Tübingen: Mohr Siebeck.

Joüon, P. (1993), *A Grammar of Biblical Hebrew*, Vols. 1–2, SubB 14, Rome: Pontifical Biblical Institute.

Juel, D. (1977), *Messiah and Temple*, SBLDS 32, Missoula: Scholars Press.

Kampen, J. (1994), 'The Eschatological Temples of 11QT', in J. C. Reeves and J. Kampen (eds.), *Pursuing the Text, Studies in Honor of B. Z. Wacholder*, JSOTS 184, Sheffield: Sheffield Academic Press.

Keel, O. (1985), *The Symbolism of the Biblical World*, New York: Crossroad.

Kerr, A. R. (2002), *The Temple of Jesus' Body*, JSNTS 220, Sheffield: Sheffield Academic Press.

Kiddle, M. (with M. Ross) (1940), *The Revelation of St. John*, MNTC, London: Hodder & Stoughton.

Kilgallen, J. (1976), *The Stephen Speech*, AnBib 67, Rome: Biblical Institute Press.

Kim, S. (1987), 'Jesus – The Son of God, the Stone, the Son of Man, and the Servant: The Role of Zechariah in the Self-Identification of Jesus', in G. F. Hawthorne and O. Betz (eds.), *Tradition and Interpretation in the New Testament, Essays in Honor of E. E. Ellis*, Grand Rapids: Eerdmans; Tübingen: Mohr Siebeck, 134–148.

Kissane, E. J. (1943), *The Book of Isaiah*, Vol. 2, Dublin: Browne & Nolan.

Kittel, G. and G. Friedrich (eds.) (1964–76), *Theological Dictionary of the New Testament*, 10 vols., Grand Rapids: Eerdmans.

Kline, M. G. (1980), *Images of the Spirit*, Grand Rapids: Baker.

————(1989), *Kingdom Prologue*, South Hamilton: Gordon-Conwell Theological Seminary.

————(2001), *Glory in Our Midst*, Overland Park, KS: Two Age Press.

Koehler L. and W. Baumgartner (1994), *The Hebrew and Aramaic Lexicon of the Old Testament*, rev. ed. by W. Baumgartner and J. J. Stamm, Leiden/New York/Cologne: Brill.

Koester, H. '*topos*', *TDNT*, 8:187–208.

Koester, C. R. (1989), *The Dwelling of God*, CBQMS 22, Washington, DC: Catholic Biblical Association of America.

Kraft, H. (1974), *Die Offenbarung des Johannes*, HNT 16a, Tübingen: Mohr Siebeck.

Krodel, G. A. (1989), *Revelation*, Augsburg Commentary on the New Testament, Minneapolis: Augsburg Publishing House.

Laansma, J. (1997), *I Will Give You Rest*, WUNT 2.98, Tübingen: Mohr Siebeck, 159–251.

Lacocque, A. (1979), *The Book of Daniel*, London: SPCK.

Lanci, J. R. (1997), *A New Temple in Cornith*, SBL 1, New York: Peter Lang.

Lane, W. L. (1991a), *Hebrews 1 – 8*, WBC 47A, Dallas, TX: Word.

———(1991b), *Hebrews 9 – 13*, WBC 47B, Dallas, TX: Word.

Larkin, W. J. (1995), *Acts*, IVPNTC, Downers Grove: IVP.

LaRondelle, H. K. (1989), 'The Middle Ages Within the Scope of Apocalyptic Prophecy', *JETS* 32, 345–354.

Larson, C. B. (1993), *Illustrations for Preaching and Teaching*, Grand Rapids: Baker.

Lauterbach, J. Z. (ed.) (1976), *Mekilta de-Rabbi Ishmael*, Vols. 1–3, Philadelphia: Jewish Publication Society of America.

Lenski, R. C. H. (1934), *The Interpretation of St. Paul's Epistles to the Colossians, to the Thessalonians, to Timothy, to Titus and to Philemon*, Minneapolis: Augsburg Publishing House.

Leupold, H. C. (1960), *Exposition of Genesis*, Vols. 1–2, Grand Rapids: Baker.

Levenson, J. D. (1976), *Theology of the Program of Restoration of Ezekiel 40 – 48*, HSMS 10, Missoula: Scholars Press.

———(1981), 'From Temple to Synagogue', in B. Halpern and J. D. Levenson (eds.), *Traditions in Transformation*, Winona Lake, IN: Eisenbrauns, 143–166.

———(1984), 'The Temple and the World', *JR* 64, 294–295.

———(1985), *Sinai and Zion*, San Francisco: Harper & Row.

———(1986), 'The Jerusalem Temple in Devotional and Visionary Experience', in A. Green (ed.), *Jewish Spirituality*, New York: Crossroad, 32–61.

———(1988), *Creation and the Persistence of Evil: The Jewish Drama of Divine Omnipotence*, San Francisco: Harper & Row.

Levertoff, P. P. (ed.) (1926), *Midrash Sifre on Numbers*, in *Translations of Early Documents*, Series 3, Rabbinic Texts, London: Golub.

Lewis, Theodore J. (1992), 'Beelzebul', *ABD* 1, 638–640.

Lichtheim, M. (1976), *Ancient Egyptian Literature: A Book of Readings*, Vol. 2, Berkeley: University of California Press.

Lincoln, Andrew T. (1990), *Ephesians*, WBC, Dallas, TX: Word.

—— (1981), *Paradise Now and Not Yet*, SNTSMS 43, Cambridge: Cambridge University Press.

Lohmeyer, E. (1970), *Die Offenbarung des Johannes*, HNT 16, Tübingen: Mohr Siebeck.

Longman, T. (2001), *Immanuel in Our Place*, Phillipsburg: Presbyterian & Reformed.

Lundquist, J. M. (1983), 'What Is a Temple? A Preliminary Typology', in H. B. Huffmon, F. A. Spina and A. R. W. Green (eds.), *The Quest for the Kingdom of God: Studies in Honor of George E. Mendenhall*, Winona Lake, IN: Eisenbrauns, 205–219.

—— (1984a), 'The Common Temple Ideology in the Ancient Near East', in T. G. Madsen (ed.), *The Temple in Antiquity*, RSMS 9, Salt Lake City, UT: Brigham Young University.

—— (1984b), 'Temple Symbolism in Isaiah', in M. S. Nyman (ed.), *Isaiah and the Prophets*, RSMS 10, Salt Lake City, UT: Brigham Young University.

Marshall, I. H. (1983), *1 and 2 Thessalonians*, CBC, Grand Rapids: Eerdmans; London: Marshall, Morgan & Scott.

—— (1989), 'Church and Temple in the New Testament', *TynB* 40, 203–222.

—— (forthcoming, c. 2006), 'The Old Testament in Acts', in G. K. Beale and D. A. Carson (eds.), *Commentary on the Use of the Old Testament in the New*, Grand Rapids: Baker.

Martin, D. M. (1995), *1, 2 Thessalonians*, NAC 33, Nashville, TN: Broadman & Holman.

Martínez, G. (1988), 'L'interprétation de la Torah d'Ézéchiel dans les MSS. de Qumrân', *RevQ* 13, 441–452.

—— (1994), *The Dead Sea Scrolls Translated*, Leiden/Boston/Cologne: Brill.

Martínez, G. and E. J. C. Tigchelaar (eds.) (2000), *The Dead Sea Scrolls Study Edition*, 2 vols., Leiden/Boston/Cologne: Brill.

Mazar, A. (1992), 'Temples of the Middle and Late Bronze Ages and the Iron Age', in A. Kempinski and R. Reich (eds.), *The Architecture of Ancient Israel*, Israel Exploration Society, Jerusalem: Ahva Press, 161–187.

McCartney, D. J. (1994), '*Ecce Homo*: The Coming of the Kingdom as the Restoration of Human Vicegerency', *WTJ* 56, 1–21.

McKelvey, R. J. (1969), *The New Temple*, Oxford: Oxford University Press.

McMahon, G. (1997), 'Instructions to Priests and Temple Officials (1.83)', in W. W. Hallo and K. L. Younger (eds.), *The Context of Scripture* 1, Leiden/Boston/Cologne: Brill, 217–221.

McNamara, M. (1995), *Targum Neofiti 1: Numbers*, ArBib, Vol. 4, Collegeville, MN: Liturgical Press.

Mealy, J. W. (1992), *After the Thousand Years*, JSNTS 70, Sheffield: Sheffield Academic Press.

Metzger, B. M. (1971), *A Textual Commentary on the Greek New Testament*, London/New York: United Bible Societies.

Meyers, C. (1976), *The Tabernacle Menorah: A Synthetic Study of a Symbol from the Biblical Cult*, ASOR, Dissertation Series 2, Missoula: Scholars Press.

———(1985a) 'Lampstand', in P. J. Achtemeier (ed.), *Harper's Bible Dictionary*, San Francisco: Harper & Row, 546.

———(1985b), 'The Tree of Life', in P. J. Achtemeier (ed.), *Harper's Bible Dictionary*, San Francisco: Harper & Row, 1094.

———(1992a) 'Sea, Molten', *ABD* 5, 1061–1062.

———(1992b), 'Temple, Jerusalem', *ABD* 6, 359–360.

Michaels, J. R. (1967), 'The Centurion's Confession and the Spear Thrust', *CBQ* 29, 102–109.

Michel, O. '*naos*', *TDNT*, 4:880–890.

Midrash on Proverbs, The (1992), translated by B. L. Visotzky, New Haven: Yale University Press.

Midrash Tanhuma-Yelammedenu: An English Translation of Genesis and Exodus from the Printed Version of Tanhuma-Yehammedenu with Introduction, Notes and Indexes (1996), translated by S. A. Berman, Hoboken, NJ: KTAV.

Milligan, G. (1908), *St. Paul's Epistles to the Thessalonians*, Old Tappan, NJ: Revell.

Mitchell, T. C. (1980), 'Altar', *IBD* 1, 34–37.

Morray-Jones, C. R. A. (1998), 'The Temple Within', in SBLSP, 1, Atlanta: Scholars Press, 400–431.

Morris, L. (1959), *The First and Second Epistles to the Thessalonians*, NICNT, Grand Rapids: Eerdmans.

Motyer, J. A. (1996), 'Urim and Thummim', in J. D. Douglas (ed.), *The New Bible Dictionary*, Grand Rapids: Eerdmans; Leicester: IVP, 1219.

Moule, C. F. D. (1950), 'Sanctuary and Sacrifice in the Church of the New Testament', *JTS* 1, 34, 29–41.

Moulton, J. H. and G. Milligan (1972), '*arrabōn*', in *The Vocabulary of the Greek New Testament*, Grand Rapids: Eerdmans.

Nelson, H. H. (1944), 'The Egyptian Temple', *BA* 7, 44–53.

Neusner, J. (ed.) (1982–), *The Talmud of the Land of Israel: A Preliminary Translation and Explanation* (the Jerusalem Talmud), Vols. 1–35, Chicago: University of Chicago Press.

Niehaus, J. J. (1995), *God at Sinai*, Grand Rapids: Zondervan.

———(forthcoming), *No Other Gods*, Grand Rapids: Baker.

Nolland, J. (1993), *Luke 18:35 – 24:53*, WBC 35C, Dallas, TX: Word.

Pagolu, A. (1998), *The Religion of the Patriarchs*, JSOTS 277, Sheffield: Sheffield Academic Press.

Pao, D. W. (2000), *Acts and the Isaianic New Exodus*, WUNT 2.130, Tübingen: Mohr Siebeck.

Parry, D. W. (1994), 'Garden of Eden: Prototype Sanctuary', in D. W. Parry (ed.), *Temples of the Ancient World*, Salt Lake City, UT: Desert Book Company, 126–151.

———(1990), 'Sinai as Sanctuary and Mountain of God', in J. M. Lundquist and S. D. Ricks (eds.), *By Study and Also by Faith, Essays in Honor of H. W. Nibley*, Salt Lake City, UT: Desert Book Company.

Patai, R. (1967), *Man and Temple*, New York: KTAV.

Peipkorn, A. C. (1933), *Historical Prism Inscriptions of Ashurbanipal I*, Chicago: Chicago University Press.

Porteous, N. W. (1965), *Daniel*, Philadelphia: Westminster.

Poythress, V. (1991), *The Shadow of Christ in the Law of Moses*, Brentwood: Wolgemuth & Hyatt.

Prigent, P. (1981), *L'Apocalypse de Saint Jean*, Paris: Delachaux et Niestle.

Pritchard, J. B. (1969), *Ancient Near Eastern Texts*, Princeton: Princeton University Press.

Pusey, E. B. (1885), *Minor Prophets* 2, New York: Funk & Wagnalls.

Rahlfs, A. (ed.) (1971), *Septuaginta*, Stuttgart: Würtembergische Bibelanstatt.

Richard, E. (1978), *Acts 6:1 – 8:4. The Author's Method of Composition*, SBLDS 41, Missoula: Scholars Press.

Richard, E. J. (1995), *First and Second Thessalonians*, SacP 11, Collegeville, MN: Liturgical Press.

Robertson, O. P. (1975–76), 'Tongues: Sign of Covenantal Curse and Blessing', *WTJ* 38, 43–53.

Rodale, J. I. (1978), *The Synonym Finder*, Emmaus, PA: Rodale.

Rodriguez, A. M. (2001), 'Ancient Near Eastern Parallels to the Bible and the Question of Revelation and Inspiration', *JATS* 12, 43–64.

Ross, A. P. (1981), 'The Dispersion of the Nations in Genesis 11:1–9', *BSac* 138, 119–137.

———(1988), *Creation and Blessing*, Grand Rapids: Baker.

Russell, D. S. (1981), *Daniel*, Edinburgh: Saint Andrew; Philadelphia: Westminster.

Sailhamer, J. H. (1992), *The Pentateuch as Narrative*, Grand Rapids: Zondervan.

Satterthwaite, P. E. (2000), 'Biblical History', in T. D. Alexander and B. Rosner (eds.), *New Dictionary of Biblical Theology*, Leicester: IVP, 43–51.

Schlier, H., *'apostasia'*, *TDNT*, 1:513–514.

Schmitt, J. W. and J. C. Laney (1997), *Messiah's Coming Temple*, Grand Rapids: Kregel.

Schneider, C., *'katapetasma'*, *TDNT*, 3:628–630.

Schrenk, G., *'hieron'*, *TDNT*, 3:234, 241.

Schultz, C., (1980), *"ēdût'*, in R. L. Harris, G. J. Archer and B. K. Waltke (eds.), *Theological Word Book of the Old Testament*, Chicago: Moody, 649–650.

Schwartz, D. B. (1979), 'The Three Temples of 4QFlorilegium', *RevQ* 10, 83–91.

Scofield, C. I. (ed.) (1967), *The New Scofield Reference Bible*, New York: Oxford.

Scott, J. M. (1995), *Paul and the Nations*, WUNT 84, Tübingen: Mohr Siebeck.

Scroggs, R. (1966), *The Last Adam*, Oxford: Blackwell.

Septuagint Version of the Old Testament and Apocrypha with an English translation, The (1972), Grand Rapids: Zondervan.

Shafer, B. E. (1997), 'Temples, Priests, and Rituals: An Overview', in B. E. Shafer (ed.), *Temples of Ancient Egypt*, Ithaca, NY: Cornell University Press.

Shiffman, L. H. (1989), 'Architecture and Laws: The Temple and Its Courtyards in the Temple Scroll', in J. Neusner, E. S. Frerichs and N. M. Sarna (eds.), *From Ancient Israel to Modern Judaism: Essays in Honor of Marvin Fox* 1, BJS 159, Atlanta: Scholars Press, 267–284.

Showers, R. E. (1982), *The Most High God*, Bellmawr, NJ: Friends of Israel Gospel Ministry.

Simon, M. (1951), 'Saint Stephen and the Jerusalem Temple', *JEH* 2.

Sjöberg, A. W., E. Bergmann and G. B. Gragg (1969), *The Collection of the Sumerian Temple Hymns*, Locust Valley, NY: J. J. Augustin.

Skinner, J. (1910), *A Critical and Exegetical Commentary on Genesis*, ICC, Edinburgh: T. & T. Clark.

Smith, G. V. (1977), 'Structure and Purpose in Genesis 1 – 11', *JETS* 20, 307–319.

Snodgrass, K. R. (1998), 'Recent Research on the Parable of the Wicked Tenants: An Assessment', *BBR* 8, 187–216.

Sparks, J. N. (1987), *The Preaching of the Apostles*, Brookline, MA: Holy Cross Orthodox Press.

Spatafora, A. (1997), 'From the "Temple of God" to God as the Temple', *Tesi Gregoriana* 27, Rome: Gregorian University Press, 72–73.

Speiser, E. A. (1982), *Genesis*, AB, Garden City, NY: Doubleday.

Sperber, A. (1962), *The Bible in Aramaic*, Vol. 3, *The Latter Prophets According to Targum Jonathon*, Leiden: Brill.

Stager, L. E. (1999), 'Jerusalem and the Garden of Eden', *ErIs* 26, Festschrift for F. M. Cross, Jerusalem: Israel Exploration Society, 183–194.

———(2000), 'Jerusalem as Eden', *BAR* 26, 36–47, 66.

Steiner, R. C. (1997), 'The Aramaic Text in Demotic Script (1.99)', in W. W. Hallo and K. Lawson Younger (eds.), *The Context of Scripture* 1, Leiden/Boston/Cologne: Brill, 309–327.

Stephanovic, R. (2002), 'Finding Meaning in the Literary Patterns of Revelation', *JATS* 13, 27–43.

Stordalen, T. (2000), *Echoes of Eden*, Leuven: Peeters.

Stott, J. R. W. (1991), *The Message of 1 & 2 Thessalonians*, BST, Leicester: IVP; Downers Grove: IVP.

Strathmann, H., *'martys ktl.'*, *TDNT*, 4:482.

Swarup, P. N. W. (2002), 'An Eternal Planting, a House of Holiness', unpublished PhD dissertation, Cambridge University (Abstract in *TynB* 54 [2003], 151–156).

Sylva, D. D. (1987), 'The Meaning and Function of Acts 7:46–50', *JBL* 106, 261–275.

Taylor, J. B. (1969), *Ezekiel*, TOTC, Leicester: IVP.

Terrien, S. (1970), 'Omphalos Myth and Hebrew Religion', *VT* 20, 315–338.

Thompson, R. C. (1976), *The Devils and Evil Spirits of Babylonia*, New York: AMS Press.

Thornton, T. C. G. (1974), 'Stephen's Use of Isaiah LXVI.1', *JTS* 25, 432–434.

Tomlinson, R. A. (1976), *Greek Sanctuaries*, New York: St Martin's.

Towner, W. S. (2001), *Genesis*, Louisville: Westminster John Knox.

Townsend, J. T. (ed.) (1982), *Midrash Tanhuma*, Vols. 1–2, Hoboken, NJ: KTAV.

Tuell, S. S. (1996), 'Ezekiel 40 – 42 as Verbal Icon', *CBQ* 58, 649–664.

Uhlschöfer, H. K. (1977), 'Nathan's Opposition to David's Intention to Build a Temple in Light of Selected Ancient Near Eastern Texts', PhD thesis, Boston University, University of Michigan Microfilms.

Ulansey, D. (1991), 'The Heavenly Veil Torn: Mark's Cosmic Inclusio', *JBL* 110, 123–125.

Van Aarde, A. G. (1991), '"The Most High God Does Live in Houses, But Not Houses Built by Men . . .": The Relativity of the Metaphor "Temple" in Luke–Acts', *Neot* 25, 51–64.

Van Dijk, H. J. (1968), *Ezekiel's Prophecy on Tyre*, BibO 20, Rome: Pontifical Biblical Institute.

van Leeuwen, C. (1997), '*ēd* witness', in E. Jenni and C. Westermann (eds.), *Theological Lexicon of the Old Testament*, Peabody, MA: Hendrikson, 838–846.

van Ruiten, J. T. A. G. M. (1999), 'Visions of the Temple in the Book of Jubilees', in B. Ego, A. Lange and P. Pilhofer (eds.), *Gemeinde ohne Tempel/Community Without Temple*, WUNT 118, Tübingen: Mohr Siebeck, 215–227.

Vance, A. B. (1992), 'The Church as the New Temple in Matthew 16:17–19: A Biblical-Theological Consideration of Jesus' Response to Peter's Confession as Recorded by Matthew', ThM thesis, Gordon-Conwell Theological Seminary.

VanGemeren, Willem A. (ed.) (1997), *New International Dictionary of Old Testament Theology and Exegesis*, 5 vols., Grand Rapids: Zondervan.

Vanhoozer, K. (1998), *Is There a Meaning in This Text?*, Grand Rapids: Zondervan.

——— (2001), 'From Speech Acts to Scripture Acts', in Bartholomew et al. (eds.), *After Pentecost: Language and Biblical Interpretation*, Carlisle: Paternoster; Grand Rapids: Zondervan, 1–49.

Vawter, B. (1977), *On Genesis*, Garden City, NY: Doubleday.

Vermes, Geza (1987), *The Dead Sea Scrolls in English*, 3rd ed., Sheffield: JSOT Press.

von Rad, G. (1962), *Old Testament Theology*, Vols. 1–2, New York: Harper & Row.

Vos, G. (1979; 1930), *The Pauline Eschatology*, Grand Rapids: Baker (originally published by Princeton University Press).

——— (2001), *The Eschatology of the Old Testament*, Phillipsburg, NJ: Presbyterian & Reformed.

Walker, P. W. L. (1996), *Jesus and the Holy City*, Grand Rapids: Eerdmans.

Waltke, Bruce K. (2001), *Genesis*, Grand Rapids: Zondervan.

Walton, J. H. (1995), 'The Mesopotamian Background of the Tower of Babel Account and Its Implications', *BBR* 5, 155–175.

—— (2001), *Genesis*, NIVAC, Grand Rapids: Zondervan.

Wanamaker, C. A. (1990), *Commentary on 1 & 2 Thessalonians*, NIGTC, Grand Rapids: Eerdmans.

Watts, R. (1997), *Isaiah's New Exodus in Mark*, Grand Rapids: Baker.

Weinfeld, M. (1981), 'Sabbath and the Enthronement of the Lord – the Problem of the Sitz im Leben of Genesis 1:1 – 2:3', in A. Caquot and M. Delcor (eds.), *Melanges bibliques et orientaux en l'honneur de M. Henri Cazelles*, Kevelaer: Butzon & Bercker; Neukirchen-Vluyn: Neukirchener Verlag, 501–512.

Wenham, G. J. (1987), *Genesis 1 – 15*, WBC, Waco, TX: Word.

—— (1994), 'Sanctuary Symbolism in the Garden of Eden Story', in R. S. Hess and D. T. Tsumara (eds.), *'I Studied Inscriptions from before the Flood'*, Winona Lake, IN: Eisenbrauns.

Westermann, C. (1995), *Genesis 12 – 36*, Minneapolis: Fortress.

Wevers, J. W. (1969), *Ezekiel*, NCB, Camden, NJ: Thomas Nelson.

Wieder, N. (1955), 'The Doctrine of the Two Messiahs Among the Karaites', *JJS* 6, 14–25.

Wiens, D. L. (1995), *Stephen's Sermon and the Structure of Luke-Acts*, North Richland Hills, TX: Bibal Press.

Wightman, G. J. (1995), 'Ben Sira 50:2: The Hellenistic Enclosure in Jerusalem', in S. Bourke and J.-P. Descoeudres (eds.), *Trade, Contact, and the Movement of Peoples in the Eastern Mediterranean, Studies in Honour of J. B. Hennessy*, Mediterranean Archaeology Supplement 3, Sydney: Meditarch, 275–283.

Wilkinson, R. H. (2000), *The Complete Temples of Ancient Egypt*, New York: Thames & Hudson.

Wilson, P. (1997), *A Ptolemaic Lexicon*, OLA 78, Leuven: Peeters.

Wise, M., M. Abegg and E. Cook (1996), *The Dead Sea Scrolls*, San Francisco: Harper.

Witherington, B. (1998), *The Acts of the Apostles*, Grand Rapids: Eerdmans.

Woudstra, M. H. (1970), 'The Tabernacle in Biblical-Theological Perspective', in J. B. Payne (ed.), *New Perspectives on the Old Testament*, Waco, TX: Word, 88–103.

Wright, C. J. H. (2001), *The Message of Ezekiel*, BST, Leicester: IVP.

Wright, N. T. (1992a), *The Climax of the Covenant*, Minneapolis: Fortress.
―――(1992b), *The New Testament and the People of God*, London: SPCK.
―――(1996), *Jesus and the Victory of God*, Minneapolis: Fortress.
Yarden, L. (1971), *The Tree of Light*, Ithaca, NY: Cornell University Press.
Young, E. J. (1996), *The Book of Isaiah*, Grand Rapids: Eerdmans.
Ziegler, J. (ed.) (1983), *Isaias*, in *Septuaginta*, Vetus Testamentum Graecum 14, Göttingen: Vandenhoeck & Ruprecht.
Zimmerli, W. (1979), *Ezekiel*, Vol. 1, Philadelphia: Fortress.
―――(1983), *Ezekiel*, Vol. 2, Philadelphia: Fortress.
Zlotowitz M. and N. Scherman, (1977), *Bereishis Genesis*, Brooklyn: Mesorah.

Index of modern authors

Index of Bible references

Index of ancient sources